ENGLISH POETRY

Select
Bibliographical Guides

Edited by A.E. Dyson

Chaucer
Spenser
Donne
Herbert
Milton
Marvell
Dryden
Pope
Blake
Wordsworth
Coleridge
Byron
Shelley
Keats
Tennyson
Browning
Arnold
Hopkins
Yeats
Eliot

ENGLISH POETRY

Select Bibliographical Guides

ENGLISH POETRY

Select Bibliographical Guides

Edited by A. E. DYSON

OXFORD UNIVERSITY PRESS

1971

Oxford University Press, Ely House, London W.1

GLASGOW NEW YORK TORONTO MELBOURNE WELLINGTON
CAPE TOWN SALISBURY IBADAN NAIROBI DAR ES SALAAM LUSAKA ADDIS ABABA
BOMBAY CALCUTTA MADRAS KARACHI LAHORE DACCA
KUALA LUMPUR SINGAPORE HONG KONG TOKYO

PRINTED IN GREAT BRITAIN
BY RICHARD CLAY (THE CHAUCER PRESS), LTD
BUNGAY, SUFFOLK

CONTENTS

ABBREVIATIONS

JOURNALS, SERIES, ETC. FREQUENTLY CITED

BNYPL   *Bulletin of New York Public Library*
C.B.E.L.   *Cambridge Bibliography of English Literature*
D.N.B.   *Dictionary of National Biography*
EIC   *Essays in Criticism*
ELH   *Journal of English Literary History*
JEGP   *Journal of English and Germanic Philology*
MLN   *Modern Language Notes*
MLR   *Modern Language Review*
MP   *Modern Philology*
N.C.B.E.L. *New Cambridge Bibliography of English Literature*
O.H.E.A.   *Oxford History of English Art*
O.H.E.L.   *Oxford History of English Literature*
PMLA   *Publications of the Modern Language Association of America*
PQ   *Philological Quarterly*
RES   *Review of English Studies*
SEL   *Studies in English Literature*
SP   *Studies in Philology*
SR   *Sewanee Review*
TLS   *Times Literary Supplement*
UTQ   *University of Toronto Quarterly*
VP   *Victorian Poetry*
VN   *Victorian Newsletter*
VS   *Victorian Studies*

INTRODUCTION

This Guide is intended for those who are embarking on a serious study of English literature. Their first concern is with the obvious questions. Which editions can be recommended, including the authoritative texts, and good cheaper ones? What critics should be read? What biographies exist of the major writers, and can any be described as standard? Are a writer's letters in print? Where do we have to look for full bibliographies? Which books throw light on authors by portraying the background against which they wrote?

Each of the chapters in this book is divided up into sections in which these questions are answered. At the end of each chapter, there is a classified list with bibliographical details of all the books and articles mentioned earlier.

The question of which critics should be read is, perhaps, the most difficult to answer. Differences of opinion naturally flourish. One problem for the student these days is the sheer quantity of criticism published. Any full bibliography bears witness to this, and the effect can be bewildering or even paralysing. Some of the criticism is ephemeral, some for specialists only, some not very good. With so many will-o'-the-wisps, how can a student keep his path?

Each contributor to this Guide has based his selection of critical material on his own experience, but has not merely indulged personal taste. The books and articles cited include those which would figure in any general consensus, and contributors have added the most valuable other articles and books known to them. It is recognized that good work may have been omitted, but a select reading list cannot satisfy everyone, and the sections on BIBLIOGRAPHIES should be complete enough to make amends.

The contributors to this book are concerned with mapping territory, pointing to landmarks, suggesting routes. Such activity is, of course, merely inaugural. The various signposts all point through the door of a library, and once the reader is there the biographies, bibliographies, texts, and works of criticism suggest directions of their own.

It should be kept in mind that the writing of this book was completed late in 1970, and that the information about books and articles relates to the situation at that time. New books of importance are reviewed in *The Times Literary Supplement*, the *New York Review of Books* and other leading literary papers, and an eye should be kept on these. Monthly visits to the periodicals room of a good library should be a normal feature of a student's life. He will soon become familiar with the literary journals most frequently listed in this book.

It is becoming increasingly common for important articles from learned journals to be collected together in paperback volumes. These enable the student to own writings which he would otherwise have to borrow from library collections of journals, and which are sometimes difficult to obtain. Some of them will be mentioned in the body of this book, but it may be convenient if I list the most important of the series here.

(a) *Collections of articles on a single author*

Twentieth Century Views. General Editor, Maynard Mack (Englewood Cliffs, N.J.: Prentice-Hall). Modern critical essays.

Modern Judgements. General Editor, P. N. Furbank (London: Macmillan). Criticism of the past twenty or thirty years.

The Critical Heritage Series. General Editor, B. C. Southam (London: Routledge & Kegan Paul; and New York: Barnes & Noble). Reviews and comments written during the author's lifetime.

Discussions Of Literature. General Editor, Joseph H. Summers (Boston, Mass.: Heath; and London: Harrap). General critical essays.

Penguin Critical Anthologies. General Editor, Christopher Ricks (Harmondsworth: Penguin). Criticism from the author's lifetime to today.

(b) *Collections of articles on a single work*

Macmillan Casebook Series. General Editor, A. E. Dyson (London: Macmillan). About one-third devoted to writings published before 1930, two-thirds to modern criticism.

Twentieth Century Interpretations. General Editor, Maynard Mack (Englewood Cliffs, N.J.: Prentice-Hall). Mainly recent criticism, in selection.

Norton Critical Editions (New York: Norton). Text, and selected criticism in section at end.

Students should know where to go for bibliographical information in addition to that which is contained in this book. *The Cambridge Bibliography of English Literature* (edited in four volumes by F. W. Bateson, with subsequent supplementary volumes edited by George Watson) is the standard work. It is now being replaced by the *New Cambridge Bibliography of English Literature*, of which one volume, edited by George Watson, is currently in print. The Modern Language Association of America publishes an annual list of the year's work in English studies in *PMLA*—comprehensive but without commentary. There is also *The Year's Work in English Studies* which is published annually by the English Association (London). This is more selective than the *PMLA* list and has worrying gaps, but it includes commentaries on the works listed, and offers some insight on the varieties of current criticism. Comprehensive and valuable bibliographies are also to be found in the various volumes of the Oxford History of English Literature. Students of literature who are particularly concerned with the historical background might well look for guidance to the appropriate volumes in the Oxford History of England, which, besides being authoritative, contain useful bibliographical material.

A note now on the bibliographical details given in this book. In the REFERENCES section at the end of each chapter, the place and date of publication of a book is almost always that of the most recent edition. Readers should distinguish between *editions* and *impressions*. The copy of a book on a library shelf may well contain the date of an impression printed more recently than the edition listed in this book; but impressions are usually unaltered, or lightly corrected, reprints of the most recent edition.

Books originally published in paperback are given places and dates of publication, but full details of paperback *reprints* are not given, because such paperbacks are normally unaltered reprints of the latest hardback editions. The phrases 'paperback, U.K.', 'paperbacks, U.K. and U.S.', and 'paperback, U.S.' signify simply that at the time of going to press paperback reprints were listed as available, in the markets shown, by *Paperbacks in Print* (U.K.) and *Paperbound Books in Print* (U.S.). However, new paperbacks appear in their thousands each year, while others go out of print, and readers who intend to buy books on a limited budget should consult up-to-date issues of the catalogues mentioned.

Journals and series cited frequently are customarily referred to by abbreviations of their names, and this practice is followed here. The abbreviations chiefly used are listed on p. vii.

A.E.D.

J. A. Burrow

TEXTS

The only large-scale edition of Chaucer's works available at present (1968) is that of W. W. Skeat, in six volumes, published first in 1894. Its glossary remains, together with the Concordance prepared by Tatlock and Kennedy, the best guide to Chaucer's word-usage; but most of Skeat's other work has, inevitably, been superseded. A new edition on a similar scale is in preparation, under the general editorship of E. T. Donaldson.

The standard single-volume edition is that of F. N. Robinson (2nd edn., 1957). This contains all Chaucer's known works, verse and prose, save for the possibly Chaucerian *Equatorie of the Planetis*, a prose treatise on an astronomical instrument discovered by D. J. Price and first edited by him in 1955. The greater part of Chaucer's poetry (not his prose) is to be found in E. T. Donaldson, *Chaucer's Poetry: An Anthology for the Modern Reader* (1958, with regularized Middle English spelling), and in A. C. Baugh, *Chaucer's Major Poetry* (1963). Both Donaldson and Baugh gloss their texts at the bottom of each page; but Donaldson's anthology has two advantages over its rival: it includes a series of distinguished critical essays by the editor, and its texts have been prepared afresh from the manuscript materials. In particular, readers should note that Donaldson, unlike Baugh or Robinson (2nd edn.), takes full account of the materials collected by Manly and Rickert in their monumental *Text of 'The Canterbury Tales'* (1940), and so offers a considerably better-grounded text of Chaucer's greatest work.

Of the numerous editions of single works, only a few can be mentioned here. R. K. Root's edition of *Troilus and Criseyde* (1926) is a standard work, pleasantly produced and full of useful information. D. S. Brewer produced an excellent edition of *The Parliament of Fowls* in 1960. In a handy volume in the Everyman series A. C. Cawley prints *The Canterbury Tales* complete (Robinson's text), with good notes and glosses on the same page as the text. J. M. Manly's student's edition of *The Canterbury Tales* (1928), though heavily bowdlerized, remains useful, especially for its material on fourteenth-century life and thought. Another edition of *The Canterbury Tales*, again less than complete, though not expurgated, is that published by R. A. Pratt in 1966. Pratt's text is, with Donaldson's, the best text of *The Canterbury Tales* now available; and it is accompanied by excellent glosses and notes. The most distinguished of the many editions of individual Tales are those of K. Sisam: *The Clerkes Tale* (1923) and *The Nun's Priest's Tale* (1926). J. A. W. Bennett's edition of *The Knight's Tale* also deserves special mention.

CRITICAL STUDIES AND COMMENTARY

Most of what was written about Chaucer from his own day until 1900 was gathered together and printed by Caroline Spurgeon in *Five Hundred Years of Chaucer Criticism and Allusion, 1357–1900*. In her Introduction Miss Spurgeon gives an account (not unprejudiced by the tastes of her own age) of how views of Chaucer have changed from age to age. The same subject is treated more briefly and dispassionately by D. S. Brewer in an essay entitled 'Images of Chaucer, 1386–1900', in *Chaucer and Chaucerians* (1966). See also J. A. Burrow (ed.), *Geoffrey Chaucer*, a Penguin Critical Anthology (1969). There is indeed much to be learned from past readings of Chaucer, particularly when they conflict with our own (as they nearly always do); but there are perhaps only three pieces from before 1900 which count as required reading for anyone interested in Chaucer nowadays. These are: Dryden's *Preface to the Fables* (1700), Blake's account, printed in his *Descriptive Catalogue* (1809), of his own picture of the Canterbury pilgrims (a picture reproduced by Spurgeon), and Matthew Arnold's essay 'The Study of Poetry', first published in 1880. Each of these pieces is a classic of Chaucer criticism in its pre-academic phase.

The professors took over from the poets round about the end of the nineteenth century. There followed what one might call the first academic phase of Chaucer criticism, which stretched, very roughly, from 1900 to 1930. Its chief American monument (and it was about this time that the United States began to dominate the subject) is G. L. Kittredge's *Chaucer and his Poetry* (1915). The style of this book may irritate modern readers; but Kittredge was a shrewd critic. His account of the dramatic interplay of pilgrims and tales in *The Canterbury Tales* (it was Kittredge who gave currency to the idea of a 'Marriage Group') still demands respectful reading, if not unqualified assent. Kittredge's opposite number in England was W. P. Ker, whose two Clark Lectures on Chaucer, published in *Form and Style in Poetry*, show his usual perspicacity. Two other books from the end of this period must be mentioned: J. Livingston Lowes,

Geoffrey Chaucer and the Development of his Genius (1934), which is especially good on matters of 'background', and G. K. Chesterton, *Chaucer* (1932), a serious but refreshingly unacademic book.

As we approach the present day, the volume of books and articles on Chaucer increases to such an extent that a whole volume of the Hammond–Griffith–Crawford bibliography (see BIBLIOGRAPHIES below) is devoted to listing work done in the ten years ending in 1963. The *Companion to Chaucer Studies* edited by Beryl Rowland (1968) gives a generally very useful bibliographical survey of current Chaucer scholarship. Under these circumstances, paperback collections of important articles from learned journals perform a useful function. There are two such collections of articles on Chaucer: *Chaucer: Modern Essays in Criticism*, edited by E. C. Wagenknecht (1959), and *Chaucer Criticism*, edited by R. J. Schoeck and J. Taylor, in two volumes—Volume I: *The Canterbury Tales* (1960), and Volume II: *'Troilus and Criseyde' & the Minor Poems* (1961). The Schoeck and Taylor collection is, on the whole, to be preferred. I shall refer to it several times in the ensuing brief survey of modern work on various aspects of Chaucer's achievement.

The English Chaucer—that is, the Chaucer who stands in relation to medieval *English* society, literature, and speech—has not, relatively speaking, benefited much from recent criticism and scholarship. His relations with the English vernacular literature still present many problems. So far as the popular romances are concerned, there is an excellent essay by E. T. Donaldson on 'The Idiom of Popular Poetry in *The Miller's Tale*' in the 1950 volume of *English Institute Essays*, reprinted in his collection of essays, *Speaking of Chaucer*. There is also a good chapter on the English sources of 'Sir Thopas' by L. H. Loomis in the standard modern work on the sources of the Canterbury Tales, *Sources and Analogues of Chaucer's 'Canterbury Tales'*, edited by W. F. Bryan and G. Dempster. Further valuable suggestions are to be found in D. S. Brewer's essay 'The Relationship of Chaucer to the English and European Traditions', in *Chaucer and Chaucerians* (1966), and also in D. Everett's admirable *Essays on Middle English Literature* (1955). But much remains to be done in this field.

Another somewhat neglected subject is Chaucer's English. There is a useful survey of Chaucer's sounds and inflections in S. Moore (revised A. H. Marckwardt), *Historical Outlines of English Sounds and Inflections* (1951); and there are also summary accounts in the major editions. But no first-rate, full-scale, philological work on Chaucer has been published for a long time—J. Mersand's *Chaucer's Romance*

Vocabulary (2nd edn., 1939) being a very doubtful exception—and
the literary critics have not been very active either. We are still
waiting for the 'inquiry into the art and language of Chaucer' that
F. R. Leavis proposed in his 'Sociology and Literature' (reprinted
in *The Common Pursuit*), though the first and last chapters of J. Speirs's
Chaucer the Maker contain some interesting (as well as some very
dubious) suggestions. Indeed, the business of studying Chaucer's
idiom, discriminating its different varieties and relating them to the
society of the day, has hardly begun, despite the work of Donaldson,
Everett, and others. Critics often seem, like Dryden, to have 'given
up the words'—the proverbs (though there is B. J. Whiting's
Chaucer's Use of Proverbs), the poetic diction, the colloquialisms, the
technical jargons, and, above all, the simple staple idiom—in their
pursuit of matters Continental and Latin.

The Continental Chaucer—the Chaucer who read French and
Italian (and perhaps Spanish?) poems—has been the subject of
much excellent work in recent decades; but there are two books
which stand out from the rest: C. S. Lewis's *Allegory of Love* (1936)
and C. Muscatine's *Chaucer and the French Tradition* (1957). Lewis's
book is still, perhaps, the most influential of all pieces of modern
Chaucer criticism. Occasionally his clear-cut manner of presentation
has proved misleading: he suggests, for example, that Courtly Love
always and everywhere meant adultery, which it did not: see
G. Mathew, 'Marriage and Amour Courtois in Late Fourteenth
Century England', in *Essays Presented to Charles Williams*, and also
Chapter XIV in the same author's *Court of Richard II* (see BACK-
GROUND READING below). But his rehabilitation of the courtly and
allegorical traditions represented in *The Romance of the Rose* has been
of prime importance. It has been followed up, in more recent years,
in essays such as J. V. Cunningham, 'The Literary Form of the
Prologue to *The Canterbury Tales*' (1952), and above all in Muscatine's clear-cut and challenging book. Muscatine distinguishes two
'styles' in medieval French literature, the Courtly and the Bourgeois,
and he studies the mutations of these in Chaucer's work. His scheme
leads him to pay more attention than did Lewis to the bourgeois or
realistic strain in Chaucer; and he has much to say about the fabliau
tales—a topic somewhat inadequately treated by W. W. Lawrence
in his otherwise useful book, *Chaucer and 'The Canterbury Tales'*
(1950). There has, in fact, been some general revival of scholarly
interest in these tales of late, witness T. W. Craik's shrewd and unpretentious discussions in *The Comic Tales of Chaucer* (1964), and such
learned articles as P. E. Beichner, 'Characterization in *The Miller's*

Tale' (to be found in Volume I of Schoeck and Taylor's collection). It may be noted that J. Bédier's standard book on the fabliau genre, *Les Fabliaux*, has recently (1957) been capped with an excellent study under the same title by P. Nykrog.

However, the poems which have profited most from recent work on 'the Continental Chaucer' are *The Book of the Duchess*, *The Parliament of Fowls*, and *Troilus*. There are valuable essays on the first of these poems in Wagenknecht (by B. H. Bronson), in Schoeck and Taylor (by J. Lawlor), and above all in W. Clemen's book, *Chaucer's Early Poetry*, translated from the German and revised in 1963. Clemen's admirable book illustrates the sympathetic treatment that contemporary critics, following Lewis (and Kittredge), are ready to accord to the earlier and more obviously conventional Chaucer. Recent work on *The Parliament of Fowls* is conveniently summed up in the valuable edition of that poem by D. S. Brewer, already mentioned above; but, unfortunately, there has been no similar separate edition of *Troilus* since that of R. K. Root (1926), and it is hard to keep up with the spate of critical essays on that poem— which is on the way to regaining its sixteenth-century standing as the greatest, or at least the most-studied, of Chaucer's works. The twelve essays printed in Schoeck and Taylor give a fair idea of recent work. One of the most interesting of the twelve, C. S. Lewis's 'What Chaucer Really Did to *Il Filostrato*', deals with a subject that has since been taken up by S. B. Meech in his massive *Design in Chaucer's 'Troilus'* (1959)—Chaucer's handling (with the help, as we now know, of a French crib) of his Italian original. The taste of Chaucer critics for source-criticism is well justified by the interest of this particular case; but it must be said that Meech's book is dull to read. One might contrast it in this respect with E. T. Donaldson's lively and penetrating essay on the poem in his anthology *Chaucer's Poetry* (see TEXTS above).

The Elizabethans admired *Troilus* as the master-work of a 'learned', 'moral' poet, as Caroline Spurgeon shows, and the increasing interest in the poem in recent years has gone along with an increasing interest in the Latin or 'clerkly' side of Chaucer—especially his rhetoric, his scientific knowledge, and his moral and philosophical thought. Chaucer's education is still something of a mystery; but he plainly read a good deal outside the French and Italian poets, and his Latin learning (classical, patristic, and medieval) is now taken seriously by most critics. The 'frolic' or 'merry' Chaucer of the eighteenth century, accordingly, is under a cloud.

The pioneer work on Chaucer's rhetoric was done by J. M. Manly, whose 'Chaucer and the Rhetoricians' (reprinted by Schoeck and Taylor, Volume I) appeared in 1926. This essay was most salutary at the time: it firmly established the idea that Chaucer's style was 'eloquent' and artful as well as 'fresh'. But Manly was too ready to accept the notion that great poets will always grow progressively more impatient of conventional methods as they get older; and his conception of rhetoric was rather narrowly based on E. Faral's collection of twelfth- and thirteenth-century rhetorical texts, published two years earlier. A broader view of rhetoric (taking account, for example, of the prescribed *topoi* or common-places) has gained currency since the publication of E. R. Curtius's seminal book, *European Literature and the Latin Middle Ages* (English edition, 1953); but the full influence of this massive and fascinating study is only just beginning to make itself felt in Chaucer studies (e.g. in Brewer's edition of *The Parliament*). An excellent pre-Curtius account of the matter is to be found in Chapter VII of Miss Everett's *Essays on Middle English Literature* ('Some Reflections on Chaucer's "Art Poetical" '). R. O. Payne's book, *The Key of Remembrance* (1963), develops out of the rhetoricians, somewhat obscurely, a Chaucerian poetic.

W. C. Curry's *Chaucer and the Medieval Sciences* is discussed under BACKGROUND READING below. It has prompted considerable interest in Chaucer's scientific knowledge. Astrology and medicine, as well as rhetoric, enter into the portraits in the General Prologue, as N. Coghill points out in his British Council pamphlet, *Geoffrey Chaucer* (1956); and Lycurgus and Emetrius, in *The Knight's Tale*, are what they are partly, at least, because Chaucer conceived them as, respectively, Saturnalian and Martial men. Curry's discussion of the character of the Wife of Bath, printed by Wagenknecht, gives a good idea of his methods.

Perhaps the most striking instance of current interest in Chaucer's moral and philosophical world-view is J. A. W. Bennett's *The Parlement of Foules: An Interpretation* (1957)—a close-packed and very learned study of *The Parliament*, and in particular of the philosophical ideas associated with the figures of Venus and Nature in that poem. The author's exposition of 'The Philosophy of Plenitude'—stemming from twelfth- and thirteenth-century French sources—is specially notable, not least for the light it throws on *The Canterbury Tales*. More recently (1968) Bennett has published an equally learned and illuminating study of *The House of Fame*, in which he attempts to establish a unity of theme and of structure. Other critics have shown an interest in the older philosophy of Boethius as it appears, particularly, in *Troilus* and *The Knight's Tale*. It is no longer usual—though still possible—to regard Troilus's long Boethian soliloquy on predestination as an unfortunate after-thought, even though it was (as Root showed) added in revision. On *The Knight's Tale* two essays, one by W. Frost, the other by C. Muscatine, have been widely influential: the former is reprinted by Schoeck and Taylor, the latter by Wagenknecht. More recently an essay by R. Neuse has raised new questions about the poem.

This is the place to mention the work on Chaucer published by the so-called 'patristic' or 'historical' critics, chief among them D. W. Robertson. A volume edited by D. Bethurum, *Critical Approaches to Medieval Literature* (1960), contains a discussion on this kind of criticism between E. T. Donaldson (con) and R. E. Kaske (pro) from which much is to be learned. Schoeck and Taylor reprint, in their second volume, a study of *Troilus* by D. W. Robertson, and this essay (entitled 'Chaucerian Tragedy') gives a good idea of the approach adopted by him and his followers—the use of biblical and patristic materials, the allegorical reading, and, generally, the 'strong moral line': Robertson sees Troilus as a 'mortal sinner', who 'subjects himself to Fortune by allowing himself to be overcome by the physical attractions of Criseyde', as Adam was overcome by Eve. Another specimen of the approach is afforded by R. P. Miller's interesting essay on the Pardoner, printed by Schoeck and Taylor in their first volume. Robertson's essay on *Troilus* has now been incorporated in his book, *A Preface to Chaucer* (1962). This is a far-ranging, learned study; but the criticism of Robertson and his followers is vitiated (despite their claim to be 'historical') by the fundamentally unhistorical supposition that the Middle Ages form a single homogeneous period, in which all significant writers, Chaucer included, may be expected to compose according to the prescriptions of St. Augustine. What we miss in Robertson's work is a sense of the individual writer and a sense of the particular period (as against the epoch)—the sense of period that we find in G. Mathew's *Court of Richard II* (see BACKGROUND READING below), or in J. Stevens's *Music and Poetry in the Early Tudor Court* (1961). Stevens provides just the right historical context for a discussion of Chaucer as the poet of 'Courtly Love'. Where Robertson (like C. S. Lewis, whom he otherwise does not much resemble) talks in general terms about the Middle Ages' view of love and about Andreas Capellanus (had Chaucer read Andreas Capellanus?), Stevens describes the social setting, and indeed the social function, of courtly love litera-ture in late medieval England.

One of the most striking features of modern Chaucer criticism, finally, has been its recurring interests in 'Chaucer the narrator', the dramatic person who tells the stories and describes the people: the dreamer-poet in the dream-poems, the pilgrim-poet in *The Canterbury Tales*. This interest can be traced in Muscatine's book, in the critical essays of Donaldson ('Chaucer the Pilgrim' and the essays in his edition), and in other recent essays. The main lines of the argument are these: the Narrator is not to be simply identified with the Poet, even though he often shares his name and characteristics; he consistently sees less than the Poet himself sees, and expects his audience to see; and he is, as Donaldson puts it, 'the chief agent by which the poet achieves his wonderful, complex, ironic, comic, serious vision of the world'.

BIOGRAPHIES

All future biographies of Chaucer will no doubt be based on Crow and Olson's *Chaucer Life-Records*, published in 1966. This definitive volume contains all known contemporary records of Chaucer's life. The records are printed together with a concise commentary, whose tendency is to suggest that nothing in Chaucer's life (nor even his burial in Westminster Abbey) need have been otherwise if he had never written a line of poetry.

Short, and for most purposes sufficient, biographies may be found in the editions of Robinson, Donaldson, Baugh, and Pratt (see TEXTS above). Donaldson's narrative is perhaps the most interesting, Pratt's the most up-to-date (he alone records the recent discovery that Chaucer was in Spain in 1366). Fuller accounts are given by Manly, in the Introduction to his edition of *The Canterbury Tales* (see TEXTS), by M. Chute in her *Geoffrey Chaucer of England* (1946), and by D. S. Brewer in *Chaucer in his Time* (1963).

BIBLIOGRAPHIES

The pioneer bibliography of Chaucer studies was E. P. Hammond's *Chaucer: A Bibliographical Manual* (1908). Despite its age, this is still a valuable work of reference (e.g. for its alphabetically arranged section on pieces printed with the works of Chaucer in early editions). It has been supplemented by D. D. Griffith, *Bibliography of Chaucer, 1908–1953*, and by W. R. Crawford, *Bibliography of Chaucer, 1954–63*. These three volumes provide between them, for the period up to 1963, a virtually complete list of books and articles bearing on Chaucer.

The Cambridge Bibliography, with its Supplement, gives quite generous coverage up to 1954. The second edition of R. D. French's *Chaucer Handbook* (1947) contains a not very selective list of books and articles. Short general bibliographies appear in editions such as those of Robinson, Donaldson, Baugh, and Pratt (see TEXTS above); and Robinson also gives select references in his notes to individual works. In this respect, however, Robinson's second edition was not brought entirely up to date. It is always necessary to consult Hammond–Griffith–Crawford on any matter of special interest.

BACKGROUND READING

J. Huizinga's *The Waning of the Middle Ages* (1924) is still, for students of Chaucer, the most helpful book on the culture of the Later Middle Ages in general, even though Huizinga does not very often refer to England. Mention should also be made of *The Flowering of the Middle Ages*, edited by Joan Evans, in which vivid illustrations are accompanied by expert text.

The standard history of England in the age of Chaucer is the *Oxford History of England* volume, *The Fourteenth Century*, by M. McKisack (1959). *Chaucer's World*, edited by E. Rickert, uses contemporary documents (translated) to build up a portrait of the times, while R. S. Loomis attempts to do the same thing with pictures in *A Mirror of Chaucer's World*. M. Bowden, in her *Commentary on the General Prologue to 'The Canterbury Tales'*, provides much useful background information, as does J. M. Manly in the course of his attempt to identify the real-life originals of some of Chaucer's pilgrims in *Some New Light on Chaucer* (1926). J. J. Jusserand's *English Wayfaring Life in the Middle Ages* may usefully be read in conjunction with *The Canterbury Tales*. D. W. Robertson's *Chaucer's London* is also valuable.

Four books on particular segments of 'Chaucer's world' deserve special mention. Each is a distinguished book in its own right; and each has something in it for the reader of Chaucer. On the court, Gervase Mathew's *The Court of Richard II* (1968); on the city, S. L. Thrupp's *The Merchant Class of Medieval London* (1948); on the country, G. C. Homans's *English Villagers of the Thirteenth Century* (1941); and on the Church, W. A. Pantin's *The English Church in the Fourteenth Century* (1955). Pantin's excellent study may be read in conjunction with G. R. Owst, *Literature and Pulpit in the Middle Ages*. It may be said in general that the reader will get a livelier sense of fourteenth-century realities from two or three first-class monographs on particular subjects than from a whole library of general introductions to the period.

The Discarded Image, by C. S. Lewis, provides the best account of the medieval 'world-picture'. Lewis's lively and imaginative account of the structure of the universe (the seven planets, etc.) brings to life many passages in Chaucer's poetry. More specialized information about Chaucer's scientific interests (which were many and various) may be found in W. C. Curry's book, *Chaucer and the Medieval Sciences*. The importance of this work is twofold: it enables one to understand the overtly difficult scientific passages in Chaucer's poetry (and there are many of them—e.g. the account of Arcite's 'lover's malady' in *The Knight's Tale*), and it enables one to see how scientific ideas helped to form his conception of characters and situations, without necessarily leaving much trace of their presence. In the Introduction to Manly's student's edition of *The Canterbury Tales* (see TEXTS above), there is a helpful short account of astronomy and astrology. E. J. Holmyard's Pelican book, *Alchemy*, provides background for *The Canon's Yeoman's Tale*.

The last chapter of G. Leff's Pelican book, *Medieval Thought from Saint Augustine to Ockham*, provides a well-informed introduction to the difficult subject of fourteenth-century philosophy (including the work of Chaucer's 'Bisshop Bradwardyn'). On Chaucer's chief philosophical authority, Boethius, the reader may consult H. R. Patch, *The Tradition of Boethius* (1935).

Some studies in Chaucer's literary backgrounds are mentioned in CRITICAL STUDIES AND COMMENTARY above.

REFERENCES

TEXTS

A. C. Baugh (ed.), *Chaucer's Major Poetry* (New York, 1963; London, 1964).

J. A. W. Bennett (ed.), *The Knight's Tale*, 2nd edn. (London, 1958).

D. S. Brewer (ed.), *The Parlement of Foulys* (London and New York, 1960).

A. C. Cawley (ed.), *Canterbury Tales* (Everyman's Library, London and New York, 1958).

E. T. Donaldson (ed.), *Chaucer's Poetry: an Anthology for the Modern Reader* (New York, 1958).

J. M. Manly (ed.), *Canterbury Tales* (New York and London, 1928).

J. M. Manly and E. Rickert (eds.), *The Text of 'The Canterbury Tales'* (8 vols., Chicago, 1940).

R. A. Pratt (ed.), *Selections from The Tales of Canterbury and Short Poems* (paperback, Boston, 1966).

D. J. Price (ed.), *The Equatorie of the Planetis* (Cambridge, 1955).

F. N. Robinson (ed.), *The Works of Geoffrey Chaucer*, 2nd edn. (Boston and London, 1957).

R. K. Root (ed.), *The Book of Troilus and Criseyde* (Princeton, N.J., 1926; paperback, U.K.).

K. Sisam (ed.), *The Clerkes Tale of Oxenford* (Oxford, 1923).

K. Sisam (ed.), *The Nun's Priest's Tale* (Oxford, 1926).

W. W. Skeat (ed.), *The Complete Works of Geoffrey Chaucer* (6 vols., Oxford, 1894), followed by a seventh vol., *Chaucerian and Other Pieces* (Oxford, 1897).

J. S. P. Tatlock and A. G. Kennedy (eds.), *A Concordance to the Complete Works of Geoffrey Chaucer* (Washington, D.C., 1927).

CRITICAL STUDIES AND COMMENTARY

Matthew Arnold, 'The Study of Poetry', Introduction to T. H. Ward's *The English Poets* (1880); reprinted in *Essays in Criticism, Second Series* (London, 1888).

J. Bédier, *Les Fabliaux*, 2nd edn. (Paris, 1895).

P. E. Beichner, 'Characterization in the *Miller's Tale*', in Schoeck and Taylor (eds.), vol. 1.

J. A. W. Bennett, *'The Parlement of Foules': An Interpretation* (Oxford, 1957).

J. A. W. Bennett, *Chaucer's Book of Fame: An Exposition of 'The House of Fame'* (Oxford, 1968).

D. Bethurum (ed.), *Critical Approaches to Medieval Literature: Selected Papers from the English Institute, 1958–9* (New York, 1960).

William Blake, *A Descriptive Catalogue of Pictures . . .* (1809).

D. S. Brewer (ed.), *Chaucer and Chaucerians: Critical Studies in Middle English Literature* (London, 1966; paperback, U.S.).

B. H. Bronson, *'The Book of the Duchess* Re-opened', *PMLA* lxvii (1952); reprinted in Wagenknecht (ed.).

W. F. Bryan and G. Dempster (eds.), *Sources and Analogues of Chaucer's 'Canterbury Tales'* (Chicago, 1941).

J. A. Burrow (ed.), *Geoffrey Chaucer* (paperback, Harmondsworth, 1969).

G. K. Chesterton, *Chaucer* (London, 1932; paperback, U.K.).

W. Clemen, *Chaucer's Early Poetry*, trans. by C. A. M. Sym (London, 1963; paperback, New York, 1964; paperback, U.K.).

N. Coghill, *Geoffrey Chaucer* (paperback, British Council, London, 1956; paperback, U.S.).

T. W. Craik, *The Comic Tales of Chaucer* (London, 1964; paperbacks, U.K. and U.S.).

J. V. Cunningham, 'The Literary Form of the Prologue to *The Canterbury Tales*', *MP* xlix (1952).

W. C. Curry, *Chaucer and the Medieval Sciences*, 2nd edn. (New York and London, 1960). Chapter on Wife of Bath reprinted by Wagenknecht (ed.).

E. R. Curtius, *European Literature and the Latin Middle Ages*, trans. by W. R. Trask (New York and London, 1953; paperback, U.S.).

E. T. Donaldson, *Speaking of Chaucer* (London, 1970).

E. T. Donaldson, 'Idiom of Popular Poetry in *The Miller's Tale*', in A. S. Downer (ed.), *English Institute Essays, 1950* (New York, 1951); reprinted in *Speaking of Chaucer*.

E. T. Donaldson, 'Chaucer the Pilgrim', *PMLA* lxix (1954); reprinted in Schoeck and Taylor (eds.), vol. i, and in *Speaking of Chaucer*.

John Dryden, Preface to *Fables Ancient and Modern, Translated into Verse from Homer, Ovid, Boccace and Chaucer* (1700).

D. Everett, *Essays on Middle English Literature*, ed. P. M. Kean (Oxford, 1955).

E. Faral, *Les Arts poétiques du XIIe et du XIIIe siècle* (Paris, 1924).

W. Frost, 'An Interpretation of Chaucer's *Knight's Tale*', *RES* xxv (1949); reprinted in Schoeck and Taylor (eds.), vol. i.

W. P. Ker, The Clark Lectures, in Ker, *Form and Style in Poetry*, ed. R. W. Chambers, with an Introduction by J. Buxton (London, 1966).

G. L. Kittredge, *Chaucer and his Poetry* (Cambridge, Mass., 1915).

J. Lawlor, 'The Pattern of Consolation in *The Book of the Duchess*', *Speculum* xxxi (1956); reprinted in Schoeck and Taylor (eds.), vol. ii.

W. W. Lawrence, *Chaucer and 'The Canterbury Tales'* (New York and Oxford, 1950).

C. S. Lewis, *The Allegory of Love* (Oxford, 1936; paperbacks, U.K. and U.S.).

C. S. Lewis, 'What Chaucer Really Did to *Il Filostrato*', *Essays and Studies*, xvii (1932); reprinted in Schoeck and Taylor (eds.), vol. ii.

J. L. Lowes, *Geoffrey Chaucer* (New York and Oxford, 1934).

J. M. Manly, 'Chaucer and the Rhetoricians', *Proceedings of the British Academy*, xii (1926); reprinted in Schoeck and Taylor (eds.), vol. i.

G. Mathew, 'Marriage and Amour Courtois in Late Fourteenth Century England', in *Essays Presented to Charles Williams* (Oxford, 1947).

S. B. Meech, *Design in Chaucer's 'Troilus'* (Syracuse, N.Y., 1959).

J. Mersand, *Chaucer's Romance Vocabulary*, 2nd edn. (New York, 1939).

R. P. Miller, 'Chaucer's Pardoner, the Scriptural Eunuch, and the *Pardoner's Tale*', *Speculum*, xxx (1955); reprinted in Schoeck and Taylor (eds.), vol. i.

S. Moore, *Historical Outlines of English Sounds and Inflections*, revised A. H. Marckwardt (Ann Arbor, Mich., 1951).

C. Muscatine, 'Form, Texture and Meaning in Chaucer's *Knight's Tale*', *PMLA* lxv (1950); reprinted in Wagenknecht (ed.).

C. Muscatine, *Chaucer and the French Tradition* (Berkeley, Calif., 1957; paperbacks, U.S. and U.K.).

R. Neuse, 'The Knight: the First Mover in Chaucer's Human Comedy', *UTQ* xxxi (1961–2).

P. Nykrog, *Les Fabliaux* (Copenhagen, 1957).

R. O. Payne, *The Key of Remembrance: A Study of Chaucer's Poetics* (New Haven, Conn., and London, 1963).

D. W. Robertson, Jr., *Chaucer's London* (paperback, New York, 1968).

D. W. Robertson, Jr., 'Chaucerian Tragedy', *ELH* xix (1952); reprinted in Schoeck and Taylor (eds.), vol. ii.

D. W. Robertson, Jr., *A Preface to Chaucer: Studies in Medieval Perspectives* (Princeton, N.J., 1962; London, 1963; paperback, U.S.).

B. Rowland (ed.), *Companion to Chaucer Studies* (Toronto, 1968—cloth and paperback; paperbacks, U.K. and U.S.).

R. J. Schoeck and J. Taylor (eds.), *Chaucer Criticism*, Volume I: *The Canterbury Tales* (paperback, Notre Dame, Ind., 1960; paperback, U.K.); Volume II: '*Troilus and Criseyde' and the Minor Poems* (paperback, Notre Dame, Ind., 1961; paperback, U.K.).

J. Speirs, *Chaucer the Maker*, 2nd edn. (London, 1960; paperback, U.K.).

C. F. E. Spurgeon, *Five Hundred Years of Chaucer Criticism and Allusion, 1357–1900* (3 vols., Cambridge, 1925).

J. E. Stevens, *Music and Poetry in the Early Tudor Court* (London, 1961).

E. C. Wagenknecht (ed.), *Chaucer: Modern Essays in Criticism* (paperback, New York, 1959; paperback, U.K.).

B. J. Whiting, *Chaucer's Use of Proverbs* (Cambridge, Mass., 1934).

BIOGRAPHIES

D. S. Brewer, *Chaucer in his Time* (London, 1963).

M. Chute, *Geoffrey Chaucer of England* (New York, 1946; paperback, U.S.).

M. M. Crow and C. C. Olson (eds.), *Chaucer Life-Records* (Oxford, 1966).

BIBLIOGRAPHIES

F. W. Bateson (ed.), *The Cambridge Bibliography of English Literature* (4 vols., Cambridge, 1940); supplementary volume, ed. G. Watson (Cambridge, 1957).

W. R. Crawford, *Bibliography of Chaucer, 1954–63* (Seattle, 1967).

R. D. French, *A Chaucer Handbook*, 2nd edn. (New York, 1947).

D. D. Griffith, *Bibliography of Chaucer, 1908–1953* (Seattle, 1955).

E. P. Hammond, *Chaucer: A Bibliographical Manual* (New York, 1908).

BACKGROUND READING

M. Bowden, *A Commentary on the Prologue to 'The Canterbury Tales'*, 2nd edn. (New York and London, 1967).

W. C. Curry, *Chaucer and the Medieval Sciences*. See above, CRITICAL STUDIES.

J. Evans (ed.), *The Flowering of the Middle Ages* (London, 1966).

E. J. Holmyard, *Alchemy* (paperback, Pelican Books, Harmondsworth, 1957; paperback, U.S.).

G. C. Homans, *English Villagers of the Thirteenth Century* (Cambridge, Mass., 1941).

J. Huizinga, *The Waning of the Middle Ages* (London, 1924; paperbacks, U.K. and U.S.).

J. J. Jusserand, *English Wayfaring Life in the Middle Ages*, trans. by L. T. Smith, 3rd edn. (London, 1925; paperbacks, U.K. and U.S.).

G. Leff, *Medieval Thought from Saint Augustine to Ockham* (paperback, Harmondsworth, 1958; paperback, U.S.).

C. S. Lewis, *The Discarded Image* (Cambridge, 1964; paperbacks, U.K. and U.S.).

R. S. Loomis, *A Mirror of Chaucer's World* (Princeton, N.J., 1965).

M. McKisack, *The Fourteenth Century, 1307–1399* (*Oxford Hist. of Eng.*, vol. v, Oxford, 1959).

J. M. Manly, *Some New Light on Chaucer* (New York, 1926).

G. Mathew, *The Court of Richard II* (London, 1968).

G. R. Owst, *Literature and Pulpit in Medieval England*, 2nd edn. (Oxford, 1962).

W. A. Pantin, *The English Church in the Fourteenth Century* (Cambridge, 1955; paperback, U.S.).

H. R. Patch, *The Tradition of Boethius: a Study of his Importance in Medieval Culture* (Oxford, 1935).

E. Rickert, *Chaucer's World* (New York and London, 1948; paperbacks, U.K. and U.S.).

S. L. Thrupp, *The Merchant Class of Medieval London (1300–1500)* (Chicago, 1948; paperback, U.S.).

2 · SPENSER   *c.* 1552–1599

Peter Bayley

TEXTS

Many editions of the complete works, notably by Hughes (1715), Todd (1805: for a century and a half the standard variorum edition), Grosart's incomplete edition of 1882–4 and the Oxford editions by Smith and de Selincourt, and in America by Child (1855) and Dodge (1908), culminated in the great Variorum Spenser of Johns Hopkins University, edited initially by Greenlaw, Osgood, and Padelford. Publication began in 1932 and concluded in 1949. This is in eleven volumes including a Life and an Index. Each volume contains long extracts from critics and commentators, as well as full critical apparatus. It is very much a reference book, and should only be used as such. It is easy to get lost in the commentary, or to find the commentary a barrier rather than a bridge to enjoyment, however much it contributes to understanding.

The three-volume Clarendon Press edition, edited by J. C. Smith (*The Faerie Queene*, 2 vols.), and E. de Selincourt (*Minor Poems*), is the most satisfactory, and indispensable for the textual study of Spenser, but without annotation or glossary. The best single-volume edition, though the text is printed in double columns, is that in the Oxford Standard Authors, by the same editors, using the same text, with a sensible Introduction by de Selincourt, and a good glossary, but again without notes. The American alternative, R. E. N. Dodge's Cambridge Edition, has the advantage of slight annotation. W. L. Renwick's Scholartis Press edition promised to be outstanding, and its introductions and notes remain indispensable, but unfortunately it was never completed.

There are no editions of *The Faerie Queene* separately which are better than these, but there are several editions of separate books. Books I and II, ed. Bayley (O.U.P.)—replacing Kitchin's editions of 1867 and 1887 (Winstanley's editions (C.U.P.) are now over fifty years old, and their emphasis, however scholarly is over-elaborate and out of date; in Book I it is on historical allegory, in Book II on the Aristotelian basis of Spenser's ethical scheme); Book v, ed. A. B. Gough (O.U.P.); Book VI, ed. T. Wolff (Macmillan); and S. P. Zitner's edition of the Mutability Cantos (Nelson). There is also an edition by R. Kellogg and O. Steele of Books I and II, with some selections from the minor poems; it has extensive analysis and commentary.

CRITICAL STUDIES AND COMMENTARY

There were many incidental comments on Spenser, beginning, at the very outset of his writing career, with Webbe's *Discourse of English Poetrie* in 1586 and Sidney's *Apologie for Poetrie*. Sir Kenelm Digby (quoted by H. S. Davies and by P. J. Alpers in their collections of essays) was probably the earliest who could be called a *commentator*. Ben Jonson criticized Spenser's language but 'would have him read for his matter'; Cowley avowed he was made a poet by reading Spenser as a boy; Milton several times declared his admiration of 'our sage and serious poet Spenser'; Dryden censured, in a famous passage, the faulty design and lack of uniformity of *The Faerie Queene*, and 'his obsolete language, and the ill choice of his stanza', but praised his verses—'So numerous, so various, and so harmonious', and said of him 'no man was ever born with a greater genius or had more knowledge to support it'. Spenser was from the beginning acknowledged as a major English poet, the first of the Renaissance, the first since Chaucer.

So his reputation came down into the eighteenth century, and in the first half of that century Spenser's work was the subject of increasing examination and comment. The poets also admired him, and his stanza, if not his style, subject-matter, or 'kind' of poetry, was often imitated. But of his imitators, who included Prior, Shenstone, Thomas Warton, James Beattie, and dozens of lesser poets, only Thomson in *The Castle of Indolence* got anywhere near a true Spenserian effect. In the others one feels the verse always striving for the eighteenth-century trot of couplets rather than Spenser's long, light, and varying stride. And in fact their attempts were not really serious. Although Prior pays tribute to Spenser's 'Height of Imagination', 'Majesty of Expression in describing the Sublime', his knowing how 'to temper those Talents, and sweeten the Description, so as to make it lovely as well as Pompous', his 'agreeable Manner of mixing Morality with [the] Story, and That *Cusiosa Felicitas* in the Choice of . . . Diction', his form, subject-matter, diction, even his stanza, are not at all Spenserian. Shenstone in *The School-Mistress* is only playing with Spenser's stanza and language, although from affection; Beattie takes it too seriously in his unfinished *The Minstrel*, but remains, if a Spenserian at all, a cottage Spenser. Only Thomson, in his far from serious *Castle of*

Indolence, shows that he has really been under Spenser's magic spell. The stanza, language, imagination, and vision of Spenser are unique, inimitable, and his would-be imitators realized it. When they wrote in 'Spenserians', they acknowledged that they were putting on fancy dress. Spenser had almost no serious or useful influence on the writers of the eighteenth century, though they were grateful for his strain of 'fancy' or 'imagination'; he opened casements for them and contributed to their taste and appetite for the past and for nature.

The first half of the eighteenth century produced some of the best Spensarian criticism, wide-ranging, humane, sympathetic, concerned with broad sweeps, not with *minutiae* or particularities. It is surprising, on first reading eighteenth-century critics, to find that many of these arbiters of the Age of Reason responded warmly to the romantic in Spenser, to his multifariousness and the astonishing fertility of his imagination. They enjoyed his work and were at pains to find excuses for the faults they could not help seeing. John Hughes, in the essays contained in his edition of 1715, especially in 'Remarks on the *Fairy Queen*', was the first to write any extended criticism or commentary. He followed some seventeenth-century neo-classical writers, Rymer, Temple, Blackmore, and Dryden, in criticizing the lack of classical unity in *The Faerie Queene*. Some of them had condemned Spenser for being led astray by Ariosto and the Italians instead of following correctly in the steps of Homer and Virgil, but Hughes found a way out of the difficulty. This was to declare that Spenser never intended his epic to conform to the practice of Homer and Virgil, that *The Faerie Queene* should 'be consider'd as a Poem of a particular kind, describing in a Series of Allegorical Adventures or Episodes the most noted Virtues and Vices', and that to compare it with the

Models of Antiquity, wou'd be like drawing a parallel between the *Roman* and the *Gothick* Architecture. In the first there is doubtless a more natural Grandeur and Simplicity; in the latter, we find great Mixtures of Beauty and Barbarism, yet assisted by the Invention of a Variety of inferior Ornaments; and tho the former is more majestick in the whole, the latter may be very surprizing and agreeable in its Parts.

He pays brief tribute to Spenser's serious purpose—'the perpetual Stories of Knights, Giants, Castles, and Enchantments, and all that Train of Legendary Adventures, wou'd indeed appear very trifling, if *Spenser* had not found a way to turn them all into Allegory, or if a less masterly Hand had fill'd up his Draught', but still says 'it is surprizing to observe how much the Strength of the Painting is superior to the Design'.

Hughes, the first editor of Spenser, is the first also to view the poet in breadth, and with that serene and sane enjoyment based on a thorough knowledge of the classical and Italian poets, and a love of literatures, which mark the early commentators. Thomas Warton is more hidebound, and more worried about unity. He is the first to make the mistake of beginning with Spenser's Letter to Ralegh and accepting it as a veracious and helpful guide to the unfinished *Faerie Queene*. But this he did in the same spirit that Spenser probably wrote it—to attempt to show a greater unity in the poem and a more careful plan than in fact existed. Yet he found that 'in reading Spenser if the critic is not satisfied, yet the reader is transported', and in so saying he spoke for most of the good critics of Spenser, Augustan and Romantic alike, and for all good readers of him. He was surprisingly obtuse about the mingling of 'the extravagancies of pagan mythology' and 'the VISIONS of God' (the poet is 'guilty of an impropriety, which, I fear, amounts to an impiety'), but he pointed to an interesting anomaly or inconsistency in the planning when he thought 'the poet might either have established TWELVE KNIGHTS without an ARTHUR, or an ARTHUR without TWELVE KNIGHTS'.

Richard Hurd takes on from Hughes the idea of *The Faerie Queene* as 'not of a classical but Gothic composition', and extends the application of the word Gothic from the structure to the ingredients of the poem, which 'derives it's [*sic*] METHOD, as well as the other characters of it's composition, from the established modes and ideas of chivalry'. The unity of *The Faerie Queene* is 'not the classic Unity . . . but it is an Unity of another Sort, an unity resulting from the respect which a number of related actions have to one common purpose. In other words, It is an unity of *design*, and not of action.'

The eighteenth-century critics, then, were chiefly concerned with the design and unity of *The Faerie Queene*. Sometimes they worried about the verse form, as the sixteenth- and seventeenth-century writers had worried about language and diction. They didn't concern themselves much with the other poems. Their successors, the Romantic and later nineteenth-century critics, were not much interested in the structure of *The Faerie Queene*. They devoted themselves chiefly to discussion of the allegory, and whether or not it was important, to the poetic effects achieved, and to the dream-like imagined world they found in the poem, something that most of them admired and enjoyed above everything else. Sweetness, fancy, charm, richness, grace, enchantment, harmony, luxury, languour, are the nouns, luxuriant, delicious, drowsy, smooth, bewitching, sensuous, are the adjectives they use (Thomas Campbell, Hazlitt, Leigh Hunt) in describing the 'endless grace and dreaming pleasure' of 'honeytongued' Spenser. Coleridge, of course, saw more, and had more to say. Although he wrote no extended or exclusive account of Spenser, his *Lectures on Shakespeare, Miscellanies,* and *Notebooks* all have interesting comments here and there, and it is always worth while using the indexes to pick up Spenser references. His third lecture in 'A Course of Lectures' contains a brief illuminating discussion of allegory, of Spenser's verse and metre, and of some aspects of his poetic powers.

Hazlitt's 'the love of beauty . . . and not of truth, is the moving principle of his mind' is a characteristic claim. It leads on to his equally famous advice to readers who are 'afraid of the allegory'. 'If they do not meddle with the allegory, the allegory will not meddle with them. Without minding it at all, the whole is as plain as a pikestaff.' Leigh Hunt took a similar view: 'let no evil reports of his "allegory" deter you from his acquaintance, for great will be your loss. His allegory itself is but one part allegory, and nine parts beauty and enjoyment.' This attitude occasions the grossest misunderstanding of the poet: 'Spenser,' Leigh Hunt declares, 'is the farthest removed from the ordinary cares and haunts of the world of all the poets that ever wrote, except perhaps Ovid'; and James Russell Lowell, in an extended study of Spenser that is often rewarding, suggests that Spenser perhaps adopted the form of allegory 'only for the reasons that it was in fashion, and put it on as he did his ruff, not because it was becoming, but because it was the only wear'. Two voices at least in the nineteenth century, however, had spoken of Spenser's intellectual strength and ethical intention. Ruskin realized how necessary it was 'to point out the profound divinity and philosophy of our great English poet', and characteristically overdid it, but always with such understanding of the Middle Ages and the Renaissance, and of religious and pictorial symbolism, that the Spenserian references in *The Stones of Venice* are of considerable value. They may be found most easily by using the index. But they are, of course, only incidental illuminations. Edward Dowden, a neglected critic, wrote 'Spenser, the Poet and Teacher', an essay in part-refutation of Lowell and of his Romantic predecessors: he claimed most strongly Spenser's attachment to and concern for 'real life', judged him 'primarily a poet, but while a poet, he also aspires to be what Milton named him—a teacher', and wrote powerfully of poetry that 'aims at something more than to decorate life'. He related Spenser's aims in *The Faerie Queene* to Sidney's *Apologie for Poetry*, especially to the claims that the end or object of the life of man is virtuous action, and that poetry must be accorded a higher place than philosophy or history in its power to lead man to an active virtue. His is a wonderful brief account of the poem. If there were a situation in which someone had time or opportunity to read for only one hour about the poet, I would unhesitatingly commend Dowden, and would feel confident that the reader had been set on the right road.

As in the eighteenth century, the poets of the nineteenth century admired and sometimes imitated Spenser, notably Scott (the 'Vision of Don Roderick'), Byron ('Childe Harold'), Shelley ('The Revolt of Islam', and, most intimately and successfully, 'Adonais', though notice how Shelley's nervous impatient speed overcomes Spenser's calm measure), and Keats ('The Eve of St. Agnes'). But, as Osgood remarked long ago:

... virtually all great poets of whatever manner or school bear witness, conscious or unconscious, to his power. Works consciously imitated from Spenser . . . though numerous enough, represent but a more superficial and less significant phase of it. In subtler and more essential ways Spenser's power exerts itself in Marlowe, Shakespeare, the Fletchers, Jonson, Milton, Dryden, Pope, Gray, Collins, Goldsmith, Chatterton, Burns, Wordsworth, Coleridge, Scott, Shelley, Keats, Tennyson, and a host of minor writers. Here it is seen in the metrical form, there in the fable or matter, now in the style, now in the single phrase or word; it appears even in the transformed aspect of things which Spenser has helped his successors to perceive.

The twentieth century had advanced over a quarter of its way before Spenser really began to come into his own. But the way was early prepared for the host of commentators, by the Oxford English Texts editions of 1909 and 1910, by C. E. Osgood's great *Concordance* of 1915, by H. E. Cory's spacious and gracious study of 1917, and by F. I. Carpenter's *Reference Guide* of 1923. In 1925 appeared W. L. Renwick's *Edmund Spenser*, modestly subtitled 'An Essay on Renaissance Poetry'. I think it remains the soundest and most comprehensive (despite its brevity) of all general books on Spenser. Renwick begins: 'An attempt is made to arrive at some understanding of what a very important poet was trying to do and why he was trying to do that and not something else, of the reasons why his poems have their peculiar form and character.' He firmly places Spenser in relation to the poetic theory and practice of the Renaissance; he establishes the character of *The Faerie Queene* as a deliberate attempt at a Heroic

Poem in English, a poem inspired by both Romance and Epic; he deals succinctly with the minor poems; he has valuable chapters on Style and Language, on Verse and Metre, and on Imitation and Allegory; and he emphasizes Spenser's sense of vocation and of the importance of the poet's calling: 'The poet was responsible for his country as a nursery of poetry; for his native tongue; for the truth and soundness of his doctrine; for the action it prompted and the desires it aroused and the thought it directed. He was responsible to the Giver that his talent was sedulously cultivated and worthily employed.' Renwick wrote before the age of close commentary. He provides background, information, comparison, pointers, suggestions, and illumination in a historical and aesthetic setting. He does not flay the text in the modern way, nor supplant it with his own ideas of what it might (or ought to) mean. Writing before the present mass professionalization of literary scholarship and comment, he could be called old-fashioned. If that term be thought of as at all pejorative, Renwick's classic study, full of knowledge, learning, humility, and piety, should refute it. H. S. V. Jones's *A Spenser Handbook* remains indispensable. It needs revision now, to bring its bibliographies up to date, and to take account in the text of the mass of work on Spenser that has appeared since it was published in 1930, but it is an exemplary and complete guide to the poet and his work. B. E. C. Davis's *Edmund Spenser: a Critical Study* follows and amplifies Renwick, treating Spenser 'first as the New Poet of that English Renaissance which sprang from the vision of classical and medieval culture, secondly as the Poet's Poet, prescribing by example to his successors a grammar of poetry that has withstood the test of time'. It is a careful comprehensive study, which is informative on Spenser's humanism, allegory, philosophical ideas, and technique.

In 1934 perhaps the most sensitive and charming of the books on Spenser appeared, Janet Spens's *Spenser's 'Faerie Queene'*. Very subjective, a little wayward, perhaps over-sensitive and over-ingenious, it is more often persuasive than convincing. Miss Spens puts forward the interesting theory that Spenser originally thought in terms of an eight book, eight-canto epic on the Seven Deadly Sins, and she illuminates not only Spenser but also Shakespeare, Milton, and Wordsworth to whom she makes continual suggestive reference. This is impressionistic interpretation at its very best. C. S. Lewis, in a remarkable chapter in *The Allegory of Love* (1936) gives in just over sixty pages a masterly analysis of the poem and a sparkling account of Italian epic (to which he apportions too exclusive an influence on

The Faerie Queene). One feels he was the best reader of *The Faerie Queene* Spenser ever had, with the possible exception of Dowden. Some of Lewis's remarks, for example on 'the flawless health' of Spenser's imagination—'To read him is to grow in mental health'— might today be considered irrelevant critical comment, but I believe they valuably point to an essential achievement in the work of this great moral poet. I think Lewis is wrong about the significance of the Bower of Bliss, and it is a pity he twists his criticism to make this chapter, the concluding chapter of the book, too patly prove his proposition that the death of the form of allegory and that of the ideal of courtly love coincide in Spenser's *Faerie Queene*. But this is still essential reading. Lewis wrote further on him in his volume of the *Oxford History of English Literature*, and three essays and a review are printed in W. Hooper's collection of Lewis's *Studies in Medieval and Renaissance Literature*. Lewis never, alas, wrote a book on Spenser, but notes of a course of lectures intended ultimately to form a book have been freely edited and supplemented in a personal reconstruction by A. D. S. Fowler.

Edmund Spenser and 'The Faerie Queene' (1948) by Leicester Bradner is a pleasant introduction, placing emphasis on Spenser's pre-occupation with instability and mutability, and suggesting that the poet sees the creative power of love as the way to conquer the destructiveness of time and change. It is unreliable in its assumptions, based on Josephine Bennett, about the order of composition of the books of *The Faerie Queene*. Also unreliable in some details, though suggestive about Spenser's affinities with Italian romance, is J. Arthos's *On the Poetry of Spenser and the Form of Romances*.

An era of detailed commentary and interpretation began in 1960. First came Sister M. Pauline Parker's *The Allegory of 'The Faerie Queene'*, a comprehensive and painstaking study contending that it is 'primarily and fundamentally a Christian poem'. The book's discursive plan makes it long and rather difficult to assimilate, but it is valuable in theological and ethical exposition, and Sister Parker's profession, together with her knowledge and sympathy, has given her unusual insight into and understanding of the moral structure of the poem. Of course, any account from a single definite attitude is likely to be exhaustive in that direction and deficient in considering others, and this book is no exception. It over-emphasizes the didactic as Spenser's overriding impulse and achievement, at the expense of his creative, designing, myth-making, romantic, and patriotic impulses, though she adds an interesting and varied chapter on 'Spenser's Poetic World'. A. C. Hamilton's *The Structure of*

Allegory in 'The Faerie Queene' is a commentary from a quite different angle, directing attention primarily to the literal level of the story and citing the authority of Sidney for what he sees as Spenser's practice.

Instead of treating the narration as a veil to be torn aside for the hidden meaning, we should allow Sidney's art of reading poetry by using the narration 'but as an imaginative ground plot of a profitable invention'. Once we allow this art of reading, then Spenser's allegory need not be read as a complicated puzzle concealing riddles which confuse the reader in labyrinths of error, but as an unfolding drama revealing more and greater significance as it brings the reader full understanding of its complex vision.

It is not an easy book (as this brief quotation may show), it contains some doubtful interpretation, and it is not very systematic, yet it has much sensitive comment and illumination, especially on Spenser's uses of the Psyche and Persephone myths and on his prosody and imagery.

Graham Hough's straightforward *A Preface to 'The Faerie Queene'* is a more reliable and useful guide. His line of sight is from the tradition of romantic epic, acknowledging C. S. Lewis as his master, and his account of the poem's literary ancestry, especially in Ariosto and Tasso, is excellent. So are the seven brief chapters of analysis. Neither a bigot nor a zealot, impervious to critical fashions, he pursues a steady even course through the work, never inclining to over-emphasis on didacticism or allegory or narrative or, indeed, on anything: a refreshingly moderate and sensible view. Perhaps a penalty is that it lacks the *aperçus* and occasional gleams of original understanding or vision that more ambitious and less level-headed books often provide, but to introduce epic Spenser plain there is nothing to beat this.

William Nelson's *The Poetry of Edmund Spenser* is the best general book on Spenser so far. It is not a long book for one that deals with the life, the prose, and all the poetry, and although packed with reference and information, a surprising amount of it original, it is not congested or difficult to read. Nelson acknowledges that he has come to see Spenser as 'a learned moralist and an eloquent, highly sophisticated artist', and perhaps he emphasizes the learning and the meaning a little at the expense of the art. But it is rich in quotation, and in comment on the quotation, and no reader could forget or ignore that Nelson's subject is a major poet, erudite and complex, but also a skilled and highly conscious artist.

Miss Kathleen Williams's *Spenser's 'Faerie Queene': The World of*

Glass is a commentary on the poem from yet another angle. She is convinced of its essential unity, and she begins also from the assumption that 'what *The Faerie Queene* is about, or is made of, is not abstract virtues and vices but human experience', and she accordingly emphasizes the relevance of Spenser's Faerie Land and its inhabitants to actual human experience. She over-emphasizes the human at the expense of the heroic, symbolic, or exemplary in the characters, often seeing them as if they were characters in a novel, and she tends to neglect Spenser's moral and exemplary purpose and his epic and patriotic intention, but this is a perceptive, original, and charming book, full of sensibility and insight.

Latest, biggest, and most expensive is *The Poetry of 'The Faerie Queene'* by P. J. Alpers. It is deliberately non-exclusive, trying to cover many different angles of approach in the course of its own approach, which is along the surface of the poetry. It has learning, insight, and understanding; it is much concerned with recent criticism of Spenser; it is often penetrating on the nature of Spenser's poetry and, in detailed exposition of passages, illuminating; and it has good accounts of the nature of some of Spenser's debts (to Ariosto especially). Alpers draws attention to the 'rhetorical' nature of Spenser's verse and claims that it is best described 'as a developing psychological experience within the reader rather than . . . an action to be observed by him', which points to an obvious but not disabling weakness in the method.

Alpers made a passing comment in which he contrasted C. S. Lewis's 'cosy accounts of Spenser's mind' with 'the severer moral and intellectual structures that characterise the American tradition of Renaissance Studies'. H. Berger's study of Book II, *The Allegorical Temper*, tends to crush Spenser and his poem beneath severe 'moral and intellectual structures'. There is no question of the great contribution American scholarship has made to Spenserian as to almost all other literary studies, but increasingly it tends to become a specialist trade, and one hesitates to recommend too much of this erudite and esoteric commentary to the ordinary student. In details of scholarship and learning, in range of reference, and in involvement in poetic theory, such books as Berger's are impressive, but sometimes the actual thesis is relatively commonplace or unoriginal. Berger's argument is that the first six cantos of Book II emphasize how different Sir Guyon is from an Everyman figure, and the last five reveal 'what they have in common—what all men inherit from Adam's defection', and the turning-point is Guyon's 'faint', which marks the transition in emphasis from Aristotelian to Christian temperance, *pietas* to *amor*, activity to passivity, Chance to Providence. But his investigation of Spenser's methods and of problems associated with them, and perhaps especially his theory of 'Conspicuous irrelevance', are always stimulating.

T. P. Roche's study of Books III and IV, *The Kindly Flame*, is shorter, less stringent, and more conscious of *The Faerie Queene* as an imaginative poem rather than a text for exegesis. He makes illuminating use of iconography, but occasionally goes too far in elaborate interpretation, most obviously in his view of the Masque of Cupid as a dramatization of Amoret's fantasies and sexual fear.

Book V has been explored in two recent books. T. K. Dunseath's *Spenser's Allegory of Justice in Book Five of 'The Faerie Queene'* breaks right away—too drastically I feel—from traditional concern with the historical allegory, placing emphasis on a fairly recent identification of Artegall as a 'type' of Hercules, on Artegall's ultimate achievement of 'internal peace' and on the Renaissance belief that the proper end of justice is peace. It is stimulating but not convincing: it is often difficult to recognize the actual narrative matter of Book V through his learned interpretation. Mrs. J. Aptekar's *Icons of Justice* as learnedly but less ambitiously examines the 'iconography and thematic imagery'. She does not aim at a complete interpretive commentary, wisely confining herself to elucidation, and we may learn much from her not only about Spenser's natural use of emblems but also about his view of justice revealed through them, notably Mercilla's Lion, Britomart's Crocodile and figures of 'Force' and 'Fraud'. D. Cheney has examined—again, to an English eye, with some disproportion of erudition to literary response—Spenser's varied way with pastoral in *The Faerie Queene* in *Spenser's Image of Nature*.

For long there was too much vague looking at and vague writing about *The Faerie Queene*. The (opposite) danger now is that it will be killed by commentary. However, the skilful and erudite commentaries of the last decade that I have discussed all bring new accretions of knowledge; and they emphasize that beneath the surface colour, fancy, and charm lies the formidable and fascinating construction of an intellectual, articulate, and very learned creator. There have been three useful brief introductions to Spenser recently, by Gransden, Sale, and Watson. There remain to be noted a number of other works on special aspects of Spenser or on the background of his thought. Miss Josephine W. Bennett's *The Evolution of 'The Faerie Queene'* is the only book devoted entirely to the composition and development of the poem. Her fascinating and often persuasive detective work sheds light on the poem, but her arguments must for ever remain challengeable. W. J. B. Owen and J. H. Walter have written good articles on the subject.

On the mythological background H. G. Lotspeich's *Classical Mythology in the Poetry of Edmund Spenser* is invaluable, and it includes an excellent essay on Spenser's use of myth. D. Bush's *Mythology and the Renaissance Tradition in English Poetry* has a valuable chapter, and in *Classical Myth and Legend in Renaissance Dictionaries* Starnes and Talbert have a chapter on Spenser's use of the dictionaries. R. Ellrodt's study of *Neoplatonism in the Poetry of Spenser* is a most scholarly investigation, which reduces the emphasis on Spenser's Platonism, and contains much convincing new interpretation. On the historical background, on sixteenth-century ideas about the historicity of Arthur, and on the Trojan and Tudor myth, E. Greenlaw's *Studies in Spenser's Historical Allegory* is the most useful, though many of his claims have been questioned; C. B. Millican's *Spenser and the Table Round* and I. E. Rathborne's *The Meaning of Spenser's Fairyland* explore other aspects of the Elizabethans' interest in the imaginative past. E. C. Wilson's *England's Eliza* is a fascinating account of the idealization of Queen Elizabeth in the poetry of her age, in which of course Spenser figures largely. Pauline Henley has written on *Spenser in Ireland*, and Raymond Jenkins articles on the subject. The best book on *Virgil and Spenser* is that by M. Y. Hughes. A. W. Satterthwaite has analysed Spenser's relationship to Ronsard and du Bellay, and in *Spenser and the Numbers of Time* A. D. S. Fowler has investigated *The Faerie Queene* in terms of its supposed arrangement according to the mystical science of numbers, and has found 'numerological significance in line-, stanza-, canto-, and book-totals; in the location of these units; and even in the numbers of characters mentioned in each episode'. He claims that 'Pythagorean number symbolism, astronomical symbolism based on orbital period figures and on Ptolemaic star catalogue totals, medieval theological number symbolism' all 'are worked into what . . . must be one of the most intricate poetic textures ever devised'. Immense erudition, stimulating conjecture, and valuable iconographic *trouvailles* do not conceal some fiddling with numbers and the basic unlikelihood of such elaborate structures ever forming a consistent part of the total frame of a romantic epic poem. (An article by A. Kent Hieatt on 'Epithalamion'—which has 24 stanzas and 365 long lines—first presented the possibility of Spenser's having used number symbolism: Hieatt's claim, for a comparatively short and very ordered poem, is convincing.)

There are few other books devoted to the minor works of Spenser. Among them J. J. Higginson's *Spenser's 'Shepherds Calendar' in Relation to Contemporary Affairs* is an older and P. E. McLane's *Spenser's 'Shepheardes Calender'* a more recent investigation. Both, especially the latter, have been and will be strenuously challenged on many points. McLane makes many new identifications, some of them convincing, but his claim that the projected marriage of Queen Elizabeth to the Duke of Alençon is the centre of Spenser's concern in 'The Shepheardes Calender' seems over-pitched. H. Stein's *Studies in Spenser's 'Complaints'*, Kent Hieatt's short masterly analysis of 'Epithalamion' in his *Short Time's Endless Monument* and Enid Welsford's detailed study of the 'Fowre Hymnes' and 'Epithalamion', in which she reinvestigates Platonic and neo-Platonic influences, should also be consulted.

Valuable essays on various aspects of Spenser's work, by Martz, Hamilton, Berger, Sherman Hawkins, Kent Hieatt, and Hallett Smith appear in W. Nelson's collection *Form and Convention in the Poetry of Edmund Spenser*; by Saunders, Kathleen Williams, Jenkins, Maxwell, Whitaker, Owen, and Neill in *That Soueraine Light*, edited by W. A. Mueller and D. C. Allen; by Woodhouse, Sale, and M. Craig in P. J. Alpers' selection *Elizabethan Poetry*. J. R. Elliott's selection, *The Prince of Poets, Essays on Edmund Spenser*, has a number of brief extracts from poets' views of Spenser, bits and pieces by Hazlitt, Lowell, Dowden, and Renwick, extracts from Hurd and Upton and from nine more recent critics. It is a useful collection, though all the critical essays have appeared elsewhere in books or in the collections mentioned above as well as in critical journals. It publishes a small portion of Dowden's admirable essay, but, beyond a brief note in the Acknowledgements, it indicates neither that it is only a small portion nor where the extensive cuts have been made. P. J. Alpers' more recent volume in the Penguin Critical Anthologies series is similar, but fuller and has more modern extracts as well as characteristically enthusiastic and discriminating comments by the editor.

Excellent, too, is *Spenser's Critics*, edited by W. R. Mueller, which prints much more of Dowden and marks the cuts, and also includes fairly large portions of Hughes, Spence, Upton, Warton, Hurd, Hazlitt, Lowell, Greenlaw, Renwick, Osgood, Davis, Lewis, and Watkins.

H. S. Davies, in his *The Poets and their Critics* (1943), collected a number of valuable comments on Spenser.

The Variorum Spenser prints extracts from important studies and

articles published up to the time of publication of the appropriate
volume of the series.

There are also valuable sections, chapters, or comments on
Spenser in various other works, which I have listed under BACK-
GROUND READING.

BIOGRAPHIES AND LETTERS

A. C. Judson's 'Life' in the variorum edition supersedes all others.
It is indispensable: very detailed on Spenser's official career and
movements, and with a full bibliography. But it is a work of factual
statement, and, disappointingly, no lively picture emerges of the
poet, his friends and associates, or his age. A little further detail
about Spenser's movements has emerged since Judson's book
appeared in 1945, but nothing significant.

The Bibliographies (below) by Carpenter and Atkinson list
events in Spenser's life and also specify the Calendars of State
Papers and other documents from which our knowledge of the
details of the poet's life as an official has gradually been built up.
They include lists of allusions to him, but there is as yet no Spenser
Allusion Book.

Spenser's exchange of correspondence with his friend Gabriel
Harvey, originally published in 1580 and thought to be part of a
deliberate publicity campaign, is published in The Oxford Standard
Authors *Spenser*, edited by Smith and de Selincourt, and in the
variorum edition. The 'Letter of the Authors expounding his whole
intention . . .' addressed to Sir Walter Ralegh is almost invariably
printed with the text of *The Faerie Queene*.

BIBLIOGRAPHIES

Students of Spenser are lucky in having excellent bibliographies,
which are up-to-date as far as 1960. They are: F. I. Carpenter's
A Reference Guide to Edmund Spenser; D. F. Atkinson's *Edmund Spenser,
a Bibliographical Supplement*; W. F. McNeir's and F. Provost's *Annotated Bibliography of Edmund Spenser, 1937–1960*. The last-named is
differently organized from the others, the number of headings (and
consequently of repetitions of citations of work) having been greatly
reduced. Like its two predecessors, it summarizes the contents of
works, and, like Miss Atkinson's, lists the chief reviews of them.

The bibliographies in the variorum edition will also be found
useful.

Professor Kathleen Williams has admirably surveyed 'The Present

State of Spenser Studies' in the University of Texas Studies in English; it is not simply a bibliography but a critical study of recent work on Spenser, books and outstanding articles.

J. Wurtsbaugh, *Two Centuries of Spenserian Scholarship* (*1609–1805*) is a useful survey.

The Year's Work in English Studies (London, annually) briefly summarizes each year's contribution to English studies, and is the most useful guide to the latest work on Spenser. Other regular bibliographical information will be found in the following: *Abstracts of English Studies*, which analyses the contents of 400 current periodicals; the annual bibliography of the *Publications of the Modern Languages Association of America*, which lists books and articles; and the annual bibliography of contributions to Renaissance scholarship in *Studies in Philology*. A *Spenser Newsletter*, issued from the University of Western Ontario made a modest début in Winter 1970.

BACKGROUND READING

This period and this author demand and reward a knowledge of the historical background, movements, and events; and although I believe *concentration* upon Spenser's possible historical and allegorical reference is usually misdirected, much in his work takes on new significance when the history is known, and some of it is incomprehensible without such knowledge. Liveliest and most engaging of histories, and often the most illuminating too, is A. L. Rowse's. Himself a literary man, he has much of interest on literary figures, not least on Spenser. He is especially valuable on education, religion, and the court, and on Ireland, but on all aspects of Elizabeth's England he is informative, and provocative. Soberer appraisal is to be found in J. B. Black's volume in the *Oxford History of England*, and in J. E. Neale. For the history of the Church of England, W. H. Frere's volume on the period is excellent, though now some details need correction. He was, of course, an Anglo-Catholic, but he understood all shades of opinion and feeling in that catholic Church. The best general book on Puritanism is P. Collinson's account. A. F. S. Pearson's study is still extremely valuable. On Roman Catholicism Meyer remains invaluable, but P. McGrath's more recent *Papists and Puritans under Elizabeth I* is excellent. Valuable reading in first-hand material is to be found in Pollard's collection of Tudor Tracts, selected from Arber's eight-volume *The English Garner*, and in McKerrow's edition of Nashe. G. B. Harrison's *The Elizabethan Journals*, 'being a record of those things most talked of during the years 1591–1603', is an imaginary diary culled from all the most valuable records, and presents a vivid picture of Elizabethan England.

On the background of ideas Hardin Craig and E. M. W. Tillyard remain invaluable, and so is Miss Nugent's anthology *The Thought and Culture of the English Renaissance*.

Louis B. Wright's *Middle-Class Culture in Elizabethan England*, H. S. Bennett's two volumes on *English Books and Readers*, and E. H. Miller's *The Professional Writer in Elizabethan England* are all required reading, rich in fact and detail, and illuminating on other aspects of Elizabethan culture as well. The same is true of P. Sheavyn's *Literary Profession in the Elizabethan Age*, revised by J. W. Saunders, whose own book *The Profession of English Letters* has also much of relevance and value. Both deal at some length with the system of patronage. On that subject John Buxton has written an excellent account of Sir Philip Sidney, his circle, and his relations. Spenser, befriended by Sidney and to some extent by Leicester, making use of every possible connection in his search for patronage, figures fairly prominently here. E. Rosenberg has written a study of *Leicester, Patron of Letters* in which, naturally, Spenser has an even greater part. Articles by Patricia Thomson, and M. C. Bradbrook should also be consulted. John Buxton's book on *Elizabethan Taste* is good; most detailed, of course, is the two-volume *Shakespeare's England*.

Though mentioned under BACKGROUND READING, much of what follows might more properly be called 'foreground reading'. It is all material in article or essay form, concerned with influence upon Spenser, which I have placed in rough categories. Details will be found below, under CRITICAL STUDIES (*c*) *Articles*.

Religious and Biblical Influences: articles by Gang, Hamilton, Landrum, Padelford, and Woodhouse; *Classical:* by De Moss, Harrison, M. Y. Hughes, McPeek, and Padelford; *Medieval:* by Crane, Greenlaw, Durr, and Friedland; *Italian;* by Blanchard, Scott, and Pope; *French*: by Harrison and Renwick; *Elizabethan:* by Gray and Jenkins. On *Language, Diction and Style:* articles by McElderry, Pope, Renwick, Rix, Ward, Wrenn, and Wyld.

REFERENCES

TEXTS

The first three books of *The Faerie Queene* were originally published in 1590. In 1596 appeared a second edition with Books IV–VI added. The Mutability Cantos, or fragmentary Book VII, did not appear until the edition of 1609. The 1590 edition, which seems to have been printed hastily, included a long list of *errata* or 'Faults Escaped in the Print'. The first three books of the 1596 edition were printed from a copy of 1590; many of the 'Faults Escaped' were corrected, but a number of new errors were made. R. E. N. Dodge follows the first editions: *The Faerie Queene* I–III of 1590, III–VI of 1596. J. C. Smith based his edition on that of 1596, incorporating the 'Faults Escaped', and correcting others by a collation of 1590 and 1596.

R. E. N. Dodge (ed.), *Complete Poetical Works of Edmund Spenser* (Boston, 1908).

E. Greenlaw, C. G. Osgood, F. M. Padelford *et al.* (eds.), *The Works of Edmund Spenser, a Variorum Edition* (9 vols., Baltimore, 1949; rev. edn., 1958). *Index*, by C. G. Osgood (1963). *Concordance*, by C. G. Osgood (republished Gloucester, Mass., 1963).

W. L. Renwick (ed.), *The Complete Works of Edmund Spenser* (incomplete; Scholartis Press, London): Vol. I: *The Complaints* (1928); Vol. II: *Daphnaida and other Poems* (1929); Vol. III: *The Shepherd's Calendar* (1930); Vol. IV *A View of the Present State of Ireland* (1934).

J. C. Smith and E. de Selincourt (eds.), *The Poetical Works of Edmund Spenser* (Oxford Standard Authors, London, 1912; paperback, U.S.).

E. de Selincourt (ed.), *Spenser's Minor Poems* (Oxford English Texts, Oxford, 1910).

J. C. Smith (ed.), *Spenser's Faerie Queene* (2 vols., Oxford English Texts, Oxford, 1909).

P. C. Bayley (ed.), *The Faerie Queene, Book I* (Oxford, 1966).

L. Winstanley (ed.), *The Faerie Queene, Book I* (Cambridge, 1915).

P. C. Bayley (ed.), *The Faerie Queene, Book II* (Oxford, 1965).

L. Winstanley (ed.), *The Faerie Queene, Book II* (Cambridge, 1914).

R. Kellogg and O. Steele (eds.), *The Faerie Queene, Books I and II* (paperback, New York, 1965).

A. B. Gough (ed.), *The Faerie Queene, Book V* (Oxford, 1921).

T. Wolff (ed.), *The Faerie Queene, Book VI* (London, 1959).

S. P. Zitner (ed.), *The Faerie Queene, The Mutabilitie Cantos* (London, 1968).

CRITICAL STUDIES AND COMMENTARY
(a) Books
P. J. Alpers, *The Poetry of 'The Faerie Queene'* (Princeton, N.J., 1967).

J. Aptekar, *Icons of Justice: Iconography and Thematic Imagery in Book V of 'The Faerie Queene'* (New York, 1969).

J. Arthos, *On the Poetry of Spenser and the Form of Romances* (London, 1956).

J. W. Bennett, *The Evolution of 'The Faerie Queene'* (Chicago, 1942).

H. Berger, *The Allegorical Temper* (New Haven, Conn., and Oxford, 1957).

L. Bradner, *Edmund Spenser and 'The Faerie Queene'* (Chicago and London, 1948).

D. Bush, *Mythology and the Renaissance Tradition in English Poetry*, rev. edn. (New York, 1963; paperback, U.S.).

D. Cheney, *Spenser's Image of Nature* (New Haven, Conn., 1966).

S. T. Coleridge, *Shakespearian Criticism*, ed. T. M. Raysor, new edn. (2 vols. Everyman's Library, London and New York, 1960); *Miscellaneous Criticism* (London and Cambridge, Mass., 1936).

H. E. Cory, *Edmund Spenser* (repr. New York, 1965).

B. E. C. Davis, *Edmund Spenser* (repr. New York, 1962).

E. Dowden, 'Spenser, the Poet and Teacher', in A. B. Grosart (ed.), *The Complete Works in Verse and Prose of Edmund Spenser* (incomplete; vol. i, privately printed, 1882).

T. K. Dunseath, *Spenser's Allegory of Justice in Book V of 'The Faerie Queene'* (Princeton, N.J., 1968).

R. Ellrodt, *Neoplatonism in the Poetry of Spenser* (Geneva, 1960).

A. D. S. Fowler, *Spenser and the Numbers of Time* (London, 1964).

R. Freeman, *Edmund Spenser* (paperback, British Council, London, 1957; paperback, U.S.).

K. W. Gransden, *A Critical Commentary on Spenser's 'Faerie Queene'* (London, 1969).

E. A. Greenlaw, *Studies in Spenser's Historical Allegory* (Baltimore and London, 1932).

A. C. Hamilton, *The Structure of Allegory in 'The Faerie Queene'* (Oxford, 1961).

W. Hazlitt, *Lectures on the English Poets* (World's Classics, London, 1924; ed. A. R. Waller, Everyman's Library, London, 1910).

P. Henley, *Spenser in Ireland* (Dublin, 1928).

A. K. Hieatt, *Short Time's Endless Monument* (New York, 1960).

J. J. Higginson, *Spenser's 'Shepherds Calendar' in Relation to Contemporary Affairs* (New York, 1912).

G. Hough, *A Preface to 'The Faerie Queene'* (London, 1962; paperback, U.S.).

J. Hughes (ed.), *The Works of Edmund Spenser* (5 vols., London, 1715). See for essays on *The Faerie Queene*, *The Shepheardes Calendar*, etc.

M. Y. Hughes, *Virgil and Spenser* (Berkeley, Calif., 1929).

Leigh Hunt, 'Imagination and Fancy', in L. H. and C. W. Houtchens (eds.), *Literary Criticism* (New York, 1956).

R. Hurd, *Letters on Chivalry and Romance* (London, 1762)., ed. E. J. Morley (London, 1911).

H. S. V. Jones, *A Spenser Handbook* (London, 1947).

C. S. Lewis, *The Allegory of Love* (Oxford, 1936; paperbacks, U.K. and U.S.).

C. S. Lewis, *Studies in Medieval and Renaissance Literature* (Cambridge, 1966).

C. S. Lewis, *Spenser's Images of Life*, ed. A. D. S. Fowler (Cambridge, 1967).

H. G. Lotspeich, *Classical Mythology in the Poetry of Edmund Spenser* (New York, 1965).

J. R. Lowell, *The Writings of James Russell Lowell* (Boston, 1891).

P. E. McLane, *Spenser's 'Shepheardes Calender'* (Notre Dame, Ind., 1961; paperback, U.S.).

C. B. Millican, *Spenser and The Table Round* (Cambridge, Mass., and London, 1969).

W. Nelson, *The Poetry of Edmund Spenser* (New York and London, 1963; paperbacks, U.K. and U.S.).

M. P. Parker, *The Allegory of 'The Faerie Queene'* (Oxford, 1960).

I. E. Rathborne, *The Meaning of Spenser's Fairyland* (repr. New York, 1965).

W. L. Renwick, *Edmund Spenser* (London, 1925).

H. D. Rix, *Rhetoric in Spenser's Poetry* (Pennsylvania State College Studies, No. 7, 1940).

T. P. Roche, *The Kindly Flame* (Princeton, N.J., 1964).

J. Ruskin, *The Stones of Venice*, in *Works*, eds. E. T. Cook and A. Wedderburn, Vols. IX and X (Library edn., London, 1903; 3 vols., Everyman's Library, London, o.p.).

R. Sale, *Reading Spenser* (paperback, New York, 1968).

Sir P. Sidney, *An Apology for Poetry*, ed. G. Shepherd (London, 1965); or *A Defence of Poetry*, ed. J. A. van Dorsten (London, 1966); also in Gregory Smith (ed.), *Elizabethan Critical Essays* (2 vols., Oxford, 1904).

J. Spens, *Spenser's 'Faerie Queene'* (London, 1934).

D. T. Staines and E. W. Talbert, *Classical Myth and Legend in Renaissance Dictionaries* (Chapel Hill, N.C., 1955).

M. Stein, *Studies in Spenser's 'Complaints'* (Oxford, 1934).

H. W. Sugden, *The Grammar of Spenser's 'Faerie Queene'* (Philadelphia, Pa., 1936).

T. Warton, *Observations on 'The Fairy Queen' of Spenser* (London, 1754; enlarged, 1762).

E. Watson, *Spenser* (London, 1967; paperback, U.K.).

W. Webbe, *A Discourse of English Poetrie* (1586; Arber Reprints, London, 1870); also in Gregory Smith (ed.), *Elizabethan Critical Essays*.

E. Welsford, *Spenser: 'Fowre Hymnes' and 'Epithalamion'* (Oxford, 1967).

V. K. Whitaker, *The Religious Basis of Spenser's Thought* (Stanford, Calif., 1950).

34 PETER BAYLEY

K. Williams, *Spenser's 'Faerie Queene': the World of Glass* (London, 1966).

E. C. Wilson, *England's Eliza* (Cambridge, Mass., and London, 1939; repr. 1966).

(b) Collections of Essays or Extracts

P. J. Alpers (ed.), *Elizabethan Poetry: Modern Essays in Criticism* (London, 1967; Oxford Paperbacks 133, 1968; New York, 1967).

P. J. Alpers (ed.), *Edmund Spenser* in Penguin Critical Anthologies (paperback, Harmondsworth, 1969).

H. S. Davies (ed.), *The Poets and their Critics* (paperback, London, 1943); (now reprinted in boards, 2 vols.) has a section on Spenser.

J. R. Elliott (ed.), *The Prince of Poets: Essays on Edmund Spenser* (paperback, New York and London, 1968).

W. R. Mueller and D. C. Allen (eds.), *That Soueraine Light* (Baltimore, 1952).

W. R. Mueller (ed.), *Spenser's Critics* (Syracuse, 1959).

W. Nelson (ed.), *Form and Convention in the Poetry of Edmund Spenser* (New York and London, 1961).

(c) Articles (some refs. are to subsection *(b)* above)

D. C. Allen, 'On Spenser's "Muiopotmos" ', *SP* 53 (1956); 'Three Poems on Eros', *Comparative Literature* 8 (1956).

P. C. Bayley, 'Order, Grace and Courtesy in Spenser's World' in J. J. Lawlor (ed.), *Patterns of Love and Courtesy* (London, 1966).

J. W. Bennett, 'The Theme of Spenser's "Fowre Hymnes" ', *SP* 28 (1931) and 32 (1935).

H. H. Blanchard, 'Spenser and Boiardo', *PMLA* 40 (1925); 'Imitations from Tasso in *The Faerie Queene*', *SP* 22 (1925).

R. S. Crane, 'The Vogue of Guy of Warwick . . .', *PMLA* 30 (1915).

M. Craig, 'The Secret Wit of Spenser's Language', in Alpers (ed.).

W. F. De Moss, 'Spenser's Twelve Moral Virtues "according to Aristotle" ', *MP* 16 (1918).

R. E. N. Dodge, 'Spenser's Imitations from Ariosto', *PMLA* 12 (1897) and 35 (1920).

J. W. Draper, 'Glosses to Spenser's "Shepheardes Calender" ', *JEGP* 18 (1919).

J. Dundas, "Allegory as a Form of Wit', *SR* 11 (1964).

R. A. Durr, 'Spenser's Calendar of Christian Time', *ELH* 24 (1957).

M. Evans, 'Platonic Allegory in *The Faerie Queene*', *RES* N.S. 12 (1961); 'The Fall of Guyon', *ELH* 28 (1961).

L. S. Friedland, 'Spenser as a Fabulist', *Shakespeare Association Bulletin*, 12 (1937).

N. Frye, 'The Structure of Imagery in *The Faerie Queene*', *UTQ* 30 (1961).

T. M. Gang, 'Nature and Grace in *The Faerie Queene*: the Problem Reviewed', *ELH* 26 (1959).

A. H. Gilbert, 'Spenser's Imitations from Ariosto', *PMLA* 34 (1919).

E. A. Greenlaw, 'Chaucer and Spenser', *PMLA* 26 (1911); 'Spenser's Fairy Mythology', *SP* 15 (1918).

A. C. Hamilton, 'The Argument of "The Shepheardes Calender" ', *ELH* 23 (1956).

T. P. Harrison, 'Spenser, Ronsard and Bion', *MLN* 49 (1934); 'Spenser and the Earlier Pastoral Elegy', *Univ. of Texas Studies in English*, 13 (1933).

S. Hawkins, 'Mutabilitie and the Cycle of the Months', in Nelson (ed.) and in J. R. Elliott (ed.).

S. K. Heninger, 'The Implications of Form for "The Shepheardes Calender" ', *SR* 9 (1962).

A. K. Hieatt, 'The Daughters of Horus: Order in the Stanzas of "Epithalamion" ', in Nelson (ed.).

M. Y. Hughes, 'Spenser and the Greek Pastoral Triad', *SP* 20 (1923); 'The Relation of *The Faerie Queene* to the *Nicomachaean Ethics*', *PMLA* 39 (1924).

A. C. Judson, 'Spenser's Theory of Courtesy', *PMLA* 47 (1932).

F. Kermode, 'The Cave of Mammon', in *Elizabethan Poetry* (Stratford-upon-Avon Studies 2, London, 1960); *Spenser and the Allegorists*, Brit. Acad. Warton Lecture (London, 1962); '*The Faerie Queene, I and V*', Bulletin of the John Rylands Library, 47 (1964).

G. M. Landrum, 'Spenser's Use of the Bible and his Alleged Puritanism', *PMLA* 41 (1926).

B. R. McElderry, 'Archaism and Innovation in Spenser's Poetic Diction', *PMLA* 47 (1932).

J. A. S. McPeek, 'The Major Sources of Spenser's "Epithalamion" ', *JEGP* 35 (1936).

L. L. Martz, 'The "Amoretti": "Most Goodly Temperature" ', in Nelson (ed.), and in J. R. Elliott (ed.).

J. C. Maxwell, 'The Truancy of Calidore', *ELH* 19 (1952); also in W. R. Mueller and D. C. Allen (eds.).

T. W. Nadal, 'Spenser's "Daphnaida" and Chaucer's "Book of the Duchess" ', *PMLA* 23 (1908).

Kerby Neill, 'The Degradation of the Red Cross Knight', *ELH* 19 (1952).

W. V. Nestrick, 'The Virtuous Discipline of Gentlemen and Poets', *ELH* 29 (1962).

W. J. B. Owen, ' "In these VII Books Severally Handled and Discoursed" ', *ELH* 19 (1952); also in W. R. Mueller and D. C. Allen (eds.).

W. J. B. Owen, 'Spenser's Letter to Ralegh', *MLR* 45 (1950); 'Spenser's Letter to Ralegh—A Reply', *MLN* 75 (1960); 'The Structure of *The Faerie Queene*', *PMLA* 68 (1953).

F. M. Padelford, 'Aspects of Spenser's Vocabulary' in *Renaissance Studies in Honor of Hardin Craig* (Stanford, Calif., 1941); 'Spenser and the Puritan Propaganda', *MP* 11 (1913); 'Spenser's "Fowre Hymnes", a Resurvey', *SP* 29 (1932); 'Spenser and the Theology of Calvin', *MP* 12 (1914); 'Spenser and the Spirit of Puritanism', *MP* 14 (1916).

W. J. B. Pienaar, 'Edmund Spenser and Jonker van der Noot', *English Studies*, 8 (1926).

E. F. Pope, 'The Critical Background of the Spenserian Stanza', *MP* 24 (1926); 'Renaissance Criticism and the Diction of *The Faerie Queene*', *PMLA* 41 (1926).

W. L. Renwick, 'Mulcaster and Du Bellay', *MLR* 17 (1922); 'The Critical Origins of Spenser's Diction', *MLR* 17 (1922).

R. Sale, 'Spenser's Undramatic Poetry', in Alpers (ed.).

J. W. Saunders, 'The Façade of Morality', in Mueller and Allen (eds.).

J. G. Scott, 'The Sources of Spenser's "Amoretti" ', *MLR* 22 (1927).

Hallett Smith, 'The Use of Conventions in Spenser's Minor Poems', in Nelson (ed.).

R. C. Strong, 'The Popular Celebration of the Accession Day of Queen Elizabeth I', *Journal of the Warburg and Courtauld Institute*, 21 (1958).

J. H. Walter, '*The Faerie Queene*: Alterations and Structure', *MLR* 36 (1941) and 38 (1943).

A. Ward, 'The Language of *The Faerie Queene*', in P. C. Bayley (ed.), *Spenser, 'The Faerie-Queene'*, Book I and Book II.

V. K. Whitaker, 'The Theological Structure of *The Faerie Queene, Book I*', *ELH* 19 (1952), and in Mueller and Allen (eds.).

K. Williams, ' "Eterne in Mutabilitie": The Unified World of *The Faerie Queene*', *ELH* 19 (1952); and in Mueller and Allen (eds.). 'The Present State of Spenser Studies', *University of Texas Studies in English* (Autumn 1965).

A. S. P. Woodhouse, 'Nature and Grace in *The Faerie Queene*', *ELH* 16 (1949), and in Alpers (ed.); see also *ELH* 27 (1960).

C. L. Wrenn, 'On Re-reading Spenser's "Shepheardes Calender" ', *Essays and Studies* (Eng. Assoc.), 29 (1943); reprinted in his *Word and Symbol* (London, 1967).

H. C. Wyld, 'Spenser's Diction and Style in Relation to Those of Later English Poetry', in *A Grammatical Miscellany offered to Otto Jespersen on his Seventieth Birthday* (Copenhagen and London, 1930).

F. A. Yates, 'Elizabeth as Astraea', *Journal of the Warburg and Courtauld Institute* 10 (1947); 'Elizabethan Chivalry: the Romance of the Accession Day Tilts', *Journal of the Warburg and Courtauld Institute* 20 (1957).

S. P. Zitner, 'Spenser's Diction and Classical Precedent', *PQ* 45 (1966).

BIOGRAPHIES AND LETTERS

A. C. Judson, *The Life of Edmund Spenser* in the Variorum edition (Baltimore, 1945).

J. W. Bennett, 'Spenser and Gabriel Harvey's *Letter-Book*', *MP* 29 (1931).

R. Gottfried, 'Spenser as an Historian in Prose', *Transactions of Wisconsin Academy of Sciences, Arts and Letters*, 30 (1937).

M. M. Gray, 'The Influence of Spenser's Irish Experiences on *The Faerie Queene*', *RES* 6 (1930).

G. Harvey, *Letter Book (1573–80)*, ed. E. J. L. Scott (London, 1884); *Works*, ed. Grosart (London, 1884).

R. Heffner, 'Spenser's *View of Ireland*, some Observations', *Modern Language Quarterly*, 3 (1942).

R. Jenkins, 'Spenser and Ireland', in W. R. Mueller and D. C. Allen (eds.).

W. J. B. Owen (see CRITICAL STUDIES).

R. M. Smith, 'The Irish Background of Spenser's *View*', *JEGP* 42 (1943).

BIBLIOGRAPHIES

D. F. Atkinson, *Edmund Spenser: a Bibliographical Supplement* (Baltimore, 1937).

F. I. Carpenter, *A Reference Guide to Edmund Spenser* (Chicago, 1923).

W. F. McNeir and F. Provost, *Annotated Bibliography of Edmund Spenser, 1937–1960* (Pittsburgh and Louvain, 1962).

K. Williams, 'The Present State of Spenser Studies', *University of Texas Studies in English* (Autumn, 1965).

J. Wurtsbaugh, *Two Centuries of Spenserian Scholarship, 1609–1805* (Baltimore, 1936).

Abstracts of English Studies (London, annually).

The Year's Work in English Studies (London, annually).

PMLA, annual bibliographies.

SP annual bibliography (the Renaissance).

BACKGROUND READING

Shakespeare's England (2 vols., Oxford, 1916).

J. W. H. Atkins, *English Literary Criticism: The Renaissance* (London, 1947).

F. W. Bateson, *English Poetry and the English Language* (Oxford, 1934).

H. S. Bennett, *English Books and Readers, 1558–1603* (2 vols., Cambridge, 1965).

J. B. Black, *The Reign of Elizabeth, 1558–1603*, 2nd edn. (Oxford History of England, vol. viii, Oxford, 1959).

M. W. Bloomfield, *The Seven Deadly Sins* (East Lansing, Mich., 1952).

M. C. Bradbrook, 'No Room at the Top: Spenser's Pursuit of Fame', in *Elizabethan Poetry* (Stratford-upon-Avon Studies 2, London, 1960).

M. C. Bradbrook, *Shakespeare and Elizabethan Poetry* (London, 1951; paperback, U.K.).

J. Buxton, *Elizabethan Taste* (London, 1963; paperback, U.K.).

J. Buxton, *Sir Philip Sidney and the English Renaissance* (London, 1954; paperback U.K.).

P. Collinson, *The Elizabethan Puritan Movement* (London, 1967).

H. Craig, *The Enchanted Glass* (Oxford, 1950).

D. Daiches, *A Critical History of English Literature* (2 vols., London and New York, 1960; 4 vols., paperback, U.K.).

M. Evans, *English Poetry in the 16th Century* (London, 1967; paperbacks, U.K. and U.S.).

R. Freeman, *English Emblem Books* (London, 1948).

W. H. Frere, *The English Church in the Reign of Elizabeth and James I* (London, 1904).

N. Frye, *Anatomy of Criticism* (Princeton, N.J., 1957; paperbacks, U.S. and U.K.).

W. W. Greg, *Pastoral Poetry and Pastoral Drama* (London, 1916).

B. Groom, *The Diction of Poetry from Spenser to Bridges* (Toronto, 1955).

G. B. Harrison (ed.), *The Elizabethan Journals* (3 vols., London, 1928–33).

E. Honig, *Dark Conceit* (Evanston, Ill., 1959; paperbacks, U.K. and U.S.).

F. Kermode (ed.), *English Pastoral Poetry from the Beginnings to Marvell* (London, 1952).

J. W. Lever, *The Elizabethan Love Sonnet* (London, 1956; paperbacks, U.K. and U.S.).

C. S. Lewis, *English Literature in the Sixteenth Century* (*O.H.E.L.*, vol. iii, Oxford, 1954).

J. L. Lievsay, *Stefano Guazzo and the English Renaissance, 1575–1675* (Chapel Hill, N.C., 1960).

P. McGrath, *Papists and Puritans under Elizabeth* ; (London, 1967; paperback, U.K.).

R. B. McKerrow (ed.), *Works of Thomas Nashe* (5 vols., London, 1904–10).

A. O. Meyer, *England and The Catholic Church under Queen Elizabeth*, trans. J. R. McKee (London, 1967).

E. H. Miller, *The Professional Writer in Elizabethan England* (Cambridge, Mass., 1959).

J. E. Neale, *Queen Elizabeth I* (London, 1934; paperbacks, U.K. and U.S.).

E. M. Nugent (ed.), *The Thought and Culture of the English Renaissance* (Cambridge, 1956).

A. F. S. Pearson, *Thomas Cartwright and Elizabethan Puritanism* (London, 1925).

A. F. Pollard (ed.) *Tudor Tracts, 1532–1588* (London, 1902).

M. Praz, *The Flaming Heart* (New York, 1954).

E. Rosenberg, *Leicester, Patron of Letters* (New York, 1955).

A. L. Rowse, *The England of Elizabeth* (London, 1951; paperbacks, U.K. and U.S.).

A. L. Rowse, *The Expansion of Elizabethan England* (London, 1955; paperback, U.K.).

A. W. Satterthwaite, *Spenser, Ronsard and Du Bellay* (Princeton, N.J. 1960).

J. W. Saunders, *The Profession of English Letters* (London, 1964).

P. Sheavyn, *The Literary Profession in the Elizabethan Age*, 2nd edn., revised by J. W. Saunders (Manchester and New York, 1967).

Gregory Smith, *Elizabethan Critical Essays* (see CRITICAL STUDIES).

Hallett Smith, *Elizabethan Poetry* (Cambridge, Mass., 1952).

J. E. Spingarn, *Literary Criticism in the Renaissance* (New York, 1899; paperbacks, U.K. and U.S.).

P. Thomson, 'The Literature of Patronage, 1580–1630', *EIC* 2 (1952).

E. M. W. Tillyard, *The Elizabethan World Picture* (London, 1943; paperbacks, U.K. and U.S.).

E. M. W. Tillyard, *The English Epic and Its Background* (London, 1954; paperbacks, U.K. and U.S.).

R. Tuve, *Allegorical Imagery* (Princeton, N.J., 1966).

W. B. C. Watkins, *Shakespeare and Spenser* (Princeton, N.J., 1950; paperbacks, U.K. and U.S.).

E. Wind, *Pagan Mysteries in the Renaissance* (London, 1958; paperbacks, U.K. and U.S.).

L. B. Wright, *Middle-Class Culture in Elizabethan England* (Chapel Hill, N.C., 1935).

3 · DONNE

W. Milgate

IN the eighteen-thirties, while Donne's literary reputation was still at its lowest point, it was possible for Henry Hallam (in his *Introduction to the Literature of Europe*) to remark that from Donne's poetry 'it would perhaps be difficult to select three passages that we should care to read again'. It is not so today, when it is a lean year that does not produce forty contributions to Donne scholarship and criticism (in books, articles, notes, and reviews), and the student will find it necessary to 'read again' in almost all the poetry quite frequently. There are few even minor, and no major, areas of Donne studies which are not controversial; and it certainly cannot be assumed that any selective guide to them will be generally found satisfactory.

TEXTS

Complete unanimity has not yet been achieved, for example, about the details of the text of the poems, nor, in respect of many, about their dates, their groupings, and the authenticity of their titles. Disagreements arise ultimately from the nature of the early texts in which the poems were preserved. Donne himself published only three poems, *The First Anniversary* and an accompanying 'Funeral Elegy' as *An Anatomy of the World* (1611), reprinted with the addition of *The Second Anniversary* ('Of the Progress of the Soul') in 1612. Three others were printed, at least with his knowledge if not all with his entire approval, during his lifetime: the Latin verses to Ben Jonson on *Volpone*, published with the play in 1607; the mock-commendatory poem 'Upon Mr. Coryate's *Crudities*', published in Coryate's book and in the associated *The Odcombian Banquet* in 1611; and the 'Elegy upon Prince Henry', included in Sylvester's *Lachrymae Lachrymarum* (3rd edn.) in 1613. But usually Donne held fast to the attitude of the Renaissance courtier, that the writing of verse was one of the lively accomplishments of a civilized man, who should apologize (as Donne apologized to friends, on the publication of the *Anniversaries*) for having 'descended to print any thing in verse'. None of his poetry (except a verse letter, found in 1970, and two brief Latin epigrams) survives in his own handwriting. Otherwise we must rely on manuscript copies—of a few poems singly, but mainly of collections—derived from transcripts of poems, or, much more frequently, of groups of poems, which Donne allowed to circulate in manuscript; and on the earliest (posthumous) collected editions. Of these last the most important are the first (1633) and second (1635); and the difficulties of the modern editor are increased by our not knowing who supplied the printer's copy or who was responsible for the fairly sophisticated and skilful editing of each volume. All later collected editions of the poems until the eighteen-seventies were based ultimately on that of 1635. The other verses published in Donne's lifetime—three of the *Songs and Sonnets* in song-books, and a few fragments of other poems—were derived from transcripts circulating among lovers of poetry. A. B. Grosart edited the *Complete Poems* in 1872–3, printing them variously from the manuscript, or other, copies which seemed the most attractive; the *Poems* were edited by J. R. Lowell and C. E. Norton in 1895, the basis of the text being the edition of 1633 for the poems it contains, and otherwise the first printed text; and E. K. Chambers made eclectic use of the readings of all seventeenth-century editions, with isolated references to the manuscript copies, in *The Poems of John Donne* (The Muses' Library, 1896; with an Introduction by G. E. B. Saintsbury). Sir Herbert Grierson's *The Poems of John Donne* (1912), however, superseded all previous editions. Grierson showed that the first edition of 1633 derived its contents (apart from poems already in print) from two main manuscripts, belonging to groups of which other examples are extant, and that *a priori* the early editions of the *Poems* had no greater authority than surviving manuscripts—indeed, that the modern editor of Donne is, in respect of most of the poems, in the same position as an editor of any ancient writer, and must examine all the surviving early texts in manuscript and in print and apply to them the techniques of textual criticism worked out by editors of the Bible, of the ancient classical authors, and of Dante. Grierson's edition of the poems was a landmark in English studies; his Introduction and commentary are still of value; and, as the standard text of the *Poems* during half a century of intensive study of Donne, it is needed by students wishing to follow up the references of other scholars and critics. With the aid of manuscripts discovered since 1912, and with a more complete and rigorous application of Grierson's principles, it has been possible to carry the editing of the *Poems* somewhat further: in Helen Gardner's editions of the *Divine Poems* and *The Elegies and the Songs and Sonnets*, in W. Milgate's edition of *The Satires, Epigrams and Verse Letters*, and in a proposed edition of the Epithalamions, *Anniversaries*, and Epicedes for which the last-named editor will be responsible. In the three volumes already pub-lished the nature and authority of the texts printed in 1633 and 1635 are examined: readings that are possibly revisions by Donne himself are isolated; the general Introductions offer new approaches in inter-preting some of the poems; and in the commentary, as elsewhere, cognizance is taken, as far as possible, of scholarship and criticism since Grierson's edition appeared. References to many contributions to Donne studies are given, and the student will find it more profit-able to follow these up, as he requires, at the relevant places than to read them listed here. Some points concerning interpretation, the date and order of the poems, and editorial procedure raised in these editions are still in dispute; nevertheless, when the whole edition is revised it will contain, it is hoped, a generally acceptable standard text.

Meantime the *Anniversaries* have been edited by F. Manley, on sounder lines than those followed by Grierson, with a large and helpful commentary; but the interpretation of the poems offered in the general Introduction has not been generally favoured. An edition of the *Songs and Sonets* by T. Redpath has a text (based on Grierson's, with departures from it) that has come under criticism; but students will find the Introduction and the commentary useful and suggestive, though Redpath would be the last to expect, or to wish, that his interpretations should stifle disagreement. Most other editions of the *Poems* and of selections from them naturally follow Grierson's text, often with some changes. Grierson himself, in a one-volume edition (1929; without commentary and with a new Introduction), made a few changes from his standard text of 1912. In J. Hayward's *Complete Poetry and Selected Prose* (1929; with some revision in successive editions), and in a reprint of Hayward's text, with some additions, edited by C. M. Coffin, a similar procedure was followed. A complete departure from Grierson's principles was, however, made in R. E. Bennett's *Complete Poems*, in which the text was modernized and the poems were printed as nearly as possible in chronological order, and great care was taken with the versifica-tion; but the principles on which its text is established are a rever-sion to Grosart's and are unacceptable; there is no commentary. A more recent one-volume edition of the *Poems* is that of J. T. Shawcross, who has made a more extensive examination of manu-script copies of the poems than other editors, though the extension is into fields—commonplace books and miscellanies—that produce little or no fruit; Shawcross's list of manuscripts in which Donne's poems occur is the most nearly complete so far published, with very few and unimportant omissions (except that indicated by A. MacColl, 'A New Manuscript of Donne's Poems'); his text is reasonably based (being a revision of Grierson's), and a chronological arrangement is attempted; but the commentary is wayward, and the explanatory notes are often enough wrong or misleading. As examples of useful selections may be mentioned H. W. Garrod's *John Donne: Poetry and Prose*; J. Hayward's *John Donne—a Selection from his Poetry*; J. Reeves's *Selected Poems*; and A. L. Clements's *John Donne's Poetry* (which includes reprints of a large number of important critical essays and comments on the poems).

Texts of the prose works are mentioned at the end of the following section.

CRITICAL STUDIES AND COMMENTARY

For the multitude of such studies and comments there are good reasons. In this century Donne's poetry has been found particularly congenial to modern poets and their readers, and criticism has often been biased in favour of its qualities understood—or misunderstood —as exhibiting Donne as a precursor or pattern of modern styles and of modern conflicts and attitudes of mind; his poetry has been at the centre of controversies about the theory of criticism; his shorter poems have proved ideal for 'explication'; and he has occupied a key position in studies of the development of literature and thought in the Renaissance. An elementary introduction to Donne's work is provided in G. Williamson's *Six Metaphysical Poets—a Reader's Guide*; and two brief general studies, both entitled *John Donne*, by K. W. Gransden and F. Kermode, will be found useful. The best account of the poetry is J. B. Leishman's *The Monarch of Wit*, which, though it does not discuss all the poems fully, provides a sound idea of the variety of Donne's work, a generally reliable discussion of his development, and a sensible critique of the basic modern controversies about his poetry. The book also discusses the audience for which Donne wrote, and his contemporary reputation.

About these last topics there is little enough evidence; they may be further studied in A. Alvarez's *The School of Donne* and in A. J. Smith's *Donne and the Metaphysical Poets*. The decline of Donne's reputation is connected with the growth of 'Augustan' taste, and of this there are several useful studies: R. L. Sharp's *From Donne to Dryden*, G. Walton's *Metaphysical to Augustan*, and G. Williamson's *The Proper Wit of Poetry*. By the eighteenth century the outlook and learning of Donne's day had in many respects become outmoded, and he figures mainly as a great but eccentric 'wit' rather than as an

eminent poet; A. H. Nethercot's studies of 'The Reputation of the
Metaphysical Poets' discuss most of the relevant pieces of evidence;
and Dr. Johnson's *Life of Cowley* is still an important document in
Donne criticism. The Romantic period, among its many revivals,
brought a renewed interest in Renaissance literature, and some at
least of Donne's poetry won the admiration of Lamb, De Quincey,
and especially of Coleridge (whose remarks are conveniently
collected in T. M. Raysor's *Coleridge's Miscellaneous Criticism* and
R. F. Brinkley's *Coleridge on the Seventeenth Century*). Until the last two
decades of the nineteenth century, however, the opinion of Donne's
verse commonly resembled that quoted at the beginning of this
chapter, but some uncommon readers like Browning and Patmore
wrote of it with enthusiasm; the two major studies of Donne's
reputation at this period are Kathleen Tillotson's 'Donne's Poetry
in the Nineteenth Century' and J. E. Duncan's *The Revival of
Metaphysical Poetry*; the latter continues the account to recent times.
The editions of the *Poems* by Grosart, Lowell and Norton, Chambers,
and (especially) Grierson, stimulated, and accompanied, an increasing appreciation of the poetry.

It was, however, Grierson's anthology *Metaphysical Lyrics and
Poems of the Seventeenth Century*, with its admirable Introduction (1921)
and T. S. Eliot's famous review of it ('The Metaphysical Poets'),
which established Donne as a major poet and a centre of lively
critical discussion. F. R. Leavis, in *Revaluation* ('The Line of Wit'),
developing Eliot's ideas, placed Donne firmly in the main stream
of English poetry; G. Williamson, in *The Donne Tradition*, applied
(without extending) Eliot's insights with a verve and enthusiasm
which are still attractive; and C. Brooks, in *Modern Poetry and the
Tradition*, and in a striking essay 'The Language of Paradox' (in
The Well-Wrought Urn), further demonstrated the importance of
Donne's verse in the reassessment of the English poetic tradition,
and in the theory of criticism. It was not surprising that critics
concentrated mainly on the aspects of Donne's poetry most akin to
those of modern 'symbolist' verse: the nature and function of the
imagery, and the working of irony and 'tensions' within the poem.
Though some of the works mentioned here might properly be included in BACKGROUND READING below, the criticism of Donne's
lyrics (especially) is inextricably bound up with studies of 'metaphysical' poetry, and others of these will be found rewarding: Sir
Herbert Read's 'The Nature of Metaphysical Poetry', J. Smith's
'On Metaphysical Poetry', E. G. Lewis's 'An Interpretation of
Donne's Elegy "The Dream" ', W. B. Smith's 'What is Metaphysical

Poetry?', J. C. Ransom's study in *The World's Body*, and Helen Gardner's Introduction to her selection, *The Metaphysical Poets*. Needless to say, it is in this area of critical study that conflicts are most hotly waged. Ideas suggested by T. S. Eliot and developed (sometimes beyond his intentions) by others are appraised by L. Unger in *Donne's Poetry and Modern Criticism*, and one of the most influential is criticized in F. Kermode's essay 'The Dissociation of Sensibility'. Theories about the nature of metaphysical poetry are questioned in J. A. Mazzeo's 'Critique of Some Modern Theories of Metaphysical Poetry' by reference to remarks of Renaissance critics upon related topics, although what they say hardly constitutes a definition of the term 'metaphysical'. Attempts to see 'metaphysical poetry' in its historical context have been made by Lu Emily Pearson in *Elizabethan Love Conventions*, by H. W. Wells in *Poetic Imagery*, and most pointedly by Rosemond Tuve in *Elizabethan and Metaphysical Imagery* (in which, despite a valuable emphasis on the necessity of interpreting poems as a whole, the relation of the metaphysical style to the logic of Peter Ramus has been damagingly criticized, and too little allowance is made for Donne's individuality). C. Brooks's approach has been questioned by W. J. Rooney, in ' "The Canonization": The Language of Paradox Reconsidered'.

A student familiar with the works so far listed will perhaps appreciate more fully the import of other discussions of Donne; such preliminary skirmishes are not, however, absolutely necessary, provided that, as everywhere in Donne studies, an alert scepticism is maintained. Mrs. N. J. C. Andreasen's study of the love poetry, *John Donne: Conservative Revolutionary*, raises the basic issues and offers useful guidance, though the classification of the poems (Ovidian, Petrarchan, Platonic) is too rigid and, more or less unintentionally, leads to the perilous suggestion that the three groups are in chronological order; and with the judgements of some of the lyrics the student will probably wish to disagree. A. J. Smith's *John Donne: the Songs and Sonets* will repay discriminating study. Two longer books adopt even more strenuously the method of 'close reading': C. Hunt's *Donne's Poetry* is lively and often penetrating, and adds to the analysis of some of the poems a general assessment of Donne's powers and limitations which has aroused the usual critical dissatisfaction; and D. Louthan's *The Poetry of John Donne* is a rather eccentric and fanciful exercise in the techniques popularized by W. Empson's *Seven Types of Ambiguity*. (In reading Hunt's book, the student will benefit from P. Legouis's dry comments on it in 'Donne, L'Amour et les Critiques'.) More important is A. Stein's

John Donne's Lyrics, which deals thoughtfully with the nature of the eloquence, integrity, and simplicity of the poems—not to everyone's complete satisfaction—and which should be read for its many valuable insights into the poems and into Donne's relation to the poetry and to the critical consciousness of today. Of the many shorter studies of the love poems may be mentioned C. S. Lewis's 'Donne and Love Poetry in the Seventeenth Century', Joan Bennett's reply to it ('The Love Poetry of John Donne'), and her chapter on Donne in *Five Metaphysical Poets*. Some chapters in *From Donne to Marvell*, edited by B. Ford, consider Donne from points of view based on those of F. R. Leavis. A different sort of critical approach is illustrated in D. W. Harding's 'Coherence of Theme in Donne's Poetry'. It is not possible to list here the numerous 'explications' of Donne's poems; but some idea of their range will be obtained from the studies already mentioned, and, for example, from Helen Gardner's 'The Argument about "The Ecstasy" ' and A. B. Chambers's 'Good-friday . . .: The Poem and the Tradition'. Four collections of essays contain much essential material for the student: *A Garland for John Donne*, ed. T. Spencer; *John Donne: a Collection of Critical Essays*, ed. Helen Gardner; *Discussions of John Donne*, ed. F. Kermode; and *Seventeenth-Century English Poetry*, ed. W. R. Keast.

There are several notable studies of material used by Donne in his poetry. E. H. Duncan discusses 'Donne's Alchemical Figures' and D. C. Allen assesses 'John Donne's Knowledge of Renaissance Medicine'. M. A. Rugoff classifies Donne's images in *Donne's Imagery*, but, as in all these studies, the information is only a starting-point for the student, who must consider the poetic use to which Donne puts his material: especially (a matter to which too little consideration has been given) the relation of the type of image to the genre of the poem. It was natural that a trained mind should show signs of the methods by which the activities of the mind are disciplined: hence such studies as 'Logic in the Poetry of John Donne' by Elizabeth L. Wiggins, 'Rhetoric in the Poetry of John Donne' by T. O. Sloan, and a consideration of the relation of Donne's poetry to the practice of formal religious meditation, undertaken independently by Helen Gardner in her edition of the *Divine Poems* and by L. L. Martz in *The Poetry of Meditation* (see, however, S. Archer's sceptical discussion, 'Meditation and the Structure of Donne's "Holy Sonnets" '). That editing Donne is more than usually a matter of critical expertise is shown by G. Williamson's study of many of the cruxes in the poems, 'Textual Difficulties in the Interpretation of Donne's Poetry' (included with other important studies of Donne's work in his *Seventeenth-Century Contexts*). Both editing and properly reading the poetry also depend on an understanding of Donne's handling of metre; and on this topic the student should begin by reading the note prefixed to the commentary in Helen Gardner's editions of the *Divine Poems* and the love poems, and then M. F. Moloney's 'Donne's Metrical Practice' and (with caution) A. Stein's article on 'Donne's Prosody'. The handling of stanza-forms is well treated in P. Legouis's *Donne the Craftsman*, which is essential reading also on Donne's dramatic technique and offers challenging interpretations of some of the lyrics. Of Donne's diction an important study, unfortunately not very accessible, has been made by Z. R. Sullens, *Neologisms in Donne's English Poems*, which shows that in his creative use of English Donne is little, if at all, inferior to Shakespeare. With H. C. Combs, Sullens has also compiled the standard *Concordance to the English Poems*.

Three other topics may also be mentioned here, namely Donne's relations to the tradition of the emblem, to the 'baroque' and to 'Petrarchanism'. Concerning the first J. Lederer in 'John Donne and the Emblematic Practice' and Rosemary Freeman in *English Emblem Books* reach different conclusions. M. Praz, in several studies of Donne (for example, *Studies in Seventeenth-Century Imagery* and *Secentismo e marinismo in Inghilterra*), relates his work both to the emblem and to the baroque; the latter relation has been taken as far as it can usefully go in M. M. Mahood's *Poetry and Humanism*. More recent points of view on Donne's alleged connection with both the tradition of the emblem and the baroque are gathered and developed in D. L. Guss's *John Donne, Petrarchist*, which, in addition to offering valuable discussions of some of the lyrics, corrects some previous notions about Donne's relation to Continental poets and most of what used formerly to be said of his 'anti-Petrarchanism'; the term 'Petrarchanism' is incidentally shown to be too amorphous in meaning to be of much service as a critical tool.

Nobody can read very far in studies of Donne's poetry without noticing how often his prose writings are called upon to interpret or to comment upon the poems. The brief compositions collected as *Juvenilia* (Paradoxes, Problems, Characters, and an Essay) were mostly gathered in two editions in 1633, and, with additions, by the poet's son John in 1652; the standard modern edition is that by G. L. Keynes, but an edition using the surviving manuscript copies is in preparation; a facsimile of the first edition was supervised by R. E. Bennett. A collection of table-talk, 'News from the Very Country' (published, like one of the Characters and the 'Essay of Valour', in various editions of Overbury's *Wife*) was included by the younger John Donne in an edition of the *Poems* in 1650, and has been reprinted in both Hayward's and Coffin's *Complete Poetry and Selected Prose* (see TEXTS). In the *Poems* of 1650 was also included a mock catalogue of books, *Catalogus Librorum Aulicorum*, edited by Evelyn M. Simpson, with a translation by P. Simpson, as *The Courtier's Library*. Probably in 1608 Donne composed his main 'problem', *Biathanatos*, a casuistical discussion of the circumstances in which suicide would not be a sin; it was first printed by Donne's son in 1646, and of this text there is a modern facsimile introduced by J. W. Hebel; a scholarly edition is in preparation. It may have been at any time between about 1608 and 1614 that Donne wrote his *Essays in Divinity*, meditations and prayers arising from the opening verses of Genesis and Exodus (printed by his son in 1651); the standard edition is that of E. M. Simpson. In *Pseudo-Martyr* (1610— never reprinted) Donne defended the King's exaction of the Oath of Allegiance from Roman Catholics. In the following year he published *Conclave Ignati* and an English translation, *Ignatius his Conclave*, a satire on the Jesuits; there are available a facsimile of the English text prepared by C. M. Coffin, a reprint of it in Hayward's (and in Coffin's) *Complete Poetry and Selected Prose*, and a scholarly edition by Fr. T. Healy. *Devotions upon Emergent Occasions*, published in 1624 by Donne, is made up of meditations on his serious illness in 1623; the standard modern edition is that of J. Sparrow. Most important of all Donne's prose works are the 160 *Sermons*, of which he published only a few himself, most of them being printed by his son in three collections (1640, 1649, and 1660); they have been edited in ten volumes by G. R. Potter and E. M. Simpson, with valuable introductions. An attractive anthology, *Donne's Sermons: Selected Passages*, was made by L. Pearsall Smith, though the book gives little idea of the architecture of the sermons from which they are extracted. Most selections from Donne's prose, therefore, include at least one sermon in full, as in the volumes edited by Hayward and Coffin just mentioned, and in the admirable *John Donne: Selected Prose*, chosen by E. M. Simpson.

Mrs. Simpson's *Study of the Prose Works* is the standard work on the subject. The prose has recently, however, attracted much detailed attention, and among the results is Joan Webber's rewarding book *Contrary Music*.

BIOGRAPHIES AND LETTERS

All biographies of Donne are heavily indebted to Izaak Walton's *Life*, which should be read not only as illuminating the poet but also as a work of art in its own right. Otherwise, accounts of Donne's life are superseded by R. C. Bald's *John Donne: A Life*, which collects all the available biographical information; here also will be found a record of scholarly studies of biographical significance. Bald wisely does not attempt a thoroughgoing interpretation of Donne's character, motives, and thought; and, indeed, any such attempt is probably out of the question until all the poet's work is re-edited and many controversies are resolved. Thus, on the question of Donne's 'mediaevalism' there are differences of interpretation, as, for example, between Mary P. Ramsay's *Les Doctrines médiévales chez Donne* and M. F. Moloney's *John Donne: his Flight from Medievalism*. The 'libertine' doctrine is discussed by R. C. Bald in ' "Thou, Nature, art my Goddess": Edmund and Renaissance Scepticism', and Donne's connection with it by L. I. Bredvold, 'The Naturalism of Donne'; concerning the latter the expected controversial note is struck in R. Ornstein's 'Donne, Montaigne, and Natural Law'. A more personal reference is made in S. E. Sprott's 'The Legend of Jack Donne the Libertine' and A. R. Benham's 'The Myth of John Donne the Rake'. C. M. Coffin's *John Donne and the New Philosophy* attempts an account of Donne's intellectual development, particularly with relation to the new science and its implications; amid much of value, however, there are many points at which Coffin's interpretations are disputed. Three useful essays with biographical implications are conveniently collected in one volume—M. Y. Hughes's 'Kidnapping Donne', G. R. Potter's 'John Donne's Discovery of Himself', and J. M. Cline's 'The Poetry of the Mind'; and D. R. Roberts's 'The Death-Wish of John Donne' considers a further aspect of Donne's cast of mind. A different line of inquiry is undertaken in E. G. Lewis's 'The Question of Toleration in the Works of John Donne', R. W. Battenhouse's 'The Grounds of Religious Toleration in the Thought of John Donne', and M. F. Moloney's 'John Donne and the Jesuits'. Of Donne's religious thought and experience several helpful discussions may be consulted: L. I. Bredvold's 'The Religious Thought of Donne', Helen C. White's *The Metaphysical Poets* and her article 'John Donne and the Psychology of Spiritual Effort', and Sister M. Geraldine's 'John Donne and the Mindes Indeavours'; while W. R. Mueller, in *John Donne: Preacher*, makes a sound study of Donne's mature religious outlook and of his methods and emphases in the pulpit. Students weak in theological knowledge will find I. Husain's *The Dogmatic and Mystical Theology of John Donne* of assistance, but they should be warned that the book makes Donne appear merely as an exact and passive supporter of established doctrine. In fact, he cannot be narrowly categorized as a member of any theological 'party' (as has been shown, for example, in two studies, E. R. Daniel's 'Reconciliation, Covenant and Election' and M. E. Heatherington's ' "Decency" and "Zeal" in the Sermons of John Donne'), for his free-ranging intellect and sympathies made him a genuinely creative force in the tradition of the English Church; it was not without reason that A. Jessopp's biographical study, *John Donne*, appeared in the 'Leaders of Religion' series. The student seeking a sound point of reference in the controversies about Donne's outlook and character will, however, find none better than the opening chapters of Mrs. Simpson's *Study of the Prose Works* (see under CRITICAL STUDIES, (*b*) *Prose*, below) and Sir Herbert Grierson's essay 'Donne and the "Via Media" '.

Donne's letters, of which a considerable number survive and of which some are very fine, are invaluable in the study of his life and thought. His son published a large proportion of them in *Letters to Several Persons of Honour*, 1651 (edited in this century by C. E. Merrill), and *A Collection of Letters made by Sir Tobie Mathews*, 1660. These, with others derived from elsewhere, were collected by Sir Edmund Gosse in his *Life and Letters of John Donne*. Gosse's book was for seventy years the standard life, and later studies have been bedevilled by his biographical interpretation of the love poems and by his errors. Nevertheless, although his text of the letters is not very accurate, Gosse's work in dating many of them and identifying the addressees was performed with considerable skill and learning, and the student will find his collection of letters indispensable, since there is no complete scholarly modern edition. For information as to where the letters not included in Gosse's book can be found, for current opinion about the dating, addressees, and text where Gosse is in error, and for references to scholarly studies of the letters, R. C. Bald's biography should be consulted.

BIBLIOGRAPHIES

From references and reading lists in many of the works so far mentioned the student will have been able to compile a formidable assemblage of works of criticism and commentary. In the standard *Bibliography* by Sir Geoffrey Keynes, as well as accounts of the early and later editions of Donne's work, a list of the surviving books once owned by him, and a collection of most of the early references to him, will be found a fairly full guide to criticism and scholarship until about 1957. This must be supplemented by the following: T. Spencer and M. Van Doren, *Studies in Metaphysical Poetry*, continued in L. E. Berry's *Bibliography of Studies in Metaphysical Poetry, 1939–1960;* W. White's *John Donne since 1900: a Bibliography of Periodical Articles* and his 'Sir Geoffrey Keynes's Bibliography . . . a Review, with Addenda'; and M. Y. Hughes's survey of recent criticism in *Contemporary Literary Scholarship* edited by L. Leary. For more recent Donne studies it is necessary to consult the annual surveys: in *The Year's Work in English Studies*, 'Recent Literature of the Renaissance' in *Studies in Philology*, bibliographies of The Modern Humanities Research Association (U.S.A.); in *Publications of the Modern Language Association of America*; in *Studies in English Literature*; in *Renaissance News* (since 1967, *Renaissance Quarterly*); and in reports at shorter intervals in *Abstracts of English Studies* and *Seventeenth-Century News*.

BACKGROUND READING

The study of the cultural and social milieu in which Donne's work was written could most profitably begin with D. Bush's *English Literature in the Earlier Seventeenth Century*, in which a general survey is supported by excellent bibliographies. A select bibliography will also be found in *English Prose, 1600–1660* (including selections from Donne), edited by V. Harris and I. Husain. The commonly shared ideas about the universe are studied, in relation to literature, in C. S. Lewis's *The Discarded Image*, and E. M. W. Tillyard's *The Elizabethan World Picture* (given a more specific reference in Tillyard's *The Metaphysicals and Milton*). Valuable guidance to studies of the thought of Donne's age will be found in H. J. C. Grierson's *Cross Currents in English Literature*, H. Craig's *The Enchanted Glass*, and B. Willey's *The Seventeenth-Century Background*. It is important to remember that Donne began writing his characteristic poetry during the reign of Elizabeth I, before the best work of Spenser and other 'Elizabethan' poets was finished; hence such an admirable study as H. Smith's *Elizabethan Poetry* is suggested as background reading. The changes from Elizabethan attitudes during Donne's lifetime are well studied in F. P. Wilson's *Elizabethan and Jacobean*, P. Cruttwell's *The Shakespearean Moment*, and S. L. Bethell's *The Cultural Revolution of the Seventeenth Century*; and the changes in social pressures upon authors are suggestively treated by L. C. Knights in his essay 'On the Social Background of Metaphysical Poetry' and by J. Danby in *Poets on Fortune's Hill*. Of more specialized studies, the student of Donne will profit by knowing the survey by J. Bamborough of Renaissance psychology in *The Little World of Man*, and L. Babb's account of *The Elizabethan Malady* (sc. melancholy); and V. Harris's

All Coherence Gone gives a full treatment of the controversy about the decay of the world, to which Donne makes extended reference in *The First Anniversary*. Two books by Marjorie Nicolson are helpful in understanding his attitude to the new developments in science: *The Breaking of the Circle* (which contains an interpretation of the *Anniversaries* that has not won much acceptance), and *Science and Imagination*. Donne's connection with sceptical thought in the seventeenth century is illuminated in Margaret Wiley's *The Subtle Knot*, and his conception of the relation of faith to reason may be studied with the aid of D. C. Allen's *The Legend of Noah*. His religious writing is placed in its context by Helen C. White in *English Devotional Literature*, and his sermons are related to the traditions of preaching in W. F. Mitchell's *English Pulpit Oratory from Andrewes to Tillotson*. Most of Donne's statements about the writing of poetry are assembled, along with the theories of other seventeenth-century poets, in L. Jonas's *The Divine Science*. The most recent account of the poetic tradition inaugurated in England by Donne and of its development during the seventeenth century is E. Miner's *The Metaphysical Mode from Donne to Cowley*. Finally, the student is urged to study the impressive volumes of R. Ellrodt, of which the title, *L'Inspiration personelle et l'esprit du temps chez les poètes métaphysiques anglais* points to a question that must always be in the mind of the reader of 'background' studies.

REFERENCES

TEXTS

R. E. Bennett (ed.), *The Complete Poems of John Donne* (Chicago, 1942).

A. L. Clements (ed.), *John Donne's Poetry: Authoritative Texts, Criticism* (paperback, New York, 1966).

C. M. Coffin (ed.), *Donne: Complete Poetry and Selected Prose* (New York, 1952).

H. Gardner (ed.), *John Donne: The Divine Poems* (Oxford English texts, Oxford, 1952).

H. Gardner (ed.), *John Donne: The Elegies and the Songs and Sonnets* (Oxford English texts, Oxford, 1965).

H. W. Garrod (ed.), *John Donne: Poetry and Prose, with Izaac Walton's Life* [1640] *and Selected Criticism* (Oxford, 1946).

H. J. C. Grierson (ed.). *The Poems of John Donne* (Oxford English texts, Oxford, 1912).

H. J. C. Grierson (ed.), *The Poems of John Donne* (Oxford, 1929; Oxford Standard Authors, London, 1933).

J. Hayward (ed.), *Donne: Complete Poetry and Selected Prose*, rev. edn. (London, 1962).

J. Hayward (ed.), *John Donne: Selected Poems* (paperback, Harmondsworth, 1950; paperback, U.S.).

A. MacColl, 'A New Manuscript of Donne's Poems', *RES* N.S. xix (1968).

F. Manley (ed.), *John Donne: the Anniversaries* (Baltimore, 1968).

W. Milgate (ed.), *John Donne: The Satires, Epigrams and Verse Letters* (Oxford English texts, Oxford, 1967).

T. Redpath (ed.), *The Songs and Sonets of John Donne* (London, 1956; paperbacks, U.K. and U.S.).

J. Reeves (ed.), *Selected Poems of John Donne* (London, 1952; paperback, U.K.).

J. T. Shawcross (ed.), *The Complete Poetry of John Donne* (paperback, New York, 1967).

CRITICAL STUDIES AND COMMENTARY

(a) Poetry

D. C. Allen, 'John Donne's Knowledge of Renaissance Medicine', *JEGP* xlii (1943).

A. Alvarez, *The School of Donne* (London and New York, 1961; paperbacks, U.K. and U.S.).

N. J. C. Andreasen, *John Donne: Conservative Revolutionary* (Princeton, N.J., 1967).

S. Archer, 'Meditation and the Structure of Donne's "Holy Sonnets"', *ELH* xxviii (1961).

J. Bennett, *Five Metaphysical Poets*, rev. edn. of *Four Metaphysical Poets* (2nd edn. 1953), with a new chapter (paperback, Cambridge and New York, 1964).

J. Bennett, *Four Metaphysical Poets*, with added anthology (paperback, U.S.).

J. Bennett, 'The Love Poetry of John Donne', in *Seventeenth-Century Studies Presented to Sir Herbert Grierson* (Oxford, 1938).

R. F. Brinkley (ed.), *Coleridge on the Seventeenth Century* (Durham, N.C., 1955).

C. Brooks, *Modern Poetry and the Tradition* (Chapel Hill, N.C., 1939; London, 1948; paperbacks, U.K. and U.S.).

C. Brooks, *The Well-Wrought Urn*, rev. edn. (New York, 1968; paperbacks, U.K. and U.S.).

A. B. Chambers, '"Goodfriday, 1613. Riding Westward": The Poem and the Tradition', *ELH* xxviii (1961).

H. C. Combs and Z. R. Sullens, *A Concordance to the English Poems of John Donne* (Chicago, 1940).

E. H. Duncan, 'Donne's Alchemical Figures', *ELH* ix (1942).

J. E. Duncan, *The Revival of Metaphysical Poetry* (Minneapolis, Minn., 1959).

T. S. Eliot, 'The Metaphysical Poets', in *Selected Essays* (New York, 1932); 3rd edn. (London, 1958).

W. Empson, *Seven Types of Ambiguity*, 3rd edn. (London, 1956; paperback, U.S.).

B. Ford (ed.), *From Donne to Marvell* (*Pelican Guide to English Literature* iii; paperback, Harmondsworth and New York, 1956).

R. Freeman, *English Emblem Books* (London, 1948).

H. Gardner (ed.), *John Donne: a Collection of Critical Essays* (paperback, Englewood Cliffs, N.J., 1962; paperback, U.K.).

H. Gardner, 'The Argument about "The Ecstasy" ', in *Elizabethan and Jacobean Studies Presented to F. P. Wilson* (Oxford, 1969).

H. Gardner (ed.), *The Metaphysical Poets*, rev. edn. (paperbacks, Harmondsworth and New York, 1966); 2nd edn. (Oxford, 1967).

K. W. Gransden, *John Donne* (London, 1954).

H. J. C. Grierson (ed.), *Metaphysical Lyrics and Poems of the Seventeenth Century* (Oxford, 1921; paperbacks, U.K. and U.S.). Introduction reprinted in *The Background of English Literature* (London, 1925; paperback, U.K.).

D. L. Guss, *John Donne, Petrarchist: Italianate Conceits and Love Theory in the "Songs and Sonets"* (Detroit, 1966).

D. W. Harding, 'Coherence of theme in Donne's Poetry', *Kenyon Review*, xiii (1951).

C. Hunt, *Donne's Poetry: Essays in Literary Analysis* (New Haven, Conn., 1954).

S. Johnson, *The Life of Cowley* (1779; many modern reprints).

W. R. Keast (ed.), *Seventeenth-Century English Poetry: Modern Essays in Criticism* (paperback, New York, 1962; paperback, U.K.).

F. Kermode (ed.), *Discussions of John Donne* (paperbacks, Lexington, Mass., and London, 1962).

F. Kermode, *John Donne* (paperback, British Council, London, 1957; paperback, U.S.).

F. Kermode, 'The Dissociation of Sensibility', *Kenyon Review*, xix (1957).

F. R. Leavis, 'The Line of Wit', in *Revaluation* (London, 1936; paperbacks, U.K. and U.S.).

J. Lederer, 'John Donne and the Emblematic Practice', *RES* xxii (1946).

P. Legouis, 'Donne, L'Amour et les critiques', *Études Anglaises* x (1957).

P. Legouis, *Donne the Craftsman* (Paris, 1928; New York, 1962).

J. B. Leishman, *The Monarch of Wit*, rev. edn. (London, 1965; paperbacks, U.K. and U.S.).

C. S. Lewis, 'Donne and Love Poetry in the Seventeenth Century', in *Seventeenth-Century Studies Presented to Sir Herbert Grierson* (Oxford, 1938).

E. G. Lewis, 'An Interpretation of Donne's Elegy "The Dream"', *MLR* xxix (1934).

D. Louthan, *The Poetry of John Donne: A Study in Explication* (New York, 1951).

M. M. Mahood, *Poetry and Humanism* (London, 1950).

L. L. Martz, *The Poetry of Meditation*, 2nd edn. (New Haven, Conn., 1962; paperbacks, U.K. and U.S.).

J. A. Mazzeo, 'A Critique of Some Modern Theories of Metaphysical Poetry', *MP* l (1952).

M. F. Moloney, 'Donne's Metrical Practice', *PMLA* lxv (1950).

A. H. Nethercot, 'The Reputation of John Donne as Metrist', *SR* xxx (1922).

A. H. Nethercot, 'The Reputation of Native versus Foreign "Metaphysical" Poets in England', *MLR* xxv (1930).

A. H. Nethercot, 'The Reputation of the Metaphysical Poets during the Age of Johnson', *SP* xxii (1925).

A. H. Nethercot, 'The Reputation of the Metaphysical Poets during the Age of Pope', *PQ* iv (1925).

A. H. Nethercot, 'The Reputation of the "Metaphysical Poets" during the Seventeenth Century', *JEGP* xxiii (1924).

A. H. Nethercot, 'The Term "Metaphysical Poets" before Johnson', *MLN* xxxvii (1922).

L. E. Pearson, *Elizabethan Love Conventions* (Berkeley, Calif., 1933).

M. Praz, *Secentismo e marinismo in Inghilterra* (Florence, 1925). Part I incorporated in *John Donne* (Turin, 1958).

M. Praz, *Studies in Seventeenth-Century Imagery*, 2nd edn. (Rome, 1964).

J. C. Ransom, *The World's Body* (New York and London, 1938; paperback, U.S.).

T. M. Raysor (ed.), *Coleridge's Miscellaneous Criticism* (London and Cambridge, Mass., 1936).

H. Read, 'The Nature of Metaphysical Poetry', *The Criterion*, i (1923); reprinted in *Collected Essays in Literary Criticism*, 2nd edn. (London, 1951; paperback, U.K.).

H. Read, *The Nature of Literature* (New York, 1956).

W. J. Rooney, ' "The Canonization": The Language of Paradox Reconsidered', *ELH* xxiii (1956).

M. A. Rugoff, *Donne's Imagery: a Study in Creative Sources* (New York, 1962).

G. E. B. Saintsbury, 'The Poetry of Donne', Introduction to E. K. Chambers's edition of the *Poems* (1896); in *Prefaces and Essays* (London, 1933).

R. L. Sharp, *From Donne to Dryden: The Revolt against Metaphysical Poetry* (Chapel Hill, N.C., 1940).

T. O. Sloan, 'The Rhetoric in the Poetry of John Donne', *SEL* iii (1963).

A. J. Smith, *Donne and the Metaphysical Poets: the Critical Heritage* (London, 1968).

A. J. Smith, *John Donne: The Songs and Sonets* (London, 1964; paperback, U.S.).

J. Smith, 'On Metaphysical Poetry', *Scrutiny*, ii (1933); reprinted in *Determinations*, ed. F. R. Leavis (London, 1934).

W. B. Smith, 'What is Metaphysical Poetry?', *SR* xlii (1934).

T. Spencer (ed.), *A Garland for John Donne* (Gloucester, Mass., 1931 and 1958).

A. Stein, 'Donne's Prosody', *PMLA* lix (1944).

A. Stein, *John Donne's Lyrics: the Eloquence of Action* (Minneapolis, Minn., and London, 1962).

Z. R. Sullens, *Neologisms in Donne's English Poems* (Rome, 1964).

K. Tillotson, 'Donne's Poetry in the Nineteenth Century', in *Elizabethan and Jacobean Studies Presented to F. P. Wilson* (Oxford, 1959; reissued 1969).

R. Tuve, *Elizabethan and Metaphysical Imagery* (Chicago, 1947; paperbacks, U.K. and U.S.).

L. Unger, *Donne's Poetry and Modern Criticism* (Chicago, 1950); reprinted in *The Man in the Name* (Minneapolis, Minn., 1956).

G. Walton, *Metaphysical to Augustan* (Cambridge, 1955).

H. W. Wells, *Poetic Imagery Illustrated from Elizabethan Literature* (Columbia, Mo., 1924).

E. L. Wiggins, 'Logic in the Poetry of John Donne', *SP* xlii (1945).

G. Williamson, *Seventeenth-Century Contexts* (London, 1960; Chicago, 1961).

G. Williamson, *Six Metaphysical Poets: a Reader's Guide* (New York, 1967; paperback, U.S.). Also *The Metaphysical Poets* (Reader's Guides, London, 1968; paperback, U.K.).

G. Williamson, *The Donne Tradition* (Cambridge, Mass., 1930; paperback, U.S.).

G. Williamson, *The Proper Wit of Poetry* (Chicago and London, 1961).

(b) Prose

R. E. Bennett (ed.), [Donne] *Iuvenilia, or Certain Paradoxes and Problems* (Facsimile Text Society, New York, 1936).

C. M. Coffin (ed.), [Donne] *Ignatius his Conclave* (Facsimile Text Society, New York, 1941).

J. Donne, *Pseudo-Martyr* (1610).

John Donne: Selected Prose, chosen by E. M. Simpson and ed. H. Gardner and T. Healy (Oxford, 1967).

T. Healy (ed.), [Donne] *Ignatius his Conclave* [English and Latin Texts] (Oxford, 1969).

J. W. Hebel (ed.), [Donne] *Biathanatos* (Facsimile Text Society, New York, 1930).

G. L. Keynes (ed.), [Donne] *Paradoxes and Problems* (London, 1923).

G. R. Potter and E. M. Simpson (eds.), *The Sermons of John Donne* 10 vols. (Berkeley, Cal., 1953–62).

E. M. Simpson, *A Study of the Prose Works of John Donne*, 2nd edn. (Oxford, 1948).

E. M. Simpson (ed.), [Donne] *Essays in Divinity* (Oxford, 1952).

E. M. Simpson (ed.), [Donne] *The Courtier's Library* (London, 1930).

L. P. Smith, *Donne's Sermons: Selected Passages* (Oxford, 1919).

J. Sparrow (ed.), [Donne] *Devotions upon Emergent Occasions* (London, 1923).

J. Webber, *Contrary Music: the Prose Style of John Donne* (Madison, Wis., 1963).

BIOGRAPHIES AND LETTERS

R. C. Bald, *John Donne: a Life* (Oxford, 1970).

R. C. Bald, ' "Thou, Nature, art my Goddess": Edmund and Renaissance Scepticism', in *J. Q. Adams Memorial Studies*, ed. J. G. McManaway *et al.* (Ithaca, N.Y., 1948).

R. W. Battenhouse, 'The Grounds of Religious Toleration in the Thought of John Donne', *Church History* xi (1942).

A. R. Benham, 'The Myth of John Donne the Rake', *PQ* xxiii; and in *Renaissance Studies in Honor of Hardin Craig* (Stanford, Calif., 1941).

L. I. Bredvold, 'The Naturalism of Donne in Relation to some Renaissance Traditions', *JEGP* xxii (1923).

L. I. Bredvold, 'The Religious Thought of Donne in Relation to Medieval and Later Traditions', in *Studies in Shakespeare, Milton and Donne* (Univ. of Michigan Pubns., i, New York, 1964).

J. M. Cline, 'The Poetry of the Mind', in *Essays in Criticism: Second Series* (Univ. of California Pubns. in English, iv, Berkeley, Calif., 1934).

C. M. Coffin, *John Donne and the New Philosophy* (New York, 1937 and 1958).

E. R. Daniel, 'Reconciliation, Covenant and Election: a Study in the Theology of John Donne', *Anglican Theological Review*, xlviii (1966).

Sr. M. Geraldine, 'John Donne and the Mindes Indeavours', *SEL* v (1965).

E. Gosse, *The Life and Letters of John Donne* (2 vols., London, 1899; repr. Gloucester, Mass., 1959).

H. J. C. Grierson, 'Donne and the "Via Media" ', *MLR* xliii (1948); reprinted in *Criticism and Creation* (London, 1959).

M. E. Heatherington, ' "Decency" and "Zeal" in the Sermons of John Donne', *Texas Studies in Literature and Language* ix (1967).

M. Y. Hughes, 'Kidnapping Donne', in *Essays in Criticism: Second Series* (see above, J. M. Cline).

Itrat Husain, *The Dogmatic and Mystical Theology of John Donne* (London, 1938).

A. Jessopp, *John Donne* (London, 1897).

E. G. Lewis, 'The Question of Toleration in the Works of John Donne', *MLR* xxxiii (1938).

C. E. Merrill (ed.), *Letters to Severall Persons of Honour* (New York, 1910).

M. F. Moloney, 'John Donne and the Jesuits', *Modern Language Quarterly*, viii (1947).

M. F. Moloney, *John Donne: His Flight from Medievalism* (Uzbana, Ill., 1944; repr. New York, 1965).

W. R. Mueller, *John Donne: Preacher* (Princeton, N.J., 1962).

R. Ornstein, 'Donne, Montaigne and Natural Law', *JEGP* lv (1956).

G. R. Potter, 'John Donne's Discovery of Himself', in *Essays in Criticism: Second Series* (see above, J. M. Cline).

M. P. Ramsay, *Les Doctrines médiévales chez Donne*, 2nd edn. (Oxford, 1924).

D. R. Roberts, 'The Death-Wish of John Donne', *PMLA* lxii (1947).

S. E. Sprott, 'The Legend of Jack Donne the Libertine', *UTQ* xix (1950).

I. Walton, *Life of Donne* (edn. of 1675), in, e.g., Walton's *Lives* (World's Classics, London, 1927).

H. C. White, 'John Donne and the Psychology of Spiritual Effort', in *The Seventeenth Century: Bacon to Pope*, by R. F. Jones *et al.* (Stanford, Calif., 1951).

H. C. White, *The Metaphysical Poets* (New York, 1956; paperbacks, U.K. and U.S.).

BIBLIOGRAPHIES

L. E. Berry, *A Bibliography of Studies in Metaphysical Poetry, 1939–1960* (Madison, Wis., 1964).

G. L. Keynes, *A Bibliography of John Donne*, 3rd edn. (Cambridge, 1958).

L. Leary (ed.), *Contemporary Literary Scholarship* (New York, 1958).

T. Spencer and M. Van Doren, *Studies in Metaphysical Poetry: Two Essays and a Bibliography* [to 1938] (New York, 1939).

W. White, *John Donne since 1900: a Bibliography of Periodical Articles* (Boston, 1942); reprinted from the *Bulletin of Bibliography*, xvii (1941–2).

W. White, 'Sir Geoffrey Keynes's Bibliography . . .: a Review with Addenda', *Bulletin of Bibliography*, xxii (1959).

BACKGROUND READING

D. C. Allen, *The Legend of Noah: Renaissance Rationalism in Art, Science and Letters* (Urbana, Ill., 1949; paperbacks, U.K. and U.S.).

L. Babb, *The Elizabethan Malady* (East Lansing, Mich., 1951).

J. Bamborough, *The Little World of Man* (London, 1952).

S. L. Bethell, *The Cultural Revolution of the Seventeenth Century* (London, 1951).

D. Bush, *English Literature in the Earlier Seventeenth Century*, 2nd edn. (*O.H.E.L.*, vol. v, Oxford, 1962).

H. Craig, *The Enchanted Glass* (New York, 1936; Oxford, 1950).

P. Cruttwell, *The Shakespearean Moment* (London, 1954, New York, 1960; paperback, U.K.).

J. Danby, *Poets on Fortune's Hill* (London, 1952); as *Elizabethan and Jacobean Poets* (London, 1964; paperback, U.K.).

R. Ellrodt, *L'Inspiration personnelle et l'esprit du temps chez les Poètes métaphysiques anglais* (2 parts, Part 1 in 2 vols., Paris, 1960).

H. J. C. Grierson, *Cross Currents in English Literature of the Seventeenth Century* (London, 1958; paperbacks, U.K. and U.S.).

V. Harris, *All Coherence Gone* (Chicago, 1949).

V. Harris and Itrat Husain, *English Prose, 1600–1660* (paperbacks, London and New York, 1965).

L. Jonas, *The Divine Science* (Columbia, Mo., 1940).

L. C. Knights, 'On the Social Background of Metaphysical Poetry', *Scrutiny*, xiii (1945).

C. S. Lewis, *The Discarded Image* (Cambridge, and paperback, New York, 1964; paperback, U.K.).

E. Miner, *The Metaphysical Mode from Donne to Cowley* (Princeton, N.J., 1969).

W. F. Mitchell, *English Pulpit Oratory from Andrewes to Tillotson* (London, 1932).

M. Nicolson, *The Breaking of the Circle*, 2nd edn. (New York, 1960; paperback, U.S.).

M. Nicolson, *Science and Imagination* (Ithaca, N.Y., 1956).

H. Smith, *Elizabethan Poetry: a Study in Conventions, Meaning and Expression* (Cambridge, Mass., 1952; paperback, U.S.).

E. M. W. Tillyard, *The Elizabethan World Picture* (London, 1943; paperbacks, U.K. and U.S.).

E. M. W. Tillyard, *The Metaphysicals and Milton* (London, 1956).

H. C. White, *English Devotional Literature (Prose), 1600–40* (Madison, Wis., 1931).

M. L. Wiley, *The Subtle Knot* (London, 1952).

B. Willey, *The Seventeenth-Century Background* (London, 1934; paperbacks, U.S. and U.K.).

F. P. Wilson, *Elizabethan and Jacobean* (Oxford, 1945).

4 · HERBERT

Margaret Bottrall

TEXTS

The standard text for the study of George Herbert is the admirable edition of *The Works* by F. E. Hutchinson in the Oxford English Texts series. Covering the whole of Herbert's extant work, poetry and prose, English and Latin, it was first issued in 1941, revised in 1945, and reprinted in 1953. Canon Hutchinson's prime concern was to establish the text of *The Temple* by a more complete and accurate collation of the two existing manuscripts than had hitherto been attempted. The Introduction, besides dealing with textual problems, gives a brief factual biography, and traces Herbert's contemporary and later reputation. The commentary on the poems is invaluable.

A convenient pocket edition is the World's Classics, *The Poetical Works of George Herbert*, of which the second edition (1961) has a good Introduction by Helen Gardner; this reproduces the Oxford text of the poems.

Until Hutchinson's more scholarly edition superseded it, G. H. Palmer's edition of *The English Works of George Herbert* was much used by students. The fruit of many years of devoted research, it was published in a three-volume edition in Boston in 1905, revised in 1907, and reissued in a single volume in 1916. The Introduction and notes contain much that is of value, but the rearrangement of the poems to suit a conjectural chronological and psychological order is indefensible.

Notes on some of the nineteenth-century editions will be found under CRITICAL STUDIES AND COMMENTARY below. Hutchinson gives full bibliographical information about the early editions.

The standard edition of *The Country Parson* is that of H. C. Beeching (Oxford, 1898). The Introduction and notes reflect his knowledge of English seventeenth-century churchmanship.

The Latin Poetry of George Herbert was edited by Mark McCluskey and Paul R. Murphy, with a page-by-page translation into modern free verse, in 1962.

Easily available Selections include *A Choice of George Herbert's Verse*, with an Introduction by R. S. Thomas; and *Selected Poems by*

George Herbert, arranged with an Introduction by Douglas Brown. This is specially suitable for school use; it includes, for purposes of comparison, some representative poems by such writers as Donne, Vaughan, and Marvell.

Herbert is well represented in Helen Gardner's anthology *The Metaphysical Poets*; and in *The Meditative Poem*, an anthology edited by Louis L. Martz, Herbert tops the list with sixty-eight poems.

Because it may be convenient to be reminded of these selections from Herbert's poetry, they have been included here; but *The Temple*, in justice to its author, needs to be studied in its entirety. It is not a massive work, and its structure is not the least interesting thing about it.

CRITICAL STUDIES AND COMMENTARY

George Herbert is known to have composed English poems from his seventeenth year onwards, but during his lifetime the only writings of his to be printed were some Latin poems and orations. Some of the lyrics contained in the *The Temple* were written before he was ordained; some belong to the time of his priesthood. While at Bemerton he also wrote a treatise on what the ministry of a country parson should ideally be, but this was not published until nearly twenty years after his death. None of his sermons survive. Undoubtedly, he circulated some of his English poems in manuscript, as might be expected, considering the courtly and learned circle to which he belonged.

On his deathbed George Herbert sent to his friend Nicholas Ferrar, of Little Gidding, a small manuscript book containing the poems that were to be issued as *The Temple*, leaving it to Ferrar's discretion whether they should be made public at all. Within a few months the volume was printed at Cambridge, in 1633.

The Temple was an immediate success. It went into four editions within three years, and by 1709 it had reached its thirteenth edition. During the seventeenth century its piety attracted men of very different churchmanship. King Charles I is said often to have read 'Herbert's divine poems' during his imprisonment; and the eminent Puritan divine, Richard Baxter, summed up his commendations in the memorable words: 'Herbert speaks to God like one that really believeth a God, and whose business in the world is most with God. Heart-work and Heaven-work make up his books.'[1] But it was not only the devotional character of the poems that commended

[1] Preface to *Poetical Fragments*, 1681.

them to contemporary readers. Poets were quick to pay tribute to Herbert; Richard Crashaw, for example, did him homage by entitling his own first book of sacred verse *Steps to the Temple*. Henry Vaughan attributed his conversion from secular to religious themes to 'the blessed man, Mr. George Herbert', and his *Silex Scintillans* is full of echoes, conscious and perhaps unconscious, of the poetry he so much admired. A much less distinguished poet, Christopher Harvey, was so ardent an imitator that his book of verse, *The Synagogue*, won the approval of devout readers and was commonly bound up with *The Temple* in editions from 1641 onwards.

Herbert's poetry seems to have held its own throughout the Protectorate and the Restoration, and even well into the reign of Queen Anne. Purcell, Blow, and Jeremiah Clark were among the musicians who composed settings to Herbert's poems—a testimony that their lyrical attractiveness long survived the age of the lutenists, to which they belong by origin. In 1714 George Ryley completed a detailed commentary on *Mr. Herbert's Temple, and Church Militant, Explained and Improved by a Discourse on Each Poem, Critical and Practical*. It was the doctrinal content of the poems that interested Ryley, who annotated them from a fund of scriptural and theological learning. His treatise survives only in manuscript,[2] but an account of it can be found in an appendix to Joseph H. Summers' book, *George Herbert: his Religion and Art* (1954), and quotations from Ryley are included in the body of the book.

Mr. Summers's introductory chapter gives a most useful survey of the vicissitudes of Herbert's poetic reputation during the seventeenth, eighteenth, and nineteenth centuries. He notes that the New England poet, Edward Taylor, who continued writing till 1725, was profoundly indebted to Herbert; and that John Reynolds (1667–1727) combined an admiration for Herbert with enthusiasm for the new science, particularly for Newton. But during the eighteenth century Herbert's literary reputation suffered an eclipse, as did those of the other metaphysical poets, whose conceit-ridden style was disparaged by Addison and Johnson. There was no new edition of *The Temple* between 1709 and 1799, when a Bristol printer put it on the market again. Not that Herbert's name was forgotten. Walton's *Life* (see BIBLIOGRAPHIES below) kept his memory green, and *The Country Parson* continued to be read when the poems were generally discredited as uncouth, homely, and lacking in lucidity. John Wesley did much to commend Herbert's devotional verse to his followers. No fewer than forty-seven of his lyrics are to be found in

[2] Bodleian MS. Rawl. D. 199.

Hymns and Sacred Poems, edited by John and Charles Wesley, and printed at Bristol in 1739. In adapting some of the poems for congregational singing, Wesley mangled both metre and diction; but in 1773 he published in their original form *Select Parts of Mr. Herbert's Sacred Poems*, including much of 'The Church Porch'. On the whole, however, eighteenth-century literary taste rejected Herbert, whatever edification devout readers, such as William Cowper, might derive from him.

It was Coleridge who rescued Herbert the poet from disrepute. In *The Friend* and in *Biographia Literaria* he emphasized Herbert's command of 'correct and natural language'. The conceits, that had for a long time been obstacles to general enjoyment, did not hinder Coleridge from perceiving the purity of his diction and his fine poetic workmanship. He also came to appreciate profoundly Herbert's treatment of religious themes, going so far as to say that only 'a devout and devotional Christian . . . an affectionate and dutiful child of the Church . . .' could fully grasp all that Herbert has to offer.[3] This estimate proved somewhat damaging. Many later commentators have presented Herbert as a mild ecclesiastical figure, with limited talents.

The appeal of Herbert's devotional poetry took on new strength at the time of the Oxford Movement, when Anglicans were rediscovering their heritage. Editions of *The Temple*, and selections, appeared with increasing frequency. It was the work of editors, rather than critics, that gave Herbert during the nineteenth century a permanent place in the ranks of English poets and divines. Pickering edited the English works, and included notes by Coleridge in the two-volume edition of 1835-6. A. B. Grosart produced in 1874 the first *Complete Works*, in three volumes, with a good deal of scholarly apparatus. He was the first editor to make use of the Williams MS. of *The Temple* for purposes of collation. Unfortunately, however, his text is very unreliable. In 1876 Grosart was responsible for a facsimile reprint of *The Temple*. G. H. Palmer's edition of the English works in 1905 was a great improvement on Grosart's; but it was not until the publication of F. E. Hutchinson's edition in 1941 that the texts were satisfactorily established.

Among the nineteenth-century writers who responded with enthusiasm to George Herbert were Christina Rossetti, Gerard Manley Hopkins, Emerson, and Thoreau. Critical studies worth consulting include Edward Dowden's chapter on Herbert and

[3] S. T. Coleridge, *Miscellaneous Criticism*, ed. T. M. Raysor (Cambridge, Mass., 1936), p. 244.

Vaughan in *Puritan and Anglican*, and Paul Elmer More's essay in *Shelburne Essays: Fourth Series*.

It was not until the 1930s that George Herbert came in for much intensive criticism. The surge of interest in Donne and his followers, precipitated by Grierson's edition of Donne's poems in 1912 and his anthology *Metaphysical Lyrics and Poems of the Seventeenth Century: Donne to Butler* (1921), naturally affected Herbert; but he was seen as a lesser luminary beside the blazing Donne. Grierson's verdict suggests, as Coleridge's had done, that Herbert is unlikely to be of much interest to anyone outside the Church of England: '*The Temple* breathes the spirit of the Anglican church at its best, primitive and modest; and also of one troubled and delicate soul seeking and finding peace.' This is undeniably true, but it does much less than justice to Herbert's originality and strength. There is a touch of condescension, too, in Grierson's assessment: 'If not greatly imaginative, Herbert is a sincere and sensitive poet, and an accomplished artist elaborating his argumentative strain of little allegories and conceits with felicitous completeness, and managing his variously patterned stanzas . . . with a finished and delicate harmony.'[4]

Sections on Herbert appear in the well-known studies of Donne and his successors that were published in the thirties. George Williamson's *The Donne Tradition* (1930), Joan Bennett's *Four Metaphysical Poets* and J. B. Leishman's *The Metaphysical Poets*, both published in 1934 at Cambridge and Oxford respectively, and Helen C. White's *The Metaphysical Poets: a Study in Religious Expression* (New York, 1936) have all established themselves as enlightening introductions to a body of verse that had never previously received so much concentrated attention from English critics.

An essay to celebrate the tercentenary of George Herbert's death, by F. E. Hutchinson, appeared in *The Nineteenth Century* in March 1933, and was subsequently included in *Seventeenth-Century Studies Presented to Sir Herbert Grierson* (1938). A brief article by T. S. Eliot in *The Spectator* in 1932 suggests that Herbert's poetry 'is definitely an *oeuvre* to be studied entire'. He also contributed short studies to *The Times Literary Supplement* in 1933 and 1941. Austin Warren's essay in *The American Review*, vii (1936), is not only attractive but important, in that it evaluates Herbert not as a satellite of Donne's but as a religious poet of intrinsic power and merit, with a quite individual style. A revised version of this essay appears in *Rage for Order: Essays in Criticism*, a volume by Austin Warren published in Chicago in 1948. Another excellent essay is that by L. C. Knights,

---

[4] *Metaphysical Lyrics and Poems*, p. xliv.

which appeared in *Scrutiny* in 1944 and was reprinted in *Explorations* three years later. This argues the case for Herbert as a poet of inner conflict, whose art is intelligible and significant to readers who may not share his religious assumptions.

A pioneer piece of close reading of an individual poem of Herbert's is to be found in William Empson's *Seven Types of Ambiguity*, first published in 1930. Empson devotes several pages to an analysis of 'The Sacrifice'. When it first appeared, this brief study did much to rescue Herbert from the charge of mere quaintness, for Empson's scrutiny of the poem's subtleties demonstrated how active and distinguished an intelligence George Herbert possessed. Twenty years later this interpretation proved to be fruitfully provocative. During 1950 Rosemond Tuve took issue with Empson in *The Kenyon Review*, contending that it was inadequate and misleading to examine a seventeenth-century religious poem with modern psycho-analytical tools, while ignoring the liturgical tradition to which it patently belonged. The first section of her extremely important book, *A Reading of George Herbert* (1952), is an expansion of this argument, and is entitled ' "The Sacrifice" and Modern Criticism'.

Before considering further Professor Tuve's contributions to Herbert studies, mention should be made of Rosemary Freeman's valuable study of *George Herbert and the Emblem Books*, which originally appeared in *Review of English Studies* in 1941 and, in a revised form, in her *English Emblem Books*. This took Herbert right outside the ambience of Donne and showed some very interesting connections with religious books popular in the early seventeenth century. Miss Freeman in 1963 contributed a study of Herbert's poem 'Dulnesse' to *Essays in Criticism*, as part of an essay entitled 'Parody as a Literary Form: George Herbert and Wilfred Owen'.

The characteristic virtue of Rosemond Tuve as an expositor of Herbert's poetry is her intimate understanding of the religious tradition within which that poetry was conceived. This, coupled with her interest in Renaissance rhetoric, and specially in Elizabethan and Jacobean imagery, makes *A Reading of George Herbert* a most illuminating book. It insists on the need to reckon with scriptural typology, Christian iconography, and the liturgy of the pre-Reformation Church in any attempt to comprehend what Herbert intended in his poems. More theological than the 1952 criticism, Miss Tuve's essay on 'George Herbert and *Caritas*', printed in the *Journal of the Warburg and Courtauld Institute* (1959), is an exploration, at once authoritative and sensitive, of Herbert's attempts to define the nature of divine love and man's response to it.

Another critic of seventeenth-century devotional poets who took as his point of departure their religious background is Louis L. Martz. Herbert is considered at length in *The Poetry of Meditation* (1954). This has proved an immensely influential book, under-mining as it does the 'School of Donne' formula for grouping to-gether sundry seventeenth-century poets. Professor Martz showed how the practice of formal meditation not only affected the structure of individual poems but also encouraged precisely that fusion of intelligence and feeling long perceived as characteristic of the 'Meta-physicals' but not satisfactorily accounted for. Herbert's affinity with S. François de Sales is the subject of one chapter; another deals with the unity of *The Temple*. The influence of Sidney is considered, and so is Herbert's general indebtedness to secular lyrics—an idea that Miss Tuve plays down, but that certainly should not be ignored.

In 1954 appeared two full-length studies; a comparatively slight one by Margaret Bottrall, *George Herbert*, and Joseph H. Summers's *George Herbert: his Religion and Art*.[5] The former, meant for the general reader, combines an account of Herbert's life with critical comment on his English writings. The latter, much more scholarly, also combines biography with criticism, and is the most satisfactory introduction to the study of George Herbert available to the serious student—apart from the admirable edition of the *Works* by F. E. Hutchinson, already referred to (in TEXTS above), which with its Introduction and commentary is indispensable.

Reference should be made to the chapter on Herbert in M. M. Mahood's *Poetry and Humanism* (1950). Malcolm M. Ross contri-buted an article on 'George Herbert and the Humanist Tradition' to the *University of Toronto Quarterly* in January 1947, which is in-corporated in his *Poetry and Dogma* (1954). This also includes a chapter on 'The Spiritual Anglicans', in which Herbert's defective eucharistic theology is emphasized, the main thesis of the book being 'the transfiguration of eucharistic symbols in seventeenth-century English poetry'. An article contributed by Elsie A. Leach to the *Huntingdon Library Quarterly* in 1953 on 'John Wesley's use of George Herbert' elaborates some points made by F. E. Hutchinson in an essay, 'John Wesley and George Herbert', published in 1936. D. J. Enright contributed a chapter on 'George Herbert and the Devo-tional Poets' to the Pelican *Guide to English Literature*, vol. III, *From Donne to Marvell* (1956).

By the mid fifties George Herbert's poetic reputation stood high.

---

[5] Chapters from both these books are reprinted in *Seventeenth-Century English Poetry*, ed. W. R. Keast (1962).

Critics had established that he was a poet abundantly worth studying in his own right. His psychological subtlety, his remarkably sure handling of colloquial language, and his exquisite craftsmanship were acknowledged strengths; and it was apparent that, in spite of his personal links with Donne, he was not his poetic disciple to any marked extent. As late as 1961, however, A. Alvarez produced a book entitled *The School of Donne*, in which the chapter on Herbert is well worth reading; and in 1959 R. Ellrodt published an excellent general study of the English Metaphysicals, with a full bibliography —*Les Poétes metaphysiques anglais*. Mention should also be made of Arno Esch, *Englische religiöse Lyrik des 17 Jahrhunderts: Studien zu Donne, Herbert, Crashaw, Vaughan* (1955).

In 1960 Agnes Latham remarked in *The Year's Work in English Studies* that 'Criticism has to a great extent exhausted the subject of metaphysical poetry', but a good many studies of individual poems by Herbert are to be found in learned periodicals during the sixties. In 1962 a brief but valuable pamphlet by T. S. Eliot, *George Herbert*, was published by Longmans in their Writers and their Work series. In it Eliot claims a place for Herbert among those poets whose work 'every lover of English poetry should read, and every student of English poetry should study, irrespective of religious belief or unbelief'. D. C. Allen's *Image and Meaning* (1960) contains some close analysis of poems by Herbert. Among the many scholarly articles on single poems may be mentioned Fredson Bowers's 'Herbert's Sequential Imagery: "The Temper" ', published in *Modern Philology* (1962); and E. B. Greenwood's 'George Herbert's Sonnet on Prayer', in *Essays in Criticism* (1965). On more general topics the following may be noted: Robert L. Montgomery, Jr., 'The Province of Allegory in George Herbert's Verse'; R. E. Hughes, 'George Herbert's Rhetorical World'; and Rosalie Colie's *'Logos* in *The Temple'*. The last has been included in the author's *Paradoxia Epidemica: The Renaissance Tradition of Paradox* (1966).

H. R. Swardson's *Poetry and the Fountain of Light* (1962), which is concerned with the conflict between Christian and classical tradition in seventeenth century poetry, has an unremarkable chapter on 'Herbert's Language of Devotion'. There is also a full-length study of Herbert's poetry by M. E. Rickey, *Utmost Art: Complexity in the Verse of George Herbert*, published in 1966. G. Williamson's *A Reader's Guide to the Metaphysical Poets* (1968) contains a chapter on Herbert.

A most valuable intensive study of Herbert's poetic art is the recently published *George Herbert's Lyrics* by Arnold Stein, from the

Johns Hopkins Press (1968). Professor Stein sets out to demonstrate that Herbert is one of the great masters of English lyric poetry, who endowed with genuine individuality the fixed theme that was his central concern: God's transforming love and man's imperfect response to it. Herbert's mastery of the art of plainness is assessed with reference to classical and Christian rhetorical principles. His prosody is examined with unprecedented thoroughness, the technique owing something to applied linguistics. The larger aspects of form and style are also subjected to careful scrutiny. But the book as a whole is by no means arid. Professor Stein is conversant with the language and psychology of religious devotion, and handles them sympathetically; and he is interested enough in the actual writing of poems to be able to comment perceptively on how Herbert's experiences are given imaginative expression.

Herbert studies have benefited from the shift of interest away from Donne, whose rich seams have been mined to exhaustion by scholars and commentators. The lyrics of George Herbert, though superficially less tough-fibred than Donne's, have proved well able to stand up to searching scrutiny, and to yield a variety of rewards. They still speak eloquently to devout Christians; they exhibit to all attentive readers the inner conflicts of a man exceptionally intelligent, honest, and sensitive; and they afford the pleasure that beautiful workmanship gives to those who care for English poetry.

BIOGRAPHIES AND LETTERS

Herbert's extant letters, both in English and Latin, some of which have biographical interest, are included in Hutchinson's edition of the *Works* (see TEXTS above). This also gives a good summary biography, though more recent research has made it incomplete.

By far the most attractive and influential biography of George Herbert is Izaak Walton's *Life*, published in 1670; but it was not the first. The earliest written record of Herbert's Life is the brief Preface to *The Temple* (1633) written by his friend Nicholas Ferrar. In 1652 'A Prefatory View of the Life of Mr. Geo. Herbert' was included in *Herbert's Remains*. The main item in this miscellany was *A Priest to the Temple, or, The Countrey Parson*. This was reissued separately in 1671, when the editor forsook his anonymity, prudently assumed during the Protectorate, and revealed himself as Barnabas Oley, a Laudian divine. He wrote a new Preface to Herbert's treatise, and the biographical sketch was relegated to the back of the volume. It presented Herbert as an exemplar of Anglican piety, the ideal parish priest; and in this Oley forestalls Walton.

The Country Parson itself, though by no means autobiographical, reveals a good deal about Herbert's activities as the rector of Bemerton. Its combination of spiritual wisdom with humour and good sense makes it a worthy complement to the poems, and it contains some important remarks on rhetoric.

Walton's *Life of Mr. George Herbert* is an indispensable text for any student of the poetry or prose. Walton had never known Herbert personally, but he was acquainted with some of his friends, and from them he culled facts, documents, and anecdotes. The biography has been censured for being too adulatory. Certainly it was written in a spirit of veneration, by a devout Churchman who looked back wistfully on pre-Cromwellian days. Certainly, too, Walton constructed conversations and worked on his material with a greater attention to literary than to historical considerations. But his delightful narrative gives an impression of Herbert's temperament, sensibility, and moral character, which the poems themselves reflect.

A. G. Hyde's *George Herbert and his Times* (1906) is not in any way authoritative. The biographical chapter in Joseph H. Summers's *George Herbert: his Religion and Art* (1954) provides a good corrective to Walton, in that it stresses the importance of Herbert's connections with the university and court. Margaret Bottrall's *George Herbert* (1954) is biographical as well as critical. Marchette Chute, in *Two Gentle Men* (1959), juxtaposes the lives of George Herbert and Robert Herrick, and provides a modern biography that is informed as well as lively. T. S. Eliot comments on Herbert's family connections and life in his introductory pamphlet, mentioned above under CRITICAL STUDIES.

BIBLIOGRAPHIES

Besides the *Cambridge Bibliography of English Literature* and its *Supplement*, the student should consult *George Herbert: a Concise Bibliography*, a cyclostyled list published by S. A. and D. R. Tannenbaum (New York, 1946) in their Elizabethan Bibliographies series.

T. S. Eliot's *George Herbert* (1962) is one of Longman's Bibliographical series of Supplements to British Book News; it contains a brief account of the early editions, and a summary list of books and articles on Herbert, very far from exhaustive.

More valuable by far is Douglas Bush's *English Literature in the Earlier Seventeenth Century* (see BACKGROUND READING below). This provides, besides a useful Herbert bibliography, general reading lists that are invaluable to all students of the period.

In Arnold Stein's *George Herbert's Lyrics* there are many useful footnote references to recent articles, particularly on individual poems, but it does not include a systematic bibliography.

A Concordance to the English Poems of George Herbert was compiled by Cameron Mann (1927).

Embracing a wider field than Herbert studies is the valuable work by Theodore Spencer and Mark van Doren, *Studies in Metaphysical Poetry: two Essays and a Bibliography* (1939). This covers the scholarly and critical comment between 1912 and 1939. A continuation of this enterprise is Lloyd E. Berry's *A Bibliography of Studies of Metaphysical Poetry* (1964).

BACKGROUND READING

The best easily available source for suggestions on background reading is Douglas Bush's *English Literature in the Earlier Seventeenth Century* (1962), which lists works bearing on the historical, religious, and literary climate in which George Herbert lived and wrote. Some of the titles mentioned above could be listed here (e.g., Louis L. Martz's *The Poetry of Meditation*), since they provide a framework in which the poetry of Herbert may fruitfully be considered. Several well-known books dealing collectively with the English metaphysical poets have already been listed because they include substantial criticism of Herbert. Obviously he cannot be understood in isolation from Donne (or, for that matter, from Sidney and the Elizabethan song-writers); nor can he be evaluated without reference to them and to Vaughan, Crashaw, Marvell, and others. The suggestions for background reading attached to the chapter on Donne should prove equally useful with reference to Herbert.

Among the innumerable articles dealing in a general way with the characteristics of metaphysical poetry, a few of the more enduring earlier ones may be noted here. Besides T. S. Eliot's brief but almost hypnotically influential critiques on 'The Metaphysical Poets' and 'Andrew Marvell', published in his *Selected Essays* (London, 1932), there are James Smith's 'On Metaphysical Poetry' and F. R. Leavis's 'The Line of Wit', the former of which appeared in *Scrutiny*, ii (1933–4), and the latter in *Scrutiny*, iv (1935–6). Dr. Leavis's essay was reprinted in *Revaluations* (1936) and Mr. Smith's in *Determinations*, ed. F. R. Leavis (1934). 'On Metaphysical Poetry' also appears in the collection of reprints from *Scrutiny* published by the Cambridge University Press in 1968. Another important essay is G. Williamson's 'Strong Lines', *English Studies*, xviii (1936), reprinted in his collection of essays, *Seventeenth-Century Contexts* (1961).

Readers interested in the life of Herbert and his friendship with the Ferrars should consult *The Ferrar Papers*, edited by Bernard Blackstone (1938). Edward Dowden's *Puritan and Anglican* (1900) has been complemented by J. F. H. New's *Anglican and Puritan* (1963). An interesting compilation is *Anglicanism*, by Paul Elmer More and F. L. Cross (1935), which illustrates the thought and practice of the Church of England by copious extracts from religious literature of the seventeenth century. Helen C. White's *English Devotional Literature (Prose), 1600–1640* (1931), is a valuable book for students of Herbert. Herschel Baker's *The Wars of Truth: Studies in the Decay of Christian Humanism* (1961) is an important book, and S. L. Bethell's *The Cultural Revolution of the Seventeenth Century* (1961) is also relevant. Books on the seventeenth-century cultural revolution do not always pay much attention to the pre-Civil-War epoch, but H. J. C. Grierson's *Cross Currents in English Literature of the Seventeenth Century* (1929) considers at some length the literary results of Anglican and Puritan attitudes. F. P. Wilson's *Elizabethan and Jacobean* (1945) deals with the transitional period to which George Herbert belonged. Basil Willey's *The Seventeenth-Century Background* (1934) does not mention George Herbert, but it devotes a chapter to the poet's very dissimilar elder brother, Lord Herbert of Cherbury. A background book of a different kind is Bruce Pattison's *Music and Poetry of the English Renaissance* (1948), which should not be neglected by students of George Herbert's lyrics.

REFERENCES

TEXTS

H. C. Beeching (ed.), *The Country Parson* (Oxford, 1898).

D. Brown (ed.), *Selected Poems of George Herbert* (London, 1960).

H. Gardner (ed.), *The Metaphysical Poets* (paperback, Harmondsworth, 1957; Oxford, 1961).

H. J. C. Grierson (ed.), *Metaphysical Lyrics and Poems of the Seventeenth Century* (Oxford, 1921; paperbacks, U.K. and U.S.).

A. B. Grosart (ed.), *The Complete Works of George Herbert* (3 vols., London, 1874).

A. B. Grosart (ed.), *The Temple* (facsimile, London, 1876).

F. E. Hutchinson (ed.), *The Works of George Herbert* (Oxford English Texts, 1941; rev. 1945); *George Herbert: Poems*, 2nd edn., O.E.T. text, with an Introduction by H. Gardner (World's Classics, Oxford, 1961).

L. L. Martz (ed.), *The Anchor Anthology of Seventeenth-Century Verse*, Vol. I: *The Meditative Poem* (New York, 1962; paperbacks, U.K. and U.S.).

M. H. McCluskey and P. R. Murphy (eds.), *The Latin Poetry of George Herbert* (Athens, Ohio, 1962).

G. H. Palmer (ed.), *The English Works of George Herbert*, 2nd edn. (3 vols., Boston, 1907).

W. Pickering (ed.), *The Works of George Herbert* (2 vols., London, 1835–6).

J. H. Summers (ed.), *Selected Poetry of George Herbert* (paperback, U.S., 1967).

R. S. Thomas (ed.), *A Choice of George Herbert's Verse* (London, 1967; paperback, U.K.).

CRITICAL STUDIES AND COMMENTARY

D. C. Allen, *Image and Meaning* (Baltimore, 1960).

A. Alvarez, *The School of Donne* (London, 1961; paperbacks, U.K. and U.S.).

J. Bennett, *Four Metaphysical Poets*, rev. edn. (Cambridge, 1953, repr. New York, 1958); reissued as *Five Metaphysical Poets* (Cambridge, 1964; paperbacks, U.K. and U.S.).

M. Bottrall, *George Herbert* (London, 1954).

F. Bowers 'Herbert's Sequential Imagery: "The Temper"', *MP* lix (1962).

S. T. Coleridge, *Miscellaneous Criticism*, ed. T. M. Raysor (London and Cambridge, Mass., 1936).

R. Colie, '*Logos* in *The Temple*', *Journal of the Warburg and Courtauld Institute*, xxvi (1963).

R. Colie, *Paradoxia Epidemica* (Princeton, N.J., 1966).

E. Dowden, *Puritan and Anglican* (London, 1900).

T. S. Eliot, *Spectator*, 12 March 1932; *TLS* 2 March 1933 and 12 July 1941.

T. S. Eliot, *George Herbert* (paperback, British Council, London, 1962; paperback, U.S.).

R. Ellrodt, *Les Poètes metaphysiques anglais* (Paris, 1960).

W. Empson, *Seven Types of Ambiguity*, rev. edn. (London and New York, 1947; paperback, U.S.).

A. Esch, *Englische religiöse Lyrik des 17 Jahrhunderts* (Halle, 1955).

R. Freeman, 'George Herbert and the Emblem Books', *RES* xvii (1941).

R. Freeman, *English Emblem Books* (London, 1948).

R. Freeman, 'Parody as a Literary form: George Herbert and Wilfred Owen', *EIC* xiii (1963).

E. B. Greenwood, 'George Herbert's Sonnet on Prayer', *EIC* xv (1965).

H. J. C. Grierson (see TEXTS above).

R. E. Hughes, 'George Herbert's Rhetorical World', *Criticism*, iii (1961).

F. E. Hutchinson, 'George Herbert: a Tercentenary', *The Nineteenth Century*, cxiii (1933); reprinted in *Seventeenth-Century Studies Presented to Sir Herbert Grierson* (Oxford, 1938).

F. E. Hutchinson, 'John Wesley and George Herbert', *London Quarterly*, clxi (1936).

W. R. Keast (ed.), *Seventeenth-Century English Poetry: Modern Essays in Criticism* (paperback, New York, 1962; paperback, U.K.).

L. C. Knights, 'George Herbert', *Scrutiny*, xii (1943–4); reprinted in *Explorations* (London, 1946, paperbacks, U.K. and U.S.).

E. A. Leach, 'John Wesley's Use of George Herbert', *Huntington Library Quarterly*, xvi (1953).

J. B. Leishman, *The Metaphysical Poets* (Oxford, 1934, New York, 1963).

M. M. Mahood, *Poetry and Humanism* (London, 1950).

L. L. Martz, *The Poetry of Meditation* (New Haven, Conn., 1954; paperbacks, U.S. and U.K.).

R. L. Montgomery, 'The Province of Allegory in George Herbert's Verse', *Texas Studies in Literature and Language*, i (1960).

P. E. More, *Shelburne Essays: Fourth Series* (New York and London, 1906).

M. E. Rickey, *Utmost Art: Complexity in the Verse of George Herbert* (Lexington, Ky., 1966).

M. M. Ross, 'George Herbert and the Humanist Tradition', *UTQ* (January 1947); incorporated in his *Poetry and Dogma* (New Brunswick, N.J., 1954).

A. Stein, *George Herbert's Lyrics* (Baltimore, 1968).

J. H. Summers, *George Herbert: his Religion and Art* (Cambridge, Mass., and London, 1954).

H. R. Swardson, *Poetry and the Fountain of Light* (London, 1962).

R. Tuve, 'On Herbert's "Sacrifice" ', *Kenyon Review*, xii (1950).

R. Tuve, *A Reading of George Herbert* (Chicago, Ill., and London, 1952).

R. Tuve, 'George Herbert and *Caritas*', *Journal of the Warburg and Courtauld Institute*, xxii (1959).

A. Warren, 'George Herbert', *American Review*, vii (1936).

A. Warren, *Rage for Order: Essays in Criticism* (Chicago, 1948; paperback, U.S.).

H. C. White, *The Metaphysical Poets* (New York, 1956; paperbacks, U.S. and U.K.).

G. Williamson, *The Donne Tradition* (Cambridge, Mass., 1930).

G. Williamson, *A Reader's Guide to Six Metaphysical Poets* (paperback, New York, 1967); British edition entitled, *A Reader's Guide to the Metaphysical Poets* (cloth and paperback, London, 1968).

BIOGRAPHIES AND LETTERS

M. Bottrall, *George Herbert* (London, 1954).

M. Chute, *Two Gentle Men* (London, 1959).

T. S. Eliot, *George Herbert* (paperback, British Council, London, 1962; paperback, U.S.).

N. Ferrar (ed.), *The Temple* (London, 1633). See his Preface.

F. E. Hutchinson, Introduction to *The Works of G. H.* (Oxford, 1945).

A. G. Hyde, *George Herbert and his Times* (London, 1906).

B. Oley (ed.), *Herbert's Remains* (London, 1652).

J. H. Summers, *George Herbert: His Religion and Art* (Cambridge, Mass., and London, 1954).

I. Walton, *The Life of Mr George Herbert* (London, 1670); in *Lives*, ed. G. Saintsbury (World's Classics, London, 1927).

BIBLIOGRAPHIES

F. W. Bateson (ed.), *The Cambridge Bibliography of English Literature* (4 vols, Cambridge, 1940); vol. v, *Supplement* ed. G. Watson (Cambridge, 1957).

L. E. Berry, *A Bibliography of Studies of Metaphysical Poetry* (Madison, Wis., 1964).

D. Bush, *English Literature in the Earlier Seventeenth Century.* (See BACKGROUND READING below.

T. S. Eliot, *George Herbert* (paperback, British Council, London, 1962; paperback, U.S.).

C. Mann, *A Concordance to the English Poems of George Herbert* (Boston and New York, 1927).

T. Spencer and M. Van Doren, *Studies in Metaphysical Poetry: Two Essays and a Bibliography* (New York, 1939).

A. Stein, *George Herbert's Lyrics* (Baltimore, 1968).

S. A. and D. R. Tannenbaum, *George Herbert: a Concise Bibliography* (Elizabethan Bibliographies 35, New York, 1946).

BACKGROUND READING

H. Baker, *The Wars of Truth: Studies in the Decay of Christian Humanism* (Cambridge, Mass., 1961).

S. L. Bethell, *The Cultural Revolution of the Seventeenth Century* (London, 1951).

B. Blackstone (ed.), *The Ferrar Papers* (Cambridge, 1938).

D. Bush, *English Literature in the Earlier Seventeenth Century, 1600–1660,* 2nd edn. (O.H.E.L., vol. v, Oxford and New York, 1962).

E. Dowden, *Puritan and Anglican* (London, 1900).

T. S. Eliot, 'The Metaphysical Poets' and 'Andrew Marvell' in *Selected Essays* (London, 1932).

B. Ford (ed.), *From Donne to Marvell* (*Pelican Guide to English Literature* iii (paperbacks, Harmondsworth and New York, 1956).

H. J. C. Grierson, *Cross Currents in English Literature of the Seventeenth Century* (London, 1929; paperbacks, U.K. and U.S.).

F. R. Leavis, 'The Line of Wit', *Scrutiny*, iv (1935–6); reprinted in *Revaluation* (London, 1936; paperbacks, U.K. and U.S.).

P. E. More and F. L. Cross (eds.), *Anglicanism* (Milwaukee, Wis., 1935).

J. F. H. New, *Anglican and Puritan* (London, 1963).

B. Pattison, *Music and Poetry of the English Renaissance* (London, 1948).

J. Smith, 'On Metaphysical Poetry', *Scrutiny*, ii (1933–4); reprinted in *Determinations*, ed. F. R. Leavis (London, 1934), and in *A Selection from Scrutiny*, ed. F. R. Leavis (2 vols., Cambridge, 1968; paperbacks, U.K. and U.S.).

H. C. White, *English Devotional Literature (Prose), 1600–1640* (Madison, Wis., 1931).

B. Willey, *The Seventeenth-Century Background* (London, 1934; paperback, U.S. and U.K.).

G. Williamson, 'Strong Lines', *English Studies*, xviii (1936); reprinted in *Seventeenth-Century Contexts* (London, 1960, and Chicago, 1961).

F. P. Wilson, *Elizabethan and Jacobean* (London, 1945).

Douglas Bush

THE limits of space and the huge bulk of material, which has grown so much in recent decades, forbid mention of many good books and countless good articles and essays.

TEXTS

The standard edition of the complete works is that of F. A. Patterson *et al.* (18 vols., 1931–8), which has full textual notes; the two-volume Index (1940) is almost a concordance of both verse and prose. Two single volumes which contain all the poetry and the greater part of the prose are *The Student's Milton*, ed. Patterson (1933), with some apparatus, and *Complete Poems and Major Prose*, ed. M. Y. Hughes (1957), with full introductions and notes. Similar volumes, with much less prose and minimal apparatus, have been edited by C. Brooks (1950) and M. H. Nicolson (1962), both paperbacks. Recent editions of the complete poems are those of H. Darbishire (2 vols., 1952–5), with textual apparatus; B. A. Wright (1956), with a textual Introduction; D. Bush (1965–6); and J. Carey and A. Fowler (1968)—the last two with full Introductions and notes. The complete English poems have been edited, with varying apparatus, by C. Williams (1940), J. H. Hanford (2nd edn., 1953), and J. T. Shawcross (1963). Volumes of selections, some in paperback, have been edited by G. and M. Bullough (1958), D. Bush (1949; rev. 1968), N. Frye (1951)—the last two with some prose—M. Y. Hughes (1937, 1962), E. Le Comte (1961), I. G. MacCaffrey and C. Ricks (companion volumes, 1966, 1968), M. Mack (1950), F. T. Prince (1957, 1962, 1968), B. Rajan (1964), and B. A. Wright (1938, often reprinted). Of all the editions cited, some retain the original spelling and punctuation; others are more or less modernized. The full notes in some older editions, e.g., those of A. W. Verity (issued and revised, 1891–1952), remain helpful.

Some special editions are: *The Latin Poems*, ed. W. MacKellar (1930), with translations and notes; *Sonnets*, edited by J. S. Smart (1921), who made signal advances in knowledge, and by E. A. J. Honigmann (1966), who added a good deal, mostly of value; *Milton's 'Lycidas'*, ed. C. A. Patrides (see CRITICISM AND COMMENTARY (*c*) below), and *Milton's 'Lycidas'*, ed. S. Elledge (1966), with copious notes and illustrative material. Among small facsimiles is *Justa Edouardo King*, ed. E. C. Mossner (1939). H. F. Fletcher's massive facsimile edition of the complete poems (4 vols., 1943–8) is very useful for its reproduction of the original printed editions and of the Cambridge manuscript, which contains most of Milton's minor poems, some of them much revised. A new concordance, edited by W. Ingram, is forthcoming from Oxford.

Scholarly editions of individual prose works are partly superseded by the *Complete Prose Works* being edited in eight volumes by D. M. Wolfe and many associates, who provide very elaborate historical introductions and notes and new translations of the Latin works. The first paragraph, above, cited the anthologies of F. A. Patterson and M. Y. Hughes, which contain a large bulk of prose. Among small collections of prose are those of M. W. Wallace (1925), M. Y. Hughes (1947), and K. M. Burton (1958). A larger body of prose has been given scholarly editing in one volume by J. M. Patrick and others (1967).

CRITICAL STUDIES AND COMMENTARY

Scholarly and critical writings are arranged below according to their subjects: (*a*) *Paradise Lost*; (*b*) total work and selected works and topics; (*c*) early poems; (*d*) *Paradise Regained*; (*e*) *Samson Agonistes*; (*f*) the prose works and Milton's thought. Mention may be made here of the Variorum Commentary on all the poetry—the first since Todd's of 1801—which is being prepared by M. Y. Hughes and others; it will contain, in half a dozen volumes, the fullest body of information, annotation, and criticism ever brought together. D. Bush and A. B. Giamatti have done vol. i (1970), on the Latin, Greek, and Italian poems.

(*a*) *Paradise Lost*, since the romantic age, has been the main battle-ground of criticism. Blake and Shelley, as revolutionary rebels against the establishment, made over Milton and the poem in their own image. Others slighted or dismissed the poet's religious theme but exalted his imaginative and artistic power. This, the predominant attitude, was eventually summed up in Sir Walter Raleigh's dictum (1900), that '*Paradise Lost* is not the less an eternal monument because it is a monument to dead ideas'. One further step in this direction was possible, the denigration of the poet's art as well as of his odious creed and personality. The loud or quiet utterances of Ezra Pound and T. S. Eliot enabled F. R. Leavis to affirm that the disenthronement of Milton had been effected with remarkably little fuss (*Revaluation*, 1936; cf. *The Common Pursuit*, 1952). The most acute counsel for the prosecution has been A. J. A. Waldock (1947); his fundamental disability was tone-deafness to Milton's Christian beliefs and values, combined with a failure to understand the method of their presentation. This approach was carried on by J. Peter (1960). The vehemently anti-Christian William Empson began and ended *Milton's God* (1961) on the text that 'the reason why the poem is so good is that it makes God so bad'.

Meanwhile, from about 1917 onward, J. H. Hanford and other scholars were replacing the nineteenth-century stereotype of the dichotomized 'sublime Puritan' with the unified conception of the Renaissance humanist. D. Saurat (1925) took that line, with aberrations. E. M. W. Tillyard (*Milton*, 1930) gave the first general survey of the humanized 'modern' Milton, though he still saw in *Paradise Lost* a cleavage between 'conscious' and 'unconscious' meanings. B. Willey (*The Seventeenth Century Background*, 1934) set forth the difficulties Milton himself faced. The conventional antinomy between Puritan and poet was opposed by C. Williams (1940) and C. S. Lewis (1942), who saw a unified Christian poem. Since then, Waldock especially has stimulated more and more satisfying expositions. (The fullest account of controversy is that of P. Murray; the Victorian Milton is described by J. G. Nelson; criticism since Lewis has in 1968 been given comprehensive and penetrating analysis by Irene Samuel). Although orthodoxy of any kind provokes automatic dissent in many modern minds, the central orthodoxy of recent decades embodies the soundest and best criticism Milton and *Paradise Lost* have ever had, because it is the first that unites informed and sympathetic understanding of his Christian beliefs and ethical principles with sophisticated and subtle aesthetic perception. It is now a matter of course that, like any work of the past, the poem must be taken on its own terms, that only by first seeing what Milton meant can we see what he still means for us. Of special value in this regard —along with its aesthetic value—was, and is, B. Rajan's '*Paradise Lost*' *and the Seventeenth-Century Reader* (1947). A short statement of this view is L. A. Cormican's chapter in *From Donne to Marvell* (1956).

While modern critics recognize the inseparable unity of Milton's theme and art, some writers have concentrated on the former, e.g., J. S. Diekhoff (1946), G. A. Wilkes (1961), D. H. Burden (1967), and, in a special way, S. E. Fish (below). These expositors have shown that, far from falling through 'blind recklessness' (Raleigh) into fatal contradictions, Milton everywhere wove a logical and coherent pattern. The alleged pitfalls are now found rather in the reader than in the poem, which is far more complex and subtle than either Milton's old friends or old and new enemies perceived. As Northrop Frye observes, apropos of Satan's superficial and rebellious view of the Son's elevation, all superficial readers of Milton are in the position of minor devils.

Thus, while traditional criticism was happy in noting Homeric and Virgilian parallels, modern critics, from Sir Maurice Bowra (*From Virgil to Milton*, 1945) to J. M. Steadman (*Milton and the Renaissance Hero*, 1967), have stressed Milton's Christian re-creation of the classical epic, especially the contrasts between Satan's egoistic pride and martial heroism and the true heroism of the Son and the regenerate Adam. In the modern Christian approach symbolism and irony are seen as pervasive elements of structure and detail: e.g. heaven, hell, and Eden are not only places but states of mind, and Satan and his fellows and Adam and Eve are alike enveloped in dramatic irony, hostile or compassionate. A. Stein (*Answerable Style*, 1953) emphasizes Milton's dramatic rendering of his theme along with the suggestiveness of his language; and the war in heaven, so long condemned as unrealistic realism, is persuasively presented as a monstrous burlesque of military force and prowess. So, too, as Rajan and others have seen, the allegory of Satan, Sin, and Death—likewise subject to age-old censure—appears as a grisly ironical parody of the Trinity (one that puts the 'heroic' Satan in his true setting). Isabel G. MacCaffrey ('*Paradise Lost*' as '*Myth*', 1959) gives a fresh exposition of archetypal motifs in a 'myth' shaped by a poet of strongly Christian and classical temper: hence the religious and moral dimensions of time and space, light and darkness, change and recurrence, indeed everything in a hierarchical and dynamic universe. For Frank Kermode, in an important essay ('Adam Unparadised', *The Living Milton*, 1960), *Paradise Lost* is 'wonderfully satisfying' as an embodiment of 'life in a great symbolic attitude'; Kermode, one may add, ended his *Romantic Image* (1957) with the prophecy that it will before long be 'read once more as the most perfect achievement of English poetry, perhaps the richest and most intricately beautiful poem in the world'.

Two critics—J. B. Broadbent in a comprehensive, energetic, and ill-written book, *Some Graver Subject* (1960), and H. R. Swardson in a chapter (*Poetry and the Fountain of Light*, 1962)—opened our decade by reviving, from different standpoints, views of the dichotomized poet and poem which modern criticism had been disposing of. B. A. Wright (*Milton's 'Paradise Lost'*, 1962) forcefully defended aspects of the poem, from fable to style, that had been commonly misunderstood. Several critics emphasize, in their several ways, Milton's continuous presence. J. H. Summers (*The Muse's Method*, 1962), through sensitive analysis of episodes, passages, and rhythms, provides illuminating lessons in the right reading of the whole poem. Anne D. Ferry (*Milton's Epic Voice*, 1963) argues that the narrator expresses and unifies his total meaning through one voice that is variously heard in statement, simile, and especially metaphor. J. Arthos (*Dante, Michelangelo and Milton*, 1963) hears in all Milton's poems and styles the unique voice of the rational sublime, celebrating divine order. L. L. Martz (*The Paradise Within*, 1964) hears the 'human, flexible, responsive voice of an individual living in a great tradition, interpreting the discoveries of his "unpremeditated Verse", and encouraging us to read the poem as the progress of an interior journey, toward the center of the soul'. Martz, like C. S. Lewis, loses sympathy in the last two books—which of late have had many able defenders, the latest B. Rajan (*Huntington Library Quarterly*, xxxi (1967–8); *The Lofty Rhyme* (1970)) and J. Reesing (*Milton's Poetic Art*, 1968, 71–104).

Helen Gardner (*A Reading of 'Paradise Lost'*, 1965), steering between the antithetical extremes of criticism, begins with Milton's own religious recognition of problems beyond human reach. She stresses the imaginative force and fervour of his very personal and very moving vision of the world, the world of beauty and love, freedom and responsibility, good and evil, in which it is the human destiny to live. N. Frye (*The Return of Eden*, 1965), also with a teacher's awareness of adverse conditioning to be met, presents a suggestive, economical survey of the total scheme, of Milton's Christian re-creation of epic conventions and his whole hierarchical structure, a 'vast symmetrical pattern . . . in which evil parodies good'. S. E. Fish (*Surprised by Sin*, 1967) meets such complaints as Waldock's with a comprehensive thesis: starting from Summers and Mrs. Ferry, he argues for Milton's ever-present consciousness of the Christian though inevitably fallen reader who at times shares the humanly natural but wrong feelings of Satan or Eve or Adam and, seeing himself thus revealed, undergoes a corrective experience. W. G. Madsen (*From Shadowy Types to Truth*, 1968) breaks new ground by applying the typological interpretation of the Old and New Testaments that was current in Milton's age: e.g., he sees (p. 111) in Raphael's account of the war in heaven 'a shadow of things to come. . . a shadow of this last age of the world and of the Second Coming of Christ', and its chief lesson for the reader is that of patience. L. Ryken (*The Apocalyptic Vision in 'Paradise Lost'*, 1970) explores the ways in which Milton presents 'transcendental, ideal experience' in heaven and prelapsarian Eden. In general, whatever the differences among critics, it is agreed that the modern reader—who is probably not a Christian but can read Dante with more or less sympathy—must see *Paradise Lost* as a Christian 'myth' of the human condition.

Some books on Milton's religious beliefs and thought are cited below in (*f*). Traditional materials and ideas about the Creation and the Fall are set forth by G. McColley (1940), A. Williams (1948), and J. M. Evans (1968). W. Kirkconnell collected and translated pre-Miltonic analogues (*The Celestial Cycle*, 1952). J. H. Sims's *The Bible in Milton's Epics* (1962) is a well-ordered survey. One may mention here Irene Samuel's *Dante and Milton* (1966), a close inquiry into what one Christian epic may have gained from the other.

Several discussions of *Paradise Lost* and the classical epics, especially Steadman's, were noted above. Some other writings in this area are: A. S. P. Woodhouse, 'Pattern in *Paradise Lost*' (1953), P. Hägin (*The Epic Hero and the Decline of Heroic Poetry*, 1964), who sets *Paradise Lost* apart from neoclassical theory, and K. W. Gransden, '*Paradise Lost* and the *Aeneid*' (1967); chapters in D. Bush, *Mythology and the Renaissance Tradition* (rev. edn., 1963), and T. Greene, *The Descent from Heaven* (1963); D. P. Harding, *The Club of Hercules* (1962); and A. B. Giamatti, *The Earthly Paradise and the Renaissance Epic* (1966).

Some books are focused on Milton's artistry. J. I. Cope (*The Metaphoric Structure of 'Paradise Lost'*, 1962)—going on from Mrs. MacCaffrey, with less clarity of presentation and style—sees 'a poem in which certain repeated metaphors mimetically express the epic theme with an unprecedented tenacity': he expounds the symbolism of time and space and manifold aspects of scenic structure and all kinds of movement. C. Ricks (*Milton's Grand Style*, 1963), with interesting citations from neglected eighteenth-century commentators, refutes modern charges against Milton's epic manner as mere grandiloquence and shows how rich and functional his syntax and language are. W. Shumaker (*Unpremeditated Verse: Feeling and Perception in 'Paradise Lost'*, 1967) analyses—more systematically than W. B. C. Watkins (see (*b*) below)—the ways in which imagery springs from and appeals to the senses in a poem that is both 'mythic' and 'rational'.

To come to more technical studies, F. T. Prince's compact *The Italian Element in Milton's Verse* (1954) demonstrated the poet's awareness, in minor as well as major poems, of Italian theories of the sublime and of stylistic devices for achieving it. R. D. Emma's *Milton's Grammar* (1964) is a concrete analysis of diction and style. Robert Bridges's *Milton's Prosody* has been amplified or modified by himself (1921), by S. E. Sprott (*Milton's Art of Prosody*, 1953), F. T. Prince (above), Ants Oras in numerous articles (e.g., 1953), R. O. Evans (*Milton's Elisions*, 1966), and others.

The many writers named in this section (and other sections) are all more or less helpful, but even Milton did not grade the nine orders of angels. For a possibly intimidated novice there is much critical wisdom in A. Rudrum's small guide, *Milton: 'Paradise Lost'* (1966).

There are very useful collections of scattered critiques. *Paradise Lost* is the theme of *Milton*, ed. L. L. Martz (1966), the main theme in *Milton*, ed. A. E. Barker (1965), and *Milton's Epic Poetry*, ed. C. A. Patrides (1967). Earlier essays and comments are assembled in *Milton Criticism*, ed. J. Thorpe (1950), *Milton: The Critical Heritage*, ed. J. T. Shawcross (1970), covering 1628–1731, and *The Romantics on Milton*, ed. J. A. Wittreich (1970). Some collections of tercentenary papers are: *Huntingdon Library Quarterly* xxxi (November 1967); *Language and Style in Milton*, ed. R. D. Emma and J. T. Shawcross (1968), mainly on *Paradise Lost*; the also Anglo-American *Approaches to 'Paradise Lost'*, ed. C. A. Patrides (1968); *New Essays on 'Paradise Lost'*, ed. T. Kranidas (1969); a Canadian volume edited by B. Rajan (1969); and *Milton Studies I*, ed. J. D. Simmonds (1969), mainly on *Paradise Lost*.

(b) With the critical biographies cited in BIOGRAPHIES below may be joined J. H. Hanford's compendious *Milton Handbook* (5th edn., 1970); D. Daiches' *Milton* (1957), an active survey of all the writings; M. H. Nicolson's *John Milton* (1963), 'A reader's guide to the poetry'; a chapter in D. Bush, *English Literature in the Earlier Seventeenth Century* (rev. 1962); and J. Carey's small and unsympathetic *Milton* (1969).

Some volumes of articles and essays or special surveys are: *John Milton: poet and humanist* (1966), a selection of Hanford's early but durable studies; E. M. W. Tillyard's *The Miltonic Setting* (1938) and *Studies in Milton* (1951), which enlarged or modified his *Milton* of 1930; I. Samuel, *Plato and Milton* (1947); D. C. Allen's enlightening and provocative *The Harmonious Vision* (1954); R. M. Adams's lively, astringent *Ikon: Milton and the Modern Critics* (1955); W. B. C. Watkins's *Anatomy of Milton's Verse* (1955), a direct response to sensuous and passionate poetry; *The Living Milton*, ed. F. Kermode (1960), containing reports from writers who are not 'Miltonists'; R. Daniells's *Milton, Mannerism and Baroque* (1963), the fullest treatment of that elusive theme (cf. the chapter in M. M. Mahood, *Poetry and Humanism*,

1950); M. Y. Hughes, *Ten Perspectives on Milton* (1965), a major authority's collected studies, e.g., 'Milton and the Symbol of Light'; *The Lyric and Dramatic Milton*, ed. J. H. Summers (1965), which has two groups of papers; two pieces in G. Williamson's *Seventeenth Century Contexts* (1961) and half a dozen in his *Milton and Others* (1965); A. E. Barker's critical anthology, *Milton* (1965); T. Kranidas, *The Fierce Equation: A Study of Milton's Decorum* (1965); varied papers by eleven authorities edited by A. P. Fiore (1967); a critical anthology, *Milton*, edited by A. Rudrum (1968); J. Reesing, *Milton's Poetic Art: 'A Mask', 'Lycidas', and 'Paradise Lost'* (1968), mentioned above; E. L. Marilla's collected studies, mainly of Milton's poetic use of the ideas of Christian humanism, *Milton and Modern Man* (1968); B. Rajan's felicitous analyses of the chief poems, collected in *The Lofty Rhyme* (1970); and *Milton Studies II*, ed. J. D. Simmonds (1970).

(c) Hanford's 'The Youth of Milton' (1925; reprinted in the 1966 volume cited in (b) above) is still good. The commentary of C. Brooks and J. E. Hardy (*Poems of Mr. John Milton*, 1951) has the virtues and defects of the 'New Criticism'. The best single book on the early poems is R. Tuve's *Images and Themes in Five Poems by Milton* (1957). Two valuable essays are A. E. Barker's on the 'Nativity' (1941) and J. B. Leishman's on 'L'Allegro' and 'Il Penseroso' and their background (1951), included in Leishman's *Milton's Minor Poems* (1969).

There are monographs on *Comus* by J. Arthos (1954) and J. Blondel (1964), a commentary, *'Comus' and 'Samson Agonistes'* (1961), by J. B. Broadbent, and a commentary on *Comus* and other poems by A. Rudrum (1967). A. S. P. Woodhouse's 'The Argument of Milton's *Comus*' (1941; supplemented in 1950), which set interpretation on a new plane, has been more or less modified by, e.g., R. M. Adams ((b) above), A. E. Dyson (1955), R. Tuve (above), W. G. Madsen ((f) below), M. H. Nicolson ((b) above), and, less directly, by C. L. Barber (1965) and B. Rajan (1968). J. S. Diekhoff's *A Maske at Ludlow* (1968) is a useful anthology of modern criticism and includes the Bridgewater text. J. G. Demaray's *Milton and the Masque Tradition* (1968) deals with formal elements.

While *Lycidas* had long been exalted as a supreme exercise in classical art, modern study in depth has seen it as probably the greatest short poem in the language. C. A. Patrides's *Milton's 'Lycidas'* (1961) is a useful collection of modern essays.

Editions of the sonnets (see TEXTS above) contain much important comment. Two substantial studies are J. H. Finley's 'Milton and Horace' (1937) and parts of Prince's *Italian Element* ((a) above).

(d) A fresh, learned, and comprehensive work on *Paradise*

Regained is B. K. Lewalski's *Milton's Brief Epic* (1966). A critical analysis occupies half of A. Stein's *Heroic Knowledge* (1957) and parts of Steadman's *Milton and the Renaissance Hero* (1967). Among numerous essays are those of W. G. Rice (reprinted in Barker, *Milton*); M. Y. Hughes (reprinted in his *Ten Perspectives*); F. Kermode (1953); A. S. P. Woodhouse (1956); N. Frye (1956); L. L. Martz (*The Paradise Within*, 1964); a chapter in M. Fixler ((*f*) below); and H. Schultz's book (ibid.).

(*e*) Some critiques of varying focus are: W. R. Parker, *Milton's Debt to Greek Tragedy in 'Samson Agonistes'* (1937); half of Stein's *Heroic Knowledge* (1957); Sister Miriam Clare, *'Samson Agonistes': A Study in Contrast* (1964); and, on Christian typology, F. M. Krouse's book (1949) and a chapter in W. G. Madsen (*From Shadowy Types*, 1968). The drama figures largely in Steadman ((*d*) above). Among essays are those of Hanford (1925; reprinted in his 1966 volume); Woodhouse (1959); W. Empson ('A Defense of Delilah', 1960–1); G. A. Wilkes (1963); and several pieces in *The Lyric and Dramatic Milton* ((*b*) above). G. M. Crump has edited *Twentieth Century Interpretations of 'Samson Agonistes'* (1968). W. Kirkconnell compiled an illustrative book of analogues, *That Invincible Samson* (1964).

(*f*) The most thorough single analysis of Milton's libertarian thought is A. E. Barker's *Milton and the Puritan Dilemma, 1641–1660* (1942). The fullest commentaries are in the *Complete Prose Works* (see TEXTS above). Some religious and political books which have Milton in the foreground or background are: W. Haller, *The Rise of Puritanism* (1938) and *Liberty and Reformation in the Puritan Revolution* (1955); A. S. P. Woodhouse, *Puritanism and Liberty* (1938); Z. S. Fink, *The Classical Republicans* (1945); M. Fixler (*Milton and the Kingdoms of God*, 1964), who analyses Milton's early millenarian hopes and his disenchantment; and histories of political thought in the period.

Milton's theological beliefs are most fully expounded by M. Kelley (*This Great Argument*, 1941) who ties *Paradise Lost* closely with *De Doctrina Christiana*, and C. A. Patrides in *Milton and the Christian Tradition* (1966), a broader study, learnedly documented. Kelley upholds the label 'Arian', traditional since the publication of Milton's treatise in 1825; Patrides endorses the recent label, 'subordinationist'. R. M. Frye (*God, Man, and Satan*, 1960) links Milton and Bunyan with old and modern religious thought. Milton's religious evolution is outlined in a chapter in Woodhouse's *The Poet and his Faith* (1965).

Milton's religious and metaphysical view of nature is treated by

W. C. Curry (*Milton's Ontology, Cosmogony, and Physics*, 1957) and, less reconditely, in W. G. Madsen's study of his 'Idea of Nature' (1958). Two opposed or complementary traditions are set forth in H. Schultz, *Milton and Forbidden Knowledge* (1955), on the century's religious fear of intemperate 'curiosity', and K. Svendsen, *Milton and Science* (1956), which turns information to critical account. A tradition quite central for Milton is the theme of R. Hoopes, *Right Reason in the English Renaissance* (1962). W. J. Grace (*Ideas in Milton*, 1968) outlines Milton's beliefs and ideas and relates them to the poems. J. M. Steadman's *Milton's Epic Characters* (1968) 'explores the intellectual background' of the two epics, 'with particular emphasis on problems of characterization'. Music, which was of more than aesthetic concern to Milton and his age, has been treated in S. G. Spaeth's pioneer work (1913) and by J. Hollander (1961) and G. L. Finney (1962).

BIOGRAPHIES AND LETTERS

Milton's private letters, in Latin and in translation, are in the standard *Works* (see TEXTS above: Patterson, vol. xii). They have been translated afresh in E. M. W. and P. B. Tillyard, *Milton: Private Correspondence and Academic Exercises* (1932), and again, with full notes, by W. A. and A. T. Turner, in successive volumes of the *Complete Prose Works* (see Wolfe in TEXTS). The first volume of this last includes that partial record of Milton's reading, his Commonplace Book, translated, with full notes, by Ruth Mohl, who carried commentary further in *John Milton and His Commonplace Book* (1969). J. S. Diekhoff collected 'Milton's utterances upon himself and his works' in *Milton on Himself* (1939).

The six early biographies, by John Aubrey and others, are in *The Early Lives of Milton*, ed. H. Darbishire (1932); her attribution of the anonymous one to Milton's nephew, John Phillips, has been disputed. The chief lives are given in *The Student's Milton* (see Patterson in TEXTS above). The foundation of modern biography is D. Masson's all-inclusive *Life* (6 vols., 1881–96); it remains valuable, though open at times to revision. There are small critical biographies by J. H. Hanford (1949), K. Muir (1955), E. Saillens (1959; trans. 1964), and D. Bush (1964–5). W. R. Parker's *Milton: A Biography* (2 vols., 1968, with copious notes and index) is a massive product of long labour and expert scholarship; it includes a few heresies. J. M. French's *Life Records of John Milton* (5 vols., 1949–58) is a documentary work of reference which chronicles every event and allusion.

Some more special books may be added. D. L. Clark made a detailed study (1948) of the classical curriculum at St. Paul's School. H. F. Fletcher's *Intellectual Development of John Milton* (2 vols., 1956–61) has a very full account of secondary and university education; it is somewhat eccentric in regard to Milton's early writings. A later phase is most fully described in J. Arthos, *Milton and the Italian Cities* (1968). In *Milton's Contemporary Reputation* (1940) W. R. Parker digests reactions to Milton's controversial prose during 1641—74 and reprints five replies to him. E. S. Le Comte's *A Milton Dictionary* (1961) is a handy 'companion'.

BIBLIOGRAPHIES

Bibliographies of editions and of scholarship and criticism are: D. H. Stevens, *Reference Guide to Milton from 1800 to the Present Day* (Chicago and London, 1930); H. F. Fletcher, *Contributions to a Milton Bibliography 1800–1930* (University of Illinois Studies XVI, 1931; reprinted, New York, 1967); C. Huckabay, *John Milton: An Annotated Bibliography 1929–1968* (Pittsburgh and Louvain, 1969; rev. from 1960 edn.); *C.B.E.L.*, ed. F. W. Bateson (1941), i. 463–73, and *Supplement*, ed. G. Watson (1957); D. Bush, *O.H.E.L.* volume (see CRITICISM (*b*) above, 1966 impression, with an updated bibliography of Milton); J. H. Hanford and C. W. Crupi, *Milton* (paperback, New York, 1966), a 52-page list, with some comments; Hanford and Taaffe, *A Milton Handbook* (5th edn., 1970); a full and briefly descriptive bibliography for all Milton's work and background in C. A. Patrides's *Milton's Epic Poetry* (paperback, New York, 1967; paperback, U.K.), pp. 383–428; and extensive references in many books, e.g., Hughes's edition of 1957 (see TEXTS above) and Barker's anthology, *Milton* (paperback 1965; paperback, U.K.). For current writing on Milton and his age there are the annual bibliographies in *SP* and *PMLA*; the *Annual Bibliography* of the modern Humanities Research Association, and the selective survey, *The Year's Work in English Studies*; and, more specially, *Seventeenth-Century News*, ed. J. M. Patrick *et al.*, and the *Milton Newsletter*, ed. R. C. Flannagan (1967 ff.), now, 1970, called *Milton Quarterly*.

BACKGROUND READING

Since space has been heavily taxed, the resolute reader must be referred to the large bibliography in D. Bush (see CRITICISM (*b*) above) on all areas of English writing, thought, history, and culture, and to Patrides (BIBLIOGRAPHIES above).

REFERENCES

TEXTS

H. C. Beeching (ed.), *The English Poems of John Milton*, in modern spelling, with Reader's Guide to Milton by Walter Skeat, and Introduction by Charles Williams (World's Classics, London and New York, 1940).

C. Brooks (ed.), *Complete Poetry and Selected Prose of John Milton* (paperback, New York, 1950). See also Brooks and Hardy, under CRITICAL STUDIES (*c*) above.

G. and M. Bullough (eds.), *Milton's Dramatic Poems* (London and Fair Lawn, N.J., 1958).

K. M. Burton (ed.), *Milton's Prose Writings* (London and New York, 1958).

D. Bush (ed.), *The Portable Milton*, rev. edn. (New York, 1968; paperbacks, U.S. and U.K.).

D. Bush (ed.). *The Complete Poetical Works of John Milton* (Boston, 1965; Oxford Standard Authors, London, 1966; paperback, U.K.).

J. Carey and A. Fowler (eds.), *The Poems of John Milton* (London and New York, 1968).

H. Darbishire (ed.), *The Poetical Works of John Milton* (2 vols., Oxford English Texts, Oxford, 1952–5).

S. Elledge (ed.), *Milton's 'Lycidas'* (New York and London, 1966).

H. F. Fletcher (ed.), *John Milton's Complete Poetical Works, Reproduced in Photographic Facsimile* (4 vols., Urbana, Ill., 1943–8).

N. Frye (ed.), *John Milton: 'Paradise Lost' and Selected Poetry and Prose* (paperbacks, U.S. and U.K., 1951).

J. H. Hanford (ed.), *The Poems of John Milton*, 2nd edn. (New York, 1953).

E. A. J. Honigman (ed.), *Milton's Sonnets* (London and New York, 1966).

M. Y. Hughes (ed.), *'Paradise Regained', the Minor Poems, and 'Samson Agonistes'* (New York, 1937).

M. Y. Hughes (ed.), *John Milton: Prose Selections* (New York, 1947).

M. Y. Hughes (ed.), *John Milton: Complete Poems and Major Prose* (New York, 1957).

M. Y. Hughes (ed.), *Paradise Lost* (paperback, New York, 1962).

W. Ingram (ed.), *A Concordance to Milton's English Poetry* (Oxford, 1971).

E. Le Comte (ed.), *John Milton: 'Paradise Lost' and Other Poems* (paperback, N.Y., 1961).

I. G. MacCaffrey (ed.), *John Milton: 'Samson Agonistes' and the Shorter Poems* (paperback, U.S. and U.K., 1966).

M. Mack (ed.), *Milton* (New York, 1950).

W. MacKellar (ed.), *The Latin Poems of John Milton* (paperback, New Haven, Conn., and London, 1930).

E. C. Mossner (ed.), *Justa Edouardo King* (facsimile, New York, 1939).

M. H. Nicolson (ed.), *Milton: Poems and Selected Prose* (paperback, U.S. and U.K., 1962).

J. M. Patrick *et al.* (eds.), *The Prose of John Milton* (paperback, New York, 1967).

C. A. Patrides (ed.), *Milton's 'Lycidas': The Tradition and the Poem* (paperback, U.S. and U.K., 1961).

F. A. Patterson *et al.* (eds.), *The Works of John Milton* (20 vols., New York, 1931–40).

F. A. Patterson (ed.), *The Student's Milton* (New York, 1933).

F. T. Prince (ed.), *Milton: 'Samson Agonistes'* (London and New York, 1957).

F. T. Prince (ed.), *Milton: 'Paradise Lost', Books I and II* (London and New York, 1962).

F. T. Prince (ed.), *Milton: 'Comus' and other Poems* (London, 1968).

B. Rajan (ed.), *John Milton: 'Paradise Lost', Books I and II* (London, 1964).

C. Ricks (ed.), *John Milton: 'Paradise Lost' and 'Paradise Regained'* (paperback, U.S. and U.K., 1968).

J. T. Shawcross (ed.), *The Complete English Poetry of John Milton* (New York, 1963; paperbacks, U.S. and U.K.).

J. S. Smart (ed.), *The Sonnets of Milton* (Glasgow, 1921; paperbacks, U.K. and U.S., 1966).

A. W. Verity (ed.), *The Cambridge Milton for Schools* (various vols., issued and reprinted, Cambridge, 1891–1952).

M. W. Wallace (ed.), *Milton's Prose* (London and New York, 1925).

D. M. Wolfe *et al.* (eds.), *Complete Prose Works of John Milton* (in progress: Vols. I–IV, New Haven, Conn., and London, 1953–66).

B. A. Wright (ed.), *Shorter Poems of John Milton* (London and New York, 1938).

B. A. Wright (ed.), *Milton's Poems* (London and New York, 1956).

CRITICAL STUDIES AND COMMENTARY

R. M. Adams, *Ikon: Milton and the Modern Critics* (Ithaca, N.Y., and London, 1955; paperbacks, U.S. and U.K.).

D. C. Allen, *The Harmonious Vision: Studies in Milton's Poetry* (Baltimore and London, 1954).

J. Arthos, *On A Mask Presented at Ludlow-Castle* (paperback, Ann Arbor, Mich., 1954).

J. Arthos, *Dante, Michelangelo and Milton* (London, 1963).

C. L. Barber, '*A Mask Presented at Ludlow Castle*: The Masque as a Masque', in J. H. Summers (ed.), *The Lyric and Dramatic Milton* and Diekhoff (ed.), *A Maske* (q.v.).

A. E. Barker, 'The Pattern of Milton's *Nativity Ode*', *UTQ* x (1940–1).

A. E. Barker, *Milton and the Puritan Dilemma, 1641–1660* (Toronto, 1942; reprinted 1956).

A. E. Barker (ed.), *Milton: Modern Essays in Criticism* (paperback, New York and London, 1965).

J. Blondel, *Le 'Comus' de John Milton: masque neptunien* (paperback, Paris, 1964).

C. M. Bowra, *From Virgil to Milton* (London, 1945, New York, 1946; paperbacks, U.K. and U.S.).

R. Bridges, *Milton's Prosody*, rev. edn. (London and New York, 1921; reprinted 1965).

J. B. Broadbent, *Some Graver Subject: An Essay on 'Paradise Lost'* (London, 1960, New York, 1960 [1961]).

J. B. Broadbent, *Milton: 'Comus' and 'Samson Agonistes'* (London, 1961; paperback, New York, 1961).

C. Brooks and J. E. Hardy, *The Poems of Mr. John Milton* (New York, 1951).

D. H. Burden, *The Logical Epic: A Study of the Argument of 'Paradise Lost'* (London and Cambridge, Mass., 1967).

D. Bush, *Mythology and the Renaissance Tradition in English Poetry*, rev. edn. (New York, 1963; paperback, U.S.).

D. Bush, *English Literature in the Earlier Seventeenth Century, 1600–1660*, rev. edn. (*O.H.E.L.*, vol. v, Oxford and New York, 1962).

D. Bush and A. B. Giamatti (eds.), *A Variorum Commentary on the Poems of John Milton*, vol. i: *Latin, Greek, and Italian Poems* (London and New York, 1970).

J. Carey, *Milton* (London, 1969; paperback, New York, 1969; paperback, U.K.).

J. I. Cope, *The Metaphoric Structure of 'Paradise Lost'* (Baltimore and London, 1962).

L. A. Cormican, 'Milton's Religious Verse', in B. Ford (ed.), *From Donne to Marvell* (paperback, Harmondsworth and New York, 1956).

G. M. Crump (ed.), *Twentieth Century Interpretations of 'Samson Agonistes'* (paperback, Englewood Cliffs, N.J., 1968; paperback, U.K.).

W. C. Curry, *Milton's Ontology, Cosmogony, and Physics* (Lexington, Ky., 1957; paperbacks, U.S. and U.K.).

D. Daiches, *Milton* (London and paperback, New York, 1957; paperback, U.K.).

R. Daniells, *Milton, Mannerism and Baroque* (Toronto, 1963).

J. G. Demaray, *Milton and the Masque Tradition* (Cambridge, Mass., and London, 1968).

J. S. Diekhoff, *Milton's 'Paradise Lost': A Commentary on the Argument* (New York and London, 1946; repr. 1958).

J. S. Diekhoff (ed.), *A Maske at Ludlow* (Cleveland, 1968).

A. E. Dyson, 'The Interpretation of *Comus*', *Essays and Studies 1955* (London).

T. S. Eliot, 'A Note on the Verse of John Milton', *Essays and Studies*, xxi (1936); reprinted in Eliot's *On Poetry and Poets* (London and New York, 1957; paperbacks, U.K. and U.S.).

T. S. Eliot, 'Milton', *Proc. of the British Academy*, xxxiii (1947); *SR* lvi (1948); reprinted with preceding essay (1957).

R. D. Emma, *Milton's Grammar* (The Hague, 1964).

R. D. Emma and J. T. Shawcross (eds.), *Language and Style in Milton: A Symposium in Honor of the Tercentenary* (New York, 1968).

W. Empson, 'A Defense of Delilah', *SR* lxviii (1960); reprinted in *Milton's God*.

W. Empson, *Milton's God* (London and New York, 1961; rev. 1965).

J. M. Evans, *'Paradise Lost' and the Genesis Tradition* (Oxford and New York, 1968).

R. O. Evans, *Milton's Elisions* (Gainesville, Fla., 1966; paperback, U.S.).

A. D. Ferry, *Milton's Epic Voice: The Narrator in 'Paradise Lost'* (Cambridge, Mass., and London, 1963).

Z. S. Fink, *The Classical Republicans: an Essay in the Recovery of a Pattern of Thought in Seventeenth Century England* (Chicago, 1945; 2nd edn., 1962).

J. H. Finley, 'Milton and Horace: A Study of Milton's Sonnets', *Harvard Studies in Classical Philology*, xlviii (1937).

G. L. Finney, *Musical Backgrounds for English Literature: 1580–1650* (New Brunswick, N.J., 1962).

A. P. Fiore (ed.), *Th'Upright Heart and Pure: Essays on John Milton* (Pittsburgh, 1967).

S. E. Fish, *Surprised by Sin: the Reader in 'Paradise Lost'* (London and New York, 1967).

M. Fixler, *Milton and the Kingdoms of God* (Chicago and London, 1964).

N. Frye, 'The Typology of *Paradise Regained*' (1956); reprinted in the anthologies of Barker and Patrides (q.v.), and (rev.) in Frye's *Return of Eden*.

N. Frye, *The Return of Eden: Five Essays on Milton's Epics* (Toronto and London, 1965).

R. M. Frye, *God, Man, and Satan: Patterns of Christian Thought and Life in 'Paradise Lost,' 'Pilgrim's Progress', and the Great Theologians* (Princeton, N.J., 1960).

H. Gardner, *A Reading of 'Paradise Lost'* (Oxford, 1965; paperback, U.K.).

A. B. Giamatti, *The Earthly Paradise and the Renaissance Epic* (Princeton, N.J., 1966; paperback, U.S.).

W. J. Grace, *Ideas in Milton* (Notre Dame, Ind., and London, 1968; paperback, U.S.).

K. W. Gransden, '*Paradise Lost* and the *Aeneid*', *EIC* xvii (1967).

T. Greene, *The Descent from Heaven: A Study in Epic Continuity* (New Haven, Conn., and London, 1963).

P. Hägin, *The Epic Hero and the Decline of Heroic Poetry: A Study of the Neoclassical English Epic with Special Reference to Milton's 'Paradise Lost'* (Bern, 1964).

W. Haller, *The Rise of Puritanism, Or, the Way to the New Jerusalem* (New York, 1938; paperbacks, U.S. and U.K.).

W. Haller, *Liberty and Reformation in the Puritan Revolution* (New York and London, 1955; paperbacks, U.K. and U.S.).

J. H. Hanford, *A Milton Handbook*, 5th edn., rev. by Hanford and J. G. Taaffe (New York, 1970).

J. H. Hanford, *John Milton: poet and humanist* (Cleveland, 1966), which includes 'The Pastoral Elegy and Milton's *Lycidas*' (1910) (also reprinted in Patrides's *Milton's 'Lycidas'*); 'The Youth of Milton' (1925); and '*Samson Agonistes* and Milton in Old Age' (1925).

D. P. Harding, *The Club of Hercules: Studies in the Classical Background of 'Paradise Lost'* (Urbana, Ill., 1962).

J. Hollander, *The Untuning of the Sky: Ideas of Music in English Poetry, 1500–1700* (Princeton, N.J., 1961).

R. Hoopes, *Right Reason in the English Renaissance* (Cambridge, Mass., and London, 1962).

M. Y. Hughes, *Ten Perspectives on Milton* (New Haven, Conn., and London, 1965).

M. Kelley, *This Great Argument: A Study of Milton's 'De Doctrina Christiana' as a Gloss upon 'Paradise Lost'* (Princeton, N.J., and London, 1941).

F. Kermode, 'Milton's Hero' [*Paradise Regained*], *RES* iv (1953).

F. Kermode, *Romantic Image* (London and New York, 1957; paperbacks, U.K. and U.S.).

F. Kermode (ed.), *The Living Milton: Essays by Various Hands* (London, 1960; paperback, U.K.).

W. Kirkconnell, *The Celestial Cycle: The Theme of 'Paradise Lost' in World Literature, with Translations of the Major Analogues* (Toronto, 1952).

W. Kirkconnell, *That Invincible Samson: The Theme of 'Samson Agonistes' in World Literature, with Translations of the Major Analogues* (Toronto, 1964).

T. Kranidas, *The Fierce Equation: A Study of Milton's Decorum* (The Hague and London, 1965).

T. Kranidas (ed.), *New Essays on 'Paradise Lost'* (Berkeley, Calif., 1969).

F. M. Krouse, *'Samson Agonistes' and the Christian Tradition* (Princeton, N.J., and London, 1949).

F. R. Leavis, 'Milton's Verse', *Revaluation* (London, 1936, New York, 1947; paperbacks, U.K. and U.S.).

F. R. Leavis, 'Mr Eliot and Milton' (1949); 'In Defence of Milton' (1938); reprinted in *The Common Pursuit* (London, 1952, New York, 1964; paperback, U.K.).

J. B. Leishman, '*L'Allegro* and *Il Penseroso* in Their Relation to Seventeenth-Century Poetry', *Essays and Studies 1951* (London).

J. B. Leishman, *Milton's Minor Poems*, ed. G. Tillotson (London, 1969).

B. K. Lewalski, *Milton's Brief Epic: The Genre, Meaning, and Art of 'Paradise Regained'* (Providence, R.I., and London, 1966).

C. S. Lewis, *A Preface to 'Paradise Lost'* (London, 1942; paperbacks, U.K. and U.S.).

I. G. MacCaffrey, *'Paradise Lost' as 'Myth'* (Cambridge, Mass., and London, 1959).

W. G. Madsen, 'The Idea of Nature in Milton's Poetry', in *Three Studies in the Renaissance*, by R. B. Young, W. T. Furniss, and W. G. Madsen (New Haven, Conn., and London, 1958).

W. G. Madsen, *From Shadowy Types to Truth: Studies in Milton's Symbolism* (New Haven, Conn., and London, 1968).

M. M. Mahood, *Poetry and Humanism* (London, 1950).

E. L. Marilla, *Milton and Modern Man* (University, Ala., 1968).

L. L. Martz, *The Paradise Within: Studies in Vaughan, Traherne, and Milton* (New Haven, Conn., and London, 1964; paperbacks, U.S. and U.K.).

L. L. Martz (ed.), *Milton: A Collection of Critical Essays* (Englewood Cliffs, N.J., 1966; paperbacks, U.S. and U.K.).

G. McColley, *'Paradise Lost': An Account of Its Growth and Major Origins* (Chicago, 1940).

Sister Miriam Clare, *'Samson Agonistes': A Study in Contrast* (New York, 1964).

P. Murray, *Milton, The Modern Phase: a Study of Twentieth-century Criticism* (London and New York, 1967).

J. G. Nelson, *The Sublime Puritan: Milton and the Victorians* (Madison, Wis., 1963).

M. H. Nicolson, *John Milton: A reader's guide to his poetry* (paperback, New York, 1963).

Ants Oras, 'Milton's Blank Verse and the Chronology of His Major Poems', *SAMLA Studies in Milton*, ed. J. M. Patrick (Gainesville, Fla., 1953).

W. R. Parker, *Milton's Debt to Greek Tragedy in 'Samson Agonistes'* (Baltimore and London, 1937).

C. A. Patrides, *Milton and the Christian Tradition* (Oxford, 1966).

C. A. Patrides (ed.), *Milton's Epic Poetry: Essays on 'Paradise Lost' and 'Paradise Regained'* (paperback, Harmondsworth, 1967).

C. A. Patrides (ed.), *Approaches to 'Paradise Lost'* (London, 1968).

J. Peter, *A Critique of 'Paradise Lost'* (London and New York, 1960).

F. T. Prince, *The Italian Element in Milton's Verse* (London and New York, 1954).

B. Rajan, *'Paradise Lost' and the Seventeenth Century Reader* (London, 1947, and New York, 1948; paperback, U.S.).

B. Rajan, *'Comus: The Inglorious Likeness'*, *UTQ* xxxvii (1967–8).

B. Rajan, *'Paradise Lost:* The Hill of History', *Huntington Library Quarterly*, xxxi (1967–8).

B. Rajan, *The Lofty Rhyme: A study of Milton's major poetry* (London and Coral Gables, Fla., 1970).

B. Rajan (ed.), *'Paradise Lost': a Tercentenary Tribute* (Toronto, Buffalo, and London, 1969).

Sir Walter Raleigh, *Milton* (London and New York, 1900; repr. 1968).

J. Reesing, *Milton's Poetic Art: 'A Mask', 'Lycidas', and 'Paradise Lost'* (Cambridge, Mass., and London, 1968).

W. G. Rice, *'Paradise Regained'* (1936), reprinted in A. E. Barker (ed.), *Milton: Modern Essays in Criticism*.

C. Ricks, *Milton's Grand Style* (Oxford, 1963; paperbacks, U.K. and U.S.).

A. Rudrum, *Milton: 'Paradise Lost'* (paperback, London, 1966).

A. Rudrum, *Milton: 'Comus' and Shorter Poems* (paperback, London, 1967).

A. Rudrum (ed.), *Milton: Modern Judgements* (London, 1968; paperback, U.K.).

L. Ryken, *The Apocalyptic Vision in 'Paradise Lost'* (Ithaca, N.Y., and London, 1970).

I. Samuel, *Plato and Milton* (Ithaca, N.Y., 1947; paperback, U.K.).

I. Samuel, *Dante and Milton: The 'Commedia' and 'Paradise Lost'* (Ithaca, N.Y., and London, 1966).

I. Samuel, *'Paradise Lost'*, in R. M. Lumiansky and Herschel Baker (eds.), *Critical Approaches to Six Major English Works: 'Beowulf' through 'Paradise Lost'* (Philadelphia, 1968).

D. Saurat, *Milton: Man and Thinker* (1925); rev. edn. (London and New York, 1944).

H. Schultz, *Milton and Forbidden Knowledge* (New York and London, 1955).

J. T. Shawcross (ed.), *Milton: The Critical Heritage* (London and New York, 1970).

W. Shumaker, *Unpremeditated Verse: Feeling and Perception in 'Paradise Lost'* (Princeton, N.J., 1967).

J. D. Simmonds (ed.), *Milton Studies I* (Pittsburgh, 1969); *II* (ibid. 1970).

J. H. Sims, *The Bible in Milton's Epics* (Gainesville, Fla., 1962).

S. G. Spaeth, *Milton's Knowledge of Music* (Princeton, N.J., 1913; paperback, U.S.).

S. E. Sprott, *Milton's Art of Prosody* (Oxford, 1953).

J. M. Steadman (ed.), *HLQ* xxxi (Nov. 1967), Milton Tercententary Issue.

J. M. Steadman, *Milton and the Renaissance Hero* (Oxford, 1967).

J. M. Steadman, *Milton's Epic Characters: Image and Idol* (Chapel Hill, N.C., 1968).

A. Stein, *Answerable Style: Essays on 'Paradise Lost'* (Minneapolis, Minn., and London, 1953; paperbacks, U.S. and U.K.).

A. Stein, *Heroic Knowledge: An Interpretation of 'Paradise Regained' and 'Samson Agonistes'* (Minneapolis, Minn., and London, 1957).

J. H. Summers, *The Muse's Method: An Introduction to 'Paradise Lost'* (Cambridge, Mass., and London, 1962; paperback, U.S.).

J. H. Summers (ed.), *The Lyric and Dramatic Milton* (New York and London, 1965).

K. Svendsen, *Milton and Science* (Cambridge, Mass., and London, 1956).

H. R. Swardson, *Poetry and the Fountain of Light: Observations on the Conflict between Christian and Classical Traditions in Seventeenth-Century Poetry* (Columbia, Mo., and London, 1962).

J. Thorpe (ed.), *Milton Criticism: Selections from Four Centuries* (New York, 1950, and London, 1951; paperbacks, U.K. and U.S.).

E. M. W. Tillyard, *Milton* (London and New York, 1930; paperbacks, U.K. and U.S.).

E. M. W. Tillyard, *The Miltonic Setting Past and Present* (Cambridge and New York, 1938).

E. M. W. Tillyard, *Studies in Milton* (London and New York, 1951).

R. Tuve, *Images and Themes in Five Poems by Milton* (Cambridge, Mass., 1957, and London, 1958).

A. J. A. Waldock, *'Paradise Lost' and its Critics* (Cambridge and New York, 1947; paperbacks, U.K. and U.S.).

W. B. C. Watkins, *An Anatomy of Milton's Verse* (Baton Rouge, La., 1955).

G. A. Wilkes, *The Thesis of 'Paradise Lost'* (paperback, Melbourne, 1961).

G. A. Wilkes, 'The Interpretation of *Samson Agonistes*', *Huntington Library Quarterly*, xxvi (1962–3).

B. Willey, *The Seventeenth Century Background: Studies in the Thought of the Age in Relation to Poetry and Religion* (London, 1934; paperback, U.S.).

A. Williams, *The Common Expositor: An Account of the Commentaries on Genesis, 1527–1633* (Chapel Hill, N.C., and London, 1948).

C. Williams: See TEXTS, H. C. Beeching, above.

G. Williamson, *Seventeenth Century Contexts* (Chicago and London, 1961).

G. Williamson, *Milton and Others* (Chicago and London, 1965).

J. A. Wittreich (ed.), *The Romantics on Milton* (Cleveland, 1970).

A. S. P. Woodhouse (ed.), *Puritanism and Liberty* (London and Chicago, 1938; reprinted 1950–51).

A. S. P. Woodhouse, 'The Argument of Milton's *Comus*', *UTQ* xi (1941–2); '*Comus* Once More', ibid. xix (1949–50).

A. S. P. Woodhouse, 'Pattern in *Paradise Lost*', *UTQ* xxii (1952–3).

A. S. P. Woodhouse, 'Theme and Pattern in *Paradise Regained*', *UTQ* xxv (1955–6).

A. S. P. Woodhouse, 'Tragic Effect in *Samson Agonistes*', *UTQ* xxviii (1958–9); reprinted in Barker, *Milton*.

A. S. P. Woodhouse, 'Milton', in *The Poet and his Faith: Religion and Poetry in England from Spenser to Eliot and Auden* (Chicago and London, 1965).

B. A. Wright, *Milton's 'Paradise Lost'* (London and New York, 1962; paperbacks, U.K. and U.S.).

BIOGRAPHIES AND LETTERS

J. Arthos, *Milton and the Italian Cities* (London, 1968).

D. Bush, *John Milton: A Sketch of his Life and Writings* (New York, 1964, and London, 1965; paperback, U.S.).

D. L. Clark, *Milton at St. Paul's School: A Study of Ancient Rhetoric in English Renaissance Education* (New York and London, 1948).

H. Darbishire (ed.), *The Early Lives of Milton* (London, 1932).

J. S. Diekhoff (ed.), *Milton on Himself* (New York and London, 1939; repr. 1965).

H. F. Fletcher, *The Intellectual Development of John Milton* (2 vols., Urbana, Ill., 1956–61).

J. M. French, *Life Records of John Milton* (5 vols., New Brunswick, N.J., 1949–58).

J. H. Hanford, *John Milton, Englishman* (New York, 1949, and London, 1950; paperback, U.S.).

E. S. Le Comte, *A Milton Dictionary* (paperback, New York, 1961).

D. Masson, *The Life of John Milton* (6 vols., i–iii rev., with an Index, London, 1881–96).

Ruth Mohl, *John Milton and His Commonplace Book* (New York, 1969).

K. Muir, *John Milton* (London and New York, 1955; rev. 1960).

W. R. Parker, *Milton's Contemporary Reputation* (Columbus, Ohio, 1940).

W. R. Parker, *Milton: A Biography* (2 vols., Oxford, 1968).

E. Saillens, *John Milton, poète combattant* (Paris, 1959); *John Milton: Man— Poet—Polemist* (Oxford and New York, 1964).

E. M. W. and P. B. Tillyard (eds.), *Milton: Private Correspondence and Academic Exercises* (Cambridge, 1932).

BIBLIOGRAPHIES

See BIBLIOGRAPHIES above, p. 86.

BACKGROUND READING

See volumes by Bush and by Patrides (BIBLIOGRAPHIES, p. 86).[1]

---

[1] [See also the BACKGROUND READING sections of the next two chapters, on Marvell and Dryden. – Ed.]

6 · MARVELL 1621–1678

D. I. B. Smith

Over the past ten years Marvell's poetry has become the focus of an extraordinary amount of critical attention. Part of the explanation for this, no doubt, is the accelerating tempo of the scholarly industry, part perhaps an elusiveness in the poet's own position—in a poem like the 'Horation Ode', for example—which defies ultimate analysis. The critical superstructure has at least a firm foundation in H. M. Margoliouth's superb edition of Marvell's *Poems and Letters* (1952). The text is sound, complete, and beautifully presented, the notes invaluable. There is no introduction, but Margoliouth's annotations contain a wealth of interpretative insights.

Less satisfactory, though convenient, are a number of paperback editions. Hugh MacDonald's *The Poems of Andrew Marvell* in the Muses Library series is a most useful text, reprinting the unique copy of Marvell's *Miscellaneous Poems* of 1681, and *To Mr. Lovelace, Upon the Death of Lord Hastings*, and *An Elegy upon the Death of My Lord Francis Villiers*. Marvell's restoration satires are not included. The Introduction gives a spare and lucid account of the poet's life, some textual information, and a selection of critical opinions. Not all Marvell's poems are securely authenticated, particularly the satires. A bold attempt to solve this problem is made by George de F. Lord in his edition, *Andrew Marvell: Complete Poetry* (1968). Using the Bodleian copy of the 1681 edition of *Miscellaneous Poems*, with manuscript additions and corrections (MS. Eng. poet. d. 49), as his authority, Lord includes as Marvell's 'The Second Advice to a Painter' and 'The Third Advice to a Painter', works not generally ascribed to the poet, and rejects as 'of doubtful authorship' the inconveniently royalist poem on 'Tom May's Death', hitherto regarded as genuine. Margoliouth and MacDonald viewed this manuscript (probably that used by Edward Thompson in his unreliable edition of 1776) with rather less enthusiasm than Professor Lord. In his Introduction Professor Lord discerns a dialectical development in Marvell's poetry and calls for a higher critical opinion of the satires. Two selections of Marvell's poetry have interesting Introductions: J. H. Summers' *Marvell* (1961) and Frank

Kermode's *Andrew Marvell: Selected Poetry* (1967). Summers emphasizes the continuity of Marvell's poetic career and the acute consciousness of genre that characterizes his work, while Kermode
outlines the tradition in which Marvell must be understood, and
inveighs against the historians of ideas who would impose upon the
poet some 'time bound, specious "unity of thought" '. James Winny
in the Introduction to yet another selection, *Andrew Marvell: Some
Poems* (1962), also sees Marvell as the spokesman of a civilized
tradition, a tradition threatened by civil war. Marvell's Latin poetry
has been edited and translated by W. A. McQueen and K. A. Rockwell: *The Latin Poetry of Andrew Marvell* (1964). Marvell's prose—the
source of his fame in his own day—is only now being re-edited, so
that the most recent edition is still A. B. Grosart's *Complete Works*
(1872–5). A selection of poetry and prose has been edited with a
useful Introduction by Dennis Davison: *Andrew Marvell: Selected
Poetry and Prose* (1952).

CRITICAL STUDIES AND COMMENTARY

While he lived, Marvell's reputation rested on the two parts of *The
Rehearsal Transpros'd* (1672–3), which Bishop Burnet described as the
'wittiest books that have appeared in this age', read 'from the king
down to the tradesman'. These works in defence of religious toleration led his contemporary Antony Wood to characterize Marvell
as the 'buffooning champion' of the Nonconformists. At the end of
his life Marvell wrote *An Account of the Growth of Popery and Arbitrary
Government in England* (1677), a work which, together with some
ferocious anti-court satires, provided the substance for the late
seventeenth-century and eighteenth-century view of Marvell as a
kind of Whig hero:

> Marvell this Island's watchful Centinel
> Stood in the gap and bravely kept his Post
> When Courtiers too in Wine and Riot slept:
> 'Twas he th'approach of Rome did first explore,
> And the grim Monster, Arbitrary Power . . .

The poems, which excite such interest today, were not published
until three years after Marvell's death, in the *Miscellaneous Poems*
(1681), and were probably not at all to general taste, although Wood
notes that they 'were then taken into the hands of many persons of
his perswassion, and by them cried up as excellent'. Johnson only
mentions Marvell in passing in the 'Life of Dryden', but his poems
were thought to be of sufficient interest to warrant three editions

in the eighteenth century, those of Cooke (1726 and 1772) and Thompson (1776). In the nineteenth century Lamb, Poe, Emerson, and Tennyson were among Marvell's enthusiastic admirers, but it was not until the twentieth-century surge of interest in the Metaphysicals that Marvell's poetry was deemed worthy of the close analysis accorded to a 'major writer'. T. S. Eliot's famous essay TLS, 1 April 1921, was chiefly responsible for this distinction; the essay has been reprinted many times, most recently in *Andrew Marvell: A Collection of Critical Essays*, edited by G. de F. Lord (1968). Eliot placed Marvell firmly in the tradition of 'Latin civilization', asserting that the poet's importance rested on the 'vast and penetrating influence of Ben Jonson'. This essay also appeared in the volume of tercentenary tributes, *Andrew Marvell, 1621–1678*, edited by W. H. Bagguley (reprinted 1965), where there are a number of other suggestive studies. Bishop Henson brilliantly delineated the nature of Marvell's faith, which he termed 'puritan citizenship'—Anglican, Erastian, and anti-clerical—while H. J. Massingham explored his character as a 'political amphibian'. Edward Wright's essay in the volume suggested an approach which has been relentlessly, perhaps unnecessarily, pursued: 'In the small world of the Fairfax estate—garden, park and river leas—he expressed into poetry a philosophy as large as that which Coleridge could not reduce into prose. He was a singing Cambridge Platonist.' Pierre Legouis's great study, *André Marvell: poète, puritain, patriote* (1928) is still the point from which any serious evaluation of Marvell must start. The poet's life, art, and relation to his age, are carefully and thoroughly examined. Not all of the questions Legouis raises are fashionable today, but they are essential to a larger understanding of the poet. The translation and abridgement of 1965 is also an invaluable work, including the biographical discoveries of the intervening years, and commenting—generally with good-humoured scorn—on the critical developments in the same period. His own comments on the poems, however, do little more than set the stage for closer examination. The learned and useful footnotes of the earlier work are gone, as is, unhappily, the exhaustive bibliography. Victoria Sackville-West's study of 1929 is superficial and patronizing. In 1940 Bradbrook and Thomas's study, *Andrew Marvell*, presented Marvell as the heir to the view of Nature transmitted by the Spenserians—the symbolic view of Nature as 'Divine Hieroglyph'.

This Platonism is seen as distilled into the emblems which characterize Marvell's poetry. Some careless generalizations follow: that Marvell stopped writing poetry when science removed the support for this view of Nature, for example. However, in seeing Marvell in terms of a literary rather than a philosophic—or 'history of ideas' —tradition, the authors seem on surer ground than a number of later critics. There is a useful examination of the prose, particularly the *Rehearsal Transpros'd*, where some pertinent comparisons with Swift are made. Ruth Wallerstein's *Studies in Seventeenth-Century Poetic* (1950), half of which is devoted to Marvell, continues to examine the Platonic and emblematic aspects of Marvell's poetry. She is particularly concerned to define the context of Marvell's thought in terms of medieval and Renaissance neo-Platonism, with St. Bonaventura as the central figure. It is difficult, however, to reconcile the large and often unwieldy body of thought with the slight and graceful poems, and the tendency to abstraction runs counter to their nature. I do not find it helpful to be told that the deepest reality for Marvell is 'where symbolic platonism coincides with moral intuition'. Miss Wallerstein is sensitive and perceptive when actually dealing with the poems. Miss Wallerstein and T. S. Eliot are good examples of two strains which appear to have become increasingly divergent in Marvell criticism: those whose approach is primarily that of 'history of ideas' and who endeavour to place Marvell's poetry in a context of patterns of thought, and those who see the poems as works of literature in a literary tradition.

The remarkable critical interest that Marvell elicits is indicated by four book-length studies (excluding the translation of Legouis) which have appeared since 1964. The first of these is the rather simple-minded *Andrew Marvell* (1964) by L. W. Hyman. Hyman provides a careful explication of each poem, but the literary background and the background of ideas are very sketchily indicated. In 1966 J. B. Leishman's *The Art of Marvell's Poetry* was published. Leishman died before the work was completed or thoroughly revised, and is therefore frequently repetitious and occasionally disjointed. It is, however, the best book available on the nature of Marvell's poetry. The method can be gathered from a remark Leishman made in another context: 'The fact is that analysis without comparison soon begins to yield diminishing returns.' Leishman wished to discover what was distinctive in Marvell's poetry, and he did so by acute comparisons between Marvell, his contemporaries, and their literary forbears in their treatment of the great commonplaces of seventeenth-century poetry. He was able to show that Marvell's poetry is a tissue of contemporary echoes, and that, contrary to frequent assertion, Marvell's descriptive and expository manner is quite unlike the characteristic manner of Donne. The influences, likenesses, and distinctions between Marvell and Crashaw, Vaughan, Wootton, Stanley, Randolph, Cowley, and others are sensitively delineated. Marvell is seen as part of a long and continuous literary tradition, to which he makes his unique contribution and is built upon in his turn. It is Marvell's decorous eclecticism which makes me profoundly doubtful that any habit of thought—Platonic, hermetic, neo-Platonic, Cambridge-Platonic— is characteristic of him. Some readers may find Leishman's constant concern with Marvell's carelessness, and his willingness to rewrite lines, a little strange, but Leishman approached his author as a fellow-craftsman whose occasional slipshod work might be improved. A less diffuse example of Leishman's critical skill may be found in his fine little pamphlet, *Some Themes and Variations in the Poetry of Andrew Marvell*, the British Academy Warton Lecture of 1961, where the 'Coy Mistress' is 'placed' with beautiful exactness.

It is the sad fate of Marvell's subtle and pellucid poems that they frequently become the prey of a criticism turgid, ingenious, and per- verse. Nothing could be less like Leishman's work than Harold Toliver's *Marvell's Ironic Vision* (1965), where a distressing jargon of abstraction raises a barrier between the reader and the poetry. Much of the work is taken up with an effort to yoke together, by violence, the heterogeneous matters of Cambridge Platonism and Marvell's lyrics. The poems become 'philosophic strategies' charac- terized by 'oppositional calculus'. There is not a great deal concern- ing the real nature of Marvell's irony in this work, though R. H. Syfret in her review (*RES* xvii (1966)) discerns Mr. Toliver's theme as the 'recurrent pattern of dualisms held in careful balance' and the 'unresolved tension between polarities' in Marvell's verse, and suggests that a new estimate of the poet should begin with *Marvell's Ironic Vision* (this work, Leishman's *Art of Marvell's Poetry* and Legouis's *Andrew Marvell* are compared by Frank Kermode in *Encounter*, November 1966).

A study very different from those previously examined is John M. Wallace's *Destiny His Choice: The Loyalism of Andrew Marvell* (1968), an acute and learned examination of the historical back- ground to Marvell's work from the 'Elegy Upon the Death of My Lord Francis Villiers' to the *Account of the Growth of Popery and Arbitrary Government*. Wallace's view is that Marvell is a 'loyalist'— one who adheres to the established form of government (cf. Donal Smith, 'The Political Beliefs of Andrew Marvell' in *UTQ*)—and it is in these terms that he would explain the 'Horation Ode'. Tracing in great detail the general transference of allegiance from Charles to Cromwell. Wallace argues convincingly for a similar transference in Marvell's sympathy. The 'Horatian Ode', then, is not impartial, but a public address following the rules of deliberative oration, in which Marvell looks forward to Cromwell's election to the constitutional dictatorship of England. *The First Anniversary* is also seen as a rhetorical exercise urging that Cromwell should accept the Crown and institute a new dynasty of kings. Power had to be turned into authority. Following his view of Marvell as loyalist, Wallace accepts Marvell's belief in the prerogatives of the King, and views with considerable scepticism the ascription to Marvell of most of the scurrilous satires. However, his examination of the 'Last Instructions' shows how difficult—and perhaps finally irrelevant—it is to interpret literature simply in terms of an imposed historical pattern. There is an adequate account of the prose, though curiously Professor Wallace does not seem to have read the context of pamphlet literature—in this case more relevant—for the prose to nearly the same extent as he had clearly done for a work like the 'Horation Ode'. The book ends with an examination of 'Upon Appleton House', welded with some difficulty on to the predominantly historical and political material that has gone before. Wallace sees the work as Marvell's own farewell to the life of retirement and his tribute to the Christian virtue of his employer.

Andrew Marvell: A Collection of Critical Essays (1968) edited by G. de F. Lord brings together a number of diverse papers of which the best is Eliot's from 1921. J. H. Summers's contribution examines Marvell's view of Nature, arguing that the poet sees man as alienated from Nature and only able to live in it as observer or destroyer. J. S. Coolidge is concerned with the Horatian elements in Marvell's work, seeing them as general influences rather than particular borrowings. Marvell, he asserts, shared Horace's concept of 'Necessity' and the 'Decorum' of war and peace (for Marvell, then, Cromwell's success comes from his awareness of this 'Decorum' or appropriateness in History). G. H. Hartman interprets 'The Garden' in the light of Romans 1:20 and 8:19 ff., arguing that the poem is concerned with the redemption of nature and man, and their related temptations. The volume concludes with an examination by Earl Miner of the 'Last Instructions to a Painter'. For him the poem is unified by its 'attitude', by the convention of the Painting as frame, and by the consideration of it as a 'historical' poem in Dryden's sense of the genre.

Though slight, two pamphlet studies of Marvell should be noted.

Dennis Davison's *The Poetry of Andrew Marvell* (1964) is clearly aimed at a student audience and has a robustly common-sense approach to the poems—they are self-contained and require no elaborate background information. The clear, elegant explications are a useful starting-point. The British Council booklet *Andrew Marvell* by John Press is a balanced short introduction, with a good biographical summary and a helpful bibliography.

Of all Marvell's poems, the 'Horation Ode' seems most to invite analysis and resist it. In 1946, in the *English Institute Essays*, Cleanth Brooks argued that in the 'Horation Ode' Marvell was able to qualify his praise of Cromwell with reservations that arose from ironies and ambivalences in the poem. Douglas Bush replied in 1952, in *Sewanee Review*, insisting that Marvell's providential view of history prevents an ironic reading of the poem, and Mr. Brooks returned to defend his position (*SR* (1953)), and to suggest that historical evidence does not solve critical problems. The three essays are conveniently printed in *Seventeenth-Century English Poetry: Modern Essays in Criticism* (1962), edited by W. R. Keast, a collection which also contains Frank Kermode's 'The Argument of Marvell's "Garden" ' and Leo Spitzer's 'Marvell's "Nymph Complaining for the Death of Her Faun": Sources versus Meaning'. Kermode makes a persuasive case for approaching the 'Garden' in terms of an awareness of the genre of the poem rather than as a nexus of ideas, while Spitzer observes that the identification of sources does not decide the meaning of the poem, which, he suggests, arises out of an understanding of the character of the nymph. To return, however, to the 'Horation Ode', in this poem the poet has been envisioned as Marxist (L. D. Lerner in *Interpretations*, edited by J. Wain (1955)) and as Machiavellian. The last view is advanced by Joseph Mazzeo in his *Renaissance and Seventeenth-Century Studies* (1964), where it is argued that Marvell saw politics 'as an activity which cannot be entirely subsumed in the categories of traditional ethics', and presented Cromwell as the complete Machiavellian prince. In his examination of *The First Anniversary* Mazzeo suggests that Marvell viewed Cromwell as continuing a Machiavellian while taking on the attributes of a Davidic king. A different approach is explored by R. H. Syfret in 'Marvell's "Horatian Ode" ', *RES* xii (1961), where Marvell's sources in Horace and Lucan (particularly Thomas May's translation of the latter) are closely examined. For Marvell and his contemporaries the civil wars of Rome afforded an obvious historical parallel to the situation in England, and Lucan and Horace offered a valuable perspective. The investigation of sources *is* valuable here, for the works of these Latin writers were immediately familiar to seventeenth-century readers.

Equally provocative and baffling are the garden poems. In *The Happy Man*, vol. i (1954), a study of the myth of rural retirement in the seventeenth century, Maren-Sofie Røstvig suggests that Marvell must be understood in the context of the *beatus ille* tradition, and points to similarities between the work of Marvell and the Polish poet Sarbiewski. In the substantially revised second edition of her work (1962) Professor Røstvig emphasizes the *hermetic* rather than the general Platonist nature of Marvell's vision, and insists on a closer literary relationship between Marvell and his employer Fairfax, who translated a commentary on Mercurius Trismegistus' *Poemander*. Marvell's green is then a *hermetic* green. In a chapter entitled 'Marvell and the Garden' from his study *The Enclosed Garden* (1966) Stanley Stewart argues that 'The Garden' must be understood as religious allegory in the tradition of the 'Song of Songs'—the poem is about the soul's attainment of the state of Grace, and union with Christ. 'Upon Appleton House', with its gravely humorous hyperbole, provides many difficulties for critics. D. C. Allen brings his encyclopedic learning to bear on the poem in his *Image and Meaning* (1960), a study of metaphoric traditions in Renaissance poetry. Allen suggests that the work is made up of a number of poems each celebrating the house in a different way, and indicates the manner in which it takes its place in a long tradition of house poems. More useful—and even more learned—is Kitty Scoular's chapter on 'Upon Appleton House' in her *Natural Magic: Studies in the Presentation of Nature in English Poetry from Spenser to Marvell* (1965). In her hands the poem becomes a thick texture of emblematic associations, familiar conceits, contemporary commonplaces of poetry, painting, landscape gardening, and science. It is difficult to perceive a controlling pattern of meaning in this 'pleasant confusion', but almost all critics are similarly defeated.

Marvell's political verses are examined in Ruth Nevo's *The Dial of Virtue*, where the 'Horatian Ode', the *First Anniversary*, and the 'Last Instructions' are placed in their context as seventeenth-century poems on affairs of state. The book traces the change from a static hierarchic society to a dynamic one where the king is shorn of his divinity. It is also concerned with the concomitant development of satire in this period. Unhappily, this last purpose tends to make Mrs. Nevo view most poems as steps towards Dryden's *Absalom and Achitophel*.

A stimulating study of the poetry of Marvell and the Metaphysicals is Robert Ellrodt's *Les Poètes métaphysiques anglais*, tome ii (1960), a brilliant attempt to define the poets and their sensibilities through their psychology and cultural environment. Professor Ellrodt places Marvell with Lord Herbert of Cherbury and Abraham Cowley, as poets in transition towards a poetry purely intellectual or purely sensual. He makes a series of acute distinctions between Donne and Marvell, but one feels that not all the poems will support the weight of argument he places on them.

Since this chapter was first written the spate of critical work on Marvell has continued undiminished. It is not possible to deal with all the articles but one should note the more important books. Rosalie Colie's '*My Ecchoing Song*' (1970) advances the attractive proposition that Marvell's poetry is a commentary on the genres and traditions that it explores and exhausts. Marvell's approach to poetry is seen as 'professional' though clearly this term is confusing, especially if one thinks of Dryden and Milton as 'professional' poets also. Much of the book is taken up with useful and learned, if rather disorganized, analyses of 'The Garden' and 'Upon Appleton House'. Earl Miner explores the shifting balance of public and private poetry in *The Metaphysical Mode from Donne to Cowley* (1969) reprinting an earlier reading of the 'Nymph Complaining' as a study in the death of innocence at both the personal and national levels. Marvell's modishness is further attested by two critical anthologies. The introduction to Michael Wilding's *Marvell* (1969) is perhaps the best extant account of the development of Marvell's poetic reputation, indicating the strength of American appreciation and the fact that esteem for the poet steadily grew in the nineteenth century. Some interesting studies are reprinted including Eliot's crotchety Johnsonian qualification of his earlier position, Christopher Hill's view of Marvell as revolutionary poet, and J. V. Cunningham's analysis of the logic of the 'Coy Mistress'. John Carey's *Andrew Marvell* (1969) one of the Penguin Critical Anthologies, questions the very basis of such collections: for him the Emperor is quite naked. His two introductions demonstrate an appropriate tough reasonableness and the critical selection spans an extraordinary variety of opinion—from the revengeful strictures of Marvell's ecclesiastical opponent Bishop Parker, to Professor Harold Toliver. Dr. Carey seems to have been more concerned to indicate the contradictions and confusions in Marvell criticism than enlighten us about the poetry.

BIOGRAPHIES AND LETTERS

There is only one adequate biography of Marvell and that is
Legouis's *Andrew Marvell*, of which mention has already been made.
Marvell was a shadowy and complex personality, whose character is
impossible to fathom. He was, as Massingham observes in the
tercentenary tribute, 'a Cromwellian who never fought in the Civil
War, a monarchist who denounced the corruptions of kingship, a
servant of two hostile parties and a factionary of neither, a politician
who did his best for both worlds'. Augustine Birrell's *Andrew Marvell*
(1905), though without the benefit of the details which recent research (by such scholars as Mrs. Elsie Duncan Jones and L. N. Wall)
has unearthed, is worth reading, if only because, like Marvell,
Birrell was a parliamentarian. The Life of Marvell by C. H. Firth,
in the *D.N.B.*, though also not up to date, is none the less a model of
lucidity and learning, written by a great historian of the period. A
contemporary 'life' of Marvell is available in O. L. Dick's edition of
Aubrey's 'Brief Lives' (1949). Not very many of Marvell's personal
letters seem to have survived, though those we do have, especially the
letters to his nephew William Popple, are revealing. As a member of
Parliament, however, he corresponded regularly with the mayor and
corporation of his constituency, Hull, and the Society of Trinity
House, Hull, from 1660 till his death in 1678, detailing his proceedings on their behalf and giving general news of parliamentary
affairs. The best edition of the letters is that of Margoliouth, already
noted. Since the second edition of this work a number of unpublished
letters have come to light, and been published by Caroline Robbins,
in *TLS*, 19 December 1958 and 20 March 1959, and *Études Anglaises*,
xvii (1964).

BIBLIOGRAPHIES

The best bibliography of Marvell is that which Legouis appended
to his study of 1928. All Marvell's works and their various editions
are listed, together with those works ascribed to him though on
doubtful authority. The prose pamphlets are listed, along with the
works that provoked them and those which they in turn provoked.
Anthologies in which the poet's poems appeared after his death are
noted, as are all books and articles on him. Each listing is accompanied by a short commentary. This may be supplemented by
Studies in Metaphysical Poetry (1939), by T. Spencer and M. Van
Doren, and Lloyd E. Berry's *A Bibliography of Studies in Metaphysical
Poetry, 1939–60* (1964). Two recent studies with full bibliographies

are H. E. Toliver's *Marvell's Ironic Vision* (see CRITICAL STUDIES above), and Klaus Hofmann's study of Marvell's imagery *Das Bild in Andrew Marvells lyrischen Gedichten* (1967). Toliver's work, in addition to a full listing of Marvell criticism to 1963, gives a general list of background reading, primarily concerned with the history of ideas, particularly Platonism in the seventeenth century. Hofmann's book lists theses on Marvell as well as published Marvell studies to 1966. The most thorough catalogue of work on the poet since 1927, however, is to be found in Dennis Donovan's helpful pamphlet *Andrew Marvell, 1927–1967* (1969).

BACKGROUND READING

The most useful starting-point for background reading is probably Douglas Bush's indispensable *English Literature in the Earlier Seventeenth Century* (1966 edn.), not only for its masterly treatment of the period but also because it has an exceptionally full and thorough bibliography. There have been a great many accounts of the breakdown of the medieval–Renaissance organic universe in the seventeenth century, the most comprehsive of which is Herschel Baker's *The Wars of Truth: Studies in the Decay of Christian Humanism in the Earlier Seventeenth Century* (1952). Also useful, and dealing with different aspects of this pervasive change, are S. L. Bethell, *The Cultural Revolution of the Seventeenth Century* (1951), Marjorie Hope Nicolson, *The Breaking of the Circle: Studies in the Effect of the 'New Science' upon Seventeenth-Century Poetry* (rev. 1960), and Margaret L. Wiley, *The Subtle Knot: Creative Scepticism in Seventeenth-Century England* (1952). Rosamund Tuve's *Elizabethan and Metaphysical Imagery* (1947) is an impressive demonstration of the continuity of the Elizabethan poetic in the seventeenth century, though it fails to account fully for the unique quality of Metaphysical poetry. In many ways the best background reading for Marvell's lyric poetry is the exploration of the poetry of his contemporaries, but a reading of history is helpful for the Cromwellian poems and necessary for the satires of the Restoration. For the Civil War and Interregnum the authoritive and detailed accounts by S. R. Gardiner are most valuable: the *History of the Great Civil War* (1893) and the *History of the Commonwealth and Protectorate* (rev. 1903); A. S. P. Woodhouse, *Puritanism and Liberty: Being the Army Debates (1647–9) from the Clarke Manuscripts with Supplementary Documents* (1950 edn.) prints a number of important documents of the struggle, and provides a trenchant analysis of the central issues. For Cromwell himself the best source is the *Writings and Speeches of Oliver Cromwell* edited by W. C. Abbott

(1937–47). Marvell's satires are best seen in their context in the extensively annotated *Poems on Affairs of State: Augustan Satirical Verse, 1660–1714*, Vol. I: *1660–1678*, edited by G. de F. Lord. The standard history of this last period is that of David Ogg, *England in the Reign of Charles II* (1955 edn.), though a better sense of the sort of day to day matters in court and country in which the satires are rooted can be gained from a reading of Pepys's *Diary* (ed. H. B. Wheatley, 1928) or the splendidly annotated *Diary of John Evelyn* edited by E. S. de Beer (1955).

REFERENCES

TEXTS

Dennis Davison (ed.), *Andrew Marvell: Selected Poetry and Prose* (London, 1952).

A. B. Grosart (ed.), *The Complete Works in Verse and Prose of Andrew Marvell* (4 vols., London, 1872–5).

G. de F. Lord (ed.), *Andrew Marvell: Complete Poetry* (New York 1968; paperback, U.S.).

Frank Kermode (ed.), *Andrew Marvell: Selected Poetry* (paperbacks, London and New York, 1967).

H. MacDonald (ed.), *The Poems of Andrew Marvell*, 2nd edn. (London, 1956; paperbacks, U.S. and U.K.).

W. A. McQueen and K. A. Rockwell (eds.), *The Latin Poetry of Andrew Marvell* (paperback, Chapel Hill, N.C., 1964).

H. M. Margoliouth (ed.), *The Poems and Letters of Andrew Marvell*, 2nd edn. (2 vols., Oxford English Texts, Oxford, 1952).

J. H. Summers (ed.), *Marvell* (paperback, New York, 1961).

J. Winny (ed.), *Andrew Marvell: Some Poems* (London, 1962).

CRITICAL STUDIES AND COMMENTARY

D. C. Allen, *Image and Meaning* (Baltimore, 1960).

W. H. Bagguley (ed.), *Andrew Marvell, 1621–1678* (London, 1922; New York, 1965).

M. C. Bradbrook and M. G. Lloyd Thomas, *Andrew Marvell* (Cambridge, corrected repr. 1962).

Cleanth Brooks, 'Marvell's "Horatian Ode"', in W. R. Keast (ed.), *Seventeenth-Century English Poetry* (paperback, New York and London, 1962).

Cleanth Brooks, 'A Note on the Limits of "History" and the Limits of "Criticism"', in Keast (above).

Douglas Bush, 'Marvell's "Horatian Ode" ', in Keast.

John Carey (ed.), *Andrew Marvell* (paperbacks, Harmondsworth and New York, 1969).

Rosalie Colie, '*My Ecchoing Song*' (Princeton, N.J., 1970).

Dennis Davison, *The Poetry of Andrew Marvell* (paperback, London, 1964).

Robert Ellrodt, *Les Poètes métaphysiques anglais*, tome ii (Paris, 1960).

L. W. Hyman, *Andrew Marvell* (New York, 1964).

Frank Kermode, 'The Argument of Marvell's "Garden" ', in Keast (above).

Frank Kermode, 'Marvell Transprosed', *Encounter*, xxvii (1966).

Pierre Legouis, *André Marvell* (Paris, 1928).

Pierre Legouis, *Andrew Marvell: Poet, Puritan, Patriot*, 2nd edn. (Oxford, 1968; paperback, U.K.).

J. B. Leishman, *Some Themes and Variations in the Poetry of Andrew Marvell* (paperback, Oxford, 1961).

J. B. Leishman, *The Art of Marvell's Poetry* (London, 1966; paperbacks, U.K. and U.S.).

L. D. Lerner, 'An Horatian Ode upon Cromwell's Return from Ireland', in J. Wain (ed.), *Interpretations* (London, 1955; paperback, U.K.).

G. de F. Lord (ed.), *Andrew Marvell: A Collection of Critical Essays* (paperback, Englewood Cliffs, N.J., 1968; paperback, U.K.).

Andrew Marvell, *The Rehearsal Transpros'd* (2 parts, London, 1672-3).

Andrew Marvell, *An Account of the Growth of Popery* (Amsterdam, 1677).

Andrew Marvell, *Miscellaneous Poems* (London, 1681).

Joseph Mazzeo, *Renaissance and Seventeenth-Century Studies* (New York and London, 1964).

Earl Miner, *The Metaphysical Mode from Donne to Cowley* (Princeton, N.J., 1969).

Ruth Nevo, *The Dial of Virtue* (Princeton, N.J., 1963).

J. Press, *Andrew Marvell*, (paperback, British Council, London, 1966; paperback, U.S.).

Maren-Sofie Røstvig, *The Happy Man*, vol. i, 2nd edn. (Oslo, 1962).

V. Sackville-West, *Andrew Marvell* (London, 1928).

Kitty Scoular, *Natural Magic* (Oxford, 1965).

D. Smith, 'The Political Beliefs of Andrew Marvell', *UTQ* xxxvi (1966).

Leo Spitzer, 'Marvell's "Nymph Complaining for the Death of Her Faun": Sources versus Meaning', in Keast (above).

Stanley Stewart, *The Enclosed Garden* (Madison, Wis., and London, 1966).

R. H. Syfret, 'Marvell's "Horatian Ode" ', *RES* xii (1961).

H. E. Toliver, *Marvell's Ironic Vision* (New Haven, Conn., 1965).

J. M. Wallace, *Destiny His Choice: The Loyalism of Andrew Marvell* (Cambridge, 1968).

Ruth Wallerstein, *Studies in Seventeenth-Century Poetic* (Madison, Wis., 1950; paperbacks, U.K. and U.S.).

Michael Wilding (ed.), *Marvell: Modern Judgements* (London, 1969; paperback, U.K.).

BIOGRAPHIES AND LETTERS

Augustine Birrell, *Andrew Marvell* (London, 1905).

O. L. Dick (ed.), *Aubrey's 'Brief Lives'* (London, 1949; paperbacks, U.S. and U.K.).

C. H. Firth, Life of Marvell, in *D.N.B.*

Pierre Legouis, *Andrew Marvell*. See author under CRITICAL STUDIES above.

H. M. Margoliouth (ed.). See under TEXTS above.

Caroline Robbins, 'Marvell Letters', in *TLS*, 19 Dec. 1958 and 20 Mar. 1959.

Caroline Robbins, 'Six Letters by Andrew Marvell', *Études Anglaises*, xvii (1964).

BIBLIOGRAPHIES

Lloyd E. Berry, *A Bibliography of Studies in Metaphysical Poetry 1939–60* (Madison, Wis., 1964).

D. G. Donovan, *Andrew Marvell, 1927–1967*, Elizabethan Bibliographies Supplements XII (paperback, London, 1969).

Klaus Hofmann, *Das Bild in Andrew Marvells lyrischen Gedichten* (Heidelberg, 1967).

Pierre Legouis, *André Marvell* (Paris, 1928).

T. Spencer and M. Van Doren, *Metaphysical Poetry* (New York, 1939).

H. E. Toliver, *Marvell's Ironic Vision* (New Haven, Conn., 1965).

BACKGROUND READING

W. C. Abbott (ed.), *The Writings and Speeches of Oliver Cromwell* (4 vols., Cambridge, Mass. 1937–47).

Herschel Baker, *The Wars of Truth* (Cambridge, Mass., 1952).

E. S. de Beer (ed.), *The Diary of John Evelyn* (6 vols., Oxford English Texts, Oxford, 1955).

S. L. Bethell, *The Cultural Revolution of the Seventeenth Century* (London, 1951).

Douglas Bush, *English Literature in the Earlier Seventeenth Century, 1600–1660*, 2nd edn. (*O.H.E.L.*, vol. v, Oxford and New York, 1962).

S. R. Gardiner, *The History of the Great Civil War* (4 vols., London, 1893).

S. R. Gardiner, *The History of the Commonwealth and Protectorate* rev. edn. (4 vols., London, 1903).

G. de F. Lord (ed.), *Poems on Affairs of State*, Vol. I: *1660–1678*, (New Haven, Conn., 1963).

Marjorie Hope Nicolson, *The Breaking of the Circle*, rev. edn. (New York, 1960; paperback, U.S.).

David Ogg, *England in the Reign of Charles II*, 2nd edn. (2 vols., Oxford, 1956; paperbacks, U.K. and U.S.).

H. E. Toliver. See BIBLIOGRAPHIES above.

Rosamund Tuve, *Elizabethan and Metaphysical Imagery* (Chicago, 1947; paperbacks, U.K. and U.S.).

H. B. Wheatley (ed.), *The Diary of Samuel Pepys* (8 vols., London, 1928).

Margaret L. Wiley, *The Subtle Knot* (Cambridge, Mass., 1952).

A. S. P. Woodhouse (ed.), *Puritanism and Liberty*, 2nd edn. (London, 1950).

James Kinsley

Most of Dryden's original verse was first published in separate printings. Some of the prologues and epilogues were first sold as half-sheets; but most of them, and almost all the songs, came out with the plays or in poetical miscellanies. The major verse translations, made for an age which saw itself as a 'noble collateral' with Greece and Rome, appeared in fine folio volumes: *The Satires of Decimus Junius . . . [and] Aulus Persius Flaccus* (1693), *The Works of Virgil Adorn'd with a Hundred Sculptures* (1697), and *Fables Ancient and Modern: Translated . . . from Homer, Ovid, Boccace, & Chaucer* (1700). But a good deal of translation from the classics was contributed to Jacob Tonson's *Miscellany Poems* (1684), *Sylvae* (the second part, 1685), *Examen Poeticum: being the Third Part of Miscellany Poems* (1693), and the miscellanies of 1694 and 1704. Small gatherings of the original verse were made in 1688 and 1692, but the first substantial collected edition, and that in which the English Augustans commonly read Dryden, was published by Tonson a year after the poet's death. Milton received a deal of editorial attention (much of which would have displeased him) in the early eighteenth century; the 'less presumptuous' Dryden, though more distinctly a founding father of Augustan poetry, had to wait till 1760 for an editor to 'unite the whole of his original poems and translations (the plays and his Virgil excepted)' in a single edition, with a biography and explanatory notes—Samuel Derrick, who helped Dr. Johnson to write Dryden's life.

The Augustan Age was over, and Dryden dead for more than a century, before his work was enshrined by Sir Walter Scott in a great library edition as that of 'one of our most eminent English classics—one who may claim at least the third place in that honoured list, and who has given proofs of greater versatility of talent than either Shakespeare or Milton'. For the serious student of Dryden this edition remains an essential piece of equipment: it is textually inaccurate and inadequate by modern standards, indeed, but it is annotated by an editor who not only was a considerable poet, antiquary, and historian, but also stood closer to Dryden in temperament and understanding than any later scholar could.

The heirs-presumptive to Scott are the consortium of scholars in California, preparing the library edition of Dryden's works which was finely inaugurated by the late E. N. Hooker in 1956. At the present rate of publication, the purchase of this edition can be recommended only to enterprising investors still at primary school, and it exemplifies the familiar defects of American scholarship—disproportion in the scale of the commentary, the supplementary employment of specialists to provide material which any editorial handyman could have got together with less fuss, and the dispersal of textual evidence in a waste of insignificance. Nevertheless, here for the first time Dryden is well served in the scrupulous treatment of his whole text and in the painstaking elucidation of his sense; and these editors show him to be more complex, and make him more intelligible, than any earlier commentator had done.

Scott served as a basis for a number of nineteenth-century editions of the poems: even in the Cambridge Poets *Dryden*, which superseded the Globe edition in 1908, G. R. Noyes went back 'to correct and condense Scott's work'. Noyes's original commentary was in many respects first-rate. His 1950 revision is a heroic attempt to take account of the resurgence in Dryden scholarship between the two World Wars. His commentary remains the best on this scale for students, and his modernized text has been given a remission—I think regrettably—as the basis of Montgomery's *Concordance*.

Reviewers have not rejected my claim that the Oxford English Texts edition (ed. James Kinsley) provides, 'for the first time, a complete text of Dryden's original poems and verse translations based on a critical review of all the early printings', with adequate literary and historical commentary. (The Oxford Standard Authors edition offers the same text—except for the *Virgil*—without commentary or the paraphernalia of textual criticism.)

Parts of the poetic corpus have been edited for students. W. B. Gardner's edition of the prologues and epilogues, though vulnerable to criticism on both textual and literary grounds, marks off an important category of verse for special consideration. (Wiley's *Rare Prologues and Epilogues* should also be consulted here.) Cyrus Day's edition of the songs does a similar service, with some musical illustrations, and with historical notes demonstrating Dryden's popularity as a lyric poet in the eighteenth century. James and Helen Kinsley's edition of *Absalom and Achitophel* has replaced that by Christie and Firth (1871, 1892). The World's Classics text of the

Virgil has been reissued, with an essay by Kinsley which attempts to set the book in the context of Dryden's career and of Augustan translation from the classics; a paperback edition of *Virgil* by Kinsley and Arvid Løsnes is in preparation. Students who wish to read the major poems with some reference to Dryden's criticism and drama can do so conveniently in Douglas Grant's elegant but lightly annotated volume in the Reynard Library. There is a shorter annotated selection from the poems, with a critical essay, by James Kinsley, in the New Oxford English Series.

Guy Montgomery's *Concordance* is convenient, comprehensive, and accurate. But students must be warned that it shares the weaknesses of Noyes's edition on which it is based. Noyes has modernized (and Americanized) the spelling, printed some poems from inferior texts, admitted some (probably or certainly) not by Dryden, and put others with a good claim into an appendix (which the *Concordance* ignores).

CRITICAL STUDIES AND COMMENTARY

Dryden established himself as a poet in the 1660s, and remained England's most prolific and magisterial man of letters down to his death in 1700. But although he was the victim of much scurrilous (and some physical) abuse and occasional burlesque—see *The Rehearsal* by Buckingham and others (1672), *The Hind and the Panther Transvers'd* by Prior and Charles Montagu (1687), and the catalogue of 'Drydeniana' in Macdonald's *Bibliography* (see below)—there was almost no contemporary criticism of his poetry. But Dryden was himself the inaugurator of English literary criticism as we understand it, and his own first considerable critic. In his prefaces, dedications, and letters he writes freely and delightfully of his artistic intentions, successes, and failures, doing himself the service of a sympathetic but judicious reviewer. Ker's Oxford edition of the main *Essays* is outdated, and is now replaced in a new paperback selection by James Kinsley and George Parfitt. Watson's complete two-volume edition in Everyman's Library, though physically graceless, is well annotated and carries a useful glossary of critical terms. Much of the non-dramatic criticism is, of course, included, with commentary, in Noyes's and Kinsley's editions of the *Poems*. For *Of Dramatick Poesie*, and related documents, the best edition is J. T. Boulton's. Aden's *Critical Opinions of Dryden*, intolerable to read but invaluable for reference, is a dictionary of passages from the prose works arranged by topic; it must be supplemented from the poems, especially from the prologues and epilogues.

Eighteenth-century criticism of Dryden is extensive.[1] Together with Milton and Pope, he provided a great quarry of illustrative material for literary discussion; and from Dennis and Addison on, his name and verses are everywhere in periodical essays and in works on the theory and practice of poetry. Critical comment on him by the poets is frequent, but usually brief and incidental: for instance, Swift's attack on his 'vicious way of rhyming' in triplets (letter of 12 April 1735), the dismissal in *A Tale of a Tub* of *The Hind and the Panther* as Dryden's 'Master-piece . . . intended for a compleat Abstract of sixteen thousand Schoolmen', and the satiric portrait of Dryden as a weakly Modern emulating Virgil in *The Battel . . . between the Antient and the Modern Books*; Pope's

> Dryden taught to join
> The varying verse, the full resounding line,
> The long majestic march, and energy divine

(*Imitations of Horace*, Ep. II. i) and comments, mostly in praise of his master, throughout his work; Gray's fine lines in *The Progress of Poesy*, his use of Dryden to demonstrate that 'our poetry has a language peculiar to itself' (letter to West, April 1742), and the famous postscript to Beattie in October 1765, 'Remember Dryden, and be blind to all his faults'; Churchill's tribute in *Gotham* III to Dryden's 'lay Which might have drawn an Angel from his Sphere'; and Burns's delighted discovery of the *Virgil*—'from everything I have seen of Dryden, I think him, in genius, and fluency of language, Pope's master' (letter of 4 May 1788).

The first sustained criticism of Dryden's poetry is to be found in his memorialists and biographers. Dennis's hostility to Pope, the 'empty eternal babbler' whose star was threatening to outshine Dryden's, detracts little from his eloquent defence of Dryden for 'the Solidity of his Thought . . . the Power, and Variety, and Fulness of his Harmony . . . the Purity, the Perspicuity, the Energy of his Expression; and . . . the Pomp and Solemnity and Majesty of his Style' (letter to Tonson, 4 June 1715)—a definition of his poetic quality which stood orthodoxly firm for almost a century. The dramatist Congreve's Dedication of Dryden's plays (1717) is the only serious 'character' of him by a contemporary; Congreve is the first, I think, to recognize Dryden's achievement in prose, and he makes a fundamental claim for the poetry which nineteenth-century critics missed or rejected: 'Take his verses and divest them of their

[1] A collection of Augustan comment on Dryden is being edited by James and Helen Kinsley for the Critical Heritage series (1971).

rhymes, disjoint them in their numbers, transpose their expressions, make what arrangement and disposition you please of his words, yet shall there eternally be poetry, and something which will be found incapable of being resolved into absolute prose: an incontestable characteristic of a truly poetical genius.' There is a full general estimate of Dryden's literary power in Derrick's biography prefixed to the *Works* (1760). But the greatest eighteenth-century study of Dryden is Dr. Johnson's in *Lives of the Poets*.

Johnson makes incidental comments on the poems as he works his way through Dryden's literary career in the first part of the Life; but it is the second part which is critically important. This is partly because he comes to the poetry from a consideration of the poet, offering us an intellectual 'character' of Dryden which (though at some points looking suspiciously like a self-portrait of Johnson) draws his works into a new coherence: 'There is scarcely any science or faculty that does not supply him with occasional images and lucky similitudes; every page discovers a mind very widely acquainted both with art and nature, and in full possession of great stores of intellectual wealth'; 'the power that predominated in his intellectual operations was rather strong reason than quick sensibility', and 'the favourite exercise of his mind was ratiocination'. But 'next to argument, his delight was in wild and daring sallies of sentiment, in the irregular and excentrick violence of wit. He delighted to tread upon the brink of meaning, where light and darkness begin to mingle'—a 'baroque' and 'metaphysical' aspect of Dryden's poetry which made Johnson uneasy, but which later critics, preoccupied with his 'prosaic' faculty for 'immense statement', overlooked. Johnson recognizes Dryden's central place in English Augustan poetry here and in the Life of Pope (where, in a finely judicious passage, he compares the two poets and allows Dryden's superiority of 'genius . . . that energy which collects, combines, amplifies, and animates'; 'Dryden is read with frequent astonishment, and Pope with perpetual delight'). He offers comment, mainly sensible and sometimes memorable, on the major poems, with more enthusiasm for the great odes than we might expect. Although as a moralist he censures Dryden for sycophancy, he perceives, below the mercenary motive, part of the aesthetic and ideological base of the panegyric poems (cf. Kinsley, 'Dryden and the Art of Praise'). His conclusion is Dryden's Augustan monument:

Perhaps no nation ever produced a writer that enriched his language with such variety of models. To him we owe the improvement, perhaps the completion of our metre, the refinement of our language, and much of the correctness of our sentiments. By him we were taught 'sapere et fari', to think naturally and express forcibly. . . . He shewed us the true bounds of a translator's liberty. What was said of Rome, adorned by Augustus, may be applied by an easy metaphor to English poetry embellished by Dryden, 'lateritiam invenit, marmoream reliquit', he found it brick, and he left it marble.

Johnson's essay provided the critical basis of Scott's much more comprehensive account of Dryden in 1808. But Scott, though less epigrammatic and magisterial (and so less liable to absurdity), is in two respects superior: he writes with clearer design and perspective, and (as Johnson advocated but failed to do) he brings powerful historical instinct and scholarship to his reading of Dryden. His assessment remains Augustan: Dryden is the father of modern English poetry, leaving to letters 'a name second only to those of Milton and Shakespeare'. But the tide of taste was turning. Blake, writing in 1810, was more prophetic than eccentric in his view that 'while the Works of Pope and Dryden are look'd upon as the same Art with those of Milton and Shakespeare . . . there can be no art in a Nation but such as is Subservient to the interest of the Monopolizing Trader who Manufactures Art by the Hands of Ignorant Journeymen' (*Public Address*, p. 60). Five years earlier, Wordsworth had told Scott: 'I admire [Dryden's] talents and genius highly—but his is not a poetical genius. The only qualities I can find in Dryden that are essentially poetical, are a certain ardour and impetuosity of mind, and an excellent ear. . . . [His] is not a language that is, in the highest sense of the word, poetical, being neither of the imagination nor of the passions' (Letter of 7 November 1805). Dryden was not entirely without admirers in the new age—Coleridge, Byron, Keats (who made a careful study of his versification), Hazlitt, and later Tennyson and Hopkins; but the main line of nineteenth-century criticism moved through Wordsworth to Arnold's judgement, that 'Dryden and Pope are not classics of our poetry, they are classics of our prose'. The scholars continued their historical and biographical services, but there is little of critical value in the editorial essays of W. D. Christie or Verrall's *Lectures*, and Walter Raleigh could still complain in 1913 that the new 'fanciful, decorative, conceited, mystical' taste in poetry was as inimical to Dryden as 'Romance' had been: 'he . . . has his admirers, but they are dwindled to an old-fashioned sect'.

A critical reformation was, however, on the way. The 1920s brought renewed interest in later seventeenth-century drama and poetry, associated with such names as Herbert Grierson, Allardyce Nicoll, D. Nichol Smith, Bonamy Dobrée, Leslie Hotson, R. F. Jones, Mario Praz, Kathleen Lynch, V. de Sola Pinto, J. W. Krutch; Mark Van Doren published the first adequate modern account of Dryden as a craftsman in poetry (still not quite superseded, though the critical approach has dated); and—possibly with even greater effect—T. S. Eliot began to pay him the homage of the new poetry. 'The depreciation or neglect of Dryden,' said Eliot, 'is due not to the fact that his work is not poetry, but to a prejudice that the material, the feelings, out of which he builds, is not poetic'; and the revaluation of Dryden's poetry owes much to this neo-metaphysical stand. But Eliot's understanding of his quality as a poet was partial. His defence is a reassessment of the ratiocinative, satiric, and rhetorical elements in Dryden's style—it is poetic just where the Romantics thought it prosaic; and he argues that 'Dryden's words state immensely, but their suggestiveness is nothing'. Later criticism has shifted ground, concerning itself (especially since 1950) with the complexity, allusiveness, and subtlety of Dryden; the range and richness of his diction and imagery (taking up Johnson's position); his transmutation of idea and argument into poetry.

Since Van Doren's, few substantial books have been devoted entirely to Dryden's poetry. William Frost attempts too much in his able but not well-organized study of the translations; but in looking at the cultural problem of how the Restoration artist 'assimilates . . . memories of a heroic past', and at the ambivalent attitude of the age to the heroic, he opens a promising new line of critical enquiry (see also the sections on Dryden and Neo-classicism in Tillyard's *English Epic*, and Kinsley's Introduction to Dryden's *Virgil*). Hoffman's study of the imagery of representative poems, though sometimes rather strained, is notable for analysing Dryden's poetic treatment of authority. In *Dryden's Poetic Kingdoms* Roper makes a fresh and sensitive study of cross-reference and analogy in the poems. In such company Nichol Smith's Clark Lectures, elegant and deceptively simple, now seem old-fashioned. Anna Maria Crinò makes a laudable but not wholly successful attempt to illustrate the range of Dryden's craftmanship in the context of '*il cosmopolitismo della cultura europea*' in his day. With one eye on Dryden, K. G. Hamilton examines later seventeenth-century notions of poetry as discourse; his book contains much useful reference and quotation, and gives a much more reliable account of the general context in which Dryden wrote than, for instance, that in Willey's *Seventeenth-Century Background*. (Bredvold's *Intellectual Milieu* is not as broad a study as the title suggests; he investigates the tradition of scepticism underlying *Religio Laici* and *The Hind and the Panther*.) The best historical introduction to the satires is Ian Jack's *Augustan Satire*. A subtler book on a broader but closely related theme, invaluable for the study of the political poems, is Ruth Nevo's *Dial of Virtue*, which brings panegyric and philippic together as two interactive modes of a single category of literature.

A great deal of criticism has been published in periodicals and gatherings of essays. Two useful collections of these are Schilling's *Dryden* and Swedenberg's *Essential Articles*. Older general essays which remain important are Raleigh's, on the political satires; the unsympathetic chapter in Grierson's *Cross Currents*; Dobrée's 'Dryden' in *A Variety of Ways*, and his 'Milton and Dryden'; C. S. Lewis's provocatively hostile 'Shelley, Dryden, and Mr Eliot' ('Dryden fails to be a satisfactory poet because being rather a boor, a gross, vulgar, provincial, misunderstanding mind, he yet constantly attempts those kinds of poetry which demand the *cuor gentil*'); and Geoffrey Tillotson's 'Eighteenth-Censury Poetic Diction'. More recent essays which express the modern concern with poetic principles and techniques are Jefferson's 'Aspects of Dryden's Imagery'; Kinsley's 'Dryden and the Art of Praise'; Lillian Feder on Dryden's classical rhetoric; Hemphill, 'Dryden's Heroic Line'; Emslie on the couplet; and Sutherland's lecture on *The Poet as Orator*.

Much of the periodical literature on the satires has been exegetical and annotative: see especially the essays by R. F. Jones, Godfrey Davies, E. S. de Beer, and James Kinsley. For critical commentary, see Schilling's *Dryden and the Conservative Myth*, the essays by Ruth Wallerstein, Christopher Ricks, and Alan Roper, the chapters in Jack's *Augustan Satire*, and the Introduction to Kinsley's student edition of *Absalom*. Critical discussions of other poems include E. N. Hooker and Kinsley on *Annus Mirabilis*; Ward, Hooker, and Chiasson (correcting Bredvold's bias) on *Religio Laici*; Brennecke, Wallerstein, Kinsley, and Fowler and Brooks on the odes; H. G. Wright on the Fables (see also the chapter in Wright's *Boccaccio in England*); and Helene Hooker, Bottkol, Brower, Proudfoot, and Løsnes on the classical translations.

BIOGRAPHIES AND LETTERS

Biographical comments on Dryden occur first in contemporary collected 'lives'—Edward Phillips's *Theatrum poetarum* (1675), Anthony Wood's *Athenae Oxonienses* (1691), Gerard Langbaine's

Account of the English Dramatick Poets (1691), *The Poetical Register* (1719); and there is Congreve's portrait in the Dedication of Dryden's plays (1717). The first true biography, based on this material and on Dryden's works, is Birch's in the *General Dictionary, Historical and Critical* (1734–41). In 1760 Samuel Derrick prefixed a life to his edition of Dryden's works, making use of new documents and family report. Johnson's biography in *Lives of the Poets* is based on Birch and Derrick, again with additional material; it lacks perspective, but it has enduring value as a critical 'character' of Dryden.

The first major life (and indeed the first full-scale literary biography in the language) is Malone's, 'grounded on Original and Authentick Documents' and prefixed to his edition of the *Prose Works* (1800). Malone set himself 'to consider the subject as wholly new', checking the traditions, searching registers, periodicals, and libraries, consulting members of the Dryden family and the manuscripts of gossips like Aubrey, Oldys, and Spence. But the result is much more than a mass of documentation. It was Malone who first gave shape to Dryden's history as a dramatist, and, eschewing literary evaluation after Johnson's 'beautiful and judicious piece of criticism', tried to see Dryden whole, not merely as a poet but as a man. For all its faults of disproportion, digressive antiquarianism, and inaccuracies in transcription, this is the fundamental Life of Dryden.

Johnson was primarily a critic, Malone an antiquary. Dryden's third great biographer was both of these, and a humane historian as well; and Scott started from the realization that 'the Life of Dryden may be said to comprehend a history of the literature of England, and its changes, during nearly half a century.' His objects were 'to enable the reader to estimate how far the age was indebted to the poet, and how far the poet was influenced by the taste and manners of the age', and in the second he was impressively successful. This is the first 'life and times' of Dryden; and the first critical biography, in which context, chronology, character, and literary assessment are worked together in one grand design.

There are several nineteenth-century biographical sketches prefixed to editions of the poems (the fullest is Christie's); and Noyes's comes in the same tradition. The only substantial Victorian life (and the first to be published on its own) is George Saintsbury's: in its day independently critical, energetic, remarkably acute on Dryden's religion and politics, and going far towards achieving Scott's first object of estimating the age's debt to the poet. The now standard modern biography by C. E. Ward attracts respect rather than admiration. It is more accurate, superficially more informative, and in many places better documented than its predecessors; but it has almost nothing of their energy, main comment, or (since it looks back beyond Saintsbury and Scott to Malone, and 'in general' excludes literary assessment) critical concern. Still, it is a diligent, scholarly, and devoted work in its own kind, and is indispensable. For an excellent survey of the lives of Dryden, and a long series of important 'Collateral Investigations', see J. M. Osborn's *Dryden: Some Biographical Facts and Problems.*

Only about sixty of Dryden's letters survive, and these belong almost wholly to the last twenty years of his life. Some were published by Derrick and Johson, but the first large gathering (forty-five) was made by Malone. The only full and critical edition is C. E. Ward's (1942).

BIBLIOGRAPHIES

The standard bibliography is Hugh Macdonald's, which must be supplemented and corrected from the reviews in *The Library* xx (341–3); *MP* xxxix (313–19); *PQ* xix (196–7); *MLN* lvi (74–5); and *RES* xvi (221–3). (There is an interleaved copy in the Bodleian Library, Oxford.) This the most valuable ancillary published for students of Dryden in this century. It has technical flaws which have seemed more serious as the science of bibliography has advanced, but it is a monumental reference work not only to Dryden but to the literature of his day. The catalogues of the scholar-bookseller P. J. Dobell, on which MacDonald's book was largely built, should not be overlooked.

New work on Dryden is listed as it appears in the *Annual Bibliography of English Language and Literature* published by Cambridge for the Modern Humanities Research Association, and, often with comment, in the bibliography for 1660–1800 published annually in *PQ*. The *Cambridge Bibliography of English Literature* (with *Supplement*, 1957) is under revision. S. H. Monk's *List of Critical Studies . . . 1895–1948* is a convenient classified guide which deserves to be brought up to date. See also the bibliographies in Noyes's edition (1950, pp. 1045–6) and in the books referred to above by Crinò, Hamilton, and Nevo.

BACKGROUND READING

Dryden not only ranged imaginatively over the whole field of 'art and nature' but also reflected the manners, religion, and philosophical and political movements of his time on a scale rivalled only by Chaucer and Shakespeare. The student is bewildered at once by the bulk and variety of his work and by the complexity of its reference. Editorial commentary is now, at least on the major poems, more adequate than it has ever been; and a new reader should not often be driven outside his texts for enlightenment. But to the more advanced, or rarely curious, some of the following may be helpful.

Good general histories of the period are G. N. Clark's *Seventeenth Century* and *Later Stuarts*. The reigns of Dryden's masters are treated superbly on a larger scale by David Ogg in *Charles II* and *James II*, and in Turner's *James II*. Clark and Ogg provide bibliographies, and give some account of the artistic achievement of the time. Nichol Smith's *Characters* is an anthology, with a good introduction, of the prose tradition which Dryden adapted so brilliantly in his political poems. Everyman's illustrated social history is Trevelyan's. The main political and social documents are available, with extensive commentary, in Browning's *Historical Documents, 1660–1714*. A critical reader will still profit from Macaulay's *History*. Some good elderly books on political ideas are Gooch's *Political Thought from Bacon to Halifax* and *English Democratic Ideas*; Figgis's *Theory of Divine Right*; and Russel Smith's *Theory of Religious Liberty*. For intellectual history, see A. O. Lovejoy's *Great Chain of Being* and *Essays*. One of the main sources of Dryden's thought is analysed in Thorpe's *Hobbes*. On the science of the time, see Lyons's *History of the Royal Society*, Butterfield's *Origins of Modern Science*, and Bush's *Science and English Poetry*.

A grand conspectus of the literature of the period is offered, with fine scholarship and critical understanding, in Sutherland's recent contribution to *O.H.E.L.* The old *Cambridge History* is still valuable (ed. Ward and Waller). For briefer accounts, see the opening of Butt's *Augustan Age* and Ford's *From Dryden to Johnson* (which contains short bibliographies), and the section by Sherburn in Baugh's *Literary History*. Beljame's fundamental literary-social survey of 1881 is available in an English translation.

For the other arts see Allen's *Tides in English Taste*; Waterhouse's *Painting in Britain, 1530–1790*, and (much more specialized) Baker's *Lely*; until the *New Oxford History of Music* reaches this period, Parry's volume in the original *History*, and (excellent introductions to a musician with whom Dryden collaborated) Westrup's and Moore's studies of Purcell; Allardyce Nicoll's *Restoration Drama* (with bibliographical notes); Summerson's *Architecture in England, 1530–1830* and *Wren*, Gotch's *English Home*, and Lenygon's two books on furniture and decoration. Iris Brooke's account of costume during the century is conveniently short and well illustrated.

REFERENCES

TEXTS

C. L. Day (ed.), *The Songs of John Dryden* (Cambridge, Mass., 1932).

Samuel Derrick (ed.), *The Miscellaneous Works of John Dryden* (4 vols., London, 1760).

W. B. Gardner (ed.), *The Prologues and Epilogues of John Dryden* (New York, 1951).

Douglas Grant (ed.), *Dryden: Poetry, Prose, and Plays* (London, 1952).

E. N. Hooker and H. T. Swedenberg (eds.), *The Works of John Dryden*, Vol. I: *Poems, 1649–1680* (Berkeley, Calif., and Los Angeles, 1956).

James Kinsley (ed.), *The Poems of John Dryden* (4 vols., Oxford English Texts, Oxford, 1958).

James Kinsley (ed.), *The Poems and Fables of John Dryden* (Oxford Standard Authors, London, 1962; paperbacks, U.K. and U.S.).

James Kinsley (ed. with Helen Kinsley), *Dryden: 'Absalom and Achitophel'* (London, 1961).

James Kinsley, Intro. to *The Works of Virgil* (London, 1961).

James Kinsley (ed.), *Dryden: Selected Poems* (London, 1963).

James Kinsley and George Parfitt (eds.), *John Dryden: Selected Criticism* (paperback, Oxford, 1970; paperback, U.S.).

Guy Montgomery and others (eds.), *Concordance to the Poetical Works of John Dryden* (Berkeley, Calif., and Los Angeles, 1957).

G. R. Noyes (ed.), *The Poems of Dryden* rev. edn. (Cambridge, Mass., 1950). With bibliography, pp. 1045–6.

Walter Scott (ed.), *The Works of John Dryden* (18 vols., London, 1808); rev. edn., George Saintsbury (1882–3).

A. N. Wiley, *Rare Prologues and Epilogues (1642–1700)* (London, 1940).

CRITICAL STUDIES AND COMMENTARY

J. M. Aden (ed.), *The Critical Opinions of John Dryden: A Dictionary* (Nashville, Tenn., 1963).

Blake. See Keynes.

J. M. Bottkol, 'Dryden's Latin Scholarship', *MP* xl (1943).

J. T. Boulton (ed.), *Dryden: 'Of Dramatick Poesie. An Essay. With . . . Defence of an Essay'* (London, 1964).

L. I. Bredvold, *The Intellectual Milieu of John Dryden: Studies in some Aspects of Seventeenth-Century Thought* (Ann Arbor, Mich., 1934; paperback, U.S.). But note Chiasson, below.

Ernest Brennecke, 'Dryden's Odes and Draghi's Music', *PMLA* xlix (1934).

R. A. Brower, 'Dryden's Epic Manner and Virgil', ibid. lv (1940).

E. J. Chiasson, 'Dryden's apparent Scepticism in *Religio Laici*', *Harvard Theological Review* (1961).

William Congreve, Dedication of *The Dramatick Works of John Dryden* (6 vols., London, 1717).

Anna Maria Crinò, *John Dryden* (Florence, 1957). Contains a bibliography.

Godfrey Davies, 'The Conclusion of Dryden's *Absalom and Achitophel*', *The Huntington Library Quarterly*, x (1946).

E. S. De Beer, '*Absalom and Achitophel*: Literary and Historical Notes', *RES* xvii (1941).

Dennis. *See* Hooker.

Bonamy Dobrée, 'Dryden', in *A Variety of Ways* (Oxford, 1932).

Bonamy Dobrée, 'Milton and Dryden: a Comparison and Contrast in Poetic Ideas and Poetic Method', *ELH* iii (1936).

T. S. Eliot, *John Dryden: The Poet, the Dramatist, the Critic* (New York, 1932).

T. S. Eliot, *The Use of Poetry and the Use of Criticism*, 2nd. edn. (London and New York, 1964; paperback, U.K.).

T. S. Eliot, 'John Dryden', in *Homage to John Dryden: Three Essays on Poetry of the Seventeenth Century* (London, 1924; paperback, U.S.; first pbl. *TLS* 9 June 1921).

McDonald Emslie, 'Dryden's Couplets: Imagery vowed to Poverty', *The Critical Quarterly*, ii (1960).

McDonald Emslie, 'Dryden's Couplets: Wit and Conversation', *EIC* xi (1961).

Lillian Feder, 'John Dryden's use of classical Rhetoric', *PMLA* lxix (1954).

Alastair Fowler and Douglas Brooks, 'The Structure of Dryden's "Song for St. Cecilia's Day, 1687" ', *EIC* xvii (1967).

William Frost, *Dryden and the Art of Translation* (New Haven, Conn., and London, 1955).

H. J. C. Grierson, *Cross Currents in English Literature of the XVIIth Century; or The World, the Flesh and the Spirit* (London, 1929; paperbacks, U.K. and U.S.).

K. G. Hamilton, *The Two Harmonies: Poetry and Prose in the Seventeenth Century* (Oxford, 1963). Contains a bibliography.

George Hemphill, 'Dryden's Heroic Line', *PMLA* lxxii (1957).

G. B. Hill (ed.), *Lives of the English Poets by Samuel Johnson, LL.D.* (3 vols., Oxford, 1905).

A. W. Hoffman, *John Dryden's Imagery* (Gainesville, Fla., 1962).

E. N. Hooker (ed.), *The Critical Works of John Dennis* (2 vols., Baltimore, 1939 and 1943).

E. N. Hooker, 'The Purpose of Dryden's *Annus Mirabilis*', *The Huntington Library Quarterly*, x (1946).

E. N. Hooker, 'Dryden and the Atoms of Epicurus', *ELH* xxiv (1957).

Helene M. Hooker, 'Dryden's *Georgics* and English Predecessors', *The Huntington Library Quarterly*, ix (1946).

Ian Jack, *Augustan Satire: Intention and Idiom in English Poetry, 1660–1750* (Oxford, 1952; paperbacks, U.K. and U.S.).

D. W. Jefferson, 'Aspects of Dryden's Imagery', *EIC* iv (1954).

Johnson. See Hill.

R. F. Jones, 'The Originality of *Absalom and Achitophel*', *MLN* xlvi (1931).

W. P. Ker (ed.), *Essays of John Dryden* (2 vols., Oxford, 1900).

Geoffrey Keynes (ed.), *The Complete Writings of William Blake* (Oxford Standard Authors, London, 1966; paperbacks, U.K. and U.S.).

James Kinsley, 'Dryden and the Art of Praise', *English Studies*, xxxiv (1953).

James Kinsley, 'Dryden and the *Encomium Musicae*', *RES* iv (1953).

James Kinsley, 'Dryden's Bestiary', ibid. iv (1953).

James Kinsley, Historical Allusions in *Absalom and Achitophel*, ibid. vi (1955).

James Kinsley, 'The Three Glorious Victories in *Annus Mirabilis*', ibid. vii (1956).

C. S. Lewis, 'Shelley, Dryden, and Mr. Eliot', in *Rehabilitations and other Essays* (London, 1939).

Arvid Løsnes, 'Dryden's *Æneis* and the Delphin *Virgil*', in M.-S. Røstvig, *The Hidden Sense* (Oslo, 1963).

Ruth Nevo, *The Dial of Virtue: a Study of Poems on Affairs of State in the Seventeenth Century* (Princeton, N.J., 1963). Contains a bibliography.

D. Nichol Smith, *John Dryden*, the Clark Lectures (Cambridge, 1950).

L. Proudfoot, *Dryden's 'Aeneid' and its Seventeenth-Century Predecessors* (Manchester, 1960).

Walter Raleigh, 'John Dryden and Political Satire', in *Some Authors* (Oxford, 1923).

Christopher Ricks, 'Dryden's *Absalom*', *EIC* xi (1961).

Alan Roper, *Dryden's Poetic Kingdoms* (London and New York, 1965).

Alan Roper, 'Dryden's *Medal* and the Divine Analogy', *ELH* xxix (1962).

B. N. Schilling, *Dryden and the Conservative Myth: A Reading of 'Absalom and Achitophel'* (New Haven, Conn., 1961).

B. N. Schilling (ed.), *Dryden: a Collection of Critical Essays* (paperback, Englewood Cliffs, N.J., 1963; paperback, U.K.).

J. R. Sutherland, *John Dryden: the Poet as Orator*, W. P. Ker Memorial Lecture (Glasgow, 1963).

H. T. Swedenberg (ed.), *Essential Articles for the Study of John Dryden* (Hamden, Conn., 1966).

Geoffrey Tillotson, 'Eighteenth-Century Poetic Diction', in *Essays in Criticism and Research* (Cambridge, 1942).

E. M. W. Tillyard, essay on 'To Anne Killigrew', in *Five Poems, 1470–1870* (London, 1948).

E. M. W. Tillyard, *The English Epic and its Background* (London, 1954; paperbacks, U.K. and U.S.).

Mark Van Doren, *The Poetry of John Dryden* (New York, 1931); entitled *John Dryden: a Study of his Poetry* (New York, 1946; paperback, U.S.).

A. W. Verrall, *Lectures on Dryden* (Cambridge, 1914).

Ruth Wallerstein, ' "On the Death of Mrs. Killigrew": The Perfecting of a Genre', *SP* xliv (1947).

Ruth Wallerstein, 'To Madness near allied: Shaftesbury [in] *Absalom and Achitophel*', *Huntington Library Quarterly*, vi (1943).

C. E. Ward, '*Religio Laici* and Father Simon's *History*', *MLN* lxi (1946).

George Watson (ed.), *John Dryden: 'Of Dramatic Poesy' and other Critical Essays* (2 vols., Everyman's Library, London, 1962).

H. G. Wright, 'Some Sidelights on the Reputation and Influence of Dryden's *Fables*', *RES* xxi (1945).

H. G. Wright, Ch. iv in *Boccaccio in England from Chaucer to Tennyson* (London, 1957).

BIOGRAPHIES AND LETTERS

W. D. Christie, biographical memoir prefixed to *Poetical Works of John Dryden* (London and New York, 1897).

Edmond Malone (ed.), *The Critical and Miscellaneous Prose Works of John Dryden, now first collected: with . . . An Account of the Life and Writings of the Author . . . and a Collection of his Letters* (3 vols. (vol. i in two parts), London, 1800).

J. M. Osborn, *John Dryden: some Biographical Facts and Problems*, rev. edn. (Gainesville, Fla., 1965).

George Saintsbury, *Dryden* (London, 1881, New York, 1902).

C. E. Ward (ed.), *The Letters of John Dryden, with Letters Addressed to Him* (Durham, N.C., 1942).

C. E. Ward, *The Life of John Dryden* (Chapel Hill, N.C., and London, 1961).

BIBLIOGRAPHIES

P. J. Dobell, *The Literature of the Restoration* (London, 1918).

P. J. Dobell, *Books of the Time of the Restoration* (London, 1920).

P. J. Dobell, *John Dryden: Bibliographical Memoranda* (London, 1922).

Hugh Macdonald, *John Dryden: a Bibliography of Early Editions and of Drydeniana* (Oxford, 1939).

S. H. Monk, *John Dryden: a List of Critical Studies published from 1895 to 1948* (Minneapolis, Minn., 1948); additions by W. R. Keast in *MP* xlvii (1951).

BACKGROUND READING

B. S. Allen, *Tides in English Taste, 1619–1800: a Background for the Study of Literature* (2 vols., Cambridge, Mass., and London, 1937).

C. H. C. Baker, *Lely and the Stuart Portrait Painters* (2 vols., London, 1912).

A. C. Baugh (ed.), *A Literary History of England* (New York, 1948).

A. Beljame, *Le Public et les hommes de lettres en Angleterre au dix-huitième siècle* (Paris, edn. of 1897); English trans. by E. O. Lorimer (London, 1948).

Iris Brooke, *English Costume of the Seventeenth Century* (London, 1950).

Andrew Browning (ed.), *English Historical Documents, 1660–1714* (London, 1953).

Douglas Bush, *Science and English Poetry* (New York, 1950; paperbacks, U.K. and U.S.).

John Butt, *The Augustan Age* (London, 1950; paperback, U.S.).

Herbert Butterfield, *The Origins of Modern Science, 1300–1800* (London, 1949; paperback, U.S.).

G. N. Clark, *The Seventeenth Century* (Oxford, 1945).

G. N. Clark, *The Later Stuarts, 1660–1714* (2nd edn. Oxford, 1956).

J. N. Figgis, *The Theory of the Divine Right of Kings* (Cambridge, 1914; paperback, U.K.).

Boris Ford (ed.), *The Pelican Guide to English Literature* Vol. 4: *From Dryden to Johnson* (paperback, Harmondsworth and New York, 1957).

G. P. Gooch, *Political Thought from Bacon to Halifax* (London, 1914).

G. P. Gooch, *The History of English Democratic Ideas in the Seventeenth Century* (Cambridge, 1927; paperback, U.K.).

J. A. Gotch, *The English Home from Charles I to George IV* (London, 1918).

Francis Lenygon, *Furniture in England, 1660–1760* (London, 1920).

Francis Lenygon, *Decoration in England, 1640–1760* (London, 1927).

A. O. Lovejoy, *The Great Chain of Being: a Study in the History of an Idea* (London and Cambridge, Mass., 1936; paperbacks, U.K. and U.S.).

A. O. Lovejoy, *Essays in the History of Ideas* (Baltimore, 1948; paperback, U.S.).

H. Lyons, *The Royal Society, 1660–1940* (Cambridge, 1944).

T. B. Macaulay, *The History of England from the Accession of James II* (3 vols., Everyman's Library, London, 1906).

R. E. Moore, *Henry Purcell and the Restoration Theatre* (London, 1961).

D. Nichol Smith (ed.), *Characters from the Histories and Memoirs of the Seventeenth Century* (Oxford, 1918).

Allardyce Nicoll, *A History of English Drama, 1660–1900*, Vol. I: *Restoration Drama, 1660–1700*, rev. edn. (Cambridge, 1952).

David Ogg, *England in the Reign of Charles II*, 2nd edn. (2 vols., Oxford, 1956; paperbacks, U.K. and U.S.).

David Ogg, *England in the Reigns of James II and William III* (Oxford, 1955; paperback, U.K.).

C. Hubert Parry, *The Oxford History of Music*, Vol. III: *The Music of the Seventeenth Century* (Oxford, 1938).

H. F. Russel Smith, *The Theory of Religious Liberty in the Reigns of Charles II and James II* (Cambridge, 1911).

J. N. Summerson, *Architecture in England, 1530–1830* (London, 1953).

J. N. Summerson, *Sir Christopher Wren* (London, 1953).

James Sutherland, *English Literature in the Late Seventeenth Century* (*O.H.E.L.*, vi, Oxford and New York, 1969).

C. W. Thorpe, *The Aesthetic Theory of Thomas Hobbes* (London, 1939).

G. M. Trevelyan, *Illustrated English Social History*, vol. ii (London, 1949; paperback, U.K.).

F. C. Turner, *James II* (London, 1948).

A. W. Ward and A. R. Waller (eds.), *C.H.E.L.* (Cambridge, 1912).

E. K. Waterhouse, *Painting in Britain, 1530–1790* (London, 1953).

J. A. Westrup, *Purcell* (London, 1937; paperback, U.S.).

Basil Willey, *The Seventeenth-Century Background: Studies in the Thought of the Age in relation to Poetry and Religion* (London, 1934; paperbacks, U.K. and U.S.).

J. H. Wilson, *The Court Wits of the Restoration* (Princeton, N.J., 1948).

Geoffrey Tillotson[1]

TEXTS

Present-day scholars have done Pope proud. Their work has superseded that of their many predecessors.

Editing Pope was a process begun by Pope himself, who in collected editions added light annotations, calling attention to variant readings, giving dates of composition, and so on. Nor did he stop at his poems. He called in his letters, and edited a large volume of them (see below). From Pope's day to our own, his poems, at least, have never been out of print.

The great nineteenth-century edition of the works—poems, letters, prose pieces—was that begun by W. Elwin in 1871 and completed by W. J. Courthope in 1889. It will always be consulted, since Elwin was an able and hard-working scholar. Otherwise it has now at last become superseded by means of various scattered editions. The Twickenham edition of the poems now stands complete, having recently received the addition of the four volumes of Homer translations. Meanwhile the letters have been edited by George Sherburn (see below).

Much of Pope's prose has now been edited—in *Prose Works* (Vol. I), where Ault made lively additions to the canon of the prose (as also to the verse); in Kerby-Miller's *Memoirs of Martinus Scriblerus*; and in E. Leake Stevens's *Peri Bathous*. (Pope's literary criticism is available in a useful paperback edited by B. A. Goldgar.)

The Twickenham edition, its annotations reduced to essentials by John Butt, general editor, has been available since 1963 in one volume; and three years later, Herbert Davis's *Pope* was added to the Oxford Standard Authors series. There have been several school editions of separate poems or groups of poems.

The surviving MSS. of Pope's poems have been the subject of study since Percy Simpson examined that of *An Essay on Criticism*

---

[1] [English scholarship suffered a great loss with the death of Professor Geoffrey Tillotson while this book was in production. Had he been able to correct the proofs himself, he would undoubtedly have wished to add certain recent books and articles. The editor and publishers are grateful to Professor Kathleen Tillotson and Mr. Brian Jenkins for reading the proofs, and to Mr. Peter Dixon for suggesting additions.—Ed.]

in his *Proof-Correcting in the Sixteenth, Seventeenth and Eighteenth Centuries* (1935). It is understood that Professor Mack is compiling an edition of them.

CRITICAL STUDIES AND COMMENTARY

Critics have quarrelled over Pope's poetry, some of them holding that it does not qualify for that honorific term, except sometimes when, almost by accident, it is something like the 'Elegy to the Memory of an Unfortunate Lady'. The quarrels began in Pope's own day, and became warm after his death (when it was too late for an offender to figure in a revision of the *Dunciad*!). Part of the quarrel was recorded by W. L. Macdonald in *Pope and His Critics* (which deals with the eighteenth-century critics only), and by J. J. Van Rennes in his *Bowles, Byron and the Pope Controversy*.

During the nineteenth century the quarrel became less fierce, partly out of common gratitude (Pope never ceased to be read and quoted), and partly out of repletion—no more could be said by either side, though Matthew Arnold did what he could to keep the quarrel alive by consigning Pope to a niche among the prose-writers.

In our own century Pope slowly emerged, after the First World War, as the poet we all now see him to be. We have recaptured the excitement of many of his first readers, whose feeling was expressed in that couplet of Swift's:

> In *Pope*, I cannot read a Line,
> But with a Sigh, I wish it mine.

As it happens, I have lived through the course of that emergence, and so perhaps may be allowed to write of it as I saw it happen.

It is an index to the low estimation in which Pope was held in the early twentieth century that, so far as I recall, two great critics, A. C. Bradley and Lascelles Abercrombie, make no mention of him. I well remember my arguments in the school playground with another boy, who was a champion of the eighteenth century as an age of good prose and of poetry that was good because it differed from prose merely by virtue of its metre. In my opinion he had no conception of what poetry really was. He had a better mind than I had for tackling the matter of solid prose works—it scarcely occurred to me then that their *manner* could be examined with equal intentness—and this in my view was a disqualification for understanding the first thing about poetry. I was a close student in those

days of Keats's poems. Clearly there was no common ground between the admirer of Gibbon and Pope and the admirer of Keats.

The poem that my opponent put up against *Endymion* was the
Essay on Man. I did not deign to touch the *Essay on Man* or anything
else of Pope's, until, a little higher up in the school, the Latin
mistress firmly remarked that I ought not to dismiss him finally till
I had read the *Rape of the Lock*. I read this poem on her recommenda-
tion, but do not remember the effect it produced upon me.

I hope it produced the right effect—an effect of the identity in
some particulars at least of Pope's poetry with Keats's. There is no
better preparation for reading Pope than a passion for Keats. I was
to try to bring the two together in my first essay on Pope. I had
already been encouraged to take that line by a remark of T. S.
Eliot's. In his Introduction to the *Selected Poems* of Ezra Pound (1928)
he remarked that the modern test for liking poetry was whether or
not you liked the poetry of Pope, whereas the immediately preceding
test had been whether or not you liked the poetry of Keats. It was
becoming clear that both Keats and Pope were poets, and it is the
establishment of Pope as a poet, as much like Keats as he is like anybody, that has been one of the achievements of twentieth-century
criticism.

Already this had been neatly demonstrated by Lytton Strachey in
a lecture he gave in Cambridge in 1925. By this time English readers
were becoming more keenly interested in pre-nineteenth-century
poetry and plays. The year before, Bonamy Dobrée had produced
his *Restoration Comedy*, a brilliant book that showed a true sense of the
witty plays that greatly helped Pope to achieve his own witty satire.
In his lecture Strachey quoted Pope's line:

Die of a rose in aromatick pain,

and asked in Johnsonian style: 'If that is not sensuously beautiful,
what is?' As it happened, the selecting of this particular line paid a
compliment to the poetry of the late seventeenth century rather
than to Pope's, the Keatsian phrase 'aromatic pain' being one of
Lady Winchelsea's, in her poem 'The Spleen'. Strachey's point did
not suffer for anybody familiar with the poetry of Lady Winchelsea,
because the line he selected from Pope was not the only Keatsian
line of an author providing at will lines such as:

To Isles of fragrance, lilly-silver'd vales,
Diffusing languor in the panting gales:
To lands of singing or of dancing slaves,
Love-whisp'ing woods, and lute-resounding waves.

And indeed—to attempt arithmetic—half Pope's genius was Keatsian. The sensuous intensity and weighty richness of both Keats and Pope are shown by the very look of the corpus of their poetry—they so much preferred to write in the weighty five-foot line that there is little of theirs in any other metre, though there is more in Keats than in Pope.

Another critic beside Strachey had shown Pope in a true light. It is surely becoming plain that G. K. Chesterton is one of the best critics of the first half of the twentieth century—perhaps his criticism will last longer than any other section of his work. In 1902 he wrote on Pope in one of the periodicals (the revised essay was included in *Twelve Types*), stating boldly that 'Pope was really a great poet', and going on to praise the combination of richness and conciseness in his couplets, and hazarding the 'dark suspicion that a modern poet might manufacture an admirable lyric out of almost every line of Pope'.

With Eliot's remark, Strachey's lecture, and this little essay of G. K. Chesterton's the stage was set and lighted for everything that has happened since.

One grave error committed by Strachey was his repetition of the old idea that Pope was detestable as a person. He accepted as proven all the charges made against the man Pope, comparing his verses to 'nothing so much as spoonfuls of boiling oil, ladled out by a fiendish monkey at an upstairs window upon such of the passers-by whom the wretch had a grudge against'. The only difference between Strachey and the earlier moral critics of Pope was that Pope's wickedness amused him. That was in accordance with the high spirits of the years that followed the First World War. It was, however, one thing for Strachey to be amused at wickedness, and another to pin wickedness on to Pope—or at least without examining the surviving evidence.

The interest of Pope for the mid-twentieth century being mainly an interest in the poetry, I devoted only a small part of my review of Sherburn's biography to praise of the biography, passing on to devote the sizeable remainder to the poetry. In it I claimed Pope as fellow of the young Milton—the Milton of the minor poems—and of Keats, and asserted that his technical mastery recalled Mozart. This claim was too much for one ageing critic, who, in his *Sunday Times* review of Sherburn, remarked: 'In delight at Pope's orderliness it is unwise to look for what cannot be found. . . . Such statements [as those of mine] are like signposts pointing in the wrong direction.' A few years later a *New Statesman* critic, a younger man, after quoting my claim that Pope was akin to Keats, exploded with 'What bosh!' These comments serve to show the sort of way in which Pope was seen even by intelligent literary people in the thirties. They had not read or re-read his work to see him as he really was, but had lazily taken over the old view of him.

In 1938 appeared two books on Pope—the first on his poetry since Joseph Warton's *Essay on the Genius and Writings of Pope* (2 vols., 1756, 1782). One of these books was Root's *Poetical Career of Alexander Pope*. Reviewing it in the *Modern Language Review*, I praised it as a readable and sensible study of the development of Pope as a poet. My one reservation was that Root's Pope turned out not quite dazzling enough to be the real Pope.

The second of the two books was my *On the Poetry of Pope*. I wrote it after completing much of the reading in seventeenth-century poetry demanded of anybody who was editing Pope. This reading taught me that while Empsonian ambiguities did crop up here and there in his poetry—*Seven Types* in 1930 had happily chosen certain passages of him for comment—much of his ambiguity existed only for readers who had acquired enough literary knowledge to see them. I tried to show what sort of ambiguities my own studies had led me to discover.

Much of this book was concerned with Pope's technique. That was where my interest lay in the first place, but I acknowledged the interest also of his matter in my first chapter, when I discussed the eighteenth-century idea that poetry should concern itself with what was of interest to the man in the street, the sort of reader Johnson was to dub the 'common reader'. That principle I came to see as constant throughout Pope's work, and my second book, accordingly, was an attempt to explore the human matter in it. I called the book *Pope and Human Nature*, and it was amusing to find critics taking me to task for not treating of rocks and stones and trees—of 'external nature', that is, nature external to man. I had of necessity said something about Pope's interest in what Huxley called 'man's place in nature', but, the author being Pope, as little as possible. Pope knew that man was very little concerned with what Wordsworth was to cherish, and his poetry had little to say about mountains and all that, for the same reason that these things were ignored in Bacon's essays.

During the eighteenth century there was a noticeable shift from this philosophy, chiefly on the part of minor writers. Joseph Warton, its main spokesman, believed that poetry was best when it left the picturing and commenting that made up satires, epistles, and moral

POPE 133

essays, and took to narrative and the more directly lyric forms. (Warton's hero was the author of the *Faerie Queene*.) This meant that to the criticism that concerned itself with Pope's character as a man there was added a criticism directed against his poetry as not of the most poetical sort. Stretching into the nineteenth century, a new battle of the books was being fought, the point at issue being the nature of poetry. At one juncture the critics were opposing a ship to a tree, as typifying the quarrel, unaware that Pope was fully aware of the distinction, and sympathetic towards the claims of the more completely natural object.

To our mid-twentieth century, when the technique of poetry has been receiving much attention, the intricacies of Pope's have proved of first-rate interest. There was a good sample of his intricacy in the line Strachey quoted. He quoted it for its sensuous richness, but did not note that the richness of 'aromatic pain' is still further complicated by the joke that precedes it—'Die of a rose' is a variant of 'die of a fever' or of a surfeit of lampreys. F. R. Leavis, in his important essay in *Revaluation*, emphasized equally Pope's debt to the 'metaphysical' wit in seventeenth-century poetry and his devotion to the civilization of his own day. In his satire Pope was seen by Leavis as combining the 'supply-varying, continually surprising play of satiric ridicule' with glowing words of devotion to the ideals of the age. He found in Pope a play of mind and flexibility of attitude that demanded from the reader a peculiar alertness of response.

Wilson Knight preferred to concentrate on what he saw as the 'total contents' of Pope's poetry. His essay 'The Vital Flame' appeared first in 1939, and was reprinted in 1954, together with four other chapters on Pope, in *Laureate of Peace*. His assumption was that 'fundamental to all religion, art, and philosophy lies the all but insoluble problem of assimilating the world of good and evil in man's experience to the divine powers.' Pope, as the poet of an age seen by Knight as one of harmony and assurance, presents us with a unified and harmonious life-view, concentrating 'on man, body and soul, felt in direct, even intimate, relation to nature, society and the cosmos', and achieving a marriage of classical-Renaissance humanism and the New Testament. (Amiel, the French thinker much liked by Matthew Arnold, held that 'what we see is our soul in things', and this theory is certainly borne out by the criticism Pope has called forth in the twentieth, as in earlier centuries!)

Meanwhile much useful criticism of the poetry was coming to exist in the introductions to the Twickenham volumes, as also in other books and essays by the editors and those who participated in the beginnings. David Nichol Smith, for example, in *Some Observations on Eighteenth-Century Poetry* (the Alexander Lectures at the University of Toronto in 1937), defended Pope's poetic diction and his handling of the heroic couplet. Some years later a volume of essays on eighteenth-century literature was presented to him in honour of his seventieth birthday. For this John Butt wrote an introduction to Pope, dwelling on the sources of his inspiration, while in 'Pope at Work' George Sherburn recorded what he had learnt of Pope's processes of composition, deducing his conclusions from a study of some of the extant manuscripts. By this time Sherburn had also shown his critical powers in his study of the intellectual quality, structure, and imagery of the fourth book of the *Dunciad*. In 1949 followed a volume of essays—this time in Sherburn's honour—*Pope and his Contemporaries*, for which Maynard Mack, editor of the Twickenham *Essay on Man*, wrote his indispensable essay on Pope's imagery, 'Wit and Poetry and Pope'. His observations on the ways by which Pope produced a metaphorical effect without using what it is customary to regard as metaphor pointed the way for much subsequent thought on the poetry. A disciple of Mack's, Mrs. Rebecca Price Parkin, followed in 1955 with her *Poetic Workmanship of Alexander Pope*, which contains much analysis, not all of it, perhaps, sensitive and knowledgeable enough. Mack's second essay, 'The Muse of Satire', insisting on the impersonality and fictionality of formal satire, finally answers those who would still see Pope's merely as personal outpourings.

I recall Sherburn's remarking to me soon after the appearance of *On the Poetry of Pope* that it was plain to see that I held the *Rape of the Lock* to be his greatest poem. His remark surprised me. How could one choose the greatest among poems so different and so excellent? Pope may have been right when he said that his rapture had tamed down as he grew older. If it did, it gave place to something equally splendid—an intensified solidity, a firmer grandeur, sometimes a marmoreal simplicity and a finality that could be called Roman—all these things coexisting with enriched luxuriance. Perhaps the wrong impression I had given Sherburn was due to my closer knowledge, in the thirties, of what Pope had written up to 1717 (the date at which he collected the first volume of his *Works*), and Sherburn had interpreted quantity of references as implying an estimation of quality. That remark of my Latin mistress, however, represented a view, two centuries old, that the *Rape of the Lock* stood out as Pope at his best. It was to give way, a decade or so after Sutherland's fine edition, to the *Dunciad*.

In 1941 a Classics don wrote an article on that mock epic in the *Modern Language Review*—an article that led one to sigh for a new *Dunciad*! He cheerfully began by proposing, since the *Dunciad* was universally known as a failure, to show why. A failure! One might as soon call the contents of the Palm House at Kew a failure. The *Dunciad* is a difficult poem because only repeated readings and accumulating knowledge bring out its daedal shape. It therefore marked an important point in the history of the poem's intelligibility when Professor Aubrey Williams in 1955 brought out his *Pope's 'Dunciad' : a Study of its Meaning*. In it Williams was able to point to a line of thought in the poem that had escaped everybody who had written about it, though it must have been obvious in the eighteenth century, when every educated person read Virgil. The *Dunciad* is shaped in imitation of the action of the *Aeneid*, and just as Aeneas migrated from Troy to Italy, so the 'Smithfield muses' Pope is attacking were now reaching the 'ears of kings' in the West End. Moreover, the significance of the strange learning displayed both in the poem and in its elaborate notes is made much clearer.

Other writers have attempted to make us understand and share Pope's feeling for the poetry of Greece and Rome, both as inspiration to write well—

> How match the Bards that none e'er matched before?

—and as practitioners in forms he and his fellow-poets wished to write in. His poetry is usually planned in some sort of relation to poems of classical, particularly Roman, antiquity. As early as 1929 Austin Warren had produced his *Alexander Pope as Critic and Humanist*, an excellent book, providing detailed information about the scope of Pope's learning. In *Pope and the Heroic Tradition* (1951), Douglas Knight examined text, Preface, and notes of Pope's translation of the *Iliad*, and found him constantly aware of a European heroic tradition and an English heroic style. Reuben Brower followed with his *Alexander Pope: the Poetry of Allusion*, which kept close to Pope's text, discussing the parallels with classical poetry that an editor would report without discussion. Brower was out to show Pope using 'the poetry of the past for his own poetic purposes'.

Though the fashionable poem was now the *Dunciad*, Pope's other satirical and moral poetry—the *Imitations of Horace* and the *Moral Essays* especially—were coming to engage American scholars and critics. Benjamin Boyce considered Pope's account of individuals or types in *The Character-Sketches in Pope's Poems*, examining in particular the way he revised them, and their relation to the satiric sketches of his predecessors and contemporaries. Boyce concluded that Pope's instinct was to particularize, to add individual detail even to portraits of types. When in 1955 R. W. Rogers's book on the *Satires* appeared, I challenged his idea that there was any change of importance in Pope's subject-matter when he resumed the writing of original poems after 1727. Pope's concerns remained the same throughout his career; his one ambition was to dig deeper and deeper into the one human matter.

Thomas R. Edwards Jr., wrote of this continuity of matter in his book *This Dark Estate: A Reading of Pope*. As a critic Mr. Edwards has something of Wilson Knight in him. He tries to see Pope's ideas *sub specie aeternitatis*—his ideas on the sum of things and the contribution made to the ideas by the way they are expressed. In the 'Conclusion' Pope is brought into relation with poets like Blake and Yeats, and at one point is found reiterating the 'rueful wisdom of Robert Frost'. My one reservation about Mr. Edwards's thoughtful book is that poets, and Pope among them, it seems to me, are like painters rather than philosophers. For me Pope's deepest wish was to produce an aesthetic effect, as I tried to argue in what I said about satire in *Pope and Human Nature*. Pope liked thoughts because they added to what, in *An Essay on Man*, he described as 'all the strength and colour of our life'.

During the last quarter of a century Pope has been the subject of numerous studies in the periodicals. It was, therefore, appropriate for Professor Mack to collect some forty of them in a mammoth anthology. These *Essential Articles* range universally, the territory being so widely inviting. Some are aesthetic and literary, some textual, and some explanatory. Professor Mack has the frankness to admit disarmingly that no writing 'about' literature can be considered 'essential', not, at least, unless it provides information for those who do not have it already. But his anthology is an impressive tribute to the interest Pope has aroused in the mid century. Of particular value are the pieces by Alpers, Auden, Brooks, Butt, Fenner, Frost, Hooker, Kernan, Leavis, Maresca, Mengel, Pettitt, and Sherburn.

Comprehensive as this anthology is, one is conscious of things there was no room for—in particular, Elder Olson's 'Rhetoric and the Appreciation of Pope', which appeared as long ago as 1940, and demonstrated the rightness for rhetorical purposes of Pope's ordering of his materials, especially in the 'Epistle to Dr. Arbuthnot'. That Olson did not know the *history* of the materials, and how Pope found a place in the poem for things written earlier, did not affect his argument.

Now at last the Twickenham edition stands complete, many of its volumes having reached what is perhaps their final shape, reprinting having made revision possible. Those last four volumes, the *Homer*, are indeed a bang-like ending. Professor Mack and his team have had an enormous task, and their two-hundred-page Introduction is masterly. My only comment is that I think they accept an accident too readily as a blessing. The importance for Pope of his translation of Homer they see as vital—whereas it appears to me that he translated the *Iliad* and *Odyssey* because they were the only great things left untranslated by a good or a great poet. In particular, Dryden had translated Virgil. If Pope could have had his choice, Virgil would have fallen to the author of the *Rape of the Lock*, the author of lines like:

> The meeting Points the sacred Hair dissever,
> From the fair Head, for ever and for ever!

and

> Or Alom-*Stypticks* with contracting Power
> Shrink his thin Essence like a rivell'd Flower,

which are so much more Virgilian than Homeric. As I began by saying, half the genius of Pope coincided with the genius of Keats: in other words, with those poets who are more like Virgil than Homer.

The other day somebody in one of the journals said that he thought Pope's reputation had now passed its peak, and was due to decline. I myself think that, like Dickens, he has found in the twentieth century his rightful place, which he no doubt had in his own day throughout Europe, and that, in Wordsworthian phrase, the heights were within his reach and he reached them. With those words I ended my first book on him. How much more argument in favour of my conclusion has been provided since 1938!

BIOGRAPHIES AND LETTERS

The biographical work of the twentieth-century scholars has been as interesting as their editorial work. Obviously nothing can supersede any biography by Dr. Johnson, simply because it exists as great literature and is as much about human nature as about any individual. But for a full and faithful account the world had to wait till George Sherburn published his *Early Career of Alexander Pope* in 1934.

Before him there had been book-length lives by Owen Ruffhead in Pope's own century, the biographical accounts which editors of his works felt themselves called on to provide by way of introduction, the rounding-off volume of Elwin and Courthope's edition of the *Works*, which was inaccurately done by Courthope, and lastly, Edith Sitwell's biographical study in 1930. The interest of this last book was that it replaced the sneers of earlier biographers by sympathetic smiles. With a woman's nose for the truth, she had looked at Pope's portraits, fallen in love with them, and suggested that the 'wasp of Twickenham' could never have existed, and that Pope was what Charles Lamb—who was right about so many things —had honoured when, after reading aloud a passage in 'An Epistle to Dr. Arbuthnot', he asked, 'Do you think I would not wish to have been friends with such a man as this?' Double dealing and subterfuge were certainly committed by Pope on occasion—he was not morally stainless to the extent that, say, Trollope was. On the other hand, he had his virtues—he was generous, benevolent, kindly—among them things that make life run smoothly, like entertainingness and brilliance, and more gaiety than could be hoped for from one who spoke accurately of 'this long disease, my life'.

Sherburn took his *Early Career* up to about 1726, when the *Dunciad* was preparing, and his study of the quarrel literature of Pope's time showed Pope as far more innocent than had appeared before, and as an injured as well as an injuring participator in the gang-warfare of the wits. Sherburn was also careful to show how full and happy Pope's social life was, and how many friends he had, friends who were both 'ordinary' and men of genius.

As almost always, the early half of a life is the more interesting. The sequel Sherburn did not write exists essentially in the head-notes that he affixed as editor to the letters of each year. And there is further biographical material in Norman Ault's *New Light on Pope*, and more in R. W. Rogers's *Major Satires of Alexander Pope*, which takes up the course of Pope's career as a poet where Sherburn's *Early Career* left off, and gives a careful account of the struggles of the years when he was writing mainly formal satire and moral verse. Rogers might be said to have written his own prefaces to the relevant volumes of the Twickenham edition, with the advantage of continuity. There is a nicely written brief account of the whole life by Bonamy Dobrée.

In 1966 W. K. Wimsatt published his splendid *Portraits of Alexander Pope*.

As mentioned earlier, Pope called in his letters and edited a large volume of them in 1737 to stand beside the two large volumes of his poems. In editing them he paid small respect to text, dating, or recipient. He presented them, not as an historian or scrupulous autobiographer might, but as a great writer conscious of great prose, which long ago had happened to have a particular audience of one, but which had really always been intended for the whole civilized world. He also wanted to impress that world with the brilliance of his personality and friends.

The authoritative modern edition of the letters is that edited by George Sherburn, to whose excellent volumes an addendum soon proved necessary: a small cache of unknown youthful letters was presented to the Bodleian Library, and described and edited by Sherburn in his *RES* article, 'Letters by Alexander Pope, chiefly to Sir William Trumbull'. A useful small selection of the letters has been made and introduced by John Butt.

BIBLIOGRAPHIES AND BACKGROUND READING

Major bibliographies and a selection of useful books for background reading are listed under REFERENCES below.

REFERENCES

TEXTS

The Twickenham Edition of the Poems of Alexander Pope. General Editor: John Butt (London and New Haven, Conn., 1939–69):

Vol. I: *Pastoral Poetry and An Essay on Criticism*, ed. E. Audra and A. L. Williams (1961).

Vol. II: *The Rape of the Lock and Other Poems*, ed. G. Tillotson, 3rd edn. (1962).

Vol. III, i: *An Essay on Man*, ed. M. Mack (1950).

Vol. III, ii: *Epistles to Several Persons (Moral Essays)*, ed. F. W. Bateson, 2nd edn. (1961).

Vol. IV: *Imitations of Horace, with An Epistle to Dr. Arbuthnot and The Epilogue to the Satires*, ed. J. Butt, 2nd edn. (1953).

Vol. V: *The Dunciad*, ed. J. Sutherland, 3rd edn. (1963).

Vol. VI: *Minor Poems*, ed. N. Ault, completed by J. Butt (1954).

Vols. VII, VIII: *The Iliad of Homer*, ed. M. Mack, with N. Callan, R. Fagles, W. Frost, and D. M. Knight (1967).

Vols. IX, X: *The Odyssey of Homer*, ed. M. Mack with N. Callan, R. Fagles, W. Frost, and D. M. Knight (1967).

Vol. XI: *Index*, ed. M. Mack (1969).

The Poems. A one-volume edition of the Twickenham text, with selected annotations, ed. J. Butt, 2nd edn. (London, 1966; paperbacks, U.K. and U.S.).

N. Ault (ed.), *The Prose of Works of Alexander Pope*, vol. I (Oxford, 1936, re-issued 1968).

H. Davis (ed.), *Alexander Pope: Poetical Works* (Oxford Standard Authors, London, 1966).

W. Elwin and W. J. Courthope (eds.), *The Works of Alexander Pope* (10 vols., London, 1871–89).

B. A. Goldgar (ed.), *Literary Criticism of Alexander Pope* (paperback, Lincoln, Nebr., 1965).

C. Kerby-Miller (ed.), *Memoirs of Martinus Scriblerus* (London and New Haven, Conn., 1950; New York, 1966).

E. Leake Stevens (ed.), *Peri Bathous, or the Art of Sinking in Poetry* (London and New York, 1952, New York, 1968).

CRITICAL STUDIES AND COMMENTARY

J. M. Aden, *Something Like Horace: Studies in the Art and Allusion of Pope's Horatian Satires* (Nashville, Tenn., 1969).

P. J. Alpers, 'Pope's *To Bathurst* and the Mandevillian State', *ELH* xxv (1958); reprinted in Mack (ed.), *Essential Articles* (see below).

W. H. Auden, 'Alexander Pope', in B. Dobrée (ed.), *From Anne to Victoria* (London), 1937; reprinted in *EIC* i (1951), and Mack (ed.).

R. A. Blanchard (ed.), *Discussions of Alexander Pope* [from Swift to M. Mack] (paperback, Boston, Mass., 1960).

B. Boyce, *The Character-Sketches in Pope's Poems* (London and Durham, N.C., 1962).

C. Brooks, 'The Case of Miss Arabella Fermor: A Re-examination', *SR* li (1943); reprinted in *The Well-Wrought Urn* (New York, 1947, London, 1949; paperbacks, U.S. and U.K.); and Mack (ed.).

R. A. Brower, *Alexander Pope: The Poetry of Allusion* (Oxford, 1959; paperbacks, U.K. and U.S.).

J. Butt, 'The Inspiration of Pope's Poetry', in *Essays on the Eighteenth Century Presented to David Nichol Smith* (Oxford, 1945).

J. Butt, 'Pope's Poetical Manuscripts', *Proceedings of the British Academy*, xl (1954); reprinted in Mack (ed.).

G. K. Chesterton, 'Pope and the Art of Satire', in *Twelve Types* (London, 1902).

P. Dixon, *The World of Pope's Satires. An Introduction to the Epistles and Imitations of Horace* (London and New Haven, Conn., 1968).

T. R. Edwards, Jr., *This Dark Estate: A Reading of Pope* (London, Berkeley, and Los Angeles, Calif., 1963).

T. S. Eliot, Introduction to *Ezra Pound: Selected Poems*, 2nd edn. (London, 1948; paperback, U.K.).

W. Empson, *Seven Types of Ambiguity*, 3rd edn. (London and Norfolk, Conn., 1963; paperbacks, U.K. and U.S.).

A. Fenner, Jr., 'The Unity of Pope's Essay on Criticism', *PQ* xxxix (1960); reprinted in Mack (ed.).

W. Frost, '*The Rape of the Lock* and Pope's *Homer*', *Modern Language Quarterly*, viii (1947); reprinted in Mack (ed.).

D. G. Greene, ' "Dramatic Texture" in Pope', in F. W. Hilles and H. Bloom (eds.), *From Sensibility to Romanticism* (New York and London, 1965; paperbacks, U.S. and U.K.).

E. N. Hooker, 'Pope on Wit: the *Essay on Criticism*', *PQ* xxxix (1960); reprinted in Mack (ed.).

G. K. Hunter, 'The Romanticism of Pope's Horace', *EIC* x (1960); reprinted in Mack (ed.).

A. B. Kernan, '*The Dunciad* and the Plot of Satire', *SEL* ii (1962); reprinted in Mack (ed.).

D. M. Knight, *Pope and the Heroic Tradition: a Critical Study of his Iliad* (New Haven, Conn., 1951, and London, 1952).

G. Wilson Knight, *Laureate of Peace: On the Genius of Alexander Pope* (London and New York, 1954); reissued as *The Poetry of Pope: Laureate of Peace*, New York (1965).

F. R. Leavis, 'Pope', in *Revaluation* (London, 1936, New York, 1947; paperbacks, U.K. and U.S.); reprinted in Mack (ed.).

W. L. Macdonald, *Pope and his Critics* (London and Seattle, Wash., 1951).

M. Mack (ed.), *Essential Articles for the Study of Alexander Pope* (Hamden, Conn., 1964, London, 1965, revised and enlarged, 1968).

M. Mack, *The Garden and the City: Retirement and Politics in the Later Poetry of Pope* (Toronto, 1969).

M. Mack, ' "Wit and Poetry and Pope": some Observations on his Imagery', in J. Butt (ed.), *Pope and his Contemporaries: Essays Presented to George Sherburn* (Oxford, 1949).

M. Mack, 'The Muse of Satire', *Yale Review*, xli (1951).

T. E. Maresca, *Pope's Horatian Poems* (Columbus, Ohio, 1966).

E. F. Mengel, Jr., 'Patterns of Imagery in Pope's *Arbuthnot*', *PMLA* lxix (1954); reprinted in Mack (ed.).

E. Olson, 'Rhetoric and the Appreciation of Pope', *MP* xxxvii (1940).

D. Nichol Smith, 'Pope—Poetic Diction', in *Some Observations on Eighteenth-Century Poetry*, 2nd edn. (London and Toronto, 1960; paperback, U.S.).

H. Pettitt, 'Pope's *Eloisa to Abelard*: An Interpretation', *University of Colorado Studies: Series in Language and Literature*, iv (1953); reprinted in Mack (ed.).

R. Price Parkin, *The Poetic Workmanship of Alexander Pope* (Minneapolis, Minn., 1955, and London, 1956; New York, 1966).

R. W. Rogers, *The Major Satires of Alexander Pope* (Urbana, Ill., 1955).

R. K. Root, *The Poetical Career of Alexander Pope* (London and Princeton, N.J., 1938; Gloucester, Mass., 1962).

G. Sherburn, '*The Dunciad*: Book IV', *Studies in English, 1944* (Austin, Tex., 1945); reprinted in Mack (ed.).

G. Sherburn, 'Pope at Work', in *Essays on the Eighteenth Century Presented to David Nichol Smith* (Oxford, 1945).

Percy Simpson, 'Autograph Copy for Pope's *Essay on Criticism*, 1711', in *Proof-Reading in the Sixteenth, Seventeenth and Eighteenth Centuries* (Oxford, 1935).

L. Strachey, *Pope* (Cambridge, 1925).

T. Tanner, 'Reason and the Grotesque: Pope's *Dunciad*', *Critical Quarterly*, vii (1960).

G. Tillotson, *On the Poetry of Pope*, (Oxford, 1938, 2nd edn. 1959).

G. Tillotson, *Pope and Human Nature* (Oxford, 1958).

M. R. Trickett, *The Honest Muse: A Study in Augustan Verse* (Oxford and New York, 1967).

J. J. Van Rennes, *Bowles, Byron and the Pope Controversy* (Amsterdam, 1927).

A. Warren, *Alexander Pope as Critic and Humanist* (London and Princeton, N.J., 1929; Gloucester, Mass., 1963).

Joseph Warton, *On the Genius and Writings of Pope* (Part I, 1756; Part II, 1782; rev. edn. in 2 vols., 1782).

A. L. Williams, *Pope's 'Dunciad': a Study of its Meaning* (London and Baton Rouge, La., 1955; Hamden, Conn., 1968).

BIOGRAPHIES AND LETTERS

(a) Biographies

N. Ault, *New Light on Pope* (London, 1949, New York, 1950; Hamden, Conn., 1967).

B. Dobrée, *Alexander Pope* (London, 1951, New York, 1952; paperbacks, U.K. and U.S.).

Samuel Johnson, 'The Life of Pope', *Lives of the English Poets*, vol. iii, ed. G. B. Hill (Oxford, 1905).

Owen Ruffhead, *The Life of Alexander Pope* (1769).

G. Sherburn, *The Early Career of Alexander Pope* (Oxford, 1934; New York, 1963).

E. Sitwell, *Alexander Pope* (London, 1935, New York, 1936; paperback, U.S.).

Joseph Spence, *Observations, Anecdotes, and Characters of Books and Men*, ed. J. M. Osborn (2 vols., Oxford, 1966).

W. K. Wimsatt, *Portraits of Alexander Pope* (New Haven, Conn., 1966).

(b) Letters

J. Butt (ed.), *Letters of Alexander Pope* (London and New York, 1960).

G. Sherburn (ed.), *The Correspondence of Alexander Pope* (5 vols., Oxford, 1956).

G. Sherburn, 'Letters of Alexander Pope, Chiefly to Sir William Trumbull', *RES* N.S. ix (1958).

BIBLIOGRAPHIES

E. A. Abbott, *A Concordance to the Works of Alexander Pope* (New York, 1875; reprinted 1965).

R. H. Griffith, *Alexander Pope: a Bibliography* (2 parts, Austin, Tex., 1922, 1926; reprinted London, 1962).

J. E. Tobin, *A List of Critical Studies published from 1895 to 1944* (paperback, New York, 1945).

BACKGROUND READING

G. N. Clark, *The Later Stuarts, 1660–1714*, 2nd edn. (*O.H.E.*, vol. x, Oxford, 1955).

A. O. Lovejoy, *The Great Chain of Being* (London and Cambridge, Mass., 1936; paperbacks, U.K. and U.S.).

B. N. Schilling (ed.), *Essential Articles for the study of English Augustan Backgrounds* (London and Hamden, Conn., 1961).

B. Willey, *The Eighteenth-Century Background: Studies on the Idea of Nature in the Thought of the Period* (London, 1940, New York, 1941; paperbacks, U.K. and U.S.).

B. Williams, *The Whig Supremacy, 1714–1760*, 2nd edn. revised by C. H. Stuart (*O.H.E.*, vol. xi, Oxford, 1962).

D. V. Erdman

TEXTS AND REPRODUCTIONS

Blake published his own works, by a process he called 'Illuminated Printing' that kept every word, every letter, every mark of punctuation—as well as the line and colour of his illustrations—under his own control. Modern editions, one might think, need only copy; indeed, excellent colour slides and facsimile volumes of many of his works are available, thanks to Micro Methods Ltd., for the strip films, and to the Blake Trust (and Trianon Press), for the handmade facsimiles. Yet the latter are very costly and the former not books in hand, and neither can be read easily. (Nor should it be supposed that facsimile-making, which often involves retouching or even retracing of letters and lines—not to speak of punctuation—is always textually faithful.)

Fortunately Blake etched and coloured many copies of his *Songs of Innocence and of Experience* and several of his small and large prophetic books, and today most of these (as well as his drawings, paintings, and separate engravings) are available for serious study in public or semi-public libraries and galleries: in Cambridge, London, Cambridge (Mass.), New Haven (Conn.), New York, Pennsylvania, Virginia, California, and Auckland. Since Blake composed ambidextrously in words and pictures, using them in combination in his Songs and Books and in his illustration of the works of others, a student must include all these among his 'texts'. When Blake asked, rhetorically, 'Are they Two & not One? can they Exist Separate?' he was referring to 'a Wife & . . . a Harlot', 'a Church & . . . a Theatre', 'Religion & Politics'; he might as well have included 'Poetry & Painting'. Only the costly Blake Trust facsimiles are adequately faithful, but others are to be found that can be used with caution. Most of Blake's manuscripts have been reproduced in half-tone: *The Notebook*, by Sir Geoffrey Keynes (1935), *The Four Zoas*, by G. E. Bentley, Jr. (1963), and *Tiriel*, with its illustrations, also by Bentley (1967). Most of the 'Visionary Portraits' that can be located have been reproduced, along with the newly discovered *Blake–Varley Sketchbook*, in a facsimile edition by Martin Butlin (1969). A new edition of the Notebook is in preparation.

Good modern texts of Blake's poetry began with the editions of selected *Poetical Works* by John Sampson in 1905 and 1913, and of all *The Writings* by Keynes in successively revised editions from 1925 to 1957; these included lyrics, epigrams, prophecies, epics, and anatomies (*An Island in the Moon* and *The Marriage of Heaven and Hell*); also Blake's genial, impulsive, often aphoristic marginal comments on the works of Lavater, Swedenborg, Bacon, Reynolds, and others; and his letters. In the present decade a large number of small and large corrections and additions, particularly to the transcriptions of manuscript material, have been made—by H. M. Margoliouth and G. E. Bentley, Jr., respectively, for editions of *Vala* and *The Four Zoas* (early and late drafts deduced from the same manuscript) —and by D. V. Erdman, with various assistance, in the preparation of a *Concordance to the Writings* (1968).

Because they incorporate some or all of these corrections and revisions, the following recent editions supersede all previous ones, including the earlier Keynes. Sir Geoffrey Keynes's *The Complete Writings . . . , with Variant Readings,* 2nd edn. (1966) is roughly chronological in arrangement, and offers variant or deleted readings of verse or prose as bracketed insertions in the main text. *The Poetry and Prose* edited by D. V. Erdman, with commentary by H. Bloom (1966), is schematic in arrangement, beginning with the canon of works in Illuminated Printing, and relegates poetic deletions and variants to the textual notes. Scholars will find a fuller presentation and discussion of textual details in the latter edition, as well as the absence of editorial improvement upon Blake's own minimal and odd punctuation, spelling, and capitalization. In substantive readings the Keynes and Erdman texts are approaching agreement with each reprinting, except that the latter will not contain all Blake's letters until the fifth printing, and the former remains unreliable in the undeleted as well as deleted text of *The Four Zoas*. (An appendix in the Blake *Concordance*—which is keyed to the pagination and line-numbering of the Keynes edition—facilitates the location of most of these recent changes, including the few readings still in dispute or doubt.)

A complete edition of the *Poetry* only is available (1970) in the Longmans Annotated Poets series, with a commentary by W. H. Stevenson and an Erdman–Stevenson text, modernized in spelling, capitalization, and punctuation.

Most volumes of selections are too meagre even for classroom use, but those of Bateson and Gardner are useful for their annotations, and Vivian de Sola Pinto's for a fine Introduction; Frye's for that.

and as the most ample edition of *Selected Poetry and Prose* (1953). A book of selected illustrations in colour is Keynes's misleadingly titled *Study of the Illuminated Books* (1964).

Several facsimile editions of Blake's type-set *Poetical Sketches* of 1783 have been issued; an annotated one is in preparation by Michael Curtis Phillips.

For a brief survey of the slow history of textual correction, see my textual notes in the *Poetry and Prose*. For a detailed account of the modern texts, with focus on the few words or passages still in doubt or in dispute, see my essay in *W. Blake: Essays for S. Foster Damon* (ed. Rosenfeld, 1969). Of technical but also psychological interest should be my illustrated scrutiny of 'The Suppressed and Altered Passages in Blake's *Jerusalem*'. For an extended but inconclusive debate over the nature and dating of the 'Vala' manuscript, see the Introduction to Bentley's edition, and my critical review, 'The Binding (et cetera) of *Vala*'. The Victorian mistreatment of Blake's text is documented in Deborah Dorfman's *Blake in the Nineteenth Century* (1969).

Reproduction of Blake's drawings, paintings, and engravings has gathered momentum in recent years, but is far from complete, even in black and white. Important collections, partly in colour, are Darrell Figgis's *The Paintings* (1925), Laurence Binyon's *Drawings and Engravings* (1922) and illustrated list of *The Engraved Designs* (1926), supplemented by Keynes's *Engravings* (1950) and his *Engravings . . .: the Separate Plates* (1956). Keynes also published a first series of *The Pencil Drawings* in 1927 (second series, 1956), material now being prepared for an enlarged edition.

In 1963, when S. Foster Damon published *Blake's 'Grave', A Prophetic Book: Being W. Blake's Illustrations for Robert Blair's* The Grave, *Arranged as Blake Directed*, he was forcefully calling attention to a note (probably by Blake's friend B. H. Malkin) in the original edition: 'These Designs, detached from the Work they embellish, form of themselves a most interesting Poem', and to the slowly dawning critical recognition that Blake's illustrations of other men's poems constitute actual prophetic works of his own. It may be true that, in the case of Blair's *Grave*, Blake's designs, as engraved by L. Schiavonetti and arranged for publication by R. H. Cromek, were 'hopelessly hampered by being tied to Blair's text', as Damon concludes. And, at the other end of the scale, it is possible to see, as Martin Butlin[1] has only just pointed out in his Tate Gallery Little Book of *William Blake* (1966), a unified conception in the twelve

[1] See also his *Works of W. Blake in the Tate Gallery*.

large colour prints of *c.* 1795 ('arguably Blake's greatest works'), despite their being tied to no one's text at all and despite their 'bafflingly wide' range of subjects. Yet most of Blake's series of designs attach themselves creatively to the work they embellish. The most familiar graphic prophetic poem in this genre is Blake's twenty-two-plate *Illustrations of the Book of Job,* frequently reprinted and excellently so in an edition by Damon in 1966. In 1953 Albert S. Roe demonstrated, in a volume of commentary and reproductions, that *Blake's Illustrations to the 'Divine Comedy'* are in the same genre. A somewhat more diffuse series are, *Blake's Designs for Gray's Poems,* issued by H. J. C. Grierson in 1922 but soon to be published in full colour; in the press is a valuable commentary by Irene Tayler. Series still awaiting commentary are the twelve illustrations to Milton's 'L'Allegro' and 'Il Penseroso', published in Adrian Van Sinderen's *Blake* of 1949; the eight to *Comus,* the six to the 'Nativity' ode, and the thirteen to *Paradise Lost* (all frequently reproduced);[1] also the twenty-eight to Bunyan's *Pilgrim's Progress,* reproduced in colour and described by Keynes in 1941.

Very few of the 537 large water-colour drawings illustrating Edward Young's *Night Thoughts* (from which forty-three engravings were published in 1797) have ever been reproduced, but a complete edition, with a suitably minute yet sweeping commentary, is being prepared by John Grant, E. J. Rose, and Michael Tolley. Also waiting to be studied in groups or series, despite much individual attention, are some two hundred tempera and water-colour paintings — or at least the 174 located and reproduced in *W. Blake's Illustrations to the Bible* (1957), compiled by Keynes and introduced by George Goyder. Slighter things are most of 'Blake's Shakespeare', a score of various drawings assembled and discussed by W. M. Merchant in *Apollo* (1964). In 1925 Thomas Wright published the eighteen *Heads of the Poets* Blake painted for Hayley; a commentary by William Wells (1969) has been issued by the Manchester Gallery.

CRITICAL STUDIES AND COMMENTARY

In *A Blake Bibliography* (1964) G. E. Bentley, Jr., and Martin K. Nurmi supply a well-documented survey of 'Blake's Reputation and Interpreters'. What little reputation Blake had before publication of the Gilchrist *Life* in 1863 is summed up in Edward Fitz-

---

[1] Now E. J. Rose has ably begun the discussion in 'Blake's Illustrations . . .' (1970).

gerald's epithet, 'A Genius with a Screw Loose'; the *Life*, crammed with sympathetic anecdote and vivid quotation (or paraphrase), and enthusiastically reviewed, 'made him sensationally well known', and thirty years of 'discovery and enthusiasm' followed, including the still impressive 'Critical Essay' of appreciation by Swinburne (1868). The next Bentley–Nurmi section tells how 'The Unreal Blake: 1893–1921' was fabricated by the contrariness of the next generation, pre-eminently by the 'misguided and misguiding' labours of Edwin John Ellis (*The Real Blake*, 1906) and William Butler Yeats—inventing and interpreting a 'Symbolic' system for Blake, editing the texts scandalously badly, and rearranging Blake's life, fundamentally by inventing for him an Irish father and mother. 'It is a fine story, but it has nothing to do with the engraver who wrote the *Songs of Innocence*.'

An early critical study of Blake's work, now quite superseded, was Pierre Berger's *W. Blake, Mysticisme et poésie* (Paris, 1907).

The period 1921–40 is marked by 'A Bibliography, a Text, and Scholarship', the descriptive scholarship of Sir Geoffrey Keynes's *Bibliography* (1921) and first complete text of Blake's *Writings* (1925); the pioneering and still important critical scholarship of Joseph Wicksteed and S. Foster Damon. In Blake's *Vision of the Book of Job* (1910, best edition 1924) Wicksteed inaugurated the close critical study of Blake's graphic poetry. In *W. Blake: his Philosophy and Symbols* (1924) Damon laid the foundations of modern interpretation of all the prophetic or philosophical poetry and painting. His recent revised presentation of Blake's 'Ideas and Symbols' in the form of *A Blake Dictionary* (1965)—though it does not, as the title might imply, record generally accepted meanings or incorporate 'digests of the works of other scholars', and though it is peppered with sweeping and often groundless assertions and unlabelled conjectures, so that it must be used with caution (see my critique in *JEGP*)—is yet a mine of information and interpretation. More or less in abeyance in the later volume is Damon's earlier, and for a time influential, assumption that 'the key to everything Blake ever wrote or painted lies in his mysticism', an assumption pretty thoroughly demolished in Helen C. White's *The Mysticism of William Blake* (1927) and by Schorer (see below).

In other studies of the 1920s and 1930s listed in Bentley and Nurmi there is little that will serve the beginning student, though at some advanced stage he may find profit in ransacking the commentary volume of the D. J. Sloss and J. P. R. Wallis edition of *The Prophetic Writings* (1926), or Wicksteed's 'often naïve and highly personal

[but] useful' study of *Blake's Innocence and Experience* (1928). Some still find value in the analysis of ideas in J. Middleton Murry's *W. Blake* (1933)[1] and in the pursuit of analogous symbolism in astrology, alchemy, and the Kabbala in Milton O. Percival's *W. Blake's Circle of Destiny* (1938).

The next section, by Nurmi, concluding the survey, is headed 'English Blake, His Setting and Sources: 1940–1962', and begins with Margaret Ruth Lowery's *Windows of the Morning* (1940), a study of the *Poetical Sketches* that was largely a pioneering and holding operation. For a corrective and fruitful approach read Robert Gleckner's 'Blake's Seasons', especially for a recognition of 'Blake's clear awareness of the poetic traditions within which he was writing and his deliberate warping, reshaping, or inverting of those traditions'. Still valuable in itself as well as for having opened the field is Ruthven Todd's chapter on 'W. Blake and the Eighteenth-Century Mythologists' in his *Tracks in the Snow* (1946; revised edition in preparation).

The problem of getting past the nineteenth- and early twentieth-century interpreters to Blake himself is partly a matter of relocating *W. Blake in This World*—the title of a short book by Harold L. Bruce (1925), still a lively exercise in debunking. For getting one's feet on the ground in 'Blake's Westminster' there is a gritty chapter in the paperback *Blake* (1968) by Stanley Gardner (followed by an oriented chapter on the *Poetical Sketches*). Heavier volumes after the Second World War elaborated and consolidated 'The Historical Approach' (title of an essay of mine in *English Institute Essays 1950*, ed. Downer); J. Bronowski's *W. Blake: a Man Without a Mask* (1944; reissued as *Blake and the Age of Revolution* in 1965, revolution having become popular again); Mark Schorer's *W. Blake: the Politics of Vision* (1946, abridged 1959); and D. V. Erdman's *Blake: Prophet Against Empire* (1954, revised 1969), with the subtitle 'A Poet's Interpretation of the History of His Own Times'. In this same period, touching but slightly on historical aspects, though recognizing, for example, that *Jerusalem* is a story of 'the struggle between the prophet and the profiteer for the soul of England', appeared Northrop Frye's *Fearful Symmetry* (1947), with an elevated, brilliantly elaborated, general theory of the unity of Blake's 'mental vision of experience'. To interpret Blake consistently in terms of his own theory of poetry as intellectual allegory is, according to Frye, to begin 'a complete revolution in one's reading of all poetry', and Frye proceeds to relate Blake to the world of thought by the study of analogues and of

[1] And see his edition of the *Visions of the Daughters of Albion*.

anagoge. (For a succinct exposition of Frye's view nineteen years later, see his 'The Keys to the Gates' (1966).)

It would be difficult to imagine more contrary approaches than these; yet it is possible to see—concretely in the critical work of a subsequent generation—that the political–historical interpretation of Bronowski, Schorer, and Erdman, and the archetypal mythological interpretation of Frye have served as true contraries inspiring progression. By the time of Blake's bicentenary, in 1957, Frye could see him 'headed for what at one time seemed his least likely fate: a genuine, permanent, and international popularity'.

Frye's new way of reading poetry, expounded in his *Anatomy of Criticism* (1957), has inspired the approach through Blake to Spenser and Milton, as to Shakespeare, Chaucer, and Pope—and in the other direction to Yeats and Joyce. The historical interpretation, carried farthest in my *Prophet Against Empire*, modified the critical understanding of 'Edward the Third', the Songs, *Visions of the Daughters of Albion* (read as a threefold vision of national, physical, and moral slavery), *America, Europe,* and the three epic prophecies.

The best way, perhaps, to indicate the scope and variety of recent studies will be to move from the more general to those dealing with particular works. To the brief introductory essays in the editions of Frye and Pinto mentioned above should be added the rather longer chapter in Harold Bloom's *A Visionary Company* (1961). A persuasive and perceptive 'reading' straight through Blake is to be found in the same author's book, *Blake's Apocalypse: a Study in Poetic Argument* (1963). Martin Price's *To the Palace of Wisdom: Studies in Order and Energy from Dryden to Blake* (1965) culminates in a chapter on Blake's vision and satire. Another survey that ends in Blake is Désirée Hirst's *Hidden Riches: Traditional Symbolism from the Renaissance to Blake* (1964), full of suggestive material, though the author tends to view Blake as a sort of doctrinal failure rather than as a creative artist. (The tradition includes Neoplatonism and Behmenism.) Anyone getting involved in the relation of Blake's thought to classical traditions, Druidism, or deism—or Paracelsus, Boehme, Plato, the Encyclopedists, Thomas Taylor—should turn for cautionary guidance to Peter Fisher's *The Valley of Vision* (1961). For example, 'Blake is the contrary, not the negation, of the political views of Plato and Dante . . . he reverses their utopian rationalism . . . and converts Plato's tyranny of desire into his own vision of the tyranny of reason.' Studies of value, yet inclined to 'explain' Blake from 'sources', are George Harper's *The Neoplatonism of W. Blake* (1961) and Kathleen Raine's *Blake and Tradition* (1969), an illustrated demonstration of improbable and probable discoveries, safest on the long poems. The basic assumption of both Harper and Raine, that Blake knew and read Taylor, is conjectural. A. L. Morton's *The Everlasting Gospel* (1958) finds approximate sources of Blake's undoubted antinomianism in seventeenth-century religious radicals, without quite bridging the chasm in between. Concerned more comparatively with the poetry of religion are Martha England's four chapters on 'Blake and the Hymns of Charles Wesley' in *Hymns Unbidden* (1966). Murray Roston's *Prophet and Poet: The Bible and the Growth of Romanticism* (1965) treats the Old Testament as 'the very source' of Blake's inspiration. Contrariwise, in *The New Apocalypse: The Radical Christian Vision of W. Blake* (1967) Thomas Altizer reads Blake as the source of 'a new and radical form of faith' transforming Western Christian tradition. Times have changed since J. G. Davies's orthodox assimilation of *The Theology of W. Blake* (1948).

Two recent studies of considerable scope are *Blake's Humanism* (1968) by John Beer and *Energy and the Imagination* (1970) by Morton D. Paley. Beer's work is primarily interpretive, with lucid explications (especially of *Milton*) and helpful blackboard paradigms of 'fourfold vision'. His sympathizing, in the prophecies not with Los but with Urizen provides a fresh, but quite limiting, point of view. The reader must also be on guard against errors of indentification and interpretation, especially of details in Blake's pictures. Paley's book, subtitled 'A Study of the Development of Blake's Thought', opens and closes with stimulating essays on the concepts of Energy and Imagination, but his best chapters focus on specific works— 'The Tyger', the Lambeth books, 'Vala', and the paintings of Pitt, Nelson, and Napoleon—placing them carefully in time and in relation to intellectual and literary traditions. Paley is excellent on Blake's transforming relation to the thought of Boehme, the Platonists, Bacon, Hobbes, et al. Chapter 4, for example, derives the zoas from Renaissance faculty psychology.

Also general in scope, though particularizing, are the several articles by Irene Chayes and by Edward Rose listed below. Hers deal judiciously with problems of archetypal criticism; with them should be considered Frye's earlier 'Blake's Treatment of the Archetype' (1951). Rose's suggest various systematic approaches to Blake's mythopoesis. A more politically and psychologically oriented study is John Sutherland's essay, 'Blake and Urizen' (1970). A minimal but sound study of Blake's prosody along conventional lines is Alicia Ostriker's *Vision and Verse in W. Blake* (1965); see also John

Hollander's 'Blake and the Metrical Contract' (1965), and Miss Raine's 'Note on Blake's "Unfettered Verse" ' (1969).

Blake's lyrics, described by Frye as 'popular poetry in the sense that they are practically foolproof introductions to poetic experience', are immediately available yet worth—and receiving—endless study. In the 1950s the critical vogue was to concentrate on the songs as poems, excluding not only biography and psychology but Blake's own explications and even his illustrations. Thus we have Stanley Gardner's *Infinity on the Anvil* (1954) and Robert Gleckner's *The Piper and the Bard* (1959), both good within the limits imposed; Gleckner, indeed, welcomes certain aspects of 'context' as defined in his 'Point of View and Context in Blake's Songs' (1957). An indispensable book and guide is Hazard Adams' *W. Blake: a Reading of the Shorter Poems* (1963). Adams studies the lyrics archetypally as attempts to organize the world of poetic symbolism, assuming 'that Blake's best lyrics do not form merely *parts* of his system, but . . . are microcosms of it'. And he supplies a very useful 'Bibliographical Appendix and Index', locating and quoting previous commentaries —selectively, but running back to Ellis and Yeats in 1893.

The trend of the 1960s was to recover Blake's illuminations as such. Inevitably 'The Tyger' continued to enthral and perturb. Morton Paley (*PMLA* lxxxi (1966)) traced the history of interpretations and refined upon Martin Nurmi's essay in the same journal ten years earlier; Paul Miner's sleuthing for tigers in London and in Blake (*Criticism*, iv (1962)), and Rodney Baine's for traditional responses to tigers (*PQ* lxvi (1967)) enlarged the context, as did Tolley's 'Remarks' (1967).

Alvin Greenburg has widened the discussion of 'The Real World of Blake's Manuscript Lyrics' (1965). John Grant's 'Interpreting Blake's "The Fly" ' (1963) culminated a long controversy over this puzzling Song of Experience that has been resumed by Jean Hagstrum (1969). William J. Keith's 'The Complexities of Blake's "Sunflower": an Archetypal Speculation' appeared in Frye's *Blake: a Collection of Critical Essays* (1966)—which conveniently reprints the Grant and Gleckner articles just mentioned, as well as Irene Chayes's 'Little Girls Lost', Nurmi's 'Fact and Symbol in "The Chimney Sweeper" ', and Adams's ' "The Crystal Cabinet" and "The Golden Net" '. A provocative minority report on 'The Clod & the Pebble' is Hagstrum's in 1963.

A poem that tests the critic's sophistication, 'The Mental Traveller', continues to show that there are infinitely more facets to a Blake poem than his diagrammatic 'threefold, fourfold' seems to imply.

Impressive, differing, modern studies are John Sutherland's (1955), Irene Chayes's 'Plato's *Statesman* Myth in Shelley and Blake' (1961), Morton Paley's ' "The Female Babe" and "The Mental Traveller" ' (1962), Nurmi's of 1964, and Frye's recent 'The Keys to the Gates'; and now along comes Gerald Enscoe, stepping free of the archetypal 'framework' with 'The Content of Vision: Blake's "Mental Traveller" ' (1968). A thoughtful study of another late poem is Grant's 'Apocalypse in Blake's "Auguries of Innocence" '. My textual study of 'The Everlasting Gospel' (' "Terrible Blake in His Pride" ', 1965), though only incidentally critical, may prompt critical study; behind it is Michael Tolley's note on 'Blake's Use of the Bible' (1962), which he followed with ' "Edens Flood" Again' (1968).

The recent study of *The Songs of Innocence and of Experience as Dramatic Poems* (1966), by D. G. Gillham, reverts to the earlier spirit of 'a patient reading of the poems themselves' with little apparent gain. A more difficult book to dismiss, since it is subtitled 'An Introduction to Blake' and since its emphasis on chronological study should be welcome, is E. D. Hirsch's *Innocence and Experience* (1964); errors of fact or deduction, omissions of relevant information, make it a confusing and misleading introduction to anything.

Blake's longer poems are extensively dealt with in chapters of the major critical and biographical books, and also in Harold Bloom's commentary in *The Poetry and Prose* (by no means a mere excerpting of his *Blake's Apocalypse*). A few special studies will be noted here. Gleckner's 'Blake's *Tiriel* and the State of Experience' (1957) is complemented by the *Tiriel* studies of Nancy Bogen and Mary Hall (1970). William Halloran clears up confusion about early symbols in '*The French Revolution*: Revelation's New Form' (1970). Studies of the centrally important *Marriage of Heaven and Hell* abound; Martin Nurmi's monograph (1957) is excerpted in Grant's *Discussions*; Bloom's 'Dialectic in *The Marriage of Heaven and Hell*' (1958) is reprinted in M. H. Abrams's collection, *English Romantic Poets* (1960). A refreshing castigation of critics for 'over-qualifying Blake's extremity' is the third chapter of Kingsley Widmer's *The Literary Rebel* (1965). Also focused on *The Marriage* is Gleckner's 'Blake and the Senses' (1965).

On *Visions of the Daughters of Albion* and on *America* my own 'Blake's Vision of Slavery' and '*America*: New Expanses' are the most thorough, though other studies are in the wings. Carmen Kreiter's 'Evolution and William Blake' (1965) opened one door to *The Book of Urizen*; W. J. T. Mitchell's 'Poetic and Pictorial Imagination' (1969) several; Robert Simmons's 'The Symmetry of Fear' (1970) is a brilliant analysis, with wide implications. Michael Tolley has written a probing study (1970) of the Biblical and Miltonic elements in *Europe*. Morton Paley has a good chapter (1970) on *Ahania*.

Karl Kiralis discusses 'Intellectual Symbolism in Blake's Later Prophetic Writings' (1959) and 'The Theme and Structure of W. Blake's *Jerusalem*' (1956). Wicksteed's volume of commentary, for the Blake Trust *Jerusalem* (1954), is highly impressionistic and personal. Frye's important 'Notes for a Commentary on *Milton*' (1957) and Edward Rose's notes on '. . . the Poet as Prophet in Blake's Design and Verse' (1964) have yet to inspire such a commentary, but some studies of what *Milton* is not, including Brian Wilkie's 'Epic Irony in Blake's *Milton*' (1970), are forthcoming. Rose has written of the structure of *Jerusalem* (1963), the symbol of 'Blake's Hand' (1964), and 'The Symbolism of the Opened Center and Poetic Theory in Blake's *Jerusalem*' (1965); and he covers all three prophecies in 'The Covenant of the Harvest in Blake's Prophetic Poems' (1970). Kenneth Johnston considers 'Romantic Forms of Urban Renewal' (1970) apropos the rival city plans for Babylon and Jerusalem in these works.

Other articles that concern Blake's illuminations as much as his verse include Paul Miner's 'The Polyp as a Symbol . . .' (1960), Henry Lesnick's two essays on '*Jerusalem*' (1969, 1970), and Irene Chayes's essay on 'The Presence of Cupid and Psyche' (1970). Northrop Frye examines 'Blake's Reading of the Book of Job' in the Damon Festschrift (1969); Anne Kostelanetz offers an interpretation of 'Blake's 1795 Color Prints'. *Blake's Visionary Forms Dramatic* edited by D. V. Erdman and J. T. Grant (1970) contains a wide range of studies of Blake's composite art, by Eben Bass, Helen McNeil, W. J. T. Mitchell, Ben Nelms, George Quasha and Janet Warner, and includes Irene Tayler's 'Metamorphoses of a Favorite Cat' from her forthcoming (1971) book on the Gray illustrations and a first report (by Grant) on the ambitious *Night Thoughts* commentary in preparation by Grant, Rose, and Tolley.

Karl Kiralis's fifty-page article (1969) on Blake as a guide to Chaucer's *Canterbury Pilgrims* deals with Blake's commentary as well as his engraving. In a category by itself is Martha England's study of *An Island in the Moon* as related to Haymarket theatricals (1969).

Much of the current study of Blake's art develops the wisdom of Frye's brief 'Poetry and Design in W. Blake' (1951), especially the recognition that it is not abstract art but hieroglyphic in tendency. Hagstrum's *Introduction to the Illuminated Verse* (1964) is much more than that; despite flaws of detail it is to be recommended for information and stimulation. Earlier studies, G. W. Digby's iconographical and Jungian *Symbol and Image* (1957) and Sir Anthony Blunt's art-historical *Art of W. Blake* (1959), remain valuable for their illustration and discussion of analogues, but are critically obsolescent. Blake's early drawings of Gothic effigies are collated with modern photographs in Miner's 'The Apprentice of Great Queen Street' (1963).

BIOGRAPHIES AND LETTERS

Still the indispensable *Life* is Alexander Gilchrist's, completed after his death by a team including his wife and William Michael Rossetti, in 1863, and considerably revised in 1880. See Deborah Dorfman, 'Blake in 1863 and 1880: The Gilchrist *Life*' (1967). Ruthven Todd's corrected and annotated edition (1942, 1945) is out of print, but an enlarged and illustrated edition is in preparation. Extensive documentary pinpointing has been supplied by the *Blake Records* (1969) compiled by G. E. Bentley, Jr. On Blake's reputation see Miss Dorfman's book (1969).

Harold Bruce's spirited *Blake in This World* is mentioned above. Quirky but still good to rummage in is Thomas Wright's *Life* of 1929. Mona Wilson's (1927, 1948) is a sort of sobered Gilchrist. Adapted to the present is Raymond Lister's pleasant *Blake: an Introduction to the Man and to his Work* (1968). The works of Bronowski, Schorer, and Erdman cited above are full of biographical matter. Bernard Blackstone's *English Blake* (1949) is primarily an eloquent plea for the acceptance of Blake's work and spirit into our educational system at every level.

Morton Paley (1970) discusses the physical basis of Blake's visions in a developed capacity for eidetic imagery. An important psychological study, concerned not with the old chestnut of Blake's madness but with his typical artistic imagination is Joanna Field's 'Psycho-Analysis and Art' (1959). An earlier 'Psychological Study' by W. P. Witcutt (1946) has little to recommend it.

Blake's letters, another one of which turns up every year or so, are available in *Complete Writings* and *Poetry and Prose* (partly), but the scholar will need to consult Keynes's *Letters of W. Blake* (1956; revised 1968) for letters to Blake, his business receipts, and notes of identification and location.

Articles of biographical relevance include my 'Blake's Early Swedenborgianism: a Twentieth-Century Legend' (1953); several of Bentley's which are now incorporated into his *Blake Records*

(1969); Keynes's 'W. Blake and John Gabriel Stedman' (1965), his *Blake Studies* (1949, 1969), and innumerable notes and prefaces; Morton Paley's 'Cowper as Blake's Spectre' and Nancy Bogen's 'The Problem of Blake's Early Religion' (1968).

BIBLIOGRAPHIES

A Blake Bibliography: Annotated Lists of Works, Studies and Blakeana, by G. E. Bentley, Jr., and Martin K. Nurmi (1964) is being brought up to date. It includes a section of 'Catalogues and Bibliographies' and a list of 'Books Owned [or possibly owned] by Blake'. It deals with editions of the writings and reproductions of the drawings and paintings, and with Blake's engravings in books. It does not attempt to cover the ground of Keynes's descriptive *Bibliography* (1921) or the Keynes and Wolf *Census of W. Blake's Illuminated Books* (1953)— both currently reprinted without change—though these need correction as to sequence and dating of copies of Blake's works, as well as information as to present whereabouts. A survey of studies up to 1964 has been published by Frye and Nurmi.

Martin Butlin is engaged on a much-needed catalogue raisonné of Blake's art; meanwhile there are partial listings in works such as Binyon's and Keynes's cited above.

Reference aids include *A Concordance* (1968) to both poetry and prose and the Damon *Dictionary* described above. Current exchanges of queries and notes will be found in the *Blake Newsletter* begun in 1967, edited by Paley.

BACKGROUND READING

See, mainly, CRITICAL section above. Suggestions here concern the social and artistic ambience. E. P. Thompson's *The Making of the English Working Class* (1964) is a humane and vivid exploration of Blake's England. Forthcoming essays by Thompson deal directly with Blake and Wordsworth. Harold Fisch's *Jerusalem and Albion: The Hebraic Factor in Seventeenth-Century Literature* (1964) enlists Blake's assistance in viewing 'his chief *dramatis personae* . . . Milton, Bacon, Locke, and Newton'. Robert Rosenblum's *Transformations in Late Eighteenth-Century Art* (1966) concerns the complex changes in the graphic arts in Blake's time. Frederick Antal's *Fuseli Studies* (1956) illuminate the career and styles of Blake's intimate friend and collaborator, as do Eudo Mason's *The Mind of Henry Fuseli* (1951) and his reprint of Fuseli's *Remarks on Rousseau*; also Gert Schiff's catalogue of *Füsslis Milton-Galerie*.

Interesting impressions of Blake and his influence may be gained

··· §0 0–2838 ···

from his youthful followers' lives, A. H. Palmer's *Life and Letters of S. Palmer* (1892), W. Calvert's *Memoirs* (1893), and Alfred Story's *Linnell* (1892). Blake's important influence on Yeats, Joyce and Shaw, is examined in Hazard Adams's *Blake and Yeats* (1955), Robert Gleckner's 'Joyce and Blake', and a thesis by Barbara Y. Newsom on 'Shaw and Blake', and see H. Bloom's *Yeats, passim*. George Harper's 'Blake's *Nebuchadnezzar* in "The City of Dreadful Night" ' is of interest. Anna Balakian has surveyed 'The Literary Fortunes of W. Blake in France'.

REFERENCES

TEXTS AND REPRODUCTIONS

F. W. Bateson (ed.), *Selected Poems of W. Blake* (London, 1957; paperback, U.K.).

G. E. Bentley, Jr. (ed.), *W. Blake's 'Tiriel'* (London, 1967).

G. E. Bentley, Jr. (ed.), *W. Blake: Vala or The Four Zoas* (Oxford, 1963).

L. Binyon, *The Drawings and Engravings of W. Blake*, 114 plates (London, 1922).

L. Binyon, *The Engraved Designs of W. Blake* (London, 1926).

J. Bunyan, *The Pilgrim's Progress*, ed. G. B. Harrison, with a new Introduction by G. Keynes, and 29 plates (New York, 1941).

M. Butlin (ed.), *The Blake–Varley Sketchbook* (London, 1969).

M. Butlin, *William Blake*, with plates (Tate Gallery Little Book series London, 1966).

M. Butlin (ed.), *The Works of W. Blake in the Tate Gallery* (London, 1957).

S. F. Damon (ed.), *Blake's 'Grave': a Prophetic Book* . . . (Providence, R.I., 1963).

S. F. Damon (ed.), *Blake's 'Job'* (Providence, R.I., 1966).

D. V. Erdman, 'The Binding (et cetera) of *Vala*', *The Library*, xix (1964 [1968]).

D. V. Erdman (ed.), *The Poetry and Prose of W. Blake*, with Commentary by H. Bloom (Garden City, N.Y., 1966; paperback, U.S.).

D. V. Erdman, 'The Suppressed and Altered Passages in Blake's *Jerusalem*', *Studies in Bibliography*, xvii (1964).

D. V. Erdman, 'they . . . took the form of books': A Temporary Report on Texts of Blake', in A. H. Rosenfeld (ed.), *W. Blake: Essays For S. Foster Damon*.

D. V. Erdman *et al.* (eds.), *A Concordance to the Writings of W. Blake* (2 vols., Ithaca, N.Y., 1968).

D. Figgis, *The Paintings of W. Blake*, 100 plates (London, 1925).

N. Frye (ed.), *Selected Poetry and Prose of W. Blake* (paperback, New York, 1953).

S. Gardner (ed.), *W. Blake: Selected Poems* (London, 1962; paperback, U.K.).

H. J. C. Grierson (ed.), *W. Blake's Designs for Gray's Poems*, 116 plates, 6 in colour (London, 1922).

G. Keynes, *Engravings by W. Blake: the Separate Plates*, a Catalogue Raisonné, 45 plates (Dublin, 1956).

G. Keynes (ed.), *The Complete Writings of W. Blake, with Variant Readings*, 2nd edn. (Oxford Standard Authors, London, 1966; paperbacks, U.K. and U.S.).

G. Keynes (ed.), *The Notebook of W. Blake Called the Rossetti Manuscript*, facsimile (London, 1935).

G. Keynes (ed.), *Pencil Drawings by W. Blake*, 1st Series, 82 plates (London, 1927).

G. Keynes (ed.), *Blake's Pencil Drawings*, 2nd Series, 57 plates (London, 1956).

G. Keynes, *A Study of the Illuminated Books of W. Blake, Poet, Printer, Prophet*, 32 colour plates (Paris, London and New York, 1964).

G. Keynes (ed.), *W. Blake's Engravings*, 1st Series, 142 plates (London, 1950).

G. Keynes (ed.), *W. Blake's Illustrations to the Bible* (Paris, 1957).

H. M. Margoliouth (ed.), *W. Blake's 'Vala': Blake's Numbered Text* (Oxford, 1956).

W. M. Merchant, 'Blake's *Shakespeare*', with 22 illus. by Blake or Blake/ Fuseli, *Apollo*, lxxix (1964).

J. Middleton Murry (ed.), *Visions of the Daughters of Albion*, facsimile in colour (London, 1958).

V. de S. Pinto (ed.), *W. Blake* [Selected Writings] (London, New York, 1965; paperbacks, U.K. and U.S.).

A. S. Roe, *Blake's Illustrations to the 'Divine Comedy'*, 112 plates (Princeton, N.J., 1953).

E. J. Rose, 'Blake's Illustrations for *Paradise Lost, L'Allegro, and Il Penseroso*: A Thematic Reading', 24 illus., Hartford Studies in Literature, ii (1970).

W. H. Stevenson and D. V. Erdman (eds.), *Poems of W. Blake* (London, 1970).

A. Van Sinderen, *Blake: the Mystic Genius*, colour plates of the *L'Allegro* and *Il Penseroso* designs (Syracuse, N.Y., 1949).

W. Wells, *W. Blake's 'Heads of the Poets'* (Manchester, 1969).

T. Wright (ed.), *The Heads of the Poets* 18 plates (Olney, Bucks., 1925).

The William Blake Trust publishes colour facsimiles of *America* (1963), *Book of Thel* (1965), *Book of Urizen* (1958), *Gates of Paradise* (1968), *Jerusalem* (A [colour], 1951; C, 1955), *Marriage of Heaven and Hell* (1960),

Milton (1967), *Songs* (1955; cheaper edn. 1968); *Visions of the Daughters of Albion* (1959).

Micro Methods, Ltd. supply colour strip films of the Illuminated Books in the Fitzwilliam Museum and the British Museum.

CRITICAL STUDIES AND COMMENTARY

M. H. Abrams (ed.), *English Romantic Poets* (paperback, London and New York, 1960).

H. Adams, ' "The Crystal Cabinet" and "The Golden Net' ", in Frye (ed.), *Blake*.

H. Adams, *W. Blake: a Reading of the Shorter Poems* (Seattle, 1963).

T. J. J. Altizer, *The New Apocalypse: The Radical Christian Vision of W. Blake* (Ann Arbor, Mich., 1967).

R. M. Baine, 'Blake's "Tyger": The Nature of the Beast', *PQ* xlvi (1967).

E. Bass, 'The Thrust of Design in *Songs of Innocence and of Experience*', in Erdman and Grant (eds.).

J. Beer, *Blake's Humanism*, 54 illus. (Manchester and New York, 1968).

P. Berger, *W. Blake, Mysticisme et poésie* (Paris, 1907).

H. Bloom, *Blake's Apocalypse: a Study in Poetic Argument* (New Haven, Conn., 1962, and London, 1963; paperback, U.S.).

H. Bloom, 'Dialectic in *The Marriage of Heaven and Hell*', *PMLA* lxxiii (1958); reprinted in Abrams (ed.), above.

H. Bloom, *The Visionary Company* (New York, 1961, and London, 1962; paperback, U.S.), pp. 1–119.

H. Bloom, Commentary, in *The Poetry and Prose*, ed. D. V. Erdman.

A. Blunt, *The Art of W. Blake* (New York, 1959).

N. W. Bogen, 'A New Look at Blake's *Tiriel*', *BNYPL* lxxiv (1970).

J. Bronowski, *W. Blake: a Man Without a Mask* (London, 1944); revised as *W. Blake and the Age of Revolution* (New York, 1965).

H. Bruce, *W. Blake in This World* (New York, 1925).

I. H. Chayes, 'Little Girls Lost: Problems of a Romantic Archetype', *BNYPL* lxvii (1963); reprinted in Frye (ed.), *Blake*.

I. H. Chayes, 'The Presence of Cupid and Psyche', in Erdman and Grant (eds.).

I. H. Chayes, 'Plato's *Statesman* Myth in Shelley and Blake', *Comparative Literature*, xiii (1961).

S. F. Damon, *A Blake Dictionary: The Ideas and Sources of W. Blake* (Providence, R.I., 1965).

S. F. Damon, *W. Blake: his Philosophy and Symbols* (Boston, repr. of 1947).

J. G. Davies, *The Theology of W. Blake* (Oxford, 1948).

G. W. Digby, *Symbol and Image in W. Blake* (Oxford, 1957).

A. S. Downer (ed.), *English Institute Essays, 1950* (New York, 1951).

M. W. England, 'Blake and the Hymns of Charles Wesley', in M. W. England and J. Sparrow, *Hymns Unbidden* (New York, 1966).

M. W. England, 'The Satiric Blake: Apprenticeship at the Haymarket?' *BNYPL* lxxiii (1969); reprinted, without appendices, in Erdman and Grant (eds.).

G. Enscoe, 'The Content of Vision: Blake's "Mental Traveller" ', *Papers on Language & Literature*, iv (1968).

D. V. Erdman, '*America:* New Expanses', in Erdman and Grant (eds.).

D. V. Erdman, *Blake, Prophet Against Empire: a Poet's Interpretation of the History of his Own Times*, rev. edn. (Princeton, N.J., 1969; paperback, U.S.).

D. V. Erdman, 'Blake: The Historical Approach', in A. S. Downer (ed.); reprinted in Grant (ed.), *Discussions*.

D. V. Erdman and J. T. Grant (eds.), *Blake's Visionary Forms Dramatic* (Princeton, N.J., 1970).

D. V. Erdman, 'Blake's Vision of Slavery', *Journal of the Warburg and Courtauld Institutes*, xv (1952); abridged in my *Blake: Prophet . . .*, and in Frye (ed.), *Blake*.

D. V. Erdman, ' "Terrible Blake in His Pride": An Essay on "The Everlasting Gospel" ', in Hilles and Bloom (eds.).

D. V. Erdman, review of S. F. Damon, *A Blake Dictionary*, in *JEGP* lxv (1966).

P. F. Fisher, 'Blake and the Druids', *JEGP* lviii (1959).

P. F. Fisher, 'Blake's Attacks on the Classical Tradition', *PQ* xl (1961).

P. F. Fisher, *The Valley of Vision: Blake as Prophet and Revolutionary* (Toronto, 1961).

N. Frye (ed.), *Blake: a Collection of Critical Essays* (paperback, Englewood Cliffs, N.J., 1966; paperback, U.K.).

N. Frye, 'Blake's Reading of the Book of Job', in Rosenfeld (ed.).

N. Frye, 'Blake's Treatment of the Archetype', in Downer (ed.); reprinted in Grant (ed.), *Discussions*.

N. Frye, *Fearful Symmetry: a Study of W. Blake* (Princeton, N.J., 1947; paperbacks, U.K. and U.S.).

N. Frye, 'The Keys to the Gates', in J.V. Logan, J. E. Jordan, and N. Frye (eds.), *Some British Romantics* (Columbus, Ohio, 1966).

N. Frye, 'Notes for a Commentary on *Milton*', in Pinto (ed.).

N. Frye, 'Poetry and Design in W. Blake', *Journal of Art and Aesthetics*, x (1951); reprinted in Frye (ed.), *Blake*, and Grant (ed.), *Discussions*.

S. Gardner, *Blake* (Literature in Perspective series, London, 1968; paperbacks, U.K. and U.S.).

S. Gardner, *Infinity on the Anvil: a Critical Study of Blake's Poetry* (Oxford, 1954).

D. G. Gillham, *Blake's Contrary States: The 'Songs of Innocence and of Experience' as Dramatic Poems* (Cambridge, 1966).

R. F. Gleckner, 'Blake and the Senses', *Studies in Romanticism*, v (1965).

R. F. Gleckner, 'Blake's Season's, *SEL* v (1965).

R. F. Gleckner, 'Blake's *Tiriel* and the State of Experience', *PQ* xxxvi (1957).

R. F. Gleckner, *The Piper and the Bard: a Study of W. Blake* (Detroit, 1959).

R. F. Gleckner, 'Point of View and Context in Blake's Songs', *BNYPL* lxi (1957); reprinted in Abrams (ed.), and in Frye (ed.), *Blake*.

J. E. Grant (ed.), *Discussions of W. Blake* (paperback, Boston, Mass., 1961).

J. E. Grant, 'Interpreting Blake's "The Fly" ', *BNYPL* lxvii (1963); reprinted in Frye (ed.), *Blake*.

J. E. Grant, 'Envisioning the First *Night Thoughts*', in Erdman and Grant (eds.).

J. E. Grant, 'Apocalypse in Blake's "Auguries of Innocence" ', *Texas Studies in Literature and Language*, v (1964).

A. Greenberg, 'The Real World of Blake's Manuscript Lyrics', *Bucknell Review*, xiii (1965).

J. H. Hagstrum, *W. Blake, Poet and Painter: an Introduction to the Illuminated Verse* (Chicago and London, 1964).

J. H. Hagstrum, 'W. Blake's "The Clod & the Pebble" ', in C. Camden (ed.), *Restoration and Eighteenth-Century Literature* (Houston, Tex., 1963).

J. H. Hagstrum, 'Blake's "The Fly" ', in Rosenfeld (ed.).

M. S. Hall; '*Tiriel*: Visionary Form Pedantic', *BNYPL* lxxiv (1970).

W. F. Halloran, '*The French Revolution*: Revelation's New Form', in Erdman and Grant (eds.).

G. M. Harper, *The Neoplatonism of W. Blake* (Chapel Hill, N.C., 1961).

F. W. Hilles and H. Bloom (eds.), *From Sensibility to Romanticism* (New York and London, 1965; paperbacks, U.S. and U.K.).

E. D. Hirsch, Jr., *Innocence and Experience: an Introduction to Blake* (New Haven, Conn., 1964).

D. Hirst, *Hidden Riches: Traditional Symbolism from the Renaissance to Blake* (London and New York, 1964).

J. Hollander, 'Blake and the Metrical Contract', in Hilles and Bloom (eds.).

K. Johnston, 'Romantic Forms of Urban Renewal', in Erdman and Grant (eds.).

W. J. Keith, 'The Complexities of Blake's "Sunflower": an Archetypal Speculation', in Frye (ed.), *Blake*.

K. Kiralis, 'Intellectual Symbolism in Blake's Later Prophetic Writings', *Criticism*, i (1959); reprinted in Grant (ed.), *Discussions*.

K. Kiralis, 'The Theme and Structure of W. Blake's *Jerusalem*', *ELH* xxiii (1956); reprinted in Pinto (ed.).

K. Kiralis, 'William Blake as an Intellectual and Spiritual Guide to Chaucer's *Canterbury Pilgrims*', *Blake Studies*, i (1969).

A. T. Kostelanetz, 'Blake's 1795 Color Prints: an Interpretation', in Rosenfeld (ed.).

C. S. Kreiter, 'Evolution and W. Blake', *Studies in Romanticism*, iv (1965).

H. Lesnick, 'Direction and Perspective in Blake's *Jerusalem*', *BNYPL* lxxiii (1969).

H. Lesnick, 'Narrative Structure and the Antithetical Vision of *Jerusalem*', in Erdman and Grant (eds.).

M. R. Lowery, *Windows of the Morning: a Critical Study of W. Blake's 'Poetical Sketches'* (New Haven, Conn., 1940).

H. T. McNeil, 'The Formal Art of *The Four Zoas*', in Erdman and Grant (eds.).

P. Miner, 'The Apprentice of Great Queen Street', *BNYPL* lxvii (1963).

P. Miner, 'The Polyp as a Symbol in the Poetry of W. Blake', *Texas Studies in Literature and Language*, i (1960).

P. Miner, ' "The Tyger": Genesis and Evolution in the Poetry of W. Blake', *Criticism*, iv (1962).

W. J. T. Mitchell, 'Blake's Composite Art', in Erdman and Grant (eds.).

W. J. T. Mitchell, 'Poetic and Pictorial Imagination in Blake's *The Book of Urizen*', *Eighteenth-Century Studies*, iii (1969).

A. L. Morton, *The Everlasting Gospel: a Study in the Sources of W. Blake* (London, 1958; paperback, U.S.).

J. M. Murry, *W. Blake* (London, 1933).

B. F. Nelms, 'Text and Design in *Illustrations of the Book of Job*', in Erdman and Grant (eds.).

M. K. Nurmi, *Blake's 'Marriage of Heaven and Hell': a Critical Study* (Kent, Ohio, 1957); excerpt in Grant (ed.), *Discussions*.

M. K. Nurmi, 'Blake's Revisions of *The Tyger*', *PMLA* lxxi (1956).

M. K. Nurmi, 'Fact and Symbol in "The Chimney Sweeper" of Blake's *Songs of Innocence*', *BNYPL* lxviii (1964); reprinted in Frye (ed.), *Blake*.

M. K. Nurmi, 'Joy, Love, and Innocence in Blake's "The Mental Traveller" ', *Studies in Romanticism*, iii (1964).

A. Ostriker, *Vision and Verse in W. Blake* (Madison, Wis., and Milwaukee, Wis., 1965).

M. D. Paley, *Energy and the Imagination: A Study of the Development of Blake's Thought*, 8 plates (Oxford, 1970).

M. Paley, ' "The Female Babe" and "The Mental Traveller" ', *Studies in Romanticism*, i (1962).

M. Paley, 'Tyger of Wrath', *PMLA* lxxxi (1966).

M. Paley (ed.), *Blake Newsletter*, journal (begun in 1967).

M. O. Percival, *W. Blake's Circle of Destiny* (New York, 1938).

V. de S. Pinto (ed.), *The Divine Vision: Studies in the Poetry and Art of W. Blake* (London, 1957).

M. Price, *To the Palace of Wisdom: Studies in Order and Energy from Dryden to Blake* (Garden City, Kans., 1965).

G. Quasha, 'Orc as a Fiery Paradigm of Poetic Torsion', in Erdman and Grant (eds.).

K. Raine, 'A Note on Blake's "Unfettered Verse" ', in Rosenfeld (ed.).

K. Raine, *Blake and Tradition* (2 vols., Princeton, N.J., and London, 1969).

K. Raine, 'Blake's Debt to Antiquity', *SR* lxxi (1963).

E. J. Rose, 'Blake's Hand: Symbol and Design in *Jerusalem*', *Texas Studies in Literature and Language*, vi (1964).

E. J. Rose, 'The Covenant of the Harvest in Blake's Prophetic Poems', in Erdman and Grant (eds.).

E. J. Rose, ' "Mental Forms Creating": "Fourfold Vision" and the Poet as Prophet in Blake's Design and Verse', *Journal of Aesthetics and Art Criticism*, xxiii (1964).

E. J. Rose, 'The Structure of Blake's *Jerusalem*', *Bucknell Review*, xi (1963).

E. J. Rose, 'The Symbolism of the Opened Center and Poetic Theory in Blake's *Jerusalem*', *SEL* v (1965).

A. Rosenfeld (ed.), *W. Blake: Essays for S. Foster Damon* (Providence, R.I., 1969).

M. Roston, *Prophet and Poet: The Bible and the Growth of Romanticism* (Evanston, Ill., 1965).

M. Schorer, *W. Blake: the Politics of Vision* (New York, 1946; paperback, abridged, U.S.).

R. E. Simmons, 'The Symmetry of Fear', in Erdman and Grant (eds.).

D. J. Sloss and J. P. R. Wallis (eds.), *Blake: the Prophetic Writings*, Vol. II: *Commentary, etc.* (Oxford English Texts, Oxford, 1926).

J. H. Sutherland, 'Blake and Urizen', in Erdman and Grant (eds.).

J. H. Sutherland, 'Blake's "Mental Traveller" ', *ELH* xxii (1955); reprinted in Grant (ed.), *Discussions*.

A. C. Swinburne, *W. Blake: a Critical Essay* (London, 1868).

I. Tayler, *Blake's Illustrations to the Poems of Thomas Gray*, with plates (Princeton, 1971).

I. Tayler, 'Metamorphoses of a Favorite Cat', in Erdman and Grant (eds.).

R. Todd, 'William Blake and the Eighteenth-Century Mythologists', in R. Todd, *Tracks in the Snow* (London, 1946).

M. J. Tolley, 'Remarks on "The Tyger" ', *Blake Newsletter*, No. 2 (October, 1967).

M. J. Tolley, 'The Form of Blake's *Europe: a Prophecy*', in Erdman and Grant (eds.).

M. J. Tolley, 'W. Blake's Use of the Bible in a Section of "The Everlasting Gospel" ', *Notes & Queries*, N.S. ix (1962).

M. J. Tolley, ' "Eden's Flood" Again', *Notes & Queries*, N.S. xv (1968).

J. Warner, 'Blake's Use of Gesture: the Outstretched Arms', in Erdman and Grant (eds.).

H. C. White, *The Mysticism of W. Blake* (Madison, Wis., 1927).

J. H. Wicksteed, *Blake's 'Innocence and Experience'* (London, 1928).

J. H. Wicksteed, *Blake's 'Vision of the Book of Job'* (London and New York, revision of 1924).

J. H. Wicksteed, *W. Blake's 'Jerusalem'* (London, 1954). A Commentary for the Blake Trust *Jerusalem*.

K. Widmer, *The Literary Rebel* (Carbondale, Ill., and Edwardsville, Ill., 1965).

B. Wilkie, 'Epic Irony in Blake's *Milton*', in Erdman and Grant (eds.).

BIOGRAPHIES AND LETTERS

J. Beer, *Blake's Humanism* (Manchester and New York, 1968).

G. E. Bentley, Jr., *Blake Records* (Oxford, 1969).

B. Blackstone, *English Blake* (Cambridge, 1949).

N. W. Bogen, 'The Problem of Blake's Early Religion', *Personalist*, xlix (1968).

H. Bruce.   See CRITICAL STUDIES above.

D. Dorfman, 'Blake in 1863 and 1880: The Gilchrist *Life*', *BNYPL* lxxi (1967).

D. Dorfman, *Blake in the Nineteenth Century: His Reputation as a Poet from Gilchrist to Yeats* (New Haven, Conn., and London, 1969).

E. J. Ellis, *The Real Blake: a Portrait Biography* (London, 1907).

D. V. Erdman, *Blake: Prophet* . . . Cited in CRITICAL STUDIES above.

D. V. Erdman, 'Blake's Early Swedenborgianism: a Twentieth-Century Legend', *Comparative Literature*, v (1953).

J. Field. See Milner (1959).

A. Gilchrist. See Todd.

G. Keynes, *Blake Studies: Notes on his Life and Works, in Seventeen Chapters* (London, 1949, reprinted 1970).

G. Keynes (ed.), *The Letters of W. Blake*, 2nd edn. (London, 1968).

G. Keynes, 'W. Blake and John Gabriel Stedman', *TLS*, 20 May 1965.

R. Lister, *W. Blake: an Introduction to the Man and to his Work* (London, 1968).

M. Milner [pseud. for Joanna Field], 'Psycho-Analysis and Art', in J. D. Sutherland (ed.), *Psycho-Analysis and Contemporary Thought* (London, 1948; New York, 1959).

M. D. Paley, 'Cowper as Blake's Spectre', *Eighteenth-Century Studies*, i (1968).

A. Symons, *W. Blake* (London, 1907).

R. Todd (ed.), A Gilchrist, *Life of William Blake*, '*Pictor Ignotus*' (London and New York, 1942; enlarged edition in progress).

M. Wilson, *Life of W. Blake* (London, reissued with additions, 1948).

T. Wright, *The Life of W. Blake*, with 135 illus. (2 vols., Olney, Bucks., 1929).

BIBLIOGRAPHIES

G. E. Bentley, Jr. and M. K. Nurmi (eds.), *A Blake Bibliography: Annotated Lists of Works, Studies, and Blakeana* (Minneapolis, 1964).

M. Butlin, *Catalogue Raisonné* . . . (in progress).

D. V. Erdman *et al.* (eds.), *A Concordance to the Writings of W. Blake*. See TEXTS above.

N. Frye and M. K. Nurmi, 'Blake', in C. W. and L. H. Houtchens (eds.), *The English Romantic Poets and Essayists: a Review of Research and Criticism*, 2nd edn. (New York, 1966).

G. Keynes, *A Bibliography of W. Blake* (New York, 1921).

G. Keynes and E. Wolf, 2nd (eds.), *W. Blake's Illuminated Books: a Census* (New York, 1953).

BACKGROUND READING

H. Adams, *Blake and Yeats: the Contrary Vision* (Ithaca, N.Y., 1955).

F. Antal, *Fuseli Studies* (London, 1956).

A. Balakian, 'The Literary Fortune of W. Blake in France', *Modern Language Quarterly*, xvii (1956).

H. Bloom, *Yeats* (New York, 1970).

S. Calvert, *A Memoir of Edward Calvert, Artist* (London, 1893).

H. Fisch, *Jerusalem and Albion: The Hebraic Factor in Seventeenth-Century Literature* (New York, 1964).

H. Fuseli, *Remarks on the Writings and Conduct of J. J. Rousseau* (London, 1767; reprinted with German translation and commentary, by E. C. Mason, illustrated, Zürich, 1962).

R. F. Gleckner, 'Joyce and Blake: Notes Toward Defining a Literary Relationship', in M. Magalaner (ed.), *A James Joyce Miscellany: Third Series* (Carbondale, Ill., 1962).

G. M. Harper, 'Blake's *Nebuchadnezzar* in "The City of Dreadful Night" ', *SP* 1 (1953).

E. C. Mason (ed.), *The Mind of Henry Fuseli*, selections from his writings, with an Introduction (London, 1951).

B. Y. Newsom, 'Shaw and Blake,' thesis, Cornell University.

A. H. Palmer, *The Life and Letters of Samuel Palmer* (London, 1892).

R. Rosenblum, *Transformations in Late Eighteenth-Century Art* (Princeton, N.J., 1966).

G. Schiff, *Johann Heinrich Füsslis Milton-Galerie* (Zürich and Stuttgart, 1963).

A. T. Story, *The Life of John Linnell* (London, 1892).

E. P. Thompson, *The Making of the English Working Class* (New York and London, 1963; paperbacks, U.S. and U.K.).

J. C. Maxwell and S. C. Gill

TEXTS

It is difficult to advise the student which text of Wordsworth to buy. There is no satisfactory text of the complete works, for reasons which are too complicated to explain in full here, but may be outlined as follows. None of the various published volumes included all the work composed to that date. Thus the *Lyrical Ballads* of 1798 does not include all the poems of that period. Wordsworth constantly revised his work, and only the latest text has his authority, although critics agree that in many cases the earlier text is to be preferred. Wordsworth devised a layout for his poems that was designed to discourage a chronological reading. Most students dislike it, but it does represent the poet's wishes. Thus it can be seen that (*a*) any complete text, including all revisions, will be very bulky; (*b*) any edition of a single volume will not include enough for a just assessment of the poetry as a whole; and (*c*) any text which prints the last and authorized text will not present the poet at his best.

A number of solutions present themselves. The standard edition of the poems in five volumes, edited by Ernest de Selincourt and Helen Darbishire, supplemented by de Selincourt's great edition of *The Prelude*, must always be at the undergraduate's side, and should be bought by any more advanced student. The undergraduate will find more than enough here, while the postgraduate will soon learn not to trust the edition completely, although he will continue to use it. For introductory work the student could either buy the excellent selection edited by W. M. Merchant in the Reynard Library, which prints early texts in chronological order, or he could buy a number of texts to give a full coverage of certain areas. The Oxford text of the 1805 *Prelude*, D. Roper's edition of *Lyrical Ballads*, with critical Prefaces, and H. Darbishire's text of *Poems Published in 1807*, would provide the student with texts of most of the well-known Wordsworth. Other important poems, such as 'The Borderers' or 'Home at Grasmere' could then be consulted in libraries in the standard de Selincourt edition. W. J. B. Owen has edited the *Lyrical Ballads, 1798*, and R. L. Brett and A. R. Jones the editions of *Lyrical Ballads* up to 1805, adding the critical Prefaces and some other relevant material. The Oxford Standard Authors Wordsworth is only complete in the sense that it includes the poems that Wordsworth authorized. It does not include many poems to be found in the de Selincourt edition, is difficult to read, and impossible to annotate. None of the many smaller selections currently available will be found adequate for university work.

The only two editions of the prose works at present available are, unfortunately, the work of extremely untrustworthy scholars, A. B. Grosart and W. A. Knight. There is a very full and thoroughly annotated edition of the Preface to *Lyrical Ballads* by W. J. B. Owen. An unannotated collection of the literary criticism by Nowell C. Smith still has its uses, and Wordsworth's critical opinions, whether expressed in prose or verse, have been arranged by Markham L. Peacock, Jr., under the three headings of 'Subjects', 'Authors and Books', and 'Wordsworth on his Own Works'. There are two editions of the *Guide through the Lakes*, by de Selincourt and by W. M. Merchant. The *Tract on the Convention of Cintra* has been edited separately by A. V. Dicey, and as part of *Political Tracts of Wordsworth, Coleridge and Shelley* by R. J. White, who brings to the task the equipment of a professional historian, but who is not wholly reliable as an editor. A most interesting 'Incomplete Wordsworth Essay upon Moral Habits' has been published by Geoffrey Little in the *Review of English Literature*.

A number of projects under way at the moment should make study a little easier for future readers of this guide. W. J. B. Owen and J. W. Smyser are preparing an edition of the complete prose writings, which will be much more full than any available now. Oxford University Press is soon to publish the first of a series of editions of Wordsworth's poetical notebooks, which will include all of the obscure material silently left out of the standard edition of the poetry. Cornell University proposes to publish a series of editions of the individual poems, which will present reading texts with full annotation, but also, for the specialist, facsimile texts of the manuscripts, or parts of them. Finally, Jonathan Wordsworth and Stephen Gill are working on an edition presenting chronologically the earliest complete text of all of the poems to 1807.

CRITICAL STUDIES AND COMMENTARY

It is an unexpected and humbling fact that much of the very best criticism of Wordsworth is also the earliest. A number of splendid phrases are well known, summed up in Jeffrey's judgement on *The Excursion*, 'This will never do.' Such, it is commonly thought, was the philistine reaction of the age to Wordsworth's art. But in remembering only the witty dismissal, we miss the genuine thoughtfulness of much of this criticism. For what all the critics are trying to consider, Jeffrey in his review of *The Excursion*, Coleridge in *Biographia Literaria*, Lamb in his letters, and Hazlitt in reviews and lectures, is how far a complex, intellectual, and philosophical poem can be a *poem* at all. Coleridge had declared Wordsworth capable of producing the '*first* and *only* true philosophical poem in existence', but others were not so sure either of the poet or the genre. For Jeffrey the doctrine of *The Excursion* was the problem. He thought it pretentious and not a little mad. For Hazlitt and Lamb, however, it was the relation between philosophy and poetry that was obscure. Lamb felt that a reader needed 'some previous acquaintance with the author's theory', before he could encounter the story of Margaret in Book I. Hazlitt, on the other hand, wanted less of the dramatic narrative which Lamb valued so highly. He wanted a 'philosophical poem altogether, with only occasional digressions or allusions to particular instances'. Hazlitt demands that the philosophy should declare itself boldly, without recourse to the machinery of plot and dialogue.

Such early criticism of the most ambitious poem Wordsworth published in his lifetime is not negligible. The student should supplement it with Keats's wonderfully perceptive letters on Wordsworth the man and the writer in order to sense how immediately and intensely Wordsworth's challenge to his age was felt. Clearly the criticism is less easy to assimilate than that written in our current literary-critical idiom, but the student will find that many of the trends of later criticism up to the present day are anticipated here. We are still asking the same questions, still puzzling over the same problems, in the complex, philosophical poetry of this great writer.

Coleridge and Hazlitt's line of thinking has been developed by many critics who are prepared to make claims for Wordsworth as a philosopher. Leslie Stephen's 'Wordsworth's Ethics' (1876), the most rigorously argued of a number of similar nineteenth-century essays, argues that the importance of Wordsworth's poetry rests on the profundity and range of the ethical system it expounds. For Stephen there is no question that the system is 'distinctive and capable of systematic exposition'. Stephen argues from within the poetry, making little of Wordsworth's specific debts to earlier thought. Arthur Beatty's very important study, however, *William Wordsworth: His Doctrine and Art*, attempts to show how much Wordsworth's poetry rests upon the associationism of David Hartley, and how far perplexing ideas, in such poems as 'Tintern Abbey' and the 'Ode: Intimations of Immortality', can be understood more easily by reference to him. Beatty's study is of first importance, especially since literary students notoriously fight shy of analytical philosophic systems. He forces us to examine how far Wordsworth, for all the originality of his genius, was a child of eighteenth-century philosophy. But the study is weakened because Beatty does not allow literary–critical intelligence enough play. Quite simply, he does not make enough of the difference between a good and a bad poem. A similar failing will be felt in two other similar studies, which can none the less be highly recommended. H. W. Piper's *The Active Universe* displays fascinating evidence that Wordsworth's belief in the One Life in man and nature was supported not only by speculative thinkers of his day but also by sober scientists. Piper's discussion of the interplay between Wordsworth and Coleridge is weakened by doubtful dating of important poems, but the study remains of great interest. Melvin Rader's *Wordsworth: A Philosophical Approach*, on the other hand, stresses, with an abundance of very illuminating quotation, Wordsworth's rejection of associationism and his leaning towards the transcendentalism usually associated with Coleridge. The truth about Wordsworth's philosophic debts can never be decided with the finality that individual scholars would like. For this reason Newton P. Stallknecht's *Strange Seas of Thought* will be found a useful, balancing survey. Stallknecht admits and examines the debts to empiricist as well as idealist philosophy, but continues carefully to examine what Wordsworth made of his debts. Again the student will find very interesting the wealth of quotation from inaccessible, and frequently unreadable, philosophic works, which anticipate and parallel the writings of Wordsworth and Coleridge. Rader is a professional philosopher. A. N. Whitehead, author of *Science and the Modern World*, is a scientist. Each testifies especially importantly to the vitality of Wordsworth's thought. Finally, E. D. Hirsch, Jr., has tried to demonstrate the interest of Wordsworth's ideas in a wider, European, context. In his *Wordsworth and Schelling* he shows the similarity of thought in the two writers, not to establish priority of influence in the usual way, but to show how the development of two contemporary thinkers who *did not* influence each other lends 'force to the view that romanticism is a meaningful historical term'. The point is so well made early on in the book, however, that the study cannot but seem too long.

Too much reading of such studies is likely to bring on a kind of delirium. Wordsworth's thought is evidently so important, but seemingly so complex, that one despairs of ever understanding it. As a corrective, two dissenting voices might be considered. Aldous Huxley's essay on 'Wordsworth in the Tropics' argues that Wordsworth's belief in the benevolent intervention of nature in man's life could not have been sustained had he seen and experienced nature in other and more hostile contexts. In 'A Minority Report' Douglas Bush argues that Wordsworth has little to say to modern man, because, in all but his very finest work, Wordsworth was in retreat from the problems of the modern world. Both essays have to be grappled with if one is to come to terms with the poetry.

A quite different approach was adopted by Arnold in his Introduction to his selection of Wordsworth. Provoked by Stephen's essay, Arnold argued that Wordsworth's power is as a poet and not as a philosopher. (See J. Dover Wilson's study of the two critics.) To Arnold Wordsworth is above all a source of refreshment and spiritual joy, not of moral guidance. There is no doubt that Arnold, anticipated in some degree by Walter Pater, pin-pointed one source of Wordsworth's power. Striking tributes in support will be found, for example, by J. S. Mill in his *Autobiography* and W. H. White in the *Autobiography of Mark Rutherford*. Both men stumbled on Wordsworth when they were exhausted, one by a utilitarian upbringing and the other by the starvation culture of dissent, and both found nourishment in Wordsworth's celebration of the 'human heart by which we live'.

Although Arnold's is a legitimate approach, however, it is a dangerous one. His emphasis on the shortness of Wordsworth's life as a great poet and on his lack of intellectual distinction, however qualified by an emphasis on his achievement *as a writer*, made possible a later and much more dubious line of inquiry. Early in this century G. M. Harper and Émile Legouis revealed the story of Wordsworth's love for Annette Vallon and of their illegitimate daughter. Shelley had described Wordsworth as a 'solemn and unsexual man', and the discovery that after all he was not so provoked much re-examination of the poetry in the light of the supposed inner turmoils caused by this youthful passion. Clearly investigation into the nature of Wordsworth's creative process is important—he conducted the first in *The Prelude*—but psycho-analytical criticism of Wordsworth to date has been positively misleading. Herbert Read's *Wordsworth*, recently reissued in paperback, and Hugh I'Anson Fausset's *The Lost Leader* attempt to demonstrate the nature of Wordsworth's early poetry, and the cause of his decline and political hardening, as if the psychological speculations so recklessly bandied about were hard fact. Neither writer shows any great acquaintance with the poetry. G. W. Meyer's more important *Wordsworth's Formative Years* is likewise damaged by an irresponsible jumbling of facts and speculation. Although much more scholarly and sensitive, F. W. Bateson's *Wordsworth: A Re-Interpretation* is essentially of this tradition. Speculating on Wordsworth's relation to Annette Vallon, to Dorothy, and to the other women in his life, Bateson calls on psychology to help literary criticism. It has not been accepted either that the psychology is sound or that its literary critical function is valid, but there is no doubt that Bateson is a sensitive judge of poetry and can write well about it.

Such are two of the main lines of Wordsworth criticism. Much valuable and interesting work, of course, cannot be fitted into these dominant critical schools, and should be mentioned here. Comments, in reviews and elsewhere, by Wordsworth's contemporaries up to 1822 are usefully collected by Elsie Smith, and are soon to be supplemented by another collection by R. S. Woof. Less interesting than his reminiscences, but still worth reading as an assessment late in the poet's life, is De Quincey's essay of 1845. Among biographical–critical accounts from the years immediately after Wordsworth's death, that by George Brimley is worth a glance. A few years later there is a characteristically vivacious essay by Walter Bagehot, contrasting Wordsworth's poetry as 'pure' with that of Tennyson ('ornate') and Browning ('grotesque'). (A couple of years before, in *On Translating Homer*, Arnold had compared Wordsworth's simplicity with Tennyson's *simplesse*.)

With the new century the number of writers that are of intrinsic and not merely historical interest increases. The beginner, and not only the beginner, is likely to get more stimulus from Raleigh's monograph and Bradley's essay than from more recent and more portentous studies. The decade of the First World War was less productive, and it is doubtful how far the conscription of the patriot benefited the poet, but there is some good criticism as well as some dated speculation on the composition of *The Prelude* in H. W. Garrod's book. C. H. Herford's short book is perhaps the last word from a critic of the older generation, and is still an excellent introduction.

T. S. Eliot never wrote at any length on the poetry, but the Wordsworth and Coleridge chapter in *The Use of Poetry and the Use of Criticism* should not be neglected. F. R. Leavis offered a basically Arnoldian reading, but less one-sided than Arnold's, and another *Scrutiny* essay, by James Smith, has valuable comments on Wordsworth's concern with the relation of the percipient to the external world, which link up with C. C. Clarke's book, mentioned later. (Clarke's 1950 essay on the great decade is also worth attention.) Wilson Knight, as usual, furnished some individual insights. Finally, from this period, there is the unpretentious but shrewd little book by J. C. Smith.

Drawing on the de Selincourt and Darbishire edition of the poetry, post-war studies are fuller and more scholarly than was previously the case. In only one area, however, has there been a real advance on earlier lines of enquiry. A number of studies have examined very fruitfully both how Wordsworth's *poetry* creates its meaning, and, while avoiding the rigidity of formal historical–philosophical studies already discussed, just what that meaning is. The earliest of these is John Jones's *The Egotistical Sublime*. The student will not find this an easy book, but it repays study. Jones follows the development of Wordsworth's thought, from its first grappling with the problems of defining man's relation to the external world and to God, through to its acceptance (which was not mere resignation) of much of the orthodox Christian scheme. Jones sees both Wordsworth and Coleridge as 'natural monists', but suggests that, whereas Coleridge craved unity, Wordsworth rested in a perception of the 'significant relation' of man and nature. The later Christian thought is seen not as a denial of this but as a redefinition. The discussion is often knotty, and in the early part of the book damagingly cryptic, but it is always well supported by examination of the finest verse. Whereas Jones is wide-ranging, David Ferry attempts in *The Limits of Mortality* to establish a subtle interpretation through close reading of only certain of the major poems. In his view Wordsworth was in fact lovingly hostile to man, so that in his work there is always a tension against the doctrine proposed in *The Prelude*: Love of Nature Leads to Love of Man. The study is heady stuff and can cause intoxication. C. C. Clarke has examined Wordsworth's key statements about the nature of perception, and by illuminating common-sense discussion leads the non-philosophic reader into an awareness of the problems inherent in the understanding of man's knowledge of the world. It is a little book on a big subject, however, and the student should beware of the feeling that each neatly parcelled section is the last word on the matter. Alex King's *Wordsworth and the Artist's Vision* likewise demonstrates that Wordsworth has something to say and that it is of continuing importance. He ranges widely in a discussion of the nature of the peculiar vision granted to certain artists, and is not afraid of broaching difficult subjects like the value and nature of the truth of Wordsworth's ideas. This is an out-of-the-ordinary book, which will not provide cut and dried information or ideas for the weekly essay, but it should be read.

Clarke and King have the great merit that they write unpretentious prose. In *The Music of Humanity* Jonathan Wordsworth likewise studies with attractive lucidity the artistic and intellectual background to the poetry up to the completion of the first great work, 'The Ruined Cottage'. The emphasis throughout is on the literary value of the poetry, which provides just the guidance the inexperienced reader needs. In his study of the poetry to 1814, however, G. H. Hartman seems to obscure the central issues by over-elaborate prose and by a complex professionalism which will daunt the beginner. In his determination to examine all the poetry in the light of the main thesis, Hartman often has to neglect what is individual and challenging in the given work. For a dissenting voice over just one area, see the appendix on Hartman in Enid Welsford's *Salisbury Plain*.

Wordsworth was not, of course, an isolated figure, and students will make a better judgement by studying him together with the other Romantics. Three studies which may help should be mentioned, with the proviso that many other surveys of the Romantic movement will be found of use at a more superficial level. Harold Bloom's *The Visionary Company* recognizes that the Romantics shared a belief now strange to us: an intense faith in the power of the imagination to create, fortify, and redeem. His examination of how each poet expressed his shifting hold on this faith is always illuminating, though one may feel that the terms Bloom uses were really minted for a discussion of Blake rather than for the other Romantics. David Perkins discusses the quest of the Romantic poets to create a new kind of imagery to support a poetry of assertion, when the certainties which had supported, for instance, Augustan rhetoric had dissolved. Perkins can never resist the grand phrase, however, and much of the energy of the book actually generates more heat than light. Edward E. Bostetter likewise discusses how the Romantic poets overcame special problems for didactic writing at that moment, but as the catch-penny title might suggest, *The Romantic Ventriloquists* is a pedestrian and not notably sensitive book.

Much of the best criticism of Wordsworth is centred on individual poems or problems, and this section must conclude with a selection from this.

The early Wordsworth: In addition to the valuable chapters in Legouis and Jonathan Wordsworth already listed, Z. S. Fink's *The Early Wordsworthian Milieu* should be noted.

The Prelude: This has been the most extensively and intensively studied of Wordsworth's poems. The exhaustive study by R. D. Havens is relevant to all Wordsworth's major works. It is too long and not always critically acute. Moreover, the fact that the Commentary which constitutes the second part presupposes and supplements de Selincourt means that, though voluminous, it is not self-contained. But it is indispensable for advanced study. More readable is Herbert Lindenberger's study, a series of linked essays on various aspects of the poem. The complicated history of composition is lucidly summarized by J. R. MacGillivray, but the student should be warned that fresh discoveries are still being made. *The Prelude* (and also 'Michael') is set in contrast with other narrative poems of the period by Karl Kroeber; an older essay by A. C. Bradley is also relevant here. Two stimulating and individual critics who deal incidentally with the poem are William Empson and Donald Davie.

Lyrical Ballads: The collection was usefully placed in its historical context by Robert Mayo, some of whose conclusions have been modified by S. M. Parrish and Charles Ryskamp. On the Preface, in its various forms, the treatment by W. J. B. Owen in his edition (see above) can be supplemented by Roger Sharrock and George Whalley (more on the Wordsworth–Coleridge relationship than on the Preface as such), and by M. H. Abrams (1954). A most important essay is that by Mark L. Reed on the growth of the idea of *Lyrical Ballads*.

On individual poems the following may be recommended: 'The Thorn': S. M. Parrish (1957) carries to excess the reading which makes the psychology of the narrator the paramount interest. Albert Gérard (1964) gives a more balanced view. 'Tintern Abbey': General accounts usually give prominence to this poem. The fullest separate study is by James Benziger. 'Nutting' is discussed by Alan Grob (1962). 'Michael' is the main subject of an essay by Peter Ure. 'The Old Cumberland Beggar' is the centre of a valuable essay by H. V. D. Dyson, and is also discussed in conjunction with 'The Ruined Cottage' by Cleanth Brooks (1965). 'Resolution and Independence' has been a key poem for many critics. Perhaps the best starting-point is the essay by W. W. Robson, which can be followed up in the discussions of Albert Gérard (1960), A. E. M. Conran (provocative on Wordsworth's development in the years after 1800, and also on Wordsworth's humour), and Alan Grob (1961). G. W. Meyer (1950) studies the poem as an 'Answer to Coleridge's "Dejection: An Ode" '.

'The Borderers', following the pioneer account by de Selincourt, accompanying his printing of the newly discovered Preface (1926), has been given a key position by a number of critics, and is the subject of a separate essay by Roger Sharrock (1964).

The 'Immortality Ode' is analysed by Lionel Trilling (1942), by T. M. Raysor, by Cleanth Brooks (1947), and by Alan Grob.

The Excursion is the subject of a monograph by J. S. Lyon.

The sonnet 'Surprised by Joy' is analysed, along with Donne and Yeats poems, by R. A. Brower.

Wordsworth's style: Although Wordsworth is known popularly as the creator of a particular *style* of writing, little has, in fact, been written on the technicalities of his verse. The student will find nothing in Wordsworth studies comparable to M. R. Ridley's *Keats' Craftmanship* or E. C. Pettet's *On the Poetry of Keats*. Marjorie L. Barstow has studied the theories of the Preface to *Lyrical Ballads*, and Josephine Miles the kind of vocabulary through which Wordsworth expresses feeling. Another full-length study is Florence Marsh's investigation of Wordsworth's imagery, but for the most part the really interesting comments are embedded in larger works. Coleridge's chapters of examination in *Biographia Literaria* are still very rewarding. The chapter on *The Prelude* in R. A. Foakes's *The Romantic Assertion* is helpful, though skimpy. In 'Wordsworth and Coleridge on Meter' S. M. Parrish (1960) examines afresh the theory and practice of the two poets. This is a valuable study which should be taken farther. In *The Quest for Permanence* and *The Simple Wordsworth* David Perkins and John Danby make many useful observations in the course of detailed discussion of particular passages. Few critics, however, have hazarded a discussion of the essential nature of Wordsworth's style, although much suggestive commentary is to be found in John Bayley's *The Romantic Survival*. Donald Davie's two very influential studies come as near as any have to isolating the peculiar strengths of Wordsworth's verse.

BIOGRAPHIES AND LETTERS

A few biographical comments from Wordsworth's own lifetime retain their interest. The earliest of these is Hazlitt's 'My First Acquaintance with Poets' (1823), describing his meeting with Wordsworth and Coleridge in 1798. Much fuller, but not factually reliable, is De Quincey's series of articles published in 1839, and later revised in his *Collected Works*. The earlier, and better, version has been edited by Edward Sackville-West. Another reference to Wordsworth occurs in

De Quincey's 'Letter to a Young Man whose Education has been Neglected' (1823; see Masson's edn.), in which he credits Wordsworth with the distinction between 'literature of power' and 'literature of knowledge'. There are also many important comments by Henry Crabb Robinson (1775–1862), collected by Edith J. Morley in *Henry Crabb Robinson on Books and their Writers*. (See below for Robinson's correspondence with the Wordsworth circle.)

The official, and very discreet, life by Wordsworth's nephew Christopher appeared only a year after the poet's death. It contains brief autobiographical memoranda. The next forty years saw little of biographical value, though there is some new material, including extracts from letters, in F. W. H. Myers's sketch in the English Men of Letters series. The most readable contribution from these years is H. D. Rawnsley's 'Reminiscences of Wordsworth among the Peasantry of Westmoreland'. Though the reminiscences are confined to the older Wordsworth, they provide a useful corrective to over-idealized pictures of him.

A great advance was made by Émile Legouis's *La Jeunesse de William Wordsworth, 1770–1798* (1896; English translation 1897). This is the first serious study of the early years, and also remains important for the relation of Wordsworth's early work to eighteenth-century poetry. From the same period dates another pioneer study of a subject that still concerns Wordsworthians, W. Hale White's *An Examination of the Charge of Apostasy against Wordsworth*.

The next major work was G. M. Harper's biography, which remained standard until recently. Both in allocation of space and in direction of sympathy, Harper's book is heavily weighted on the side of the early Wordsworth. More recent work has perhaps gone too far in redressing the balance. Harper was the first to reveal the facts about Annette Vallon and Wordsworth's illegitimate daughter —a subject on which Harper himself (1921) and Legouis (1922) later wrote at greater length. In the next few years Annette tended to receive disproportionate attention from critics (see above, CRITICAL STUDIES, on Read and Fausset). A partly successful attempt to rehabilitate the later Wordsworth was made by Edith C. Batho, who presented him as something of a Tory radical. George W. Meyer redirected attention to the early years, adopting a rather inquisitorial attitude to *The Prelude* as a biographical document. Harper's life has at last been superseded by the two-volume biography of Mary Moorman. Though not entirely reliable, this gives a balanced and sympathetic account, though the interest tends to flag in the uneventful later years. H. M. Margoliouth gives a very perceptive account of an important relationship in his *Wordsworth and Coleridge*. For the specialist, and also for the more general student who wants ready access to evidence on biographical problems, Mark Reed's study of the chronology will be invaluable. The first volume, up to 1799, has already appeared.

For most of the letters, there is no need to go beyond the edition of *The Letters of William and Dorothy Wordsworth* by Ernest de Selincourt. Two collections, however, were deliberately excluded from this edition, and are to be found in Edith J. Morley's edition of the *Correspondence of Henry Crabb Robinson with the Wordsworth Circle*, yielding more than a hundred letters by Dorothy and William, most of them to Crabb Robinson himself; and L. N. Broughton's edition of William's correspondence with his American editor, Henry Reed. The Dorothy–William portions of both these volumes will, however, be incorporated in the revision of the de Selincourt edition, the first three volumes of which have already appeared. There is a brief selection edited by Philip Wayne. The wonderfully vivid journals kept by Dorothy supplement the more stodgy qualities of William's letters. Ernest de Selincourt has edited the standard edition, and there are smaller editions of the Grasmere years by Helen Darbishire and Colette Clark. To complete an acquaintance with the human warmth and the intellectual energy of the Wordsworth circle, the student should read at least the first two volumes of Coleridge's letters, edited by E. L. Griggs.

BIBLIOGRAPHIES

The relevant section in the *N.C.B.E.L.* will be adequate for the bibliographical needs of most students not embarked on advanced work. Advanced students, however, will soon discover the remarkable fact that there is no full bibliography of Wordsworth and that they will have to rely on the catalogues of the *Cornell Wordsworth Collection*, ed. G. H. Healey, and of the *Amherst Wordsworth Collection*, ed. C. H. Patton. Bibliography of criticism is, however, a different matter. J. V. Logan's *Wordsworthian Criticism* lists the major critical works up to 1944, and prefaces the lists with most valuable chapters of discussion of such topics as Wordsworth's early reputation and of critical trends. This bibliography has been supplemented by E. F. Henley and D. H. Stam in their *Wordsworthian Bibliography, 1945–1964*. For studies of the Wordsworth circle, and of the Romantic Movement more generally, students should consult the annual bibliography of the Romantic Movement in *PQ* and, since 1965, in *English Language Notes*. T. M. Raysor's *The English Romantic Poets:*

A Review of Research will seem less frightening to the inexperienced student than any of the bibliographies mentioned above, as will E. Bernbaum's pedestrian but invaluable *Guide Through the Romantic Movement*. Finally, G. H. Hartman introduces each section of the notes to his *Wordsworth's Poetry, 1787–1814* with a critical bibliography. These will be found most useful, but the student should remember that the selections are part of a book with a strong thesis to propound, and so cannot be expected to be inclusive or colourlessly uncritical.

BACKGROUND READING

An original writer in many ways, Wordsworth was none the less responsive to his age and indebted to cultural tradition. A number of background studies may help the student to place Wordsworth in his milieu and to assess both his indebtedness and his originality. Three studies, of a considerable number, may be recommended as introductions to the political situation. E. J. Hobsbawm's *The Age of Revolution* sets the radicalism of the English Romantics in an international context. Crane Brinton's *The Political Ideas of the English Romantics* is narrower in historical information, but very useful on individual writers. The extent to which Wordsworth was subjected to revolutionary influence while at his most impressionable age is revealed by Benn Ross Schneider, Jr., in his study of *Wordsworth's Cambridge Education*, and F. M. Todd has outlined Wordsworth's developing attitudes to political affairs in *Politics and the Poet*.

Revolution was the issue, in action, of ideas which had been fermenting throughout the eighteenth century. Their vitality and importance can be discovered in such studies as Basil Willey's *The Eighteenth-Century Background*, J. W. Beach's *The Concept of Nature in Nineteenth-Century Poetry*, and C. B. Tinker's *Nature's Simple Plan*. Important shifts of taste which affected Wordsworth are traced in W. J. Bate's *From Classic to Romantic*. M. H. Abrams's very influential *The Mirror and the Lamp* and P. W. K. Stone's *The Art of Poetry, 1750–1820* document changes of both poets and readers over the Romantic period. Russell Noyes has followed up one aspect of contemporary taste in *Wordsworth and the Art of Landscape*.

In studying a phenomenon like the Romantic Movement it is difficult to give due emphasis to national characteristics without becoming insular. A. O. Lovejoy and René Wellek raise the question of how useful the term Romantic is in two wide-ranging essays, 'On the Discrimination of Romanticisms', and 'The Concept of

Romanticism in Literary History'. H. G. Schenk's *The Mind of the European Romantics* and Anthony Thorlby's compilation *The Romantic Movement* are stimulating antidotes to narrow-mindedness. The English Romantics, however, do have a marked character. M. H. Abrams has written well on 'English Romanticism: the Spirit of the Age', and has isolated an area for brilliant discussion in his 'The Correspondent Breeze: A Romantic Metaphor'. Also in M. H. Abrams's *English Romantic Poets* is the Lovejoy essay and W. K. Wimsatt's 'The Structure of Romantic Nature Imagery'. A. E. Powell has examined other common areas of Romantic thought in *The Romantic Theory of Poetry*, establishing a unity which Douglas Bush has discerned through a study of *Mythology and the Romantic Tradition*.

Knowledge of the reception given to an original talent like Wordsworth's can also tell us much concerning his age and the pressure against which he had to struggle. What Wordsworth meant to Arnold, and through him to a whole generation of readers, is discussed in Leon Gottfried's very interesting book *Mathew Arnold and the Romantics*. R. A. Foakes's *Romantic Criticism, 1800–1850* collects the documents which formed the tastes both popular and intellectual by which the Romantics were judged.

REFERENCES

TEXTS

H. Darbishire (ed.), *Poems in Two Volumes, 1807*, 2nd edn. (Oxford, 1952).

E. de Selincourt and Helen Darbishire (eds.), *The Poetical Works of William Wordsworth* (5 vols., Oxford English Texts, Oxford, 1940–9); vol. ii, 2nd edn. (1952); vol. iii, 2nd edn. (1954).

E. de Selincourt (ed.), *The Prelude, Text of 1850*, 2nd edn. rev. by Helen Darbishire (Oxford English Texts, Oxford and New York, 1959).

E. de Selincourt (ed.), *The Prelude, Text of 1805*, revised by Stephen Gill (Oxford Standard Authors, London, 1970; paperbacks, U.K. and U.S.).

E. de Selincourt (ed.), *Wordsworth's 'Guide through the Lakes'* (London, 1906).

A. V. Dicey (ed.), *Wordsworth's 'Tract on the Convention of Cintra'* (London, 1915).

A. B. Grosart (ed.), *The Prose Works of William Wordsworth* (3 vols., London, 1876).

W. A. Knight (ed.), *Prose Works of William Wordsworth* (2 vols., London, 1896).

G. L. Little, 'An Incomplete Wordsworth Essay upon Moral Habits', *Review of English Literature*, ii (1961).

W. M. Merchant (ed.), *A Guide Through the District of the Lakes* (London, 1951; Bloomington, Ind., 1952).

W. M. Merchant (ed.), *Wordsworth: Poetry and Prose* (London and Cambridge, Mass., 1955; paperbacks, U.K. and U.S.).

W. J. B. Owen (ed.), *Wordsworth's Preface to 'Lyrical Ballads'* (Copenhagen, 1957).

W. J. B. Owen (ed.), *Wordsworth and Coleridge: 'Lyrical Ballads' 1798* (Oxford, 1967).

Markham L. Peacock Jr. (ed.), *The Critical Opinions of William Wordsworth* (Baltimore, 1950).

D. Roper (ed.), *Lyrical Ballads* (London, 1968).

N. C. Smith (ed.), *Wordsworth's Literary Criticism* (London, 1905).

R. J. White (ed.), *Political Tracts of Wordsworth, Coleridge and Shelley* (Cambridge, 1953).

CRITICAL STUDIES AND COMMENTARY

M. H. Abrams, 'Wordsworth and Coleridge on Diction and Figures', in *English Institute Essays 1952* (New York, 1954).

M. H. Abrams (ed.), *English Romantic Poets: Modern Essays in Criticism* (paperback, New York, 1960; paperback, U.K.).

M. Arnold, *On Translating Homer, Last Words* (London, 1862).

M. Arnold, 'Wordsworth' (1879), in *Essays in Criticism: Second Series* (London, 1888).

W. Bagehot, 'Wordsworth, Tennyson, and Browning; or, Pure, Ornate, and Grotesque Art in English Poetry' (1864), in E. D. Jones (ed.), *English Critical Essays: Nineteenth-Century* (World's Classics, London, 1916).

M. L. Barstow, *Wordsworth's Theory of Poetic Diction* (New Haven, Conn., and London, 1917).

F. W. Bateson, *Wordsworth: A Re-Interpretation*, rev. edn. (London, 1956; paperback, U.K.).

J. Bayley, *The Romantic Survival* (London, 1957; paperback, U.K.).

A. Beatty, *William Wordsworth: His Doctrine and Art in their Historical Relations* 2nd edn. (Madison, Wis., 1927; paperbacks, U.K. and U.S.).

J. Benziger, ' "*Tintern Abbey*" Revisited', *PMLA* lxv (1950).

H. Bloom, *The Visionary Company* (New York, 1961; London, 1962; paperback, U.S.).

E. E. Bostetter, *The Romantic Ventriloquists* (Seattle, Wash., 1963).

A. C. Bradley, 'Wordsworth', in *Oxford Lectures on Poetry* (London, 1909; paperbacks, U.K. and U.S.).

182   J. C. MAXWELL AND S. C. GILL

A. C. Bradley, 'The Long Poem in the Age of Wordsworth', in *Oxford Lectures on Poetry* (London, 1909; paperbacks, U.K. and U.S.).

G. Brimley, 'Wordsworth's Poems' (1851), in *Essays* (Cambridge, 1858).

C. Brooks, 'Wordsworth and the Paradox of the Imagination', in *The Well-Wrought Urn* (New York, 1947; paperback, U.S.).

C. Brooks, 'Wordsworth on Human Suffering: Notes on Two Early Poems', in Hilles and Bloom (eds.).

R. A. Brower, 'The Sinewie Thread', in *The Fields of Light* (New York, 1951; paperback, U.K.).

A. E. M. Conran, 'The Dialectic of Experience: A Study of Wordworth's *Resolution and Independence*', *PMLA* lxxv (1960).

D. Bush, 'Wordsworth: A Minority Report', in G. T. Dunklin (ed.), *Wordsworth: Centenary Studies* (Princeton, N.J., 1951).

C. C. Clarke, 'Loss and Consolation in the Poetry of Wordsworth (1798–1805), *English Studies* (Amsterdam), xxxi (1950).

C. C. Clarke, *Romantic Paradox* (London, 1962).

S. T. Coleridge, *Biographia Literaria; or Biographical Sketches of My Literary Life and Opinions* (1817), ed. J. Shawcross (Oxford, 1907); ed. G. Watson, Everyman's Library (London, 1956).

J. F. Danby, *The Simple Wordsworth* (London, 1960 and New York, 1961).

D. Davie, 'Diction and Invention: A View of Wordsworth', in *Purity of Diction in English Verse*, 2nd edn. (London, 1967; paperback, U.K.).

D. Davie, 'Syntax in the Blank Verse of Wordsworth's *Prelude*', in *Articulate Energy* (London, 1955).

T. De Quincey, 'On Wordsworth's Poetry' (1845), in D. Masson (ed.), *De Quincey's Collected Writings*, vol. xi (London, 1897).

E. de Selincourt, 'The Hitherto Unpublished Preface to Wordsworth's "Borderers" ' (1926), in *Oxford Lectures on Poetry* (London, 1934).

H. V. D. Dyson, ' "The Old Cumberland Beggar" and the Wordsworthian Unities', in *Essays on the Eighteenth Century Presented to David Nichol Smith* (Oxford, 1945).

T. S. Eliot, *The Use of Poetry and the Use of Criticism* (London, 1933; paperback, U.K.).

W. Empson, ' "Sense" in *The Prelude*', in *The Structure of Complex Words* (London, 1951; paperback, U.S.).

H. I'A. Faussett, *The Lost Leader* (London, 1933).

D. Ferry, *The Limits of Mortality* (Middletown, Conn., 1959).

Z. S. Fink, *The Early Wordsworthian Milieu* (Oxford, 1958).

R. A. Foakes, *The Romantic Assertion* (London, 1958).

H. W. Garrod, *Wordsworth*, 2nd edn. (Oxford, 1927).

A. Gérard, ' "Resolution and Independence": Wordsworth's Coming of Age', *English Studies in Africa*, iii (1960).

A. Gérard, 'Of Trees and Man: the Unity of Wordsworth's "The Thorn" ', *EIC* xiv (1964).

A. Grob, 'Wordsworth's "Immortality Ode" and the Search for Identity', *ELH* xxxii (1965).

A. Grob, 'Process and Reminiscence in "Resolution and Independence" ', *ELH* xxviii (1961).

A. Grob, 'Wordsworth's "Nutting" ', *JEGP* lxi (1962).

G. H. Hartman, *Wordsworth's Poetry, 1787-1814* (New Haven, Conn., 1964; paperbacks, U.K. and U.S.).

W. Hazlitt, 'Mr. Wordsworth', in *The Spirit of the Age* (1825), ed. E. D. Mackerness (London, 1969).

W. Hazlitt, 'Observations on Mr. Wordsworth's Poem *The Excursion*' (1814), in *The Round Table* (1817); *Works*, ed. P. P. Howe (London, 1930-4), vol. iv.

R. D. Havens, *The Mind of a Poet* (Baltimore, 1941).

C. H. Herford, *Wordsworth* (London, 1930).

F. W. Hilles and Harold Bloom (eds.), *From Sensibility to Romanticism: Essays Presented to Frederick A. Pottle* (New York, 1965).

E. D. Hirsch, Jr., *Wordsworth and Schelling* (New Haven, Conn., 1960).

Aldous Huxley, 'Wordsworth in the Tropics', in *Do What You Will* (London, 1929).

F. Jeffrey. See D. N. Smith (ed.).

J. Jones, *The Egotistical Sublime* (London, 1954).

J. Keats, *Letters of John Keats*, ed. H. E. Rollins (Cambridge, Mass., 1958).

A. King, *Wordsworth and the Artist's Vision* (London, 1966).

G. W. Knight, 'The Wordsworthian Profundity', in *The Starlit Dome: Studies in the Poetry of Vision* (London, 1941; paperback, U.K.).

K. Kroeber, 'Wordsworth: The Personal Epic', in *Romantic Narrative Art* (Madison, Wis., 1960; paperback, U.S.).

C. Lamb, *Letters of Charles and Mary Lamb*, ed. E. V. Lucas (2 vols., Everyman's Library, London, 1935).

F. R. Leavis, 'Wordsworth', in *Revaluation* (London, 1936; paperbacks, U.K. and U.S.).

H. Lindenberger, *On Wordsworth's 'Prelude'* (Princeton, N.J., 1963; paperbacks, U.K. and U.S.).

J. S. Lyon, *'The Excursion': a Study* (New Haven, Conn., 1950).

J. R. MacGillivray, 'The Three Forms of *The Prelude*', in Millar MacLure and F. W. Watt (eds.), *Essays in English Literature from the Renaissance to the Victorian Age Presented to A.S.P. Woodhouse* (Toronto and London 1964).

F. G. Marsh, *Wordsworth's Imagery* (New Haven, Conn., 1952).

R. Mayo, 'The Contemporaneity of the *Lyrical Ballads*', *PMLA* lxix (1954).

G. W. Meyer, ' "Resolution and Independence": Wordsworth's Answer to Coleridge's "Dejection: An Ode" ', *Tulane Studies in English* ii (1950).

J. Miles, 'Wordsworth: The Mind's Excursive Power', in C. D. Thorpe, C. Baker, and B. Weaver (eds.), *The Major English Romantic Poets: a Symposium in Reappraisal* (Carbondale, Ill., 1957).

J. S. Mill. *Autobiography* (London, 1873), ed. H. J. Laski (World's Classics, London, 1924; paperbacks, U.K. and U.S.).

S. M. Parrish, 'Dramatic Technique in the *Lyrical Ballads*', *PMLA* lxxiv (1959).

S. M. Parrish, ' "The Thorn": Wordsworth's Dramatic Monologue', *ELH* xxiv (1957).

S. M. Parrish, "Wordsworth and Coleridge on Meter", *JEGP* lix (1960).

W. Pater, 'Wordsworth' (1874), in *Appreciations* (London, 1889).

D. Perkins, *The Quest for Permanence* (London and Cambridge, Mass., 1959).

H. W. Piper, *The Active Universe: Pantheism and the Concept of Imagination in the English Romantic Poets* (London, 1962).

M. M. Rader, *Wordsworth: a Philosophical Approach* (Oxford, 1967).

W. Raleigh, *Wordsworth* (London, 1903).

T. M. Raysor (ed.), *The English Romantic Poets: a Review of Research*, 2nd edn. (New York, 1956).

T. M. Raysor, 'The Themes of Immortality and Natural Piety in Wordsworth's "Immortality Ode" ', *PMLA* lxix (1954).

H. Read, *Wordsworth* (London, 1930; paperback, U.K.).

M. L. Reed, 'Wordsworth, Coleridge, and the "Plan" of the *Lyrical Ballads*', *UTQ* xxxiv (1965).

M. L. Reed, *Wordsworth: The Chronology of the Early Years, 1770–1799* (Cambridge, Mass., 1967).

W. W. Robson, 'Wordsworth's "Resolution and Independence" ' (1955), in *Critical Essays* (London, 1966).

C. Ryskamp, 'Wordsworth's *Lyrical Ballads* in their Time', in Hilles and Bloom (eds.).

R. Sharrock, ' "The Borderers": Wordsworth on the Moral Frontier', *Durham University Journal*, lvi (1964).

R. Sharrock, 'Wordsworth's Revolt Against Literature', *EIC* iii (1953).

R. Sharrock, 'Speech and Prose in Wordsworth's Preface', *EIC* vii (1957).

D. Nichol Smith (ed.), *Jeffrey's Literary Criticism* (London, 1910).

E. Smith, *An Estimate of William Wordsworth by his Contemporaries* (Oxford, 1932).

J. C. Smith, *A Study of Wordsworth* (Edinburgh, 1944).

James Smith, 'Wordsworth: A Preliminary Survey', *Scrutiny*, vii (1938).

N. P. Stallknecht, *Strange Seas of Thought* (Durham, N.C., 1945); 2nd edn. (Bloomington, Ind., 1958).

L. Stephen, 'Wordsworth's Ethics' (1876), in *Hours in a Library: Third Series* (London, 1879).

L. Trilling, 'The Immortality Ode' (1942), in *The Liberal Imagination* (New York and London, 1950; paperback, U.S.); and in Abrams (ed.).

P. Ure, 'Wordsworth; "Michael": the Picture of a Man', *Durham University Journal*, xliv (1951).

E. Welsford, *Salisbury Plain* (Oxford, 1966).

G. Whalley, 'Preface to *Lyrical Ballads*: A Portent', *UTQ* xxv (1956).

A. N. Whitehead, *Science and the Modern World* (New York, 1925; Cambridge, 1926; paperbacks, U.K. and U.S.).

J. Dover Wilson, *Leslie Stephen and Matthew Arnold as Critics of Wordsworth* (Cambridge, 1939).

J. Wordsworth, *The Music of Humanity* (London, 1969).

BIOGRAPHIES AND LETTERS

E. C. Batho, *The Later Wordsworth* (Cambridge, 1933).

L. W. Broughton (ed.), *Wordsworth and Reed: The Poet's Correspondence with his American Editor, 1836–1850* (Ithaca, N.Y., 1933).

C. Clark (ed.), *Home at Grasmere* (paperback, Harmondsworth, 1960).

H. Darbishire (ed.), *Dorothy Wordsworth: Journals* (World's Classics, London, 1958).

T. De Quincey, 'Literary and Lake Reminiscences' (1839), in *Recollections of the Lake Poets*, ed. Edward Sackville-West (London, 1948); also in De Quincey's final version, *Reminiscences of the English Lake Poets*, ed. J. E. Jordan (Everyman's Library, London, 1961).

E. de Selincourt (ed.), *The Letters of William and Dorothy Wordsworth* (Oxford, 1935–9); rev. edn., Vol. I, by C. L. Shaver (1967); Vol. II, by Mary Moorman (1969); Vol. III, by Mary Moorman and Alan G. Hill (1970).

E. de Selincourt (ed.), *The Journals of Dorothy Wordsworth* (London, 1941).

E. L. Griggs (ed.), *Collected Letters of Samuel Taylor Coleridge* (Oxford and New York, 1956–   ).

G. M. Harper, *William Wordsworth: His Life, Works and Influence*, 3rd edn. (London, 1929).

G. M. Harper, *Wordsworth's French Daughter* (London, 1921).

W. Hazlitt, 'My First Acquaintance with Poets' (1823), in E. D. Jones (ed.), *English Critical Essays, Nineteenth Century* (World's Classics, London, 1916).

É. Legouis, *La Jeunesse de William Wordsworth, 1770–1798* (1896), English trans., 2nd edn., London, 1921).

É. Legouis, *William Wordsworth and Annette Vallon* (London, 1922).

H. M. Margoliouth, *Wordsworth and Coleridge. 1795–1834* (London, 1953).

G. W. Meyer, *Wordsworth's Formative Years* (Ann Arbor, Mich., 1943).

M. Moorman, *William Wordsworth* (2 vols., Oxford, 1957–65; paperback, U.K.).

E. J. Morley (ed.), *Correspondence of Henry Crabb Robinson with the Wordsworth Circle* (Oxford, 1927).

E. J. Morley (ed.), *Henry Crabb Robinson, 'On Books and their Writers'* (London, 1938).

F. W. H. Myers, *Wordsworth* (London, 1881).

H. D. Rawnsley, 'Reminiscences of Wordsworth among the Peasantry of Westmoreland' (1882), in W. Knight (ed.), *Wordsworthiana* (London, 1889); with Introduction by G. Tillotson (London, 1969).

M. Reed, *Wordsworth: the Chronology of the Early Years, 1770–1799* (Cambridge, Mass., 1967).

P. Wayne (ed.), *The Letters of William and Dorothy Wordsworth* (World's Classics, London, 1954).

W. Hale White ('Mark Rutherford'), *The Autobiography of Mark Rutherford* (London 1881).

W. Hale White, *An Examination of the Charge of Apostasy against Wordsworth* (London, 1898).

C. Wordsworth, *Memoirs of William Wordsworth* (London, 1851).

BIBLIOGRAPHIES

G. Watson (ed.), *N.C.B.E.L.*, vol. iii: 1800–1900 (Cambridge and New York, 1969).

E. Bernbaum, *Guide Through the Romantic Movement*, 2nd edn. (New York, 1949).

E. Bernbaum and James V. Logan, Jr., 'Wordsworth', in Raysor (ed.).

G. H. Healey, *The Cornell Wordsworth Collection* (Ithaca, N.Y., 1957).

E. F. Henley and D. H. Stam, *Wordsworthian Bibliography, 1945–1964* (New York, 1965; paperback, U.S.).

J. V. Logan, *Wordsworthian Criticism* (Columbus, Ohio, 1947).

C. H. Patton, *The Amherst Wordsworth Collection* (Amherst, Mass., 1936).

BACKGROUND READING

M. H. Abrams, *The Mirror and the Lamp* (New York, 1953; paperback, U.S.).

M. H. Abrams, 'The Correspondent Breeze: A Romantic Metaphor' (1957); 'English Romanticism: the Spirit of the Age', in Abrams (ed.), p. 181 above.

W. J. Bate, *From Classic to Romantic* (Cambridge, Mass., 1949; paperbacks, U.K. and U.S.).

J. W. Beach, *The Concept of Nature in Nineteenth-Century Poetry* (New York, 1936).

C. Brinton, *The Political Ideas of the English Romanticists* (London, 1926; paperback, U.S.).

D. Bush, *Mythology and the Romantic Tradition* (Cambridge, Mass., 1937; paperback, U.K.).

R. A. Foakes, *Romantic Criticism, 1800–1850* (London, 1968; paperback, U.K.).

L. Gottfried, *Matthew Arnold and the Romantics* (London and Lincoln, Neb., 1963).

E. J. Hobsbawm, *The Age of Revolution* (London, 1962; paperbacks, U.K. and U.S.).

A. O. Lovejoy, 'On the Discrimination of Romanticisms' (1924), in *Essays in the History of Ideas* (Baltimore, 1948; paperback, U.S.); and in Abrams (ed.).

R. Noyes, *Wordsworth and the Art of Landscape* (Bloomington, Ind., 1968; paperback, U.S.).

A. E. Powell, *The Romantic Theory of Poetry* (London, 1926).

H. G. Schenk, *The Mind of the European Romantics* (London, 1966; paperback, U.S.).

B. R. Schneider, Jr., *Wordsworth's Cambridge Education* (Cambridge, 1957).

P. W. K. Stone, *The Art of Poetry 1750–1820* (London, 1967).

A. Thorlby, *The Romantic Movement* (paperback, London, 1966; paperback, U.S.).

C. B. Tinker, *Nature's Simple Plan* (Princeton, N.J., 1922).

F. M. Todd, *Politics and the Poet* (London, 1957).

R. Wellek, 'The Concept of Romanticism in Literary History', in *Concepts of Criticism* (New Haven, Conn., 1963; paperbacks, U.K. and U.S.).

B. Willey, *The Eighteenth-Century Background* (London, 1940; paperbacks, U.K. and U.S.).

W. K. Wimsatt, 'The Structure of Romantic Nature Imagery', in *The Verbal Icon* (Lexington, Ky., 1954; paperbacks, U.K. and U.S.); and in Abrams (ed.).

John Beer

TEXTS

Although Coleridge is one of the most rewarding of English poets, he is also one of the most difficult to approach initially. In the case of most major writers there is a sizeable corpus of important works with which the student can grapple, providing a firm base for preliminary judgement. With Coleridge there is no such large centre: once the student has read some of the major poems ('The Ancient Mariner', 'Kubla Khan', 'Christabel', 'Frost at Midnight', 'Dejection: An Ode', say) he is left to make his own way through Coleridge's works in prose and verse, with many possible approaches available.

For the student who wishes to tackle Coleridge's work in an ambitious manner the path has been greatly eased in recent years by a series of editions transforming the whole face of Coleridge scholarship. The complete edition of the *Letters* by Earl Leslie Griggs is almost complete; the *Notebooks* are being edited for the first time by Kathleen Coburn. *The Collected Coleridge*, a new edition now in progress, will complete the presentation of his entire writings, whether printed or left in manuscript.

The student who is coming to Coleridge for the first time, with more limited purposes, still needs to have a sense of the full range of Coleridge's writings. The Nonesuch edition (edited by Stephen Potter) and the Viking edition, *The Portable Coleridge* (edited by I. A. Richards) both contain generous selections from the full range of Coleridge's writings in a single volume. The standard edition of the *Poems* at present is that in the Oxford English Texts series.[1] A shorter collection appears in the World's Classics series; my recently revised Everyman edition contains a number of poems (such as the important first version of 'Dejection') that have not hitherto been collected, and arranges the poems against passages of commentary giving the pattern of Coleridge's own development. *Biographia Literaria* also appears in a convenient edition in Everyman's Library; for detailed annotation and other matter, however, Shawcross's sixty-year-old Oxford edition remains indispensable, at least until the

[1] Of same date is Oxford Standard Authors edn. (also ed. E. H. Coleridge).

appearance of the Collected Coleridge edition. For those notebooks that have not yet been edited, similarly, *Anima Poetae*, the selection made by E. H. Coleridge in the last century, remains an important source: other important general prose works, such as *Aids to Reflection* and H. N. Coleridge's record of the *Table Talk* are available only in Victorian editions until the appropriate volumes in the Collected Coleridge appear. The seven-volume American *Collected Works*, edited by Shedd in the nineteenth century, contains some rare works, such as the *Theory of Life*; writings, both published and unpublished, which bear on the seventeenth century have been collected by Florence Brinkley in *Coleridge on the Seventeenth Century*; a *Concordance* to the poetry has been produced by Sister Eugenia Logan. Texts of more specialized works by Coleridge are discussed under the relevant headings in the following section.

CRITICAL STUDIES AND COMMENTARY

(*a*) *Nineteenth Century*

In his own lifetime, and particularly in his early life, Coleridge stimulated an excitement among his contemporaries which, since it seems to have been sparked off rather by his conversation and presence than by the large body of his writings, is now not easy to recapture. The student who has looked at the best of Coleridge's poems should turn to such contemporary documents as Hazlitt's essays 'My First Acquaintance with Poets' and 'Mr. Coleridge'; De Quincey's chapter in *Reminiscences of the English Lake Poets*; Lamb's essay 'Christ's Hospital Five and Thirty Years Ago' (in *The Essays of Elia*), and Wordsworth's tributes in *The Prelude* (1850 edn., xi, 370–470; xiv, 275–414); other contemporary impressions of the sort may be found in the collection *Coleridge the Talker*, edited by Armour and Howes.

Coleridge was regarded by most contemporaries as a fascinating, rather exotic, figure with whom they found it difficult to come to terms. His literary reputation was at its height during the Regency period, when his lectures in London were a fashionable attraction. In the last decade or so of his life, when he produced mainly theological works, he appealed particularly to the serious-minded young men of the time who were looking for a way to reconcile traditional Christian teaching with the problems raised by the growth of radical critical methods in theology. The changing public reaction to his works during his lifetime may be seen at first hand in the reviews collected in J. de J. Jackson's volume on him in the 'Critical Heritage' series.

After his death, however, writers in the major Victorian intellectual tradition found it harder to accept his doctrines as a guide, feeling that something more physically grounded and positive was needed in order to meet the complex problems of society which surrounded them. Carlyle (in the eighth chapter of his *Life of John Sterling*) gives a fascinating account of the later Coleridge, presenting him as a man of unrivalled gifts who had failed by a lack of practical sense and of will to action. Newman's few direct references to him make it clear that Coleridge's doctrine that the traditional Christian positions could be defended by regarding them as great symbols was a prime factor in driving him to assert the importance of the Church as a body which must be accepted as real in more positive terms. The age, he felt, demanded something more than symbols. A more sympathetic account of Coleridge during this period was given by John Stuart Mill, who in his essays 'Bentham' (1838) and 'Coleridge' (1840) argued that these figures were, respectively, the great 'seminal minds' of the nineteenth century. The last two essays are brought together by F. R. Leavis, with an introductory essay, in his *Mill on Bentham and Coleridge*: they are also the basis of an important chapter in Raymond Williams's *Culture and Society*. Further discussion of the various questions mentioned here may be found in Basil Willey's *Nineteenth-Century Studies* and in the essays 'Coleridge and the Victorians' and 'Newman and the Romantic Sensibility' contributed by Graham Hough and myself to the collection *The English Mind*, edited by Davies and Watson.

Later Victorian attitudes continued to crystallize around this combination of fascination and disquiet. Although, as F. J. A. Hort's essay shows, his religious beliefs remained a potent force in the Broad Church movement (see below), and a few writers, like George Eliot, betrayed a more profound influence, there was a general tendency to acknowledge the charm and delicacy of Coleridge's writings while deploring his moral failure as a man. Even when, towards the end of the century, the growth of aestheticism awakened new interest in his artistic achievements, the Victorian insistence on strength of character prohibited any real enthusiasm. Thus while Swinburne's account in his *Essays and Studies* (1875) expresses well the contemporary feeling for the 'charm' and 'music' of his verse, Leslie Stephen (*Hours in a Library: III*), who also has some perceptive comments on the poetry, embeds them in a long discussion of Coleridge's moral thought and its relationship to his moral status, speaking finally of 'early promise blighted and vast powers all but running hopelessly to seed'. Walter Pater's influential essay in

Appreciations, similarly, while giving a long and sympathetic account of Coleridge's poetry, characterizes him disparagingly (and questionably) by 'his passion for the absolute, for something fixed where all is moving, his faintness, his broken memory, his intellectual disquiet', claiming for him no more than a rank 'among the interpreters of one of the constituent elements of our life'.

(b) Modern Studies of Coleridge's Poetry

The twentieth century, rejecting extremer forms of aestheticism, has found it necessary to come to terms with Coleridge in a new way. After the First World War a number of studies appeared which laid greater stress on the role of the imagination in his poetry and thought. The pre-eminent of these, J. L. Lowes's *The Road to Xanadu*, clearly owed something to the stimulus of the Imagist movement in poetry, which had sought to cut through problems of poetic diction by asserting the primacy in poetry of the simple, direct image. To such writers, 'The Ancient Mariner' and 'Kubla Khan' provided grand exemplars of the way that poetry ought to be written: the first flashing a series of isolated vividnesses on the reader, the second weaving a kaleidoscope of exotic imagery before his eyes. Lowes developed the Imagist thesis, arguing that the process of image-making could be pursued still further by tracing their sources in books which Coleridge had previously read. 'Coleridge', he wrote, '. . . was reading with a falcon's eye for details in which lurked the spark of poetry.' He demonstrated that in some cases this reading had left a series of scattered images in his subconscious, to re-emerge, at the moment of composition, in a new, magical crystallization.

Lowes's book is a classic of its kind: written as a record of literary detection, it transmits the excitement of successful literary scholarship in action. At the same time, his stress on the impact of the poem's imagery, and his unwillingness to consider questions of meaning, did much to devalue Coleridge's intellectual status. Stephen Potter's *Coleridge and S.T.C.*, though more ready to come to terms with Coleridge's intelligence, also insisted on splitting him into 'Coleridge', the sincere, spontaneous imaginative writer, and 'S.T.C.', the religious, obscurantist humbug—a dichotomy which, while earning some justification as a generalization, also does violence to Coleridge's pervasive aspirations after a unified view of human existence. Nevertheless, Potter's study deserves to be read for the sake of its positive understanding, which is both suggestive and stimulating.

Lowes's book was persuasive enough to dominate critical attitudes to Coleridge for a generation. In time, however, a number of critics, working from widely separated positions, came to sense that the question of meaning in Coleridge's poetry could not be so easily cast aside. George Wilson Knight's chapter in *The Starlit Dome* is particularly valuable, since, though relying largely on an intuitive approach, it is the work of a mind that is unusually responsive to the images of radiance which recur throughout Coleridge's poetry. Maud Bodkin, pursuing an archetypal view of poetry, found in Coleridge's major works a fruitful field of universal images. Robert Penn Warren set forth the grounds for a symbolic interpretation of *The Ancient Mariner* in an essay which was to be highly influential. Kenneth Burke, in *The Philosophy of Literary Form*, used Coleridge's poetry as a major point of reference for his discussion of language as symbolic action. Ideally, each of these approaches should be examined, since each has its individual quality, which cannot be summarized; good general summaries can, however, be found in Humphry House's Clark Lectures, where the discussion is also continued intelligently. My own study, *Coleridge the Visionary*, which follows the lead of those who look for symbolic meaning, challenges Lowes's method more directly, arguing that the great poems are intimately related to ranges of speculation which preoccupied Coleridge all his life, and that the previous reading which Lowes discusses can be seen, on re-examination, to reflect not merely a dilettante quest for vivid poetical images but a search for patterns of meaningful symbolism which might interpret human experience, Coleridge's quest taking him naturally to the imagery of various religions and mythologies in search of a common 'mind of man'. Under this approach, the succession of associated images is further linked by large subterranean patterns of meaning.

The study of meaning in the great poems has not gone unquestioned. The existence of symbolic structures in the poetry has been denied by E. E. Stoll, Elder Olson, and Elisabeth Schneider. A thoughtful essay by E. E. Bostetter also takes issue with the symbolists (particularly as represented by Penn Warren) for suggesting that the symbolic structure of 'The Ancient Mariner' makes it sacramental of the 'one Life'. He draws attention to incidents such as the game of dice in the poem, and suggests that such elements of arbitrariness make its central impact one of nightmare rather than sacrament, the reader's feeling at the end being one of a qualified relief rather than of having assisted at a celebration of life.

Three further studies of the poem may be mentioned; R. L. Brett's essay, in a long and clear-headed discussion, relates it to Coleridge's critical ideas. M. Gardner's *Annotated Ancient Mariner* gives a useful range of factual information; the Doré illustrations reproduced in it form in themselves an unusual series of visual criticisms. William Empson is more idiosyncratic, approaching the poem with his usual blend of logic and kindliness. Although his essay takes the poem to logical extremes, which for many readers are resisted by its own form and content, the essay is perceptive and witty, meeting our primary demand that the critic should respond to Coleridge's work with an enlivening intelligence of his own.

Other studies have dwelt on the personal element in the poem. George Whalley, who has elsewhere added to our knowledge of 'Dejection: an Ode' and a number of poems surrounding it, by his examination of Coleridge's love for Sara Hutchinson, in his *Coleridge and Sara Hutchinson and the Asra Poems*, suggests in an essay that the Mariner is a figure with close correspondences to Coleridge himself, drawing attention to many parallels between the Mariner's deprivations and isolation and Coleridge's own progress through life, which again and again deprived him of love and affection, leaving him 'alone on a wide, wide sea'. The article, which is persuasive and well-documented, should be read in conjunction with the end of Geoffrey Yarlott's chapter on the poem in *Coleridge and the Abyssinian Maid*. Yarlott, discussing the large number of references to the poem in Coleridge's notebooks (a phenomenon to which R. C. Bald first drew attention in 1940), points out that the suggestions of self-identification belong particularly to the 1804 voyage to Malta (the first long sea journey, presumably, that Coleridge had undertaken), and that some observations on that occasion, together with the emotions that accompanied them, prompted new touches in later editions of the poem itself—notably the stanza describing the ghostly light from the helmsman's lamp. His account provides an interesting modification of Whalley's theory, suggesting that Coleridge, while not having primarily written the poem as a personal myth, came to find it tragically relevant to his own later sufferings and desolations, particularly when, in going to Malta, he undertook a voluntary exile from the people whom he loved most.

'Kubla Khan' raises particular problems of its own. Although the poem was sometimes read symbolically in the nineteenth century, Lowes's interpretation has encouraged many to read it simply as a shifting kaleidoscope of glamorous images. Marshall Suther's study *Visions of Xanadu*, though heavily laboured, corrects some of these assumptions by drawing attention to the pervasiveness of the imagery of the poem in other poetry written by Coleridge before and after. Elisabeth Schneider has discussed the question from another point of view in *Coleridge, Opium and Kubla Khan*. Her study throws valuable light on his opium-taking, showing that Coleridge's illnesses in connection with the drug were mostly, in fact, withdrawal symptoms, associated with his attempts to free himself from addiction. Her further theory that the poem is little more than a conscious pastiche, drawing on a new fashion set by Southey and Landor, demands a late date, which she finds it practically impossible to justify, in view of a fairly clear reference to the poem in Dorothy Wordsworth's *Journals*; and her general point that the poem is devoid of symbolic meaning discounts too readily the range of significant parallels in Coleridge's own imagery. My own study sees the poem in a tradition of 'problem-solving' dreams, in which the elements of a problem, transformed into images, dance themselves into a pattern which resolves it. On this reading, every image in the poem is highly charged with significance, and the poem itself is, among other things, a 'cover-story' for a pattern of symbolic images which grows in complexity as one contemplates it, though never entirely losing touch with the immediate sensuous effects of the language. Whether or not this view of the poem is accepted, however, it is clearly important that we should first read 'Kubla Khan' as a poetic structure in the most straightforward sense and Miss Schneider presents an excellent short reading of the poems (extracted in Miss Coburn's collection—see (*g*) below) which does precisely that. Her invitation to regard the poem as no more than a simple verbal structure is, however, undermined by Kenneth Burke's excellent essay, 'Kubla Khan', which, while not a definitive discussion, succeeds in showing, through the ambiguities of the actual words and images, how hard it is to hold this poem in the mind as a simple verbal and metrical structure, since the effect of the persistent ambivalences is to draw the reader, quite naturally, into side-eddyings of the imagination at every stage.

'Christabel' was the object of an investigation on the lines of Lowes's by A. H. Nethercot (*The Road to Tryermaine*) some years ago, but proved more resistant to such an approach. It is clearly a more 'conscious' poem than 'The Ancient Mariner' and needs to be examined more directly in terms of Coleridge's own ideas and poetic aims. The fragmentary nature of the poem leaves certain questions unanswered—particularly those concerning Geraldine. That she is straightforwardly evil is assumed by critics such as Charles Tomlinson and argued more intricately by R. A. Bostetter (1963); while R. H. Fogle (who discusses the poem in the conclusion to his *The Idea of Coleridge's Criticism*) would agree with my own view that she is a more complicated figure, expressing Coleridge's sense that evil (like the small dull moon and the small dull eye of the snake in the poem) is a diminished and mean form of a power which in itself is essential to the health of human experience.

Some more recent studies have resisted the tendency to restrict discussion to a few major poems, arguing that it is now time for Coleridge's entire poetic achievement to be examined afresh. George Watson's *Coleridge the Poet*, which begins from this point of view, draws attention to the neglected question of traditional form in the poetry: thus 'The Ancient Mariner' *is* a ballad, 'Dejection' *is* an ode—and even the 'fragment' has a respectable literary history. Coleridge's achievement is seen largely in terms of his powers of imitation, and emerges as paradoxical ('His own poetry never seems so much itself as when it is pretending to be something else'): as a result, questions of meaning are played down. The successive states in 'The Ancient Mariner' are seen as states in an evolving pastiche; the main point of 'Christabel' is that it 'offered Coleridge a new metre and a Gothic language;' and although 'Kubla Khan' does have a meaning, that meaning is literary in a more narrow sense: it is 'a poem about poetry'. It is a refreshingly literary approach, but it leans rather heavily on some of Coleridge's later (and suspect) suggestions that the ideas in his poetry were not to be taken very seriously.

Patricia Adair's *The Waking Dream*, another attempt to look at the poetry more generally, is uneven in effect. At worst it falls into a patronizing coyness which is the bane of Coleridge criticism; at its best it shows a very real feeling for Coleridge's poetry. Miss Adair has a sense of Coleridge's European background—particularly in Greek myth and Italian literature—combined with a sense of his interest in, and ability to use, the unconscious: this sometimes gives her interpretations of Coleridge's poetry a range and suggestiveness which is lacking from narrower readings.

There is still room for a more comprehensive study of Coleridge's poetry as a whole, nevertheless. Modern critics still tend to dismiss large areas of his poetry as 'bad' by means of a quotation or two unaccompanied by further discussion: this may be good enough for the general reader but not for the more discriminating one who wants to look at Coleridge more closely against his background. One approach which comes closer to the poetry may be found in Max Schulz's *The Poetic Voices of Coleridge*, which examines some of the different styles used by Coleridge in his poetry. His book also discusses Coleridge's relationship to some contemporary German poems. Albert Gérard's *English Romantic Poetry* contains a chapter in which some of the conversation poems are examined structurally, and seen to follow a pattern of alternating contraction and expansion (a 'systole' and 'diastole'), concluding in a 'return' of some kind. The relationship between Coleridge's pantheistic leanings and his Kierkegaardian sense of 'otherness' is explored in another chapter of the same study.

(c) Coleridge's Ideas

Coleridge was fond of describing himself as being primarily a philosopher or metaphysician, and spoke often of the great philosophical work which he hoped to write. As a result—and although his friends and opponents alike agreed that his teachings did not, and could not, form the basis of a 'school'—most early treatments of his thought viewed it against the orthodox development of European philosophy, and particularly German philosophy of the Romantic period. (The question of his debt to the latter philosophers is a vexed one, which still needs further investigation.) J. H. Muirhead's *Coleridge as Philosopher*, one of the first modern studies, attempts to see Coleridge in the context of British Idealism; many statements in it would now need to be modified, however, in view of articles such as A. O. Lovejoy's 'Coleridge and Kant's Two Worlds' (*Essays*), and of the further evidence since provided by the *Philosophical Lectures* (ed. Coburn), the *Letters* and the *Notebooks*, along with other manuscript material still to appear. Thomas MacFarland, in *Coleridge and the Pantheist Tradition*, a study which takes account of the new evidence, evaluates Coleridge's relationship to the Germans afresh from the standpoint of his long engagement with pantheism, arguing that his over-all attempt to bring together the philosophy of 'I am' and that of 'it is' is a wider enterprise than some of his detailed debts might suggest, and the source of his true originality as a thinker. The book, which is fully and lucidly argued, provides an excellent long introduction to Coleridge's thought and its context. Other writers have taken Coleridge's major contribution to lie in his study of the organic (see, e.g., Gordon Mackenzie's *Organic Unity in Coleridge*). Herbert Read's essay, 'The Notion of Organic Form: Coleridge' (*The True Voice*), briefly shows the idea at work in his poetry, and Dorothy Emmet's 'Coleridge on the Growth of the Mind', an extremely perceptive essay, relates it to his psychological speculations. Stephen Prickett's *Coleridge and Wordsworth* surveys the idea at greater length, relating it in particular to Coleridge's theory of human growth and education.

Some of the most interesting studies of Coleridge are those which do not try to fit him to a particular framework but simply to explore the development of his ideas with no preconceived pattern in mind. Although such studies may lack intellectual discipline and make Coleridge seem a looser thinker than he actually is, their response to Mill's sense of him as a 'seminal mind' focuses attention on the operation of his intelligence. An early and important example of this approach was I. A. Richards's *Coleridge on Imagination*. This was one of the first studies to approach Coleridge's ideas directly, without a long preliminary excursus into the problem of his personality: the result is a book which still stands head and shoulders above most studies, by virtue of its ability to present Coleridge's ideas as an exciting and important display of independent human intelligence in action. An article by F. R. Leavis a few years later, on the other hand, had a strong influence in turning critical opinion against Coleridge. While paying many tributes to Coleridge's powers and describing him as 'more brilliantly gifted than Arnold', the article came down in favour of Arnold as the greater critic, and declared that '(Coleridge's) currency as an academic classic is something of a scandal.' It was this last dismissive phrase that stuck. At the same time, the earlier endeavours of Stephen Potter and I. A. Richards to present Coleridge as a mind whose perceptions were still as alive as ever were being slowly assisted by the new editing of his works. His Victorian editors, though devoted and by no means unperceptive, had often tidied his writing into a prose more 'charming' than the original, losing on the way the bare nervous outline that has only become generally apparent again with the publication of the *Letters* and *Notebooks*. The new material has also made it possible to examine Coleridge's own early development in greater depth, a task under-taken, for example, by Paul Deschamps in *La Formation de la pensée de Coleridge*.

The reaction against over-ready formalizations is particularly strong in the work of Kathleen Coburn, who approaches Coleridge with the open-mindedness of a scholar who believes that Coleridge's importance lies first of all in the ranging and seminal power of his mind. Her collection *Inquiring Spirit* makes no effort to organize Coleridge or to appropriate him to any particular school or point of view: she simply groups together extracts which exhibit his mind in action on a variety of topics. Her editing of the *Notebooks* is another, larger, attempt to achieve the same end, this time showing the com-prehensiveness of Coleridge's mind. Some striking new patterns which emerge from this editing may be found in her article 'Re-flexions in a Coleridge Mirror'.

William Walsh's work extends this tradition. His early essays in *The Use of Imagination* dwell on the relevance of Coleridge's ideas to the growth of intelligence in childhood. His longer study, *Coleridge: the Work and the Relevance*, presents a Coleridge who is of significance to the twentieth century largely by reason of his power to exhibit the subtle operations and growths of the mind and its perceptions without previous prejudice. He relies on a loose, largely unstructured presentation, interspersing Coleridge's own achievements with sensitive and acute commentary of his own. Since his concern is with the minute delicacy of Coleridge's mind in action, he is at his best when discussing work such as 'Frost at Midnight', where the sense of a mind in action, delicately establishing one position after another without hectoring or fuss, is particularly evident; on the other hand, a reader returning to Coleridge with Walsh's enthusiasm in his mind might well be disturbed by the amount of obsessional writing in the original. Walsh shies nervously away from Coleridge's own insistences that he was moved by large and general ideas or principles; he finds the point of *Biographia Literaria* not in its enunciations of principle but in its detailed criticisms. As a result he presents us with an attractive but rather lightweight Coleridge.

J. A. Appleyard's *Coleridge's Philosophy of Literature* is, by contrast, an attempt by a writer with a strong philosophical background to find a framework for Coleridge's thought. By focusing his attention on Coleridge's attitude to literature he is able to explore his philosophy at a point where it is particularly significant; and the breadth of his philosophic interests, coupled with his willingness in some chapters to let Coleridge speak for himself, make this a densely argued, unusually thorough study.

(d) Coleridge as Literary Critic

Apart from *Biographia Literaria*, Coleridge's critical work is difficult of access, being mainly scattered through a variety of lecture reports, marginal annotations, notebooks, and so on. Collections of the *Shakespearean Criticism* and the *Miscellaneous Criticism* have, however, been assembled by T. M. Raysor; the newcomer will also receive help from J. V. Baker's *The Sacred River*, which, by presenting a large range of Coleridge's critical comments in the framework of a loose argument, offers a good first guide through the maze.

If we turn to Coleridge's theory of criticism, important discussions may be found in I. A. Richards's *Coleridge on Imagination* and J. A. Appleyard's *Coleridge's Philosophy of Literature* (both discussed above).

R. H. Fogle, in *The Idea of Coleridge's Criticism*, concentrates on the presence of his theories of the organic in his criticism, concluding with a chapter in which he offers to show these ideas at work in a particular poem, 'Christabel'. J. de J. Jackson's *Method and Imagination in Coleridge*, by contrast, is more concerned with the relevance to his theories of his concept of 'method'.

Among brief studies, Herbert Read's *Coleridge as Critic* may be recommended for its clarity and insight. Basil Willey's *Coleridge on Imagination and Fancy* presents a sympathetic account of his most famous critical distinction, placing it in a historical and intellectual context, while George Whalley, in 'The Integrity of *Biographia Literaria*', suggests the organizing pattern of his most important critical work by tracing its growth in letters and notes over fifteen years. L. C. Knights, in 'Idea and Symbol: Some Hints from Coleridge', shows the seminal power with which a single passage from *The Statesman's Manual* indicates some essential elements of the poetic symbol as it operates in the work of the greatest writers.

(e) Coleridge as Political Thinker

Coleridge's political thinking, while affecting a few minor poems and providing a theme for 'France: an Ode', is only marginally relevant to his poetic achievement (the degree of relevance is examined in detail in Carl Woodring's *Politics in the Poetry of Coleridge*). But no study of the man can ignore this side of his activity; apart from writing two 'Lay Sermons' and conducting two journals (*The Watchman* and *The Friend*), which contained a good deal of political reference, he contributed a large number of essays to contemporary journals, some of which were collected after his death under the title *Essays on his own Times*. Among early studies of Coleridge's contribution to political thought Alfred Cobban's *Edmund Burke and the Revolt against the Eighteenth Century* sets it in contemporary perspective, while R. J. White, in *The Political Thought of Samuel Taylor Coleridge*, gives a generous selection of Coleridge's statements on the subject from the larger range of his work, and, in an introductory essay, sums up succinctly many of the main themes.

(f) Coleridge as Religious Thinker

Although always important to him, Coleridge's religious preoccupations grew with the years. His main works in the field of religious thought are *Aids to Reflection* (1825), *On the Constitution of Church and State* (1830), and the posthumous *Confessions of an Inquiring*

Spirit. The response to his ideas is best studied at first hand in F. D. Maurice's 1842 Dedication to *The Kingdom of Christ*, and in F. J. A. Hort's essay 'Coleridge': the value of both essays extends well beyond the bounds of strict theology. A long general account of Coleridge's religious thought and its influence on some subsequent writers is given by C. R. Sanders in *Coleridge and the Broad Church Movement*.

Coleridge's American influence, notably on the New England Transcendentalists, has been the subject of several essays. Alice Snyder's 'American Comments on Coleridge a Century ago' gives a good account, with references to many previous discussions. Modern judgements of his religious thinking range from H. N. Fairchild's account in *Religious Trends in English Poetry*, which judges it by the canons of orthodoxy and (not surprisingly) finds it wanting, to Marshall Suther's *The Dark Night of Samuel Taylor Coleridge*, which, considering the religious significance of Coleridge's career in more general terms, aligns him with poets such as Baudelaire and Rimbaud as an early existentialist poet-voyager. The most detailed recent study of his religious thought is J. D. Boulger's *Coleridge as Religious Thinker*.

(g) General Introductory Studies

Many readers coming to Coleridge for the first time will find that Humphry House's Clark Lectures (mentioned earlier) offer a good first approach to his achievement: of the large range of introductory essays and chapters available, those by John F. Danby, Graham Hough, D. G. James, Kathleen Raine, and L. G. Salingar may be particularly recommended. A useful collection of essays assembled by Kathleen Coburn for the Twentieth-Century Views series brings together conveniently a number of studies, some of which (asterisked in REFERENCES) have been discussed in earlier sections.

A reader who has a fair knowledge of Coleridge's writings and has read some of the more obvious critical works might wish to find a simple way of acquainting himself with the stronger lines of recent scholarship. He could hardly do better than begin by consulting *The Major English Romantic Poets* (edited by C. D. Thorpe *et al.*), in which he will find three attractive essays on Coleridge: J. M. McLuhan tries to relate Coleridge's poetic sensibility, to the twentieth-century consciousness; D. G. James gives a lucid, rounded picture of the main lines of Coleridge's thought; and Kathleen Coburn demonstrates the light that can be thrown on Coleridge's work by a sensitive reading of the *Notebooks*. It is by bringing together a number of approaches such as these, rather than by consulting any one scholar or critic, that the diverse qualities of his achievement can best be appreciated.

BIOGRAPHIES AND LETTERS

The standard edition of the *Letters* is by Earl Leslie Griggs, publication of which will shortly be completed. Those who find this too bulky for their immediate needs may prefer the shorter representative selection which has been produced by Kathleen Raine; other selections may be found in the Nonesuch and Viking editions mentioned earlier. Although the letters as a whole contain some dull patches and many daunting descriptions of medical symptoms, the complete collection is, however, indispensable for anyone who wishes to come to terms with Coleridge's mind in any important way.

It is harder to recommend a biography of Coleridge. The significance of his career is hardly reflected in the events of his life; for this reason a short study such as that provided by I. A. Richards for his Viking edition is as helpful as any. Longer narrative biographies necessarily tend to distort on a larger scale, and it is perhaps significant that every writer who has so far attempted a long biography has, in one sense or another, lost patience. Lawrence Hanson's volume describing his life up to 1800 is, after thirty years, without its promised successor. E. K. Chambers, who did persevere to the end, hounds Coleridge through his later pages for 'instability of character' and for not taking his share of the economic burdens of mankind. Geoffrey Yarlott's *Coleridge and the Abyssinian Maid* approaches the problem more successfully, cutting across the chronological contours and ignoring much biographical detail in order to present a thesis about the personality of his subject; but he too cannot resist the temptation to hound Coleridge, arguing that, since he only wrote poetry when he was happy, and was happiest when living with his wife and child under the aegis of Tom Poole, at Nether Stowey (both questionable hypotheses), he would have achieved more if he had not followed Wordsworth to the Lake District and not fallen in love with Sara Hutchinson. Although there are some perceptive observations in this volume, as in some of the more specifically psycho-analytic studies, such as David Beres's article 'A Dream, a Vision and a Poem: A Psychoanalytic Study of the origin of the "Rime of the Ancient Mariner" ', and Beverly Fields's *Reality's Dark Dream*, it is difficult to avoid the conclusion that moralists and psycho-analysts alike miss the main point of Coleridge's career. W. J. Bate's short study is a more generous piece of work, and the most successful attempt yet made to see Coleridge's life and work together. We still need a full-length biography which will take full account of his own self-knowledge, however; we need even more a biographer who will respond to Henry James's challenge and accept the

general responsibility of rising to the height of accepting (Coleridge) for what he is, recognizing his rare, anomalous, magnificent, interesting, curious, tremendously suggestive character, vices and all, with all its imperfections on its head, and *not* being guilty of the pedantry, the stupidity, the want of imagination, of fighting him, deploring him in the details— failing to recognise that one *must* pay for him and that on the whole he is magnificently worth it.

Notebooks (New York, 1947), p. 152

BIBLIOGRAPHIES

There has been no comprehensive separate bibliography of Coleridge for over sixty years, and those by J. L. Haney (1903), and T. J. Wise (1913–19) are long out of date. The recent *New Cambridge Bibliography of English Literature* (vol. iii), however, contains a section which aims to include all significant studies. Richard Haven is at present preparing a bibliography of nineteenth-century studies.

A complete bibliography of work on Coleridge is somewhat daunting: unless he is looking for some particular specialized subject, the student will often do better to consult the excellent select bibliography in Kathleen Coburn's collection of essays, which will direct him to most of the main studies. W. L. Renwick's volume in the *O.H.E.L.* has a helpful bibliographical supplement, giving a guide to individual poets and to the period in general.

Select bibliographies referring to particular aspects of Coleridge's work appear in a number of books. D. P. Calleo and John Colmer both list studies of his political thought, J. A. Appleyard of his philosophy (with particular reference to the theory of criticism). W. W. Beyer has a bibliography of studies of his poetry (particularly useful for a student pursuing its relationship to German poetry); J. V. Baker has a long list of studies of Coleridge as critic. The bibliography in H. W. Piper's *The Active Universe* is a good guide to the intellectual scientific background; M. H. Abrams's *The Mirror and the Lamp* lacks a bibliography but its notes serve as a similar guide to the literature of literary criticism in Coleridge's time.

BACKGROUND READING

Coleridge's range of interests is too wide for any single work to offer an adequate idea of his 'background'. W. L. Renwick's volume in the *O.H.E.L.* gives a good picture of the general prevailing conditions in the political and literary scene of his time, while M. H. Abrams's *The Mirror and the Lamp* is indispensable as a guide to the prevalent critical ideas in the eighteenth century which provided a matrix for the development of Coleridge's own literary criticism and critical theory. Certain important ideas of Coleridge's can be placed in context by reading particular specialized studies: his interest in science, for example, is illuminated by H. W. Piper's *The Active Universe*, his interest in the unconscious by L. L. Whyte's *The Unconscious before Freud*. Geoffrey Grigson's essay 'The Harp of Aeolus' shows, at a more factual level, some of the contemporary bases for a single potent image in his poetry. A. S. Byatt's *Wordsworth and Coleridge in their Time* provides a good, ranging, introduction to the social and political background of the two poets, with some sensitive comments on their life and work.

It is impossible to appreciate the impact of certain ideas, or the individual blend of them which Coleridge created for himself, without consulting contemporary works at first hand. Apart from familiarizing himself with the English and German philosophical traditions generally, anyone studying Coleridge in depth should read Hartley's *Observations on Man* (1749), Darwin's *Botanic Garden* (1791) and *Zoönomia* (1794–6), and Godwin's *Political Justice* (1793). The literary tradition in which Coleridge developed, similarly, can be explored by reading the poems of Gray and Collins, Cowper's *Task*, and one or two Gothic novels—especially Ann Radcliffe's *The Mysteries of Udolpho* (1794) and Matthew Lewis's *The Monk* (1796). A student requiring some further sense of the intellectual tradition within which Coleridge worked as a young man could hardly do better than look through the works of Joseph Priestley in a complete edition: as he turns the pages and looks at the subjects dealt with, he will see something of the range of ideas with which an educated man of the time could expect to be familiar, including science, politics, and theology. At the same time, a return to Coleridge's own writing will suggest something of the original 'shaping powers' which he himself brings to his own investigations and which give his most characteristic writing its unique qualities of intelligence and imagination.

REFERENCES

(Items marked with an asterisk appear in Kathleen Coburn's collection of essays under CRITICAL STUDIES (g) below; some others appear there in an abridged form.)

TEXTS

J. B. Beer (ed.), *Coleridge's Poems*, with Introduction and commentary (Everyman's Library, London and New York, 1963).

R. F. Brinkley (ed.), *Coleridge on the Seventeenth Century* (Durham, N.C., 1955).

Kathleen Coburn (ed.), *The Notebooks of Samuel Taylor Coleridge* (London and New York, 1957–   ).

E. H. Coleridge (ed.), *Anima Poetae: from the Unpublished Notebooks of Samuel Taylor Coleridge* (London and New York, 1895).

E. H. Coleridge (ed.), *S. T. Coleridge: Poetical Works* (Oxford English Texts, 2 vols., Oxford and New York, 1912).

E. H. Coleridge (ed.), *The Poems of S. T. Coleridge* (Oxford Standard Authors, London, 1912; paperbacks, U.K. and U.S.).

H. N. Coleridge (ed.), *Specimens of the Table Talk of the Late Samuel Taylor Coleridge* (London and New York, 1835, etc.).

S. T. Coleridge, *The Friend* (London, 1818, etc.; New York, 1831, etc.).

E. L. Griggs (ed.), *Collected Letters of Samuel Taylor Coleridge* (Oxford and New York, 1956–   ).

Sister Eugenia Logan (ed.), *Concordance to the Poetry of Samuel Taylor Coleridge* (St. Mary of the Woods, Ind., 1940; repr. Magnolia, Mass.).

L. Patton (ed.), *The Collected Coleridge*, Vol. 2: *The Watchman* (London and Princeton, N.J., 1970).

S. Potter (ed.), *Coleridge: Select Poetry and Prose* (Nonesuch edn., London and New York, 1933).

A. Quiller-Couch (ed.), *The Poems of Samuel Taylor Coleridge* (World's Classics, London and New York, 1912).

I. A. Richards (ed.), *The Portable Coleridge* (paperback, New York, 1950; paperback, U.K.).

B. Rooke (ed.), *The Collected Coleridge*, Vol. 4: *The Friend* (London and Princeton, N.J., 1969).

J. Shawcross (ed.), *Coleridge's 'Biographia Literaria'* (2 vols., Oxford and New York, 1907).

W. G. Shedd (ed.), *Coleridge's Complete Works* (7 vols., New York, 1853).

G. G. Watson (ed.), *Coleridge's 'Biographia Literaria'* (Everyman's Library, London and New York, 1960).

CRITICAL STUDIES AND COMMENTARY

(a) *Nineteenth Century*

R. W. Armour and R. F. Howes (eds.), *Coleridge the Talker* (Ithaca, N.Y., 1940).

Thomas Carlyle, *Life of John Sterling* (London, 1851, etc.; Boston, 1852, etc.; World's Classics, London and New York, 1907).

H. S. Davies and G. G. Watson (eds.), *The English Mind: Studies in the English Moralists, Presented to Basil Willey* (Cambridge and New York, 1964).

Thomas De Quincey, *Reminiscences of the English Lake Poets* (Everyman's Library, London and New York, 1909).

William Hazlitt, 'My First Acquaintance with Poets', in *The Spirit of the Age* (1825) (World's Classics, London, 1904, and other selections).

William Hazlitt, 'Mr Coleridge' in *Winterslow* (London, 1850, etc. and other selections).

F. J. A. Hort, 'Coleridge' in *Cambridge Essays:* II (London, 1856).

J. de J. Jackson (ed.), *Coleridge: the Critical Heritage* (London, 1970).

Charles Lamb, *Essays of Elia* (Everyman's Library, London and New York, 1906; paperback, U.K.).

F. R. Leavis (ed.), *Mill on Bentham and Coleridge*, with an Introduction (London, 1950; New York, 1951; Mill's text in paperback, U.S.).

Walter Pater, *Appreciations* (London and New York, 1889 etc.).

Leslie Stephen, *Hours in a Library: III* (London, 1879, etc.; New York, 1894 etc.).

A. C. Swinburne, *Essays and Studies* (London, 1875 etc.).

Basil Willey, *Nineteenth-Century Studies: Coleridge to Matthew Arnold* (London, 1949; paperbacks, U.K. and U.S.).

Raymond Williams, *Culture and Society, 1780–1950* (London and New York 1958; paperbacks, U.K. and U.S.).

William Wordsworth, *The Prelude* (1850 text), ed. E. de Selincourt, 2nd edn., revised by Helen Darbishire (Oxford English Texts, Oxford and New York, 1959). Also Oxford Standard Authors edn. of 1805 text revised by S. Gill (London, 1970; paperbacks, U.K. and U.S.)

(b) *Modern Studies of Coleridge's Poetry*

Patricia Adair, *The Waking Dream* (London, 1967).

R. C. Bald, 'Coleridge and "The Ancient Mariner": Addenda to *The Road to Xanadu*', in *Nineteenth-Century Studies*, ed. H. Davis, W. C. De Vane, and R. C. Bald (Ithaca, N.Y., 1950).

J. B. Beer, *Coleridge the Visionary* (London and New York, 1959; paperback, U.S.).

H. Bloom, *The Visionary Company* (London and New York, 1962; paperback, U.S.).

M. Bodkin, *Archetypal Patterns in Poetry: Psychological Studies of Imagination* (London, 1934; New York, 1941; paperbacks, U.K. and U.S.).

*E. E. Bostetter, 'The Nightmare World of "The Ancient Mariner"', *Studies in Romanticism*, i (1962).

E. E. Bostetter, *The Romantic Ventriloquists* (Seattle, 1963).

R. L. Brett, *Reason and Imagination: a Study of Form and Meaning in Four Poems* (Oxford and New York, 1960; paperback, U.K.).

Kenneth Burke, *The Philosophy of Literary Form*, 2nd edn. (Baton Rouge, La., 1967; paperback, U.S.).

W. Empson, 'The Ancient Mariner', *Critical Quarterly*, vi (1964).

R. H. Fogle. See (*d*) below.

M. Gardner (ed.), *The Annotated 'Ancient Mariner'*, with illustrations by Gustav Doré (New York and London, 1966).

A. Gérard, *English Romantic Poetry: Ethos, Structure and Symbol in Coleridge, Wordsworth, Shelley, and Keats* (Berkeley and Los Angeles, Calif., and London, 1968).

A. H. House, *Coleridge*, the Clark Lectures, 1951–2 (London, 1953).

J. L. Lowes, *The Road to Xanadu*, 2nd edn. (Cambridge, Mass., and London, 1930; paperback, U.S.).

A. H. Nethercot, *The Road to Tryermaine* (Chicago, 1939; repr. New York, 1962).

Elder Olson, 'A Symbolic Reading of "The Ancient Mariner"', in *Critics and Criticism*, ed. R. S. Crane (Chicago, 1952; paperbacks U.K. and U.S.).

R. Penn Warren, *Selected Essays* (New York, 1958, London, 1964; paperback, U.S.).

S. Potter, *Coleridge and S.T.C.* (London, 1935).

Elisabeth Schneider, *Coleridge, Opium and 'Kubla Khan'* (Chicago, 1953; repr. New York, 1966).

M. F. Schulz, *The Poetic Voices of Coleridge* (Detroit, 1963).

E. E. Stoll, 'Symbolism in Coleridge', *PMLA* lxiii (1948).

M. Suther, *Visions of Xanadu* (New York and London, 1965).

C. Tomlinson, 'Christabel', in *Interpretations*, ed. J. B. Wain (London, 1955; paperback, U.K.).

G. G. Watson, *Coleridge the Poet* (London and New York, 1966).

G. Whalley, *Coleridge and Sara Hutchinson and the Asra Poems* (London, 1955).

G. Whalley, 'The Mariner and the Albatross', *UTQ* xvi (1946–7).

G. Wilson Knight, *The Starlit Dome*, 2nd edn. (London, 1959; New York, 1960).

G. Yarlott. See BIOGRAPHIES below.

(c) *Coleridge's Ideas*

J. A. Appleyard, *Coleridge's Philosophy of Literature* (Cambridge, Mass., 1965).

Kathleen Coburn (ed.), *Inquiring Spirit: A New Presentation of Coleridge from his Published and Unpublished Prose Writings* (London and Princeton, N.J., 1951).

Kathleen Coburn (ed.), *Coleridge's Philosophical Lectures, 1818–19* (London and New York, 1949).

Kathleen Coburn, 'Reflexions in a Coleridge Mirror', in *From Sensibility to Romanticism: Essays Presented to F. A. Pottle*, ed. F. W. Hilles and H. Bloom (New York and London, 1965).

P. Deschamps, *La Formation de la pensée de Coleridge, 1772–1804* (Paris, 1964).

Dorothy Emmet, 'Coleridge on the Growth of the Mind', *Bulletin of the John Rylands Library*, xxxiv (1952).

F. R. Leavis, 'Coleridge in Criticism', *Scrutiny* ix (1940); reprinted in *A Selection from 'Scrutiny'* (Cambridge and New York, 1968; paperbacks, U.K. and U.S.).

A. O. Lovejoy, *Essays in the History of Ideas* (Baltimore, 1948; paperback, U.S.).

T. McFarland, *Coleridge and the Pantheist Tradition* (Oxford and New York, 1969).

G. Mackenzie, *Organic Unity in Coleridge* (Berkeley, Calif., 1939).

J. H. Muirhead, *Coleridge as Philosopher*, corr. edn. (London and New York, 1939).

S. Prickett, *Coleridge and Wordsworth: the Poetry of Growth* (Cambridge and New York, 1970).

H. Read, *The True Voice of Feeling* (London and New York, 1953; paperback, U.K.).

I. A. Richards, *Coleridge on Imagination* (London 1934); reprinted, with essay by K. Coburn (Bloomington Ind., 1950).

W. Walsh, *The Use of Imagination* (London and New York, 1959; paperbacks U.K. and U.S.).

W. Walsh, *Coleridge: the Work and the Relevance* (London and New York, 1967).

(d) *Coleridge as Literary Critic*

J. A. Appleyard. See (c) above.

J. V. Baker, *The Sacred River: Coleridge's Theory of the Imagination* (Baton Rouge, La., 1957).

R. H. Fogle, *The Idea of Coleridge's Criticism* (Berkeley, Calif., 1962).

J. de J. Jackson, *Method and Imagination in Coleridge's Criticism* (London and Cambridge, Mass., 1969).

*L. C. Knights, *Further Explorations* (London and Stanford, Calif., 1965).

T. M. Raysor (ed.), *Coleridge's Miscellaneous Criticism* (London and Cambridge, Mass., 1936).

T. M. Raysor (ed.), *Coleridge's Shakespearean Criticism*, new edn. (2 vols., Everyman's Library, London and New York, 1960).

I. A. Richards. See (*c*) above.

H. Read, 'Coleridge as Critic', *SR* lvi (1948); reprinted in *Lectures in Criticism* (New York, 1949); and in *The True Voice of Feeling.* ((*c*) above).

G. Whalley, 'The Integrity of *Biographia Literaria*', in *Essays and Studies by Members of the English Association*, N.S. vi (1953).

B. Willey, 'Coleridge on Imagination and Fancy,' *Proceedings of the British Academy* (1946).

(e) Coleridge as Political Thinker

D. P. Calleo, *Coleridge and the Idea of the Modern State* (New Haven, Conn., 1966).

A. Cobban, *Edmund Burke and the Revolt against the Eighteenth Century*, 2nd edn. (London and New York, 1960).

S. T. Coleridge, *Lay Sermons* (1816, 1817), partly reprinted in R. J. White's *Political Tracts of Wordsworth, Coleridge and Shelley* (Cambridge and New York, 1953).

Sara Coleridge (ed.), *Coleridge's Essays on his own Times* (London, 1850).

J. A. Colmer, *Coleridge: Critic of Society* (Oxford and New York, 1959).

R. J. White, *The Political Thought of Samuel Taylor Coleridge: a Selection* (London, 1938).

C. Woodring, *Politics in the Poetry of Coleridge* (Madison, Wis., 1961).

(f) Coleridge as Religious Thinker

J. D. Boulger, *Coleridge as Religious Thinker* (New Haven, Conn., 1961).

S. T. Coleridge, *Aids to Reflection in the Formation of a Manly Character* (1825, etc.).

S. T. Coleridge, *On the Constitution of Church and State* (London, 1830, etc.).

H. N. Fairchild, *Religious Trends in English Poetry: III* (New York and London, 1949).

H. St. J. Hart (ed.), *Coleridge's 'Confessions of an Inquiring Spirit'* (London and New York, 1956; paperbacks, U.K. and U.S.).

F. J. A. Hort. See (*a*) above.

F. D. Maurice, *The Kingdom of Christ*, ed. A. R. Vidler (2 vols., London 1958; Naperville, Ill., 1959).

C. R. Sanders, *Coleridge and the Broad Church Movement* (Durham, N.C., 1942).

Alice Snyder, 'American Comments on Coleridge a Century Ago', in *Coleridge: Studies . . .*, ed. E. Blunden and E. L. Griggs (London, 1934).

M. Suther, *The Dark Night of Samuel Taylor Coleridge* (New York and London, 1960).

(g) General Introductory Studies

W. J. Bate, *Coleridge*. See BIOGRAPHIES (below).

Kathleen Coburn (ed.), *Coleridge: A Collection of Critical Essays* (paperback, Englewood Cliffs, N.J., 1967; paperback, U.K.).

J. F. Danby, *S. T. Coleridge: Anima Naturaliter Christiana* (Burning Glass Papers No. 29, Shorne, Kent, n.d.).

G. G. Hough, 'Wordsworth and Coleridge', in *The Romantic Poets* 3rd edn. (London and New York, 1967; paperbacks, U.K. and U.S.).

A. H. House. See *(b)* above.

D. G. James, *The Romantic Comedy* (Oxford and New York, 1948; paperback, U.K. and U.S.).

Kathleen Raine, *Coleridge* (paperback, British Council, London, 1953; paperback, U.S.).

L. G. Salingar, 'Coleridge: Poet and Philosopher', in *The Pelican Guide to English Literature*, vol. v (paperback, London and New York, 1957); reprinted in hardback as *Guide to English Literature* (London and New York, 1961–5).

C. D. Thorpe, C. Baker, and B. Weaver (eds.), *The Major English Romantic Poets: A Symposium in Reappraisal* (Carbondale, Ill., 1957).

BIOGRAPHIES AND LETTERS

W. J. Bate, *Coleridge* (Masters of World Literature, New York, 1968; London, 1969).

D. Beres, 'A Dream, a Vision and a Poem: A Psychoanalytic Study of the Origins of the "Rime of the Ancient Mariner" ', *International Journal of Psycho-analysis*, xxxii (1951).

E. K. Chambers, *Coleridge* (Oxford and New York, 1938).

E. L. Griggs (ed.), *Collected Letters*. See TEXTS (above).

Beverly Fields, *Reality's Dark Dream: Dejection in Coleridge* (Evanston, Ill., 1967).

L. Hanson, *The Life of S. T. Coleridge: The Early Years* (London, 1938; repr. New York, 1962).

Kathleen Raine (ed.), *Coleridge's Letters*, selected, and with an Introduction (London, 1952).

I. A. Richards, Introduction to *The Portable Coleridge* (see TEXTS above).

D. Sultana, *Samuel Taylor Coleridge in Malta and Italy* (Oxford, 1969).

G. Yarlott, *Coleridge and the Abyssinian Maid* (London and New York, 1967).

BIBLIOGRAPHIES

M. H. Abrams. See following section.

J. A. Appleyard. See *(c) Ideas* above.

J. V. Baker. See (*d*) *C. as Critic* above.

W. W. Beyer, *The Enchanted Forest* (Oxford and New York, 1963).

D. P. Calleo. See (*e*) *Political* above.

K. Coburn. See following section.

J. A. Colmer. See (*e*) above.

M. Gardner. See (*b*) *Modern Studies* above.

J. L. Haney, *A Bibliography of Samuel Taylor Coleridge* (Philadelphia, Pa., 1903).

H. W. Piper. See following section.

W. L. Renwick. See following section.

G. G. Watson (ed.), *N.C.B.E.L.*, vol. iii (Cambridge and New York, 1969).

T. J. Wise, *A Bibliography of the Writings . . . of Samuel Taylor Coleridge* (London 1913); and *Supplement* (1919).

BACKGROUND READING

M. H. Abrams, *The Mirror and the Lamp: Romantic Theory and the Critical Tradition* (New York and Oxford, 1953; paperback, U.S.).

A. S. Byatt, *Wordsworth and Coleridge in their Time* (London and Camden, N.J., 1970).

E. Darwin, *The Botanic Garden* (London, 1789–91, etc.; New York, 1798, etc.).

E. Darwin, *Zoönomia* (London, 1794–6; New York, 1796 etc.).

W. Godwin, *Political Justice* (London, 1793; Philadelphia, 1796, etc.; facs., edn., Toronto, 1946).

G. Grigson, '*The Harp of Aeolus*' *and other Essays* (London, 1948).

D. Hartley, *Observations on Man* (London, 1749; Gainesville, Fla., 1966).

M. G. Lewis, *The Monk* (London, 1795, etc.; paperbacks, U.S. and U.K.).

H. W. Piper, *The Active Universe* (London and New York, 1962).

J. Priestley, *Theological and Miscellaneous Works* (London, 1817–31).

W. L. Renwick, *English Literature, 1789–1815* (*O.H.E.L.*, vol. ix, Oxford and New York, 1963).

Ann Radcliffe, *The Mysteries of Udolpho*, ed. B. Dobrée, (London and New York, 1966; paperbacks, U.K. and U.S.).

L. L. Whyte, *The Unconscious before Freud* (New York, 1960, London, 1962; paperback, U.K.).

John Jump

UNTIL fairly recently it was common to hear readers of Byron's poetry complain that there was available for their assistance but one half-pennyworth of literary criticism to an intolerable deal of biography. The output of biography has not declined, nor has the proportion of genuinely illuminating works that it includes. But during the last few decades there has been a notable increase in the quantity of literary criticism devoted to Byron's writings, and a notable improvement in its quality. This being so, it is natural that the emphasis in the present article should fall upon the most recent period.

TEXTS

The standard edition of Byron's works is still that published, at the turn of the century, in thirteen volumes: seven containing the *Poetry* edited by E. H. Coleridge, six the *Letters and Journals* edited by R. E. Prothero. Coleridge annotates freely, usually serviceably, but sometimes digressively; he also supplies from Byron's manuscripts a generous selection of variant readings, many of them fascinatingly illustrative of stages in the creative process. As far as *Don Juan* is concerned, his work has been superseded by that of T. G. Steffan and W. W. Pratt. Their Variorum edition comprises one volume describing Byron's composition of the poem; two supplying the text and recording all legible manuscript readings that differ from it; and a fourth containing explanatory and other notes, followed by a survey of critical commentary on *Don Juan* down to the middle of the twentieth century. Though very full, Pratt's notes are not exhaustive: for example, contributors to *Notes and Queries*, August 1967, draw attention to literary parallels which he missed. Nevertheless, serious students of *Don Juan* will find this Variorum edition an invaluable tool.

E. H. Coleridge's one-volume edition of the complete poems has helpful short notes. Other one-volume editions include that in the Oxford Standard Authors series and that edited by P. E. More in the Cambridge Edition of the Poets. Of the many volumes of selections from Byron's poetry, two are especially well introduced and annotated: *Don Juan and Other Satiric Poems*, edited by L. I. Bredvold, and *Childe Harold's Pilgrimage and Other Romantic Poems*, edited by S. C. Chew. Four-fifths of Peter Quennell's Nonesuch selection consists of satiric poetry, including *Don Juan*, I—III, XI–XVII, and of prose, both supplied with occasional notes. L. A. Marchand provides fuller notes in his paperback edition of the whole of *Don Juan*. A plain text of *Don Juan* occupies one volume of the Everyman's Library *Byron*.

CRITICAL STUDIES AND COMMENTARY

The publication of *Childe Harold's Pilgrimage*, I and II (1812), made Byron famous overnight. Readers greeted the works which followed, the Turkish tales, with mounting enthusiasm, until in 1814 10,000 copies of *The Corsair* were sold on the day of publication and 25,000 in a little over one month. Through these early poems Byron popularized the romantic figure of the noble outlaw. The heroes of his dramatic poem, *Manfred* (1817), and of *Childe Harold's Pilgrimage*, III (1816) and IV (1818), illustrate further developments of this character-type. From the early protagonists, generally, the popular imagination shaped a composite Byronic hero and succumbed to his attractions. T. B. Macaulay, reviewing Thomas Moore's *Life of Byron* (1830), describes this hero as 'a man proud, moody, cynical, with defiance on his brow, and misery in his heart, a scorner of his kind, implacable in revenge, yet capable of deep and strong affection'. The most distinguished of his British progeny is Emily Brontë's Heathcliff.

The serio-comic poems of Byron's Italian years, *Beppo* (1818), *Don Juan* (1819 onwards), and *The Vision of Judgment* (1822), entertained and scandalized contemporary readers. While their popularity did not equal that of his earlier romantic poems, his works generally continued in high esteem. A boy of fourteen, Alfred Tennyson, was so moved by the news of his death in 1824 that he climbed up to a quarry near his home and scratched the words 'Byron is dead' upon the sandstone. Byron's self-sacrifice in the cause of Greek independence deeply affected public opinion throughout Europe. Without it, the British, French, and Russian navies might never have united in the same cause at Navarino in 1827. Goethe had Byron and his last adventure in mind when he introduced Euphorion into the second part of *Faust*.

For Byron's reputation was more than merely British. It spread rapidly over the whole of Europe and throughout the English-speaking world. Musset was his disciple in France, Pushkin in Russia. During the nineteenth century at least forty-one translations of one or more cantos of *Childe Harold's Pilgrimage* appeared in no fewer than ten different languages, and as many as thirty-four translations of *Manfred* in twelve different languages. These two works inspired musical compositions by Berlioz, Schumann, and Tchaikovsky. Painters, too, took subjects from them and from other poems by Byron.

In Great Britain itself, however, Byron's reputation declined during the early Victorian period, then rose slowly from about 1870 onwards. In the Preface to his volume of selections from Byron's work Swinburne wrote appreciatively of him in 1866. But, when Matthew Arnold ranked Byron above Keats and Shelley, the current favourites, in the essay introducing his own selection (1881), Swinburne switched from eloquent appreciation to shrill abuse. Nevertheless, Arnold's praise, together with that of Ruskin, Alfred Austin, and others, ensured a steady, if slow, rise in Byron's stock. In his compendious Critical Heritage anthology of nineteenth-century writings on Byron, Andrew Rutherford documents the main shifts of taste during the period.

In the twentieth century Byron has still not regained anything like the reputation he once enjoyed; and such reputation as is his derives not from the works that gave rise to the Byronic hero but from the serio-comic poetry of his later years. It has come to be generally accepted that he vacillated between going along with contemporary romantic trends and remaining loyal to eighteenth-century classical principles; that the former tendency was dominant during his years of fame in England, and that the latter tendency prevailed when he found contentment in his Italian exile. W. J. Calvert in *Byron: Romantic Paradox* (1935) has been influential in establishing this view. He regards *Don Juan* as Byron's masterpiece, in that it is the work in which his strength and sincerity at last found adequate expression.

In varying degrees, this preference for the serio-comic writings is shared by all four of the critics who during the 1960s published full-length general studies of Byron's poetry. Paul West sees Byron as a sensitive and strangely contradictory man, with 'the insecure person's fierce need of elimination', and consequently as a poet who does his best work in a comic, derisive manner, in the manner of a spoiler or wrecker. He finds *Don Juan* a more thoroughly negative poem than do many other readers. His book, intelligent, showy, lively, suggestive, and bewildering, differs strikingly from Andrew

Rutherford's, which is serious, consistent, sensible, and judicious. Whereas West is ingenious enough to devise ways of speaking with some appreciation of the early tales in verse and of the plays, Rutherford sternly dismisses nearly all of these. He finds 'a strong element of silly self-dramatisation' in the presentation of the early heroes, and he sees the plays as the result of Byron's having temporarily strayed from his true path of development. Nor does he relax his severity when he turns to the serio-comic works. *Don Juan*, while indubitably a very great poem, with a power and range to which *Beppo* does not aspire, is, he thinks, flawed by a fundamental ambiguity of outlook: 'Byron really wants to have it both ways—to be both a moral satirist and an amusingly cynical man of the world.' Reflecting as it does Byron's intellectual and moral confusion, the poem can succeed as a loose, baggy monster, but not as a fully coherent work of art. The poem of Byron's which best combines coherence with power is *The Vision of Judgment*. Rutherford regards this as his author's masterpiece, 'aesthetically perfect, intellectually consistent, highly entertaining, and morally profound'.

M. K. Joseph prefers *Don Juan*. He spends more time than does either West or Rutherford on setting each of Byron's more considerable works in the context of the literary and cultural traditions to which it relates, and he never loses sight of the critics who have preceded him. Careful consideration of Byron's earlier works does not prevent him from devoting just over one-half of his book to *Don Juan*. He argues that Byron had a master-plan in writing this poem, that he kept his serious purposes steadily in mind, and that he employed, consistently but not inflexibly, methods that were well adapted to serve those purposes. In his view, Byron's use of the myth of the Fall, associated as it is with the myth of recurrence (derived from Cuvier's catastrophism) and with other myths and symbols, gives the poem an important unifying principle; Byron's employment of a narrator, enabling him to be simultaneously involved in the action and detached from it, confirms the unity of the work; and Byron's serious and coherent, if unsystematized, moral attitudes sustain this unity. Joseph will not convince everybody. But even those who persist in thinking of *Don Juan* as a magnificent improvisation will learn much from a challenge as cogent as his.

L. A. Marchand also follows Calvert in seeing Byron as drawn to the writing of two different kinds of poetry: a satirical and realistic eighteenth-century kind, and a subjective romantic kind. Byron achieves a fusion of the two in *Don Juan*, when he comes to terms— reluctantly, for he is still in part a romantic—with an imperfect world. Marchand's is the least novel of the four full-length studies now under consideration. Declaring itself an 'Introduction', it gives a clear and straightforward description, with numerous illustrative quotations, of each poem of any importance. But for the quotations, it might seem a little tame.

In addition to these full-length general studies, two general essays call for mention here. T. S. Eliot's 'Byron', first printed in 1937, is the one important non-Scottish attempt to find significance in Byron's early connection with Scotland. W. W. Robson's 'Byron as Poet' was originally delivered as a lecture to the British Academy in 1957. 'The doubt that afflicts us, after we have mentally gone over our impressions of Byron's poetry,' writes Robson, 'crystallizes into the question: how much of it *is* poetry? And this leads to the further question: has Byron as poet enough self-knowledge and command of his experience to be judged a *great* poet?' In Byron's best poetry Robson finds, following Swinburne and Arnold, sincerity and strength. But the sincerity is that of an actor, for whom success 'is a matter of being able to mobilize emotions which one has either had, or can imagine having, without necessarily having them at the moment'. Robson's is one of the most sensitive and discriminating studies of Byron written in this century.

Understandably, most of those who have recently written at length on particular works of Byron's have taken *Don Juan* as their subject. G. M. Ridenour—like Joseph, who acknowledges his debt to him—sees the poem as coherent and unified. He discerns three structural principles in it. The first of these is the classical rhetorical theory of the styles. Byron couches his satire in the pedestrian, or low, style; but such is his dedication to truth that he periodically soars to the heroic level, and by so doing justifies his claim to be writing an 'Epic Satire'. Flight is a manifestation of pride, however, and can lead to a fall. In consonance with this, Ridenour names the Christian myth of the Fall as the second structural principle. Recurrent allusions to it, he argues, help Byron to organize in his poem the conflicting elements which compose the world as he knows it. The third structural principle is the character of the poet himself as this is presented in the poem he is writing. In a paper published in 1968 the present writer suggests that the preoccupations of this implied author result in the development of specific thematic patterns in the poem. But these do not suffice to unify *Don Juan* for him. It remains in his eyes a rather casually assembled work—and none the worse for that.

Most useful of all, however, to the reader who is looking for an informative introduction to *Don Juan* is E. F. Boyd's thorough study of the personal and literary elements that went to its making. This appeared in the same year as the monograph in which P. G. Trueblood sets out to demonstrate Byron's increasing seriousness of purpose as *Don Juan* proceeds. The two studies overlap to some extent, but they also supplement each other.

Further books that deal with particular aspects or parts of Byron's achievement include R. F. Gleckner's suggestive discussion of the earlier poems, T. G. Steffan's exhaustive consideration of *Cain*, E. J. Lovell's *Byron: the Record of a Quest*, a survey of his concept and treatment of nature, and P. L. Thorslev's *The Byronic Hero*. Thorslev combats Mario Praz's view that a perverted erotic sensibility is a central characteristic of nineteenth-century romanticism and that the Byronic hero exhibits such a sensibility. He argues that the Byronic hero is not like that, and that there is no single Byronic hero anyhow. The hero of the first two cantos of *Childe Harold's Pilgrimage* is distinct from the hero of the Turkish tales, who is quite unlike the hero of the last two cantos of *Childe Harold's Pilgrimage*, who in his turn differs appreciably from the hero of the dramas. Nor is the Byronic hero in his various manifestations the offspring of a single line of ancestry stretching back through Mrs. Ann Radcliffe's Schedoni to Milton's Satan, as Praz and others allege. Thorslev traces his descent from various eighteenth-century and romantic hero-types: from the child of nature, the hero of sensibility, and the Gothic villain in the earlier period, and from the noble outlaw and the other 'fundamentally and heroically rebellious' characters represented by Faust, Cain (or Ahasuerus), and Satan (or Prometheus) in the later. Thorslev's book serves the important critical purpose of exploding facile generalizations.

Paul West reprints an extract from Praz's book and thirteen extracts or complete essays by other hands in his *Byron* in the Twentieth-Century Views series. A number of the critics already mentioned in the present article contribute to it, and they are joined by G. Wilson Knight, F. R. Leavis, Helen Gardner, Edmund Wilson, Bertrand Russell, John Wain, and others. Since this stimulating and varied anthology can be warmly recommended, particular comments on its component items may be dispensed with. In a similar anthology devoted to the English Romantic poets generally, M. H. Abrams reprints the influential essay, 'Byron and the Colloquial Tradition in English Poetry', that Ronald Bottrall contributed to *The Criterion* in 1939. 'The amazing variety of tone and tremendous rhythmic energy of *Don Juan*,' writes Bottrall, 'come from Byron's complete understanding of the spoken language.'

The Byron Foundation Lectures at the University of Nottingham constitute in their printed form a useful series of short papers. Naturally, they vary widely in quality. Among the best are L. C. Martin's *Byron's Lyrics*, Bonamy Dobrée's *Byron's Dramas*, and G. Wilson Knight's *Byron's Dramatic Prose*. Another recent critical study of the prose is the present writer's 'Byron's Letters' in *Essays and Studies 1968*.

Before turning from critical studies to biographies, it will be appropriate to mention R. Escarpit's brilliant *Lord Byron: un Tempérament littéraire*. This is not a formal literary analysis of the poet's achievement. Nor is it strictly speaking a biography. Escarpit believes that we cannot read Byron profitably without liking or disliking him personally, without entering into a man-to-man relationship with him. So his subject is the poet's literary temperament.

BIOGRAPHIES AND LETTERS

L. A. Marchand's *Byron: a Biography* supersedes most of the earlier biographical studies; it is detailed, accurate, and judicious. Among such predecessors as it has not totally eclipsed, Iris Origo's *The Last Attachment* claims notice as an account of the poet's liaison with Teresa Guiccioli and of his life in Italian society, and Harold Nicolson's *Byron: the Last Journey* as a cool but finally sympathetic appraisal of his Greek enterprise of 1823–4. In the same year as Marchand's biography, there appeared G. Wilson Knight's *Lord Byron's Marriage*. Five years earlier, Wilson Knight had published his panegyric, *Lord Byron: Christian Virtues*, and had promised to follow it up with a book on the poet's vices. *Lord Byron's Marriage* is this book. The principal vice turns out to have been sodomy, and Lady Byron's belated realization of the irregularity of the practice to have been the cause of her insistence upon a total separation from her husband. This theory may or may not be correct; it is difficult to see how anyone can be very positive about what went on in the Byrons' bed.

Naturally, Wilson Knight's theory stimulated discussion of the marriage. Before long, books by Doris Langley Moore and Malcolm Elwin made available some previously unpublished material bearing on this and other aspects of Byron's life. The new material does not explain the separation once and for all, but it does augment the evidence that the Byrons were so ill-matched that the really puzzling question is not why they separated but why they ever came together in the first place. Malcolm Elwin's is one of the two most useful and scholarly of the biographical studies published since the appearance of Marchand's standard work in 1957. The other is John Buxton's *Byron and Shelley*, a history of the friendship between the two poets.

Eight volumes contain most of Byron's published letters: the six volumes of *Letters and Journals*, edited by R. E. Prothero and published at the turn of the century as part of what is still the standard edition of the works, and the two volumes of *Lord Byron's Correspondence*, edited by John Murray and published in 1922. The earlier of these has great virtues. It contains many letters not previously printed, and it gives full texts of many previously printed only in part; it presents in appendices a large number of important supplementary documents, such as the texts of Byron's speeches to the House of Lords and those of his writings in literary and personal controversy; and the editorial notes are copious, lively, and scholarly. But Prothero sometimes bowdlerizes what Byron wrote, as may be seen by comparing his version of the letter dated 12 August 1819 (*Letters and Journals*, iv, 341–2) with that given by Marchand (*Byron : a Biography*, p. 807). Murray is liable to do this, too. His volumes contain some of Byron's most interesting and entertaining letters—those to Lady Melbourne, for example—but their editing leaves a great deal to be desired.

We urgently need a scholarly edition of all of the letters of Byron that are now known to us. Such an edition would include not only those assembled by Prothero and by Murray but also those contained in certain smaller collections and those not yet collected at all. Among the smaller collections, that in Iris Origo's *The Last Attachment* has unusual importance. It consists of 156 letters and short notes, most of them addressed to Teresa Guiccioli, and most of them written in fluent, if not quite flawless, Italian. There are English translations of nearly all the Italian items.

Peter Quennell's *Byron : a Self-Portrait* is mainly a selection from the letters that were already available, accompanied by the whole of Byron's journals. In addition, it contains some previously unpublished letters, though not as many as Quennell supposes. Nor is his text of the letters as accurate as readers have a right to expect. Nevertheless, the two handsome volumes of his edition offer an attractive introduction to Byron's prose. An easily obtainable single-volume selection, also offering an attractive introduction to this material, is R. G. Howarth's in Everyman's Library. Peter Quennell's Nonesuch selection, while consisting mainly of verse, contains most of the journals and 127 well-chosen letters.

Byron evidently talked to his friends and acquaintances very much as he wrote in his letters and journals. So much is clear from *His Very Self and Voice*, the substantial volume in which E. J. Lovell has assembled all the major first-hand accounts in English of Byron's conversation, except for those contained in the poet's own letters and journals, and those published in Thomas Medwin's *Conversations of Byron at Pisa* (1824) and Lady Blessington's *Conversations of Lord Byron* (1832–3). Lovell feels that these records by Medwin and Lady Blessington are of such importance that they deserve to stand on their own. His edition of Medwin's book appeared in 1966, three years after his publication of his interesting biography of its author, and his edition of Lady Blessington's book in 1969.

In *His Very Self and Voice*, he summons no fewer than 150 witnesses and arranges their sometimes numerous reports in chronological order. As a result, his book can be read continuously, as a new kind of biography. In his Introduction he characterizes his various witnesses, and by so doing helps the reader to make allowance for the kind of bias to which each of them was subject. Both as a whole and in detail, *His Very Self and Voice* is one of the most stimulating and entertaining of the books on Byron the man.

BIBLIOGRAPHIES

The New Cambridge Bibliography of English Literature provides an extensive bibliography of Byron's works, of translations of his works, and of biographical and critical studies down to the middle of the 1960s. A more selective list accompanies Herbert Read's short essay in the Writers and their Work series. Many of the books reviewed in earlier sections of the present article contain bibliographies: volume vii of Coleridge's edition contains the best general bibliography of the poems, and the bibliographies appended to the books by Marchand, Joseph, and other recent writers usefully supplement the lists of biographical and critical publications given in *N.C.B.E.L.*

S. C. Chew contributes an excellent descriptive article on the bibliographical, biographical, and critical studies, and on the editions of Byron's works, to *The English Romantic Poets: a Review of Research*, edited by T. M. Raysor.

BACKGROUND READING

A man as active in his living, as wide in his interests, and as mobile in his temperament as was Byron can naturally be seen with advantage against a number of different social, intellectual, and cultural backgrounds. But such an account as is offered here must be severely selective. Given the special interest felt today in the poems of Byron's Italian years, the background of Italian culture is perhaps the one that most merits attention.

C. P. Brand, in *Italy and the English Romantics*, gives an attractive and scholarly account of the widespread fashionable British interest in Italy which grew during the latter part of the eighteenth century, reached its height immediately after the Napoleonic Wars, and was already in decline by 1840. Many scholars and artists and, above all, creative writers felt this interest deeply. Brand shows what Shelley, Byron, and others found in the Italian literature that they read and how their own work was affected. His discussion of Byron's indebtedness to the Italian serio-comic poets is distinctive and especially valuable in its elucidation of what Byron learned from Casti. Brand acknowledges that he owes much to R. D. Waller's edition of the poem by J. H. Frere that is usually known either as *Whistlecraft* or as *The Monks and the Giants*. This is the poem that opened Byron's eyes to the possibilities of the metrical stanza, *ottava rima*, that he employs in *Beppo*, *Don Juan*, and *The Vision of Judgment*. Waller's Introduction to his edition is an informative monograph on the Italian medley poems and on *The Monks and the Giants* and other imitations of them in English. It does much to clarify Byron's relationship to the great tradition of which Frere made him aware.

REFERENCES

TEXTS

L. I. Bredvold (ed.), *'Don Juan' and Other Satiric Poems* (New York, 1935).

Byron, *Poetical Works*, reset edn. (Oxford Standard Authors, London, 1945; paperbacks, U.K. and U.S.).

S. C. Chew (ed.), *'Childe Harold's Pilgrimage' and Other Romantic Poems* (New York, 1936).

E. H. Coleridge (ed.), *The Poetical Works of Lord Byron* (London, 1905).

E. H. Coleridge (ed.), *The Works of Lord Byron: Poetry* (7 vols., London, 1898–1904, reprinted New York, 1966).

L. A. Marchand (ed.), *Don Juan* (paperback, Boston, Mass., 1959).

P. E. More (ed.), *The Complete Poetical Works of Lord Byron* (Cambridge Poets edn., Boston, Mass., 1905).

V. de Sola Pinto (ed.), *Byron: Poems* (3 vols., Everyman's Library, London and New York, 1963).

Peter Quennell (ed.), *Byron: Selections from Poetry, Letters, and Journals* (Nonesuch edn., London and New York, 1949).

T. G. Steffan and W. W. Pratt (eds.), *Byron's 'Don Juan'* (4 vols., Austin, Tex., and Edinburgh, 1957).

CRITICAL STUDIES AND COMMENTARY

Matthew Arnold (ed.), Introduction to his *Poetry of Byron* (London, 1881).

Alfred Austin, *The Poetry of the Period* (London, 1870).

Ronald Bottrall, 'Byron and the Colloquial Tradition in English Poetry', in M. H. Abrams (ed.), *English Romantic Poets* (paperbacks, New York and London, 1960).

E. F. Boyd, *Byron's 'Don Juan': a Critical Study* (New Brunswick, N.J., 1945; London, 1958).

W. J. Calvert, *Byron: Romantic Paradox* (New York, 1935).

Bonamy Dobrée, *Byron's Dramas*, Byron Foundation Lecture (Nottingham, 1962).

T. S. Eliot, 'Byron', in *On Poetry and Poets* (London and New York, 1957; paperbacks, U.K. and U.S.).

Robert Escarpit, *Lord Byron: un Tempérament littéraire* (2 vols., Paris, 1957).

R. F. Gleckner, *Byron and the Ruins of Paradise* (Baltimore and London, 1967).

M. K. Joseph, *Byron the Poet* (London and Mystic, Conn., 1964).

J. D. Jump, *Byron's 'Don Juan': Poem or Hold-All?* (Swansea, 1968).

J. D. Jump, 'Byron's Letters', in Simeon Potter (ed.), *Essays and Studies, 1968* (London, 1968).

G. Wilson Knight, *Byron's Dramatic Prose*, Byron Foundation Lecture (Nottingham, 1953).

E. J. Lovell, *Byron: the Record of a Quest* (Austin, Tex., 1949).

L. A. Marchand, *Byron's Poetry: a Critical Introduction* (Boston, Mass., and London, 1965; paperback, U.S.).

L. C. Martin, *Byron's Lyrics*, Byron Foundation Lecture (Nottingham, 1948).

Mario Praz, *The Romantic Agony*, trans. A. Davidson (London and Magnolia, Mass., 1933; paperbacks, U.K. and U.S.).

G. M. Ridenour, *The Style of 'Don Juan'* (New Haven, Conn., and London, 1960).

W. W. Robson, 'Byron as Poet', in *Critical Essays* (London and New York, 1966).

John Ruskin, 'Fiction, Fair and Foul', in *On the Old Road*, ii (3 vols., London, 1885).

Andrew Rutherford, *Byron: a Critical Study* (Edinburgh, London, and Stanford, Calif., 1961; paperback, U.K.).

Andrew Rutherford (ed.), *Byron: the Critical Heritage* (London and New York, 1970).

T. G. Steffan, *Lord Byron's 'Cain'* (Austin, Tex., and London, 1969).

A. C. Swinburne (ed.), Preface to his *Selection from the Works of Lord Byron* (London, 1866).

P. L. Thorslev, *The Byronic Hero: Types and Prototypes* (Minneapolis, Minn., and London, 1962).

P. G. Trueblood, *The Flowering of Byron's Genius* (Stanford, Calif., 1945).

Paul West (ed.), *Byron: a Collection of Critical Essays* (paperbacks, Englewood Cliffs, N.J., 1963; paperback, U.K.).

Paul West, *Byron and the Spoiler's Art* (London, 1960).

BIOGRAPHIES AND LETTERS

John Buxton, *Byron and Shelley* (London, 1968).

Malcolm Elwin, *Lord Byron's Wife* (London, 1962, New York, 1963).

R. G. Howarth (ed.), *The Letters of Lord Byron* [selected] (Everyman's Library, London and New York, 1936).

G. Wilson Knight, *Lord Byron: Christian Virtues* (London and New York, 1952).

G. Wilson Knight, *Lord Byron's Marriage* (London and New York, 1957).

E. J. Lovell, *Captain Medwin: Friend of Byron and Shelley* (Austin, Tex., 1962, London, 1963).

E. J. Lovell (ed.), *His Very Self and Voice: Collected Conversations of Lord Byron* (New York, 1954).

E. J. Lovell (ed.), *Lady Blessington's Conversations of Lord Byron* (Princeton, N.J., and London, 1969).

E. J. Lovell (ed.), *Medwin's Conversations of Lord Byron* (Princeton, N.J., and London, 1966).

L. A. Marchand, *Byron: a Biography* (3 vols., New York and London, 1957).

Doris Langley Moore, *The Late Lord Byron* (London and Philadelphia, 1961).

John Murray (ed.), *Lord Byron's Correspondence* (2 vols., London and New York, 1922).

Harold Nicolson, *Byron: the Last Journey*, new edn. (London, 1948).

Iris Origo, *The Last Attachment* (London and New York, 1949).

R. E. Prothero (ed.), *The Works of Lord Byron: Letters and Journals* (6 vols., London, 1898–1904; New York, 1966).

Peter Quennell (ed.), *Byron: a Self-Portrait* (2 vols., London and New York, 1950).

BIBLIOGRAPHIES

G. Watson (ed.), *N.C.B.E.L.* vol. iii: 1800–1900 (Cambridge and New York, 1969).

S. C. Chew, 'Byron', in T. M. Raysor (ed.), *The English Romantic Poets: a Review of Research* (New York, 1956).

Herbert Read, *Byron* (paperback, British Council, London, 1951 ; paperback, U.S.).

BACKGROUND READING

C. P. Brand, *Italy and the English Romantics* (Cambridge and New York, 1957).

R. D. Waller (ed.), *The Monks and the Giants, by John Hookham Frere* (Manchester and New York, 1926).

R. B. Woodings

TEXTS

If he is not the most controversial of English poets, Shelley is certainly unique for producing editors whose scholarship is blunted by the controversy and legends that his name inspires. Almost 150 years after his death there still does not exist an authoritative edition of his complete poetry and prose. The reasons for this are many: Shelley himself saw few of his poems into print, and left many works, including almost all the prose and many of the lyrics, in manuscript when he died; until comparatively recently his editors have not had direct access to all the manuscript sources, and when available these pose real problems of decipherment and interpretation; and, of course, the image of the inspired dreamer has not prepared the way for the minutiae of textual scholarship. As a result, editors have had to take on trust the labours of their predecessors, all of whom worked under the same disabilities. Thus even the Julian edition of *The Complete Works*, edited in ten volumes by Ingpen and Peck, is far from being complete or accurate, although it remains the basis of all serious Shelley scholarship. The first four volumes of this edition are devoted to the Poetry, volumes 5 to 7 to the Prose, and the remainder to the Letters. Sections of these have been replaced by subsequent editions, but, since this work has been done piecemeal, the Julian notes must be continually consulted to check the textual authority of any poem or essay.

The standard single-volume text of the complete poems is that edited by Thomas Hutchinson. But it must be stressed that, as this was compiled in 1904, it is less trustworthy than the Julian edition, and, in its reliance on previous publications, is more a compilation of available printed texts than a new edition. In his documentation Hutchinson draws heavily on the dating supplied by Mary Shelley, much of which was guesswork, and his variant readings are untrustworthy as they are based on an uncritical selection from manuscripts then published. Hutchinson's misprints, and some of his headings and headnotes, have been revised by G. M. Matthews in the recent Oxford Paperbacks reprint (1970); but this is in no sense a new edition, as it is misleadingly described on the title-page. Notwithstanding, until the appearance of the definitive Oxford edition to be edited by Neville Rogers, and that of G. M. Matthews in the Longmans Annotated English Poets series, Hutchinson's will have to remain the most accessible complete edition.

Individual poems, however, have been issued in revised texts, although divergent editorial practice among these may cause confusion. G. M. Matthews uses his preliminary studies for his proposed Longman's edition in *Shelley: Selected Poems and Prose* to provide sound texts of *Adonais* and some of the lyrics. But his own text of 'The Triumph of Life' has already been challenged by Donald H. Reiman's new edition. *Prometheus Unbound* has received equally rigorous treatment from L. J. Zillman: in 1959 he issued a 'Variorum Edition', based on Shelley's original 1820 volume, but in 1968, having altered his views on the reliability of this edition, he produced a new text, honestly subtitled 'toward a modern definitive edition'. In the first of what is anticipated as a series of monographs published by the Keats–Shelley Memorial Association (1970), W. J. McTaggart has produced a new text, with full apparatus and Introduction, of the ballad previously entitled 'Young Parson Richards'.

Ironically, the poems that have been most carefully edited are some of the least rewarding, the so-called Esdaile poems written between 1805 and 1814. As witness to the problems of Shelley editors these poems were brought out in two separate editions within two years. The more satisfactory of these as regards its textual premises is that of Neville Rogers, *The Esdaile Poems*, intended as part of his forthcoming Oxford edition. His object has been to produce a readable text, and to this end he has sacrificed the arbitrary details of manuscript punctuation and spelling. His notes are brief but relevant. The other edition, issued for the Pforzheimer Library, offers 'a minimum clean-up text' which, in adhering to Shelley's manuscript vagaries, is trying to read. But, as with other Cameron editions, over half of the book is given to notes, valuable for the biographical information they provide.

Such textual commentary may sound pedantic, but in Shelley's case it is unavoidable, since so much criticism of his poetry is limited by the very fact that it is founded on hopelessly inadequate texts. As any scholar who has studied the text knows to his cost, Shelley does, editorially, set an exceptional problem. For quite apart from the difficulties of manuscript decipherment already mentioned, it is impossible to establish a uniform approach, each poem having to be treated as a particular 'case', with its own manuscript and printing history. Even poems that appeared in Shelley's lifetime cannot be simply reprinted, as the poet did not greatly concern himself with their accuracy, and for those published posthumously there are frequently real difficulties in establishing from the manuscripts what his intentions really were. No wonder, then, that different editions of the same poem reveal such divergencies in readings and punctuation!

Save for *A Defence of Poetry* and the Greek translations, the Julian edition still provides the only text of Shelley's essays and prose fragments. *Shelley's Prose, or, The Trumpet of a Prophecy*, edited by David L. Clark, claims to be reliable, but its readings are derived from those of Ingpen and Peck. No explanations are provided for the variants that creep into its pages, and the editor's rearrangements of essay fragments have as little justification as his erroneous ascription of origins and dates. The standard edition of *A Defence of Poetry* is that by H. F. B. Brett-Smith, which includes a summary of the manuscript problem (the essay was not printed until 1840), and useful notes that draw on Shelley's other essays. Other editions of *A Defence*, such as that by J. E. Jordan, rely on his conclusions, supplemented by those of the Julian editors, and to date no critical study of the existing manuscripts has been produced. McElderry's edition of *Shelley's Critical Prose* usefully collects together *A Defence* and the various prefaces to separate poems, and also includes the anonymous article, probably genuine, 'Byron and Shelley on the Character of Hamlet'. Shelley's longest discussion of social policy, *A Philosophical View of Reform*, is reprinted in a truncated form in R. J. White's *Political Tracts of Wordsworth, Coleridge and Shelley*. Rediscovered at roughly the same date, the translations from Plato have been brought together by J. A. Notopoulos to form Part III of his *The Platonism of Shelley*, a text now supplemented and corrected by the same editor in an article, 'New Texts of Shelley's Plato'.

Only the final part of the Julian edition has been completely superseded, by the publication of the two volumes of F. L. Jones, *The Letters of Percy Bysshe Shelley*. This provides a largely accurate, intelligently edited text of the known letters, together with reliable notes on correspondents and references, and transcriptions of many of the letters written to Shelley, including those of Godwin and Elizabeth Hitchener. As an appendix, Jones reprints the yearly lists of Shelley's reading kept by his wife, but supplemented by the additional details given in the letters. But this list is far from complete, omitting the evidence in the Bodleian notebooks and elsewhere. Unhappily, since the critical legend has to run true to form, even this standard collection is incomplete owing to the refusal of the

Pforzheimer Library to allow the inclusion of those autograph letters that it owns. Eventually all the Pforzheimer Shelleyana will be issued in the expensive series, *Shelley and his Circle, 1773–1822*, under the editorship of K. N. Cameron. The actual texts are very unhelpful, as shown by the first four volumes to appear, since they are simply literal holograph transcriptions, but the comprehensive notes that accompany these are essential to the scholar for their wealth of commentary.

Although not including anything written by Shelley himself, three other modern editions are of prime importance for the study of the poet and his work. *The Letters of Mary Shelley* and *Mary Shelley's Journal*, both edited and annotated by F. L. Jones, provide sound texts of his wife's personal correspondence and memoranda, although the former is incomplete. *The Journals and Letters* relating to Maria Gisborne and Edward Williams, again edited by F. L. Jones, include important information about Shelley's final months at Lerici. The long awaited *Journals* kept by Claire Clairmont proved to be of little interest when they were published at last in 1968.

For the reasons already given, the only textually reliable selection of Shelley's poetry is that of G. M. Matthews. His selection, that includes *Adonais*, extracts from *Prometheus Unbound* and 'The Triumph of Life', and a group of lyrics, is excellent, and his Introduction and commentary are informative, if over-simplified in the account of Shelley's beliefs. In comparison, Neville Rogers's *Selected Poetry*, although inspired by admirable principles, is marred by the kind of errors that affect so much of what he has undertaken. His Introduction rightly emphasises the need 'to see his poetry and his ideas in their fullness', but the notes, which are of such varied quality, lend the reader only a single pair of spectacles – the Platonic – and too readily impress a single reading upon each poem. Having once decided to rely on the Hutchinson text, it seems arbitrary to introduce the occasional altered reading as Rogers does, and the bibliography deserves far more attention than he pays it. Of the English school editions, that by John Holloway, *Selected Poems of Percy Bysshe Shelley* includes an outstanding introductory essay on the poet and the problems he sets for the general reader. Admitting his own difficulties, Holloway points out some of the misconceptions that interfere between the poetry and the public, particularly those related to Shelley's cliché-ridden language. Indeed, he concludes that the fundamental limitation is not the result of any linguistic failure, but stems from the very intensity of the writing, which expects too much of any five-sensed reader. Unfortunately Holloway's selection of poems is inadequate, and he takes unjustified liberties in his editing. An editor may concern himself with offering an extended plain text, as does A. S. B. Glover for the Nonesuch *Shelley, Selected Poetry, Prose and Letters*, but the very range of reference and syntactical structures that Shelley uses makes notes essential. Alternatively, he may, like A. M. D. Hughes in *Shelley: Poems Published in 1820*, reprint one of the original volumes with detailed commentary. To find adequate selections one must turn to the American college series, and of these the best (and certainly the most imaginative edition currently in print) is that of K. N. Cameron. Stressing Shelley's political involvement, he includes extracts from the essays in his choice of texts, and provides substantial notes. The Modern Library edition by Carlos Baker offers an even fuller text, but without footnotes.

CRITICAL STUDIES AND COMMENTARY

The Shelley legend has coiled itself around all aspects of Shelley studies and, like any legend, has proved to be self-duplicating. But a commentary on the available critical studies is vexed further by the heritage of the legend of Shelley criticism itself. Polemicism is never far away in any account, whether in the form of a swingeing attack on Leavis, Matthew Arnold, or Harold Bloom, or in the deliberate omission of all such names. Shelley represents his own chameleon poet, being, through the complexity of his poetry, all things to all critics. Because his poems work on several levels, critics have been able to pare his lines down to the desired layer, and so present a distinct critical portrait at odds with that produced by fellow critics, and especially with what has become the respectable critical orthodoxy. Despite attempts to identify paradox, ambiguity, and linguistic dexterity, Shelley remains aloof from the expected details of such analysis, just as he insists on the availability of source studies and the resultant extra-textual explication. Modern interpretation is made difficult by the very fact that sympathetic critics feel the need to approach his poetic achievement through a freshly defined poetics, which simultaneously produces complicated readings and the suspicion of special pleading. For this reason the progress of Shelley criticism is largely that of evolving literary theory, chronicling the emergence of, for example, the school of Northrop Frye or that of the neo-Aristotelians. Rather than any question-begging evaluation of Shelley criticism, therefore, this commentary can most usefully offer an account of the principal critical approaches, particularly as each has been pursued in more recent criticism.

Many of the problems are evident in the work of the first generation of Shelley critics; the periodical reviewers who wrote during Shelley's lifetime, and whose notices have been collected together in N. I. White's *The Unextinguished Hearth*. White shows that one tradition, that of Shelley as the victim of hatred and misunderstanding, was in fact fabricated by the poet himself, since his poetry was accorded a surprising degree of attention. When harshly attacked, it was either because he departed from Augustan canons, so producing lines that were disorganized and unsatisfying, or from accepted moral standards, which stamped him as an anarchist, libertine, or starry-eyed reformer. Significantly for what was to follow, any sympathetic critic tended to praise him for his poetry and condemn him for his ideas.

Although no adequate account of Shelley's reputation in the Victorian period has been written, the main attitudes can be seen in Roland A. Duerksen's *Shelleyan Ideas in Victorian Literature* and Sylva Norman's *Flight of the Skylark*. The former, directed to the influence Shelley exerted on such writers as Browning, Disraeli, George Eliot, and Shaw, traces how their individual responses, changing during their careers, reflect the larger pattern of Shelley's acceptance and/or rejection by their age. The other describes some of the episodes that befell Shelley's reputation, especially at the hands of his family and friends.

Inevitably the heritage left to the twentieth century was a divided one. The radicals exploited the doctrines of *Queen Mab* and *Prometheus Unbound* until Shelley came to stand for a left-wing challenge to the *status quo*; while the admirers, setting aside such pernicious doctrines, elevated Shelley the lyricist, and their admiration, chronicled in Palgrave's *Golden Treasury*, produced an Ariel, the archetype of the other-worldly Romantic. The unavoidable conflict between the two tributes produced the divided poet, a division expressed in the contradiction between the luxuriance of poetic language and the realism of political creed. Stirred in with the biographical revelations, this produced the brew served up to the twentieth-century reader.

Fundamentally the legacy resolves itself into the problem of how to read Shelley, of the supposed abstractedness of the language and the immaturity of the concepts. These issues are helpfully illustrated in an exchange in *Essays in Criticism* (1954). (See under Erdman). Opposing the view that Shelley's imagery, in a passage from *Prometheus Unbound*, is confused and unrealistic, W. Milgate argues that his words rely upon their truth to experience, but D. Erdman, seeing the looseness of principle this involves, stresses the logic and interconnectedness of the imagery. This account is substantiated by G. M. Matthews, who points to the sources of Shelley's words in current scientific lore, and shows how Shelley consistently employs his imagery according to the actuality of these terms. This discussion is supplemented by C. C. Clarke's 'Shelley's "Tangled Boughs" ', a brief commentary on a much debated image in 'Ode to the West Wind', showing how the imagery works on several levels, literal, allegorical, analogical, and symbolic. The finest description of this simultaneous functioning is G. M. Matthew's 'A Volcano's Voice in Shelley'. Although this article concentrates on the central acts of *Prometheus Unbound*, its conclusions are equally important for what they reveal of Shelley's poetic methods. Taking the recurrent imagery of volcanoes and volcanic activity, Matthews shows how, in common with most Shelleyan symbolism, this is neither restricted to some single application nor a metaphor on the road to mysticism. Instead, it provides the focal point for a series of 'vague' adjectives, being firmly located in the developing interest in scientific phenomena in the later eighteenth century. By relating volcanic imagery to the quickening of social and political movements, as well as to the human response to love, Shelley establishes a consistent metaphoric structure expressive on each of the levels of experience with which he is concerned, and, at the same time, maintaining a firm association with the non-poetic world of experience. This emphasis on the actuality of Shelley's poetry is of central importance, and can effectively counter not only the excesses of the mythopoeists, to be discussed shortly, but also the more obvious charges against Shelley's 'weak grasp on the actual'.

This phrase of F. R. Leavis is taken from the most legendary, quotable, and unrelenting of the attacks delivered during the 1930s. Tate, Cleanth Brooks, Penn Warren, *et al.*, contributed their dismissive epitaphs, but it was Leavis who summarized in *Revaluation* the full circle of literary and moral condemnation: Shelley's language is unrealized and deceptive, his entire poetic manner forbids the control of the critical sensibility, and his indulgence in sentimental commonplaces betrays a radical lack of self-knowledge. T. S. Eliot had added the final nails to this coffin in his 1933 lecture 'Shelley and Keats', when he judged Shelley's ideas as not only adolescent (and therefore appropriate only for adolescent readers) but borrowed, unassimilated, and 'shabby'. In their judgements both critics reveal an over-zealous interest in Shelley the man, an interest shared by those who have accepted their revaluations. But neither of the popularized essays by Stephen Spender and D. W. Harding add any new barbs, and both were badly out of date at the time they were written. The most sophisticated version of such denunciation is that of Edward E. Bostetter in *The Romantic Ventriloquists*. His central thesis, that the Romantic poets, by defining the world as centring on themselves, believed that they had access to truth, runs perilously close to defining them as precocious adolescents, and, though veiled, the hoary legends of Shelley biography are smuggled into the account. Shelley's ideals are shown as escapist fantasies, inspired by a morbid hatred of humanity, and his intellect as unresponsive to logic and so antagonistic to poetry itself. In this account Bostetter reveals a not uncommon tendency among critics to impose an unambiguous logical argument on to a poem, and then let the inevitable deviation of the poem from this prove the illogicality of the poet.

Although most appraisals of Shelley implicitly refute such arguments, a perspective for the debate is provided by two more general essays. In 'Shelley, Dryden and Mr Eliot' C. S. Lewis, rating *Prometheus Unbound* as the greatest of nineteenth-century poems, suggests that modern distaste stems from the unacceptability of many of Shelley's concepts. More specifically, F. A. Pottle's 'The Case of Shelley' explains the attack in terms of the critical prejudices of the 1930s, particularly the distaste for vatic poets, even if, as with Shelley, they can be shown to handle their language with due reverence.

The responsibility of Shelley criticism is therefore twofold: to offer commentary on the significance of his key terms, and set him firmly within traditions by now largely displaced; and to justify the very form of the poetry, explaining almost physically the attention the language requires. The finest criticism, of course, discharges both tasks in the same discussion. But because of this very burden there are few introductory books that, by over-emphasizing one of these aspects, do not strengthen the legendary prejudices. Desmond King-Hele's *Shelley: his Thought and Work* is intended for the general reader, providing a commentary on the important texts within a biographical framework, but the discussion is sometimes inept and frequently superficial. The author's professional interest in science, however, qualifies him to make useful points on the scientific detail of the imagery, and by drawing on the body of previous criticism the book defines a standard, respectable approach to the poetry. Similar qualifications must be made for Peter Butter's *Shelley's*

Idols of the Cave. This concentrates on the recurrent symbols, boats, caves, winds, veils, and so on, showing how these constitute 'a short-hand language for expressing ideas as well as feelings'. Inevitably the symbols become over-defined to imply a greater similarity between the poems than in fact exists. The discussion itself is confused by Butter's need to stress the 'normality' of Shelley, and the criterion of truth to human experience interferes with the direction of the criticism. However, Butter has good chapters on Shelley's scientific reading and *Prometheus Unbound*. The most scholarly of these general accounts remains the best, Carlos Baker's *Shelley's Major Poetry*. This gives a chronological chapter-by-chapter account of the longer poems, identifying the sources on which Shelley drew and demonstrating his development of a symbolic system within the poems. The psyche/epipsyche search provides a firm thematic unity, although attention to his themes does make Baker imperceptive to the poetry itself. But in emphasizing certain themes Baker blazed for contemporary students trails whose various turnings are still being explored: the movement from Necessity to Love (Godwin to Plato), and the phases of elevation to the ideal. The earlier part of this route is charted from a heavily biographical viewpoint by A. M. D. Hughes in *The Nascent Mind of Shelley*, a book especially good on the contradictory attitudes forced together in *Queen Mab*.

Respectability was lent to Shelley's symbolism through Yeats's essay of 1900, 'The Philosophy of Shelley's Poetry'. This idiosyncratic account valuably stresses the importance of Shelley's symbolism, suggesting that achievement of this represents the goal of the poetry. As might be expected, Wilson Knight in *The Starlit Dome* seizes this insight, and expands it to produce a complete symbolic system. Unapproachable as his analyses can be, he does point out the recurrent Coleridgean symbols and demonstrates how they give definite form to the poetry.

The tension implicit in Baker's account between the Platonic and revolutionary creeds has been developed by several critics who have seen Shelley's reliance on symbol within the context of this Romantic dilemma. Thus David Perkins's influential chapter in *The Quest for Permanence* describes a Shelley frustrated by the necessity to establish a valid symbolic code at the very time when the traditionally inherited symbols had lost their general relevance. Perkins fears that Shelley's over-concern with the transcendental possibilities of this ambition undermines his very sense of language, which must remain locked in the world of temporality. With other critics who hound images into contradictions, Perkins is over-literal in his analyses, but he makes some intelligent points and emphasizes the detail of Shelley's style. His final conclusion, however, refurbishes the sentimental portrait of a dishonest Shelley. As stimulating is Milton Wilson's pursuance of a related theme in *Shelley's Later Poetry*. With *Prometheus Unbound* as his focal point, he associates Shelley's stylistic peculiarities with the unresolved confusion in his dialectic, in which the temporal reformer struggles against the desired attainment of Platonic perfection. According to this view, only *Adonais* is true to its idealistic terms, though even here Shelley saves himself by sacrificing the mourners to 'cold mortality'. But a thorough knowledge of the poetry is a necessary preliminary to the appreciation of Wilson's subtle arguments.

This is certainly required for Harold Bloom's accounts in *Shelley's Mythmaking* and *The Visionary Company*, to disentangle his own idiosyncratic allusions from plausible interpretations of Shelley. Bloom is the examplar, armed with terms patented by Northrop Frye and Martin Barber, of the mythopaeic interpretation. For him Shelley is a mythmaker, related to Blake and the Old Testament prophetic books in his religious vocation, but formulating his own prophetic creed in the actual composition of poetry. 'Mont Blanc', *Prometheus Unbound*, 'The Witch of Atlas', and 'The Triumph of Life' are accordingly poems spun out of their own entrails, and Shelley's final achievement is to give these objective creations a subjective existence. Bloom's existential analyses of an 'It' transmuting into a 'Thou' have constantly to be checked against the argument and details of the poems, particularly when the transition is achieved with the aid of mythic figures borrowed from Hebraic or Blakean sources. Bloom's fallacious reading of 'The Triumph of Life', erroneous both in its rejection of Shelley's consistent use of certain symbols and the course of Shelley's poetry, must stand as a warning of the temptation to mythopaeic remodelling of poems in terms of one's own argument. Since *Shelley's Mythmaking* is discursive and confusingly written, a safer introduction to this school of criticism is Bloom's own summary of his argument in *The Visionary Company*. In this version Bloom is content to substitute Imagination for his earlier theology, and regards the poems as attempts to emancipate the self-sustaining imaginative vision. Certainly Bloom insists on an uncompromising acceptance of Shelley on the poet's own terms, making no concessions to critical disdain of the numinous in poetry; and by studying him within the European literary tradition he redirects attention to poems such as 'The Witch of Atlas' which have been mislaid during thematic drives. Because his scholarship is so much more reliable, it is perhaps unfair to bracket R. G. Woodman's *The Apocalyptic Vision in the Poetry of Shelley* with Bloom's criticism, but, shorn of its source in Shelley's debt to Orphism, his thesis is a related one. He sees Shelley as striving towards a coherent vision beyond the boundaries of his materialism, a vision only achieved in *Adonais*. Like Bloom, he interprets 'The Triumph of Life' as negative, a depiction of the imagination's failure before the omnipresence of a debasing reality. Woodman's discussion of the tradition within which Shelley was working is illuminating, both for the comments it enables him to pass on particular poems, and for his summaries of Shelley's response to other writers, especially Milton and Dante.

Although these critics insist upon their concern for the details of Shelley's poetry, their pursuance of the visionary poet who surmounts the barrier of language belies this in practice. But their realization of the cultural crisis within which Shelley was writing is the departure point for the most probing analysis of the poetry yet attempted. In his essays on *Adonais*, 'Mont Blanc', and 'The Sensitive Plant', printed in *The Subtler Language*, Earl R. Wasserman argues that Shelley's poems possess a unique complexity of imagery and syntactical structure, because he was faced as a poet with the simultaneous need to establish a world view, and to organize the very poetry in which the view is elaborated in terms of that perspective. Although this Shelley, as borne out by the evidence of his reading and prose projects, displays a remarkable breadth of knowledge, Wasserman rejects the notion that the poems were written to accord with any available philosophic system. The poems are 'dramatic' in their very enactment of the argument that gives them form, an operation that is present on several different levels. Wasserman's distinctive approach has already influenced Shelley criticism, both through his argument that the poems are autonomous in their referential details, and for his exploitation of such critical terms as 'irony', 'drama', and 'paradox'. D. J. Hughes is an example of a critic who has applied this methodology. He labels Shelley's major poems as 'self-reflexive', concerned more with the potential of their own poetic activity than with any definable themes. His article 'Kindling and Dwindling: The Poetic Process in Shelley' records the appearance of verbs descriptive of the art of writing in the poetry; while two more local articles, 'Coherence and Collapse in Shelley, with particular reference to *Epipsychidion*' and 'Potentiality in *Prometheus Unbound*', apply his insight to the structure of two particular poems. However, because both Wasserman and Hughes feel the need to define Shelley as a unique poetic case, their defence of Shelley's language may leave many unconvinced. Less oppressive in their handling of the reader are two studies of Shelley's imagery by R. H. Fogle and Glenn O'Malley, both concerned to demonstrate how the elements that compose the imagery are the components of the poetic themes. Through a comparison of the types of imagery employed by Keats and Shelley, Fogle is able to demonstrate the consistency of Shelley's poetic world, thus refuting the more insidious charges against his 'vacancy'. He admits Shelley's fondness for 'abstract' imagery, though he shows that this is more firmly located in his style and grasp of the sensory than is often admitted; but claims that he resorts to this because of his unusual awareness of the mind as a separate entity, and his constant attempt to connect the finite and the infinite. O'Malley's *Shelley and Synaesthesia* demonstrates how much farther Fogle's arguments may be exploited; taking the image syndrome of the colours of the spectrum, music, and the evening star Venus, he shows how Shelley draws on their traditional values to reveal unity in multineity and the interconnection of earthly and spiritual within human consciousness.

To some Shelley scholars such intensive critical navel-gazing is false to the very spirit of Shelley; his aspirations are committed to the general and universal, never to the minutiae of text or experience. This distrust is certainly experienced by J. A. Notopoulos and Neville Rogers, analysts of Shelley's indebtedness, in fact and essence, to Plato. The former's *The Platonism of Shelley* (see TEXTS) is basically a source study containing a detailed inventory of Shelley's borrowings, although it does warn that 'Platonism' is as much a mode of experience as a prerogative dependent on Plato's dialogues. Accepting this assessment of the indebtedness, Rogers's *Shelley at Work* traces the Platonic journey past the shadows of cave, river, boat, veil, and so on. The book disappoints because its thesis relies so little on the author's researches among the 'workshop' notebooks, although there are interesting accounts of the genesis of 'Ode to the West Wind' and other lyrics, and a stimulating discussion of Shelley's intellectual pilgrimage in the mind's 'wilderness of intricate paths'. However much this particular reliance on Plato is questioned, no critic can doubt that Shelley's reading was rivalled only by that of Coleridge in scope, and that he is the only major English philosophic poet. Consequently there have been many similar attempts to press his writing into some single intellectual mould, such as the Platonic, even though such accounts have been compelled either to omit certain works or conclude that Shelley held contradictory views.

A valuable book here is C. E. Pulos's *The Deep Truth*, which affirms Shelley's consistency as a thinker by identifying Hume as his mentor and the sceptical tradition as his school.

There remains one final approach in this survey, that which considers Shelley as a social commentator. Shelley stands out from his fellow-Romantics as the one who wrote political verse and essays throughout his career. But this fact has been largely ignored save as the decadent temptation of materialism resisted in Shelley's more spiritual moments. G. M. Matthews's 'A Volcano's Voice in Shelley' shows how unwarranted this critical affected superiority is, since the revolution never lies far from his thoughts. The most detailed study of this is K. N. Cameron's *The Young Shelley*. Primarily the biography of a political radical, this traces the development of Shelley's social views into the poetry of *Queen Mab*. The detailed footnotes analyse the evidence for such an interpretation. Such studies are limited, unavoidably it would seem on the evidence of this book and McTaggart's monograph mentioned above (see TEXTS), because of the disparity between the scholar's ability as a literary critic and his knowledge as a student of history. This state of affairs can only be remedied when critics are prepared to discard their specialist shells, and recognize that interpretations change as radically over the years in other disciplines as in their own. Otherwise accounts of Shelley, the politically committed radical, will remain untrue to their subject, being out of touch with historical scholarship.

As noted before, these books have helped to establish the directions of Shelley criticism as well as providing substantial analyses of individual works. In supplementing these I have deliberately restricted myself to articles that, through their scholarship, have established a particular reading, or to more controversial criticism that has assisted subsequent discussion.

An influential interpretation of 'Mont Blanc' is offered by I. J. Kapstein's 'The Meaning of "Mont Blanc" ', where it is claimed that Shelley is, virtually in the same breath, trying to affirm the freedom and authority of the mind and the universal control of an external religious power. Charles H. Vivian's refutation of this, 'The One "Mont Blanc" ', is less conclusive, but Vivian does assert the important premiss that the poem is experimental rather than conclusive, concerned with the experience of grappling with such metaphysical problems. But both accounts have been recently superseded by E. B. Murray's 'Mont Blanc's Unfurled Veil', which, taking a single textual crux as its point of departure, goes on to offer a stimulating reading of the poem in terms of Shelley's poetry as a whole. The same contradiction, however, between idealist and empiricist in Shelley has been noted in *Alastor*, specifically between Shelley's declaration in the Preface and the argument of the poem itself. The classic case for the poem's unity is put by E. K. Gibson, in '*Alastor*: An Interpretation', which summarizes the theme as 'the temptation of the idealist to live a solitary life rather than find partial ideals of love and human companionship in this present world'.

The Revolt of Islam (1818) has received little attention outside the chronoligical surveys, with the important exception of Brian Wilkie's discussion in *Romantic Poets and Epic Tradition*. In this study of the Romantics' epic aspirations Wilkie defines Shelley's attitudes to epic, and shows how, with his strong historical sense, he can offer his cantos as both objectively true to the past and yet faithful to human truth. A central theme is that of Shelley consciously working within the epic tradition.

G. M. Matthews's ' "Julian and Maddalo": the Draft and the Meaning' replaces much earlier speculation on origins and identities by being based on manuscript study. He demonstrates that the poem was carefully planned by Shelley, and, more important, that though biographical elements are present they do not limit the meaning: the maniac is *the* poet and not any particular writer. Matthews also notes the connection with *Prometheus Unbound*, being written at the same time. The temptation of 'every critic his own allegorist' has made this lyric drama central to any thesis, and stimulating inter-pretations are offered by Bloom, Wilson, Woodman, and Matthews. The most detailed account is certainly Earl R. Wasserman's *Shelley's 'Prometheus Unbound'*, though this is also credited with being the most difficult work of Shelley criticism. As elsewhere, Wasserman assumes the internal consistency of the play and applies Shelley's own theories to his poetic practice. Many of his illustrations—of Shelley's employment of unconnected myths within a mythopaeic structure, of his ironic juxtaposition of the original Aeschylean play, of his allegorical treatment of characters that allows their comprehensive identification—have implications beyond *Prometheus* itself. But the reader must recognize the problems in his account of Shelley's philosophic position and the dangers in such a sophisticated inter-pretation. A much older book, and one currently being given a new lease of life, is Carl Grabo's *A Newton Among the Poets*. The theme is defined in the subtitle, 'Shelley's Use of Science in *Prometheus Unbound*'. Quoting what is known about Shelley's interest in science, especially chemistry and electricity, Grabo analyses various difficult passages in the play in terms of contemporary scientific theories. In addition to explicating seemingly impenetrable lines, Grabo suggests the significance within this scientific setting of the recurrent imagery of light, and invisible forces. Shelley's actual indebtedness to science is assessed more sensibly in King-Hele's chapter concerning this.

Although not directly dealing with *Prometheus Unbound*, M. M. Rader's 'Shelley's Theory of Evil Misunderstood' makes an important contribution to destroying the tradition that the drama is statically optimistic, lacking a climax, because of the belief, originally established by Mary Shelley's note, that 'mankind had only to will that there would be no evil, and there would be none'. Radar demonstrates the errors that Mary's statement has proliferated, and cogently argues that Shelley at the same time saw evil as both operating subjectively in human minds and liable to removal only in time and through violent revolution.

A study akin to that of G. M. Matthews is Joseph Raben's 'Shelley's *Prometheus Unbound*: Why the Indian Caucasus?' The two critics share the conviction that Shelley consciously relied on current pseudo-scientific doctrines to define and universalize his themes. Raben shows that the Indian Caucasus, the setting for the play, were commonly held to be the original centre of human civilization and that geologically they still dominated the world. For K. N. Cameron, however, such insistence on the actual must lead to political allegory, and in 'The Political Symbolism of *Prometheus Unbound*' he identifies the drama's characters and events in the French Revolution and post-war Europe. An obvious limitation is Cameron's sidestepping of the poetry's complexity to make Shelley's political creed consistent.

The most detailed account of *Adonais* (1821) is that by E. R. Wasserman in *The Subtler Language*. In *Shores of Darkness*, the classic account of the Romantic rediscovery of classical myth, Edward B. Hungerford distinguishes the different levels to which the poem's myths have to apply and the conflict set up between these. R. A. Foakes (1958) handles related material in his demonstration of how Shelley framed his own myth through the use of traditional words and narratives. This general assumption that the poem draws on the available literature for its context is not new, however, and John Taafe's annotations, transcribed by R. H. Fogle with a brief commentary, reveal how much one of Shelly's more scholarly friends recognized this.

In recent years the evaluation of Shelley's final, unfinished poem 'The Triumph of Life' has been much debated. Helpful contexts are established by two articles: in 'The Secrets of an Elder Day: Shelley after *Hellas*' J. J. McGann argues that by 1822 Shelley was approaching a near-Keatsian humanism with 'an affirmation of the possibility of Imaginative Life in a world that will not support a perfection of the type urged in *Prometheus Unbound*'; while in ' "A Devil of a Nut to Crack": Shelley's *Charles the First*' R. B. Woodings analyses the motives involved in the attempt to write this historical drama, and suggests how these prepared Shelley for the vision of the final poem. Specific accounts of 'The Triumph' must start with A. C. Bradley's still valuable 'Notes on Shelley's "Triumph of Life" ', in which he identifies the 'imitations' of Dante and Petrarch. The neatest interpretation of the poem is found in Kenneth Allott's 'Bloom on "The Triumph of Life" ', written as a refutal of Bloom's eccentric pleading, but greater complexity is allowed the poem in P. H. Butter's 'Sun and Shape in Shelley's "The Triumph of Life" '. Butter considers the poem in terms of the other late lyrics, an approach followed by G. M. Matthews. Unfortunately, part of the latter's succinct account, 'On Shelley's "The Triumph of Life" ', is invalidated by the dubious manuscript readings he accepted in 'Shelley and Jane Williams' to associate the poem with Shelley's love affair with his friend's wife. These questionable readings were exposed by D. H. Reiman in 'Shelley's "The Triumph of Life": The Biographical Problem', which, for all its brevity, makes a more satisfactory case for Shelley's indebtedness to Rousseau's *La Nouvelle Héloise* than does his depressingly expanded account in the Introduction to his edition. Despite this unsupported stress on Shelley's personal predicament, Matthews' account remains central to an understanding of the poem: his perceptive analysis brings out the relation between the narrator and Rousseau, Shelley's evaluation of Rousseau, and the failure of Life's victims through surrender to their acquisitive instincts.

Although many articles have been devoted to Shelley's lyrics, their significant conclusions have been utilized in such substantial accounts as those by Rogers and King-Hele. Peter Mortensen's 'Image and Structure in Shelley's Longer Lyrics' parallels his lyric organization with that outlined by Martz as distinctive of the metaphysical religious poets, noting Shelley's reliance on a 'core image' and the firm progressive development of each lyric. R. H. Fogle in 'The Imaginal Design of Shelley's "Ode to the West Wind" ', and S. C. Wilcox in 'The Sources, Symbolism, and Unity of Shelley's "Skylark" ', offer readings of two of the finest lyrics, while D. H. Reiman examines the flexibility of imagery in 'Lines written among the Eugenean Hills'. More generally, Donald Davie's chapter on 'Shelley's Urbanity' in his *Purity of Diction in English Verse* demonstrates the range of tone that Shelley can achieve when he avoids the pretentious and prurient. In a much more obvious way N. F. Ford demonstrates that critics have been too ready to expect a seriousness of statement in Shelley that the verbal detail will not support in 'The Wit in Shelley's Poetry' and 'Paradox and Irony in Shelley's Poetry'. Clearly all these critics are bothered by the continuing prominence of Shelley's reputation as a predominantly lyric poet. In a fine essay that treats the subject in the tone it merits G. M. Matthews (1969) points to the obvious but so often overlooked fact that, compared with other poets, Shelley wrote very few lyrics for publication, and of these even fewer were intended as the self-expression of personal predicaments. Having discussed several of the so-called 'personal' poems, Matthews bravely remarks that no critic should make 'any pronouncement on a given poem's qualities until the *nature* and *function* of the poem have been inquired into'. Like a contemporary poet such as W. H. Auden, Shelley was a professional who was expected to, and did, produce truly occasional verse, 'not self-expression but artifice, creative play'. It is this same ability to suit the tone to the audience that J. M. Hall in part illustrates in his clear analysis of the *Letter to Maria Gisborne*, although his main thesis is that in this poem, as elsewhere, Shelley is concerned with his constant preoccupation, by the problems confronting the poet in a world hostile to art.

Yet another critical legend is tackled in E. E. Bostetter's 'Shelley and the Mutinous Flesh', ultimately a vindication of the poet's healthy sexuality. But the picture of the inspired dreamer is being most effectively displaced by the growing respect for Shelley's intelligence, analysed through studies of his reading and critical response to other writers. A fascinating analysis of the stimulus they provided is given in Joseph Raben's 'Milton's Influence on Shelley's Translation of Dante's "Matilda Gathering Flowers" '. As the title indicates, Raben shows in detail how Shelley strives to achieve the spirit of the original Italian through his own comprehension of another prophetic poet, and thus claim his rightful place in what he saw as the living European literary tradition. Once again, as Judith Charnaik shows in her article 'The Figure of the Poet in Shelley', his apparent self-dramatizations are in fact conscious fictions, drawn to tackle the complex relationship between the personal and traditional; for Shelley envisaged the artist's function with the same seriousness as critics have allowed for so long to an Arnold or Henry James.

Although quotations are ferreted from Shelley's prose writings, even *A Defence of Poetry* remains more mentioned than analysed—and then for its *non-sequiturs* and implausible declarations. The most detailed account of the essay is that by E. R. Wasserman, 'Shelley's Last Poetics: a Reconsideration'. Accepting Shelley's own terms as he defined them in other essay fragments, Wasserman shows how he surmounts the contradictions of a mimetic theory by the elaboration of a system that can embrace more limited theoretical concepts: the imagination is envisaged entirely as an organizing principle, and his poetic ideal is defined as more completely holistic than any envisaged by his modern detractors. More relevant, because it traces the impact of the theory on the actual poetry, is Earl J. Schulze's *Shelley's Theory of Poetry: a Reappraisal*. He discusses how Shelley sees poetry, metaphoric in its essence, as presenting unique experience, and given unity through its reliance on the functioning of human consciousness. The integrity with which he credits Shelley may be seen as the key to much contemporary criticism, criticism that has sought to justify his distinctive imagery and language within an increased understanding of the poetic themes.

The survival of many of the critical legends is proven by the controversy that still surrounds Shelley, but gradually the various approaches described above, restricted as many are by their jargon and thesis-imposing nature, have begun to produce a more comprehensive view of the poet. The briefest such account, and probably the best general introduction to Shelley, is the pamphlet contributed by G. M. Matthews to the British Council series, 'Writers and their Work'. By drawing on the knowledge accumulated as a Shelley specialist, Matthews finely integrates criticism with scholarship, textual interpretation with biographical documentation. Although less elegantly written, Gerald McNeice's *Shelley and the Revolutionary Idea* represents a similar tendency, for he too takes for granted the unity of the poetry, refusing to segment Shelley or his work. McNeice's Shelley does tread the humble earth, and his poetry is successful because of Shelley's very humanity: 'although to our confused age he may still look an outmoded optimist, the poet's passionate advocacy was never without its reaction into near despair.'

BIOGRAPHIES AND LETTERS

The skeletons that haunt Shelley's biography have certainly contributed to the most insistent of the legends: his impracticability, amorality, and intellectual hypocrisy in the treatment of his women-folk. Because it confronted these tales, N. I. White's biography,

Shelley, with its detailed impartial documentation, is a landmark in Shelley scholarship. Through his own researches and his careful sifting of the available evidence White charts Shelley's behaviour during the major crises. As well as presenting a more realistic portrait of Shelley (complete with a sense of social responsibility, personal honour, and humour), White corrects the chronology of the poems and draws attention, through his critical summaries, to writings, such as the essays, that have tended to get ignored. Of other accounts, C. L. Cline's *Byron, Shelley, and their Pisan Circle* and W. H. Marshall's *Byron, Shelley, Hunt, and 'The Liberal'* concentrate on the final years, although without providing much new information. Restressing Shelley's personal qualities, John Buxton's *Byron and Shelley, the History of a Friendship* offers a very readable account of the relationship between the two poets. He argues that this friendship is the most significant personal contact that either enjoyed, providing not a mutual source of literary borrowing but a stimulation that provoked each to produce new poetry as the result of their meetings and their acute perception of each other's poetic qualities. As is frequently declared, Edmund Blunden's *Shelley, a Life Story* is the most readable of the general biographies, though limited in its critical comments. For the present, White's biography remains essential reading (and he himself reissued it in a more popular format as *Portrait of Shelley*), but many of its details concerning Shelley's activities and the dating of individual poems must be emended as a result of the emergence of material that has come to light since 1940.

It would be wrong, however, to suggest that the controversies have been silenced by White's labours. For example, Louise Boas in *Harriet Shelley* sets about a vindication of Shelley's first wife with an ardour that must have repercussions on more than the reputation of the Shelley family. Still very helpful, despite the autobiographic inspiration and occasional deliberate fabrications of the truth, are the memoirs of Shelley's own friends, especially Hogg's *The Life of Shelley*, Edward Trelawney's *Recollections of Shelley, Byron and the Author*, and Peacock's *Memoirs of Shelley*. These were brought together in a two-volume edition, *The Life of Shelley*, by Humbert Wolfe. Although a psychological and not a biographical account, Herbert Read's analysis of Shelley's personality in *In Defence of Shelley*, reprinted in *The True Voice of Feeling*, must be mentioned, since his description of the innate narcissism and unconscious homosexuality has found its way into more respectable critical accounts.

BIBLIOGRAPHIES

The New Cambridge Bibliography of English Literature provides a complete list of books and articles on Shelley up to 1967 compiled by G. M. Matthews, and includes a summary of the original editions. For items after that date the reader has to consult the relevant sections in one of the annual bibliographies (e.g. *PMLA*, and *English Language Notes*). The most comprehensive bibliography of Shelley studies, with entries usually accompanied by a brief explanatory note, is that annually published in the *Keats–Shelley Journal*. The *Journal's* lists for 1950–62 have been republished in a single volume edited by D. B. Green and E. G. Wilson. A selective uncritical account of Shelley studies for the graduate student is provided by B. Weaver in the *Modern Language Association's* collection, *The English Romantic Poets*, and an intelligent summary list by R. H. Fogle in his bibliographical guide, *Romantic Poets and Prose Writers*.

BACKGROUND READING

Romanticism Reconsidered (ed. N. Frye), a collection of papers delivered to the English Institute, provides a most provocative discussion of the Romantic poets which makes frequent reference to Shelley. M. H. Abrams contributes an historical interpretation, 'English Romanticism: The Spirit of the Age', in which he shows how the French Revolution was received as an apocalyptic revelation heralding a new age, complete with prophetic poets. He notes that even after the disillusionment that followed 1793 the ardour was not lost, but channelled from regeneration of the nations to recreation of the inner life. This discussion is particularly relevant to Shelley, as is Northrop Frye's essay, 'The Drunken Boat: The Revolutionary Element in Romanticism'. Too often, of course, such explanations are truer to their own terms than to the poets themselves, but the more searching essays do throw out ideas that illuminate particular aspects. Key essays in this endeavour are collected together by Gleckner and Enscoe in *Romanticism: Points of View*, and these and many other features of European Romanticism are summarised in A. K. Thorlby's anthology, *The Romantic Movement*.

A classic study of the shift of critical perspective that occurred during the later eighteenth century is M. H. Abram's *The Mirror and the Lamp*. This is particularly good on Romantic theories of poetry and their relation to the types of poetry that, as a result, could be written. The account of Shelley's poetics, however, is disappointing. Writing within a more deliberate 'history of ideas' framework, E. R. Wasserman (1953 and 1964) traces the collapse of the analogical code of reference before the advance of empiricism, and speaks of the Romantic need, in the resultant uncertainty, to establish how 'the subjective and objective worlds carry on their transactions'. This same change in the concept of Nature is discussed in Basil Willey's *The Eighteenth-Century Background*, an account particularly relevant for understanding such influential thinkers as Hume, Hartley, and Godwin. J. Barrell, in his frequently cited *Shelley and the Thought of his Time*, sets his sights on the same goal of providing the 'background of ideas'. But although he summarizes the empiricist tradition and the rediscovery of the Greek thinkers, his discussion is embarrassingly superficial, doing as little justice to Plato as to Shelley. A. E. Rodway's selection, *Godwin and the Age of Transition*, is restricted to a single influence, but, allowing for the inevitable over-simplification, he offers useful, and readable, extracts from Godwin's prose.

Rodway's work for this obviously contributed to the formation of the views he advances in *The Romantic Conflict*, a stylistically infuriating book, but one which sets itself a rewarding objective— to offer a sociological analysis of major Romantic poetry. For his sources Rodway draws heavily on A. Cobban's anthology, *The Debate on the French Revolution*. A study of a more limited influence is offered by C. P. Brand's *Italy and the English Romantics*, an account of the factors that attracted Shelley and other writers to Italy and Italian culture.

Shelley's own involvement with contemporary politics provides a most suitable conclusion to this section. The most comprehensive presentation of the period remains that of Halévy, in *England in 1815* and *The Liberal Awakening, 1815–1830*, but the tensions of the period can be more immediately understood through R. J. White's *From Waterloo to Peterloo* and G. Carnall's *Robert Southey and His Age*. Both these accounts, however, must be consulted alongside E. P. Thompson's brilliant *The Making of the English Working Class*, a book which reveals to the attentive student the sources for many of Shelley's images. R. D. Altick's *The English Common Reader* provides a background for understanding Shelley's struggle to achieve an audience, while R. W. Harris's *Romanticism and the Social Order*, infuriating though it is to the trained student of literature, excellently conveys something of the excitement, 'the cloud of mind . . . discharging its collected lightning', that compelled Shelley to continue to write.

REFERENCES

References to Ridenour and to Woodings are to the collections of critical essays cited below under CRITICAL STUDIES.

TEXTS

C. Baker (ed.), *The Selected Poetry and Prose of Percy Bysshe Shelley* (paperback, New York, 1951).

H. F. B. Brett-Smith (ed.), *Peacock's 'Four Ages of Poetry', Shelley's 'Defence of Poetry', Browning's 'Essay on Shelley'* (Oxford, 1921).

K. N. Cameron (ed.), *Percy Bysshe Shelley: Selected Poetry and Prose* (paperback, New York, 1951; paperback, U.K.).

K. N. Cameron (ed.), *Shelley and his Circle, 1773–1822* (London and Cambridge, Mass., 1961–).

K. N. Cameron (ed.), *The Esdaile Notebook: a volume of early poems* (London and New York, 1964).

D. L. Clark (ed.), *Shelley's Prose, or, the Trumpet of a Prophecy* (Albuquerque, N. Mex., 1954; paperback, U.S.).

A. S. B. Glover (ed.), *Shelley: Selected Poetry, Prose and Letters* (Nonesuch edn., London, 1951).

J. Holloway (ed.), *Selected Poems of Percy Bysshe Shelley* (London, 1960; paperback, U.K.).

A. M. D. Hughes (ed.), *Shelley: Poems published in 1820*, 2nd edn. (Oxford, 1957).

T. Hutchinson (ed.), *The Complete Poetical Works of Percy Bysshe Shelley*, reset edn. (Oxford Standard Authors, London, 1943; paperback, U.S.); rev. G. M. Matthews (Oxford Paperback, London, 1970).

R. Ingpen and W. E. Peck (eds.), *The Complete Works of Percy Bysshe Shelley* (10 vols., London and New York, 1926–30 and 1965).

F. L. Jones (ed.), *The Letters of Percy Bysshe Shelley* (2 vols., Oxford, 1964).

F. L. Jones (ed.), *The Letters of Mary W. Shelley* (2 vols., Norman, Okla., 1944).

F. L. Jones (ed.), *Mary Shelley's Journal* (Norman, Okla., 1947).

F. L. Jones (ed.), *Maria Gisborne and Edward E. Williams, Shelley's Friends: their Journals and Letters* (Norman, Okla., 1951).

J. E. Jordan (ed.), *Shelley: 'A Defence of Poetry'* (paperback, Indianapolis, Ind., 1965).

W. J. McTaggart (ed.), *England in 1819: Church, State and Poverty* (paperback, London, 1970).

G. M. Matthews (ed.), *Shelley: Selected Poems and Prose* (London, 1964).

B. R. McElderry, Jr. (ed.), *Shelley's Critical Prose* (paperback, Lincoln, Nebr., 1967).

J. A. Notopoulos, *The Platonism of Shelley* (Durham, N.C., 1949 and Cambridge, 1950).

J. A. Notopoulos, 'New Texts of Shelley's Plato', *Keats–Shelley Journal*, xv (1966).

D. H. Reiman, *Shelley's 'The Triumph of Life': a Critical Study* (Urbana, Ill., 1965).

N. Rogers (ed.), *The Esdaile Poems* (Oxford, 1966).

N. Rogers (ed.), *Percy Bysshe Shelley: Selected Poetry* (paperback, Boston, Mass., 1968; paperback, U.K.).

M. K. Stocking (ed.), *The Journals of Claire Clairmont* (Cambridge, Mass., 1968).

R. J. White, *Political Tracts of Wordsworth, Coleridge and Shelley* (Cambridge, 1953).

L. J. Zillman (ed.), *Shelley's 'Prometheus Unbound': a Variorum Edition* (Seattle, Wash., 1959).

L. J. Zillman (ed.), *Shelley's 'Prometheus Unbound': the Text and the Drafts* (New Haven, Conn., and London, 1968).

CRITICAL STUDIES AND COMMENTARY

K. Allott, 'Bloom on "The Triumph of Life" ', *EIC* x (1960).

C. Baker, *Shelley's Major Poetry: The Fabric of a Vision* (Princeton, N.J., 1948, and 1961; paperbacks, U.K. and U.S.).

H. Bloom, *Shelley's Mythmaking* (New Haven, Conn., 1959; paperbacks, U.K. and U.S.).

H. Bloom, *The Visionary Company* (New York, 1961, and London, 1962; paperback, U.S.).

E. E. Bostetter, *The Romantic Ventriloquists* (Seattle, Wash., 1963).

E. E. Bostetter, 'Shelley and the Mutinous Flesh', *Texas Studies in Literature and Language*, i (1959); and Woodings.

A. C. Bradley, 'Notes on Shelley's "Triumph of Life" ', *MLR* ix (1914).

P. H. Butter, 'Sun and Shape in Shelley's "The Triumph of Life" ', *RES* N.S. xiii (1962).

P. H. Butter, *Shelley's Idols of the Cave* (Edinburgh, 1954).

K. N. Cameron, *The Young Shelley: Genesis of a Radical* (New York, 1950, and London, 1951; paperbacks, U.K. and U.S.).

K. N. Cameron, 'The Political Symbolism of *Prometheus Unbound*', *PMLA* lviii (1943); and Woodings.

J. S. Charnaik, 'The Figure of the Poet in Shelley', *ELH* xxxv (1968).

C. C. Clarke, 'Shelley's "Tangled Boughs" ', *Durham University Journal*, liv (1961).

D. Davie, *Purity of Diction in English Verse*, 2nd edn. (London, 1967; paperback, U.K.).

R. A. Duerkson, *Shelleyan Ideas in Victorian Literature* (The Hague, 1966).

T. S. Eliot, *The Use of Poetry and the Use of Criticism*, 2nd edn. (London and New York, 1964; paperback, U.K.).

D. Erdman, W. Milgate, G. M. Matthews, *et al.*, 'Shelley's Grasp upon the Actual', *EIC* iv (1954).

R. A. Foakes, *The Romantic Assertion* (London, 1958).

R. H. Fogle, *The Imagery of Keats and Shelley* (Chapel Hill, N.C., 1949 and 1962; paperback, U.S.).

R. H. Fogle, 'John Taafe's annotated copy of *Adonais*', *Keats–Shelley Journal*, xvii (1968).

R. H. Fogle, 'The Imaginal Design of Shelley's "Ode to the West Wind" ', *ELH* xv (1948).

N. F. Ford, 'The Wit in Shelley's Poetry', *SEL* i (1961).

N. F. Ford, 'Paradox and Irony in Shelley's Poetry', *SP* lvii (1960).

E. K. Gibson, '*Alastor*: A Reinterpretation', *PMLA* lxii (1947).

C. Grabo, *A Newton Among the Poets* (Chapel Hill, N.C., 1930).

J. M. Hall, 'The Spider and the Silkworm: Shelley's "Letter to Maria Gisborne"', *Keats–Shelley Memorial Bulletin*, xx (1969).

D. W. Harding, 'Shelley's Poetry' in B. Ford (ed.), *Pelican Guide to English Literature: From Blake to Byron* (paperbacks, Harmondsworth and New York, 1957).

A. M. D. Hughes, *The Nascent Mind of Shelley* (Oxford, 1947).

D. J. Hughes, 'Potentiality in *Prometheus Unbound*', *Studies in Romanticism*, ii (1963); and Woodings.

D. J. Hughes, 'Coherence and Collapse in Shelley, with particular reference to *Epipsychidion*', *ELH* xxviii (1961).

D. J. Hughes, 'Kindling and Dwindling: The Poetic Process in Shelley', *Keats–Shelley Journal*, xiii (1964).

E. B. Hungerford, *Shores of Darkness* (New York, 1941 and 1963).

I. J. Kapstein, 'The Meaning of Shelley's "Mont Blanc" ', *PMLA* lxii (1947).

D. King-Hele, *Shelley: his Thought and Work* (London and New York, 1960).

G. Wilson Knight, *The Starlit Dome: Studies in the Poetry of Vision*, 2nd edn. (London, 1959).

F. R. Leavis, *Revaluation* (London, 1936; paperbacks, U.K. and U.S.).

C. S. Lewis, *Rehabilitations and Other Essays* (London, 1939).

G. M. Matthews, 'A Volcano's Voice in Shelley', *ELH* xxiv (1957); and Woodings, and Ridenour.

G. M. Matthews, 'Shelley and Jane Williams', *RES* N.S. xii (1961).

G. M. Matthews, ' "Julian and Maddalo": the Draft and the Meaning', *Studia Neophilologia*, xxxv (1963).

G. M. Matthews, 'On Shelley's "The Triumph of Life" ', *Studia Neophilologia*, xxxiv (1962).

G. M. Matthews, *Shelley* (paperback, British Council, London, 1970; paperback, U.S.).

G. M. Matthews, 'Shelley's Lyrics', in D. W. Jefferson (ed.), *The Morality of Art: essays presented to G. Wilson Knight* (London, 1969).

J. J. McGann, 'The Secrets of an Elder Day: Shelley after *Hellas*', *Keats–Shelley Journal*, xv (1966); and Woodings.

G. McNiece, *Shelley and the Revolutionary Idea* (Cambridge, Mass., 1969).

P. Mortenson, 'Image and Structure in Shelley's Longer Lyrics', *Studies in Romanticism*, iv (1964).

E. B. Murray, 'Mont Blanc's Unfurled Veil', *Keats–Shelley Journal*, xviii (1969)

S. Norman, *Flight of the Skylark: The Development of Shelley's Reputation* (Norman, Okla. and London, 1954).

G. O'Malley, *Shelley and Synaesthesia* (Evanston, Ill., 1964).

D. Perkins, *The Quest for Permanence: the symbolism of Wordsworth, Shelley and Keats* (Cambridge, Mass., 1959).

F. A. Pottle, 'The Case of Shelley', *PMLA* lxvii (1952); and Woodings.

C. E. Pulos, *The Deep Truth: A Study of Shelley's Scepticism* (Lincoln, Nebr., 1954; paperback, U.S.).

J. Raben, 'Shelley's *Prometheus Unbound:* Why the Indian Caucasus?', *Keats–Shelley Journal*, xii (1963).

J. Raben, 'Milton's Influence on Shelley's Translation of Dante's "Matilda Gathering Flowers" ', *RES* N.S. xiv (1963); and rev. Woodings.

M. M. Rader, 'Shelley's Theory of Evil Misunderstood', *Western Reserve University Bulletin*, 23 (1930); and rev. Ridenour.

D. H. Reiman, 'Structure, Symbol, and Theme "in Lines Written among the Euganean Hills" ', *PMLA* lxxvii (1962).

D. H. Reiman, 'Shelley's "The Triumph of Life": the Biographical Problem', *PMLA* lxxviii (1963).

G. M. Ridenour (ed.), *Shelley: A Collection of Critical Essays* (Englewood Cliffs, N.J., 1965; paperbacks, U.K. and U.S.).

N. Rogers, *Shelley at Work*, 2nd edn. (Oxford, 1967).

E. J. Schulze, *Shelley's Theory of Poetry: a Reappraisal* (The Hague, 1966).

S. Spender, *Shelley* (paperback, British Council, London, 1952; paperback, U.S.).

C. H. Vivian, 'The One "Mont Blanc" ', *Keats–Shelley Journal*, iv (1955).

E. R. Wasserman, *Shelley's 'Prometheus Unbound': a Critical Reading* (Baltimore, 1965).

E. R. Wasserman, *The Subtler Language: Critical Readings of Neoclassic and Romantic Poems* (Baltimore, 1959; paperbacks, U.S. and U.K.).

E. R. Wasserman, 'Shelley's Last Poetics: a Reconsideration', in F. W. Hilles and H. Bloom (eds.), *From Sensibility to Romanticism* (New York and London, 1965).

N. I. White, *The Unextinguished Hearth: Shelley and his Contemporary Critics* (Durham, N.C., 1938 and 1968).

S. C. Wilcox, 'The Sources, Symbolism, and Unity of Shelley's "Skylark"', *SP* xlvi (1949).

B. Wilkie, *Romantic Poets and Epic Tradition* (Madison, Wis., 1965).

M. Wilson, *Shelley's Later Poetry: a Study of his Prophetic Imagination* (New York, 1959).

R. B. Woodings (ed.), *Shelley: Modern Judgements* (London, 1968; paperback, U.K.).

R. B. Woodings, ' "A Devil of a Nut to Crack": Shelley's *Charles the First*', *Studia Neophilologia*, xl (1968).

R. G. Woodman, *The Apocalyptic Vision in the Poetry of Shelley* (Toronto, 1964).

W. B. Yeats, 'The Philosophy of Shelley's Poetry', repr. in *Essays and Introductions* (London and New York 1961; paperback, U.S.).

BIOGRAPHIES AND LETTERS

E. Blunden, *Shelley, a Life Story* (London, 1946; paperbacks, U.K. and U.S.).

L. S. Boas, *Harriet Shelley: Five Long Years* (London, 1962).

J. Buxton, *Byron and Shelley* (London, 1968).

C. L. Cline, *Byron, Shelley, and their Pisan Circle* (London and Cambridge, Mass., 1952).

W. H. Marshall, *Byron, Shelley, Hunt, and 'The Liberal'* (London and Philadelphia, 1960).

H. Read, *The True Voice of Feeling* (London and New York, 1953; paperback, U.K.).

N. I. White, *Shelley* (2 vols., New York, 1940, and London, 1947).

N. I. White, *Portrait of Shelley* (New York, 1945).

H. Wolfe (ed.), *The Life of Percy Bysshe Shelley* (2 vols., London and New York, 1933).

BIBLIOGRAPHIES

R. H. Fogle (ed.), *Romantic Poets and Prose Writers* (paperback, New York, 1967).

D. B. Green and E. G. Wilson (eds.), *Keats, Shelley, Byron, and their Circles: a Bibliography, 1950–1962* (Lincoln, Nebr., 1964).

G. G. Watson (ed.), *N.C.B.E.L.*, vol. iii (Cambridge and New York, 1969).

B. Weaver, in T. M. Raysor (ed.), *The English Romantic Poets*, 2nd edn. (Mod. Lang. Assoc., New York, 1956).

BACKGROUND READING

M. H. Abrams, *The Mirror and the Lamp: Romantic Theory and the Critical Tradition* (London and New York, 1953; paperback, U.S.).

R. D. Altick, *The English Common Reader: A Social History of the Mass Reading Public, 1800–1900* (Chicago, Ill., and London, 1957; paperbacks, U.S. and U.K.).

J. Barrell, *Shelley and the Thought of his Time* (New Haven, Conn., 1947, and London, 1948).

C. P. Brand, *Italy and the English Romantics* (Cambridge, 1957).

G. Carnall, *Robert Southey and his Age: the Development of a Conservative Mind* (Oxford, 1960).

A. Cobban (ed.), *The Debate on the French Revolution 1789–1800*, 2nd edn. (London, 1960).

N. Frye (ed.), *Romanticism Reconsidered* (New York, 1963; paperbacks, U.S. and U.K.).

R. F. Gleckner and G. E. Enscoe (eds.), *Romanticism: Points of View* (paperback, Englewood Cliffs, N.J., 1962).

E. Halévy, *England in 1815*, 2nd edn. (London, 1949; paperbacks, U.K. and U.S.).

E. Halévy, *The Liberal Awakening, 1815–1830*, 2nd edn. (London, 1949; paperbacks, U.K. and U.S.).

R. W. Harris, *Romanticism and the Social Order, 1780–1830* (London, 1969; paperback, U.K.).

A. E. Rodway (ed.), *Godwin and the Age of Transition* (London, 1952).

A. E. Rodway, *The Romantic Conflict* (London, 1963).

E. P. Thompson, *The Making of the English Working Class* (London and New York, 1963); 2nd edn. (paperback, Harmondsworth, 1968).

A. K. Thorlby, *The Romantic Movement* (paperback, London, 1966; paperback, U.S.).

E. R. Wasserman, 'The English Romantics: the Grounds of Knowledge', *Studies in Romanticism*, iv (1964).

E. R. Wasserman, 'Nature Moralised: The Divine Analogy in the Eighteenth Century', *ELH* xx (1953).

R. J. White, *Waterloo to Peterloo* (London and New York, 1957; paperback, U.K.).

B. Willey, *The Eighteenth-Century Background* (London, 1940, and New York, 1941; paperbacks, U.K. and U.S.).

Robert Gittings

JOHN KEATS attracts annually more books and articles than any
other poet of the Romantic period; even Byron cannot beat his
record. Recent suggestions by critics that too much is written about
him do not seem to diminish 'that strange personal interest in all
that concerns him', first noted by his own publisher. The word
'personal' is both a clue and a warning. The staunch and attractive
personality that shines through the events of his life, the accounts by
his friends, and, above all, his own letters, has led to much self-
identification by those who have written on all aspects of the poet,
and invades texts, critical studies, biography, and background commentary. As one who has contributed to all these categories, I am
only too well aware of my own dangers in this direction. I have
therefore found it best in this bibliographical study to dispose, as
briefly and objectively as possible, of my own work first.

My *Selected Poems and Letters of John Keats* attempts to introduce,
with the major poems, a number of pieces not usually printed in such
selections, including the tragedy fragment 'King Stephen' and an
extract from 'The Cap and Bells'. Another innovation which may be
found helpful is that a representative selection of Keats's letters is
interspersed, in chronological order, with the poems, to which they
act as a supplement and sometimes commentary. It should be noted
that one of the major poems, 'Isabella', is only represented by an
extract. In the field of critical biography *John Keats: The Living Year*
first put forward, and demonstrated, through the greatest creative
year of Keats's life, the thesis that his general method of composition
was an almost instantaneous transmutation of impressions of all kinds
into poems, so that attention to the most ephemeral occasions of his
life may lead to a deeper appreciation of his work. This I still believe to be true, though I should severely prune and correct the book
for details which now seem erroneous or merely irrelevant. Part of the
object of my far larger *John Keats* was to do this, to extend the range
of study over the whole life, and to provide, factually at least, some
sort of final accuracy over many disputed or clouded questions, by
going to neglected original manuscript sources in England and the
United States. This produced what was recognized as a 'comprehen-

sive' life, the term used by B. Ifor Evans. On the other hand, as regards criticism, the book does little more than provide what I hope is an accurate summary of the main schools of thought, only adding what I realize are my own subjective insights as a poet. Though Lionel Trilling has called it 'impressive . . . . in critical perception', it has been found less satisfactory by some other American academic critics.

As specialized background to Keats, *The Mask of Keats* is a collection of essays, of which two only, 'Keats's Debt to Dante' and 'The Cap and Bells', have any stature, while *The Keats Inheritance* is a small, detailed study, providing, I hope, a full explanation of Keats's tragic and tangled finances, based on unpublished material at Keats House, Hampstead, and in the Public Record Office.

TEXTS

(*a*) *Poems*

The first attempt at a critical edition of Keats's poems is *The Poetical Works and Other Writings of John Keats* (1883), edited in four volumes by Harry Buxton Forman, and later revised with a supplementary volume added in 1890. Even if we put aside the various subsequent publications of Keats's writings in which Harry Buxton Forman and his son Maurice had a hand, no student, even today, can neglect this pioneer work of the elder Buxton Forman. He was the first to give, though with a somewhat unmethodical description of his sources, a mass of variant manuscript readings and of information regarding the composition of the poems, which are mainly collected in the first two volumes. Much valuable additional material includes Croker's review of 'Endymion' in the *Quarterly Review* (see below). Forman's single-volume Oxford edition of the poems lacks all this critical apparatus; but, reprinted eighteen times, it has much more in the way of variant readings than is usual in such editions, and is one of the best small collections ever produced.

After fifty years it was superseded by the edition of H. W. Garrod in the Oxford Standard Authors, which is, in turn, the best short complete edition in print. It has, however, none of Forman's critical apparatus, substituting a 'sheaf' of critical notes, in which Garrod is often impish rather than illuminating. The full scholarly Variorum edition (Oxford English Texts) is also Garrod's. Though in the main accurate and workmanlike, this edition needs treating with a certain amount of care, owing to the same tendencies as those which appear in the 'sheaf' of the O.S.A. edition. There are, even in the second edition, a number of obvious misprints (though not in the text itself) and failures to record or use accurately all available material. 'Lamia' probably comes off worst, as the editor quite deliberately neglected to collate one important source, while his conjectural account of Keats's revision of the final lines contains an elementary mistake. A prime omission is his failure to notice a first draft of stanzas 1 and 2 of the 'Ode on Melancholy', which has existed in photographic reproductions ever since 1895, while more recent documentary evidence has exposed the inherent fallacies of his dating of the composition of the various books of *Endymion*. For all its faults, particularly the wilful refusal, irritating to American scholars, to call the great sections of Keats MSS. in the Houghton Library, Harvard, by their proper catalogue designations, this is a fine and useful edition; yet it is a pity that Ernest de Selincourt's *The Poems of John Keats* has not been re-edited since 1926. Although necessarily now incomplete, it contains a great deal of wisdom and helpful suggestion in its very full notes. An excellent American edition, with some selected prose, is that of C. D. Thorpe; while a recent and brilliant piece of textual work by an American scholar is to be found in Literary Monographs, Vol. 1,: 'Richard Woodhouse's Interleaved and Annotated Copy of Keats's *Poems* (1817)', by Stuart M. Sperry, Jr. Among many selections, the most reliable and useful are those of J. H. Walsh and Roger Sharrock. M. R. Ridley's *Keats' Craftmanship* provides a detailed analysis of the stages of composition of 'The Eve of St. Agnes'.

(b) Letters

Keats's letters are now regarded as the indispensable accompaniment to his poems, and are so often printed with them, wholly or in part, that it is appropriate to consider them next. A brief selection was published in Monckton Milnes's first biography of the poet; thirty years later, Harry Buxton Forman aroused a Victorian furore by printing *Letters of John Keats to Fanny Brawne*, and continuing to do so in his further editions of Keats's work, despite a storm of abuse: 'Mr. Forman', as *Macmillan's Magazine* remarked, 'is apparently impenitent.' Since these letters have been dispersed and sold, the elder Forman's printing is now our sole source for many of them. He defiantly included them in his first single-volume edition of Keats's letters, in answer to Sir Sidney Colvin, who purposely omitted them in his deliberately titled *Letters of John Keats to his Family and Friends*, and who continued to do so in all reprints. Colvin also silently removed the poet's occasional excursions into lighthearted bawdy, and helped to create one of the most curious personal legends about Keats, that of the poet as a total innocent, a technique he also employed with the letters of Robert Louis Stevenson.

In 1931 Maurice Buxton Forman produced *The Letters of John Keats*, extended from his father's original edition of 1895; the fourth and last edition of Maurice's work appeared in 1952. The debt of all Keats readers to the Formans should not be lessened by the fact that their editions have now been superseded by that of a great American scholar, the late Hyder E. Rollins. Rollins's notes are full and deeply interesting. He also provides what is virtually a thirty-page diary of the events of Keats's life, with detailed source references. The only objection for the general reader is size—two large volumes—and price. A partial aid to overcoming these difficulties is the World's Classics volume, *Letters of John Keats*, selected by myself. Though not complete, it contains the larger part of Keats's letters in pocket format, and the Rollins text has been compared with originals and sometimes corrected.

CRITICAL STUDIES AND COMMENTARY

Owing to the voluminous background provided by the letters, there has always been a tendency to mix pure criticism with biography. There is, however, a clear line of books and articles which at any rate attempt to treat the poetry itself, without too much speculation about the life. Excluding the critical battles of Keats's own time and the damaging articles by J. G. Lockhart (*Blackwood's Edinburgh Magazine*, August 1818) and by John Croker (*Quarterly Review*, April 1818, but not published until September), the earliest work of this sort is in De Quincey's *Essays on the Poets and other English Writers*, whose perceptive praise of the poet is mixed with remarkable statements, such as "And yet upon his mother tongue, upon this English language, has Keats trampled as with the hoofs of a buffalo." Some equally remarkable and self-contradictory statements occur in Matthew Arnold's *The English Poets: Selections*, Vol. IV: *Wordsworth to Dobell*. Blinded by indignation at the very recently printed letters of Keats to Fanny Brawne, Arnold exploded on 'the sort of love-letter of a surgeon's apprentice which one might hear read out in the breach of promise case, or in the Divorce Courts', and continued, in the same vein, to condemn Keats's poetry for mere sensuousness. He then went on, altering his tone completely, to recognize the spiritual greatness of Keats, and to compare him with Shakespeare.

These conflicting views, reprinted by Arnold in *Essays in Criticism*, have continued to haunt many later attempts at Keats criticism; opposed sides on this topic were taken by Coventry Patmore and Gerard Manley Hopkins. Critical study less fiercely partisan, though often equally idiosyncratic, has come with our own century. H. W. Garrod's lectures as Professor of Poetry at Oxford, which he revised into his *Keats*, look more clearly at the poems than many more elaborate studies have succeeded in doing, though a few characteristic prejudices, such as Garrod's dislike of lady biographers, peep out.

The 1930s provided a trilogy of useful studies in T. S. Eliot's *The Use of Poetry and the Use of Criticism*, F. R. Leavis's *Revaluation*, and Douglas Bush's *Mythology and the Romantic Tradition in English Poetry*. Eliot briefly and a little grudgingly approves of the poetry, but highly praises the letters as a source of true poetic judgement, applicable as criticism to all types of poetry. Leavis's essay is a largely approving analysis of the major odes of Keats, with somewhat irrelevant asides on some previous critics. His major contribution is to pin-point something that has since become generally accepted, the 'profound tragic impersonality' of parts of 'The Fall of Hyperion', in which he saw farther than Eliot that 'poet and letter-writer are at last one'. For general purposes, apart from these special insights, the most full, considered and well-based article is the third, from Bush, which judiciously stresses both the traditional background and the unique creative quality of Keats.

The same type of study, emphasizing the background of Keats's thought and its philosophic nature, is found in an excellent book by D. G. James, *The Romantic Comedy*. More recent critical works have mostly come from America, but few are really satisfactory in their attempts to fit Keats to the Procrustean bed of New Criticism, though E. R. Wasserman's *The Finer Tone* is impressive, if discursive. Notable successes, however, are Lionel Trilling, with his intensely perceptive view of Keats's poetic character and personal philosophy, in his essay 'The Poet as Hero: Keats in his Letters' from *The Opposing Self*; and Cleanth Brooks's admirable analysis of the 'Ode on a Grecian Urn' in *The Well-Wrought Urn*. A book of studies from Liverpool University, edited by Kenneth Muir, *John Keats: a Reassessment*, provides essays of varying value, including some good comments by the editor himself on Keats and Hazlitt. Five interesting essays on Keats, by W. J. Bate, Cleanth Brooks, Douglas Bush, R. H. Fogle, and E. R. Wasserman, appear in *English Romantic Poets: Modern Essays in Criticism*, edited by M. H. Abrams. D. Perkins's *The Quest for Permanence* is also worth consulting.

BIOGRAPHIES AND LETTERS

Biographies of Keats have often displayed a tendency, bewildering to the reader, to ignore factual evidence and to rely on some scheme of insight allied with the biographer's own emotional relationship with the poet. This is perhaps accentuated by the 'chameleon' nature which Keats attributed to himself, the lack of 'identity', which has led to so many flatly contradictory interpretations of his character and his work, both in his own lifetime and since. Any biography of Keats has been bedevilled from the start by an accident part historical, part temperamental—the quarrels that broke out among his friends almost immediately after his death, and which prevented any Life by a contemporary. Monckton Milnes's *Life, Letters, and Literary Remains of John Keats* (1848; author created Lord Houghton in 1863) is in many ways an excellent performance; but, first appearing nearly thirty years after the poet's death, it regards the Regency Keats through Victorian spectacles, though this did not escape the keen eyes of an actual contemporary of Keats, Charles Wentworth Dilke. Milnes's picture of a gentlemanly and public-school Keats set the tone for almost every succeeding biography, and was partly responsible for a curious incident nearly thirty years later, in 1887, when two new biographies appeared simultaneously, Sidney Colvin's in the English Men of Letters series and W. M. Rossetti's in the Great Writers series. Rossetti wrote with considerably more realism than Colvin, and his criticism is worth noting, in particular his analysis of the 'Ode to a Nightingale'. His work, however, lacked a sense of proportion, and he made one fatal mistake with the Victorian reading public. He accepted the view, now supported by much contemporary medical evidence, that Keats had suffered from venereal disease. As an almost direct result, his *Life* has never been reprinted, while Colvin's, after several reprints, formed the basis for his *John Keats: his Life and Poetry, his Friends, Critics, and After-Fame*, which is a more detailed study in the Monckton Milnes manner.

Brash, dictatorial, and long-winded, Amy Lowell's *John Keats* nevertheless shows particular sensitivity to the younger Keats, and makes good use of what was then (1925) new material. A more modest and useful contribution by a woman writer is Dorothy Hewlett's *A Life of John Keats*. This work by a historical novelist is based on her earlier *Adonais*, whose main aim was 'to set Keats against the Georgian background'. In this it redresses some of the influence of Milnes and Colvin, though its use of authorities is vague, and some of its statements are fictional. One of the most exhaustive works on Keats and his poetry is Claude L. Finney's *The Evolution of Keats's Poetry*, which first saw some connection between the life and the works in a painstaking search for the source for almost every poem that Keats ever wrote. Though weak on the biographical side, and reprinted without reference to a mass of later evidence, it has great and continuing value as a reference book. In spite of some perversely wrong conclusions, notably about the relation between 'Hyperion' and 'The Fall of Hyperion'—Amy Lowell falls into the same error—its thoroughness has paved the way for many subsequent studies.

J. Middleton Murry's *Keats and Shakespeare* is a virtual biography, allied with themes which he continued to pursue through several differently titled studies in Keats, whose final version was his *Keats* of nearly thirty years after. Full of brilliant insights, Murry's work is about equally helped and harmed by its author's self-identification with Keats. Perhaps the best judgement on it was made by Murry himself as his own imaginary and sceptical critic: 'Mr. Murry insists that Keats means what he says, but when Keats says something that does not fit with Mr. Murry's theory, he has no compunction in declaring that Keats means the very opposite of what he says.' To be fair, Murry's insistence that Keats 'means what he says' outweighs a great deal of his own more personal and arbitrary interpretations. A very sound work which hovers between biography and criticism is E. C. Pettet's *On the Poetry of Keats*; while a similar study, Bernard Blackstone's *The Consecrated Urn*, mixes some moments of perception with a great amount of by-play with Erasmus Darwin and others, laying the author open to Keats's own criticism of those who 'jumble together Shakespeare and Darwin'.

Two large-scale biographies by American authors appeared within weeks of each other during the present decade; both had been in preparation for many years, though they were undoubtedly spurred to completion by Rollins's edition of the letters in the previous decade. It is tempting, therefore, to discuss *John Keats: the Making of a Poet* by Aileen Ward and *John Keats* by Walter Jackson Bate together. In fact, they each offer such different treatments of the poet that they are best appreciated apart.

Professor Ward has written a beautifully integrated book, in which biography and criticism are most aptly blended. Her own delightful style is perhaps a handicap, since it draws attention away from the soundness of much of her scholarship; her critical judgements are generalized, but often penetrating. She has been attacked, often unfairly and sometimes inaccurately, for trying to fit Keats into a Freudian casebook. Actually, this approach frequently succeeds, except where she allows it to obscure a clear reading of the text of the poems; for example, 'the languid sick' of the end of 'I Stood Tip-toe' does not mean 'a sick woman' (Keats's mother, according to Professor Ward)—'sick' is plainly a collective plural. She also falls into the traditional trap of sentimentalizing, and therefore Victorianizing, Fanny Brawne. Yet for narrative force, and effective use of what is sometimes the most tenuous material, this biography can be strongly recommended.

Its weakness lies in the one thing it has in common with Professor Bate's book. Both, while usually scrupulous in documentary sources for their criticism on the texts, accept as biographical evidence a strange and inconsistent variety of second-hand and even third-hand sources. This shows to particular disadvantage in Professor Bate, since he tends to separate the narrative of the life from his critical comments on the poems; the thirty-page chapter on 'Hyperion', containing elaborate and even diagrammatic discussions of prosody, leaves the story of Keats himself precisely where the previous chapter ended. It would be an over-simplification to recommend the book solely for its critical chapters, such as this, since on the occasions when Bate does use genuine first-hand biographical material he handles it honestly and acutely; yet one cannot agree with the American reviewer who found the biographical parts as 'superlative' as the critical, though one can genuinely endorse the same reviewer's verdict that Bate 'provides the best general analysis of Keats's poems to be found in any one book'. The two aspects of the book, in fact, do not coalesce; they seem written in different keys and even on different principles. For all this, the book triumphs as a monumental attempt to place Keats against a larger background of philosophic history and poetic tradition than any other writer seems to have seen.

Both these books are of very considerable length. A more recent work by another American, Douglas Bush, *John Keats: his Life and Writings*, achieves brevity in a comprehensive survey, unadventurous on the biographical side, but with much that is newly expressed on the critical. A genuinely brief and still valid biography is *Keats*, in the Great Lives series, by B. Ifor Evans.

BIBLIOGRAPHIES

The mass of material on Keats, confusing in its tangles of controversy and in its numerous revisions and fresh editions, has been fortunate to have so clear-headed a bibliographer as J. R. MacGillivray. He has not only provided a list of great accuracy, with frequent and helpful abbreviations of contents, but has added, in his *Keats: a Bibliography and Reference Guide*, a modest but profound Foreword which is the best essay on what Colvin called Keats's 'After-Fame'. An annual current bibliography is a regular department of the *Keats–Shelley Journal*, published by the Keats–Shelley Association of America. Its completeness and scholarship is another instance of the professional standards of that Journal, which make the English *Keats–Shelley Memorial Bulletin* look sadly amateur by contrast, though valuable work has made its first appearance in both. Ward's biography provides a good selective bibliography.

BACKGROUND READING

There remain an exceptional number of books which provide a background for Keats, by enlarging our knowledge of his friends, his circumstances, and his times. At the head of this section is the book which best allows Keats's friends to speak for themselves, *The Keats Circle: Letters and Papers, 1816–1878*, edited by Hyder E. Rollins. This record of the Harvard Keats Collection in the Houghton Library, supplemented by extracts from Keats material in another American collection, the Pierpont Morgan Library in New York, is as invaluable as the same editor's *Letters* for our knowledge of Keats, though a fresh edition including material that Rollins was unable to observe in both Harvard and New York would now make it even more valuable.

Among individual studies of more than incidental worth, Edmund Blunden's *Keats's Publisher* takes a high place, though several interesting aspects of the Taylor manuscripts, on which it is based, remain to be explored. After her over-enthusiastic *Fanny Brawne*, Joanna Richardson produced a well-balanced book in *The Everlasting Spell: A Study of Keats and his Friends*, the friends of the title being mainly Charles Brown and C. W. Dilke, whose disastrous quarrel she documents convincingly. Marie Adami's *Fanny Keats* is a charming study of the poet's sister, while the letters written to her after Keats left England by his fiancée Fanny Brawne, and now in Keats House, Hampstead, were edited by Fred Edgcumbe. D. H. Bodurtha and W. B. Pope edited Charles Armitage Brown's manuscript *Life of Keats*, which has since appeared in *The Keats Circle*.

Definitive work on Keats as a doctor remains to be done, though Charles W. Hagelman, Jr., has an unpublished University of Texas dissertation on 'John Keats and the Medical Profession', cited very effectively in Professor Ward's biography. As I have demonstrated in *John Keats* (Appendix 3), W. Hale-White's *Keats as Doctor and Patient* needs to be treated with some critical reserve as an account of the medical history of the time; a far better source for Keats's medical background is the lectures of his surgeon, Sir Astley Paston Cooper, printed in full in the first year's issue of *The Lancet*. Keats's own *Anatomical and Physiological Notebook*, edited by Maurice Buxton Forman is useful, though it has been shown to need some re-editing. The liveliest account of Keats's hospital days, though its references to Keats himself are fragmentary, is the *Memorials* of his fellow-student John Flint South (ed. C. L. Feltoe).

The friends of Keats have not, on the whole, been too fortunate in their biographers. John Hamilton Reynolds still awaits one, and so does Benjamin Bailey, a much more interesting character than most writers have allowed. There is no biography that does justice to Benjamin Robert Haydon, though his own *Autobiography* has been introduced by Edmund Blunden, and his immense *Diary* at last edited, though not very illuminatingly, by W. B. Pope, in an edition whose size and price intimidates. Edmund Blunden has painted *Leigh Hunt and his Circle* in a work full of sympathy and atmosphere, but weak on fact, while Hunt's own *Autobiography* (ed. J. E. Morpurgo) is more vague and airy about Keats than one would have hoped. Various monumental works on William Hazlitt fail to produce a spark of the man who, Keats said, had 'a demon'. Joseph Severn, whose own memories of Keats were highly untrustworthy, was rewarded with an even less trustworthy biographer himself in William Sharp, and later biographies have unfortunately followed Sharp rather than the Severn manuscript material at Harvard. Only *The Cowden-Clarkes*, Keats's schoolmaster and his wife Mary Victoria Novello, have been delightfully dealt with by Richard Altick, while Charles Cowden-Clarke's own memoir of Keats in his and his wife's *Recollections of Writers*, though shaky on chronology, reconstructs memorably the great moments, such as the composition of the sonnet 'On First Looking Into Chapman's Homer'. The political background of the whole of Keats's writing life is admirably covered by R. J. White's *Waterloo to Peterloo*.

Finally, as purely general background, Ian Jack's *English Literature, 1815–1832* fulfils several functions admirably. It gives a well-documented survey of the literary and social scene in the years when Keats wrote, a sensible essay on the poet himself, a most useful chronological table, and a wide bibliography. Dr. Jack's special study, *Keats and the Mirror of Art*, is also relevant to the aesthetic ideas of Keats's time; an excellent work on another aspect of these is Bernice Slote's *Keats and the Dramatic Principle*. Though Garrod's general contention that 'Of no other poet do we know so well both what he is and how he came to it' may seem to preclude much further work, the fascination exerted by Keats, noted at the beginning of this article, will undoubtedly continue to expand the bibliography. The open and engaging, and yet ultimately enigmatic, character of his life and work tempts each generation to interpret its own Keats.

REFERENCES

TEXTS

(*a*) *Poems*

E. de Selincourt, *The Poems of John Keats*, 5th edn. (Methuen, 1926).

H. B. Forman (ed.), *The Poetical Works and Other Writings of John Keats* (2 vols., London, 1883).

H. B. Forman (ed.), *The Complete Poetical Works of John Keats* (Oxford, 1907).

H. W. Garrod (ed.), *The Poetical Works of John Keats* (Oxford Standard Authors, London, 1956; paperbacks, U.K. and U.S.).

H. W. Garrod (ed.), *The Poetical Works of John Keats*, 2nd edn. (Oxford English Texts, Oxford, 1958).

R. Gittings (ed.), *Selected Poems and Letters of John Keats* (London, 1966; paperback, 1967).

M. R. Ridley, *Keats' Craftmanship* (London and New York, 1933 and 1962; paperbacks, U.K. and U.S.).

R. Sharrock (ed.), *Keats: Selected Poems and Letters* (Oxford, 1964).

S. M. Sperry, Jr., 'Richard Woodhouse's Interleaved and Annotated Copy of Keats's *Poems* (1817)' (Literary Monographs, vol. i, Madison, Wis., 1967).

C. D. Thorpe (ed.), *John Keats: Complete Poems and Selected Letters* (New York, 1935).

(*b*) *Letters*

S. Colvin (ed.), *Letters of John Keats to his Family and Friends*, 6th edn. (London and New York, 1928).

H. B. Forman (ed.), *Letters of John Keats to Fanny Brawne*, 2nd edn. (London, 1889).

M. B. Forman (ed.), *The Letters of John Keats*, 4th edn. (London, 1952).

R. Gittings (ed.), *Letters of John Keats, a New Selection* (paperback, Oxford, 1970).

H. E. Rollins (ed.), *The Letters of John Keats* (2 vols., Cambridge, Mass., and Cambridge, 1958).

J. H. Walsh (ed.), *Keats: Selected Letters and Poems* (London, 1954; paperback, U.K.).

CRITICAL STUDIES AND COMMENTARY

M. H. Abrams (ed.), *English Romantic Poets: Modern Essays in Criticism* (paperback, New York and London, 1960).

M. Arnold, 'John Keats', in *Essays in Criticism: Second Series* (London, 1888).

C. Brooks, 'Keats's Sylvan Historian: History Without Footnotes', in *The Well Wrought Urn* (New York, 1947; paperbacks, U.K. and U.S.).

D. Bush, 'Keats', in *Mythology and the Romantic Tradition in English Poetry* (Cambridge, Mass., 1937; paperback, U.S.).

T. De Quincey, 'John Keats', in *Essays on the Poets and Other English Writers* (Boston, 1853).

T. S. Eliot, 'Shelley and Keats', in *The Use of Poetry and the Use of Criticism*, 2nd edn. (London and New York, 1964; paperback, U.K.).

H. W. Garrod, *Keats*, 2nd edn. (Oxford, 1939).

D. G. James, 'Purgatory Blind', in *The Romantic Comedy* (London and New York, 1948; paperbacks, U.K. and U.S.).

F. R. Leavis, 'Keats', in *Revaluation: Tradition and Development in English Poetry* (London, 1936; paperbacks U.K. and U.S.).

K. Muir (ed.), *John Keats: a Reassessment* (Liverpool, 1958).

D. Perkins, *The Quest for Permanence: The Symbolism of Wordsworth, Shelley and Keats* (Cambridge, Mass., 1959).

L. Trilling, 'The Poet as Hero: Keats in his Letters', in *The Opposing Self: Nine Essays in Criticism* (London, 1955; paperback, U.S.); also as Introduction to *Selected Letters of John Keats* (New York, 1956).

E. R. Wasserman, *The Finer Tone: Keats's Major Poems* (Baltimore, 1953; paperbacks, U.K. and U.S.).

BIOGRAPHIES

(*For* LETTERS, *see* TEXTS *above*)

W. J. Bate, *John Keats* (Cambridge, Mass., 1963; paperbacks, U.K. and U.S.).

B. Blackstone, *The Consecrated Urn* (London, 1959).

D. Bush, *John Keats: his Life and Writings* (Boston, Mass., and London, 1966; paperback, U.S.).

S. Colvin, *Keats* (London and New York, 1887).

S. Colvin, *John Keats: his Life and Poetry, his Friends, Critics and After-Fame*, 3rd edn. (London, 1920).

B. I. Evans, *Keats*, 2nd edn. (London, 1938).

C. L. Finney, *The Evolution of Keats's Poetry* (New York, 1936; reprinted 1963).

R. Gittings, *John Keats: the Living Year* (London and Cambridge, Mass., 1954; paperback, U.K.).

R. Gittings, *John Keats* (London and Boston, 1968; paperbacks, U.K. and U.S.).

D. Hewlett, *A Life of John Keats*, 2nd edn. (London, 1949 and New York, 1950).

Lord Houghton (Richard Monckton Milnes), *Life and Letters of John Keats 1848* (London, 1951; paperback, U.K.).

A. Lowell, *John Keats* (2 vols., New York and London, 1925).

J. M. Murry, *Keats and Shakespeare* (London, 1925).

J. M. Murry, *Keats* (London, 1955; paperback, U.S.).

E. C. Pettet, *On the Poetry of Keats* (London, 1957).

W. M. Rossetti, *Life of John Keats* (London, 1887).

A. Ward, *John Keats: the Making of a Poet* (New York and London, 1963; paperbacks, U.K. and U.S.).

BIBLIOGRAPHIES

D. Hewlett (ed.), *Keats-Shelley Memorial Bulletin*, i–xxi (1900–70).

J. R. MacGillivray, *Keats: a Bibliography and Reference Guide*, (Toronto, 1949).

M. A. E. Steele (ed.) and others, *Keats-Shelley Journal*, i–xviii (1900–70).

BACKGROUND STUDIES

M. Adami, *Fanny Keats* (London, 1937).

R. Altick, *The Cowden-Clarkes* (London, 1948).

E. Blunden, *Keats's Publisher: A Memoir of John Taylor*, 2nd edn. (London, 1940).

E. Blunden, *Leigh Hunt and his Circle* (London, 1930).

D. H. Bodurtha and W. B. Pope (eds.), *Life of John Keats, by Charles Armitage Brown* (Oxford, 1937).

C. and M. Cowden-Clarke, *Recollections of Writers* (London, 1878; repr. 1969).

A. P. Cooper, 'Surgical Lectures', in *The Lancet* (1823–4).

F. Edgcumbe (ed.), *Letters of Fanny Brawne to Fanny Keats (1820–1824)* (Oxford, 1936).

C. L. Feltoe (ed.), *Memorials of John Flint South* (London, repr. of 1969).

M. B. Forman (ed.), *John Keats's Anatomical and Physiological Note Book* (Oxford, 1934).

R. Gittings, *The Keats Inheritance* (London and New York, 1964).

R. Gittings, *The Mask of Keats: a Study of Problems* (London and Cambridge, Mass., 1956).

W. Hale-White, *Keats as Doctor and Patient* (Oxford, 1938).

B. R. Haydon, *Autobiography*, with an Introduction by Edmund Blunden (Oxford, 1927).

I. Jack, *English Literature, 1815–1832* (O.H.E.L., vol. x, Oxford, 1963).

I. Jack, *Keats and the Mirror of Art* (Oxford, 1967).

J. E. Morpurgo (ed.), *The Autobiography of Leigh Hunt* (London, 1949).

W. B. Pope (ed.), *The Diary of Benjamin Robert Haydon* (5 vols. Cambridge, Mass., 1960–3).

J. Richardson, *Fanny Brawne* (London, 1952).

J. Richardson, *The Everlasting Spell* (London, 1963).

H. E. Rollins (ed.), *The Keats Circle: Letters and Papers, 1816–78*, 2nd edn. (2 vols., Cambridge, Mass., and Oxford, 1965).

W. Sharp, *The Life and Letters of Joseph Severn* (London, 1892).

B. Slote, *Keats and the Dramatic Principle* (New York, 1958).

R. J. White, *Waterloo to Peterloo* (London and New York, 1957; paperback, U.K.).

John Dixon Hunt

TEXTS

The best text of the poetry so far, and certainly the standard text
for some years to come, is that edited by Christopher Ricks. For the
first time in one volume are all known poems by Tennyson, including his juvenilia and various items suppressed during his career.
The text is annotated, alterations between editions noted, and each
poem provided with a commentary that seeks to explain allusions,
establishes important cross references to other poems or biographical
material, and generally provides the contextual and critical apparatus hitherto lacking for Victorian poets. Ricks's edition thus supersedes the volume in the Oxford Standard Authors, which nevertheless is still the most accessible text (double-columned) of the plays.
Earlier editions worth consulting for their notes are the Eversley
(ed. Hallam Tennyson) and the Cambridge Poets (ed. W. W. Rolfe).
There have inevitably been many selections of Tennyson's poetry,
each trying in some way to promote or save his reputation by selecting what each editor considered the essential or most respectable
Tennyson. The poet himself supervised some *Selections*, issued by his
publisher Moxon in 1865; among later examples the following are
interesting for their critical introductions and for the image of the
poet that the selections project—by F. L. Lucas, T. S. Eliot, W. H.
Auden, Douglas Bush, J. H. Buckley, H. M. McLuan, and B. C.
Southam: this last is especially recommended for its Introduction
and notes.

CRITICAL STUDIES AND COMMENTARY

Some idea of how Tennyson was treated by critics during his lifetime may conveniently be gathered in *Tennyson: the Critical Heritage*,
edited by John D. Jump. The collection of reviews and articles includes the early attacks by J. W. Croker and John Wilson ('Christopher North'), as well as other important essays by J. S. Mill, A. H.
Hallam, W. E. Gladstone, and Walter Bagehot. But it contains
little on *In Memoriam*, and does not entirely represent the extent of
Victorian scepticism with the later poetry. For although Tennyson
remained an extremely popular poet (Queen Victoria's taste is here

perhaps representative) from the publication of *In Memoriam* in 1850 to his death in 1892, he never entirely satisfied the professional critics, who grew increasingly disillusioned, especially with the *Idylls of the King*. Before his death Tennyson had come under fire from Swinburne, Bagehot, and Hopkins (all collected by Jump). Frederick Harrison (not used by Jump) is typical of this Victorian reaction: he resents the Laureate's eminence that places him beyond criticism, argues that Tennyson merely gives a graceful, but un-original shape to commonplaces of nineteenth-century thought, and complains of the *Idylls* that a 'fierce, lusty epic gets emasculated into a moral lesson for an academy of young ladies'. Victorian criticism, in fact, anticipates most modern strictures and initiates several misconceptions.

An account of modern criticism might begin with Yeats's judgements of Tennyson. In his *Autobiographies* he complains that the poetry is filled 'with what I called "impurities", curiosities about politics, about science, about history, about religion'; these extinguished the 'central flame' in Tennyson's poetry, according to another aside in 'The Symbolism of Poetry'. These remarks rehearse an assumption about Tennyson that still lingers in modern criticism: that the demands of his age steadily and insidiously encroached upon his genius, until finally he became a kind of official mouthpiece for Victorian orthodoxy. The symbolist enthusiasm of the turn of the century, and its continuance in modern poetry under the aegis of Eliot, Yeats, and Pound contributed most to the decline in Tennyson's reputation. An aesthetic that valued 'invisible essences', unseen mysteries behind all logical, material, and external phenomena, and that celebrated the poet's own introspection found little immediate appeal in a poet who seemed to have sold out to the superficial, bourgeois, tastes of his age and surrendered his imagination's integrity before the advance of science.

Modern criticism is slowly beginning to see that the apparent decline is less real than Yeats imagined and that Tennyson stands much closer to the symbolist tradition than was recognized. E. H. Waterson's account of 'Symbolism in Tennyson's Minor Poems' shows the poet's attempt to communicate his own private experience through public images; while Howard W. Fulweiler, in 'Tennyson and the "Summons from the Sea" ', discusses his sea symbolism and its continuous use in the revelation of his inner private development and in the connection of this to his public themes. Both Waterson and Fulweiler are interested in Tennyson's psychological states and in the poet's very real interest in his own psychology, a theme and a critical tendency that may be found in a good deal of Tennyson criticism: Lionel Stevenson, for example, in 'The "High-Born Maiden" Symbol' offers a Jungian interpretation of Tennyson's use of a woman to articulate his soul. The poet's grandson, Sir Charles Tennyson, considers the incidence of dreams in Tennyson's poetry and suggests, what Yeats would certainly have approved, that his grandfather found dreams the best means of communication with an unseen world and the best articulation of it in his poetry.

These and other studies, to be mentioned later, work to restore a more intricate reading of the poetry against the symbolist rejection of it. But the legacy of prejudice that Yeats represents has proved hard to evade. In 1923 appeared two critical biographies by Hugh l'Anson Fausset and Sir Harold Nicolson, both of which chronicled Tennyson's decline into Victorian orthodoxy. Nicolson postulated the poet's progress from the 'unhappy mystic of the Lincolnshire wolds' to the 'prosperous Isle of Wight Victorian'. In an attempt to rescue something from the decline he suggested selecting only the poetry which sustained the image of Tennyson as England's best poet of melancholy. Nicolson was rebuked in two subsequent books—by C. H. O. Scaife and Humbert Wolfe—that insisted there was other poetry than the 'pure', and argued that the poet's decline into 'tired aphorisms' and mild, middle-class apprehensions was fallacious; but even Wolfe, who defends *Maud* so ably, baulks at the *Idylls of the King*.

Another reason, besides symbolist prejudice, for Tennyson's continuing unpopularity in the twentieth century was that his poetry seemed unable to provide opportunities for the close analysis of tensions and complexities, of which irony was the most obvious mode, practised by the New Criticism. Yet, inevitably, there followed an attempt to reclaim Tennyson by the very critical method which generally dismissed him. Rather to his surprise Cleanth Brooks in *The Well-Wrought Urn* found 'Tears, Idle Tears' was of that subtle and intricate order of the imagination that worked via ambiguity and paradox and was consequently hospitable to close scrutiny. Brooke's essay, which is reprinted in John Killham's collection of critical essays on Tennyson, together with two other discussions of that fine poem, was a welcome reminder that the poetry was not always simple and straightforward. Nineteen years later Jerome H. Buckley can be found classifying various modes of irony that Tennyson uses, and claiming for him the 'verbal adroitness and intellectual control of the satirist'. The best modern criticism of Tennyson continues to discover his complexities without neglecting his

Victorian context—after all, Brooks's analysis of 'Tears, Idle Tears' paid no attention to the uniquely Victorian work, *The Princess*, from which the lyric was taken.

The two most valuable modern discussions of Tennyson are E. D. H. Johnson's *The Alien Vision of Victorian Poetry* and Jerome H. Buckley's *Tennyson: the Growth of a Poet*. The first argues that Tennyson, like Arnold and Browning, was in crucial matters at odds with his age, locating his enthusiasms and authority in resources of individual being rather than in an existing social order; that he sought to accommodate private insights to contemporary currents of thought without materially falsifying them; that his concern to communicate with the age and not retire into private fantasy and introspection led him to perfect techniques for such accommodation. Johnson's all too few pages on Tennyson make other important points: that he was by temperament a mystic, seeking to communicate this realm of insight by such devices as the dream, trance, and vision, and that through these he was able to say things which his readers might otherwise ignore or reject; that his early poems may be seen as a dialogue between an inner, timeless, fixed core of apprehension and an outer world of activism and energy. Johnson is especially good on *In Memoriam* and *Idylls of the King*, revealing how the art of both is an often very successful adjudication between the author's interior imaginative resources, and a means of directing these to an age generally alien to them.

Buckley's full-length study also sees Tennyson's career as that of a man trying to translate into the language of sensation and public symbol both his private visions and the vagueness endemic to them. Buckley distinguishes between uncommitted, perfunctory, 'contrived exercises in objectivity' (this, a more subtle and useful version of Tennyson's surrender to Victorianism) and the poetry which engages with the burden of self and does not evade personal involvement. Buckley is especially rewarding on the *Idylls of the King*, which he reads as Tennyson's account of the role of idealism in the context of human, physical environment. This account is challenged by Donald Smalley's 'A New Look at Tennyson—and especially the *Idylls*', where some intelligent close-reading of the Arthurian poems provides an important correction of Buckley's enthusiasm by separating the symbolist aspects of the *Idylls* from the elements more obviously designed to satisfy a large middle-class public.

There are six other full-length studies to mention. As far back as 1901 Andrew Lang tried to read the poems without interference from the legend of the Laureate or from the reaction to it; he is most rewarding on the *Idylls of the King*, which he defends from Harrison's strictures, and on Tennyson's attitudes towards Arthurian materials. Paull F. Baum's *Tennyson Sixty Years After* is a labour more of misplaced duty than of genuine interest, but its hostility is based on close readings of the poetry; inasmuch as its reservations are still those shared by many students of Tennyson, its case is worth a hearing. Valerie Pitt's *Tennyson Laureate* seems to take up the main ideas of Johnson and Buckley in its discussion of the tension between Tennyson's solitary insights and his public inclinations. The problem she sets herself—not the failure of the later poetry, but how the early private became the later public poetry—is the one that has, probably rightly, come to dominate modern criticism; but, despite occasional insights, her case is not presented with enough care for the clarity and structure of its arguments. E. E. Smith's *The Two Voices: a Tennyson Study* also rehearses, as its title implies, the tensions out of which the poetry is drawn; while it cannot be commended for consistent critical skill, it nevertheless offers a useful survey of the poet's interior dialogues and disturbs any notions of a 'simple' poetry. As a compact and alert introduction to Tennyson and his work, J. B. Steane's can be recommended for its identification of Tennyson's 'distinctive voice' and its keen sense of the critical problems raised for modern readers by the Victorians. Clyde de L. Ryals's *Theme and Symbol in Tennyson's Poems to 1850*, though occasionally mechanical, reviews Tennyson's major concerns and their continuity of expression up to *In Memoriam*; its value lies in the attention to essentially literary matters in a poetry that has sometimes seemed inimical to such a concern.

Edgar Finley Shannon, Jr., has studied the reception of the poetry by Victorian critics, and the influence of this upon subsequent poetry and upon Tennyson's concepts of his poetic role. Sir Charles Tennyson followed his biography of the poet (to be mentioned in the next section) with *Six Tennyson Essays*: these, besides discussing the manuscripts of the *Idylls* and his abilities as narrator, consider the poet as humorist, his politics, and his religion. These last essays are especially valuable for their relation of Tennyson to an astonishing range of Victorian ideas, relating to anything from biology to psychical research. There are further books on these important matters which, as well as providing conventional 'background material', reveal Tennyson's continuous involvement with contemporary issues and the consequence of this for his poetry. Charles F. G. Masterman's *Tennyson as a Religious Thinker*, despite its title and date (1900), is less concerned to claim any ethical role for the poet than to explore the nature of his spiritual beliefs; it is still the best book on the subject, though the relevant sections in H. N. Fairchild's *Religious Trends in English Poetry* should also be consulted. Similarly important is the Lockyers' book on *Tennyson as a Student and Poet of Nature*, especially its suggestions on how the 'truest poetry' uses the 'most accurate science'. Much has since been added to the Lockyers' maybe over-enthusiastic account: there is Douglas Bush, *Science and English Poetry*, Basil Willey in *More Nineteenth-Century Studies*, Lionel Stevenson's *Darwin Among the Poets*, and an essay by W. R. Rutland. Two articles which are concerned to show the imaginative uses to which Tennyson put his considerable scientific knowledge are one by W. David Shaw and C. W. Gartlein on auroral metaphors, and another by Walter Gibson on the distinctions between the language of Lyell and Darwin and Tennyson's usages.

The chapter on politics in Stephen Gwynne's *Tennyson: a Critical Study* of 1899 is most valuable, probably the best in the volume. Robert Preyer's long article on the poetry and politics of Tennyson's 'conservative vision' has, in fact, little to say about his politics, although what there is is excellent. Preyer's larger concern, a concern that at times seems too ambitious for the length of his article and forces him into rather daunting generalities, is an account of Tennyson's response to traditional thinking; he argues that the poet 'relied for his significances, for placing experience, on the traditional and inherited structure of meanings symbolized and made manifest in the Christian humanist poetic tradition', and yet in the face of his own age he was unable to utilize this tradition as a means of clarifying and enriching his experience. Despite the formidable generalizing premise, there is much excellent close analysis, especially of Tennyson's instabilities of feeling and attitude, and of his success in relating the cosmic and natural to the human.

There have been other accounts of Tennyson's relationship with the past, especially with his Romantic predecessors: notably, R. A. Foakes's *The Romantic Assertion*, which explores the informing visions of nineteenth-century poetry and the language needed to sustain them; Foakes's discussion is mainly of *In Memoriam*, but has usefully wider relevance. George H. Ford in *Keats and the Victorians* notes Tennyson's displeasure at being said to be influenced by Keats, but shows various parallels between them. Hallam, of course, in an essay that Jump reprints, was among the first to defend Tennyson by linking him with a Keatsian school of poetry. Both Robert Langbaum in *The Poetry of Experience* and Patricia Ball in her article on 'Tennyson and the Romantics' consider the use of dramatic monologue: Patricia Ball suggests that he avoided or exploited the monologue to suit his imaginative intentions; and Langbaum, in a book of fascinatingly wider scope, discusses the poet's use of monologue as a vehicle for his interest in the 'pathology of the emotions'. W. E. Fredeman has also examined Tennyson's psychological interests, especially as displayed in such a poem as "St. Simeon Stylites". Larger and longer poetic traditions are dealt with by Douglas Bush in the relevant chapter of *Mythology and the Romantic Tradition*; this is just as valuable for its incidental insights as for its ostensible interest in Tennyson's use of classical myths, moulding them for his own poetry.

A few other general studies deserve mention before those on specific aspects of Tennyson's work. Arthur J. Carr, under the title 'Tennyson as a Modern Poet' (available in Killham's collection), notes first how Tennyson 'shows and hides, as if in embryo', many twentieth-century themes and interests, and then moves on to examine how his career is permeated with anxieties about 'objective foundations', Carr's is one of the few really distinguished accounts of Tennyson in modern criticism: his suggestion that the poet's 'ideas flow in the current of his melancholic sensibility', that the definitive Tennysonian theme is 'a dreamlike sense of loss that becomes idyllic self-assurance', that the essential modernity of Tennyson lies in his poetry of the 'divided will' and a frustration with the romantic tradition, represents an emphatic contribution to our reading of Tennyson; it is the more valuable for leaving the reader much to explore for himself. Another stimulating examination of some wider themes is James Kissane's on the poet's constant longing for the past, and the consequences for the poetry of this sense of loss.

Discussion of metrics and diction may be found in Bernard Groom's *The Diction of Poetry*, which recognizes how Tennyson attempted the reconciliation of traditional poetic diction with new terms of the nineteenth century, and J. F. A. Pyre's *The Formation of Tennyson's Style*, where he considers the poet's handling of language, especially the 'deliberate and often learned artifice of phrasing'. Some of Pyre's assumptions and conclusions are modified by Alicia Ostriker's 'The Three Modes of Tennyson's Poetry'. Francis Berry in *Poetry and the Physical Voice* makes a unique and tenacious, if sometimes slightly tendentious, attempt to understand how the best poetry is the direct outcome of the physical qualities of Tennyson's voice; this topic is approached in other ways by Gordon Ray's 'Tennyson Reads *Maud*'. M. Dodsworth, in an essay contributed to Isobel Armstrong's *Major Victorian Poets*, discusses the characteristic repetitiousness of Tennyson's poetry and the relationship between the 'technical accomplishments' and his 'frames of mind'.

The most profitable direction of modern criticism of Tennyson has been towards understanding the early poetry and rescuing it from the realm of mere sensation. It began, not surprisingly, with an inquiry into Tennyson's adolescent reading and psychology, W. D. Paden's *Tennyson in Egypt*. Confessedly inspired by *The Road to Xanadu*, Paden probes the poet's psychic development, but we end by learning much about the poetry itself, moving in that 'mixed atmosphere' that Carr has prescribed as essential for Tennyson scholarship, 'neither wholly aesthetic nor wholly biographical'. The more formalist criticism continued in Joyce Green's 'Tennyson's Development during the Ten Years' Silence'; her main concern is the effect of early reviews on Tennyson's revisions for the 1842 volumes, the details of which are tabulated in an appendix, but she was one of the earliest to see a poem like 'The Lady of Shalott' as an expression of aesthetic principle rather than mere decorative medievalism. Most of the other fine early poems have been similarly discussed. G. Robert Stange's essay on 'Tennyson's Garden of Art: a Study of *The Hesperides*' (collected by Killham) rescues a fine poem, suppressed by the poet, and shows 'a difficult and meaningful subject' treated with a 'strength and freedom that he did not always display'. Tennyson's other dialogue on the responsibilities of the artist is considered by A. C. Howell in 'Tennyson's Palace of Art—an Interpretation'; he suggests, not only how central and important a statement it was for both the poet and his readers, but that the poem may also be legitimately read as an allegory of the poet's impatience with Cambridge. William Cadbury notes the pattern of involvement and withdrawal initiated in 'The Palace of Art' and then follows it through several later poems like *In Memoriam*, *Maud*, and the *Idylls*.

'Ulysses' has probably provided the most rewarding text for modern exploration of the early Tennyson. Two critics in particular see it as a test case: W. W. Robson (in Killham) locates the 'incongruity' of the poem in 'the responsible social being, the admirably serious and "committed" Victorian intellectual, ... uttering strenuous sentiments in the accent of Tennyson the most un-strenuous, lonely, and poignant of poets'. Edgar Hill Duncan first provides a survey of modern criticism of Tennyson, and then tests certain current assumptions and some of his ideas against a close reading of 'Ulysses'; the poem becomes another example of Tennyson dialogue—the mythic figure used as a dramatic mouthpiece for private sensibility, with all the enriching ambiguities of that strategy. J. H. Prynne also examines the interior universe of various poems, including 'Ulysses', where the 'irreconcilable vagueness of the horizontal images is part of their functional strength; they too are feasible only at a distance ... Incantation has taken the place of description.' Another critic who places his discussion of 'Ulysses' in the context of various modern critical attitudes is John Pettigrew; again, the dramatic rather than the lyric structure is emphasized, and the whole question raised of the relation of Tennyson's figure to Dante's Ulisse; it is one of the more thorough and rewarding accounts of the poem.

Further explorations of Tennyson's early dialectical mode have been offered by John R. Reed's 'The Design of Tennyson's "The Two Voices" ', also mainly concerned with its dramatic form, and by Alan Grob's 'Tennyson's "Lotos-Eaters": Two Versions of Art', which examines the detailed meaning beneath the 'narcotic' mood. Paul Turner's main purpose in 'Some Ancient Light on Tennyson's *Oenone*' is a detailed exploration of the classical allusions in the poem, but he moves to discuss the success of the poem's mozaic of such imitations—he sees Tennyson as a 'connoisseur in poetical sensations' broken only by the intrusive 'brains trust' of philosophical dialogue.

Finally, two pieces that range more widely among the early poems are Carl Robinson Sonn's 'Poetic Vision and Religious Certainty' and Robert Preyer's 'Tennyson as an Oracular Poet'. Sonn argues that what dominates Tennyson up to the 1840s is a need for 'deeper self-realization which would produce both an assured poetic vision and a degree of religious conviction'; he plausibly suggests that Tennyson looked analogically at intimations of God, infinite vision, and personal omnipotence, and that to achieve any was to facilitate all. Moving in similar territory, Preyer identifies Tennyson's oracular stance—a 'landscape of vision and the images of a new apocylypse', for which syntax, diction, and metre are all deliberately rarified and complicated; he examines 'The Kraken' as a central example of this mode, a fine analysis that is followed by a brief, less convincing, explanation of why Tennyson felt obliged to desert the 'condition of vision [that] is a radical detachment from actuality'.

John Killham's *Tennyson and 'The Princess': Reflections of an Age* is a fascinating account of how the poem came to be written, and of its relationship to such intellectual and social issues of the age as the new feminism, female education, evolution (a most valuable section), and the genre of 'Persian' tale. If Killham does not readily move towards any critical evaluation of this extraordinary poem, a 'test-case' of Tennyson appreciation today as it was in 1847, he has certainly provided all the materials with which it can be done. Buckley's chapter on *The Princess* is probably the best critical account of the poem. Another, recent, account is B. Bergonzi's 'Feminism and Feminity in *The Princess*' (in the Armstrong collection), which provides insights of a wider range than the title would suggest.

On *In Memoriam* there is inevitably a vast literature. The present writer has collected a dozen of the best modern essays in *A Casebook on 'In Memoriam'*, and these include T. S. Eliot's famous celebration of it as a poem of doubt, two pieces by Graham Hough and John D. Rosenberg on the poet's use of evolutionary ideas, Carlisle Moore's 'Faith, Doubt, and Mystical Experience', and a brilliant account by J. C. C. Mays of the poem's form. Beyond this collection, E. B. Mattes's study of some of the influences that shaped *In Memoriam* is essential reading, since it opens the huge hinterland of ideas (especially and significantly those of Hallam himself), reading, and personal contact upon which Tennyson drew. Miss Mattes also gives some account of Tennyson's final attempts to reorder and attain a final balance for the poem. Valerie Pitt discusses various manuscripts and the light they cast upon the composition; she demonstrates its very important literary, as opposed to autobiographical, structure. A. C. Bradley's *Commentary*, despite changes in critical taste and strategies, is still very useful for its attention to the theme of love, and for its section-by-section analysis of a suggested structure. But Bradley's version of the structure should be tested against that offered by Tennyson himself, which forms the basis of Martin J. Svaglic's 'A Framework for Tennyson's *In Memoriam*'. Another early study of the poem besides Bradley's which repays reading is John Franklin Genung's *Tennyson's "In Memoriam": its Purpose and its Structure*; Genung, a Baptist theologian by training, is obviously absorbed by the religious ideas, but he is equally valuable on the poetic consequences of Tennyson's refusal to employ traditional literary or philosophical ideas, and on the role of the poet that is canvassed in *In Memoriam*. On this last topic he anticipates the good modern treatment of the theme by E. D. H. Johnson in an essay on 'The Way of the Poet', also available in the *Casebook*. K. W. Gransden writes of *In Memoriam* in the Arnold Studies in English Literature series, and this can be recommended as a modest introduction to the poem and its critical problems. Finally, seven articles visit the poem with variously interesting results: Jonathan Bishop traces through the shifting combinations of the poem a unity that derives from the theme of change; J. M. Cohen, in '*In Memoriam* a Hundred Years After', and Stephen Allen Grant, 'The Mystical

Implications of *In Memoriam*', discuss the quality and imaginative resources of the poet's mysticism, Grant especially making useful comparisons with other mystical writing and analysis; in 'The "Heavenly Friend": The "New Mythus" of *In Memoriam*' Clyde de L. Ryals, like J. M. Cohen, explores the poem's identification of Hallam with Christ; Alan Sinfield's 'Matter-Moulded Forms of Speech: Tennyson's Use of Language in *In Memoriam*' (in Armstrong collection) attends, not to the surface accomplishment of language, but to its essential role in focusing the poet's super-natural experiences; a similar inquiry informs the present writer's reading of the symbolist modes and structures of *In Memoriam*; E. R. August, in 'Tennyson and Teilhard', shows how the poem anticipates modern religious views.

An interesting defence of *Maud* forms the core of Humbert Wolfe's essay on Tennyson. E. D. H. Johnson's article on *Maud*, allowing some similarities to symbolist poetry, traces the images of lily and rose and suggests that the poem becomes meaningful only in terms of its symbolic content. A more substantial and illuminating inquiry into the function of the imagery in *Maud*, emphasizing psychological rather than ideological aspects of the poem, is that by John Killham, included in his collection of *Critical Essays*. In *Hateful Contraries* W. K. Wimsatt also considers its connections with the symbolist poetry of T. S. Eliot: as a 'monodrama of frustration and melancholy *Maud* is one of the many precursors of *Prufrock*', yet Wimsatt is equally aware of the peculiar Victorian *timbre* that the plot provides. And, as if in collaboration, R. W. Rader's *Tennyson's 'Maud': the Biographical Genesis* identifies the roots of that plot in Tennyson's own life, and reveals the generally unconscious bearings of autobiography upon *Maud* and other poems. Roy P. Basler recommends and illustrates Tennyson's extraordinary psychological insights in *Maud* in the course of his general study of *Sex, Symbolism and Psychology in Literature*; a similar interest in the poem's psychological insights informs S. R. Weiner's 'The Chord of Self'. Gordon Ray, 'Tennyson Reads *Maud*', and A. S. Byatt, 'The Lyric Structure of Tennyson's *Maud*' (Armstrong collection), both provide helpful entries into what seems, after the *English Idylls*, the most awkward poem for modern criticism to encounter.

Two articles only provide much assistance with the *English Idylls*, a section of Tennyson's work that has met with little modern interest or favour. Thomas J. Assad is concerned with the narrative scope and 'sentimental satire' of the *Enoch Arden* volume. Philip Drew raises the whole descriptive and evaluative difficulties readers have with these poems in ' "Aylmer's Field": A Problem for Critics'; he suggests that there is common ground here between Tennyson and Victorian novelists, but that the poetry is distinguished by the varying pace and scale of the narrative, variations Tennyson introduced to accommodate his peculiar sense of the complexities of modern life.

Some attempts have been made to redeem the poetry of Tennyson's last years from its relegation by Nicolson and others to the limbo of Victorian orthodoxy. The most challenging piece is by Francis Golffing, 'Tennyson's Last Phase: The Poet as Seer'. Goffling sees the poet developing new resources of style and subject in order to evade the prison of his refined inwardness; from 1880 onwards Tennyson turns to a vision of mankind's future that will unite a rational technology and a humanized science. Two articles a little more alert to the critical problems raised by this body of verse are G. Robert Stange's study of 'Demeter and Persephone' (collected by Killham), which finds the poet still using myth as metaphor for his own doubts and conflicts, and Gordon S. Haight's 'Tennyson's Merlin', which links the late poem 'Merlin and the Gleam' to the early poetry's inquiries into aesthetics.

The *Idylls of the King* proved a stumbling block even before they were completed in 1885: Carlyle thought them 'superlative lollipops' and Hopkins wanted to entitle them *Charades from the Middle Ages*. Modern criticism has begun, a little defensively, to modify those judgements. Ryals, already a prolific commentator on Tennyson, attempts the most extensive treatment in *From the Great Deep*; his most rewarding inquiries are into the theme of illusion, and into the consequences to Camelot of Arthur's exercising his will against others in efforts to relate himself to an objective world. Similarly in 'Tennyson's Tragic Vitalism' William R. Brashear finds the poet testing Nietzschean heroic illusions against a world inhospitable to them. Edward Engelberg traces the imagery of beasts through the *Idylls*, noting its gradual ascendency as man's selfishness and indiscipline doom himself and his values. Samuel C. Burchell revisits the vexed problem of 'Tennyson's Allegory in the Distance', suggesting that the narrative progress and the mythic account of a crumbling civilization are seldom in sufficient accord. F. E. L. Priestley (in Killham) also sees the true nature of the *Idylls* as a dramatic allegory devoted to revealing how materialism, naturalism, and utilitarianism undermine all idealism. The use of landscape to focus human feeling is the concern of David Palmer in 'The Laureate in Lyonnesse', while R. B. Wilkenfeld treats the poem's design in 'Tennyson's Camelot: the Kingdom of Folly'; he finds one source of the complex 'rhythmic structure' centres on Tennyson's concern with the 'mythology of folly', and traces the varieties of folly that inhabit the world of Camelot. Finally, there is still much valuable light thrown on the changing scheme of the whole poem as Tennyson worked on it in Richard Jones's *The Growth of 'The Idylls of the King'*. Very recently the *Idylls* seem to be absorbing critical attention, though with relatively meagre rewards; among the flurry of essays, W. D. Shaw's 'Dialectical Reading' stands out for its discussion of the philosophical integrity of the poem.

BIOGRAPHIES AND LETTERS

The 'official' biography is that by the poet's grandson, Sir Charles Tennyson; he has elsewhere also offered an extended account of 'The Somersby Tennysons', which provides further background for the life. Joanna Richardson in *Tennyson: Pre-Eminent Victorian* narrates the life from 1850, drawing upon some material Sir Charles did not use; it is worth consulting for its deft impressions of how the Victorians regarded their Laureate. Of much slighter value at this stage of Tennyson studies, but of peculiarly historical interest, are the two critical biographies by Fausset and Nicolson, listed in the previous section; the latter is much the superior.

All accounts of Tennyson's life and work will have drawn upon five indispensable memoirs. Especially valuable, despite the filial piety, is Hallam's *Memoir* of his father, which in its turn is based upon the more extensive *Materials for a Life of A.T.*, which Hallam collected, printed privately, and deposited in the British Museum. The other recollections of Tennyson can be found in *Tennyson and his Friends*, also edited by Hallam Tennyson; in James Knowles's 'A Personal Reminiscence'; and in H. D. Rawnsley, *Memories of the Tennysons*.

No edition of Tennyson's letters exists, but Cecil Lang and Edgar Shannon are at work on one which should be ready in 1970. Meanwhile various letters are cited throughout the materials already mentioned.

BIBLIOGRAPHIES

The *New Cambridge Bibliography* has a much expanded section on Tennyson by W. D. Paden and Donald Low; it contains for the first time a list of manuscripts' locations, besides the canon in detail up to 1967. Less extensive, but with critical comments, is the bibliography of *The Victorian Poets*, edited by Faverty. A recent volume is Charles Tennyson's and Christine Fall's *Alfred Tennyson: an Annotated*

Bibliography. A special list of periodical reviews of Tennyson up to November 1851 appears at the end of Shannon's *Tennyson and the Reviewers* (see CRITICAL section above). Three journals, *Victorian Poetry*, *Victorian Studies*, and *Victorian Newsletter*, publish annual bibliographies through which students may keep in touch with scholarship and criticism. A general *Concordance* to Tennyson by A. E. Baker is available, and the same author has published one to 'The Devil and the Lady'. The valuable and important collection of Tennyson MSS. at Trinity College, Cambridge, were released by the Tennyson Trustees in 1969, and for the first time made available for transcription and publication. Christopher Ricks's account of the collection, together with some examples, appeared in the *Times Literary Supplement*.

BACKGROUND READING

G. M. Young's famous and still most valuable essay on 'The Age of Tennyson' is available both in Killham's collection (see CRITICAL section above) and in Young's *Victorian Essays*, which, together with his *Victorian England: Portrait of an Age* are essential reading. Humphrey House's talk on 'Tennyson and the Spirit of the Age' is reprinted in *All In Due Time*. Walter E. Houghton brings to his account of emotional, intellectual, and moral attitudes in *The Victorian Frame of Mind* a formidable range of reading; it is both a most readable survey of intellectual and moral history and a useful work of reference. Fifteen years of Victorian history, 1852–67, during which Tennyson was Laureate, are explored by W. L. Burn in *The Age of Equipoise*, a most important book on the social and legal forces that sustained a remarkable and satisfied society.

REFERENCES

TEXTS

W. H. Auden (ed.), *Tennyson: an Introduction and a Selection* (London, 1946).

J. H. Buckley (ed.), *Poems of Tennyson*, selected, with an Introduction (Boston, 1958).

D. Bush (ed.), *Tennyson: Selected Poetry*, edited, with an Introduction (New York, 1956; paperback, U.S.).

T. S. Eliot (ed.), *Poems of Tennyson* (London, 1936).

F. L. Lucas (ed.), *Alfred, Lord Tennyson: an Anthology* (Cambridge, 1932).

H. M. McLuan (ed.), *Tennyson: Selected Poetry* (New York, 1956; paperbacks, U.K. and U.S.).

C. Ricks (ed.), *The Poems of Tennyson* (London, 1968).

W. J. Rolfe (ed.), *The Poetic and Dramatic Works of Alfred Lord Tennyson* (Cambridge Poets, Boston and New York, 1898).

B. C. Southam (ed.), *Selected Poems* (London, 1964; paperback, U.K.).

Hallam Tennyson (ed.), *Tennyson: Poems, Annotated by Alfred, Lord Tennyson* (Eversley edn., 9 vols., London 1907).

T. H. Warren (ed.), *Poems of Tennyson, 1830–1870* (Oxford Standard Authors, London, 1912); new edn., *The Complete Poetical Works* (1953); since 1965 entitled *Tennyson: Poems and Plays*.

CRITICAL STUDIES AND COMMENTARY

I. Armstrong (ed.), *The Major Victorian Poets: Reconsiderations* (London, 1969).

T. J. Assad, 'On the Major Poems of Tennyson's *Enoch Arden* Volume', *Tulane Studies in English*, xiv (1966).

E. R. August, 'Tennyson and Teilhard: The Faith of *In Memoriam*', *PMLA* lxxxiv (1969).

P. Ball, 'Tennyson and the Romantics', *VP* i (1963).

R. P. Basler, *Sex, Symbolism and Psychology in Literature* (New Brunswick, N.J., 1948).

P. F. Baum, *Tennyson Sixty Years After* (1948; Hamden, Conn., 1963).

F. Berry, *Poetry and the Physical Voice* (London, 1962).

J. Bishop, 'The Unity of *In Memoriam*', *VN* xxi (1962).

A. C. Bradley, *A Commentary on Tennyson's 'In Memoriam'* (1901; London, 1966).

W. R. Brashear, 'Tennyson's Tragic Vitalism: *Idylls of the King*', *VP* vi (1968).

J. H. Buckley, *Tennyson: the Growth of a Poet* (Cambridge, Mass., 1960; paperback, U.S.).

J. H. Buckley, 'Tennyson's Irony', *VN* xxxi (1967).

S. C. Burchell, 'Tennyson's Allegory in the Distance', *PMLA* lxviii (1953).

D. Bush, *Mythology and the Romantic Tradition in English Poetry* (New York, 1957; paperback, U.S.).

D. Bush, *Science and English Poetry: a Historical Sketch, 1590–1950* (New York, 1950; paperbacks, U.K. and U.S.).

W. Cadbury, 'Tennyson's "Palace of Art" and the Rhetoric of Structures', *Criticism*, vii (1965).

J. M. Cohen, '*In Memoriam* a Hundred Years After', *Cornhill Magazine*, clxiv (1949).

P. Drew, ' "Aylmer's Field": a Problem for Critics', *The Listener*, lxxi (1964).

E. H. Duncan, 'Tennyson: a Modern Appraisal', *Tennessee Studies in Literature*, iv (1959).

E. Engelberg, 'The Beast Image in Tennyson's *Idylls of the King*', *ELH* xxii (1955).

H. N. Fairchild, *Religious Trends in English Poetry* (6 vols., New York, 1939–68).

H. l'A Fausset, *Tennyson: a Modern Portrait* (London, 1923).

R. A. Foakes, *The Romantic Assertion: a Study of the Language of Nineteenth-Century Poetry* (London, 1958).

G. H. Ford, *Keats and the Victorians* (Hamden, Conn., 1962).

W. E. Fredeman, '"A Sign Betwixt the Meadow and the Cloud": Tennyson's "St Simeon Stylites"', *UTQ* xxxviii (1968).

H. W. Fulweiler, 'Tennyson and the "Summons from the Sea"', *VP* iii (1965).

J. F. Genung, *Tennyson's 'In Memoriam': its Purpose and its Structure* (Leipzig, 1881).

W. Gibson, 'Behind the Veil: A Distinction between Poetic and Scientific Language in Tennyson, Lyell, and Darwin', *VS* ii (1958).

F. Golffing, 'Tennyson's Last Phase: the Poet as Seer', *The Southern Review*, N.S. ii (1966).

K. W. Gransden, 'Tennyson: In Memoriam', *SEL* xxii (1964).

S. A. Grant, 'The Mystical Implications of *In Memoriam*', *SEL* ii (1962).

J. Green, 'Tennyson's Development During the Ten-Year Silence', *PMLA*, lxvi (1951).

A. Grob, 'Tennyson's "Lotos-Eaters": Two Versions of Art', *MP* lxii (1964).

B. Groom, *The Diction of Poetry from Spenser to Bridges* (Toronto, 1955).

S. Gwynn, *Tennyson: a Critical Study* (London, 1899).

G. S. Haight, 'Tennyson's "Merlin"', *SP* xliv (1947).

F. Harrison, *Tennyson, Ruskin, Mill and Other Literary Estimates* (London, 1900).

A. C. Howell, 'Tennyson's "Palace of Art"—an Interpretation', *SP* xxxiii (1936).

J. D. Hunt (ed.), *A Casebook on Tennyson's 'In Memoriam'* (London, 1970; paperback, U.K.).

J. D. Hunt, 'The Symbolist Vision of *In Memoriam*', *VP* viii (1970).

E. D. H. Johnson, *The Alien Vision of Victorian Poetry* (Princeton, N.J., 1964).

E. D. H. Johnson, 'The Lily and the Rose: Symbolic Meaning in Tennyson's *Maud*', *PMLA* lxiv (1949).

R. Jones, *The Growth of the 'Idylls of the King'* (Philadelphia, 1895).

J. D. Jump (ed.), *Tennyson: the Critical Heritage* (London and New York, 1967).

J. Killham, *Tennyson and 'The Princess': Reflections of an Age* (London, 1958).

J. Killham (ed.), *Critical Essays on the Poetry of Tennyson* (London, 1964; paperbacks, U.K. and U.S.).

J. Kissane, 'Tennyson: The Passion of the Past and the Curse of Time', *ELH* xxxii (1965).

A. Lang, *Alfred Tennyson* (Edinburgh and London, 1901).

R. Langbaum, *The Poetry of Experience: The Dramatic Monologue in Modern Literary Tradition* (New York, 1957; paperback, U.S.).

N. and W. L. Lockyer, *Tennyson as a Student and Poet of Nature* (London, 1910).

C. F. G. Masterman, *Tennyson as a Religious Thinker* (London, 1900).

E. B. Mattes, '*In Memoriam; the Way of a Soul*': *a Study of Some Influences that Shaped Tennyson's Poem* (New York, 1951).

H. Nicolson, *Tennyson: Aspects of his Life, Character and Poetry* (London, 1923).

A. Ostriker, 'The Three Modes in Tennyson's Poetry', *PMLA* lxxxii (1967).

W. D. Paden, *Tennyson in Egypt: a Study of the Imagery in his Earlier Work* (Lawrence, Kan., 1942).

D. Palmer, 'The Laureate in Lyonnesse', *The Listener*, lxxvii (1967).

J. Pettigrew, 'Tennyson's "Ulysses": a Reconciliation of Opposites', *VP* i (1963).

V. Pitt, *Tennyson Laureate* (London, 1962; paperback, U.S.).

R. Preyer, 'Tennyson as an Oracular Poet', *MP* lv (1958).

R. Preyer, 'Alfred Tennyson: the Poetry and Politics of Conservative Vision', *VS* ix (1966).

J. H. Prynne, 'The Elegiac World in Victorian Poetry', *The Listener*, lxix (1963).

J. F. A. Pyre, *The Formation of Tennyson's Style* (Madison, Wis., 1921).

R. W. Rader, *Tennyson's 'Maud': the Biographical Genesis* (Berkeley, Calif., and Los Angeles, 1963).

G. Ray, 'Tennyson Reads *Maud*', Sedgewick Memorial Lecture, University of British Columbia (Vancouver, 1968).

J. R. Reed, 'The Design of Tennyson's "The Two Voices" ', *UTQ* xxxvii (1968).

W. R. Rutland, 'Tennyson and the Theory of Evolution', *Essays and Studies by Members of the English Association* xxvi (1940).

C. de L. Ryals, *Theme and Symbol in Tennyson's Poems to 1850* (Philadelphia, 1964).

C. de L. Ryals, 'The "Heavenly Friend": The "New Mythus" of *In Memoriam*', *The Personalist*, xliii (1962).

C. de L. Ryals, *From the Great Deep: Essays on 'Idylls of the King'* (Athens, Ohio, 1967).

C. H. O. Scaife, *The Poetry of Alfred Tennyson: an Essay in Appreciation* (London, 1930).

E. F. Shannon, Jr., *Tennyson and the Reviewers: a Study of his Literary Reputation and of the Influence of the Critics upon his Poetry, 1827–1851* (Cambridge, Mass., 1952, and 1967).

E. F. Shannon, Jr., 'The Critical Reception of Tennyson's *Maud*', *PMLA*, lxviii (1953).

W. D. Shaw, *Idylls of the King*: A Dialectical Reading'. *VP* vii (1969).

W. D. Shaw and C. W. Gartlein, 'The Aurora: a Spiritual Metaphor in Tennyson', *VP* iii (1965).

D. Smalley, 'A New Look at Tennyson—and especially the *Idylls*', *JEGP* lxi (1962).

E. E. Smith, *The Two Voices: a Tennyson Study* (Lincoln, Nebr., 1964).

C. R. Sonn, 'Poetic Vision and Religious Certainty in Tennyson's Earlier Poetry', *MP* lvii (1959).

J. B. Steane, *Tennyson* (paperback, London and New York, 1966).

L. Stevenson, *Darwin Among the Poets* (New York, 1963).

L. Stevenson, 'The "High-Born Maiden" Symbol in Tennyson', *PMLA* lxiii (1948).

M. Svaglic, 'A Framework for Tennyson's *In Memoriam*', *JEGP* lxi (1962).

Charles Tennyson, *Six Tennyson Essays* (London, 1954).

Charles Tennyson, 'The Dream in Tennyson's Poetry', *Virginia Quarterly Review*, xl (1964).

P. Turner, 'Some Ancient Light on Tennyson's "Œnone" ', *JEGP* lxi (1962).

E. H. Waterston, 'Symbolism in Tennyson's Minor Poems', *UTQ* xx (1951).

S. R. Weiner, 'The Chord of Self: Tennyson's *Maud*', *Literature and Psychology* xvi (1967).

R. B. Wilkenfeld, 'Tennyson's Camelot: the Kingdom of Folly', *UTQ* xxxvii (1968).

B. Willey, *More Nineteenth-Century Studies* (London, 1956).

W. K. Wimsatt, *Hateful Contraries: Studies in Literature and Criticism* (Lexington, Ky., 1965; paperbacks, U.S. and U.K.).

H. Wolfe, *Tennyson* (London, 1930).

W. B. Yeats, *Autobiographies* (London and New York, 1927; paperback, U.S.).

W. B. Yeats, 'The Symbolism of Poetry', in *Essays and Introductions* (London and New York, 1961; paperback, U.S.).

BIOGRAPHIES AND LETTERS

J. Knowles, 'A Personal Reminiscence', *Nineteenth Century*, xxxiii (1893).

H. D. Rawnsley, *Memories of the Tennysons* (London, 1900).

J. Richardson, *Tennyson: Pre-Eminent Victorian* (London, 1962).

Charles Tennyson, *Alfred Tennyson* (London, 1950; paperback, U.K.).

Charles Tennyson, 'The Somersby Tennysons: a Postscript', *VS* ix (1966).

Hallam Tennyson, *Alfred Lord Tennyson: a Memoir* (2 vols., London, 1897).

Hallam Tennyson (ed.), *Materials for a Life of A.T.* (4 vols., privately printed. Copy in the British Museum, London, n.d.).

Hallam Tennyson (ed.), *Tennyson and his Friends* (London, 1911).

BIBLIOGRAPHIES

A. E. Baker (ed.), *A Concordance to the Poetical and Dramatic Works of Tennyson* (1914; New York, 1966).

A. E. Baker (ed.), *A Concordance to 'The Devil and the Lady'* (London, 1931).

F. E. Faverty (ed.), *The Victorian Poets: a Guide to Research*, 2nd edn. (Cambridge, Mass., 1968).

C. Ricks, 'The Tennyson MSS. at Trinity College, Cambridge', *TLS* no. 3521 (21 Aug. 1969).

Charles Tennyson and C. Fall (eds.), *Alfred Tennyson: an Annotated Bibliography* (Athens, Ga., 1968).

G. G. Watson (ed.), *N.C.B.E.L.*, vol. iii (Cambridge and New York, 1969).

Journals publishing annual biblios.: *Victorian Poetry, V. Studies*, and *V. Newsletter.*

BACKGROUND READING

W. L. Burn, *The Age of Equipoise: A Study of the Mid-Victorian Generation* (London, 1967; paperbacks, U.K. and U.S.).

W. E. Houghton, *The Victorian Frame of Mind, 1830–1870* (New Haven, Conn., 1957; paperbacks, U.K. and U.S.).

H. House, *All In Due Time* (London, 1955).

G. M. Young, *Victorian England: Portrait of an Age*, 2nd edn. (London, 1953; paperback, U.S. and U.K.).

G. M. Young, *Victorian Essays* (paperback, London, 1962).

16 · BROWNING 1812–1889

Ian Jack

IN many ways Browning's reputation between the wars resembled that of John Donne twenty or thirty years before. A few of his poems were known—well-known; and he had a handful of knowledgeable and enthusiastic supporters. He was—many were willing to concede—'the first poet in the world in some things' (as Ben Jonson had said of Donne); but against his strengths were set the weaknesses supposed to follow from his 'optimism' and an alleged coarseness of sensibility. Browning's mastery of the 'dramatic monologue' was seen as a sort of special skill, and not as a development of central importance in the English poetic tradition. In spite of his own debt to Browning, the leader of critical opinion in the 1930s and 40s, T. S. Eliot, habitually slighted him in his critical writings, and a hundred lesser critics were content to leave Browning's work unexplored.

Eliot's master, Ezra Pound, has always taken a very different view, describing Browning as 'the soundest of all the Victorians'. The common reader, having encountered Browning at school, was never in doubt that the author of 'My Last Duchess' and 'The Bishop Orders his Tomb' was a major poet of some kind. In this continuing popularity with the common reader (indeed) lies the greatest difference between Browning's reputation and Donne's. Only the critics have been confused. Now the position is changing, and Robert Langbaum's brilliant book, *The Poetry of Experience*, is a sign of the times. It seems certain that the revaluation of Browning's poetry will coincide with a reconsideration of his place in the English poetic tradition.

TEXTS

The last of the four collected editions of his work which Browning himself saw through the press, *The Poetical Works*, appeared in sixteen volumes in 1888–9. This edition is to be found in most libraries, and in many respects it remains the best for the modern reader. In 1894 a seventeenth volume was added, which contains *Asolando* (the collection of poems published on the day of the poet's death in 1889), along with indexes and useful biographical and historical notes to the poems. In 1914 Sir Frederic Kenyon, who had been a close friend of the Brownings, published a further volume in a binding uniform with that of the previous volumes: *New Poems by Robert and Elizabeth Barrett Browning*. This includes brief and sometimes unhelpful replies by Browning to questions about the interpretation of certain of his poems, and some information about manuscripts.

The first collected edition that Browning had published, the two-volume *Poems . . . A New Edition* of 1849, had included only *Paracelsus* and the contents of eight pamphlets published between 1841 and 1846 under the general title *Bells and Pomegranates*: seven plays and two collections of short poems. In the three-volume *Poetical Works* of 1863 *Sordello* was restored to the canon, while Browning made an interesting attempt to classify his shorter poems as (Dramatic) Lyrics, (Dramatic) Romances, and 'Men and Women' poems. This classification was retained in the six-volume *Poetical Works* of 1868 and in the edition of 1888–9, which gives Browning's final revision of his text. It should be noted that while the two *Bells and Pomegranates* pamphlets containing the shorter poems bear the titles *Dramatic Lyrics* (1842) and *Dramatic Romances and Lyrics* (1845), and while *Men and Women* is the title of the great collection of new poems which Browning published in 1855, the shorter poems were completely re-shuffled when he decided to use 'Dramatic Lyrics', 'Dramatic Romances' and 'Men and Women' as categories of his shorter poems, in 1863 and subsequently.

In 1863 there appeared *Selections from the Poetical Works of Robert Browning*, chosen by John Forster with the poet's concurrence. Two years later *A Selection from the Works of Robert Browning* was published in the series 'Moxon's Miniature Poets': a prefatory note, signed 'R.B.', makes it clear that the poems have been chosen by the poet himself, and mentions that 'not a single piece' duplicates anything in the previous *Selections*. The poet published two further volumes of *Selections*, in 1872 and 1880.

There exist several later collected editions of Browning's poems, none of them wholly satisfactory. The Centenary edition, edited by Kenyon in ten volumes in 1912, contains brief introductions to the poems less important than those now available in William Clyde DeVane's invaluable *Handbook* (see p. 288 below). Kenyon's is sometimes referred to as the standard edition. *The Complete Works*, edited by Charlotte Porter and Helen A. Clarke in twelve volumes in 1898, claimed to be the 'first fully annotated edition of the complete works', but the notes are neither full nor outstandingly useful. This edition is often called the 'Arno' or 'Florentine' edition.

A useful one-volume edition is *The Complete Poetical Works* edited by Augustine Birrell in 1915, and including the handful of poems first published by Kenyon the previous year. Since 1929 John Murray has continued to reprint what is substantially Birrell's edition. *The Complete Poetic and Dramatic Works* (Cambridge, Mass., 1895) omits one or two minor poems but includes Browning's important 'Essay on Shelley'.

The old Oxford Standard Authors edition contains everything that Browning published up to 1864 (including his plays), rather confusingly rearranged. The new Oxford Standard Authors edition, edited by the present writer, should prove more agreeable to use: it includes everything that Browning wrote until 1864, but for the plays, and avoids the ugly double columns of its predecessor. The short poems are printed in the order in which they appeared when they were first published in volume form, though the text of each poem is that of Browning's final edition.

Two editions of Browning's poetry aiming at completeness are under way at the moment. One, which is planned to consist of thirteen volumes, is being published at Athens, Ohio, under the general editorship of Professor Roma King. The first volume, containing *Pauline* and *Paracelsus*, appeared in 1969. The other edition, which will exclude the plays (but for *Pippa Passes*), will be published in the Oxford English Texts series and will be edited by John Bryson and the present writer. Each of these editions will contain full textual apparatus, and will aim at establishing an accurate text of Browning's poems. The Ohio edition will also contain explanatory notes.

The five-volume edition of *Robert Browning's Poems and Plays* in Everyman's Library is complete to 1864, but selective after that. Of the first three volumes, which are edited by John Bryson, the first goes as far as 1844, the second to *Dramatis Personæ*, while the third gives the first-edition text of *The Ring and the Book*. Vol. IV, edited by Mildred M. Bozman, contains *Balaustion's Adventure*, *Aristophanes' Apology* and *Prince Hohenstiel-Schwangau*. Vol. V, which bears no editor's name, contains selections from the later poems.

A Choice of Browning's Verse, edited by Edward Lucie-Smith (1967), contains a sensitive Introduction by a poet who himself writes dramatic monologues. It is interesting to notice his verdict that Browning, 'more than any other Victorian, is responsible for the direction taken by our own literature, and foreshadows many of its characteristics. Browning is a kind of quarry, from which modern poetry continues to be hewn.'

The Ohio editors aim at full annotation. Meanwhile readers may consult the notes in the last volume of *The Poetical Works* (1894, noted above), DeVane's *Handbook*, the edition of *Paracelsus* edited by Margaret L. Lee and Katharine B. Locock (1909), and that of *Men and Women* edited by G. E. Hadow (1911). A. K. Cook's *Commentary upon Browning's 'The Ring and the Book'* is mentioned elsewhere. The notes in A. J. Whyte's edition of *Sordello* provide some assistance. A facsimile of the original edition of *Pauline* was published in 1886, and in 1931 N. Hardy Wallis edited 'the text of 1833, compared with that of 1867 and 1888'.

Browning's *Essay on Shelley* was edited by L. Winstanley in 1911. It is also available in a volume containing Shelley's *Defence of Poetry* and Peacock's *Four Ages of Poetry*, edited by H. F. B. Brett-Smith (1921), and in several editions of the Poems. (Two articles on this essay may be noticed here: one by Philip Drew in *Victorian Poetry*, 1963 (*LK*)[1], the other by T. J. Collins in the same periodical in the following year.)

In 1948 Donald Smalley edited *Browning's Essay on Chatterton*, with introductory chapters and notes. In a study which carries the imprimatur of DeVane Smalley convincingly attributes to Browning an article which appeared in *The Foreign Quarterly Review* for July 1842, and presents it as 'in reality a creative work of a curious and hybrid sort, an initial exercise of power in a province of writing that Browning was later to make peculiarly his own . . . the art of special pleading'. Claiming that the *Essay* 'affords fresh insight into the ways of Browning's creative thinking', Smalley relates it particularly to *The Ring and the Book*.

CRITICAL STUDIES AND COMMENTARY

(a) *Books*

Browning's early reputation was that of a promising young poet unknown to the general public. *Paracelsus* and *Strafford* enjoyed a very modest degree of success, but the publication of *Sordello* in 1840 was a disaster, and the scarcity of the *Bells and Pomegranates* pamphlets in which Browning published his plays and poems during the next few years is evidence of the general lack of interest in his work. It was soon evident that he could expect little success as a dramatist: Macready was so disappointed with *The Return of the Druses* that he confided to his diary his fear that the poet's intellect was 'not quite clear'. Although *Men and Women* (1855) is the most distinguished collection of shorter poems to be published by any Victorian poet—

---

[1] *LK* = Litzinger and Knickerbocker (eds.), *The Browning Critics* (see REFER-ENCES, CRITICAL STUDIES).

Tennyson's *Poems* of 1842 being the only possible rival—its critical reception was lukewarm at the best. Young men were reading Browning, however, and *Dramatis Personæ*, published nine years later, became the first of his volumes to reach a genuine second edition. After the publication of *The Ring and the Book* in 1868-9 Browning began to come before a rather wider reading public as a major literary figure. In May 1872, writing a prefatory note to his own *Selections* from his work (First Series), he commented on the development of his reputation in this way:

A few years ago, had such an opportunity presented itself, I might have been tempted to say a word in reply to the objections my poetry was used to encounter. Time has kindly co-operated with my disinclination to write the poetry and the criticism besides. The readers I am at last privileged to expect, meet me fully half-way. . . . Nor do I apprehend any more charges of being wilfully obscure, unconscientiously careless, or perversely harsh.

From that time to his death in 1889 Browning's reputation rose steadily, fostered by the Browning Society, a characteristic feature of the late Victorian scene which was to be immortalized by Max Beerbohm in his delightful illustration of 'Mr. Robert Browning taking tea with the Browning Society'—in which the poet himself appears as a vigorous old man surrounded by pale and earnest 'interpreters' of his work.

About the turn of the century Browning was beginning to influence a number of English and American poets (Kipling, Hardy, Pound), yet at the same time (and particularly in England) his reputation was in decline, partly in reaction against the humourless concentration on his 'message' that spread from the parent Society to Browning Societies as far afield as Texas and Japan. In America and on the Continent interest in Browning has never altogether waned, but in England it is only in the last decade or two that there have been signs of a serious revival of interest.

It is appropriate that the most valuable of all aids to the study of Browning's poetry should be the work of an American scholar: *A Browning Handbook* by William Clyde DeVane (1935; 2nd edn., 1955). After a useful biographical summary, DeVane devotes a section to each volume that Browning published, summarizing all available information about the publication of the book, the sources and date of composition of each poem, and the reception given the work by contemporary critics. From time to time DeVane's work will need to be brought up to date, but it remains a model of its kind, and only close students of Browning's work require to consult the earlier books of the same kind. *A Handbook to the Works of Robert Browning*, by Mrs. Sutherland Orr, which was first published in 1885 and several times revised, is the work of a friend of Browning's, and certainly contains material supplied by the poet himself. Yet some of Mrs. Orr's interpretations of individual poems are so limited and misleading that it is hard to believe that they were Browning's own, and impossible to accept them as finally binding. *An Introduction to the Study of Browning*, by Arthur Symons (1886), is the work of a more intelligent reader of poetry, and remains impressive as an early guide to the work of a perplexing poet. In an appendix Symons reprints the discarded prefaces to certain of Browning's works (e.g. *Paracelsus*). *The Browning Cyclopaedia*, by Edward Berdoe (1892) is much less valuable. *Robert Browning: How to Know Him*, by William Lyon Phelps (1915), is by no means as helpful a book as certain others in the same series—William P. Trent's handbook to Defoe, for example.

The *Papers* of the Browning Society, published between 1881 and 1895, are still occasionally worth consulting. *Browning's Message to his Time: his Religion, Philosophy, and Science* by Edward Berdoe (1890), consists of lectures and papers of which several had been read to the Society. J. T. Nettleship's *Essays on Robert Browning's Poetry* (1868), expanded as *Browning: Essays and Thoughts* (1890), is of greater interest. *Browning as a Philosophical and Religious Teacher*, by Sir Henry Jones (*LK*), was first published in 1891 and several times reprinted. Professor of Moral Philosophy (latterly) at the University of Glasgow, Jones was a man of ability who knew (and emphasized) that 'Browning was, first of all, a poet; it is only as a poet that he can be finally judged'. His own concern, however, was to 'discover Browning's philosophy of life', and accordingly he offers professorial considerations on Browning's optimism, the relationship between optimism and ethics, Browning's idealism and his attitude to love, 'Browning's Solution of the Problem of Evil', and related topics. In a conclusion which anticipates a famous phrase of T. S. Eliot's, Jones states that 'The severance of feeling and intelligence is Browning's fundamental error, destructive of both his moral theory and of his optimism'. Philip Drew has criticized Jones in an interesting essay in *Victorian Poetry* (*LK*), yet Jones's work has too often been disregarded or depreciated by critics of half his intelligence. His study of Browning as a thinker, with the limitations which such an approach necessarily brings with it, is an abler book than most recent investigations of comparable scope.

The title of Stopford A. Brooke's study, *The Poetry of Robert*

Browning (1902), proclaims a welcome shift of emphasis, and although he is an unexciting critic Stopford Brooke still repays occasional consultation. G. K. Chesterton's book in the 'English Men of Letters' series (*LK*) is the work of a very different sort of writer. Chesterton was a remarkable man, who approached Browning (as he approached everything) from a highly idiosyncratic point of view, and the result is an unusually illuminating study, which contains few facts but a wealth of penetrating and provocative comment. *The Early Career of Robert Browning*, by Thomas R. Lounsbury (1911), contains four lectures in which the author surveys Browning's career and reputation from *Pauline* to the end of the *Bells and Pomegranates* series. This remains a valuable book, by an able man, concerned not only with the early course of Browning's reputation but also with the development of his curiously incomplete dramatic gifts: Lounsbury's comments on the plays make a good starting-point for further study.

The work of a lifelong student of Browning, *The Infinite Moment and Other Essays in Robert Browning*, by William O. Raymond (1950, revised edn. 1965; *LK*), takes its title from Browning's remark to Ruskin, that the problem of poetry is the problem of 'putting the infinite within the finite'. The volume contains a sensitive study of Browning's relations with Isabella Blagden, three important essays on *The Ring and The Book*, a study of *Fifine at the Fair*, a consideration of 'Browning's Conception of Love as Represented in *Paracelsus*', and a well-known essay on 'Browning's Casuists'.

Another influential book, *The Alien Vision of Victorian Poetry*, by E. D. H. Johnson (1952), sees Browning in the context of Victorian literature as a whole. Johnson argues that 'the important writing of the Victorian period is to a large extent the product of a double awareness . . . a conflict, demonstrable within the work of the writers themselves, between the public conscience of the man of letters who comes forward as the accredited spokesman of his world, and the private conscience of the artist who conceives that his highest allegiance must be to his own aesthetic sensibilities'. Although this thesis is more obviously applicable to Tennyson, Johnson uses it persuasively in a suggestive sketch of Browning's poetic career. This discussion of Browning in relation to the problem of the Writer and Society has been deservedly influential.

The ablest and most interesting of all modern studies of Browning, *The Poetry of Experience: The Dramatic Monologue in Modern Literary Tradition*, by Robert Langbaum (1957), has already been mentioned. Langbaum's book contains penetrating and original interpretations of many of the shorter poems ('My Last Duchess' and 'Childe Roland to the Dark Tower Came', for example), as well as an admirable critique of *The Ring and the Book* as a 'relativist poem', but its true importance is due to Langbaum's realization that a reassessment of Browning's stature as a poet must be associated with a fresh understanding of his position in the development of English poetry. He sets Browning in a new perspective, and demonstrates conclusively that his major work is in no sense peripheral to the English poetic tradition.

Criticism worthy to be placed beside Langbaum's, though of a very different nature, is to be found in *The Disappearance of God: Five Nineteenth-Century Writers*, by J. Hillis Miller (1963). The opening paragraphs, describing the world of Browning's poetry, are reminiscent of certain passages in Wilson Knight's Shakespearian criticism: impressionistic in a sense, they derive from a remarkably close and perceptive reading of the poetry. Such reading enables Hillis Miller to make some most valuable generalizations about Browning's work:

There is a close relation between the metaphysical or psychological problems which are dominant in Browning and the specific form his language takes. The language of 'Sordello' or the 'Parleyings' suggests that Browning does not really want to be clear, precise, and comprehensible. The incoherent particulars of the historical background of 'Sordello' are intentionally obscure. They are obscure because it is not the history which Browning seeks to express. Rather, using this, he wants to express, as he says, 'the development of a soul', but, one should add, the development of a soul which does not develop, which remains close to the inexhaustible murmur of the language behind language, the formlessness prior to all form (p. 90).

Hillis Miller is particularly interesting on the long early poems, which he reads as perceptively as anyone has ever done:

When Browning's early heroes try to escape from the 'clay prisons' of themselves, and reach divine knowledge, they experience merely the dissipation of their powers into a murky emptiness. The expansiveness of Paracelsus, Sordello, and the protagonist of 'Pauline', their attempts to know and be everything at once, leads not to an intensification of life, but rather to just the opposite, a rarefaction, a thinning out, an evaporation of immense energies into the intense inane. The dramatic climax of Browning's three earliest poems is the failure of romantic Prometheanism (p. 97).

Hillis Miller insists on the links connecting Browning's early poetry with his latest, in another passage which it would be pleasant to quote. But his long chapter is full of passages that demand to be quoted, and the moral is simply that anyone seriously interested in Browning's work should turn for guidance to his remarkable study. What he gives us may not be the whole truth about Browning; but it is a very important part of the truth.

Three books of minor importance may be merely mentioned here: *L'Art et la pensée de Robert Browning*, by Paul de Reul (1929), the much briefer *Robert Browning*, by J. M. Cohen (1952), and *Amphibian: A Reconsideration of Browning*, by H. C. Duffin (1956).

The next five books that call for attention are all the work of American scholars: a fair comment on the interest in his work in the United States. *The Bow and the Lyre: The Art of Robert Browning*, by Roma A. King, Jr. (1957; *LK*), is the work of a disciple of Austin Warren who has become an authority on Browning's poetry. In this study he concentrates on 'Andrea del Sarto', 'Fra Lippo Lippi', 'The Bishop Orders his Tomb', 'Bishop Blougram's Apology', and 'Saul'; but although the book contains many interesting comments, the value of the criticism is limited by the author's unwillingness to go beyond the bare text of his poems—the words on the page. Another study of Browning by Professor King has recently appeared. *Browning's Characters: A Study in Poetic Technique*, by Park Honan (one of King's co-editors in the Ohio edition), is a courageous full-scale attempt to trace Browning's methods of characterization from the early poems and plays to the great monologues. Honan is concerned with some of the central problems that confront the critic of Browning, and although his comments do not always command our assent his book remains both stimulating and valuable. In *The Triple Soul: Browning's Theory of Knowledge* (1963) Norton B. Crowell sets out to oppose Henry Jones's statement that man is forced to 'reject the testimony either of the heart or of the head . . . [and that] Browning unhesitatingly adopts the latter alternative'. Crowell's combative book is a defence of Browning against the charge of anti-intellectualism. *The Central Truth: The Incarnation in Robert Browning's Poetry*, by William Whitla (1963), is an intelligent yet eccentric study. It contains a folding diagram, with 'Robert Browning: Poet Prophet King' in the middle of a sort of family tree; with 'Cupiditas, The Incarnation of Caritas and Amor' at the top of the page, and 'Death and Life' at the bottom; and with the main monologues arranged in a pattern round the centre. Whitla comments as follows:

The book is organized so that Browning's attempt to achieve the moment of spiritual unity through the Incarnation is examined first in the religious monologues. Then to this theme is added Browning's attempt to realize the moment of aesthetic unity in the art monologues. Both of these subjects, religion and art, have their minor roles in the third aspiration, for physical unity in the love poems. The culmination of Browning's genius is *The Ring and the Book*. Here the three themes . . . reach their fruition (p. v).

Although Whitla is aware that his scheme is imposed on Browning's poetry, and not inherent in it, he allows himself to be led by his own interests into some very questionable critical statements or implications:

Neither duke nor bishop is able to face the point of time, the critical moment in each life . . . by wedding love to power and knowledge. We should not be surprised at this serious moral defect; Browning had not yet come to write *Christmas-Eve and Easter-Day* . . . 'My Last Duchess' and 'The Bishop Orders his Tomb' . . . are fragments of the unified picture of the Renaissance that Browning could present after the solidification of his religious experience (pp. 56–7).

Robert Browning: a Study of his Poetry, by Thomas Blackburn (1967), starts from the accurate observation that there is still no standard critical book on Browning's work, but quite fails to remedy this deficiency. *Browning's Poetry of Reticence*, by Barbara Melchiori (1968), is a study of 'The Bishop Orders his Tomb', 'Andrea del Sarto', 'Childe Roland', 'Caliban upon Setebos', *Fifine*, and one or two other poems. Mrs. Melchiori is more concerned with the imaginative processes which produced Browning's poems than with their 'philosophy', and she is convinced that Freudian psychology provides a key to much that is puzzling in his life and work. Although her book remains a collection of articles rather than a comprehensive study, she has thrown most interesting light on a number of the principal poems, notably 'The Bishop Orders his Tomb'. In *The Dialectical Temper: The Rhetorical Art of Robert Browning* (1968), W. David Shaw is concerned, above all, with Browning's 'ability to engage an audience and control its responses by employing dialectical irony and the devices of legal and religious rhetoric'. His book illuminates not only the technique of Browning but also the ideas which he used his technique to express.

It is now time to mention work on *The Ring and the Book*, and one or two books on specialized aspects of Browning's poetry. *A Commentary upon Browning's 'The Ring and the Book'*, by A. K. Cook (1920), contains a great deal of information and other helpful background material. It includes a useful appendix on the text of the poem, and a full index. Charles W. Hodell's facsimile reproduction of *The Old Yellow Book* (1908), which also contains a translation, is indispensable for anyone who wishes to see how Browning handled his sources. John Marshall Gest's later translation (1927) is the work of a lawyer who is exclusively concerned with the legal aspects of the case. *Sidelights on Robert Browning's 'The Ring and the Book'*, by Louise Snitslàar (1934), is a careful thesis which sheds occasional light. *Curious Annals*, by Beatrice Corrigan (1956), contains (as the sub-title indicates) 'New Documents relating to Browning's Roman Murder Story'. Further material—unknown to Browning—may be found in E. H. Yarrill's translation of *Browning's Roman Murder Story as Recorded in a hitherto Unknown Italian Contemporary Manuscript* (1939). An important recent study is *Browning's Roman Murder Story*, by Richard D. Altick and James F. Loucks (1968), a reading of the poem that is particularly welcome because it directs attention away from the old subject of Browning's handling of his sources. The authors are concerned with the poem as a poem, with the poet's purpose, and with the way in which he strove to achieve it: their careful study throws a good deal of light on a very complicated poem.

An essential book is *Browning's Parleyings: the Autobiography of a Mind*, by William Clyde DeVane (1927). As the sub-title suggests, DeVane saw the true importance of one of the later poems which had received little attention, and he studies it less in itself than as evidence of Browning's development as a poet and as a thinker. A briefer study, *Browning and his English Predecessors in the Dramatic Monolog* [sic], by Benjamin Willis Fuson, consists primarily of long enumerations of earlier English poets who wrote in something resembling Browning's chosen form. Although there are few ideas in this pamphlet, and although those who search will be able to find earlier monologues overlooked by Fuson, there is merit in the persevering survey which leads him to the conclusion that Browning was 'not pioneer but past master' of the monologue form. *Browning's Star-Imagery: the Study of a Detail in Poetic Design*, by C. Willard Smith (1941), is the work of a scholar who began by studying Browning's versification, and was then impressed by the importance of certain other aspects of his poetic technique. It is a modest book which retains a certain value. *Robert Browning's Moral-Aesthetic Theory, 1833–1855* (1967), by Robert J. Collins, is another useful study. Sidelights on Browning are provided by *William Edmondstoune Aytoun and the Spasmodic Controversy*, by Mark A. Weinstein (1968), which deals with the gifted author of *Firmilian*.

The course of Browning's reputation is considered in many general books, and particularly in Lounsbury's *Early Career* (p. 290 above). *Browning and the Twentieth Century*, by A. Allen Brockington (1932), is 'A study of Robert Browning's Influence and Reputation' which has been censured for the fact that Ezra Pound's name does not occur in the index. It is interesting to notice that the author feels it necessary to state that the poetry of Browning 'has not perished', and internal evidence suggests that his study began as a thesis before or during the First World War. Although it might have been a better book if it had been written a decade or two later, it contains sensible remarks on the influence of Browning in Hardy, Kipling, Eliot, and other writers to the late 1920s. *Time's Revenges: Browning's Reputation as a Thinker, 1889–1962*, by Boyd Litzinger (1964), traces its theme in a manner which is informative and occasionally entertaining. *Browning: The Critical Heritage* by Litzinger and D. Smalley, gives generous selections from the criticism published up to the time of the poet's death.

(b) Essays and Articles

Anyone looking for important essays and articles on Browning should begin with two collections of critical writing published in 1965 and 1966, the one in America and the other in England. Fortunately there is little overlapping between *The Browning Critics*, edited by Boyd Litzinger and K. L. Knickerbocker, and *Robert Browning: a Collection of Critical Essays*, edited by Philip Drew—only three pieces appear in both collections. Litzinger and Knickerbocker begin with Henry Jones and give twenty-two further essays. Drew's selection, which is slightly briefer, covers a similar field with a rather different arrangement and emphasis. Litzinger and Knickerbocker include a most useful bibliography of writing on Browning from 1951 to early 1965. In the following citations of articles *LK* is used (as mentioned on a previous page) to indicate that the article is given in whole or in part in the one collection just mentioned, while *D* refers to the other.

The twentieth century began badly for Browning, with the publication of George Santayana's *Interpretations of Poetry and Religion* (1900). In the section entitled 'The Poetry of Barbarism' (*LK, D*) Santayana wrote as follows: 'Our poets are things of shreds and patches; they give us episodes and studies, a sketch of this curiosity, a glimpse of that romance; they have no total vision, no grasp of the whole reality, and consequently no capacity for a sane and steady idealization' (*D*, p. 17). In an influential attack which is extracted at length in both collections of essays, Santayana attacks Walt Whitman and Browning as pre-eminent examples of the barbaric poet. A further attack was delivered in 1905, when Paul Elmer More wrote as follows, in an essay entitled 'Why is Browning Popular?': 'It is not pleasant to be convicted of throwing stones at the prophets, as I

shall appear to many to have done. My only consolation is that, if
the prophet is a true teacher, these stones of the casual passer-by
merely raise a more conspicuous monument to his honour; but if he
turns out in the end to be a false prophet (as I believe Browning to
have been)—why, then, let his disciples look to it.' (*LK* p. 119).

There were still some who took Browning seriously, as may be seen
by a glance at the names of books on him published during the early
part of this century—or by looking into Percy Lubbock's article in
the *Quarterly Review*, published in 1912 and extracted at length in
Drew's collection. Ezra Pound's respectful comments are conveniently
accessible in his *Literary Essays*, edited by T. S. Eliot (1954). But we
are on the threshold of the 1940s before interest in Browning seems
to enter its second period.

Between 1939 and 1954 H. B. Charlton, the Shakespearian critic,
published a series of articles in the *Bulletin of the John Rylands Library*.
No doubt intended for a book, these unpretentious and helpful
articles have the following titles: 'Browning as Dramatist', 'Browning's Ethical Poetry', 'Browning as Poet of Religion', 'Poetry and
Truth: an Aspect of Browning's *Ring and the Book*', and 'Browning:
the Making of the Dramatic Lyric'.

In 1949 Edwin Muir published a brief but outstanding comment
on Browning in his *Essays on Literature and Society* (D). A single paragraph may serve to illustrate the perceptiveness of this essay:

If we judge Browning by his best work, then it is as absurd to call him an
optimist as it would be to call Dante an optimist because the *Divine Comedy*
begins in Hell and ends in Heaven. What happened to him when he spoke
directly of his hopes was that he forgot the more formidable elements in his
imaginative world. He had to enter into the lives of people quite unlike
himself before he could realise all the obstacles to his easy faith in things.
But this is what he did; his work consisted in this. (pp. 105–6)

Only a handful of the numerous general essays on Browning which
have appeared in the last twenty years can be mentioned here.
Hoxie N. Fairchild's 'Browning: the Simple-Hearted Casuist' (*LK*)
is the work of a man who made a lifelong study of the religious and
philosophical views of the major English writers. His essay, which
also appeared in 1949, concludes as if it had been designed as a reply
to Edwin Muir:

Some may prefer to say the 'real' Browning is genuinely dramatic, and
that his soul-saving giveways are reluctant concessions to the Victorian
appetite for wholesome messages. But he was a very honest man, and when
the writings of an honest man reek with purpose the logical conclusion is

that he is honestly purposeful. His naive didacticism represents the 'real' Browning no less faithfully than his psychological sophistication. He was inwardly divided against himself, though to some extent the conflict was his personal share of a prevalent nineteenth-century confusion. (p. 228)

In 1965 Robert Preyer endeavoured to distinguish between 'Two Styles in the Verse of Robert Browning'. The following year Robert Langbaum wrote interestingly on 'Browning and the Question of Myth', arguing that Browning sometimes uses myth and symbol in the modern manner.

The present writer's 1967 Warton Lecture, *Robert Browning*, discusses Browning's place in the English poetic tradition, and the different ways in which he employs the dramatic principle in his shorter poems. Earlier studies of Browning's use of the dramatic monologue, rendered largely obsolete by Langbaum's book and other subsequent work, include 'The Monologue of Browning' by G. H. Palmer, 'The Dramatic Monologue' by I. B. Sessions, and 'The Dramatic Monologue in the Victorian Period' by M. W. Mac-Callum. Studies rather wider in their bearing than their titles might suggest include *Browning and the Modern Novel* (*D*), a lecture by Hugh Sykes Davies which deserves to be better known; 'The Virgin and the Dragon' (*LK, D*) by W. C. DeVane, a study which shows the importance of the Andromeda myth to Browning's life and poetry; and 'The Intellectual Kinship of John Donne and Robert Browning' by J. E. Duncan.

The appearance of numerous articles on individual poems has been one of the welcome signs of the renewal of interest in Browning's work during the last ten or fifteen years. For the most part the reader must be referred to other bibliographies for lists of these writings, but a handful of representative articles will be mentioned here, with the caution that it is always best to begin by looking at DeVane's comments on a poem in his *Handbook*.

'Robert Browning: a Reading of the Early Narratives', by Robert Preyer, is one of the three pieces reprinted in both collections of criticism: evidence not only that it is an intelligent piece of work, but also that there is no abundance of illuminating criticism on Browning's difficult early poems. On *Pauline*, however, we may consult Mill's *marginalia* in Drew's anthology, and compare the estimates of their importance and influence by Masaó Miyoshi ('Mill and *Pauline*: the Myth and some Facts') and O. P. Govil ('A Note on Mill and Browning's *Pauline*'). T. J. Collins has written on 'Shelley and God in Browning's *Pauline*: Unresolved Problems'.

F. E. L. Priestley has written interestingly on 'The Ironic Pattern of Browning's *Paracelsus*'. *Sordello* has been discussed by a number of writers, notably W. C. DeVane ('Sordello's Story Retold'), S. W. Holmes ('The Sources of Browning's *Sordello*'), Earl Hilton ('Browning's *Sordello* as a Study of the Will'), R. R. Columbus and Claudette Kemper ('Sordello and the Speaker: a Problem in Identity'), and Daniel Stempel ('Browning's *Sordello*: the Art of the Makers-See').

On poems between *Sordello* and *Men and Women* one may consult 'The Meaning and Structure of *Pippa Passes*' by Margaret E. Glen, 'The Manichee in the Cloister: a Reading of Browning's "Soliloquy of the Spanish Cloister" ' by M. K. Starkman, 'Browning's Duke as Theatrical Producer' by David Shaw, 'Ferrara and "My Last Duchess" ' by L. S. Friedland, 'Browning's Witless Duke' (*LK*) by B. R. Jerman, and 'Browning's Shrewd Duke' (*LK*) by Laurence Perrine—these four last articles being evidence of the fascination exercised by one of Browning's first great poems. J. W. Tilton and R. D. Tuttle have written on 'Count Gismond', as has Sister M. M. Holloway. 'Touchstones for Browning's Victorian Complexity', by Karl Kroeber, contains an interesting brief study of 'Meeting at Night' and 'Parting at Morning'. Phyllis J. Guskin has written well on a neglected poem, *Christmas-Eve and Easter Day*.

Turning to the poems published in *Men and Women* in 1855, we find that Richard D. Altick has written provocatively on ' "A Grammarian's Funeral": Browning's Praise of Folly?' (*D*), claiming that the poem may be read as a satire on a man who has chosen wrongly in life. Several writers have opposed this view, notably M. J. Svaglic in an article in *Victorian Poetry*. A number of other critics have explored the obscurities of 'Childe Roland', notably Harold Golder, Barbara Melchiori, John Willoughby and T. P. Harrison, who associates the poem with Wordsworth's 'Peter Bell'. 'The Shaping of *Saul*', by J. A. S. McPeek, relates that poem to Wyatt's *Penitential Psalms*, while W. David Shaw (in 'The Analogical Argument') studies 'Saul' as a visionary poem. Another intelligent article is Ward Hellstrom's 'Time and Type in Browning's *Saul*'. Among articles on 'Bishop Blougram's Apology', that by Boyd Litzinger questions the usual view that Cardinal Wiseman himself reviewed the poem; see also F. E. L. Priestley (*LK*). William Irvine discusses four of the 1855 monologues in *Victorian Poetry* (1964). There is a brief but interesting discussion of 'In a Balcony' by an expert on the drama, Edgar Elmer Stoll (*D*). Roma A. King's essay, 'Browning: "Mage" and "Maker"': a study in Poetic

Purpose and Method' (*D*) is an illuminating discussion of 'Cleon'. Richard D. Altick has related 'Karshish' to St. Paul.

The poems published in *Dramatis Personæ* in 1864 have also been discussed by a number of critics. In ' "James Lee's Wife"— and Browning's' Glenn Sandstrom discusses the possible biographical background. 'Caliban upon Setebos' has been studied by E. K. Brown, who shows that the style is admirably adapted to the poet's dramatic purpose, while C. R. Tracy holds that the poem illustrates Theodore Parker's thesis on the early emergence of religious belief in the history or pre-history of man. John Howard sees no satire in the poem, which he regards as 'part of Browning's way of showing that God reveals to each creature only what he is capable of under-standing'. Isobel Armstrong has an interesting treatment of 'Mr. Sludge, "The Medium"' in *Victorian Poetry* (*D*). The important 'Epilogue' to *Dramatis Personæ* was examined by Watson Kirk-connell in 1926, and sensibly described as 'a brief deliverance of Browning's mature beliefs in religion and philosophy' (*D*).

Only a few of the articles on Browning's later poems can be mentioned here. In 'The Harlot and the Thoughtful Young Man' (*LK*) DeVane explored the background of *Fifine at the Fair*, a poem more recently illuminated by C. C. Watkins in an article entitled 'The "Abstruser Themes" of Browning's *Fifine at the Fair*'. The same critic has written interestingly on 'Browning's *Red Cotton Night-Cap Country* and Carlyle'. In 'A Parleying with Aristophanes' Donald Smalley relates *Aristophanes' Apology* to the *Parleyings*. Henry James wrote on *The Inn Album*: his essay may be found in his *Views and Reviews* (1908). On *La Saisiaz* one may consult F. E. L. Priestley's 'A Reading of *La Saisiaz*' (*D*), and H. N. Fairchild's '*La Saisiaz* and *The Nineteenth Century*'. *Browning's Mind and Art*, edited by Clarence Tracy (1968), is a collection of essays by F. E. L. Priestley, Geoffrey Tillotson, George Ridenour, Richard Altick, Archibald A. Hill, and others.

BIOGRAPHIES AND LETTERS

(a) Books

At the time of writing a new biography by William Irvine and Park Honan is awaited, and there is certainly room for it. If there is a 'standard' biography at the moment, it is still *The Life of Robert Browning, with Notices of his Writings, his Family, and his Friends* by W. Hall Griffin, completed and edited by Harry Christopher Minchin and first published in 1910 (slightly revised in 1938).

This is a balanced biography of the old type, containing a great deal of useful information, free from psychological hypothesis and daring speculation. Occasionally it tantalizes by failing to give evidence for statements that may be perfectly correct—the rather unlikely statement, for example, that Browning wrote 'Johannes Agricola in Meditation' and 'Porphyria's Lover' during his brief visit to Moscow in the Spring of 1834. In any case, a great deal of further information has come to light since the book was published, and many hundreds of letters are available to the modern biographer to which Griffin and Minchin had no access.

The best of the early biographical studies is the *Life and Letters of Robert Browning*, by Mrs. Sutherland Orr, who knew Browning well. It first appeared in 1891, and was issued with revisions by F. G. Kenyon in 1908: it remains important. Edmund Gosse's *Personalia* (1890) contains some interesting first-hand impressions, as does *Records of Tennyson, Ruskin and Browning* (1891) by Anne Ritchie (Anne Thackeray-Ritchie). Edward Dowden's *Life of Robert Browning*, first published in 1904 in a series called the Temple Biographies and later reprinted in Everyman's Library, deserves a further reprint today. Its scope is indicated by the opening sentence of the Preface: 'An attempt is made in this volume to tell the story of Browning's life, including, as part of it, a notice of all his books, which may be regarded as the chief of "his acts and all that he did".' A reader of Griffin and Minchin will not find new facts in Dowden's book, but he will find the course of Browning's career described intelligently and suggestively. G. K. Chesterton's volume in the English Men of Letters series has been mentioned above (p. 290). C. H. Herford's *Robert Browning* (Modern English Writers series, 1905) is a less brilliant study of Browning's life and work which is still worth consulting. *The Brownings: their Life and Art*, by Lilian Whiting (1911), throws light on Browning's friendship with Mrs. Bronson: its author was also the first person to correct the story that Elizabeth Barrett showed her husband *Sonnets from the Portuguese* at Pisa in 1847—in fact the disclosure was made two years later, at Bagni di Lucca. In *Browning: Background and Conflict* (1931) F. R. G. Duckworth emphasizes the apparent inconsistency between Browning the man and Browning the poet (a discrepancy which helped to inspire Henry James's short story, 'The Private Life'). He maintains that Browning, who found poetic composition painful, to some extent deliberately dissociated his poetry from his life. *La Jeunesse de Robert Browning*, by Henri-Léon Hovelaque (1932), is an intelligent and thorough study which is the more valuable because the poems on which it concentrates—*Pauline, Paracelsus, Sordello*—have not been as carefully studied as they deserve. *Shelley and Browning: A Myth and Some Facts*, by F. A. Pottle (1923), has a special niche in Browning studies. In this admirable piece of detective work Pottle identifies the copy of Shelley which belonged to Browning (*Miscellaneous Poems*, published by Benbow in 1826), showing (as he does so) that Mrs. Orr and William Sharp (in his *Life of Robert Browning*, 1890) had given an inaccurate account of the way in which Browning first encountered the poetry of Shelley.

One of the most provocative of recent books on Browning is *Robert Browning: a Portrait*, by Betty Miller (1952), a biography which has been described as 'glittering' and 'unsympathetic', but which undoubtedly provided stimulus to the study of the poet. While the author's interpretations of certain of the poems will strike most readers as unduly autobiographical, her psychological speculations about the poet's relations with his mother, with Elizabeth Barrett, and with the other women in his life, are both interesting and intelligent. *Robert Browning and his World: the Private Face (1812–1861)*, by Maisie Ward (1967), deals with Browning's life to the year in which his wife died and he returned to England. Mrs. Ward, who is the author of popular biographies of G. K. Chesterton and of the young Newman, describes Mrs. Miller's book as 'wonderfully ingenious and brilliantly written', commenting disapprovingly that it 'received the reviews usually accorded a best-selling novel, which indeed it notably resembles'. Unfortunately her own handling of evidence is sometimes wilful, her comments on the poems are often ingenuous, while the absence of detailed references (for which she apologizes) is bound to be irritating to the scholar. A second volume, *Two Robert Brownings?*, appeared in 1969.

(b) Articles and Essays

As in CRITICAL STUDIES (*b*) above, the reader who wishes to find a full listing of articles and essays bearing on the life of Browning must be referred to the fuller BIBLIOGRAPHIES section on p. 314 below. 'The Ancestry of Robert Browning, the Poet', by Sir Vincent Baddeley, is the most thorough investigation so far of a tantalizing subject. The character and influence of his father have been surprisingly little investigated. 'Joseph Arnould and Robert Browning: New Letters (1842–50) and a Verse Epistle', by Donald Smalley, throws light on an important phase in Browning's development and on his friendship with Alfred Domett and other able young men. 'Browning and Macready: the Final Quarrel', by Joseph W. Reed, Jr., deals with the poet's break with his producer over *A Blot in the 'Scutcheon*.

The mysteries of Browning's character are fair game for psychological analysis, and two articles by S. W. Holmes are well-known for their attempt to apply Jungian analysis. In 'Browning's *Sordello* and Jung: Browning's *Sordello* in the Light of Jung's Theory of Types' Holmes argues that the composition of *Pauline* helped Browning to diagnose his own psychic condition, and discusses the value to the poet himself of writing *Sordello*. In 'Browning: Semantic Stutterer' Holmes gives a modern twist to the old observation that Browning is great when he writes dramatically, obscure and puzzling when he writes in his own person as a prophet. In 'The Private Life of Robert Browning' (*LK*) R. D. Altick argues that Browning's almost aggressive healthiness was a symptom of mental sickness: a view opposed by K. L. Knickerbocker in 'A Tentative Apology for Browning' (*LK*).

Two articles by Betty Miller provide postscripts to her biography. 'This Happy Evening' describes Browning's meeting with Macready after the performance of Talfourd's *Ion* in 1836. 'The Séance at Ealing: A Study in Memory and Imagination' (*Cornhill Magazine*, 1957) deals with the séance in 1855 which led to disagreement between the Brownings and the writing of 'Mr. Sludge, the "Medium"'. 'An Echo from Browning's Second Courtship', by K. L. Knickerbocker, relates the poem 'Saint Martin's Summer' to Browning's unsuccessful courtship of Lousia, Lady Ashburton. In 'Browning's Grotesque Period' J. H. Hitner argues that *Red Cotton Night-Cap Country* and *The Inn Album* express the poet's depression and bitterness in the period after his rejection. 'Euripides Browningized: The Meaning of *Balaustion's Adventure*', by K. L. Knickerbocker, investigates the apparently autobiographical features in that poem. Two articles throw light on Browning's relations with his son, Pen: 'Robert Browning and his Son' by Gertrude Reese, and 'The Child of Casa Guidi' by Betty Miller. 'Browning's Heresies', by C. R. Tracy, is another article of importance.

(c) *Letters*

Although Browning was not a good letter-writer, a collected edition of his letters is greatly to be desired. Two courageous scholars, Philip Kelley and Ronald Hudson, are hoping to be able to publish a complete edition, with Mrs. Browning's letters, in a series of some thirty volumes. Meanwhile the student of Browning has to make do with a miscellaneous shelf-full of volumes, some notably inaccurate and almost all of them inadequately indexed—and to remember that letters which have still to be printed may considerably modify our picture of the poet.

The volume to begin with is certainly *The Letters of Robert Browning and Elizabeth Barrett Barrett*, published in two volumes in 1899 (and in one volume in 1923). Elvan Kintner's new edition is well annotated and indexed, and must be consulted by all serious students of Browning. Other early letters are to be found in Mrs. Sutherland Orr's *Life and Letters* (above, p. 300) and in *Robert Browning and Alfred Domett* (1906), edited by F. G. Kenyon—an interesting little volume which gives us a glimpse of Browning and his circle shortly before he met Elizabeth Barrett.

Two sizeable collections of letters are *Letters of Robert Browning, Collected by Thomas J. Wise*, edited by T. L. Hood (1933), and *New Letters of Robert Browning*, edited by W. C. DeVane and K. L. Knickerbocker (1950).

A great many other volumes contain collections of Browning letters.[2] The contents of *Twenty-Two Unpublished Letters of Elizabeth Barrett Browning and Robert Browning* (1935) were written to Henrietta and Arabella Moulton-Barrett between 1846 and the 1850s. *The Browning Box*, edited by H. W. Donner (1935), contains letters to T. F. Kelsall and his wife about the manuscripts of the poet Beddoes that had been entrusted to Browning. Of greater importance is the volume entitled *Robert Browning and Julia Wedgwood: a Broken Friendship as revealed in their Letters*, edited by Richard Curle in 1937: unfortunately these letters, which throw valuable light on the composition of *The Ring and the Book*, are by no means accurately edited. E. C. McAleer has edited two volumes of letters: *Dearest Isa: Robert Browning's Letters to Isabella Blagden* (1951), and *Learned Lady: Letters from Robert Browning to Mrs. Thomas FitzGerald, 1876–1889*: the letters in the former collection, which begin in 1857, are the more interesting. *Letters of the Brownings to George Barrett*, edited by Paul Landis and Ronald E. Freeman (1958), contains a good deal of information about 'Pen', among other subjects. *Browning to his American Friends*, edited by Gertrude Reese Hudson (1965), contains letters between the Brownings, the Storys, and James Russell Lowell, written between 1841 and 1890.

Hundreds of Browning's letters remain unpublished (many of them of very slight interest), while a great many others have been published, in whole or part, in volumes of Victorian memoirs and biography. The 'Calendar of Letters' in the Broughton–Northup–

[2] *The Brownings: their Life and Art*, by Lilian Whiting (1911) quotes many late letters to Mrs. Bronson.

Pearsall *Bibliography* lists 2,068 letters, and many others are now known to exist.

BIBLIOGRAPHIES

Much the most useful bibliography is *Robert Browning: a Bibliography, 1830–1950*, by L. N. Broughton, C. S. Northup, and Robert Pearsall (1953), which gives details of editions, manuscripts, biographical and critical studies, and other relevant material. Although the listing of letters is very incomplete, this is a volume of primary interest for anyone who wishes to study Browning's career and the course of his reputation. In most respects it renders obsolete F. J. Furnivall's *A Bibliography of Robert Browning, from 1833 to 1881* (published in the *Browning Society Papers* in 1881–2, and reprinted separately the following year), although the latter contains fuller extracts from contemporary reviews. Some useful information may be found in *Literary Anecdotes of the Nineteenth Century*, edited by W. R. Nicoll and T. J. Wise (1895–6), but it seems appropriate to consign the other works of Wise to a footnote.[3]

The fullest critical account of editions of Browning, biographical and critical studies, and the other material valuable to a serious student, is to be found in an article to which the present account is indebted, the Browning chapter (by Park Honan) in *The Victorian Poets: a Guide to Research*, 2nd edition, edited by Frederic E. Faverty (1968).

The Browning Critics (p. 295 above) contains a list which aims at including 'everything which has been published on Browning since 1950', and therefore forms a most useful supplement to the Broughton bibliography. Nearly 300 items are listed.

There is no need to emphasize the value of *The Browning Collections*, the illustrated *Catalogue of Oil Paintings, Drawings & Prints; Autograph Letters and Manuscripts; Books; etc.*, published by Sotheby, Wilkinson and Hodge to advertise the sale of 'Pen's' possessions in May 1913.

An invaluable *Concordance to the Poems of Robert Browning*, by L. N. Broughton and B. F. Stelter, was published in two volumes in 1924–5.

A Note on Elizabeth Barrett Browning

During her lifetime Elizabeth Barrett Browning was much better known as a poet than was her husband. A brief and highly selective

---

[3] *A Complete Bibliography of the Writings in Prose and Verse of Robert Browning* (1897), and *A Browning Library* (1929): both contain some useful information, but are highly unreliable because of their inclusion of Wise's own forgeries.

listing of her writings, and of studies of her work, is included here as a reminder of their importance to the reader of Robert Browning. They form a 'background' to his work which has been slighted or overlooked by most modern students of his poetry.

Mrs. Browning's *Last Poems* appeared posthumously in 1862. Her *Poetical Works* were published five years after her death, in 1866, in five volumes; and again in six volumes in 1889 and subsequently. There is a Prefatory Note by Browning. Charlotte Porter and Helen A. Clarke published their edition in 1900, while an Oxford edition made its appearance in 1904. In 1863 there had appeared *The Greek Christian Poets and the English Poets*, a reprint of a series of articles first published in *The Athenaeum* in 1842.

Many letters by Elizabeth Barrett are contained in the collections mentioned above, on pp. 302–3. Mention should also be made of *The Letters of Elizabeth Barrett Browning Addressed to Richard Hengist Horne*, edited by S. R. Townshend Mayer (2 vols., 1877); *The Letters of Elizabeth Barrett Browning*, edited by Frederic G. Kenyon (2 vols., 1897); *Elizabeth Barrett Browning: Letters to her Sister, 1846–1859*, edited by Leonard Huxley (1929); *Letters from Elizabeth Barrett to B. R. Haydon*, edited by Martha Hale Shackford (1939); *Elizabeth Barrett to Miss Mitford*, edited by Betty Miller (1954); and *Elizabeth Barrett to Mr. Boyd*, edited by Barbara P. McCarthy (1955). *Elizabeth Barrett Browning in her Letters*, by Percy Lubbock (1906), is an admirable interpretation made through a judicious selection of her letters.

There is an early French study of Mrs. Browning which retains some interest: *La Vie et l' Œuvre d'Elizabeth Barrett Browning*, by Germaine-Marie Merlette (1905). *The Family of the Barretts: a Colonial Romance*, by Jeanette Marks (1938), is a quarry of valuable information about her home background, her relations with her father, and other matters too often shrouded in legend. *Elizabeth Barrett Browning*, by Dorothy Hewlett (1953), makes use of some previously unpublished materials, but the standard biography is *The Life of Elizabeth Barrett Browning* by Gardner B. Taplin (1957), a sound and reliable study.

Mrs. Browning: a Poet's Work and its Setting, by Alethea Hayter (1962), discusses the poetry sensibly, and on occasion stimulatingly, without ever quite convincing us of its high merit. Of several brief treatments of *Aurora Leigh* perhaps the most interesting is that by J. M. S. Tompkins, in her 1961 Fawcett Lecture; valuable material is also to be found in *Chroniclers of Life*, by Amalendu Bose (1962). There is a *Descriptive Bibliography* by Warner Barnes (1968).

REFERENCES

TEXTS

Books and articles which have not been mentioned in the text are enclosed in square brackets.

(a) Collected Works

A. Birrell (ed.), *Browning: The Complete Poetical Works* (London, 1915; revised reprints since 1929).

Robert Browning, *The Poetical Works* (16 vols., London, 1888–9, 17th vol. 1894).

Robert Browning, *The Complete Poetic and Dramatic Works* (Cambridge, Mass., 1895).

J. Bryson and M. M. Bozman (eds.), *Robert Browning's Poems and Plays* (5 vols., Everyman's Library, London, many reprints).

I. Jack (ed.), *Browning: Poetical Works 1833–64* (Oxford Standard Authors, London, 1970).

F. G. Kenyon (ed.), *New Poems by Robert Browning and Elizabeth Barrett Browning* (London, 1914).

F. G. Kenyon (ed.), *The Works of Robert Browning* (Centenary edn., 10 vols., London, 1912; repr. 1967).

R. A. King, Jr., M. Peckham, P. Honan, and G. Pitts (eds.), *The Complete Works of Robert Browning* (Athens, Ohio, 1969–: vol. i, 1969).

C. Porter and H. A. Clarke (eds.), *The Complete Works of Robert Browning* (12 vols., New York, 1898).

(b) Selections and Separate Works

G. E. Hadow (ed.), *Browning's 'Men and Women', 1855* (reprint of the 2 vols. in one, Oxford, 1911). With Introduction and notes.

M. L. Lee and K. B. Locock (eds.), *Browning's 'Paracelsus'* (London, 1909).

E. Lucie-Smith (ed.), *A Choice of Browning's Verse* (paperback, London, 1967).

[S. Nowell-Smith (ed.), *Robert Browning, Poetry and Prose* (London, 1950; paperback, U.K.).]

D. Smalley (ed.), *Browning: 'Essay on Chatterton'* (Cambridge, Mass., 1948).

N. H. Wallis (ed.), *Browning: 'Pauline', The Text of 1833 compared with that of 1867 and 1888* (London, 1931).

A. J. Whyte (ed.), *Browning: 'Sordello'* (London, 1913).

L. Winstanley (ed.), *Browning: 'Essay on Shelley'* (London, 1911). Also in a volume ed. by H. F. B. Brett-Smith with Shelley's *Defence* and Peacock's *Four Ages* (Percy Reprints, Oxford, 1921).

T. J. Wise (ed.), *Pauline . . . A Reprint of the Original Edition of 1833* (London, 1886).

T. J. Wise (ed.), *Browning: 'Bells and Pomegranates', First Series*, I–V (London, 1896).

T. J. Wise (ed.), *Browning: 'Bells and Pomegranates', Second Series*, VI–VIII (London, 1897).

CRITICAL STUDIES AND COMMENTARY

R. D. Altick, and J. F. Loucks, *Browning's Roman Murder Story* (Chicago, 1968).

R. D. Altick, 'Browning's "Karshish" and Saint Paul', *MLN* lxxii (1957).

R. D. Altick, ' "A Grammarian's Funeral": Browning's Praise of Folly?', *SEL* iii (1963).

I. Armstrong, 'Browning's *Mr. Sludge, "The Medium"* ', *VP* ii (1964).

[K. Badger, ' "See the Christ Stand!": Browning's Religion', *Boston University Studies in English*, i (1955–6).]

[W. Bagehot, 'Wordsworth, Tennyson and Browning', in his *Literary Studies* (1895).]

E. Berdoe, *Browning's Message to his Time: His Religion, Philosophy, and Science* (London, 1890).

E. Berdoe, *The Browning Cyclopaedia*, 2nd edn. (London, 1897; still in print).

[J. Berlin-Lieberman, *Robert Browning and Hebraism* (Jerusalem, 1934).]

T. Blackburn, *Robert Browning: a Study of his Poetry* (London, 1967).

[J. K. Bonnell, 'Touch Images in the Poetry of Robert Browning', *PMLA* xxxvii (1922).]

[J. A. Boulton, 'Browning: a Potential Revolutionary', *EIC* iii (1953).]

A. A. Brockington, *Browning and the Twentieth Century* (London, 1932).

Stopford A. Brooke, *The Poetry of Robert Browning* (London, 1902).

E. K. Brown, 'The First Person in "Caliban upon Setebos" ', *MLN* lxvi (1951).

[J. Bryson, *Browning* (Writers and their Work series, paperback, London, 1959; paperback, U.S.).]

[L. Burrows, *Browning the Poet* (W. Australia and London, 1969.)]

H. B. Charlton, 'Browning: The Poet's Aim', *Bulletin of the John Rylands Library Manchester*, xxii (1938).

H. B. Charlton, 'Browning as Dramatist', ibid. xxii (1939).

H. B. Charlton, 'Browning's Ethical Poetry', ibid. xxvii (1942).

H. B. Charlton, 'Browning as Poet of Religion', ibid. xxvii (1943).

H. B. Charlton, 'Poetry and Truth: An Aspect of Browning's *The Ring and the Book*', ibid. xxviii (1944).

H. B. Charlton, 'Browning: The Making of the Dramatic Lyric', ibid. xxxv (1952–3).

G. K. Chesterton, *Robert Browning* (London, 1903; paperback, U.K.).

J. M. Cohen, *Robert Browning* (London, 1952).

R. J. Collins, *Robert Browning's Moral-Aesthetic Theory 1833–1855* (Lincoln, Nebr., 1967).

T. J. Collins, 'Shelley and God in Browning's *Pauline*: Unresolved Problems', *VP* iii (1965).

R. R. Columbus, and C. Kemper, 'Sordello and the Speaker: a Problem in Identity', *VP* ii (1964).

A. K. Cook, *A Commentary upon Browning's 'The Ring and the Book'* (London, 1920).

B. Corrigan (ed.), *Curious Annals: New Documents relating to Browning's Roman Murder Story* (Toronto, 1956).

[M. B. Cramer, 'Browning's Friendships and Fame before Marriage (1833–46)', *PMLA* lv (1940).]

[M. B. Cramer, 'What Browning's Literary Reputation Owed to the Pre-Raphaelites, 1847–56', *ELH* viii (1941).]

[M. B. Cramer, 'Browning's Literary Reputation at Oxford, 1855–9', *PMLA* lvii (1942).]

N. B. Crowell, *The Triple Soul: Browning's Theory of Knowledge* (Santa Fé, N. Mex., 1963).

[P. Cundiff, 'Robert Browning "Our Human Speech" ', *VN*, no. 15 (1959).]

[P. Cundiff, 'Robert Browning: "Indisputable Fact" ', *VN* no. 17 (1960).]

H. Sykes Davies, *Browning and the Modern Novel*, (Hull, 1962).

P. de Reul, *L'Art et la pensée de Robert Browning* (Brussels, 1929).

W. C. DeVane, *A Browning Handbook* 2nd edn. (1955).

W. C. DeVane, *Browning's 'Parleyings': the Autobiography of a Mind* (New Haven, Conn., 1927).

W. C. DeVane, 'Sordello's Story Retold', *SP* xxvii (Jan. 1930).

W. C. DeVane, 'The Harlot and the Thoughtful Young Man', *SP* xxix (1932).

[W. C. DeVane, 'Browning and the Spirit of Greece', in *Nineteenth-Century Studies*, ed. H. Davis, W. C. DeVane, and R. C. Bald (Ithaca, New York, 1940).]

W. C. DeVane, 'The Virgin and the Dragon', *Yale Review*, n.s. xxxvii (1947).

[P. Drew: *The Poetry of Browning*, London, 1970.]

P. Drew (ed.), *Robert Browning: a Collection of Critical Essays* (London, 1966; paperback, Boston, Mass., 1966).

P. Drew, 'Browning's *Essay on Shelley*', *VP* i (1963); and T. J. Collins, ii (1964).

P. Drew, 'Henry Jones on Browning's Optimism', *VP* ii (1964).

[A. E. DuBois, 'Robert Browning, Dramatist', *SP* xxxiii (1936).]

H. C. Duffin, *Amphibian: a Reconsideration of Browning* (Cambridge, 1956).

J. E. Duncan, 'The Intellectual Kinship of John Donne and Robert Browning', *SP* l (1953).

[G. R. Elliott, 'Shakespeare's Significance for Browning', *Anglia* (1909).]

[D. V. Erdman, 'Browning's Industrial Nightmare', *PQ* xxxvi, 1957.]

H. N. Fairchild, 'Browning: the Simple-Hearted Casuist', *UTQ* xviii (1949).

H. N. Fairchild, "*La Saisiaz* and *The Nineteenth Century*', *MP* xlviii (1950).

L. S. Friedland, 'Ferrara and "My Last Duchess" ', *SP* xxxiii (1936).

B. W. Fuson, *Browning and his English Predecessors in the Dramatic Monolog* (Iowa, 1948).

J. M. Gest (ed.), *The Old Yellow Book* (Boston, 1925).

M. E. Glen, 'The Meaning and Structure of *Pippa Passes*', *UTQ* xxiv (1955).

H. Golder, 'Browning's *Childe Roland*', *PMLA* xxxix, 1924.

O. P. Govil, 'A Note on Mill and Browning's *Pauline*' *VP* iv (1966).

[H. E. Greene, 'Browning's Knowledge of Music', *PMLA* lxii (1947).]

[B. Groom, *On the Diction of Tennyson, Browning and Arnold* (Society for Pure English, Tract no. 53, Oxford, 1939).]

P. J. Guskin, 'Ambiguities in the Structure and Meaning of Browning's *Christmas-Eve and Easter-Day*' *VP* iv (1966).

[T. P. Harrison, 'Birds in the Poetry of Browning', *RES* N.S. vii (1956).]

T. P. Harrison, 'Browning's "Childe Roland" and Wordsworth', *Tennessee Studies in Literature*, vi (1961).

[H. H. Hatcher, *The Versification of Robert Browning* (Columbus, Ohio, 1928).]

W. Hellstrom, 'Time and Type in Browning's *Saul*', *ELH* xxxiii, (1966).

E. Hilton, 'Browning's *Sordello* as a Study of the Will', *PMLA* lxix (1954).

C. W. Hodell (ed.), *The Old Yellow Book* (Washington, 1908).

Sister M. M. Holloway, 'A Further Reading of "Count Gismond" ', *SP* lx (1963).

S. W. Holmes, 'The Sources of Browning's *Sordello*', *SP* xxxiv (1937).

P. Honan, *Browning's Characters: a Study in Poetic Technique* (New Haven, Conn., 1961).

[T. L. Hood, 'Browning's Ancient Classical Sources', *Harvard Studies in Classical Philology*, xxxiii (1922).]

J. Howard, 'Caliban's Mind', *VP* i (1963).

W. Irvine, 'Four Monologues in Browning's *Men and Women*', *VP* ii (1964).

I. Jack, *Robert Browning*, Warton Lecture, 1967 (Oxford, 1968).

Henry James, 'The Private Life' (1892).

Henry James, 'The Novel in *The Ring and the Book*', *Notes on Novelists*, 1914.

Henry James, *Views and Reviews* (1908).

B. R. Jerman, 'Browning's Witless Duke', *PMLA* lxxii (1957).

E. D. H. Johnson, *The Alien Vision of Victorian Poetry* (Princeton, N.J., 1952).

[E. D. H. Johnson, 'Robert Browning's Pluralistic Universe: A Reading of *The Ring and the Book*', *UTQ* xxxi (1961).]

H. Jones, *Browning as a Philosophical and Religious Teacher* (Glasgow, 1891).

R. A. King, Jr., *The Bow and the Lyre: The Art of Robert Browning* (Ann Arbor, Mich., 1957; paperback, U.S.)

R. A. King, Jr., 'Browning: "Mage" and "Maker": a Study in Poetic Purpose and Method', *VN*, no. 20 (1961).

[R. A. King, Jr., *The Focusing Artifice* (Ohio, 1969).]

W. Kirkconnell, 'The Epilogue to *Dramatic Personæ*', *MLN* xli (1926).

[K. L. Knickerbocker, 'A Tentative Apology for Browning', *Tennessee Studies in Literature*, i (1956).]

K. Kroeber, 'Touchstones for Browning's Victorian Complexity', *VP* iii (1965).

R. Langbaum, *The Poetry of Experience: The Dramatic Monologue in Modern Literary Tradition* (London, 1957; paperack, U.S.).

R. Langbaum, 'Browning and the Question of Myth', *PMLA* lxxxi (1966).

R. Langbaum, 'The Importance of Fact in *The Ring and the Book*', *VN*, no. 17 (1960).

B. Litzinger and K. L. Knickerbocker (eds.), *The Browning Critics* (Lexington, Ky., 1965; paperbacks, U.K. and U.S.).

B. Litzinger, 'Did Cardinal Wiseman review *Men and Women*?' *VN*, no. 18 (1960).

B. Litzinger, *Time's Revenges: Browning's Reputation as a Thinker, 1889–1962* (Knoxville, Tenn., 1964).

[B. Litzinger, *Robert Browning and the Babylonian Woman* (Waco, Tex., 1962).]

B. Litzinger and D. Smalley, *Browning: The Critical Heritage* (London, 1970).

T. R. Lounsbury, *The Early Literary Career of Robert Browning* (New York, 1911, London, 1912).

P. Lubbock, 'Robert Browning', *Quarterly Review*, ccxvii (1912).

M. W. MacCallum, *The Dramatic Monologue in the Victorian Period*, Warton Lecture, 1924 (Oxford, 1925).

[J. F. Macdonald, 'Inhibitions of Browning's Poetry', in *Studies in English by Members of University College Toronto*, collected by Malcolm W. Wallace (Toronto, 1931).]

[B. R. McElderry, Jr., 'Browning and the Victorian Public in 1868–9', in *Research Studies of the State College of Washington* (Dec. 1937).]

[B. R. McElderry, ibid. 'Victorian Evaluation of *The Ring and the Book*', *Research Studies of the State College of Washington*, viii (June 1939).]

J. A. S. McPeek, 'The Shaping of *Saul*', *JEGP* xliv (1945).

B. Melchiori, *Browning's Poetry of Reticence* (Edinburgh and London, 1968).

J. Hillis Miller, *The Disappearance of God: Five Nineteenth-Century Writers* (Cambridge, Mass., 1963; paperback, U.K.).

M. Miyoshi, 'Mill and *Pauline*: the Myth and some Facts', *VS* ix (Dec., 1965).]

[P. E. More, 'Why is Browning Popular?' in his *Shelburne Essays: Third Series* (New York, 1905; paperback, U.K.).]

E. Muir, 'Robert Browning', in *Essays on Literature and Society* (London, 1949).

J. T. Nettleship, *Browning: Essays and Thoughts* (1890; first published as *Essays on Robert Browning's Poetry*, 1868).

Mrs. S. Orr, *A Handbook to the Works of Robert Browning* (London, 1885; and rev. edns).

G. H. Palmer, 'The Monologue of Browning', *Harvard Theological Review*, xi (1918).

L. Perrine, 'Browning's Shrewd Duke', *PMLA* lxxiv (1959).

[H. P. Pettigrew, 'The Early Vogue of *The Ring and the Book*', *Archiv* clxix (1936).]

W. L. Phelps, *Robert Browning: How to Know Him* (Indianapolis, Ind., 1915; London, 1916).

[L. S. Poston, 'Ruskin and Browning's Artists', *English Miscellany* (Rome, 1964).]

E. Pound, *Literary Essays*, ed. T. S. Eliot (London, 1954; paperback, U.K.).

R. Preyer, 'Two Styles in the Verse of Robert Browning', *ELH* xxxii (1965).

R. Preyer, 'Robert Browning: a Reading of the Early Narratives', *ELH* xxvi (1959).

F. E. L. Priestley, 'Blougram's Apologetics', *UTQ* xv (1946).

F. E. L. Priestley, 'The Ironic Pattern of Browning's *Paracelsus*', *UTQ* xxxiv (1964).

F. E. L. Priestley, 'A Reading of *La Saisiaz*', *UTQ* xxv (1955).

W. O. Raymond, *The Infinite Moment and Other Essays in Robert Browning*, (Toronto, 1950, rev. edn., 1966; paperback, U.S.).

Reul: See de Reul.

[G. M. Ridenour, 'Browning's Music Poems: Fancy and Fact', *PMLA* lxxviii (1963).]

[G. Roppen and R. Sommer, *Strangers and Pilgrims: An Essay on the Metaphor of Journey* (Oslo and Oxford, 1964.)—Chapter on 'Childe Roland'.]

G. Sandstrom, ' "James Lee's Wife"—and Browning's', *VP* iv (1966).

G. Santayana, *Interpretations of Poetry and Religion* (New York, 1900; paperback, U.K.).

I. B. Sessions, 'The Dramatic Monologue', *PMLA* lxii (1947).

W. D. Shaw, *The Dialectical Temper: The Rhetorical Art of Robert Browning* (Ithaca, N.Y., 1968).

W. D. Shaw, 'Browning's Duke as Theatrical Producer', *VN* no. 29 (1966).

W. D. Shaw, 'The Analogical Argument of Browning's "Saul" ', *VP* ii (1964).

D. Smalley, 'A Parleying with Aristophanes', *PMLA* lv (1940).

[D. Smalley, 'Browning's View of Fact in *The Ring and the Book*', *VN*, no. 16 (1960).]

C. W. Smith, *Browning's Star-Imagery: the Study of a Detail in Poetic Design* (Princeton, N.J., 1941).

L. Snitslàar, *Sidelights on Robert Browning's 'The Ring and the Book'* (Amsterdam, 1934).

[E. Snyder and F. Palmer, 'New Light on the Brownings', *Quarterly Review* (July, 1937).]

M. K. Starkman, 'The Manichee in the Cloister: A Reading of Browning's "Soliloquy of the Spanish Cloister" ', *MLN* lxxv (1960).

D. Stempel, 'Browning's *Sordello*: the Art of the Makers-See', *PMLA* lxxx (1965).

[L. Stevenson, 'Tennyson, Browning, and a Romantic Fallacy', *UTQ* xiii (1944).]

[L. Stevenson, 'The Pertinacious Victorian Poets', *UTQ* xxi (1952).]

E. E. Stoll, 'Browning's *In a Balcony*', in his *From Shakespeare to Joyce* (New York, 1944); repr. from *MLQ* iii (1942).

[M. R. Sullivan, *Browning's Voices in 'The Ring and the Book'* (Toronto, 1969.)]

M. J. Svaglic, 'Browning's Grammarian: Apparent Failure or Real', *VP*, vol. v, no. 2, Summer 1967.

A. Symons, *An Introduction to the Study of Browning* (London, 1886).

J. W. Tilton and R. D. Tuttle, 'A New Reading of "Count Gismond" ', *SP* lix (1962).

[C. R. Tracy, 'Browning's Heresies', *SP* xxxiii (1936).]

C. R. Tracy (ed.), *Browning's Mind and Art* (Edinburgh and London, 1968).

C. R. Tracy, ' "Caliban upon Setebos" ', *SP* xxxv (1938).

[C. C. Watkins, 'Browning's "Fame within those four years" (1862–4)', *MLR* lii (1958).]

C. C. Watkins, 'The "Abstruser Themes" of Browning's *Fifine at the Fair*', *PMLA* lxxiv (1959).

C. C. Watkins, 'Browning's *Red Cotton Night-Cap Country* and Carlyle', *VS* vii (1964).

M. A. Weinstein, *William Edmonstone Aytoun and the Spasmodic Controversy* (New Haven, Conn., 1968).

W. Whitla, *The Central Truth: The Incarnation in Robert Browning's Poetry* (Toronto, 1963).

J. Willoughby, 'Browning's "Childe Roland to the Dark Tower Came', *VP* i (1963).

E. H. Yarrill (trans.), *Browning's Roman Murder Story as Recorded in a hitherto Unknown Italian Contemporary MS.* (Waco, Tex., 1939). Introduction by W. O. Raymond.

BIOGRAPHIES AND LETTERS

[R. D. Altick, 'The Private Life of Robert Browning', *Yale Review* xli (1951).]

[V. Baddeley, 'The Ancestry of Robert Browning, the Poet', *Genealogists' Magazine*, viii (1938).]

[Browning, *The Letters of Robert Browning and Elizabeth Barrett Barrett* (2 vols., 1899; 1 vol., 1923).]

Browning, *Twenty-Two Unpublished Letters of Elizabeth Barrett Browning and Robert Browning* (New York, 1935).

G. K. Chesterton, *Browning* (London, 1903; paperback, U.K.).

[R. Curle, *Robert Browning and Julia Wedgwood: a Broken Friendship as Revealed in their Letters* (London, 1937).]

[W. C. DeVane and K. L. Knickerbocker (eds.), *New Letters of Robert Browning* (New Haven, Conn., 1950; London, 1951).]

[H. W. Donner (ed.), *The Browning Box* (London, 1935).]

E. Dowden, *Life of Robert Browning* (London, 1904).

F. R. G. Duckworth, *Browning, Background and Conflict* (London, 1931).

E. Gosse, *Robert Browning: Personalia* (London, 1890).

W. Hall Griffin, *The Life of Robert Browning, with Notices of his Writings, his Family, & his Friends*, completed and ed. by H. C. Minchin (1910); rev. edn., (1938).

[A. B. Harlan and J. L. Harlan (eds.), *Letters from Owen Meredith (Robert, First Earl of Lytton) to Robert and Elizabeth Barrett Browning* (Waco, Tex., 1936).]

C. H. Herford, *Robert Browning* (London, 1905).

[J. H. Hitner, 'Browning's Grotesque Period', *VP* iv (1966).]

[S. W. Holmes, 'Browning's Sordello and Jung: Browning's *Sordello* in the Light of Jung's Theory of Types', *PMLA* lvi (1941).]

[S. W. Holmes, 'Browning: Semantic Stutterer', *PMLA* lx (1945).]

[T. L. Hood (ed.), *Letters of Robert Browning, Collected by Thomas J. Wise* (1933).]

[E. A. Horsman (ed.), *The Diary of Alfred Domett, 1872–1885* (London, 1953).]

H. – L. Hovelaque, *La Jeunesse de Robert Browning* (Paris, 1932).

[G. R. Hudson (ed.), *Browning to his American Friends* (London, 1965).]

[F. G. Kenyon (ed.), *Robert Browning and Alfred Domett* (London, 1906).]

[R. A. King, Jr., *Robert Browning's Finances from his own Account Book* (Waco, Tex., 1947).]

[E. Kintner, *The Letters of Robert Browning and Elizabeth Barrett Barrett, 1845–6*, (2 vols., Cambridge, Mass., 1969.)]

[K. L. Knickerbocker, 'Euripides Browningized: The Meaning of *Balaustion's Adventure*', *VP* ii (1964).]

[K. L. Knickerbocker, 'An Echo from Browning's Second Courtship', *SP* xxxii (1935).]

[P. Landis and R. E. Freeman (ed.), *Letters of the Brownings to George Barrett* (Urbana, Ill., 1958).]

[E. C. McAleer (ed.), *Dearest Isa: Robert Browning's Letters to Isabella Blagden* (Austin, Tex., 1951).]

[E. C. McAleer, *Learned Lady: Letters from Robert Browning to Mrs. Thomas FitzGerald, 1876–1889* (Cambridge, Mass., 1966).]

B. Miller, *Robert Browning: a Portrait* (London, 1952).

[B. Miller, 'This Happy Evening,' *Twentieth Century* cliv (1953).]

[B. Miller, 'The Séance at Ealing a Study in Memory and Imagination', *Cornhill Magazine*, clxix (1957).]

[B. Miller, 'The Child of Casa Guidi', *Cornhill Magazine* (1949).]

Mrs. S. Orr, *Life and Letters of Robert Browning* (1891); rev. edn., by F. G. Kenyon (London, 1908).

F. A. Pottle, *Shelley and Browning: a Myth and some Facts* (Chicago, 1923; repr. 'Archon Books' New York, 1965).

[J. W. Reed, Jr., 'Browning and Macready: the Final Quarrel', *PMLA* lxxv (1960).]

G. Reese, 'Robert Browning and his Son', *PMLA* lxi (1946).

A. Ritchie (Anne Thackeray-Ritchie), *Records of Tennyson, Ruskin and Browning* (1891).

W. Sharp, *Life of Robert Browning* (London, 1890).

[D. Smalley, 'Joseph Arnould and Robert Browning: New Letters (1842–50) and a Verse Epistle', *PMLA* lxxx (1965).]

M. Ward, *Robert Browning and his World: the Private Face* (London, 1967).

M. Ward, *Robert Browning and his World: Two Robert Brownings?* (London, 1969).

L. Whiting, *The Brownings: their Life and Art* (Boston, Mass., 1911).

BIBLIOGRAPHIES

W. Barnes, *Catalogue of the Browning Collection* [at] *The University of Texas* (Austin, Tex., 1966).

[A. E. Brooks, *Browningiana in Baylor University* (Waco, Tex., 1921).]

L. N. Broughton and B. F. Stelter, *A Concordance to the Poems of Robert Browning* (2 vols., New York, 1924–5).

L. N. Broughton, C. S. Northup and R. Pearsall, *Robert Browning: a Bibliography, 1830–1950* (Ithaca, N.Y., 1953).

F. E. Faverty (ed.), *The Victorian Poets: a Guide to Research*, 2nd edn. (Cambridge Mass., 1968). The chapter on Browning is the work of Park Honan.

F. J. Furnivall, *A Bibliography of Robert Browning, from 1833 to 1881* (Browning Society *Papers*, 1881–; and separate publication).

W. R. Nicoll and T. J. Wise, *Literary Anecdotes of the Nineteenth Century*, (2 vols., 1895–6).

Sotheby, Wilkinson, and Hodge (auctioneers), *The Browning Collections: Catalogue of Oil Paintings, Drawings and Prints; Autograph Letters and Manuscripts; Books, etc.*, 1913.

[G. Watson (ed.), *N.C.B.E.L.*, vol. iii: 1800–1900 (Cambridge and New York, 1969).]

[G. E. Wilson, *Robert Browning's Portraits* (Waco, Tex., 1943).]

Elizabeth Barrett Browning

Elizabeth Barrett Browning, *Diary, 1831–2*, ed., P. Kelly and R. Hudson, (New York, 1969.)

Elizabeth Barrett Browning, *Poetical Works* (5 vols., London, 1866).

Elizabeth Barrett Browning, *Poetical Works* (6 vols., London, 1889).

Elizabeth Barrett Browning, *Complete Works*, ed. C. Porter and H. A. Clarke (6 vols., New York, 1900).

W. Barnes, *Elizabeth Barrett Browning: A Descriptive Bibliography* (Austin, Texas, 1968).

A. Bose, *Chroniclers of Life: Studies in Early Victorian Poetry*, (Orient Longmans, 1962).

A. Hayter, *Mrs Browning: a Poet's Work and its Setting* (London, 1962).

D. Hewlett, *Elizabeth Barrett Browning* (London, 1953).

L. Huxley (ed.), *Elizabeth Barrett Browning: Letters to her Sister, 1846–1859* (London, 1929).

F. G. Kenyon (ed.), *The Letters of Elizabeth Barrett Browning* (2 vols., London, 1897).

P. Lubbock, *Elizabeth Barrett Browning in her Letters* (London, 1906).

B. P. McCarthy, *Elizabeth Barrett to Mr. Boyd* (London, 1955).

J. A. Marks, *The Family of the Barretts: A Colonial Romance* (New York, 1938).

S. R. Townshend Mayer (ed.), *Letters of Elizabeth Barrett Browning Addressed to Richard Hengist Horne* (2 vols., 1877).

G.-M. Merlette, *La Vie et l'Œuvre d'Elizabeth Barrett Browning* (Paris, 1905).

B. Miller (ed.), *Elizabeth Barrett to Miss Mitford* (London, 1954).

M. H. Shackford, *Letters from Elizabeth Barrett to B. R. Haydon* (London and New York, 1939).

G. B. Taplin, *The Life of Elizabeth Barrett Browning* (New Haven, Conn., 1957; repr. Archon Books, N.Y., 1970).

J. M. S. Tompkins, *Aurora Leigh*, Fawcett Lecture, Bedford College (London, 1961).

James Bertram

> *Vir dulcissime et lucidissime . . .*
>   Lord Salisbury to Matthew Arnold at Oxford, 1870

> *Il est admis que la vérité d'un homme,*
> *c'est d'abord ce qu'il cache.*
>   André Malraux, *Antimémoires*

'Fret not yourself to make my poems square in all their parts, but like what you can my darling', Arnold wrote to his favourite sister 'K' in 1849. 'The true reason why parts suit you while others do not is that my poems are fragments—i.e. that I am fragments. . . . I shall do better some day I hope.' This was in a moment of unusual candour, to one of the two persons (the other was Clough) he most aimed to please by his writings. Twenty years later, when Clough was eight years dead and his own spring of poetry had dried, Arnold brought out the two volumes of the first collected edition of his *Poems*. To his mother he confided the verdict of a mature critic on work which lay behind him:

My poems represent, on the whole, the main movement of mind of the last quarter of a century, and thus they will probably have their day as people become conscious to themselves of what that movement of mind is, and interested in the literary productions which reflect it. It might fairly be urged that I have less poetical sentiment than Tennyson, and less intellectual vigour and abundance than Browning; yet, because I have perhaps more of a fusion of the two than either of them, and have more regularly applied that fusion to the main line of modern development, I am likely enough to have my turn, as they have had theirs.

The young Matthew Arnold *was* fragments, behind his protective disguise of dandyism: it was difficult to be both Dr. Arnold's son and an artist. The fragments might have flown apart, as they so nearly did with his younger brothers Tom and William, before these two restless temperaments found their different kinds of peace—the one in Roman Catholicism, the other in premature death as a crusader in his father's cause. Matthew, who always preferred 'a distinct

seeing of my way as far as my own nature is concerned', managed
to steer clear of romantic sirens and the rocks of dogma: his literary
career is as much a triumph of conscious mastery, or of compromise,
as his private life. No man knew better how to turn loss to gain. The
foiled lover of Marguerite became the hard-working inspector of
schools and devoted family man; the moody, introspective young
poet became the urbane Professor of Poetry, with the self-imposed
mission of civilizing the taste of his age. Arnold's second vocation as
critic arose directly out of his primary concern with poetry, and
allowed full play to the wit, vivacity, and cool common sense his
earlier romantic yearning had threatened to smother. He moved on
to the disputed ground of social and religious criticism, and became
—inevitably—a Victorian sage. On any view, he is the completest
man of letters of his time—one of its chief poets, unquestionably
the first of its literary critics, and probably the most persuasive of
its polemical writers on cultural matters. If there were serious
limitations to his practice in all three fields, the total achievement is
impressive, and has commanded more continuing scholarly attention in the last forty years than the work of any of his contemporaries.
And though the emphasis here must be on the poetry, clearly the
prose cannot be ignored—for the extent to which poetry and prose
conflict, or complement and reinforce each other, is really the central
problem of Arnold criticism.

TEXTS

Most readers make their first acquaintance with Arnold's verse in
anthologies—something he could hardly object to, since he was a
notable anthologist himself. The selection he made from his poems
for the Golden Treasury Series is still valuable as a pointer to his
own preference, though it cuts up 'Empedocles', favours some in-
different later work, and has nowhere the surgical precision of his
selections for the same series from Wordsworth and Byron. Of modern
selections the best is Allott's in the Penguin Poets, which is prefaced
by a lively dialogue about the nature of Arnold's poetry and its
interest to the modern reader that has continuing point. There have
been a number of one-volume selections from the verse and prose,
of which the three most easily accessible are Trilling's *Portable
Matthew Arnold* (1949), Mulhauser's selection in the Rinehart
Editions (1953), and Bryson's *Poetry and Prose* (1954) in the Reynard
Library. The first of these has the fullest Introduction, and a valuable
selection from the letters to Clough, but is light on the poetry.

Mulhauser has more poems, but no letters. Bryson's volume, with a clean text, brief notes on the poems, and an admirable choice from the prose works and letters, is the most comprehensive and probably the most satisfactory.

The serious student of Arnold's verse needs a complete text, and has the choice of two. Tinker and Lowry's edition in the Oxford Standard Authors (1950) gives the text and arrangement of the Library edition of 1888 (first pub. 1885), the last collection to be revised by Arnold himself, with an additional section of cancelled and uncollected pieces. This is a well-printed book with full textual variants in footnotes, Arnold's own sparse notes at the end, and the controversial Prefaces of 1853 and 1854 rather uncomfortably prominent at the beginning. Ten years earlier the same editors had brought out their invaluable *Commentary* on Arnold's poetry, which made full use of the Yale Collection of papers, and gave a great deal of illuminating background material on individual poems. The *Commentary* was always intended to be a companion volume to the Oxford text; though now out of print, it is in most libraries. A new edition is projected.

The most comprehensive edition of Arnold's poetry is that by Allott in Longmans Annotated English Poets (1965). Here the poems (with the exception of juvenilia and fragments gathered at the end) are given in carefully argued—and generally convincing—order of composition, with an elaborate apparatus of headnotes on dating and sources, footnotes for literary parallels, and textual or critical commentary. Though it sounds unwieldy, this is in practice a very workable arrangement, and the compression of relevant detail is masterly. The Prefaces are given in appendix, where they cannot so readily distort an approach to the earlier poems; and the text of a Fox How poem written by Dr. Arnold in 1839 has obvious relevance to some of his son's favourite poetic effects with streams, cities, and 'resolution by water'.

Both editions are admirable in their kind: the first gives us the poems as Arnold arranged them, the second a full picture of Arnold's poetic development. A reader can make do with either, a student will require both.

For Arnold's published prose the fountain-head is still the fifteen-volume edition of the collected *Works* (1903–4), though additions to the canon were made subsequently, notably by Allott and Neiman. Certain prose works—in particular the *Essays in Criticism* and *Culture and Anarchy*—have been steadily reprinted; some useful scholarly editions and selections are listed in the REFERENCES. All earlier editions, however, are now being superseded by the splendid *Complete Prose Works* (University of Michigan Press, begun 1960) edited by R. H. Super, of which six volumes have already appeared. This is a major work of modern scholarship, aiming at a definitive edition of the critical prose (excluding letters) in chronological order of composition, with full commentary on text, sources, and references. Super's notes are valuable, not just in themselves but for their careful listing of specialist studies on Arnold.

CRITICAL STUDIES AND COMMENTARY

In poetry, Arnold was his own first and severest critic. He argued his way, against some of his deepest instincts, to an extreme theory favouring an objective poetry of tonic moral uplift, committed to the 'great subject' and a plain dignified presentation of it. This theory is enshrined in the 1853 Preface, and Arnold tried hard to make his earlier as well as his later work conform to it. Hence the rejection of 'Empedocles' in favour of 'Sohrab and Rustum', hence such determined efforts to apply the theory in 'Balder Dead' and *Merope*. (If Arnold seems here to be running counter to his own special gift, he was also in opposition to the views of fellow-poets: it was 'Empedocles' that ravished the young Swinburne, and won Browning's enduring support; it was 'The Scholar-Gipsy' that Clough liked, rather than 'Sohrab' or 'Balder'.) Public response to Arnold's poetry was slow, and he himself did not feel it was at all general until 1878; this is in marked contrast to the intelligent appreciation his prose writing had already gained by 1861. The most interesting early reviews of Arnold's verse are W. M. Rossetti's in *The Germ* (1850), and Clough's in *The North American Review* (1853); the most enthusiastic is Swinburne's review of *New Poems* (1867); the most balanced, R. H. Hutton's essay in 1877. There is a full modern study of Arnold's contemporary reputation by Wilkins (see REFS.: BIBLIOGRAPHIES).

The first full-length study came from Saintsbury eleven years after Arnold's death; though capricious in minor judgements, it seems just in its general estimate: 'Mr. Arnold may never, in prose, be read with quite the same keenness of delight with which we read him in poetry; but he will yield delight more surely.' Russell, Arnold's first editor and a personal friend, made no strong claim for the poetry in his affectionate memoir of 1904: it was not simple, sensuous, or passionate, it was 'altogether remote from the stir and stress of popular life', and too melancholy ever to have popular appeal. Yet through the first quarter of the new century Arnold steadily won new readers, while Tennyson lost them, and Browning remained the poet of a clique. It was Arnold's melancholy the new public preferred, and it seems to have saved him in the general post-war debunking of Victorian manners led by Lytton Strachey (who made Dr. Arnold of Rugby one of his prime targets). Something of the irreverent tone of the twenties may be seen in Kingsmill's provocative sketch ('the collapse of the poet into the prophet'); but the appreciation of such scholarly critics as Paul, Quiller-Couch, Ker, and Grierson had already confirmed Arnold's position. Garrod is the most sympathetic and perceptive of these academic critics, and should still be read: for him Arnold was unquestionably the greatest of Victorian poets. Few others would make the same deliberate claim, but Arnold grew more complex and interesting as new facts about his early life emerged.

In 1932 Lowry's edition of the *Letters of Arnold to Clough* (first instalment of the original collection of Clough Papers, of which the balance has since been deposited in the Bodleian Library) began a revolution in Arnold studies. Here for the first time, in what Allott has described as a correspondence surpassed only by the letters of Keats and Hopkins in English literature 'for its sharp insights and its fascinating glimpse at the ellipitical gambolling of a free intelligence', it was possible to find an authentic portrait of the younger Arnold, and of his developing ideas about the function of poetry, including his own. Lamentably, this correspondence remains one-sided (Arnold destroyed letters, while Clough kept them); but Lowry's introductory chapters do much to fill the gap, and the subsequent revival of interest in Clough has provided much new material to help us reconstruct the outline of the long debate between these two friends—so close in intellectual sympathies, so opposed in poetic practice, and with such curious blind spots about each other's work. Arnold's 'gloriously excited' letters to Clough are his most revealing personal writing, and an indispensable document for the study of his poetry. The book is again available in print, after a disconcerting lapse.

Two of the most influential of twentieth-century critics, Eliot and Leavis, had dealings with Arnold in the 1930s. Eliot's *Use of Poetry* (1933) is rather grudgingly just to Arnold as critic, less than just to the man and the poet; but Eliot on Arnold must be read, and to his more open provocations every student must find his own answers. Leavis—who, like Eliot, seems in so many ways a continuator of Arnold's mission in the *Essays in Criticism* and *Culture and Anarchy*—

is even cooler towards Arnold's poetry: it 'comes between Wordsworth and the Georgian week-enders; for all its dilute distinction, it belongs in ethos with them'. About his critical achievement Leavis has no doubts: 'If Arnold is not one of the great critics, who are they?'

On either side of the Second World War—and clearly influenced in tone by that crisis—came two solid studies in interpretation which are still of major importance. Trilling's *Matthew Arnold* (1939) was claimed by Auden to be 'the full and final word on Arnold' for his generation, and it remains the most substantial work of an American critic temperamentally much closer to Arnold than Leavis could ever be. Trilling set out 'to show the thought of Matthew Arnold in its complex unity and to relate it to the historical events of his time'; the measure of his success is to be found both in the comprehensive sweep of his book, and its sense of continuing moral urgency. It is hard to overpraise the brilliance of his earlier chapters, or the humane balance of his summing-up: one regrets only the limited, documentary treatment he gives to the poetry. Appropriately (if with some irony, in view of Arnold's low opinion of French verse) the most detailed study of his poetry is by a Frenchman. Bonnerot's *Matthew Arnold, Poète* (1947) is a specialist study of the formidable length and detail prescribed for a Sorbonne thesis: it is matched in these respects only by Veyriras's more recent work on Clough. Bonnerot's book is valuable as biography—it offers an acute psychological study of its subject, and is fairly convincing on the Marguerite episode—but its chief importance to the student lies in its detailed analysis of key poems, notably 'Resignation', 'Empedocles', 'Tristram', and the Marguerite and Obermann poems. Bonnerot is not easy reading, but is well worth the effort.

Later critical work on Arnold is on a less heroic scale; but detailed studies of his ideas and his technique, often taking off from points of disagreement with Trilling and Bonnerot, have since multiplied, with the weight of American armament making itself increasingly felt.

Sir Edmund Chambers's *Matthew Arnold*—a spry performance by a great scholar in an unaccustomed field—had the expected terseness, lucidity, and strong detective instinct, but hardly broke new ground. This was done cogently in Brown's *Arnold: a Study in Conflict* the following year, a book which challenged Arnold's claim to the 'disinterested play of consciousness' and raised serious doubts about his consistency and integrity. E. D. H. Johnson's *Alien Vision of Victorian Poetry* was an important preliminary examination of the influence of the Victorian public in changing the poetic attitudes of Tennyson, Browning, and Arnold; in Arnold's case, by attempting to assert poetry as a *magister vitae* in 1853, he set an impossible goal both for himself and his readers; 'The Scholar-Gipsy', which creates a personal myth of the alienated artist, is his most truly original poem. Later interpretations of this poem—for example, the strikingly contrasted views of Wilson Knight and Dyson, in two fine individual studies—suggest some vagueness in Arnold's handling of the myth, but Culler provides a plausible resolution. Jump's *Matthew Arnold*, by contrast, takes a severely restrictive view of the poetry, and argues for the manifest superiority of the prose: this honest and forthright little book, building on hints from Eliot and Leavis, has had considerable vogue as a modern introduction to Arnold, but its particular emphasis is perhaps no longer needed.

Arnold's debt to the romantic poets, his quarrel with them and with the romantic in himself, have been treated at length in a number of useful studies. Jamison's *Arnold and the Romantics* reviews Arnold's judgement of five major romantic English poets, Baum's *Ten Studies* offers detailed critical readings of central and characteristic poems, and W. S. Johnson's *Voices of Matthew Arnold* is a discussion of the whole body of the poetry, concentrating on 'tone' and emphasizing the calculated presentation of opposite viewpoints in soliloquy and dialogue. Gottfried's *Matthew Arnold and the Romantics* is a thorough and learned work of comparative scholarship. Classical sources and influences in Arnold had been treated first by R. E. C. Houghton; in 1965 Anderson's admirable *Matthew Arnold and the Classical Tradition* came as a notable contribution of American scholarship, to meet the needs of less instructed generations.

Three recent general interpretations of Arnold's poetry are also American. The most important and comprehensive of these is Culler's *Imaginative Reason*, which traces a basic pattern of three symbolic landscapes ('The Forest Glade', 'The Burning Plain', 'The wide glimmering Sea') underlying the development of Arnold's poetry. Culler is particularly helpful on 'Tristram', 'Empedocles', 'The Scholar-Gipsy', and 'Thyrsis'. His mythological framework is more suggestive and rewarding in application than Madden's rather arbitrary categories for the verse, in a treatment which sees Arnold as a lifelong aesthete who moved naturally from the patterns of verse into a new sphere of critical prose. Stange, in *The Poet as Humanist*, emphasizes the influence of Goethe and Schiller, and suggests (with little evidence) that the 'Marguerite poems' were composed on the model of the German *lieder*-cycle. Beside these elaborate commentaries, Frykman's modest essay is refreshingly direct and straightforward.

Specialist articles on Arnold's poetry fall into three main groups: those which add new facts of significance, however small; those which offer new interpretations; and those which discuss influences. Here it is possible only to suggest a few names. In the first group, Garrod, Knickerbocker, Mrs. Sells, Mrs. Tillotson, Allott, Coulling, and Super; in the second, Brown, Curgenven, W. E. Houghton, W. S. Johnson, Knight, Dyson, and Gottfried; in the third, Orrick, Broadbent, Brooks, Nagarajan, Knoepflmacher, and DeLaura. Detailed references to articles are given in the REFERENCES below (CRITICAL STUDIES).

Arnold knew that his poetry came from an inward spring that was mysterious to himself, and that it was dangerous to force it: prose was easier, because it made less painful demands. Coulling has convincingly demonstrated the close relation between the 1853 Preface and Arnold's first Oxford lecture, 'On the Modern Element in Literature': 'If the Preface could not sustain Arnold the poet, the reaction to it had nevertheless helped to direct Arnold the critic toward becoming the most adequate of the Victorians.' He did not reach the wider public he was hoping for until the publication of the lectures *On Translating Homer* in 1861; from this point on he was sure of intelligent appreciation, and with *Literature and Dogma* (1873) he became a best-seller. Arnold's prose—literary, educational, social, and religious—has retained interest in varying degree. The directly professional reports on schools at home and abroad have been appreciated by educationalists, and the religious writings deplored by theologians, since they first appeared: the best of the literary and social criticism is as secure as anything of its kind in English.

Arnold as critic had distinguished admirers and detractors in his lifetime—they included Hopkins and Henry James, F. H. Bradley and Harrison and Sidgwick; but at his death the studies of Robertson and Stephen confirmed his major contribution. Dislike of his mannerisms persisted into the present century (for example, in Raleigh's *Some Authors*), but most of his main judgements on English poetry had been widely accepted until the lines were re-drawn by Eliot and Leavis, with a new emphasis on the seventeenth and eighteenth centuries, in the 1930s. Leavis's important *Scrutiny* essay on 'Arnold as Critic' in 1938 is something of a landmark, with its tribute to Arnold's distinction as a propagandist for criticism, and its endorsement of his relative valuation of the English Romantic poets. Scholarly work continued on the prose texts, on Arnold's prose techniques, and on the relation of his ideas to the thought of his age. Brown's *Studies in the Text* were preliminary to his *Study in*

Conflict; in the 1950s came Connell's excellent study of Arnold's *Educational Thought and Influence*, Faverty's *Arnold the Ethnologist* (which explores in detail the background to *On the Study of Celtic Literature*), and Holloway's *Victorian Sage*, with its illuminating essay on Arnold's methods of argument. The work of G. and K. Tillotson (now conveniently collected in *Mid-Victorian Studies*) opens new views on Arnold that have stimulated further research: for example, Mrs. Tillotson's 'Arnold and Carlyle', and DeLaura's extension of the same topic in 1964. D. G. James's *Arnold and the Decline of English Romanticism* is a rather petulant distortion of Arnold's views, but has some suggestive comments on his temperament. Recent valuable comparisons of ideas include DeLaura's 'Arnold and Newman', and Alexander's *Arnold and J. S. Mill*, which finds some striking correspondences between Mill's liberalism and Arnold's humanism. Day has a stimulating monograph on Arnold and Vico which links very neatly with the more elaborate 'mythological' interpretations of his whole creative effort.

Arnold's general significance as a literary critic is well summed up in Watson's *The Literary Critics*, Buckley's *Poetry and Morality*, and Wellek's *History of Modern Criticism*. His religious views are discussed in Willey's *Nineteenth-Century Studies* and Cockshut's *The Unbelievers*, his social intention briefly but effectively in Williams's *Culture and Society*. J. H. Raleigh has written a study of *Arnold and American Culture*; and McCarthy's *Arnold and the Three Classes* presents an interesting American view of Arnold's personal contacts with Barbarians, Populace, and Philistines—the weak link here being the middle term. The book has a good social bibliography.

BIOGRAPHIES AND LETTERS

Like many Victorians, Arnold asked that no biography of him should be written; his family agreed only to make available two volumes of carefully censored letters, to be edited by a trusted friend. The most intimate of these are to his mother and sisters, whom he always treated as intellectual equals: to his wife he wrote at length from his Continental expeditions: letters to friends like Lady de Rothschild and to literary acquaintances show the pattern of his social and public life in later years. The *Letters* are agreeable and often illuminating, but very different in tone from the urgent, intense letters to Clough. Additions to Russell's original collection have been made over the years, the most important being Whitridge's publication of 1923, which gave the interesting series to

Newman. A full check-list of Arnold's known letters has been pre-pared by Davis and published by the Bibliographical Society of the University of Virginia; but until there is an adequate modern edition of the letters, a satisfactory biography of Arnold is hardly possible.

Early private papers and journals—including the 'Fox How Magazine' edited by the Arnold children—remain unpublished, though some of this material was drawn on by Wymer in his *Dr. Arnold of Rugby*, a well-illustrated book with several of Jane Arnold's early drawings. A selection from Matthew Arnold's *Notebooks* was published as early as 1902; fifty years later Lowry, Young, and Dunn completed their monumental *Note-Books of Matthew Arnold*, an edited transcription from the working diaries and commonplace-books kept from 1852 onwards, with Arnold's reading-lists and his favourite passages from six great literatures. More clearly than any of his critical pronouncements, these *Note-Books* prove Arnold's commitment to 'high seriousness' and the practice of strenuous devotional reading: they show him as 'a strategic reader who made what he read his own'. In 1957 Guthrie completed his transcription and commentary for the remaining unpublished *Diaries*, and the following year Buckler's monograph on *Matthew Arnold's Books* gave a very different demonstration of Arnold's shrewdness and practicality in dealing with his publishers (Macmillan, and Smith, Elder) after becoming an established writer. These are the chief materials for a Life: the student who cannot consult them fully may be advised to rely on Russell's memoir, and some sampling from the letters and notebooks, to supplement the convenient modern outlines given by Trilling (Introduction to the *Portable Arnold*), Allott (Writers and their Work, No. 60), and Jump's *Matthew Arnold*.

Impressions and recollections of Arnold by those who knew him well are obviously helpful: these may be found in various writings by his brother Thomas, his niece Mrs. Humphry Ward, and such Oxford friends as Clough and Shairp. Tom Arnold's *Passages in a Wandering Life* is an important early source, and his *New Zealand Letters* (ed. Bertram) have some useful references; Mulhauser's *Correspondence of Arthur Hugh Clough*, though it does not include Matthew's letters, fills in many points of detail. Butler's *The Three Friends*, fictional reminiscence, sketches Arnold as a young master at Rugby; Mrs. Tillotson's 'Rugby 1850' (in *Mid-Victorian Studies*) is a scholarly and sympathetic expansion of one of its incidents. Miss Macdonald's *The Buried Self* treats discreetly, in the guise of romantic fiction, Arnold's encounter with Marguerite and his courtship of his wife, and well evokes the settings of Thun, Fox How, Lansdowne

House, and Bowood. Allott, in a recent article in *Notes and Queries*, draws attention to the special tenderness Arnold showed for the young writer and translator, Mary Claude.

BIBLIOGRAPHIES

Four years after his death Arnold's work was admirably surveyed by Smart in a pioneer bibliography which covered the poems (with a synoptical index to trace the course of any one poem through successive editions), the prose in periodicals and separate volumes, and some 300 items of contemporary criticisms and reviews. Smart's bibliography was several times reprinted, and was included in the *Works* (1904) in expanded form; it is still more convenient to use for early references than the valuable section on Arnold in Ehrsam, Deily, and Smith's *Bibliographies of Twelve Victorian Authors*, which builds on Smart and brings the record down to 1934. Wilkins's *The English Reputation of Matthew Arnold, 1840–1877* adds to the list of known writings about Arnold, and Houghton's valuable *Wellesley Index* helps to identify many formerly unknown contributors to Victorian periodicals.

Trilling's *Matthew Arnold* has an excellent general bibliography of background reading, and Bonnerot has a very good working list of Arnold studies to 1947. More recently, Allott's British Council pamphlet (Writers and their Work, No. 60) has an outstanding historical bibliography, and Culler's *Imaginative Reason* has a full select bibliography on Arnold's poetry. For current work on Arnold, in addition to standard annual records and digests, the annual bibliographies in *Victorian Studies* should be consulted. Parrish's *Concordance to the Poems* is invaluable for reference, and for the study of Arnold's verbal patterns.

BACKGROUND READING

An adequate appreciation of Arnold's cultivated humanism requires some knowledge of 'the best that has been thought and said in the world'—a tall order, not easily to be met by any five-foot shelf of books. The Bible and Homer stand first; after these the poets and philosophers of several great ages; then the modern writers Arnold made peculiarly his own, like George Sand and Senancour, Leopardi and Heine, Joubert and Amiel. The notebooks and letters point the way, and particular links are signposted in Allott's edition of the poems and Super's edition of the prose.

Arnold acknowledged a special debt to four men: Goethe,

Wordsworth, Sainte-Beuve, and Newman. To this short list should be added his father certainly, and probably Carlyle as well as Clough. Anyone who wants to understand Arnold's style and manner must in some degree understand theirs. Orrick's *Matthew Arnold and Goethe* is helpful, and Bonnerot prints Arnold's letters to Sainte-Beuve. Harding's *Matthew Arnold the Critic and France* is a thorough exploration of Arnold's intellectual debt to French writers, and complements Mrs. Sells's earlier book on Arnold the poet and France.

The social and intellectual climate in which Arnold lived was brilliantly outlined in Young's *Victorian England*; Houghton's *The Victorian Frame of Mind* is a closer charting. Boase's volume in the Oxford History of Art is valuable for its evidence of the main stream of Victorian taste in painting and sculpture. The Oxford Movement is gracefully outlined in Faber's *Oxford Apostles*, and later religious controversy in Willey's *More Nineteenth-Century Studies* and Cockshut's *Anglican Attitudes*; but the immediate impact of the continuing Victorian crisis of belief is perhaps best conveyed by such documentary novels as Newman's *Loss and Gain*, J. A. Froude's *Nemesis of Faith*, Hughes's *Tom Brown* books, and Mrs. Ward's *Robert Elsmere*. For the general social background, Clark's *The Making of Victorian England* may be strongly recommended. There are a number of useful collections of background essays, of which two are available in paperback in the United States: *The Victorian Age* (ed. Langbaum), and *Backgrounds to Victorian Literature* (ed. Levine).

REFERENCES

TEXTS

K. Allott (ed.), *The Poems of Matthew Arnold* (London, 1965).

K. Allott (ed.), *Matthew Arnold: a Selection of his Poems* (paperback, Harmondsworth, 1954).

K. Allott (ed.), *Five Uncollected Essays of Matthew Arnold* (Liverpool, 1953; paperback, U.K.).

M. Arnold, *Selected Poems* (London, 1878).

M. Arnold, *Poems*, Library Edition, 3 vols. (London, 1885 and 1888).

M. Arnold, *The Works of Matthew Arnold*, De Luxe edn. (15 vols., London and New York, 1903–4). Poems, Prose, Letters and Bibliography.

J. Bryson (ed.), *Matthew Arnold: Poetry and Prose* (London, 1954; paperback, U.K. and U.S.).

F. L. Mulhauser (ed.), *Matthew Arnold: Selected Poetry and Prose* (paperback, New York, 1953; paperback, U.K.).

C. A. Miles and L. Smith (eds.), *Essays in Criticism* (Oxford, 1918).

F. Neiman (ed.), *Essays, Letters, and Reviews by Matthew Arnold* (Cambridge, Mass., 1960).

R. H. Super (ed.), *The Complete Prose Works of Matthew Arnold* (Ann Arbor, Mich., and Toronto, 1960–). Already published: Vol. I: *On the Classical Tradition* (1960); Vol. II: *Democratic Education* (1962); Vol. III: *Lectures and Essays in Criticism* (1962); Vol. IV: *Schools and Universities on the Continent* (1964); Vol. V: *Culture and Anarchy* (1965); Vol. VI: *Dissent and Dogma* (1967).

C. B. Tinker and H. F. Lowry (eds.), *The Poetical Works of Matthew Arnold* (Oxford Standard Authors, London and New York, 1950).

C. B. Tinker and H. F. Lowry (eds.), *The Poetry of Matthew Arnold: a Commentary* (London and New York, 1940).

L. Trilling (ed.), *The Portable Matthew Arnold* (paperback, New York, 1949; paperback, U.K.).

J. D. Wilson (ed.), *Culture and Anarchy* (Cambridge, 1932: paperbacks, U.K. and U.S.).

CRITICAL STUDIES AND COMMENTARY

E. Alexander, *Matthew Arnold and J. S. Mill* (London, 1965).

K. Allott, *Matthew Arnold* 2nd edn. (Writers and their Work, No. 60, London, 1962).

K. Allott, 'Matthew Arnold's Original Version of "The River" ', *TLS* (1958).

K. Allott, 'Matthew Arnold's Reading-Lists in Three Early Diaries', *VS* ii (1959).

K. Allott, 'Matthew Arnold's "Stagirius" and Saint-Marc Girardin', *RES* N.S. ix (1958).

K. Allott, 'A Background for "Empedocles on Etna"' in S. Potter (ed.), *Essays and Studies* (London, 1968).

W. D. Anderson, *Matthew Arnold and the Classical Tradition* (Ann Arbor, Mich., 1965).

P. F. Baum, *Ten Studies in the Poetry of Matthew Arnold* (Durham, N.C., 1958).

L. Bonnerot, *Matthew Arnold, Poète: essai de biographie psychologique* (Paris, 1947).

J. B. Broadbent, 'Milton and Arnold', *EIC* vi (1956).

R. L. Brooks, 'The Genesis of Matthew Arnold's "Thyrsis" ', *RES* N.S. xiv (1963).

R. L. Brooks, 'A New Source for Matthew Arnold's "Sohrab and Rustum" ', *PQ* xlii (1963).

R. L. Brooks, 'The Strayed Reveller Myth', *The Library*, 5th Ser. xviii (1963).

E. K. Brown, *Studies in the Text of Matthew Arnold's Prose Works* (Paris, 1935).

E. K. Brown, *Matthew Arnold: a Study in Conflict* (Toronto and Chicago, 1948).

E. K. Brown, 'The Scholar-Gipsy: an Interpretation', *Revue anglo-américaine*, xii (1935).

V. Buckley, *Poetry and Morality: Studies on the Criticism of Matthew Arnold, T. S. Eliot and F. R. Leavis* (London, 1959).

E. K. Chambers, *Matthew Arnold* (Oxford, 1947).

A. H. Clough, 'Recent English Poetry': review of some poems by Alexander Smith and Matthew Arnold, *North American Review*, lxxvii (1853); reprinted in *Poems and Prose Remains of Clough*, vol. i (London, 1869); and in B. B. Trawick (ed.), *Selected Prose Works of Clough* (Alabama, 1964).

A. O. J. Cockshut, *The Unbelievers* (London, 1964).

W. F. Connell, *The Educational Thought and Influence of Matthew Arnold* (London, 1950).

S. M. B. Coulling, 'Matthew Arnold's 1853 Preface: its origin and aftermath', *VS* vii (1964).

A. D. Culler, *Imaginative Reason: The Poetry of Matthew Arnold* (New Haven, Conn., 1966).

J. P. Curgenven, '*The Scholar Gipsy*: a Study of the Growth, Meaning, and Integration of a Poem', *Litera* (Istanbul), 2 (1955); 3 (1956).

J. P. Curgenven, ' "Thyrsis" IV: Models, Sources, Influences; the Landscape Hellenized', *Litera* (Istanbul), 4 (1957): 5 (1958); 6 (1959).

P. W. Day, *Matthew Arnold and the Philosophy of Vico*, (Auckland, 1964).

D. J. DeLaura, 'Arnold and Carlyle', *PMLA* lxxix (1964).

D. J. DeLaura, 'Matthew Arnold and John Henry Newman: the "Oxford Sentiment" and the Religion of the Future', *Texas Studies in Literature and Language*, vi (1965).

P. Drew, 'Matthew Arnold and The Passage of Time: a Study of "The Scholar-Gipsy" and "Thyrsis"', in I. Armstrong (ed.), *The Major Victorian Poets: Reconsiderations* (London, 1969).

A. E. Dyson, 'The Last Enchantments' (on 'The Scholar-Gipsy'), *RES* N.S. viii (1957).

T. S. Eliot, *Selected Essays* (London, 1932).

T. S. Eliot, *The Use of Poetry and the Use of Criticism*, 2nd edn. (London and New York, 1964; paperback, U.K.).

F. E. Faverty, *Matthew Arnold the Ethnologist* (Evanston, Ill., 1951).

E. Frykman, *'Bitter Knowledge' and 'Unconquerable Hope': A Thematic Study of Attitudes towards Life in Matthew Arnold's Poetry, 1849–1853* (Göteborg, N.S. xi (1966).

H. W. Garrod, *Poetry and the Criticism of Life* (Oxford, 1931).

H. W. Garrod, 'Matthew Arnold's 1853 Preface', *RES* xvii (1941).

L. A. Gottfried, 'Matthew Arnold's "The Strayed Reveller" ', *RES* N.S. xi (1960).

L. A. Gottfried, *Matthew Arnold and the Romantics* (London, 1963).

F. J. W. Harding, *Matthew Arnold the Critic and France* (Geneva, 1964).

J. Holloway, *The Victorian Sage: Studies in Argument* (London, 1953; repr. U.S. 1962; paperback, U.S.).

R. E. C. Houghton, *The Influence of the Classics on the Poetry of Matthew Arnold* (Oxford, 1923).

W. E. Houghton, 'Arnold's "Empedocles on Etna" ', *VS* i (1958).

W. E. Houghton, *The Poetry of Clough: an Essay in Revaluation* (New Haven, Conn., and London, 1963).

R. H. Hutton, *Literary Essays*, 2nd edn. (London, 1877).

D. G. James, *Matthew Arnold and the Decline of English Romanticism* (Oxford, 1961).

H. James, *Views and Reviews* (London, 1908).

W. A. Jamison, *Arnold and the Romantics* (Copenhagen, 1958).

E. D. H. Johnson, *The Alien Vision of Victorian Poetry* (Princeton, N.J., 1952).

W. S. Johnson, 'Matthew Arnold's Sea of Life', *PQ* xxxi (1952).

W. S. Johnson, *The Voices of Matthew Arnold: an Essay in Criticism* (New Haven, Conn., and London, 1961).

J. D. Jump, 'Matthew Arnold and the *Spectator*', *RES* xxv (1949).

J. D. Jump, *Matthew Arnold*. rev. edn. (London, 1965).

H. Kingsmill, *Matthew Arnold* (London, 1928).

W. S. Knickerbocker, 'Matthew Arnold at Oxford: the Natural History of a Father and Son', *SR* xxxv (1927).

W. S. Knickerbocker, 'Semaphore: Arnold and Clough', *SR* xli (1933).

G. W. Knight, ' "The Scholar-Gipsy": an Interpretation', *RES* N.S. vi (1955).

U. C. Knoepflmacher, 'Dover Revisited: the Wordsworthian Matrix in the Poetry of Matthew Arnold', *VP* i (1963).

F. R. Leavis, *New Bearings in English Poetry*, 2nd edn. (London, 1950; paperbacks, U.K. and U.S.).

F. R. Leavis, 'Arnold, Wordsworth, and the Georgians', in *Revaluation* (London, 1936; paperbacks, U.K. and U.S.).

F. R. Leavis, 'Arnold as Critic', in *A Selection from 'Scrutiny'*, Vol. I (Cambridge, 1968; paperbacks, U.K. and U.S.).

H. F. Lowry (ed.), *The Letters of Matthew Arnold to Arthur Hugh Clough* (Oxford, 1932; reissue 1968).

W. A. Madden, *Matthew Arnold: a Study of the Aesthetic Temperament in Victorian England* (Bloomington, Ind., 1967).

S. Nagarajan, 'Arnold and the *Bhagavad Gita:* a Reinterpretation of *Empedocles on Etna*', *Comparative Literature*, xii (1960).

J. B. Orrick, 'Matthew Arnold and Goethe', *Publications of the English Goethe Society*, N.S. iv (1928).

H. W. Paul, *Matthew Arnold* (London, 1902).

G. Pearson, 'The Importance of Arnold's *Merope*', in I. Armstrong (ed.), *The Major Victorian Poets: Reconsiderations* (London, 1969).

J. H. Raleigh, *Matthew Arnold and American Culture* (Berkeley and Los Angeles, Calif., 1957; paperbacks, U.K. and U.S.).

W. Raleigh, *Some Authors* (Oxford, 1923).

W. M. Rossetti, Review of *The Strayed Reveller, and Other Poems*, *The Germ*, no. 2 (February 1850); reprinted in facsimile (London, 1901).

G. Saintsbury, *Matthew Arnold* (London, 1899).

I. E. Sells, *Matthew Arnold and France: the Poet* (Cambridge, 1935).

G. R. Stange, *Matthew Arnold: the Poet as Humanist* (Princeton, N.J., and London, 1967).

R. H. Super, 'Emerson and Arnold's Poetry', *PQ* xxxiii (1954).

R. H. Super, 'Arnold's "Tyrian Trader" in Thucydides', *Notes and Queries*, 201 (1956).

R. H. Super, 'The First Publication of "Thyrsis" ', *Notes and Queries*, 206 (1961).

A. C. Swinburne, *Essays and Studies* (London, 1875). Contains his review of *New Poems* (1867).

G. Tillotson, *Criticism and the Nineteenth Century* (London, 1951).

K. Tillotson, 'Arnold and Johnson', *RES* N.S. i (1950).

G. and K. Tillotson, *Mid-Victorian Studies* (London, 1965).

L. Trilling, *Matthew Arnold*, 2nd edn. (London and New York, 1949; paperbacks, U.K. and U.S.).

P. Veyriras, *Arthur Hugh Clough* (Paris, 1964).

G. Watson, *The Literary Critics* (paperback, Harmondsworth, 1962).

R. Wellek, *A History of Modern Criticism, 1750–1950* (4 vols., London, 1966).

BIOGRAPHY AND LETTERS

K. Allott, 'Matthew Arnold and Mary Claude', *Notes and Queries*, xv (1968).

T. Arnold, *Passages in a Wandering Life* (London, 1900).

J. Bertram (ed.), *New Zealand Letters of Thomas Arnold the Younger, with Letters of A. H. Clough* (Wellington and London, 1966).

W. E. Buckler, *Matthew Arnold's Books: Towards a Publishing Diary* (Paris and Geneva, 1958).

A. G. Butler, *The Three Friends: a Story of Rugby in the Forties* (Oxford, 1900).

W. B. Guthrie, 'Matthew Arnold's Diaries, the Unpublished Items: a Transcription and Commentary' (4 vols., Ann Arbor, Mich., 1957). Microfilm.

H. F. Lowry, K. Young, and W. H. Dunn (eds.), *The Note-Books of Matthew Arnold* (London, New York, and Toronto, 1952).

P. J. McCarthy, *Matthew Arnold and the Three Classes* (New York and London, 1964).

I. Macdonald, *The Buried Self: A Background to the Poems of Matthew Arnold, 1848–1851* (London, 1949).

F. Mulhauser (ed.), *The Correspondence of Arthur Hugh Clough* (2 vols., Oxford, 1957).

R. H. Ronson, 'The Death of Matthew Arnold', *TLS* 3,476, 10 Oct. 1968; and subsequent correspondence.

G. W. E. Russell, *Matthew Arnold* (London, 1904).

G. W. E. Russell (ed.), *Letters of Matthew Arnold, 1848–1888*, 2nd edn. (2 vols., London and New York, 1901).

J. C. Shairp, 'Balliol Scholars', in *Glen Desseray and Other Poems* (London, 1888).

L. Strachey, *Eminent Victorians* (London, 1918; paperback, U.S.).

Mrs. H. Ward, *A Writer's Recollections* (London, 1918).

A. Whitridge (ed.), *Unpublished Letters of Matthew Arnold* (New Haven, Conn., 1923).

N. Wymer, *Dr. Arnold of Rugby* (London, 1953).

BIBLIOGRAPHIES

A. K. Davis, *Matthew Arnold's Letters: a Descriptive Checklist* (Charlottesville, Va., 1969).

T. G. Ehrsam, R. H. Deily, and R. M. Smith, *Bibliographies of Twelve Victorian Authors* (New York, 1936).

F. E. Faverty (ed.), *The Victorian Poets: a Guide to Research* 2nd edn. (Cambridge, Mass., 1968).

W. E. Houghton (ed.), *The Wellesley Index to Victorian Periodicals* (New Haven, Conn., 1966).

S. M. Parrish (ed.), *A Concordance to the Poems of Matthew Arnold* (Ithaca, N.Y., 1959).

T. B. Smart, *The Bibliography of Matthew Arnold* (London, 1892). See also *Works*, vol. xv.

C. T. Wilkins, *The English Reputation of Matthew Arnold, 1840–1877* (Ann Arbor, Mich., 1959). Microfilm.

Annual bibliographies in *VS*

BACKGROUND READING

T. S. R. Boase, *English Art, 1800–1870* (*O.H.E.A.*, vol. x, Oxford, 1959).

F. H. Bradley, *Ethical Studies* (1876), 2nd edn. (Oxford, 1927; paperbacks, U.K. and U.S.).

G. K. Clark, *The Making of Victorian England* (London, 1962; paperbacks, U.K. and U.S.).

G. Faber, *Oxford Apostles* (London, 1933; paperback, U.K.).

J. A. Froude, *The Nemesis of Faith* (London, 1849).

F. Harrison, *The Choice of Books* (London, 1886).

W. E. Houghton, *The Victorian Frame of Mind, 1830–1870* (New Haven, Conn., and London, 1957; paperbacks, U.K. and U.S.).

T. Hughes, *Tom Brown's School-Days* (1857; paperbacks, U.K. and U.S.).

T. Hughes, *Tom Brown at Oxford* (1861).

A. P. Kelso, *Matthew Arnold on Continental Life and Literature* (Oxford, 1914).

R. Langbaum (ed.), *The Victorian Age* (paperback, New York, 1967).

R. A. Levine (ed.), *Backgrounds to Victorian Literature* (paperback, San Francisco).

Mrs. H. Ward, *Robert Elsmere*, 26th edn. (London, 1889).

B. Willey, *Nineteenth-Century Studies: Coleridge to Matthew Arnold* (London, 1949; paperbacks, U.K. and U.S.).

B. Willey, *More Nineteenth-Century Studies* (London, 1956).

R. Williams, *Culture and Society, 1780–1950* (London, 1958; paperbacks, U.K. and U.S.).

G. M. Young, *Victorian England* (Oxford, 1936; paperback, U.S.).

Graham Storey

TEXTS

THE standard edition of Hopkins's poems is that edited by W. H. Gardner and N. H. Mackenzie (*The Poems of Gerard Manley Hopkins*, 4th edn., 1967). Although not published until nearly eighty years after Hopkins's death, it is the first complete edition, based, like its two predecessors (edited by Charles Williams and Gardner, respectively), on Robert Bridges's first edition of 1918, but revised and enlarged to incorporate all his known poems and fragments. It gives a more accurate chronological order of the poems than was formerly known. Meanwhile, N. H. Mackenzie is working on an Oxford English Texts Variorum edition, which will give, for the first time, the full array of Hopkins's elaborate metrical marks.

Most of Hopkins's early verse, embedded in his two Oxford diaries, was published in his *Journals and Papers*, edited by Humphry House and completed by Graham Storey (1959, reprinted 1966). This, together with his *Sermons and Devotional Writings*, edited by Christopher Devlin (1959), constitutes the second edition, much enlarged, of his *Note-Books and Papers*, edited by House in 1937. It exhibits the remarkable range of Hopkins's gifts, containing—besides his diaries and Journal—essays, sketches, drawings, and music.

Several inexpensive selections of Hopkins's works are available: *A Selection of Poems and Prose*, edited by W. H. Gardner (1953, revised and enlarged 1966), in Penguin; *A Hopkins Reader*, containing prose and poetry, edited by John Pick (1953, revised and enlarged 1966); *Selected Poems*, edited by James Reeves (1953, latest reprint 1964), which gives none of Hopkins's stress marks; *Hopkins: Selections* (poems and prose, 1967), edited by G. Storey, in the New Oxford English Series.

CRITICAL STUDIES AND COMMENTARY

There have been few more dramatic instances of changing poetic taste than the growth of Hopkins's reputation. In his lifetime both 'The Wreck of the Deutschland' and 'The Loss of the Eurydice' were rejected by the Jesuit periodical *The Month*; and the 750 copies of the first edition of his poems, 1918, took ten years to sell. Of the second and third editions (1930 and 1948) no less than sixteen reprints and new impressions were called for. The attitudes of the three friends—Bridges, R. W. Dixon, and Coventry Patmore— all poets themselves, who saw his poems in his lifetime, are therefore of peculiar interest. They can be studied in detail in the three volumes of letters listed below. Of the three, Bridges, the faithful custodian of the manuscripts of his poems, was his only critic: he discussed his experiments in detail, but remained on the whole uncomprehending and unconvinced. Their friendship, nevertheless, was of the greatest importance to Hopkins: it can be studied in J.-G. Ritz, *Robert Bridges and Gerard Hopkins, 1863–1889* (1960). Although Dixon's letters show little detailed understanding, he was the most appreciative: he read the poems with 'delight, astonishment, & admiration', and used of them the often-quoted phrase 'the terrible crystal' (Ezekiel 1 : 22). Patmore admired Hopkins intensely as a man, but was not really comfortable with his poems: 'to me', he wrote to Bridges, 'his poetry has the effect of veins of pure gold embedded in masses of impracticable quartz'.

Bridges's most formidable criticism of his friend came in the Preface to Notes appended to the first edition of Hopkins's poems, which he edited with such care. His charges of 'faults of taste' ('affectation of metaphor' and 'perversion of human feeling'), and 'faults of style' ('Oddity and Obscurity'), read strangely now that Hopkins's reputation is so secure, and they have had the effect of obliterating the praise Bridges also gave—for his 'very forcible and original effects, and his 'rare masterly beauties'. After its reprinting in subsequent editions, the fourth edition has wisely omitted part of Bridges's Preface, but retained the remainder for its historical interest.

Reviews of the first edition of the poems, expectedly contradictory, are now mainly of historical interest too. Serious and original criticism begins with an article by I. A. Richards in *The Dial*, 1926 (reprinted in *A 'Dial' Miscellany*, edited by W. Wasserstrom, 1963). Richards claims that Hopkins's 'difficulty' is essential to the complex responses he demands: we have to wrestle with his poems to grasp them in their entirety. He returned to Hopkins in *Practical Criticism* (1929), showing again the richness that yields to sensitive examination. In *Seven Types of Ambiguity*, the following year, William Empson took the two poems that Richards had made his central examples— 'The Windhover' and 'Spring and Fall'—and analysed them to show

how much of their power springs from their multiplicity of meaning. What Bridges had characterized as 'oddity' and 'obscurity' are now being seen as Hopkins's true strengths. Laura Riding and Robert Graves had already included him in their *Survey of Modernist Poetry* (1927), and defended one striking image against Bridges's charge of 'affectation in metaphor'. With the publication of the second edition of the poems in 1930, with a highly sympathetic Introduction by Charles Williams, the way was open to acclaim Hopkins as a major poet.

That he became established as such within a very few years owes a great deal to F. R. Leavis's substantial essay in *New Bearings in English Poetry* (1932; enlarged edn., 1950). The more enthusiastic critics of the 1920s had hailed Hopkins as a revolutionary, 'modernist' ally against Victorian and Georgian decorum. Leavis examines his finest poems—'The Wreck of the Deutschland', 'Spelt from Sibyl's Leaves', some of the final Sonnets—to show that he uses the full resources of the language in the same way as Shakespeare and the Metaphysicals had done: 'his strength was that he brought poetry much closer to living speech.' His essay is still one of the best introductions to a reading of Hopkins.

The following year appeared the first full-length study of Hopkins's poems: Miss E. E. Phare's *The Poetry of G. M. Hopkins: a Survey and Commentary*. Miss Phare attempts to 'place' him by means of several comparisons, of which the longest is with Wordsworth. She examines many of the poems sympathetically, but in the small group dealing with other people—'The Bugler's First Communion', 'Felix Randal', 'Brothers', 'The Handsome Heart'—she finds an exaggerated emotional response.

The implicit assumption underlying the criticism of Hopkins's early defenders—Richards, Empson, and Leavis—is that his greatest poems are primarily poems of tension. The importance of his religious beliefs is accepted: but essentially as part of a conflict with his feelings that produced—or intensified—his poetry. This view is stated fully and explicitly by Sir Herbert Read in an essay in *English Critical Essays: Twentieth Century* (edited by P. M. Jones, 1933; reprinted in his *Collected Essays in Literary Criticism*, 1938). As interest in Hopkins's life and character grew, with the publication of his letters and Journal in the 1930s, the existence or not of such a conflict became a question of considerable controversy. The view that Hopkins's religious experience, far from opposing his poetry, gave it its true life, was put forward by Humphry House in *New Verse* (April, 1935, Hopkins issue); and it underlies the views of the majority of his critics from then on. The religious experience itself was more precisely defined, in terms of the *Spiritual Exercises* of St. Ignatius, in an article by Christopher Devlin (*Blackfriars*, 1935); and its influence on Hopkins's poetry explored by John Pick in *G. M. Hopkins: Priest and Poet* (1942), and, more recently, by D. A. Downes in *G. M. Hopkins: a Study of his Ignation Spirit* (1959). In *Metaphor in Hopkins* (1961) Robert Boyle claims that Hopkins's imagery can only be fully understood as expressing divine activity in human life.

The contrary view, which saw Hopkins's art and religion as irreconcilable, must gain some support from the obvious agony that pervades the Dublin sonnets. Attempts to explain Hopkins's sense of desolation there have differed wildly: from seeing him as the victim of frustrated creative impulses to arguing that his 'aridity' is a state fully prepared for in the *Spiritual Exercises*. Some critics, following G. F. Lahey (*Hopkins*, 1930), have seen in the self-torment of the sonnets the experience described by St. John of the Cross as the 'Dark Night of the Soul'. But neither his poetry nor his Retreat Notes (now published in full in *Sermons and Devotional Writings*) are mystical in the true sense of the word. The most convincing explanation seems to be C. Devlin's in *Sermons* (above): that, in his search for personal sanctity and sacrifice, Hopkins exaggerated the distinction between nature and duty, between his 'affective' and his 'elective' will.

The issue of *New Verse*, April 1935, devoted to Hopkins, initiated several fresh and interesting lines of inquiry. The importance of House's 'Note on Hopkins's Religious Life' has been mentioned already. Charles Madge and Geoffrey Grigson wrote on his language and imagery (Grigson stresses the exactitude of his nature-images in his later British Council pamphlet, 1955); and Christopher Devlin contributed the first of three important articles on the influence of Duns Scotus (the others are in *The Month*, 1949 and 1950).

Two other collections of essays did much to establish Hopkins's reputation in the 1940s with widely different readers. *G. M. Hopkins*, by 'the Kenyon Critics' (1945), reprinted six articles specially written for the *Kenyon Review* (1944, Hopkins's centenary) by Austin Warren, Robert Lowell, H. M. McLuhan, J. Miles, A. Mizener, and H. Whitehall, with the addition of a biographical sketch by Warren, and an essay by F. R. Leavis from *Scrutiny* (1944), retitled 'Metaphysical Isolation'. (Leavis's essay did not appear in the English edition of 1949, owing to copyright difficulties, but is reprinted in *The Common Pursuit* (1952)). All the essays are original and provocative, all treat Hopkins with great respect, and together they constitute an impressive tribute. Both Warren ('Instress of Inscape') and Mizener ('Victorian Hopkins') offer a firm corrective to critics who had divored Hopkins from his own period. The long essay on Hopkins's sprung rhythm by Harold Whitehall claims that it is, like much of Patmore's verse, dipodic not accentual; although this remains controversial, Whitehall's emphasis on a Hopkins poem as an organic whole—the technical devices intensifying, 'over-stressing', the rhythm—was very valuable. Hopkins's organic power was stressed again by Walter Ong in 'Hopkins' Sprung Rhythm and the Life of English Poetry', the most substantial of the essays in *Immortal Diamond*, edited by Norman Weyand (1949, another cen-tenary tribute, delayed by the War). Ong, moreover, maintains that in using sprung rhythm Hopkins was drawing on a tradition in-herent in English poetry: a claim Hopkins himself had made tentatively, when he wrote of his 'new rhythm' to Dixon in October 1878. A thorough examination of his metrical theories is made by Sister M. M. Holloway in *The Prosodic Theory of G. M. Hopkins* (1947). The contributors to *Immortal Diamond* were all American Jesuits; and, besides the editor's Bibliography and R. V. Schoder's Glossary, referred to below, the most useful articles are probably those which draw on specialist knowledge (e.g., M. J. Carroll's 'Hopkins and the Society of Jesus' and R. R. Boyle's 'The Thought Structure of "The Wreck of the Deutschland" ').

W. H. Gardner's two-volume study, *G. M. Hopkins: a Study of Poetic Idiosyncrasy in Relation to Poetic Tradition*, of which Volume I was published in 1944 (rev. edn., 1948) and Volume II in 1949, is still the most comprehensive critical work on Hopkins. It gives a full survey of his poetry; deals extensively with his imagery, vocabulary, and syntax; devotes two detailed chapters to his prosody, insisting (like Whitehall and Ong) on its organic nature; and contains a good deal of biographical material. Gardner's main purpose is clearly indicated by his sub-title, and it can best be given in his own words: 'It is, in effect, to show that Hopkins, at first sight so odd, eccentric, even revolutionary in the matters of style and rhythm, is actually and eminently as legitimate an offspring of the great European poetic tradition as any English poet before him.' He therefore dis-cusses in detail the influences on him of Greek, Latin, Old English, and Welsh poetry. Unfortunately, the exigencies of war-time publica-tion led to a selection of chapters being published in the first volume and the remainder in the second. This detracts from the study's organization, but not from the importance of the material.

In *G. M. Hopkins: a Critical Essay towards the Understanding of his Poetry* (1948) W. A. M. Peters considerably extends earlier studies of the influence of Duns Scotus on Hopkins, and explains Hopkins's poetic idiosyncrasies as the outcome of his metaphysical view of the world. He finds the basis of this in Hopkins's theory of 'inscape' (the individual essence of an object: what Duns Scotus had called '*haecceitas*', 'this-ness'); and, after a chapter on the meanings of 'inscape' and 'instress', devotes the rest of his book to showing the intimate connection between Hopkins's search for inscape and his highly individual use of vocabulary, grammar, and syntax. It is not an easy book; but it is an impressive and closely documented attempt to find a single, unifying principle binding together Hopkins's religious experience and his peculiar poetic techniques.

Most of the criticism of the 1940s was highly favourable to Hopkins. But in two long articles in the *Hudson Review* (1949; reprinted in *The Function of Criticism*, 1957) Yvor Winters attacked him as obscure, over-emotional, and 'romantic': the tone is, of course, totally different, but there are echoes throughout of Bridges's charges of lack of decorum and 'purely artistic wantonness'. Specific replies to Winters can be read in two issues of *Renascence*: by J. H. Johnston in 1950, and by T. P. McDonnell in 1961.

Much more subtle, but still sharply critical, is an essay by Donald Davie, 'Hopkins as a Decadent Critic', in his *Purity of Diction in English Verse* (1952; 2nd edn., 1961). Davie genuinely admires Hopkins; but he finds his ingenuity 'decadent' and his poetic theory over-individualistic: 'his is the poetry and the criticism of the egotistical sublime'. Hopkins's criticism—most of it in his letters—has been acclaimed by several critics, and surveyed by, e.g., Gardner in his *Hopkins*, and, most recently, by M. Ochshorn (*Yale Review* (1965)), who relates it to its Victorian context.

Alan Heuser's *The Shaping Vision of G. M. Hopkins* (1958) is an ambitious and interesting attempt to trace a developing vision in all Hopkins's artistic activity; it is also one of the few studies to consider seriously the place of both his drawings and his music in that development. In another thematic study—a long and suggestive essay in *The Disappearance of God* (1963)—J. Hillis Miller examines Hopkins as one of five nineteenth-century writers whose central problem is to escape their own spiritual isolation through finding God again and restoring harmony to the world.

The most systematic attempt to fit Hopkins into a traditional (as against an intuitive or revolutionary) context is T. K. Bender's study, *Hopkins: the Classical Background and Critical Reception of his*

Work (1966). Drawing support from Hopkins's unpublished notes, Bender suggests that many of his apparent innovations in structure and syntax derive from the classical texts in which he had read extensively, especially from Pindar's Odes and from Martial.

A useful collection of reprinted critical essays has been edited by G. H. Hartman for the Twentieth-Century Views series (paperback, 1966): besides essays already mentioned—by F. R. Leavis (from *New Bearings*), Yvor Winters, H. M. McLuhan, W. J. Ong, and Austin Warren—it includes two essays by the editor and pieces by John Wain, J. Hillis Miller, G. Melchiori, and F. O. Matthiessen.

The last ten years have seen an increasing flow of periodical articles on Hopkins, the majority probably on individual poems (not unexpectedly, Hopkins is a favourite in the *Explicator*'s series of exegeses; and 'The Windhover' must be the most discussed poem in the language). An explanatory commentary on the main poems has recently been published by Donald McChesney (*A Hopkins Commentary* (London, 1968)). In discussion of the other arts that Hopkins practised, John Stevens's Introduction to his music, in *Journals and Papers*, remains the best account of him as a musician; but his drawings have—at any rate in detail—been surprisingly neglected: besides their attractiveness, they have a quality of intense particularity that throws considerable light on his poetic technique.

BIOGRAPHIES AND LETTERS

There is still no definitive biography of Hopkins. Of those available, the first published, by G. F. Lahey in 1930, is appreciative but sketchy; and that by Eleanor Ruggles (1944), though much fuller and very readable, suffers from being over-dramatized. There is an excellent short account by M. C. D'Arcy in *Great Catholics*, edited by C. C. H. Williamson (1938). Although not a detailed biography, John Pick's *Hopkins: Priest and Poet* (1942; 2nd edn., paperback, 1966) is of great help in exploring the relationship between his life, religion, and poetry, and is still the best introductory study. Hopkins's most recent biographer, J.-G. Ritz (*Le Poète G. M. Hopkins*, 1964), was able to draw on the new material published in *Journals and Papers* ¶ and in *Further Letters* (1956). In *Hopkins the Jesuit* (1969) Alfred Thomas published the manuscript journal Hopkins kept as Porter during his noviciate, as part of a detailed study of his Jesuit training. But there is still further unpublished material; and a full Life, equally authoritative on his pre-Jesuit years and on his life as a Jesuit, remains to be written.

Virtually all Hopkins's known letters are published in *The Letters of G. M. Hopkins to Robert Bridges* (1935), *The Correspondence of G. M. Hopkins and R. W. Dixon* (1935), and *Further Letters of G. M. Hopkins* (1956, including his correspondence with Coventry Patmore and letters to his family), all edited by C. C. Abbott (the first two re-printed 1955). They both establish Hopkins as a great letter-writer and are of very considerable help towards understanding his poetry. Bridges's destruction of his own letters to Hopkins is a major loss.

BIBLIOGRAPHIES

There are comprehensive bibliographies in Weyand's *Immortal Diamond* (1949) and in the *New C.B.E.L.* (1969, G. Storey). The best critically selective bibliographies are those by M. Charney ('Bibliographical Study of Hopkins Criticism, 1918–1949', in *Thought* (1950)), and J. Pick (in *The Victorian Poets: a Guide to Research*, edited by F. E. Faverty (1956)). *Immortal Diamond* also contains the useful 'An Interpretive Glossary of Difficult Words in the Poems' (dialectical, archaic, coined, etc.), by R. V. Schoder.

The Hopkins manuscripts in Campion Hall, Oxford, are listed in *Journals and Papers*; and a catalogue of his then unpublished manuscripts, together with their history, is given by D. A. Bischoff in *Thought* (1952).

BACKGROUND READING

Whatever view is finally taken of Hopkins's poetry, his historical background is indisputably Victorian: among the numerous studies of the age, G. M. Young's *Victorian England* (1936) and Walter Houghton's *The Victorian Frame of Mind* (1957) are particularly recommended. Liddon's *Life of Pusey* (1893–7) and G. C. Faber's *Benjamin Jowett* (1957) throw much light on very different sides of the Oxford of his period; and Owen Chadwick's *The Mind of the Oxford Movement* (1960) on the ideas and beliefs that most formed Hopkins's mind there. The important influence of both St. Ignatius Loyola and Duns Scotus on his poetry has been referred to already: the standard translation of *The Spiritual Exercises* of St. Ignatius, with commentary, is by W. H. Longridge (4th edn., 1950); E. Betoni, *Duns Scotus: the Basic Principles of his Philosophy* (1946), translated by B. Bonansea (1961), gives a useful summary of Scotist thought.

REFERENCES

TEXTS

R. Bridges (ed.), *The Poems of G. M. Hopkins*, 1st edn. (Oxford, 1918); C. Williams (ed.), 2nd edn. (1930); W. H. Gardner (ed.), 3rd edn. (1948); Gardner and N. H. Mackenzie (eds.), 4th edn. (1967; paperbacks, U.K. and U.S.).

H. House (ed.), *The Note-Books and Papers of G. M. Hopkins* (Oxford, 1937); 2nd edn., rev. and enlarged: H. House (ed.), completed by G. Storey, *The Journals and Papers of G. M. Hopkins* (Oxford, 1959; re-printed 1966); C. Devlin (ed.), *Sermons and Devotional Writings of G. M. Hopkins* (Oxford, 1959).

W. H. Gardner (ed.), *G. M. Hopkins: A Selection of Poems and Prose*, 2nd edn. (Penguin, Harmondsworth and New York, 1966).

J. Pick (ed.), *A Hopkins Reader*, 2nd edn. (London, 1966; paperback, U.S.).

J. Reeves (ed.), *Selected Poems* (London, 1953; paperback, U.K.)

G. Storey (ed.), *Hopkins: Selections* (Oxford, 1967).

CRITICAL STUDIES AND COMMENTARY

T. K. Bender, *G. M. Hopkins: the Classical Background and Critical Reception of his Work* (Baltimore, 1966).

R. Boyle, *Metaphor in Hopkins* (Chapel Hill, N.C., 1961).

D. Davie, 'Hopkins as a Decadent Critic', in *Purity of Diction in English Verse*, 2nd edn. (London, 1967; paperback, U.K.).

C. Devlin, 'The Ignatian Spirit of G. M. Hopkins', *Blackfriars*, xiv (1935); 'Hopkins and Duns Scotus', *New Verse*, xiv (1935); 'Time's Eunuch', *Month* (May 1949); 'The Image and the Word', *Month* (February–March 1950).

D. A. Downes, *G. M. Hopkins: a Study of his Ignatian Spirit* (New York, 1959).

W. Empson, in *Seven Types of Ambiguity*, rev. edn. (London, 1947; paperback, U.S.).

W. H. Gardner, *G. M. Hopkins: a Study of Poetic Idiosyncrasy in Relation to Poetic Tradition* (2 vols., London, 1944 and 1949; New York, 1948 and 1949).

G. Grigson, 'Blood or Bran', *New Verse*, xiv (1935); *G. M. Hopkins* (paperback, British Council, London, 1955; paperback, U.S.).

G. H. Hartman (ed.), *Hopkins: a Collection of Critical Essays* (paperback, Englewood Cliffs, N.J., 1966; paperback, U.K.). Contains essays by F. R. Leavis, Y. Winters, J. Wain, R. Bridges, R. Guardini, H. M. McLuhan, J. H. Miller, G. H. Hartman, G. Melchiori, F. O. Matthiessen, W. J. Ong, S. Burkhardt, and A. Warren.

A. E. Heuser, *The Shaping Vision of G. M. Hopkins* (Oxford, 1958).

M. M. Holloway, *The Prosodic Theory of G. M. Hopkins* (Washington, 1947).

H. House, 'A Note on Hopkins's Religious Life', *New Verse*, xiv (1935).

J. H. Johnston, 'Reply to Yvor Winters', *Renascence*, 2 (1950).

The Kenyon Critics, *G. M. Hopkins* (Norfolk, Conn., 1945). Contains essays by A. Warren, R. Lowell, H. M. McLuhan, J. Miles, A. Mizener, and H. Whitehall.

F. R. Leavis, 'G. M. Hopkins', in *New Bearings in English Poetry* (London, 1932; enlarged edn., 1950; paperbacks, U.K. and U.S.); 'G. M. Hopkins', *Scrutiny*, xii (1944); reprinted in *The Common Pursuit* (London, 1952; paperback, U.K.).

D. McChesney, *A Hopkins Commentary* (London, 1968).

T. P. McDonnell, 'Hopkins as a Sacramental Poet: a Reply to Yvor Winters', *Renascence*, xiv (1961).

J. H. Miller, 'G. M. Hopkins', in *The Disappearance of God: Five Nineteenth-Century Writers* (Cambridge, Mass., 1963).

M. Ochshorn, 'Hopkins the Critic', *Yale Review*, liv (1965).

W. Ong, 'Hopkins' Sprung Rhythm and the Life of English Poetry', in N. Weyand (ed.), *Immortal Diamond* (see below).

W. A. M. Peters, *G. M. Hopkins: a Critical Essay towards the Understanding of his Poetry* (Oxford, 1948).

E. E. Phare [Mrs. A. Duncan-Jones], *The Poetry of G. M. Hopkins: a Survey and Commentary* (Cambridge, 1933).

H. Read, 'The Poetry of Hopkins', in P. M. Jones (ed.), *English Critical Essays: Twentieth Century* (Oxford, 1933); reprinted in his *Collected Essays in Literary Criticism* (London, 1938; paperback, U.K.).

I. A. Richards, 'G. M. Hopkins', *The Dial*, cxxxi (1926); reprinted in W. Wasserstrom (ed.), *A 'Dial' Miscellany* (Syracuse, N.Y., 1963); included in *Practical Criticism* (London, 1929; paperbacks, U.K. and U.S.).

L. Riding and R. Graves, *A Survey of Modernist Poetry* (London, 1927).

J. G. Ritz, *Robert Bridges and Gerard Hopkins, 1863–89: a Literary Friendship* (Oxford, 1960).

J. E. Stevens, 'Hopkins as a Musician', in *Journals and Papers* (see above).

N. Weyand (ed.), *Immortal Diamond: Studies in G. M. Hopkins* (London, 1949). Essays by members of the Society of Jesus.

Y. Winters, 'The Poetry of G. M. Hopkins', *Hudson Review*, i–ii (1949); reprinted in *The Function of Criticism* (Denver, Colo., 1957; paperback, U.S.).

BIOGRAPHIES AND LETTERS

C. C. Abbott (ed.), *Letters of G. M. Hopkins to R. Bridges*; *Correspondence of G. M. Hopkins and R. W. Dixon* (2 vols., Oxford, reprinted 1955); *Further Letters of G. M. Hopkins*, 2nd edn. (Oxford, 1956).

M. C. D'Arcy, 'G. M. Hopkins', in C. C. H. Williamson (ed.), *Great Catholics* (London, 1938; paperbacks, U.K. and U.S.).

G. F. Lahey, *G. M. Hopkins* (Oxford, 1930).

J. Pick, *G. M. Hopkins: Priest and Poet* (Oxford, 1942); 2nd edn. (paperback, Oxford and New York, 1966).

J.-G. Ritz, *Le poete G. M. Hopkins, 1844–89; l'homme et l'oeuvre* (Paris, 1964; paperbacks, U.K. and U.S.).

E. Ruggles, *Hopkins: a Life* (London, 1944; reprinted New York, 1969).

A. Thomas, *Hopkins the Jesuit: the Years of Training* (Oxford, 1969).

BIBLIOGRAPHIES

D. A. Bischoff, 'The Manuscripts of G. M. Hopkins', *Thought*, xxvii (1952).

M. Charney, 'A Bibliographical Study of Hopkins Criticism, 1918–49', *Thought*, xxv (1950).

J. Pick, 'G. M. Hopkins', in F. E. Faverty (ed.), *The Victorian Poets: a Guide to Research* (Cambridge, Mass., 1956).

R. V. Schoder, 'An Interpretive Glossary of Difficult Words in the Poems', in N. Weyand (ed.), *Immortal Diamond: Studies in G. M. Hopkins* (London, 1949).

G. Storey, 'G. M. Hopkins', in *N.C.B.E.L.*, vol. iii: 1800–1900, ed. G. Watson (Cambridge and New York, 1969).

N. Weyand, 'A Chronological Hopkins Bibliography', in *Immortal Diamond* (see above).

BACKGROUND READING

E. Betoni, *Duns Scotus: the Basic Principles of his Philosophy* (Brescia, 1946); trans. by B. Bonansea (Washington, 1961).

W. O. Chadwick, *The Mind of the Oxford Movement* (London, 1960).

G. C. Faber, *Benjamin Jowett* (London, 1957).

W. E. Houghton, *The Victorian Frame of Mind, 1830–70* (New Haven, Conn., 1957; paperbacks, U.K. and U.S.).

St. Ignatius Loyola, *The Spiritual Exercises*, trans. from the Spanish, with Commentary and a trans. of the *Directorium in Exercitia*, by W. H. Longridge, 4th edn. (London, 1950).

H. P. Liddon, *The Life of E. B. Pusey*, ed. by J. O. Johnston, R. J. Wilson, and W. C. E. Newbolt (4 vols., London, 1893–7).

G. M. Young, *Victorian England: Portrait of an Age*, 2nd edn. (London, 1953; paperbacks, U.K. and U.S.).

Jon Stallworthy

YEATS dedicated his *Reveries over Childhood and Youth* 'To those few people, mainly personal friends, who have read all that I have written'. That was in 1914, six years after he had published his *Collected Works* in eight volumes. The twenty-five years of life remaining to him were hardly less productive, as is shown by Allan Wade's admirable *Bibliography* which lists, for example, thirty-six books and periodicals edited by Yeats and twenty-eight others with an Introduction or Preface by him. Several groups of letters, like those to Lady Gregory (edited by D. T. Torchiana and G. O'Malley in *A Review of English Literature*), have been published since the second edition of Wade's *Bibliography*; other collections are now being discovered and edited, as are the work-sheets of his poetry, plays, and prose. A handful of scholars may have read all that Yeats ever published—though, if one counts such ephemera as letters to newspapers, I doubt if any scholar has read all. Clearly no one will ever read all that Yeats ever wrote. Nevertheless, the Dedication to *Reveries over Childhood and Youth* was no gesture of idle vanity: Yeats sometimes laid himself open to charges of vanity, but seldom idle vanity. There was little that he wrote—even in his letters—that gives the impression of being unconsidered. 'One day when I was twenty-three or twenty-four,' he wrote, 'this sentence seemed to form in my head, without my willing it, much as sentences form when we are half-asleep: "Hammer your thoughts into unity." ' The remarkable extent to which he achieved this can be appreciated best by those who have read most of all that he has written.

BIOGRAPHIES AND LETTERS

It would, of course, be foolish to suggest that one cannot appreciate Yeats's work until one is familiar with his whole output, but his life, his poetry, his plays, his stories, his philosophy, and his politics, are so inextricably interwoven that some knowledge of each docs undoubtedly shed light on the others.

The fullest factual biography at present is Joseph Hone's *W. B. Yeats, 1865–1939*. Curtis Bradford, who probably knows more than anybody else about Yeats's prose manuscripts, says that 'Hone . . . missed a great opportunity, for Mrs. Yeats made all Yeats's papers available to him and told him he could print anything he wanted to. He found it easier on page after page to quote Yeats's "First Draft of Autobiographies" almost verbatim without indicating that he was doing this.' Hone's biography certainly has many shortcomings—he has, for example, little to say that is very perceptive about the poems, prose, and plays—but his book is none the less indispensable. A. N. Jeffares in *W. B. Yeats: Man and Poet* does relate the life to the work, and his discussion of the latter is more detailed and illuminating than Hone's. Even so, a definitive biography that will do justice to the work and throw light on the many unexplored corners of the life remains to be written. It presents a challenge even more formidable than that so triumphantly answered by Richard Ellmann's masterly *James Joyce*, and perhaps cannot be satisfactorily undertaken until much unpublished material, now scattered from California to Tokyo, has been made available.

In the course of his long life Yeats wrote a great many letters. Though by modern literary standards a reserved man, who signed his correspondence to a sister or a former mistress 'W. B. Yeats', he was an excellent letter-writer and *The Letters of W. B. Yeats*, edited by Wade, is a necessary adjunct to the *Autobiographies*. The long essays that make up the latter are examples of his prose at its resonant best, but the voice of the living man—trenchant, informative, flamboyant—can be heard more distinctly in the letters, which are also, incidentally, a good deal more factual than much of the *Autobiographies*. The authentic accent of his public, as opposed to his private, voice is strikingly preserved in *The Senate Speeches of W. B. Yeats*, recovered from the columns of *Seanad Eireann* and edited by Donald R. Pearce. Wade's selection from the letters can be supplemented by five other volumes: *Florence Farr, Bernard Shaw and W. B. Yeats*, edited by Clifford Bax; *W. B. Yeats: Letters to Katherine Tynan*, edited by Roger McHugh; *Ah, Sweet Dancer—W. B. Yeats, Margot Ruddock: A Correspondance*, edited by Roger McHugh; *W. B. Yeats and T. Sturge-Moore: their Correspondence*, edited by Ursula Bridge; and *Letters on Poetry from W. B. Yeats to Dorothy Wellesley*, edited by her. The last of these is the most revealing, and essential to an understanding of the *Last Poems*. Whilst on the subject of letters, those by Yeats's remarkable and gifted father, collected in *J. B. Yeats: Letters to his Son W. B. Yeats and Others*, edited by Hone, explain the influence of the father on the son and shed light on much in the poet's early development.

TEXTS

Turning from the life to the work, the *Collected Poems* and *Collected Plays* have been superseded, as far as scholars are concerned, by *The Variorum Edition of the Poems*, edited by Peter Allt and Russell K. Alspach, and *The Variorum Edition of the Plays*, edited by Alspach. Not only do these set out all the changes in the printed texts of the collected poems and plays but they also give the texts and variants of poems and plays published in magazine or volume form and not included in the *Collected Poems* and *Collected Plays*. Also of great value to scholars is *A Concordance to the Poems of W. B. Yeats*, edited by S. M. Parrish and programmed by J. A. Painter, which will tell one more of Yeats's use of language than several critical studies. Due for early publication is *A Concordance to the Plays of W. B. Yeats* (2 volumes), edited by Eric Domville and programmed by J. A. Painter. The use of these two concordances in conjunction should enable scholars to learn a good deal more about the relationships between Yeats's poetry and plays.

Yeats's prose has been less well served than his poetry and plays. The bulk of it is now available in three volumes uniform with *Autobiographies*, and in a fourth, *A Vision*, uniform with the *Collected Poems* and *Collected Plays*. *Mythologies* brings together, with a few exceptions, the contents of *The Celtic Twilight* (1893), *The Secret Rose* (1897), *The Tables of the Law; The Adoration of the Magi* (1897), and *Per Amica Silentia Lunae* (1917). *Essays and Introductions* consists, again with a few exceptions, of the contents of *Ideas of Good and Evil* (1903), *The Cutting of an Agate* (2nd edn., 1919), and twelve later essays and introductions published between 1912 and 1937. *Explorations* comprises a further selection, made by Mrs. Yeats, of essays and introductions and the text of *On the Boiler* (1939), omitting the verse play *Purgatory*. The fourth volume, *A Vision*, is a reissue with corrections of the second (1937) edition, but there is nothing in this text (as there should be) to tell one that it is such a radical recasting of the first (1925) edition, with so much omitted and so much added, as to be almost a new book. A similar lack of bibliographical information—essential in an author whose work went through so many revised editions—makes the three other prose volumes unsatisfactory for scholarly use. The first volume of *The Uncollected Prose of W. B. Yeats*, edited by John P. Frayne, is now in the press and should shed new light on the man, his work, and his view of his contemporaries.

Readers who do not want, or cannot afford, the collected edition of Yeats's work may find more to their purpose *Selected Poetry of W. B. Yeats, Selected Prose of W. B. Yeats, Selected Criticism of W. B. Yeats*,[1] and *Selected Plays of W. B. Yeats*, all edited—with useful annotations—by Jeffares.

CRITICAL STUDIES AND COMMENTARY

The first book on Yeats, H. S. Krans's *William Butler Yeats and the Irish Literary Revival*, was published in 1904, but Forrest Reid's *W. B. Yeats: a Critical Study* (1915) is perhaps of more interest today for the view it gives of the poet in mid career. Reid voiced a general opinion in regretting the transition from the sensuous to the spare style, though (more perceptive than most of Yeats's readers in 1915) he found '*Responsibilities* . . . a remarkable recovery from the rather feeble and arid *Green Helmet*'. Another interesting contemporary, or near contemporary, view is that of Louis MacNeice's *The Poetry of W. B. Yeats*. As a guide to its subject it has long been superseded, but many of MacNeice's judgements are perceptive. Of more lasting importance are the essays by Sir Maurice Bowra—in *The Heritage of Symbolism*—and Graham Hough—in *The Last Romantics*—which examine, respectively, Yeats's use of symbols in the context of the European Symbolist movement, and the development of his ideas and beliefs in relation to those of Ruskin, Rosetti, Morris, and Pater. In a later essay, *Romantic Image*, Frank Kermode extends Bowra's line of inquiry with a penetrating study of Yeats's images of the dancer and the tree.

Probably the most influential of Yeats's critics have been, and are likely to remain, Richard Ellmann and T. R. Henn. Ellmann's *W. B. Yeats: the Man and the Masks*, an intellectual and spiritual biography, is complemented by *The Identity of Yeats*, which examines the work as perceptively as its predecessor examined the interaction of biography and intellectual development. Asked, however, to recommend one critical study that offers more than a brief critical introduction (and of these there are several that I shall touch on later), I should select Henn's *The Lonely Tower* for its profound understanding of Yeats, his country, and his times. Henn has made a special study of the influence of paintings on Yeats's imagination—it should be remembered that his father and brother were famous artists and that he himself attended art school—and has traced a number of poems back to pictorial sources.

Hone, Jeffares, Ellmann, and Henn all in their books quote

[1] This contains, of course, criticism written by Yeats; not criticism of his work.

briefly from the extensive manuscript and typescript drafts of Yeats's poems and plays. A number of other critics and commentators, following in their footsteps, have since explored this material in greater detail and often with illuminating results. Jeffares appears to have been the foremost pioneer in this field of textual scholarship. His article 'W. B. Yeats and His Methods of Writing Verse' (in *The Permanence of Yeats*, first item under BIBLIOGRAPHIES) offers a good general account and prints manuscript drafts and variants of 'The Fisherman', 'Among School Children', 'A Coat', and 'The Ghost of Roger Casement'. The writing and rewriting of the early verse is more fully examined in Thomas Parkinson's *W. B. Yeats: Self Critic*. He shows how from 1899 to 1911 'the theatre acted as a critic of his early verse, compelling an objectification and realization of thematic possibilities, an expansion and refinement of his diction and prosody'. From 1925 to 1933 Yeats rewrote his early lyrics 'in accord with the metrics, diction, and persistent patterns of structure characteristic of his later, or dramatic, lyrics'. A second book by Parkinson, *W. B. Yeats: The Later Poetry*, considers the principles underlying the composition of such poems as 'After Long Silence', 'Among School Children', and 'Mohini Chatterjee', as well as what he terms their 'passionate syntax'. Parkinson, himself a poet, rounds off his study with a chapter on 'Yeats and Contemporary Poetry'. Marion Witt, author of 'The Making of an Elegy: Yeats's "In Memory of Major Robert Gregory" ', perceptively charts the post-publication revisions of the later poetry in a second article, 'A Competition for Eternity'. To date, however, the most detailed examination of the genesis of individual poems has been *Between the Lines* by Jon Stallworthy. This gives transcriptions of the manuscript and typescript drafts of eighteen poems, from 'The Sorrow of Love' to 'The Black Tower'. A sequel, *Vision and Revision in Yeats's Last Poems*, sets out the development of thirteen poems; and, by way of a pendant to this, the same author has edited and introduced *Yeats: Last Poems*, a 'casebook' of contemporary reviews and later criticism. The genesis of other poems is discussed elsewhere: 'Leda and the Swan' (by Ellmann in *The Identity of Yeats*); 'Sailing to Byzantium' and 'Byzantium' (by Curtis Bradford in *Yeats: a Collection of Critical Essays*, edited by John Unterecker). Bradford, in *Yeats at Work*, considers—as the title of his book suggests—the composition of every section of Yeats's output: poetry, plays, and prose. Perhaps because so much has already been written on the first topic, Bradford is at his best discussing the plays (*At the Hawk's Well*, *The Words upon the Window Pane*, *The Resurrection*, *A Full Moon in March*, and *Purgatory*) and the prose of *The Celtic Twilight*, *The Secret Rose*, *Discoveries*, *Autobiographies*, and *On the Boiler*. Such transcriptions of Yeats's work-sheets throw light not only on the technical aspects of his composition but also on ideas and incidents that prompted him to take up his pen. The fabric of the finished work is often so complex and compressed that these strands are invisible or altered beyond recognition, and there is a good deal to be learnt from watching their interweaving on the loom.

A more conventional, though no less rewarding, avenue of approach to a work of literature is by way of its author's sources, and where Yeats is concerned there can be little doubt that the most successful explorer has been F. A. C. Wilson. His *W. B. Yeats and Tradition* is primarily a study of the last five plays Yeats wrote, together with a number of poems related thematically. These Wilson interprets by reference to alchemy and Kabbalism, and to the works of such philosophers as Plato, Plotinus, Heraclitus, Nietzsche, and Swedenborg. Yeats thought 'that any symbol which at some time or other in the world's history had been a part of religion would retain for ever, through Anima Mundi, a peculiar depth and power of communication'. Wilson's investigation of certain dominant image-clusters in Yeats's verse provoked some criticism—notably from Dame Helen Gardner. Of this Wilson took account in the American edition of *W. B. Yeats and Tradition* and in an 'Appendix to Part Three' of its sequel, *Yeats's Iconography*. Where his earlier book examined such symbols as sphere and zodiac, harlot and beggar, island, tower and cave, *Yeats's Iconography* considers the symbolism of shell and fountain, sea and statue, bird and beast, in the *Four Plays for Dancers*, *The Cat and the Moon*, and twelve related poems. Giorgio Melchiori, in *The Whole Mystery of Art*, shows how Yeats brought together the separate strands of visual influence, the influence of Blake, neo-Platonism, and Irish legend into the pattern that is a poem. He illustrates most skilfully 'the accumulation and assimilation of different images within the narrow compass of a single sonnet', 'Leda and the Swan'. In *Yeats's Autobiography* Joseph Ronsley demonstrates, through an examination of the work internally, and in relation to other published and unpublished works of Yeats, that in spite of its fragmentary genesis it is a carefully devised and unified book. Yeats did not merely chronicle and document the facts of his life and the lives of his friends, but reserved for himself the freedom to select and alter those facts in a way that would evince his sense of the symbolic pattern they made.

In general, Yeats's contemporaries and first commentators had

much less sympathy with his plays—especially the later ones—
than with his poetry and prose: Louis MacNeice was not alone in
dismissing *The Herne's Egg* as 'nonsense satire'. More recent critics,
however, have become increasingly convinced of the unity of Yeats's
work and, exploring the interrelation of its parts, have turned their
attention to the plays. Certain of these, it must be said, lend themselves more to academic dissection than to performance. In her
Preface to *Yeats's 'Vision' and the Later Plays* Helen Hennessy Vendler
says that 'readers of Yeats usually come to *A Vision* by way of something else—the poetry, the essays, or the plays. To understand most
of the essays and a good part of the poetry it is not essential to know
A Vision, but for the late plays I think it is.' The first half of her book
is a lucid analysis of Yeats's philosophical system, centred on those
parts of it relating to the creative process. She then offers a reading,
based on her interpretation of *A Vision*, of the symbolism of *The
Player Queen*, *The King of the Great Clock Tower*, *A Full Moon in March*,
The Herne's Egg, *Calvary*, *Resurrection*, *The Dreaming of the Bones*,
Purgatory, *At the Hawk's Well*, *The Only Jealousy of Emer*, and *The
Death of Cuchulain*. A more comprehensive view of Yeats as a dramatist
is offered by Peter Ure in *Yeats the Playwright*. *The Countess Cathleen*,
The King's Threshold, and *Deirdre* he considers separately, the later
plays in groups according to theme and subject-matter; and lets
himself into each group with a different key. Particularly revealing
is his discussion of the Cuchulain cycle and of the irony that is the
mainspring of each of these five plays. The great merit of *Yeats the
Playwright* is the case it makes for the *dramatic* qualities of the plays.

As with the poems, there is more to be learnt of the plays from a
study of their drafts and revisions than from the work of many
critics. Bradford, as I have said, examines the growth of five plays
from prose 'scenario' to final text. Ure considers Yeats's post-
publication revisions of certain of the earlier plays, as does S. B.
Bushrui, in much greater detail, in *Yeats's Verse Plays*. His study of
The Shadowy Waters, *On Baile's Strand*, *The King's Threshold*, and *The
Green Helmet* skilfully traces the development of Yeats's dramatic
powers and the part played by his experience of the theatre in the
forging of his later style. The manuscript drafts of *The Shadowy
Waters* are to be found in *Irish Renaissance*, edited by Robin Skelton
and David R. Clark, author of *W. B. Yeats and the Theatre of Desolate
Reality*.

Three 'critical introductions' deserve to be mentioned, because
each is well written while compressing a formidable amount of information into a small compass, and each offers a degree of original

insight denied to many a more ambitious study. My own favourite is *W. B. Yeats* by Balachandra Rajan, who is especially perceptive in his discussion of the poetry. He provides an exposition of *A Vision*, as Ure—in *Yeats*—does not. This, the shortest and cheapest of the three critical introductions, gives more space to the plays, and provides a critical bibliography. A. G. Stock's *W. B. Yeats* brings out well the relation of the earlier work to the later, and the widening of the historical vision.

A reader new to the poetry and unfamiliar with its biographical, literary, and historical background will find Unterecker's *A Reader's Guide to W. B. Yeats* useful. Though he occasionally and inevitably presents interpretations that oversimplify what the poet wrote, Unterecker is, within his self-imposed limitations, a sound and sensitive guide. He brings out particularly well the thematic relationship of poem with poem in Yeats's collections, a feature too often overlooked. No less useful to the general reader, and of greater value to the student and scholar, is Jeffares's *Commentary on the Collected Poems of W. B. Yeats*. This offers detailed annotation that includes quotation from manuscript and typescript drafts, glosses from Yeats's letters and prose writings, and parallels from other poems.

The flow of books on Yeats shows no sign of diminishing; on the contrary, the number seems likely to increase as more detailed studies of particular aspects of Yeats's work begin to appear. For example, Allen R. Grossman's *Poetic Knowledge in the Early Yeats* concentrates on one volume of the poetry: *The Wind among the Reeds*. Grossman places special emphasis on the search for wisdom, symbolized by the pursuit of the 'white woman'. This search gives rise to 'a drama of poetic knowledge', presented in Freudian terms in which the principal actors are the self (or child or creative fire), the beloved (a maternal symbol), and the guardian of the beloved. The reward for the winner of the struggle between the poetic self and the guardian is the possession of the white woman (poetic knowledge). By contrast, Robert Beum's *The Poetic Art of William Butler Yeats* directs our attention to more technical aspects of the poetry, especially that of the middle and later periods. Beum examines in some detail the metrical basis of Yeats's poetry and his use of certain stanza forms, especially the *ottava rima*. He has some interesting comments upon Yeats's use both of full rhyme and of 'slant rhyme'. More in keeping with the 'mainstream' of Yeatsian criticism is *Yeats* by Harold Bloom, which surveys the poet's output in order of publication. Professor Bloom's extensive knowledge of the Romantic poets enables him to trace clearly the abiding influences of Blake and Shelley. The early part of the book is helpful in indicating links between Yeats and such writers as Pater, Wilde, and the members of the 'Tragic Generation'. A fuller treatment of Yeats's reciprocal literary relationships with other writers is Richard Ellmann's *Eminent Domain*, containing chapters on Yeats and the following: Wilde, Joyce, Pound, Eliot, and Auden.

BIBLIOGRAPHIES

Complementary to the much expanded third edition of Wade's *Bibliography* are G. B. Saul's *Prolegomena to the Study of Yeats's Poems* and *Prolegomena to the Study of Yeats's Plays*. These list the relevant books and articles that had appeared up to their respective dates of publication, and give the printings of every poem and every play, together with brief explanatory notes and references to critical discussion. Select bibliographies appear in many of the critical studies already mentioned; one particularly strong in reviews of Yeats's books is to be found in *The Permanence of Yeats*, a good collection of essays (by such names as Auden, Blackmuir, and Eliot), edited by James Hall and Martin Steinmann. K. G. W. Cross, co-editor with Jeffares of *In Excited Reverie*, contributed to that centenary symposium 'The Fascination of What's Difficult: a Survey of Yeats Criticism and Research' considerably longer and more comprehensive than that attempted here.

BACKGROUND READING

To start with Yeats's background in its most literal sense—and the work of few English poets is so closely related to a particular landscape—Sheelah Kirby's *The Yeats Country* is a useful illustrated guide to those parts of the West of Ireland associated with his writings. A more detailed account of the topographical background to much of the later poetry is to be found in *Thoor Ballylee—Home of William Butler Yeats*, edited by Liam Miller from a paper given by Mary Hanley to the Kiltartan Society. This includes a number of striking photographs taken in 1926 of the interior of the tower: but by far the richest source of illustrative material relating to Yeats is *Images of a Poet* by D. J. Gordon (with contributions by Ian Fletcher and Frank Kermode). This originated as the catalogue of an impressive Yeats exhibition held at Reading and Manchester Universities, and, in addition to its photographs of the poet, his family and friends, the actors and settings of his *Four Plays for Dancers*, it has a lively and scholarly commentary. One of the most important books so far published on Yeats and his background is Torchiana's *W. B. Yeats and Georgian Ireland*, which is a study of the poet's identification during the last twenty years of his life with Protestant Ireland, the Ireland of Swift and Berkeley, Goldsmith and Grattan, and its heritage. Drawing on much original material and many of Yeats's uncollected —indeed long-lost—essays and reviews, speeches and interviews, Torchiana examines his 'richly biased, highly imaginative, yet strangely fair' interpretation of Irish history. A very different, but no less illuminating, study of literary influence is Ellmann's *Eminent Domain*. In six brilliant essays he demonstrates the rapacity of creative genius, examining Yeats's response to Wilde, Joyce, Pound, Eliot, and Auden; their response to him; and what each plundered from the other.

As regards Yeats's more remote literary background, his debt to Blake is explored by M. Rudd in *Divided Image* and, in greater detail, by Hazard Adams in *Blake and Yeats*; and to Irish mythology in A. D. M. Hoare's *The Works of Morris and of Yeats in Relation to Early Saga Literature* and Birgit Bjersby's *The Cuchulain Legend in the Works of W. B. Yeats*. Of more specialist interest is Alspach's article, 'Some Sources of Yeats's *The Wanderings of Oisin*'. The body of critical literature relating to the Irish literary renaissance is far too extensive for me to offer more than a token selection here. Standish O'Grady's *History of Ireland* should be mentioned as an important source book; and three books by Lady Gregory: *Cuchulain of Muirthemne, Gods and Fighting Men*, and her *Journals, 1916–1930*. Of the numerous biographies and autobiographies by friends and associates of Yeats, the most entertaining (if not necessarily the most accurate) are Oliver St. John Gogarty's *As I Was Going Down Sackville Street* and George Moore's trilogy, *Hail and Farewell*. *Scattering Branches*, edited by Stephen Gwynn, contains some vivid recollections of Yeats by Lennox Robinson, W. G. Fay, Edmund Dulac, Maud Gonne MacBride, and others. Madame MacBride's own auto-biography, *A Soldier of the Queen*, is of interest for the significant fact that it only twice refers to the poet who made her famous.

As the centenary of Yeats's birth was celebrated with a royal salute of symposia, I should perhaps close this survey with a mention of some of these tributes. Inevitably they have their misfires, but there are a number of important essays in *The Dolmen Press Yeats Centenary Papers*, edited by Liam Miller; *The World of W. B. Yeats*, edited by Robin Skelton and Ann Saddlemyer; *W. B. Yeats, 1865–1965*, edited by D. E. S. Maxwell and S. B. Bushrui; and *An Honoured Guest*, edited by Denis Donoghue and Ronald Mulryne. *In*

Excited Reverie, edited by Jeffares and Cross, received rather more attention from the reviewers than its fellow-symposia, largely on account of Conor Cruise O'Brien's controversial article 'Passion and Cunning: an Essay on the Politics of W. B. Yeats'.

REFERENCES

BIOGRAPHIES AND LETTERS

C. Bax (ed.), *Florence Farr, Bernard Shaw and W. B. Yeats* [Letters] (Dublin, 1941, London, 1946).

U. Bridge (ed.), *W. B. Yeats and T. Sturge Moore: their Correspondence, 1901–1937* (London, 1953).

J. Hone (ed.), *J. B. Yeats: Letters to his Son W. B. Yeats and Others* (London, 1944, New York, 1946).

J. Hone (ed.), *W. B. Yeats, 1865–1939* (London, 1942, New York, 1943; paperbacks, U.K. and U.S.).

A. N. Jeffares, *W. B. Yeats, Man and Poet* (London and New Haven, Conn., 1949; paperbacks, U.K. and U.S.).

R. McHugh (ed.), *Ah, Sweet Dancer—W. B. Yeats, Margot Ruddock: A Correspondence* (London and New York, 1970).

R. McHugh (ed.), *W. B. Yeats: Letters to Katharine Tynan* (Dublin and New York, 1953).

D. R. Pearce (ed.), *The Senate Speeches of W. B. Yeats* (Bloomington, Ind., 1960, London, 1961).

D. T. Torchiana and G. O'Malley (eds.), 'Some New Letters from W. B. Yeats to Lady Gregory', *REL* IV (July 1963).

A. Wade (ed.), *The Letters of W. B. Yeats* (London, 1954, New York, 1955).

D. Wellesley (ed.), *Letters on Poetry from W. B. Yeats to Dorothy Wellesley* (London and New York, 1940; paperbacks, U.K. and U.S.).

W. B. Yeats, *Autobiographies* (in the U.S. *Autobiography*) (London and New York, 1927; paperback, U.S.).

TEXTS

The Collected Poems of W. B. Yeats, 2nd edn. (London, 1950, New York, 1951).

The Collected Plays of W. B. Yeats, 2nd edn. (London, 1952, New York, 1953).

The Variorum Edition of the Poems of W. B. Yeats, ed. P. Allt and R. K. Alspach (New York and London, 1957).

The Variorum Edition of the Plays of W. B. Yeats, ed. R. K. Alspach (New York, 1965; London, 1966).

A Concordance to the Poems of W. B. Yeats, ed. S. M. Parrish, programmed by J. A. Painter (New York and London, 1963).

Mythologies (London and New York, 1959; paperback, U.S.).

Essays and Introductions (London and New York, 1961; paperback, U.S.).

Explorations, selected by Mrs. W. B. Yeats (London, 1962; New York, 1963).

On the Boiler (Dublin, 1939).

A Vision (1925), 2nd edn., reissued with corrections (London and New York, 1962; paperback, U.S.).

Selected Poetry of W. B. Yeats, ed. A. N. Jeffares (London, 1964; paperback, U.K.).

Selected Plays of W. B. Yeats, ed. A. N. Jeffares (London, 1964; paperback, U.K.).

Selected Prose of W. B. Yeats, ed. A. N. Jeffares (London, 1964; paperback, U.K.).

Selected Criticism of W. B. Yeats, ed. A. N. Jeffares (London, 1964; paperback, U.K.).

CRITICAL STUDIES AND COMMENTARY

R. Beum, *The Poetic Art of William Butler Yeats* (New York, 1969).

H. Bloom, *Yeats* (London and New York, 1970).

C. M. Bowra, *The Heritage of Symbolism* (London and New York, 1943; paperback, U.K.).

C. Bradford, *Yeats at Work* (Carbondale and Edwardsville, Ill., 1965).

S. B. Bushrui, *Yeats's Verse Plays: their Revisions, 1900–1910* (Oxford and New York, 1965).

D. R. Clark, *W. B. Yeats and the Theatre of Desolate Reality* (Dublin, 1965).

R. Ellmann, *Eminent Domain: Yeats among Wilde, Joyce, Pound, Eliot, and Auden* (New York and London, 1967; paperback, U.S.)

R. Ellmann, *The Identity of Yeats* (London and New York, 1954; paperbacks, U.K. and U.S.).

R. Ellmann, *Yeats: the Man and the Masks* (New York, 1948, London, 1949; paperback, U.K.).

A. R. Grossman, *Poetic Knowledge in the Early Years* (Charlottesville, Va., 1969).

T. R. Henn, *The Lonely Tower: Studies in the Poetry of W. B. Yeats*, 2nd edn. (London and New York, 1965; paperbacks, U.K. and U.S.).

G. Hough, *The Last Romantics* (London, 1949, New York, 1961; paperbacks, U.K. and U.S.).

A. N. Jeffares, *A Commentary on the Collected Poems of W. B. Yeats* (London, 1968, Stanford, Calif., 1969).

A. N. Jeffares, 'W. B. Yeats and His Methods of Writing Verse', in Hall and Steinman (eds.), *The Permanence of Yeats* (see BIBLIOGRAPHIES below).

F. Kermode, *Romantic Image* (London, 1957, and New York, 1964; paperbacks, U.K. and U.S.).

H. S. Krans, *William Butler Yeats and the Irish Literary Revival* (London and New York, 1904).

L. MacNeice, *The Poetry of W. B. Yeats* (London and New York, 1941; paperbacks, U.K. and U.S.).

G. Melchiori, *The Whole Mystery of Art: Pattern into Poetry in the Work of W. B. Yeats* (London and New York, 1960).

T. Parkinson, *W. B. Yeats, Self-Critic* (Berkeley, Calif., 1951).

T. Parkinson, *W. B. Yeats: the Later Poetry* (Berkeley, Calif., 1964).

B. Rajan, *W. B. Yeats: a Critical Introduction* (London and New York, 1965; paperback, U.K.).

F. Reid, *W. B. Yeats: a Critical Study* (London, 1915).

J. Ronsley, *Yeats's Autobiography: Life as Symbolic Pattern* (Cambridge, Mass., and London, 1968).

R. Skelton and D. R. Clark, *Irish Renaissance* (Amherst, Mass., and Dublin, 1965).

J. Stallworthy, *Between the Lines: W. B. Yeats's Poetry in the Making*, 2nd impr., with corrections (Oxford and New York, 1965).

J. Stallworthy (ed.), *Yeats: Last Poems* (London and New York, 1968; paperbacks, U.K. and U.S.). Contemporary reviews and criticism.

J. Stallworthy (ed.), *Vision and Revision in Yeats's Last Poems* (Oxford and New York, 1969).

A. G. Stock, *W. B. Yeats; his Poetry and Thought* (Cambridge and New York, 1961; paperbacks, U.K. and U.S.).

J. Unterecker (ed.), *Yeats: a Collection of Critical Essays* (New York and London, 1963; paperbacks, U.K. and U.S.).

J. Unterecker, *A Reader's Guide to W. B. Yeats* (London and New York, 1959; paperback, U.S.).

P. Ure, *Yeats* (Edinburgh and London, 1963, and New York, 1965; paperback, U.K.).

P. Ure, *Yeats the Playwright: a Commentary on Character and Design in the Major Plays* (London and New York, 1963; paperback, U.K.).

H. H. Vendler, *Yeats's 'Vision' and the Later Plays* (Cambridge, Mass., and London, 1963).

F. A. C. Wilson, *W. B. Yeats and Tradition* (London and New York, 1957; paperback, U.K.).

F. A. C. Wilson, *Yeats's Iconography* (London and New York, 1960; paperback, U.K.).

M. Witt, 'A Competition for Eternity: Yeats's Revision of His Later Poems', *PMLA* lxiv (1949).

BIBLIOGRAPHIES

J. Hall and M. Steinmann (eds.), *The Permanence of Yeats* (New York and London, 1950; paperbacks, U.K. and U.S.).

A. N. Jeffares and K. G. W. Cross (eds.), *In Excited Reverie: A Centenary Tribute, W. B. Yeats, 1865–1939* (London and New York, 1965).

G. B. Saul, *Prolegomena to the Study of Yeats's Plays* (Philadelphia and London, 1958).

G. B. Saul, *Prolegomena to the Study of Yeats's Poems* (Philadelphia and London, 1957).

A. Wade, *A Bibliography of the Writings of W. B. Yeats*, 3rd edn., rev. and ed. by R. K. Alspach (London, 1968).

BACKGROUND READING

H. Adams, *Blake and Yeats: the Contrary Vision* (New York, 1955).

R. K. Alspach, 'Some Sources of Yeats's *The Wanderings of Oisin*', *PMLA* lviii (1943).

B. Bjersby, *The Interpretation of the Cuchulain Legend in the Works of W. B. Yeats* (Uppsala and Dublin, 1950).

D. Donoghue and R. Mulryne (eds.), *An Honoured Guest: New Essays on W. B. Yeats* (London and New York, 1965).

O. St. J. Gogarty, *As I Was Going Down Sackville Street* (London, 1937; paperbacks, U.K. and U.S.).

D. J. Gordon, *W. B. Yeats: Images of a Poet* (Manchester, 1961).

Lady Gregory, *Cuchulain of Muirthemne: The Story of the Men of the Red Branch of Ulster, Arranged and Put into English*, with a Preface by W. B. Yeats (London, 1902, New York, 1903).

Lady Gregory, *Gods and Fighting Men: The Story of the Tuatha De Danaan and of the Fianna of Ireland, Arranged and Put into English*, with a Preface by W. B. Yeats (London and New York, 1904).

Lady Gregory, *Journals, 1916–1930* (London and New York, 1946).

S. L. Gwynn (ed.), *Scattering Branches* (London and New York, 1940).

M. Hanley (ed. L. Miller), *Thoor Ballylee—Home of William Butler Yeats* (Dublin, London, and Chester Springs, Pa., 1965; paperbacks, U.K. and U.S.).

D. M. Hoare, *The Works of Morris and of Yeats in Relation to Early Saga Literature* (Cambridge, 1937).

A. N. Jeffares and K. G. W. Cross (eds.). See BIBLIOGRAPHIES.

S. Kirby, *The Yeats Country: A Guide to Places in the West of Ireland Associated with the Life and Writings of William Butler Yeats* (Dublin, London, and New York, 1962).

[Maud Gonne] MacBride, *A Servant of the Queen* (London, 1938).

D. E. S. Maxwell and S. B. Bushrui, *W. B. Yeats, 1865–1939: Centenary Essays on the Art of W. B. Yeats* (London and New York, 1965).

L. Miller (ed.), *The Dolmen Press Yeats Centenary Papers* (Dublin, London, and Chester Springs, Pa., 1965–8).

George Moore, *Hail and Farewell* (London and New York, 1911–14).

Standish O'Grady, *History of Ireland* (London, 1878–80).

M. Rudd, *Divided Image: A Study of William Blake and W. B. Yeats* (London, 1953).

R. Skelton and A. Saddlemyer (eds.), *The World of W. B. Yeats: Essays in Perspective* (Victoria, Dublin, and London, 1965; paperbacks, U.K. and U.S.).

D. T. Torchiana, *W. B. Yeats and Georgian Ireland* (Evanston, Ill., and London, 1966).

Anne Ridler

(a) Poetry

IN the course of his Introduction to Ezra Pound's *Selected Poems* Eliot remarked that the poet who wishes to continue to write must practise his art, 'not by forcing his inspiration, but by good workmanship on a level possible for some hours' work every week of his life'. This pronouncement caused some anxiety to younger contemporaries, who were accustomed to take Eliot's every word as guidance, and they had difficulty in reconciling it with the sparseness of his own output—in poetry, that is, for in prose he was a prolific writer. But without taking those words literally, one can assume that his published work represents only a proportion of the poetry he composed, and indeed the manuscript which has lately appeared in New York (see CRITICAL STUDIES) is said to contain several of these suppressed poems.

Eliot's first book, of a dozen poems, was published when he was twenty-nine, and the first Collected edition, appearing nearly twenty years later, contains only 144 pages, if we exclude the dramatic verse. This book brought together sundry pieces which had appeared only in periodicals or in pamphlet form, also the dramatic fragments of *Sweeney Agonistes* and the choric verse from his pageant play *The Rock*. The book also contained one new poem, 'Burnt Norton', with no indication that it was to become the first of a sequence, the *Four Quartets*—indeed, it was not until some years later that Eliot, frustrated by the war from his intention of writing another play, took up the form again and realized its full possibilities. The remaining Quartets, after separate publication in various ways, appeared with 'Burnt Norton' in their sequence in 1943. After this, Eliot published only half a dozen minor lyrics, expending his main energies on his plays. These lyrics, as well as the Quartets, are included in the 1963 edition of his Collected Poems, but the verse for children of 1939, *Old Possum's Book of Practical Cats*, is not included there, though it is to be found in the American *Collected*

Poems and Plays. This volume was published in 1952, and does not, therefore, contain his last two plays. A volume containing all the previously collected poems and plays is announced for publication in 1969, in England but not in America. (This is now in print.)

The early poems which Eliot contributed to school and college magazines have now been collected. (They are to be included as an Appendix in the new English Complete edition.) These are well worth study, for they show the abrupt change of style that followed his reading of Arthur Symons's book on the French Symbolists (see BACKGROUND READING), and they contain one poem, 'The Death of St. Narcissus' (set up in type for publication in *Poetry*, Chicago, but not printed), whose opening lines were used almost verbatim in 'The Waste Land'. Here may be mentioned another discarded poem, 'Ode', which is only to be found in the volume of 1919, *Ara vos Prec*.

In addition to his original work, Eliot has published one translation (1930) from the French of the long poem *Anabasis* by St.-J. Perse.

As Eliot exerted such a rigorous censorship on his own work, his poems should be read complete. However, a selection, chosen by himself, is available. Unlike Yeats and Auden, he seldom tinkered with his work after it had appeared in print, and so there are almost no significant variants to be found in successive editions of the poems.

Eliot's first full-length drama, *The Rock*, was an affair of collaboration, written largely in prose, and only the verse-choruses have been kept in print. Of his next, most often-acted play, *Murder in the Cathedral*, six versions exist, if we include the acting text of 1935 and the film script of 1952. After *The Family Reunion*, produced and published in 1939, came the interval of the war, but in 1949 there followed *The Cocktail Party*, the first of the three comedies, which were seen at the Edinburgh Festival before publication. The collected edition of the five full-length verse plays appeared in 1962, with a dedicatory poem to the author's second wife.

A curiosity worth mentioning is the sketch of a final scene for *Sweeney Agonistes* which Eliot sent to Hallie Flanagan, and which is printed in her book *Dynamo*.

(b) Prose

Eliot is one of the great critic-poets, whose prose (the by-product of his poetry workshop, as he has called it) is important for anyone who wants to understand his verse. Three collections of essays are essential reading: the final (1951) edition of the *Selected Essays*, which adds five essays to those contained in the first edition of 1932; *On Poetry and Poets* (1957); and *To Criticize the Critic*, posthumously published in 1965. To these we must add Eliot's one book on an extended literary theme, the relation of criticism to poetry in England: *The Use of Poetry and the Use of Criticism*; also his criticism of Dryden, additional to that in the *Selected Essays* (see REFS.: TEXTS).

There remain many interesting essays as yet uncollected: until a definitive edition appears, it must suffice to suggest lines of possible inquiry for those who have access to one of the great libraries. The two books from which the first Selected Essays were culled, *The Sacred Wood* (1920) and *For Lancelot Andrewes* (1928), have prefaces and some other good essays which were not reprinted. Other prefaces of great interest are those which Eliot wrote for his selection from Ezra Pound's poems and from Marianne Moore's, for a bilingual edition of Valery's poem *Le Serpent*, and for *The Wheel of Fire* by J. Wilson Knight. His late essay on *George Herbert* was written as a British Council pamphlet, and his 'Experiment in Criticism' was a lecture given at the City Literary Institute.

Eliot edited the quarterly *Criterion* for the whole of its span, 1922–39, and some of his 'Commentary' and other articles are worth searching out, though he reprinted in the *Selected Essays* those he himself thought most important. In the first and fourth volumes he gave his idea of what a literary review should be; his obituary pieces on A. R. Orage and on Irving Babbitt are of interest. For his early criticism, the files of the *Egoist*, *Athenaeum*, *New Statesman*, *Little Review*, and *Dial* will all yield fruit: of this remarkable work Hugh Kenner has written: 'In the five years, 1917–1921, Eliot, in some seventy pieces of critical prose, some of them hasty, some peripheral, many of them incidental to a long struggle to live by his pen, carried out . . . nothing less than a rethinking, in the specific terms exacted by conscientious book reviewing, of the traditional heritage of English letters' (*The Invisible Poet*, p. 81).

For those who are studying Eliot's thought in general, his two books of social criticism must be added to the list: *The Idea of a Christian Society* and *Notes Towards the Definition of Culture*. His early thesis on the philosophy of F. H. Bradley is more usefully classified for this survey under BACKGROUND READING. A good selection of his prose, under the headings of Literary Criticism, Dramatic Criticism, and Religion and Society, was made by his friend John Hayward: it contains one or two pieces which are not available in the other collections.

CRITICAL STUDIES AND COMMENTARY

'The creative artist in England finds himself compelled, or at least tempted, to spend much of his time and energy in criticism that he might reserve for the perfecting of his proper work: simply because there is no one else to do it.' So Eliot complained, in one of the essays collected in 1920 under the title of *The Sacred Wood*. Now whether or not his poetry was robbed by it, there is no doubt that this parallel activity, carried on over a lifetime, won general acceptance for work that might otherwise have remained a poetry for intellectuals. (Among them, its acceptance came early, as George Watson has shown in an article in the *Critical Quarterly*.) Thus, in 1949, Helen Gardner could write: 'Mr. Eliot has by now created the taste by which he is enjoyed.' From such undisputed authority, some reaction was inevitable—as with the Greek who was tired of hearing Aristides called 'the just'—but the formal beauties of the poems will ensure that they survive the fickleness of fashionable taste, as well as the honeycomb-tunnelling of the thesis writer.

The two best books on Eliot were written many years ago: both are concerned primarily with the poems as works of art, and not as literary conundrums or as political or religious documents. Helen Gardner's title is *The Art of T. S. Eliot* (1949), and she more than any other critic has placed his work in its relation to the whole body of English poetry, not merely to that of contemporaries or the immediate past. Taking as her starting-point the *Four Quartets*, which she considers his masterpiece, she applies to his work his own concept of the 'auditory imagination', tracing the development of his prosody (including that of the early plays), and returning finally to the Quartets to display more clearly their beauty of imagery and form. He is, she concludes, 'neither a prophet nor a visionary primarily, but a poet, a great "maker".' The prosodic discussion is continued in her Nottingham lecture of 1965, where she links Eliot with Milton and with Pope in his preoccupation with craft, and his use of the storehouse of poetry. A lecture of the following year is devoted to Eliot as a poet of places.

F. O. Matthiessen's book first appeared in 1935, when sociological criticism was in vogue, and his different approach to the work 'through close attention to its technique' is emphasized in the Preface. The book is avowedly not a commentary on the whole of Eliot's work; it is 'an estimate not so much of particular poems as of Eliot's poetic method', and it draws freely on the poet's own critical utterances, both published and unpublished, for illumination.

Matthiessen had the benefit of talks with Eliot at Harvard during 1932–3, and his book is probably the richest source for the artist's own opinions. The edition of 1958 has two additional chapters on the later poetry by Matthiessen, and a final chapter by C. L. Barber.

Two other American writers, Hugh Kenner and Leonard Unger, have contributed valuable books on the whole *œuvre*, and a single essay by Louis Martz, 'the Wheel and the Point', exploring Eliot's symbol of 'the still point', penetrates to the heart of the poetry. Kenner's *The Invisible Poet* is specifically not a handbook, but 'an attempt to relate the work to the personality', disposing of the prevailing notion of its elusiveness. Kenner was one of the first to see how long-lasting was the influence on Eliot of F. H. Bradley's thought: his chapter on this is reprinted in the symposium he edited in 1962. (In this connection, see also J. Hillis Miller's discussion in *Poets of Reality*.) Kenner is especially interesting on the evolution of the five-part form of 'The Waste Land' and the Quartets. 'That form, originally an accident produced by Pound's cutting, Eliot would seem by tenacious determination to have analysed, mastered, and made into an organic thing.' More light will be thrown on this 'accident of Pound's cutting' when the original manuscript of 'The Waste Land', hidden until recently by the New York Public Library, is published: the *Times Literary Supplement* for 7 November 1968 contains an account of it by Donald Gallup.

Leonard Unger's main critical work is contained in his book *Moments and Patterns*, where he examines the sources, themes, and imagery, and devotes a chapter to Eliot's critics. He makes some interesting comparisons with Conrad, and points out that verbal echoes of Laforgue appear in Eliot's work long after his conscious discipleship was outgrown.

Unger is the editor of a fat volume of critical essays written between 1919 and 1948, which includes some of the early and influential criticism by F. R. Leavis, I. A. Richards, and Edmund Wilson; a collection of some twenty essays, edited by Hugh Kenner, extends the span to 1962. (Leavis's latest essay, 'Eliot's Classical Standing', is in his *Lectures in America*.) The eight essays which B. S. Rajan collected in 1947 were designed as a general introduction to Eliot's work. Two Festschrift volumes, of essays, poems, and reminiscences, were published in Eliot's lifetime, and one similar collection appeared soon after his death: the first, edited by Richard March and M. J. Tambimuttu, was put together for Eliot's sixtieth birthday, and the second, edited by Neville Braybrooke, was for his seventieth. The posthumous collection was edited by Allen Tate, and appeared first as a special number of the *Sewanee Review* for Winter 1966. A shorter 'special Eliot number' was that of *The Review*, in November 1962. Good things can be found in all these collections, and some of the essays will be mentioned under separate headings below.

The best popular introduction to the whole of Eliot's work is that of Northrop Frye (1963). His summary of Eliot's thought, though masterly given the limits of space, makes it appear cruder and more dogmatic than it actually is, and even distorts some judgements, but Frye is helpful on the vexed question of poetry and belief, on Eliot's relation to Bradley and to Indian philosophy, and on the imagery of the poems, to which he gives two chapters. Though he is appreciative of the comedies ('Sheridan crossed with John Wesley'), he holds, as some others have done, that 'The Waste Land' is 'closer to what Eliot really means by poetic drama than any of his plays'.

A more simplified introduction, in the series 'Literature in Perspective', is by T. S. Pearce; it contains a good select bibliography for the study of Eliot. M. C. Bradbrook's study, a British Council pamphlet, also provides a good introduction and bibliography, but only for the work written before 1950, when it was published. George Williamson's *A Reader's Guide* (1953) is sub-titled 'a poem-by-poem analysis'; it does not deal with the plays or the criticism, except in passing references. He assumes that the structure of 'The Waste Land' was more consciously designed than we now know it to have been (see Kenner, *The Invisible Poet*, and Pound, under BACKGROUND READING), but there is some clear exegesis, and his treatment of 'Prufrock' in the light of its epigraph adds something to the analysis of Matthiessen and others. Study of the epigraphs is for him a fruitful line of enquiry, and this may be the place to mention a short study devoted entirely to Eliot's epigraphs as an aid to understanding the poems, by Jane Worthington.

In *T. S. Eliot: the Design of his Poetry* Elizabeth Drew relates Eliot's poetry to Jung's theories about myth and the 'collective unconscious', and finds a relation between the sequence of images as they arise in the course of his poetry, and the sequence of archetypal images as traced by Jung. Kristian Smidt's *Poetry and Belief in the Work of T. S. Eliot* is another useful book with an extra-literary approach, using the background of beliefs and ideas to help understanding.

An admiring, but somewhat heavy-footed, study is by D. E. S. Maxwell (1952). He considers the poetry, including drama, and its importance in the literary history of the twentieth century. Four years earlier, Frank Wilson published 'six essays on the development' of the poetry, intended as prefaces to readings, and uneven in value. He too, misled by the precedent of the Quartets, assumes that the form of 'The Waste Land' was consciously planned, and treats it as an even-too-technical experiment in the form of the symphony.

On 'The Waste Land' alone, perhaps the clearest exposition is that of Cleanth Brooks in an essay reprinted in Unger's anthology of criticism. Its very clarity makes for some distortion of the poem, of course, but he is careful to point out that his exegesis is meant only as a scaffolding. The essay was intentionally a corrective to those critics, such as Edmund Wilson, who saw the poem as a statement of pure disillusion. The early essays of Leavis and others are still valuable today, but they need to be read with recent discoveries about the growth of the poem in mind; only Conrad Aiken, perhaps, of early critics, was aware of Eliot's method of composition (see his review, reprinted in Tate's collection).

On 'Gerontion', John Crowe Ransom has a perceptive study (in Tate); on 'Ash Wednesday' the fullest and best study is still that of E. Duncan Jones (in Rajan). Vincent Buckley, in *Poetry and the Sacred* (1968), thinks poorly of 'Ash Wednesday' and, by and large, of 'The Dry Salvages', but writes of Eliot's whole work as that of 'a great religious poet'. Hugh Kenner, whose account of the individual Quartets is one of the least satisfactory parts of his book, seems to have set a fashion for the denigration of 'The Dry Salvages'. The hint he gave is pushed to an extreme by Donald Davie in an essay called 'T. S. Eliot: the End of an Era' (in Kenner's symposium), where he treats the 'Salvages' as successful *parody* verse—surely an instance of theory run mad. Denis Donoghue's essay on the Quartets 'A New Reading' (in the quarterly *Studies*) is interesting, but sometimes seems in danger of losing sight of the poetry: his remarks, especially on Part IV of 'East Coker', need to be read with Helen Gardner as a corrective. The same is true of a piece of straightforward exegesis by Raymond Preston, *'Four Quartets' Rehearsed*. Comments on the Quartets by F. R. Leavis and D. W. Harding are included by Kenner, and by B. S. Rajan in his own symposium.

On Eliot's drama two useful books come from America. Carol H. Smith (*T. S. Eliot's Dramatic Theory and Practice*) is especially interesting on the Sweeney fragments in relation to Aristophanes, but sometimes in her later chapters seems to ignore the author's own warning that he used the Greek plays only as points of departure, not as models. David E. Jones (*The Plays . . .*) explains that he is an academic who has produced and acted in the plays he writes about, and he is particularly illuminating on *The Family Reunion*. Maud Bodkin has made a detailed study of this play in its relation to Aeschylus' trilogy, and is interesting on the treatment of the Eumenides, showing how their transformation from avengers to well-wishers is achieved for the public weal in the old drama, and for the private salvation of the hero in the modern. Helen Gardner, in an essay contributed to Tate's collection, considers Eliot's comedies in relation to the tradition which he deliberately took up: 'At the moment these plays are dated, but as they recede into history their social verisimilitude will be as much a source of strength as is the social truth of Restoration Comedy.' John Bayley (*The Review*) sees the plays as entirely cut off from the springs of Eliot's poetry, though he allows a certain success to *The Cocktail Party*; Denis Donoghue, in his study of this play (reprinted in Kenner) is much more sympathetic towards the genre, but thinks this a less successful example than *The Confidential Clerk*. Martin Browne and Robert Speaight have both written of the plays from the point of view of producer and actor (see March, Braybrooke and Tate; also Browne's lecture on the development of *The Cocktail Party*, and *The Making of T. S. Eliot's Plays*).

On Eliot's sources, that happy hunting-ground, the prime authority is Grover Cleveland Smith, whose industry has carried him so far that his indispensable book ought possibly to be included in BACKGROUND READING rather than in this section; his critical conclusions, moreover, are much less reliable than his facts. In a narrower field, a useful book is that of E. J. H. Greene: he examines in detail Eliot's debt to French poets and to the criticism of Rémy de Gourmont and Julien Benda, and discusses the style of Eliot's four French poems. S. Musgrove, in *T. S. Eliot and Walt Whitman*, is on more debatable ground, his thesis being that in Eliot's very repudiation of Whitman he was acknowledging a deep influence. Mario Praz, in an important essay, shows how the qualities Eliot prized in Dante are not necessarily those which would first strike an Italian, but 'What matters for us is not to ascertain to what extent Dante's style can be considered *simple* (in fact . . . examples of all kinds of style can be found in him), but to know that to T. S. Eliot that style *seems* simple.'

Eliot's own comments on his development as a poet are to be found in various interviews, notably those which he gave to Donald Hall and to John Lehmann, and in his Preface to a reading in a radio programme (N.B.C.), where he explains the intention behind the unfinished 'Coriolan'. And in one of the essays reprinted in *On Poetry and Poets* we have his own critique of his dramatic development.

Turning to the prose, *The Criticism of T. S. Eliot* by Victor Brombert is a clear account of Eliot's critical position, and the extent to which his practice as a critic has contradicted his theories. On the problem of belief and poetry, he traces the change in Eliot's ideas as shown in seven essays written between 1916 and 1941. John Crowe Ransom (in an essay in Unger's *Critique*) seeks—but not quite convincingly—to prove that the drift of Eliot's criticism, which he admires, was strongly against the drift of his poetry. M. C. Bradbrook (in Rajan) explains that the earlier criticism had such intensity because Eliot, in exploring the poets he then wrote about, was discovering his own style. In the Braybrooke symposium there are good essays by J. M. Cameron on Eliot as a political writer, and by Iris Murdoch on Eliot as a moralist. Richard Ellmann, in 'Yeats and Eliot' traces the growth of appreciation in Eliot's criticism of Yeats.

Among hostile critics, Yvor Winters is the most weighty. He attacks the poetry of Pound and Eliot as being chaotic, a 'poetry of revery', not of true meditation. He gives grudging admiration to 'Gerontion', but is utterly insensitive to 'The Waste Land', whose metre he describes as 'a broken blank verse interspersed with bad free verse and rimed doggerel'. His attempt to prove that Eliot is a determinist is not convincing; he does convict him of inconsistencies of statement, but Victor Brombert's analysis is clearer. A more reluctant adversary is G. Rostrevor Hamilton (*The Tell-Tale Article*), who admires Eliot's poetry and shows that he can appreciate its qualities. His thesis is that the frequency of the definite article in modern poetry is a symptom of a degeneracy in syntax, and he relates this to the disease of the age, 'an inadequate sense of the greatness of man'. In this, he is typical of those who feel that out of 'the boredom, the horror and the glory' of life, only the last is a fit theme for poetry. An attack from a very different quarter is in *Men Without Art*, where Wyndham Lewis, writing of 'T. S. Eliot: Pseudoist', executes a satirical dance round about the figures of Eliot and Pound. *Eliot in Perspective*, a critical symposium edited by Graham Martin, was published after these notes were compiled. There are also two recent Casebooks gathering critical material and background on *The Waste Land* and *Four Quartets*: the first edited by C. B. Cox and Arnold Hinchliffe, the second by Bernard Bergonzi.

BIOGRAPHIES

Eliot directed that his executrix, Mrs. Valerie Eliot, should not authorize any official biography. Despite this discouragement, there will always be those who 'peer lasciviously between the lines [of poetry] for biographical confession' (as he put it in his Introduction to Valéry's *Le Serpent*), and print their guesses.

The chief events of his life are well known, and can be found in biographical sketches included in some of the books mentioned in the previous section—e.g. Matthiessen, Grover Smith. But for a full treatment of the poet's American origins and his public life the reader should turn to Herbert Howarth's *Notes On Some Figures Behind T. S. Eliot*. Personal reminiscences are included in the Festschrift collections (see CRITICAL STUDIES), those by Conrad Aiken, Frank Morley, and Herbert Read being of especial interest; affection and bitterness are mingled in Aiken's account of their friendship in his autobiography, *Ushant*, where Eliot appears as 'Tsetse'. Richard Aldington, on the other hand, another early associate, though he wrote bitterly and unfairly of Eliot in criticism and verse in the thirties, is only mildly mocking in his book of reminiscences, *Life for Life's Sake*. Two other autobiographies in which Eliot makes a brief appearance are those of Leonard Woolf and Bertrand Russell, and there are some pages on him (with certain inaccuracies) in the second volume of Michael Holroyd's Life of Lytton Strachey.

Autobiographical asides occur here and there in Eliot's writings, notably in an address on American literature and language, in his Preface to Mowrer's *This American World*, and (on pre-war Paris) in the *Criterion*. Louis Martz, in the essay mentioned in the CRITICAL STUDIES section, quotes from an interesting reminiscence of Eliot's boyhood concerning the 'little door' into the school playground next door to his home in St. Louis, and printed in the centennial issue of the school's publication *From Mary to You*. An edition of his letters is being prepared by Mrs. Valerie Eliot.

BIBLIOGRAPHIES

There is a complete bibliography of all Eliot's published work compiled by Donald Gallup, which includes foreign translations. This was first issued in 1952, and a revised edition is now (1968) in the press. For those who do not want the elaborate detail of a full bibliography, there is a Check List of published writings at the end of the Rajan symposium, but this only covers work published up to 1945. The notes to each chapter in Grover Smith's book contain bibliographical details. A very full list of criticism on Eliot's drama is given in David E. Jones's book, and on his prose in Victor Brombert's; more general lists are in Leonard Unger (*Moments and*

Patterns), T. S. Pearce, and M. C. Bradbrook. All these books are described in the CRITICAL STUDIES section, and in the REFERENCES for that section.

BACKGROUND READING

Herbert Howarth's book, mentioned under BIOGRAPHIES, provides a useful sketch-map of the poet's American background, and F. O. Matthiessen's *American Renaissance* surveys the literary field, with studies in Emerson, Hawthorne, James, Melville, and Whitman, and many references to Eliot in his relation to them. The life, by Eliot's mother, of his celebrated grandfather William Greenleaf Eliot, is for those who want to look farther into his origins, but no English edition is available. Mrs. Eliot's long dramatic poem 'Savonarola' was introduced to English readers by her son: his Preface, adroitly non-committal about literary value, is interesting as an early statement of his thoughts about verse drama. Another preface of about this date was written for a book about the Massachusetts fishermen by James B. Connolly, which explains the fascination their life held for Eliot.

The poet drew nourishment from such varied literary sources that a list even of the most important would be too long for this survey. But Arthur Symons's *The Symbolist Movement in Literature*, with the quotations which first influenced Eliot's writing, is vital. Enid Starkie's *From Gautier to Eliot* gives the French literary background, and explains Eliot's relation to the Imagist movement. The *Letters, 1907–1941* of Ezra Pound are of great interest, both for the history of his and Eliot's early years in London, and for their exchanges on 'The Waste Land'. His *Literary Essays*, too, have a bearing on Eliot's critical work, and they contain his 1917 review of *Prufrock*, and his rejoinder to Eliot's observations on *vers libre*.

Several critics have remarked on Eliot's debt to F. H. Bradley's *Appearance and Reality*, both for his style and his approach to experience. His doctoral thesis on Bradley's philosophy (never presented for a degree, and not published until the end of his life, when he said he was no longer able to understand it), has won praise from philosophers; the two articles on Leibniz which are included with it are probably more useful for non-specialists—like the present writer —who want to understand Eliot's way of approach, for they are less technical than the thesis.

The notes to 'The Waste Land' direct the reader to Jessie Weston's *From Ritual to Romance*, and those who take this up will find Chapter

II especially relevant. An interesting essay by Francis Noel Lees (in Tate) implies that the Loeb edition of Petronius may have played a more important part in the creation of 'The Waste Land' than has hitherto been realized. Lastly, as Eliot himself has said that Dante's poetry was 'the most persistent and deepest influence' upon his own, these suggestions for 'background reading' should end by recommending *The Divine Comedy*.

REFERENCES

TEXTS

Ara vos Prec (London and New York, with slightly different contents, 1920).

Collected Poems, 1909–1962 (London and New York, 1963).

The Complete Poems and Plays, 1909–1950 (New York, 1952).

The Complete Poems and Plays (London, 1969).

Four Quartets (New York, 1943, and London, 1944; paperbacks, U.K. and U.S.).

Old Possum's Book of Practical Cats (London and New York, 1939; paperbacks, U.K. and U.S.).

Poems Written in Early Youth (London and New York, 1967; paperback, U.S.).

Selected Poems, 2nd edn. (London, 1954; paperbacks, U.K. and U.S.).

'The Waste Land' and Other Poems (paperback, New York, 1955).

The Cocktail Party (London and New York, 1950; paperbacks, U.K. and U.S.).

Collected Plays (London, 1962).

The Confidential Clerk (London and New York, 1954; paperbacks, U.K. and U.S.).

The Elder Statesman (London and New York, 1959; paperbacks, U.K. and U.S.).

The Family Reunion (London and New York, 1939; paperbacks, U.K. and U.S.).

Murder in the Cathedral, 5th edn. (London and New York, 1938; paperbacks, U.K. and U.S.). Also edited with notes by Nevill Coghill (London, 1965).

T. S. Eliot with George Hoellering, *The Film of 'Murder in the Cathedral'* (London and New York, 1952).

The Rock (London and New York, 1934).

After Strange Gods (London and New York, 1934).

Articles in *The Criterion* (London, 1922–1939): 'The Function of a Literary Review, I (1922); 'The Idea of a Literary Review', IV (1926); 'Commentary', XIII (1933), p. 115; and XIV (1935), p. 260.

'An Experiment in Criticism', essay in a collection by various authors entitled *Tradition and Experiment in Present-Day Literature* (London and New York, 1929).

For Lancelot Andrewes (London, 1928, New York, 1929).

George Herbert (Writers and their Work series, No. 152, London, 1962, and Lincoln, Nebr., 1964; paperback, U.S.).

The Idea of a Christian Society (London, 1939, and New York, 1940; paperback, under title *Christianity and Culture*, U.S.).

Address given at Mary Institute, St. Louis, 1959, printed in the school's publication *From Mary to You* (reference taken from L. L. Martz's essay).

John Dryden (New York, 1932); see also three broadcast talks printed in the *Listener* (London), 15, 22, and 29 April 1931.

Notes Towards the Definition of Culture (London, 1948, and New York, 1949; paperbacks, U.K., and, under title *Christianity and Culture*, U.S.).

On Poetry and Poets (London and New York, 1957; paperbacks, U.K. and U.S.).

The Sacred Wood (London, 1920, and New York, 1921; paperbacks, U.K. and U.S.).

Selected Essays. The third English edition (London, 1951) is the fullest; the second American edition (New York, 1950) lacks one essay, 'John Marston'. Parts of this collection are issued separately in paperback: *Dante* (U.K.), and *Elizabethan Dramatists* (U.K. and U.S.).

Selected Prose, ed. John Hayward, new edn. (London, 1953; paperbacks, U.K. and U.S.).

'To Criticize the Critic' and Other Writings (London and New York, 1965; paperback, U.S.).

The Use of Poetry and The Use of Criticism, 2nd edn. (London and New York, 1964; paperback, U.K.).

Hallie Flanagan, *Dynamo* (New York, 1943).

G. Wilson Knight, *The Wheel of Fire*, with an Introduction by T. S. Eliot, 4th edn. (London, 1959, and New York, 1960; paperbacks, U.K. and U.S.).

Marianne Moore, *Selected Poems*, with an Introduction by T. S. Eliot (London and New York, 1935).

St.-J. Perse, *Anabasis*, with a trans. by T. S. Eliot, 3rd edn. (New York, 1949); rev. edn. (London, 1959).

Ezra Pound, *Selected Poems*, with an Introduction by T. S. Eliot, new edn. (London and New York, 1948; paperbacks, U.K. and U.S.).

Paul Valery, *Le Serpent*, with an Introduction by T. S. Eliot (London, 1924).

CRITICAL STUDIES AND COMMENTARY

J. Bayley, 'The Collected Plays', *The Review*, 4 (November, 1962).

B. Bergonzi, (ed.), Casebook on *'Four Quartets'* (London, 1969; paperback, U.K.).

M. Bodkin, *The Quest for Salvation in an Ancient and a Modern Play* (London, 1941).

M. C. Bradbrook, *T. S. Eliot* (Writers and their Work series, London, 1950; paperback, U.S.).

N. Braybrooke (ed.), *T. S. Eliot: a Symposium for his Seventieth Birthday* (London and New York, 1958).

V. Brombert, *The Criticism of T. S. Eliot: Problems of an Impersonal Theory of Poetry* (New Haven, Conn., and London, 1949).

E. M. Browne, *The Making of a Play*, Judith Wilson Lecture (Cambridge, 1966). Concerns *The Cocktail Party*.

E. M. Browne, *The Making of T. S. Eliot's Plays* (London and New York, 1969).

V. Buckley, *Poetry and the Sacred* (London, 1968).

C. B. Cox and A. Hinchliffe (eds.), Casebook on *The Waste Land* (London, 1968; paperback, U.K.).

D. Donoghue, 'T. S. Eliot's Quartets: A New Reading', *Studies*, lxiv (1965).

E. Drew, *T. S. Eliot: the Design of his Poetry* (London and New York, 1950; paperback, U.S.).

T. S. Eliot, interviewed by Donald Hall, *Paris Review*, xxi (Spring–Summer 1959).

T. S. Eliot: 'T. S. Eliot talks about himself', an interview with John Lehmann, *New York Times Book Review*, 29 November 1953.

The Poetry of T. S. Eliot, an N.B.C. Radio Discussion (Chicago, 1950).

R. Ellmann, 'Yeats and Eliot', *Encounter*, xxv (July 1965).

N. Frye, *T. S. Eliot* (paperback, London, 1963, and New York, 1964).

D. Gallup, 'The Manuscript of "The Waste Land" ', *TLS*, 7 November 1968.

H. Gardner, *The Art of T. S. Eliot*, 6th impr. (London and New York, 1968; paperbacks, U.K. and U.S.).

H. Gardner, 'The Landscapes of Eliot's Poetry', being the Robert Spence Watson lecture for 1966, printed in *The Critical Quarterly*, X, 4 (1968).

H. Gardner, *T. S. Eliot and the English Poetic Tradition*, Byron Foundation Lecture, Nottingham, 1966.

E. J. H. Greene, *T. S. Eliot et la France* (Paris, 1951).

G. R. Hamilton, *The Tell-Tale Article* (London, 1949, and New York, 1950).

D. E. Jones, *The Plays of T. S. Eliot* (Minneapolis, Minn., and London, 1963; paperback, U.S.).

H. Kenner (ed.), *T. S. Eliot: a Collection of Critical Essays* (paperback, Englewood Cliffs, N.J., 1962; paperback U.K.).

H. Kenner, *The Invisible Poet: T. S. Eliot* (London and New York, 1960; paperbacks, U.K. and U.S.).

F. R. Leavis and Q. D. Leavis, *Lectures in America* (London and Toronto, 1969; paperback, U.K. 1969).

P. Wyndham Lewis, *Men Without Art* (London and Toronto, 1934).

R. March and M. J. Tambimuttu (eds.), *T. S. Eliot: a Symposium* (London, 1948, and Chicago, 1949).

G. Martin (ed.), *Eliot in Perspective* (London, 1970).

L. L. Martz, *The Poem of the Mind* (New York, 1966; paperbacks, U.S. and U.K.).

F. O. Matthiessen, *The Achievement of T. S. Eliot*, 3rd edn. (London and New York, 1959; paperbacks, U.K. and U.S.).

D. E. S. Maxwell, *The Poetry of T. S. Eliot* (London, 1952; paperback, New York, 1959; paperback, U.K.).

J. H. Miller, *Poets of Reality* (Cambridge, Mass., 1966).

S. Musgrove, *T. S. Eliot and Walt Whitman* (paperback, Wellington, N.Z., 1952, and Cambridge, 1953; paperback, U.S.).

T. S. Pearce, *T. S. Eliot* (paperback, London, 1967; paperback, U.S.).

M. Praz, 'T. S. Eliot and Dante', *The Southern Review*, ii (1937).

R. Preston, *Four Quartets Rehearsed* (London, 1946; paperback, U.S.).

B. Rajan (ed.), *T. S. Eliot: a Study of his Writings by Several Hands* (London, 1947, and New York, 1948).

K. Smidt, *Poetry and Belief in the Work of T. S. Eliot* (Norway, 1949; rev. edn., London, 1961).

C. H. Smith, *T. S. Eliot's Dramatic Theory and Practice from 'Sweeney Agonistes' to 'The Elder Statesman'* (Princeton, N.J., and London, 1963; paperbacks, U.K. and U.S.).

G. C. Smith, *T. S. Eliot's Poetry and Plays: a Study in Sources and Meaning* (paperback, Chicago, 1956).

A. Tate (ed.), *T. S. Eliot: the Man and his Work* (New York and London, 1967; paperback, U.S.).

L. Unger, *Moments and Patterns* (Minneapolis, Minn., and London, 1966; paperbacks, U.K. and U.S.).

L. Unger (ed.), *T. S. Eliot: a Selected Critique* (New York, 1948).

G. Watson, 'The Triumph of T. S. Eliot', *The Critical Quarterly*, vii, 4 (1965).

G. Williamson, *A Reader's Guide to T. S. Eliot* (New York, 1953, and London, 1955; paperbacks, U.K. and U.S.).

F. Wilson, *Six Essays on the Development of T. S. Eliot* (London, 1948).

Y. Winters, *In Defense of Reason* (New York, 1947, and London, 1960; paperback, U.S.).

J. Worthington, 'The Epigraphs to the Poetry of T. S. Eliot', *American Literature*, xxi (March, 1949).

BIOGRAPHIES

C. Aiken, *Ushant: an Autobiographical Narrative* (New York, 1952, and London, 1963; paperback, U.S.).

R. Aldington, *Life for Life's Sake* (New York, 1940, and London, 1968).

T. S. Eliot, 'American Literature and the American Language', an address delivered at Washington University in 1953, and printed in *To Criticize the Critic* (see TEXTS).

T. S. Eliot, 'Commentary' (a propos *Souvenirs* by Henri Massis), *The Criterion*, xiii (1934), p. 451.

M. Holroyd, *Lytton Strachey: a Critical Biography*, vol. ii (London, 1968).

H. Howarth, *Notes on Some Figures Behind T. S. Eliot* (New York, 1964, and London, 1965).

E. A. Mowrer, *This American World*, with an Introduction by T. S. Eliot (London, 1928).

Bertrand Russell, *Autobiography*, vol. i (London, 1967; paperback, U.S.).

L. Woolf, *Beginning Again* and *Downhill All the Way* (London and New York, 1964 and 1967).

BIBLIOGRAPHIES

D. C. Gallup, *T. S. Eliot: a Bibliography, Including Contributions to Periodicals and Foreign Translations* (London, 1952, and New York, 1953; rev. edn. 1969).

BACKGROUND READING

J. B. Connolly, *Fishermen of the Banks*, with a Publishers' Preface, anonymously, by T. S. Eliot (London, 1928).

C. C. Eliot, *William Greenleaf Eliot* (Boston, 1904).

C. C. Eliot, *Savonarola: a Dramatic Poem*, with an Introduction by T. S. Eliot (London, 1926, and on sale in U.S.A.).

T. S. Eliot, *Knowledge and Experience in the Philosophy of F. H. Bradley* (London and New York, 1964).

F. O. Matthiessen, *American Renaissance* (London and New York, 1941; paperbacks, U.K. and U.S.).

Ezra Pound, *The Letters of Ezra Pound, 1907–1941*, ed. D. Paige (New York, 1950, and London, 1951; paperback, U.S.).

Ezra Pound, *Literary Essays*, edited with an Introduction by T. S. Eliot (London and New York, 1954; paperbacks, U.K. and U.S.).

E. Starkie, *From Gautier to Eliot: The Influence of France on English Literature, 1851–1939* (London, 1960, and New York, 1961).

A. Symons, *The Symbolist Movement in Literature*, 2nd edn. (London, 1908; paperback, U.S.).

J. L. Weston, *From Ritual to Romance* (Cambridge, 1920; paperbacks, U.K. and U.S.).

NOTES ON THE CONTRIBUTORS

Peter Bayley is a Fellow of University College, Oxford, and a University Lecturer in English. He has edited Books I and II of *The Faerie Queene* for Oxford University Press, and is now engaged on a book on Spenser for Hutchinson University Library.

John Beer is a Fellow of Peterhouse, Cambridge, and a University Lecturer in English. His books include studies of Coleridge, Blake, and Forster.

James Bertram is an Associate Professor of English at the Victoria University of Wellington, New Zealand. He edited *New Zealand Letters of Thomas Arnold the Younger, with Letters of Arthur Hugh Clough*.

Margaret Bottrall teaches at Hughes Hall, Cambridge, and is a University Lecturer in the Faculty of Education. Her books include *George Herbert* (1964) and a Macmillan Casebook on Blake's *Songs of Innocence and Experience* (1969).

J. A. Burrow is a Fellow of Jesus College, Oxford, and a University Lecturer in English. His books include *A Reading of 'Sir Gawaine and the Green Knight'* (1965), and *Geoffrey Chaucer* (ed.) in the 'Penguin Critical Anthologies'.

Douglas Bush is Professor of Literature at Harvard. His best-known book is *English Literature in the Early Seventeenth Century 1600–1660* (vol. V in the Oxford History of English Literature, 2nd edn. 1962), and he is the editor of *Milton: Poetical Works* (1966).

D. V. Erdman, Professor of English at the State University of New York, Stony Brook, and Editor of Library Publications of the New York Public Library, is the author of *Blake: Prophet Against Empire*.

S. C. Gill holds a Fellowship in English Literature at Lincoln College, Oxford, and has published articles on Wordsworth.

Robert Gittings, sometime Fellow of Jesus College, Cambridge, was in 1966 Visiting Professor in English at Vanderbilt University, Tennessee. Of his many studies of Keats, the biography *John Keats* (1968) is now the best known.

John Dixon Hunt is a Lecturer in English at the University of York. His book *The Pre-Raphaelite Imagination 1848–1900* was published in 1968, and his Macmillan Casebook on Tennyson's *In Memoriam* in 1969.

Ian Jack is a Fellow of Pembroke College, Cambridge, and a University Lecturer in English. His publications include the 1967 Warton Lecture, *Robert Browning*, studies of Augustan satire and Keats, and *English Literature 1815–1832* (vol. x of the *Oxford History of English Literature*).

John Jump is John Edward Taylor Professor of English Literature in the University of Manchester. His books include *Tennyson: The Critical Heritage* (1967), a study of Matthew Arnold, and two Macmillan Casebooks, on *Hamlet* and *Dr. Faustus*.

James Kinsley is Professor of English Studies in the University of Nottingham. His many contributions to scholarship include the Oxford English Texts of Dryden and Burns.

J. C. Maxwell is a Professorial Fellow of Balliol College, Oxford, and University Reader in English Literature; before this, he was Professor of English in the University of Newcastle. He edits *Notes and Queries*, and is the editor of *The Collected Papers of Sir Walter W. Greg* (1966) and several volumes in the *New Cambridge Shakespeare*.

W. Milgate is Reader in English at the Australian National University, and edited the Oxford English Text *John Donne: The Satires, Epigrams, and Verse Letters* (1967). He also completed for publication R. C. Bald's definitive biography, *John Donne: A Life* (1970).

Anne Ridler was for some years secretary to T. S. Eliot and *The Criterion*. She is a well-known poet; her latest volume in England is *A Matter of Life and Death* (1959) and in America, *Selected Poems* (1961).

D. I. B. Smith is Professor of Literature at the University of Toronto. He is editor of *Editing Eighteenth Century Texts* (1968).

Jon Stallworthy, who works in publishing, is the author of *Between the Lines: Yeats's Poetry in the Making* (1963), *Vision and Revision in Yeats's Last Poems* (1969), the Macmillan Casebook on Yeats's Last Poems, and several volumes of poetry, the most recent of which is *Root and Branch* (1969).

Graham Storey is a Fellow of Trinity Hall, Cambridge, and a University Lecturer in English. He completed the late Humphry House's work on Hopkins's *Journals and Papers* (1959), and is now working with Madeline House on the definitive edition of the Letters of Charles Dickens.

Geoffrey Tillotson was Professor of English in the University of London, at Birkbeck College, from 1944 until his death in 1969. He was particularly well known for his editorial and critical work on Pope and Thackeray.

R. B. Woodings, a Lecturer in English at the University of East Anglia, edited *Modern Judgements on Shelley* (1968).

THE EDITOR

A. E. Dyson, Senior Lecturer in English in the University of East Anglia, is general editor of the Macmillan Casebooks on Literature, and editor (with C. B. Cox) of *The Critical Quarterly*. His publications include *The Crazy Fabric: Essays on Irony* (1965) and *The Inimitable Dickens* (1970).